THE
ARMED CONFLICT SURVEY
2021

The worldwide review of
political, military and humanitarian
trends in current conflicts

published by

 **Routledge**
Taylor & Francis Group

for

The International Institute for Strategic Studies

The International Institute for Strategic Studies
Arundel House | 6 Temple Place | London | WC2R 2PG | UK

THE ARMED CONFLICT SURVEY 2021

First published September 2021 by **Routledge**
4 Park Square, Milton Park, Abingdon, Oxon, OX14 4RN

for **The International Institute for Strategic Studies**
Arundel House, 6 Temple Place, London, WC2R 2PG, UK

Simultaneously published in the USA and Canada by **Routledge**
52 Vanderbilt Avenue, New York, NY 10017

Routledge is an imprint of Taylor & Francis, an Informa business

© 2021 The International Institute for Strategic Studies

DIRECTOR-GENERAL AND CHIEF EXECUTIVE Dr John Chipman
EDITOR Dr Irene Mia
ASSOCIATE EDITORS Nikini Arulanandam, Jack May
GRAPHICS COORDINATOR Mubasil Chaudhry
EDITORIAL Flora Bell, Gregory Brooks, Mubasil Chaudhry, Nick Fargher, Natalia Forrest
DESIGN AND PRODUCTION John Buck, Carolina Vargas, Kelly Verity
CONFLICTS Adam Weinstein (Afghanistan and Pakistan), Dr Ryan Berg (Brazil), Ladd Serwat (Cameroon and Democratic Republic of the Congo), Thierry Vircoulon (Central African Republic), Gustavo Orozco (Colombia), Hafsa Halawa (Egypt), Douglas Farah and Alexa Tavarez (El Salvador and Honduras), Sandy Wade (Ethiopia), Dr Alex Waterman (India–Central (Maoist) and India–Northeast), Dr Ben Robin (Iraq), Dr Mohd Tahir Ganie (Kashmir), Dr Andrea Carboni (Lake Chad Basin, Nigeria and Somalia), Dr Umberto Profazio (Libya), Rodrigo Aguilera (Mexico), Olivier Milland (Mozambique and the Sahel), Morgan Michaels (Myanmar), Dr Laurence Broers, Jenny Tobias and Eva Rosenthal (Nagorno-Karabakh), Michael Hart (Philippines (NPA) and Philippines (ASG & Moro)), Tsion Belay Alene (Sudan), Nuray Atmaca (Syria), Jeremy Walden-Schertz (Thailand), Dr Samir Puri (Ukraine), Eleonora Ardemagni (Yemen)
REGIONAL ESSAYS Dr Irene Mia and Juan Pablo Bickel (Americas), Adam Weinstein and Viraj Solanki (Asia), Dr Francesco Milan (Europe and Eurasia), Dr Umberto Profazio (Middle East and North Africa), Dr Benjamin Petrini (sub-Saharan Africa)
GLOBAL TRENDS Niels V.S. Harild (Economic Migration, Forced Displacement and Armed Conflict in a COVID-19 World), Dr Samir Puri (Interventions in Armed Conflicts: Waning Western Dominance), Dr Benjamin Petrini (The Long Aftermath of Armed Conflicts)
THE CHART OF ARMED CONFLICT Erica Pepe, Juan Pablo Bickel
RESEARCH CONTRIBUTIONS Bryony Essex, Thierry Geiger, Dr Gary Milante, Philipp Schweers (Armed Conflict Global Relevance Indicator), Juan Pablo Bickel, Erica Pepe (The Long Aftermath of Armed Conflicts), Ricardo Fuentes (Economic Migration, Forced Displacement and Armed Conflict in a COVID-19 World), Henry Boyd, Aaron Connelly, Dr Nigel Gould-Davis, Emile Hokayem, John Raine, Dr Clionadh Raleigh
COVER IMAGES Getty

British Library Cataloguing in Publication Data
A catalogue record for this book is available from the British Library

Library of Congress Cataloguing in Publication Data

ISBN 978-1-032-17185-2
ISSN 2374-0973

Taliban militants and villagers in
the Alingar district of Laghman
province, Afghanistan

Contents

National League for Democracy supporters during an election rally in Naypyidaw, Myanmar

Editor's Introduction

2020 has been an unprecedented year for the world in many ways, with the coronavirus pandemic spreading across all geographies and creating havoc for populations and economies alike. Lockdown measures and disruptions to global supply chains have caused major recessions and a deterioration in socio-economic indicators around the world, adding fuel to social and political instability in many already fragile and conflict-ridden countries. The legacy of the pandemic will be felt for years to come, reinforcing root causes of conflict through its nefarious impact on development, poverty, state capacity and political stability as well as on available international aid resources.

However, in the period covered by *The Armed Conflict Survey 2021*, the pandemic did not disrupt ongoing conflicts as much as it did other activities, despite mobility restrictions and calls from the United Nations for a global ceasefire. In 2020 and early 2021, conflict continued unabated across the world and even accelerated in instances such as Ethiopia, Mozambique, Myanmar, Nagorno-Karabakh and the Sahel. Non-state armed groups (NSAGs) across the globe also leveraged the pandemic-induced strains on government resources and attention to strengthen their territorial control, their activity in illegal trafficking and, in some cases, even their legitimacy with the general population.

The global conflict landscape remained dominated by the same complex and upward trends (see Figure 1) highlighted by *The Armed Conflict Survey* since its inception in 2015. In 2020 and early 2021 most armed conflicts remained internal in their essence, but have become increasingly internationalised, featuring interventions from a growing number of regional and global powers in pursuit of their

Figure 1: Global conflict trends, 1990–2020[1]

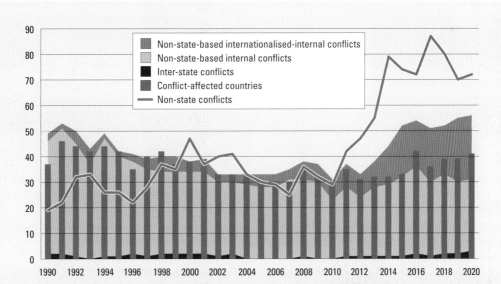

Sources: UCDP/PRIO Armed Conflict Dataset version 21.1; UCDP Non-State Conflict Dataset version 21.1; Nils Petter Gleditsch et al., 'Armed Conflict 1946–2001: A New Dataset', *Journal of Peace Research*, vol. 39, no. 5, September 2002, pp. 615–37; Ralph Sundberg, Kristine Eck and Joakim Kreutz, 'Introducing the UCDP Non-State Conflict Dataset', *Journal of Peace Research*, vol. 49, no. 2, March 2012, pp. 351–62; Therése Pettersson et al., 'Organized Violence 1989–2020, with a Special Emphasis on Syria', *Journal of Peace Research*. vol. 58, no. 4. July 2021. pp. 809–25.

foreign-policy agendas. Third-party intervention, which currently is at a record high, further complicates internal confrontations that already often spill over into neighbouring countries, feature transnational linkages and actors (e.g., jihadist Islamism) and involve multiple and overlapping drivers. Similarly, NSAGs have proliferated in number, nature and motives, exacerbate conflict dynamics and obstruct prospects for peace. Related to this, the duration of conflict has also extended, reaching an average of 30 years in 2020,[2] amid blurring boundaries between war and post-war and frequent conflict relapses. A glance at the start date and typology indicated for each of the 34 conflicts included in *The Armed Conflict Survey 2021* confirms these trends, with most internal confrontations being long-standing and involving elements of localised insurgency, intercommunal violence or organised crime.

The Armed Conflict Survey 2021 aims to capture and make sense of this complexity against the backdrop of pandemic-driven uncertainties. To do so, a strategic analysis of conflict drivers at the domestic, regional and global levels is complemented by an in-depth assessment of current developments and future trends in the conflict landscape, including potential hotspots and political risks. To shed further light on conflict dynamics we also map conflict parties and their interlinkages, focusing not only on NSAGs but also on direct/proxy third-party state interventions and global influences, which, as already stated, is one of the most notable current conflict trends.

Furthermore, *The Armed Conflict Survey 2021* introduces a new methodological tool to prioritise analysis around the global relevance of the different conflicts: the Armed Conflict Global Relevance Indicator (ACGRI). The focus on global relevance aligns with the research ethos of the International Institute for Strategic Studies (IISS) and represents our unique filter for the study of conflicts.

The global filter is also highlighted in the inclusion of comprehensive regional essays, identifying crucial trends for the active conflicts in each geographical area, including key economic, military and geopolitical drivers as well as regional influences and connections. These essays also provide an outlook for the regional conflict landscape in the year ahead, outlining the prospects for peace but also key political risks and areas of fragility to monitor.

As in previous years, the analysis of conflicts is complemented by an assessment of selected global trends of particular relevance, which were present or emerging in the period under review, to further enhance understanding of the global conflict landscape.

The data-rich analysis throughout *The Armed Conflict Survey 2021* is visually complemented by multiple graphic elements, including regional and conflict-specific maps, charts and tables, illustrating core trends or developments (including military events, interventions and data on humanitarian impact and forced displacement), regional and global links and spillovers, and potential future conflict hotspots.

Mapping the global significance of armed conflicts

The increasing complexity of the global conflict landscape, featuring the interplay of domestic, regional and international factors, calls for additional tools to help guide analysis and identify priority areas. Global relevance is a particularly important filter for the IISS given its global character and its strategic and geopolitical research focus.

The Armed Conflict Survey 2021 therefore focuses deeper analysis on those conflicts considered most globally significant while offering an overview assessment of the remaining ones: accordingly, the conflict analysis section consists of (longer) Conflict Reports and (shorter) Conflict Summaries.

Our assessment of global relevance is based on the internal expertise of our research team as well as a new composite indicator that attempts to capture quantitatively the main drivers of such significance. The ACGRI innovates from existing country-level measures of armed conflict and instability, which are largely built around endemic factors and domestic-level political, economic and security indicators. In contrast, geopolitical and global security issues underpin the ACGRI's methodological framework and definition of global relevance, together with human impact and intensity of conflict.

The ACGRI is built on three pillars of relevance, covering the following dimensions:

- The **human impact** of conflict, in terms of human losses and hardship. The rationale for including this dimension stems from the inextricable link connecting conflict-related fatalities and forced displacement to further domestic social, economic and political instability with spillover effects on regional and global stability.

- The **incidence** of conflict, as a measure of intensity and related security implications and potential negative externalities on neighbouring countries and beyond.
- The **geopolitical impact** of conflict, measured by a number of variables we created to capture the involvement of third parties and interventions by the international community based on IISS proprietary data and other international sources.

The confluence of these three pillars, using the country in which conflict takes place as the unit of analysis, provides a good proxy of the global salience of the armed conflicts included in *The Armed Conflict Survey 2021*. The ACGRI is not meant to create a ranking of the most relevant armed conflicts, but rather to guide our identification of priority conflicts for analysis and to provide a visual snapshot of their different global dimensions. The scores of the three pillars are displayed throughout *The Armed Conflict Survey 2021* and used to highlight geopolitical significance in the Chart of Armed Conflict. More details on the ACGRI's methodological framework and computation are included in the Notes on Methodology and the Data Appendix.

Delving into global relevance trends

Strategic and geopolitical considerations, coupled with those around human cost, have also informed our choice of the featured topics in the Global Trends section.

The essay 'Interventions in Armed Conflicts: Waning Western Dominance' expands on the geopolitical and strategic dimensions of third-party countries intervening in armed conflicts. It pays close attention to non-Western powers, including Iran, Israel, Russia, Saudi Arabia, Turkey and the United Arab Emirates. Over the past two decades, these powers have increasingly adopted an extrovert foreign-policy stance, intervening and shaping conflicts to advance their strategic goals, with important implications for geopolitical balance, conflict outlook and conflict resolution. This trend has occurred together with signs of intervention fatigue from traditional major players, notably the United States, as highlighted by the withdrawal of

US troops from Afghanistan after two decades in the country. The essay extrapolates on the possible evolution of non-Western intervention and whether fatigue will similarly affect these newer actors. It also contemplates the future drivers and nature of such interventions, outlining possible new extrovert players who could enter the great-power competition game, as well as developments including the potential combination of uninhabited land, sea and air combat vehicles with inhabited platforms and traditional military formations, and a more generalised use of private military companies alongside or on behalf of third-party states.

'The Long Aftermath of Armed Conflicts' essay delves into another notable contemporary trend: the increasing protractedness of conflicts and the blurring lines between their active and post-conflict phases. Using the Afghanistan and Colombia conflicts as case studies for the long aftermath of war, with a parallel trajectory of armed conflict and post-conflict reconstruction, the essay analyses this trend's strategic and policy implications for effective, timely and time-bound interventions to build durable peace in conflict-torn countries.

The last essay in this section, titled 'Economic Migration, Forced Displacement and Armed Conflict in a COVID-19 World', seeks to unpack the interlinkages between armed conflict, forced displacement and economic-migration trends and to distil the possible impact of the coronavirus pandemic on these dynamics. The essay shows how the issues of armed conflict, pandemics, climate and development economics are intertwined, requiring both integrated solutions and more localised approaches. It finds that the pandemic acts as a multiplier of existing conflict drivers and related challenges, exposing the latter in an unprecedented way and highlighting the urgency for radical corrective action and effective global governance on issues of economic and forced migration. The pandemic also heralds an entirely new phase for the developed and developing world, with a new set of challenges and opportunities for conflict prevention and resolution.

The Chart of Armed Conflict: A geopolitical snapshot of armed conflicts across the world

In line with the IISS's emphasis on global relevance of conflict, the accompanying Chart of Armed Conflict draws attention to the geopolitical impact of the 34 active conflicts included in *The Armed Conflict Survey 2021* to further enrich the insights generated by the Global Trends and Conflict Analysis sections.

In addition to presenting information on conflict start dates (according to IISS analysis), typologies and relevant refugee flows, the Chart also provides a visual overview of each conflict's geopolitical relevance, looking at resolutions adopted by the UN Security Council in 2020, multilateral missions and the involvement of third-party countries (see Data Appendix for further details).

The scores of the ACGRI's geopolitical-impact pillar are used to shade the countries in which conflicts take place in a continuum colour scale from red to yellow, providing a visual map of geopolitical importance.

Projections for the future

The Armed Conflict Survey 2021 builds on its strategic assessment of conflict drivers and trends at the domestic, regional and global levels to extrapolate future evolutions in the global conflict landscape, including prospects for peace, political risks and future hotspots to monitor. This extra layer of analysis aims to respond to the need for forward-looking insight of our audience of policymakers, practitioners, academics and corporates operating in or near countries affected by conflicts.

Conflict in the **Americas** will continue to mix organised crime and political violence with little prospect for durable peace amid deteriorating socio-economic conditions post-COVID-19, the erosion of government effectiveness and rule of law, and the increasing legitimacy of criminal groups with local populations. The regional conflict landscape will continue to be determined mainly by the policies and developments of Colombia, Venezuela and the US, particularly the latter's policies on drugs, access to firearms and migration. Further instability is expected across Central America's Northern Triangle (particularly the Dry Corridor), along the US border with Mexico and in the border regions between Colombia and Venezuela. Haiti and Venezuela, both engulfed in deepening political and economic crises, spiralling crime and collapsing institutions, are also important areas of fragility, with likely relevant regional migration and conflict spillovers.

The conflicts in eastern Ukraine and Nagorno-Karabakh in **Europe and Eurasia** will continue to simmer, with ongoing risks of escalation. Possible Russian military intervention in the region to protect Russian-speaking minorities remains a long-standing concern for Baltic states and NATO more broadly, which could create new crises.

In the **Middle East and North Africa**, the United States' likely return to the Joint Comprehensive Plan of Action (JCPOA) with Iran could have important ramifications in Iraq, reducing tensions and paving the way for a new government following general elections scheduled for October 2021. The establishment of a new executive authority in February 2021 in Libya provides an opportunity to end the long-standing conflict in the country, although risks abound, including around the intentions of Russia and Turkey. The Biden administration is also likely to embark on a new balancing act between Israel and the Palestinian Territories, where elections will be crucial in determining the way forward.[3] Potential regional flashpoints to monitor include the frozen conflict in the Western Sahara, which shows signs of re-igniting, and potential escalation risks in the eastern Mediterranean Sea. Socio-economic tensions may create further social unrest in Iraq and Lebanon amid a negative economic outlook in both countries. Prospects for peace also remain particularly slim in Syria, where the humanitarian catastrophe and the economic collapse will continue to drive conflict.

Conflict resolution in **sub-Saharan Africa** depends on the effectiveness of ongoing multilateral, regional and bilateral initiatives focusing on peacekeeping, countering violent extremism (CVE), traditional peacemaking, security and development. The escalation of conflict observed in 2020 and early 2021 has opened the door for further instability. Transnational regional wars in several countries in West Africa and the Sahel could spill into Côte d'Ivoire and Senegal. Similarly, the accelerating conflict in northern Mozambique threatens Tanzania's ability to contain the spillover from the insurgent threat. In the Horn of Africa, the war in Tigray and Ethiopia's continuing insecurity has the potential to destabilise the whole sub-region. Eritrea's military involvement in Tigray is already a concern. Parliamentary and presidential election results in Ethiopia and Somalia respectively will also be an important driver of future regional trends.

The outlook for sustainable peace in **Asia** is fairly negative, despite efforts to broker long-term ceasefires in Afghanistan, Myanmar, Kashmir along the Line of Control (LoC), and in northeast India. Overall violence levels are likely to decrease in Afghanistan due to the withdrawal of foreign troops and the rapid increase in the Taliban's territorial control, including in Kabul. Pockets of anti-Taliban resistance may still occur, especially in the Panjshir Valley. Incidents of targeted killings and violence against civilians by the Taliban will also likely continue, as will terrorist attacks by groups such as Islamic State in Khorasan Province. In Myanmar violence levels are likely to increase due to the prospects for a multi-front civil war following the February 2021 coup. Political conditions do not yet exist for a resolution of the Kashmir conflict, although the February 2021 announcement by the Indian and Pakistani militaries of a renewed ceasefire along the LoC might herald a fragile improvement in relations between the two countries. Intervention of external powers in conflicts is likely to become more regionalised in the short term following the United States' and NATO's withdrawal from Afghanistan. Asian powers, including China and India, will likely be forced to play a larger role in supporting efforts for regional stability, including in Afghanistan and Myanmar, but will face significant challenges.

Notes

[1] UCDP disaggregates between state-based (i.e., at least one conflict party is a state) and non-state-based armed conflicts (i.e., conflict parties are exclusively NSAGs), and defines an armed conflict as the 'use of armed force between two parties' that 'results in at least 25 battle-related deaths in one calendar year'. Conflict 'parties' can be either state- or non-state-based depending on the type of conflict under consideration. Based on this definition, each country can have several different ongoing conflicts per year. This methodology explains the larger number of conflicts accounted for by UCDP compared to the 11 conflicts covered in *The Armed Conflict Survey 2021*, which adopts the country as primary unit of analysis. See UCDP/PRIO Armed Conflict Dataset, version 21.1; and UCDP, 'UCDP Non-State Conflict Dataset version 21.1', UCDP Dataset Download Center. See also Nils Petter Gleditsch et al., 'Armed Conflict 1946–2001: A New Dataset', *Journal of Peace Research*, vol. 39, no. 5, September 2002; Therése Pettersson et al., 'Organized Violence 1989–2020, with a Special Emphasis on Syria', *Journal of Peace Research*, vol. 58, no. 4, July 2021; and Ralph Sundberg, Kristine Eck and Joakim Kreutz, 'Introducing the UCDP Non-State Conflict Dataset', *Journal of Peace Research*, vol. 49, no. 2, April 2012, pp. 351–62.

[2] IISS analysis based on UCDP/PRIO Armed Conflict Dataset version 21.1.

[3] The sustained fighting that broke out in April 2021 and the subsequent ceasefire signed in May are not covered in detail in this report as they fall outside the scope of the reporting period for *The Armed Conflict Survey 2021*.

Notes on Methodology

The Armed Conflict Survey 2021 reviews and analyses events, dynamics and trends related to active armed conflict around the world. We define an armed conflict as a sustained military contest between two or more organised actors making purposive use of armed force. The inclusion of a conflict in the book is based on this definition and the methodology detailed below.

Armed conflicts in 2020–21

The Armed Conflict Survey 2021 includes 34 armed conflicts that were ongoing in the period under review, running between 1 January 2020 and 28 February 2021, with some limited exceptions.[1] Five world regions are considered (Americas, Asia, Europe and Eurasia, Middle East and North Africa, and sub-Saharan Africa), as we have regrouped the two sections that previously covered the Asia-Pacific and South Asia separately into a single Asia section. New regional essays provide comprehensive analysis at the beginning of each regional section, identifying underlying drivers and crucial trends in ongoing conflicts during the review period and assessing the regional outlook and potential future conflict hotspots for the year ahead. Coverage of individual conflicts takes two formats: longer Conflict Reports and shorter Conflict Summaries depending on their global relevance as assessed by our analysis.

The list of conflicts in the 2021 edition differs slightly from the 2020 edition. *The Armed Conflict Survey 2021* includes the conflict in Mozambique for the first time. Since 2017, when the insurgency began in the country's northern Cabo Delgado province, the conflict has progressively accelerated. 2020 was the deadliest year on record as the main non-state armed group (NSAG), Ahlu al-Sunnah wal-Jamaah (locally known as 'al-Shabaab'), continued its expansion north and south of Cabo Delgado's coast and scaled up its military and organisational capabilities. The analysis of the Sahel conflict also covers Niger, in addition to Mali and Burkina Faso, given the former's increasing involvement in the regional

conflict. We have adjusted the Americas section to reflect the most relevant trends in organised armed violence in the period under review. In this vein, the Brazil chapter centres on organised violence in Rio de Janeiro and Amazonas (rather than Rio de Janeiro and Ceará, as was the case for *The Armed Conflict Survey 2020*) given the increased strategic significance of Amazonas state as a major point of criminal contestation between NSAGs against the backdrop of its vast river network and shared borders with major coca-producing countries. The focus of the Colombia chapter has also been broadened from *bandas criminales* (or BACRIMs) to other types of NSAGs, including the dissident groups of the Revolutionary Armed Forces of Colombia (FARC), the National Liberation Army (ELN) and drug cartels.

Criteria for inclusion and removal

Defining armed conflict as a military or violent phenomenon means *The Armed Conflict Survey 2021* does not aim to determine the applicability of international humanitarian law to different conflict situations (as in the Geneva Conventions or the Rome Statute).

The Armed Conflict Survey includes armed confrontations that meet our criteria in terms of *duration, intensity* and *organisation of the conflict parties*.

We require an armed conflict to run for at least three months and feature violent incidents on a weekly or at least fortnightly basis. *The Armed Conflict Survey*'s definition of armed conflict does not involve a numerical threshold of battle-related deaths, contrary to conflict datasets such as the Uppsala Conflict Data Program (UCDP). For wars between states – which feature substantial levels of military mobilisation, simultaneous and numerous armed clashes, or significant fatalities – the duration threshold may be relaxed.

The organisation of the conflict parties refers to their ability to plan and execute military operations or violent attacks. The scale of such attacks is not a factor in this determination – for the purpose of inclusion in *The Armed Conflict Survey 2021*, for example, planting improvised explosive devices (IEDs) is equivalent to battlefield clashes. For armed conflicts that involve state parties, the deployment of armed forces or militarised (not regular) police is required. NSAGs must demonstrate some logistical and operational capacity, such as access to weapons and other military equipment, or an ability to devise strategies and carry out operations, coordinate activities, establish communication between members, and recruit and train personnel. Territorial control or a permanent base in an area is not required. *The Armed Conflict Survey 2021* also remains agnostic about the type of organisational structure adopted by armed groups. Not all NSAGs have a distinct and effective chain of command – such as many of those operating in sub-Saharan Africa – but can be highly decentralised, maintain an amorphous structure, rely on a transnational network, or have a global reach. A hierarchical military structure is therefore not an inclusion criterion. In each conflict chapter, the Conflict Parties table lists the main organisational capabilities of the actors involved.[2]

The Armed Conflict Survey 2021 excludes cases of one-sided application of lethal force, terrorist attacks and public protests. Regardless of scale, instances of government repression, ethnic cleansing or genocide that occur outside of a conflict situation are not included until the population displays a capacity to fight back through an armed, organised resistance, or another state wages war – as in the case of the Khmer Rouge regime in Cambodia when Vietnam invaded in 1979. While terrorist attacks may lead to the domestic deployment of armed forces, the rarity of these events means they fail the intensity test. Situations with widespread but unorganised criminal activity are also excluded.

Our definition takes an inclusive approach to the different motivations that drive armed conflict. Indeed, *The Armed Conflict Survey 2021* includes conflicts with drivers that are political, socio-economic, ideological, religious or criminal. This is particularly evident in featured conflicts in Mexico or Central America where the main parties are criminal groups with elusive political or ideological motives.

The Armed Conflict Survey 2021 applies two criteria for removal. Armed conflicts that have lost the above-defined characteristics for inclusion are removed after two years. An armed conflict terminated through a peace agreement also ceases to be included following the military demobilisation of all conflict parties.

Classification and categorisation of armed conflicts: scope and actors

The unit of analysis in *The Armed Conflict Survey 2021* remains the conflict itself, that is, the military or violent confrontation between armed actors. In most cases, conflicts take place within the boundaries of a state and are therefore listed under those country names. One exception to this rule is when multiple conflicts coexist in the same country, such as in the Philippines, where the government is simultaneously fighting the Moro Muslim rebels in western Mindanao and the Maoist rebels of the New People's Army (NPA). In these instances, the name of the country is listed along with the name of the main insurgent group. Other conflicts have a regional scope, unfolding across multiple states. This is the case for the insurgency in the Lake Chad Basin – which involves parts of Cameroon, Chad, Niger and Nigeria – or the multifaceted and inter-related conflicts in the Sahel, spanning Burkina Faso, Mali and Niger. Conflicts that have elements of inter-state confrontation either take the name of the disputed region (Nagorno-Karabakh or Kashmir) or the parties involved (Israel–Palestinian Territories).

Conflicts may involve state or non-state actors. According to the types of actors involved and the interactions between them, armed conflicts have been grouped into one of three categories: inter-state (or international) conflicts, internal conflicts or internationalised-internal conflicts.

An *inter-state* conflict involves two or more states (or a group of states) and takes place on the territory of one or several states, as well as in the global commons.

An *internal* conflict takes place in the territory of one state and is either fought by a government (and possibly allied armed groups) against one or more NSAGs, or between two or more NSAGs without the direct participation of state forces. Within this category, we include the sub-categories of localised insurgencies (such as the one ongoing in southern Thailand), intercommunal conflicts (such as the one in Sudan) and organised crime (such as most of the conflicts in the Americas). However, these groupings are not necessarily mutually exclusive, and many internal conflicts feature characteristics of two or more sub-categories.

Lastly, *internationalised-internal* conflicts are confrontations in which the kernel of the dispute remains domestic, but which feature military intervention by one or more external states. Such involvement may include training, equipping or providing military intelligence to a conflict party or participating in the hostilities, either directly or through local proxies and sponsored actors.

The Armed Conflict Global Relevance Indicator (ACGRI)

As an additional tool for analysis and prioritisation, *The Armed Conflict Survey 2021* introduces a new composite indicator to assess the global significance of armed conflicts (see Editor's Introduction for details).

Given data availability and comparability challenges at the conflict level, the Armed Conflict Global Relevance Indicator (ACGRI) uses the country in which conflicts happen as the unit of analysis rather than the conflicts themselves. This methodological choice is justified by the fact that most of the 34 armed conflicts covered are internal (internationalised or not), meaning the conflict can be assimilated to the country in which it takes place. Wherever there are multiple insurgencies taking place at once in the same country (namely the cases of India and the Philippines), the country score encompasses all of those. On the other hand, it will not be possible to

differentiate the global significance of each domestic insurgency in isolation. In a similar fashion, conflicts that spill over national borders and affect several countries (such as those in the Sahel and Lake Chad Basin) are not given a regional score, with global relevance assessed instead at the level of each country involved.

In contrast, for the conflicts in Nagorno-Karabakh and Israel–Palestinian Territories, the unit of analysis is the conflict itself. India and Pakistan are treated separately in the case of the conflict in Jammu and Kashmir due to the presence of other localised insurgencies in both countries. Geopolitical indicators relevant to Kashmir (such as the number of United Nations Security Council (UNSC) resolutions) are attributed to both countries to ensure that the final score reflects the geopolitical impact of the inter-state conflict.

The ACGRI is organised around the three pillars of *human impact*, *incidence* and *geopolitical impact* and is composed of a total of eight variables (see Table 1). These variables are good proxies of the dimensions of global relevance we seek to cover, considering the availability of reliable data.

As a preliminary step to combine variable scores into pillar and ACGRI scores, data for each variable

Table 1: ACGRI pillars and variables

Pillar	Variable	Description	Source
Human impact	Fatalities	Number of fatalities due to conflict events, by country, 1 January 2020 to 25 February 2021[3]	Armed Conflict Location & Event Data Project (ACLED) www.acleddata.com
	Refugees	Number of refugees (total), by country of origin, as of 31 December 2020	UN High Commissioner for Refugees, UN Relief and Works Agency for Palestine Refugees in the Near East
	Internally displaced persons (IDPs)	Number of IDPs (total), by country, as of 31 December 2020	Internal Displacement Monitoring Centre
Incidence	Conflict events	Number of conflict events, by country, 1 January 2020 to 25 February 2021[4]	Armed Conflict Location & Event Data Project (ACLED), www.acleddata.com
Geopolitical impact	Interventions by major geopolitical powers	Number of interventions by major geopolitical powers within the G20 in conflict-affected countries, by country, 2020[5]	Military Balance+
	Deployments by major geopolitical powers	Number of personnel deployed by major geopolitical powers in conflict-affected countries, by country, 2020	Military Balance+
	UN Security Council resolutions	Number of UNSC resolutions concerning conflict-affected countries, by country, 2020	UN Security Council
	Peacekeeping and other multilateral missions	Number of peacekeeping and other multilateral missions present in conflict-affected countries, by country, 2020	UN, European Union, regional organisations, ad hoc coalitions and the Stockholm International Peace Research Institute (SIPRI)

is normalised on a 0–10 scale, through the following approach:

Eq.1   (indicator data-0)/(y-0) × 10 = variable score

where the indicator data refers to continuous data, y refers to the maximum value from the target countries, and 0 is used as the minimum value.

Each pillar score is the arithmetic mean of the composing variable, multiplied by 10, giving a pillar score between 0 and 100. The ACGRI score is, in turn, the arithmetic mean of the three pillars.

The scores of the ACGRI and its composing pillars are displayed throughout the book in a continuous colour progression (using conditional formatting) in order to respect the (cardinal instead of ordinal) distance between countries and to reflect more precisely the differentiation of conflicts' global relevance based on the continuum of the ACGRI scores for the full sample.

Data for all the variables included in the ACGRI is listed in the Data Appendix, along with detailed source information and the underlying calculation methodology for each variable.

Selected data from the ACGRI is also featured in the 'Key Conflict Statistics' boxes in each conflict chapter, as well as other background variables relevant to the context under analysis, such as the Gini index, GDP per capita (based on purchasing power parity in current prices–international dollars) and the Functioning of Government pillar of the Economist Intelligence Unit's Democracy Index. Full data for all these background variables is also contained in the Data Appendix.

The Chart of Armed Conflict

The Chart of Armed Conflict provides relevant data and information for the 34 conflicts included in *The Armed Conflict Survey 2021*, such as the start date (according to IISS analysis), conflict typology, number of refugees and UNSC resolutions, as well as flags corresponding to multilateral missions and third-party foreign countries deemed to be involved in the conflict.[6]

Multilateral missions included are conflict-related multilateral peace operations – either conducted under the aegis of the UN or a regional organisation, or ad hoc coalitions of states authorised by the UN – that support the peace process and facilitate peacebuilding and conflict prevention. Civilian and political missions, which do not involve armed forces, are also listed at the bottom of the Chart.[7] Data is obtained from the Military Balance+, SIPRI, and the official websites of the UN, regional organisations and ad hoc coalitions.

Foreign countries are deemed to be 'involved' as third parties in a conflict if they meet the following criteria:

Either:
- Deployment of military capabilities (outside of a multilateral mission as defined above)

Or all of the following:
- Presence of intelligence assets
- Provision of military financial support
- Role in an advisory or in operational command-and-control capacity
- Sale or transfer of military equipment.

Notes

[1] In an effort to make *The Armed Conflict Survey 2021* as timely as possible, we have extended the period of review until 30 April 2021 in a number of exceptional cases (including Myanmar, Mozambique and Ukraine) which experienced a notable acceleration of the conflict after the February cut-off date. In other cases, events after the end of February 2021 will be covered in the 2022 edition of *The Armed Conflict Survey*. The sustained fighting and subsequent ceasefire in April/May 2021 for the Israel–Palestine Territories conflict, and the Taliban's swift victory and takeover of Afghanistan in August 2021, are similarly not covered in detail in this edition as they fall outside the reporting period for *The Armed Conflict Survey 2021*.

[2] Unless otherwise stated, all figures related to military strength and capability, defence economics and arms equipment in the Conflict Parties table of conflict chapters are from the Military Balance+.

[3] Conflict fatalities include those that result from the event types of battles, explosions/remote violence and violence against civilians.

[4] Conflict events include battles, explosions/remote violence and violence against civilians.

[5] This is calculated by looking at the number of G20 countries deploying unilaterally or as part of a coalition (but not in a mission under the aegis of an international organisation) into the conflict-affected countries.

[6] In the case of interventions by coalitions of countries, such as the United States-led Combined Joint Task Force–*Operation Inherent Resolve* in Iraq, only the flag of the country leading the coalition is displayed, with an asterisk denoting the involvement and military deployment of other countries. The same ordering of conflicts on the Chart of Armed Conflict has been used to organise the internal ordering in *The Armed Conflict Survey 2021*.

[7] The estimated strength of the mission refers to the military strength, unless otherwise stated. An asterisk indicates international civilian staff.

GLOBAL TRENDS

Russian peacekeepers near Kalbajar
during the conflict between Armenia and
Azerbaijan over Nagorno-Karabakh

Interventions in Armed Conflicts: Waning Western Dominance

One of the most notable geopolitical trends of the last five years has been the growing number of states intervening in and shaping conflicts to advance their own foreign policies and strategic agendas. What used to be the preserve of the United States and its Western European allies in the post-Cold War and post-9/11 eras has become a more generalised trend, with powers such as Iran, Israel, Russia, Saudi Arabia, Turkey and the United Arab Emirates (UAE) intervening in multiple conflicts across the world.

These interventions have taken a variety of forms, ranging from the episodic use of airstrikes to the deployment of land and maritime expeditionary forces. Some have been mounted unilaterally, skirting below the radar of international scrutiny, while others have sought wider legitimacy by assembling 'coalitions of the willing', such as Saudi Arabia's intervention in the war in Yemen. Most have supported local allies or partners or proxies. Irrespective of the minutiae of specific interventions, this trend has been on full display in several armed conflicts in 2020 and early 2021.

Armed conflicts amid changing geopolitics

The nature of war has not fundamentally changed in recent years since conflicts are still predominantly internal affairs, in which non-state armed groups play a prominent role. Declared inter-state wars remain rare.[1] What has changed is the increasingly multipolar global context in which armed conflicts are being fought.[2] Other powerful countries, besides the US, are now trying to resolve or influence the outcome of wars abroad to further their own national goals. Compared to the peak of its unipolarity, characterised by interventions in the Balkans, Africa, the Middle East and Asia, the US has gradually become a distracted hegemon. The shift began under the administration of Barack Obama (2009–17) and continued under his successor, Donald Trump (2017–21), who expressed disdain for US involvement in foreign wars amid a general sense of war

weariness in the domestic discourse. There were exceptions, including the US role in the territorial defeat of the Islamic State (also known as ISIS or ISIL) in the Middle East and the US military presence that accompanied efforts to broker an end to the war in Afghanistan ahead of its military withdrawal there.[3] Global counter-terrorism missions remained a US priority, albeit with a smaller military footprint than previous interventions. Notwithstanding these, however, US foreign- and defence-policy priorities shifted towards 'great-power contests' with China and Russia, alongside the containment of Iran and North Korea. The US duly accorded prominence to conventional, nuclear and cyber deterrence, as well as alliance politics and defence diplomacy in regions of strategic contestation.

Trump was also uninterested in censuring other states' own military interventions as long as these did not disturb his administration's core interests, a stance that opened further space for other extrovert powers to fill. Joe Biden's presidency has stemmed this policy drift in one instance: in February 2021, he announced the end of US support to offensive operations in the war in Yemen, including relevant arms sales – a pointed reference to Saudi Arabia.[4] However, censuring a country with which the US has enjoyed close relations over its military intervention is one matter, and the extent to which the US is still able and willing to assert its influence in other armed conflicts remains to be seen.

Military interventions as foreign-policy tool

The Armed Conflict Survey 2021 reports that military interventions by major geopolitical powers have taken place in armed conflicts as diverse as those in Afghanistan, the Central African Republic (CAR), Iraq, Libya, Nagorno-Karabakh, the Sahel, Somalia, Syria, Ukraine and Yemen. What constitutes a 'major geopolitical power' is subjective, and the criterion used in this report is to include the wealthiest states (per the G20) that have mounted

Table 1: Major geopolitical powers participating as conflict parties, either directly or through local proxies and sponsored actors, in third parties' wars			
2011		**2020–21**	
Armed conflict	**Interventions by major geopolitical powers**	**Armed conflict**	**Interventions by major geopolitical powers**
Afghanistan	US, NATO International Security Assistance Force (ISAF)	Afghanistan	US (withdrawal under way)
Iraq	US (withdrawal under way)	CAR	Wagner Group/Russia
Libya	France, UK, US	Iraq	Iran, Turkey, UK, US
Pakistan	x70 US drone strikes	Nagorno-Karabakh	Turkey
Yemen	x12 US drone strikes	Libya	Wagner Group/Russia, Turkey
		The Sahel	France, UK (under *Operation Barkhane*)
		Somalia	US
		Syria	Iran, Israel, Russia, Turkey, US
		Ukraine	Wagner Group/Russia
		Yemen	Iran (in support of the Houthis), Saudi Arabia

Source: IISS analysis

military interventions in armed conflicts, such as France, Russia, Saudi Arabia, Turkey, the United Kingdom and the United States. To feature balanced assessments of the wars in Yemen and Syria, military interventions by Iran and Israel are also covered in this essay.

Military interventions are understood here to involve sustained military operations in which the state's armed forces fight independently, augment or fully supplant the combat power of one or more warring factions. These interventions feature expeditionary forces in declared deployments or combat operations conducted from afar with stand-off weapons and can include both declared and undeclared operations. They are distinct from dedicated training or peace-support missions, and from the sale of military equipment, although they may encompass such activities.

Changing Western interventions

Military interventions in 2020 and early 2021 by Western states reflect trends that began after the 9/11 attacks, with Western armed forces deployed alongside local partner states in operations against Islamist armed groups. However, the nature of the threat – and the nature of interventions – has changed. In 2019 the ISIS 'caliphate' in the Middle East was defeated and evicted from the territory it held by an international coalition of intervening

powers, while the Sahel has grown in importance as a locus of Western military intervention against ISIS-affiliated groups. Moreover, the US will withdraw its armed forces from Afghanistan in 2021.

Exhaustion now characterises US domestic discourse around the utility and wisdom of sustaining large military interventions abroad. As large military counter-terrorism missions decrease, the US engagement in such operations is through its special forces, the training of local security partners and, in some instances, airstrikes by inhabited and uninhabited aerial vehicles (UAVs).[5]

The UK and France remain the most extrovert of Europe's military powers. The UK is substantially less engaged in military interventions compared to a decade ago, but the Royal Air Force (RAF) remains in Iraq via *Operation Shader* (part of *Operation Inherent Resolve*), which marked its sixth year in 2020 and involves *Typhoon* aircraft conducting airstrikes against ISIS targets.[6] In the Sahel, France's military leads the multi-state *Operation Barkhane*, which also entered its sixth year in 2020. French forces are headquartered in N'Djamena, Chad, and mount operations against Islamist armed groups in cooperation with partner states organised under the G5 Sahel group (Burkina Faso, Chad, Mali, Mauritania and Niger). The US and UK militaries have also contributed to training the armed forces of Sahelian countries.

Russia's and Turkey's many-fronted interventions
Russia and Turkey have recently adopted more assertive stances, intervening in conflicts close or contiguous to their borders, but occasionally stretching further afield (Russia in Syria and the CAR; Turkey in Libya). Rivalry between Russia and Turkey has also shaped their interventions in Nagorno-Karabakh and Syria.

Irrespective of their specific motivations, Russia's military interventions are all underpinned by an extrovert foreign policy unafraid of challenging or breaching international norms to accrue influence in countries Moscow deems strategically important. Russia has displayed strategic flexibility by pursuing different kinds of intervention depending on its goals and the conflict in question. In Syria, it opted for an overt intervention, deploying a military task force in 2015 that remains in action, as well as using an air base in Latakia and a naval base in Tartus. Conversely, in Ukraine's Donbas region, the ongoing Russian intervention has been conducted in a superficially deniable way to allow Moscow to undermine Ukrainian sovereignty.[7] Russia has used private (Russian) military company Wagner Group in the CAR since 2018, supplementing it in 2020 with the deployment of at least 300 Russian military instructors.[8] Wagner Group personnel have also deployed to Libya, although this intervention has not shaped the Libyan (or CAR) conflict as decisively as those in Syria or Ukraine.

Across the Black Sea from Russia, the Turkish military has also become increasingly interventionist across several fronts to accrue influence in ongoing armed conflicts or to pursue the Kurdistan Workers' Party (PKK). In Syria and Iraq, Turkey continued its long history of cross-border military operations against the PKK and its affiliates, with *Operation Claw-Eagle* in Iraq comprising ground and air operations in 2020 and 2021. By deploying land, air and naval forces to Libya in January 2020 in support of the Government of National Accord (GNA), Turkey stepped up its interventionist ambition, driven by the desire to bolster its future claims on Libya's natural resources and shore up its influence in the Mediterranean Sea. This intervention has placed Turkey in opposition to General Khalifa Haftar's Libyan National Army (LNA), which receives support from Russia and France. In Nagorno-Karabakh, Turkish support, in the form of UAVs and intelligence, enabled Azerbaijan to mount a successful offensive against Armenia in 2020.

As of February 2021, Russia and Turkey do not appear to be experiencing intervention fatigue. Some of their interventions are relatively recent, and neither country has deployed a very large land army abroad that would require maintenance, instead using various combinations of airstrikes, contractors, local allies, task forces and other methods to reduce risk and offset the material costs of deployments. Intervention fatigue may develop in the future, but for now, Russia and Turkey remain enthusiastic armed-conflict interventionists.

The interventions of Iran, Israel and Saudi Arabia
Middle Eastern armed conflicts remain characterised by high levels of external intervention that have exacerbated key regional inter-state rivalries, notably those that pit Iran and its local partners against both Saudi Arabia and Israel. Competition is especially intense between Tehran and Riyadh, with each viewing the other's influence in the Middle East conflict zones in zero-sum terms.

As part of its campaign for greater regional influence, over several years Iran has expanded its involvement in armed conflict across the region, notably in Iraq, Syria and Yemen. Tehran has sponsored local partners and allies, often augmenting their capabilities with deployments of Islamic Revolutionary Guard Corps (IRGC) Quds Force personnel. As explained in the IISS Strategic Dossier *Iran's Networks of Influence in the Middle East*, Iran employs a mix of ideological, strategic, political and logistical links to a myriad of non-state actors, but 'Tehran has made no attempt to formalise the status of any of these relationships or the network as a whole'.[9] It persisted with this approach in 2020 and early 2021 despite the killing of its main strategist, Quds Force commander General Qasem Soleimani, in a US airstrike in January 2020. Iran's rivalries with Israel and Saudi Arabia also continued in this period.

Israel's intervention in Syria is driven by a defensive calculation that Iranian influence so close to its borders must be challenged and eroded, prompting it to maintain the tempo of its offensive air operations against IRGC and Hizbullah targets, with approximately 50 airstrikes in 2020 and more in January and February 2021.[10]

Saudi Arabia's intervention in Yemen's civil war began in 2015 and featured a coalition of

Arab countries fighting on behalf of the United Nations-recognised Yemeni government against the Iranian-backed Houthi movement (Ansarullah). A motivating factor to intervene was Riyadh's concerns that Tehran was consolidating its influence in the country. Over time, Saudi Arabia's intervention ground to a stalemate. In 2019, the UAE withdrew its military contribution to the coalition; in 2021, the US announced the end of its diplomatic support of and arms sales to Saudi Arabia in connection to the Yemen war. International efforts have instead refocused on empowering efforts to broker a political resolution to the conflict. However, Saudi airstrikes against Houthi targets have continued, while Houthi missiles have been fired at Saudi cities and oil-production facilities. Nonetheless, the Saudi stance in Yemen is increasingly characterised by the fatigue of an inconclusive intervention.

Implications for conflict resolution

As a broadening range of states mount armed-conflict interventions, some of them have gained significant stakes in brokering ceasefires and peace deals in pursuit of their national interests, often circumventing or ignoring both Western states and the UN.

For example, the Russian and Turkish governments have sought prominent roles in the Syrian peace processes. At the height of the Syrian civil war in January 2017, Russia convened the Astana talks with Iran, Turkey and the regime of Bashar al-Assad. Repeat sessions of the Astana talks began to overshadow the parallel UN-run Geneva process. While UN mediation teams dealt with the fractured Syrian opposition and tried to deliver progress on humanitarian issues, the Astana talks were elevated to the level of major-power diplomacy, as Russia, Iran and Turkey hashed out their spheres of influence. In February 2021 in Sochi, Russia convened the 15th meeting of the Astana process as the Syrian conflict entered its tenth year.

In the 2020 Nagorno-Karabakh war, Turkey's military (backing Azerbaijan's military offensive) and diplomatic interventions (subsequently playing a key role in the peace negotiations) were designed both to consolidate its role as a military partner to Azerbaijan and to increase its regional influence.[11] Russia also benefited from helping to broker the deal, securing a five-year peacekeeping involvement for 1,960 Russian military personnel, which

will occupy observation points, including in the Lachin corridor that connects Armenia to Nagorno-Karabakh. Major-power diplomacy, conducted at the behest of the warring states' patrons, has allowed Ankara and Moscow to embed their regional influence and define their spheres of influence in the South Caucasus.

The UN is responsible for mediation efforts to resolve the war in Yemen, but the leverage to end the conflict is distributed between the fighting parties and their external sponsors. Saudi Arabia and the UAE are likely to demand concessions in a future peace deal to reflect their military and financial investment during their five-year intervention. To complicate matters further, the two powers favour different approaches to settling the conflict. The Houthis remain potential spoilers, seeing no need to compromise and receiving continued support from Iran, which is unlikely to end during attempted peace talks.

The presence of powerful intervening states has implications for multilateral bodies involved in conflict resolution. The Syrian case has highlighted the setbacks faced by the UN Security Council (UNSC) as a forum for ending armed conflicts, with Russia repeatedly using its veto to protect Assad's regime and to continually block resolutions calling for investigations into the latter's use of chemical weapons. Regional conflict-resolution bodies are also affected, particularly when key member states are involved in the fighting. The Organization for Security and Co-operation in Europe (OSCE) is a pertinent example. While it remains a platform for managing the Nagorno-Karabakh and Ukraine conflicts, member states Russia and Turkey can exert their influence in accordance with their national priorities. In Ukraine, Russia agreed to the remit of the OSCE Special Monitoring Mission (SMM). However, Moscow would never endorse an OSCE mission that runs contrary to its national interests in the country. In Nagorno-Karabakh, although the OSCE has kept talks going for 30 years, Turkey and Russia were able to sideline the process when pursuing their 2020 ceasefire agreement.[12]

Outlook

In an era of intensifying inter-state competition, the evolution of armed-conflict interventions by powerful states is an important trend to follow. The evidence so far suggests that there is a significant expansion in the number of powerful countries that are willing and able to intervene, albeit with varying outcomes.

Intervention fatigue has set in for Saudi Arabia in Yemen due to the fracturing of its coalition, the loss of US support and the failure to secure a decisive outcome. Other intervening powers seem to have learned valuable lessons from observing the US-led interventions in Iraq and Afghanistan, which involved large deployments on the ground. Russia has so far avoided these circumstances in its own interventions, no doubt also drawing on the wisdom of the Soviet Union's earlier failed intervention in Afghanistan. Turkey meanwhile appears to have mounted a relatively quick intervention in the Nagorno-Karabakh war, although its Libya intervention may yet prove inconclusive given the complexity of the conflict and the involvement of multiple external players. Its interventions in Iraq and Syria mark the continuation of its long-standing and intractable war against the PKK, to which it appears committed for the long term.

The prevalent trends suggest that the geopolitical conditions could prompt yet more major geopolitical powers to become interventionist. China remains prominently absent from the list; despite its history of border wars, it lacks substantial experience in expeditionary warfare in either the modern or the imperial era, having avoided waging colonial warfare far outside its immediate environs. India is also absent: aside from fighting Pakistan over the disputed Kashmir, its only precedent is its failed intervention in Sri Lanka's civil war in the 1980s. While China and India both contribute personnel to UN peacekeeping missions, they seem to lack a nascent appetite for mounting interventions in pursuit of national objectives. It is difficult to hypothesise credible circumstances in which this might change. For the sake of conjecture, if Chinese or Indian troops were sent to stabilise a future deterioration in the security of Afghanistan or Myanmar, current evidence would point more to involvement via a UN mission than through unilateral action.

A more credible scenario involving the unilateral deployment of Chinese forces would be to protect and secure Chinese nationals and economic investments in Africa, perhaps using China's military base in Djibouti, or possibly to assist Pakistan against future security threats to Chinese-funded infrastructure projects there.

Germany and Japan continue to face considerable domestic restraints to deploying even in multilateral missions that may face combat. Australia is engaged in a public debate over whether its military would intervene in a hypothetical war involving China, Taiwan and the US, but this discussion is worst-case speculation and scenario planning, not policy. The unofficial club of geopolitically powerful and wealthy states intervening in armed conflicts in pursuit of national goals is likely therefore to remain selective.

A final variable concerns the nature of intervention itself. The rising ubiquity of uninhabited combat vehicles on land, sea and air may change the cost calculus of interventions for militaries that can afford sufficiently sized formations of these technologies and develop practical doctrines to deploy them alongside inhabited platforms and traditional military formations. Another trend is the increasing use of state-backed private military companies to intervene in conflict-riven countries to secure political and economic influence alongside or on behalf of their client.[13] Russia's use of the Wagner Group to test the waters in the CAR and Libya conflicts serve as examples, and Libya's conflict has also featured mercenaries recruited by Turkey from armed groups it supported in Syria. At the height of their interventions in Iraq and Afghanistan, the US and UK relied extensively on private military contractors to supplement their armed forces. The ways in which contractors are used in future interventions may yet evolve in different directions. The range of powerful countries choosing to engage their services may also widen. More broadly, the changing geopolitics of inter-state competition will continue to influence both the opportunities and the stakes surrounding armed-conflict interventions.

Notes

[1] Samir Puri, *Fighting and Negotiating with Armed Groups: Strategies for Securing Strategic Outcomes*, IISS *Adelphi* 459 (Abingdon: Routledge for the International Institute for Strategic Studies, 2016), pp. 7–8.

[2] Alexander Cooley and Daniel Nexon, *Exit from Hegemony: The Unravelling of the American Global Order* (Oxford: Oxford University Press, 2020).

[3] The US has not abandoned stabilisation entirely, and its Global Fragility Act (2019) restated US inter-agency approaches to assist war-to-peace transitions. See US Department of State, 'Report to Congress Pursuant to Section 504(c) of the Global Fragility Act', 17 September 2020.

[4] White House, 'Remarks by President Biden on America's Place in the World', 4 February 2021.

[5] For instance, in Somalia, US Africa Command (AFRICOM) reported that it had conducted an airstrike against an al-Shabaab compound in January 2021, which followed 52 US airstrikes there in 2020. See AFRICOM, 'US Africa Command Conducts Strikes on al-Shabaab Compound', 2 January 2021; and Harm Venhuizen, 'US Airstrikes in Somalia Continue at Rapid Pace Even After Force Relocation', *Military Times*, 26 January 2021.

[6] RAF, 'Six Years of Operation Shader', 29 August 2020.

[7] See IISS, *Russia's Military Modernisation: An Assessment* (London:

IISS, 2020), pp. 28–33. Moscow officially denies responsibility for the fighting in the Donbas, despite evidence that Russian soldiers have been heavily involved since the outbreak of the war in 2014. The Russian armed forces have a clear interest in the fighting in east Ukraine, as demonstrated by the Russian military build-up that took place in March and April 2021 in occupied Crimea and alongside Ukraine's eastern border.

[8] 'Russia's Use of its Private Military Companies', IISS *Strategic Comments*, vol. 26, no. 39, 15 December 2020.

[9] IISS, *Iran's Networks of Influence in the Middle East* (London: IISS, 2019), pp. 8–9, 19.

[10] Israel Defense Forces, '2020 in Numbers: A Whole Year in One Article'.

[11] For context regarding the extent of Turkish military support, see Ece Toksabay, 'Turkish Arms Sales to Azerbaijan Surged Before Nagorno-Karabakh Fighting', Reuters, 14 October 2020.

[12] Pamela Aall, Chester A. Crocker and Fen Osler Hampson, 'A New Concert? Diplomacy for a Chaotic World', *Survival: Global Politics and Strategy*, vol 62., no. 6, December 2020–January 2021, pp. 89–90.

[13] Sean McFate, *Goliath: Why the West Isn't Winning. And What We Must Do About It* (London: Penguin Random House UK, 2020), pp. 132–8.

The Long Aftermath of Armed Conflicts

The protracted nature of internal armed conflicts is well documented: more often than not, civil wars trap countries in cyclical spirals of violence in which conflict relapse is a recurring event.[1] Countries are mired in 'post-conflict' phases for increasingly long periods; the term itself has become more difficult to define because of its overlap with active conflict and the expanded scope of post-conflict interventions. The last few decades have witnessed increasing interventions focused on post-conflict recovery and peacebuilding, often undertaken in parallel with moments of active conflict. This dynamic is evident in Afghanistan and Colombia (see Box 1), and in other long-standing wars in the Sahel, Somalia and Syria, among others.

The aftermath of war presents pressing security, development and humanitarian issues. A strategic analysis of these areas is essential to understand contemporary armed conflicts and identify appropriate responses and paths to durable peace.

The changing nature of armed conflict

The progressive increase in the number of armed conflicts during the Cold War came to a halt with the dissolution of the Soviet Union. A cooperation momentum within the United Nations Security Council led to an intense period of conflict resolution and a parallel decline in the number of wars over the following two decades. This trend was abruptly reversed with the 2011 Arab Spring and

Figure 1: Global conflict trends, 1946–2020

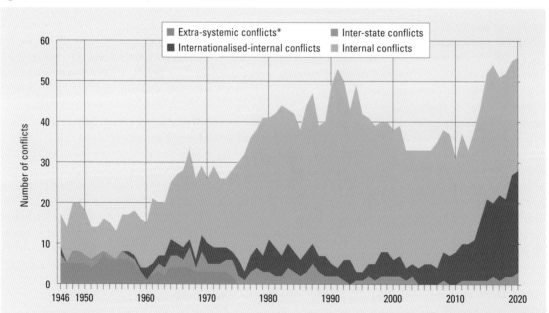

*According to UCDP/PRIO, extra-systemic conflict refers to a confrontation between a state and a non-state actor outside the state territory or system. This category applies primarily to colonial conflicts, the last of which ended in 1974.

Sources: UCDP/PRIO Armed Conflict Dataset version 21.1; UCDP Non-State Conflict Dataset version 21.1; Nils Petter Gleditsch et al., 'Armed Conflict 1946–2001: A New Dataset', *Journal of Peace Research*, vol. 39, no. 5, September 2002, pp. 615–37; Ralph Sundberg, Kristine Eck and Joakim Kreutz, 'Introducing the UCDP Non-State Conflict Dataset', *Journal of Peace Research*, vol. 49, no. 2, March 2012, pp. 351–62; Therése Pettersson et al., 'Organized Violence 1989–2020, with a Special Emphasis on Syria', *Journal of Peace Research*, vol. 58, no. 4, July 2021, pp. 809–25.

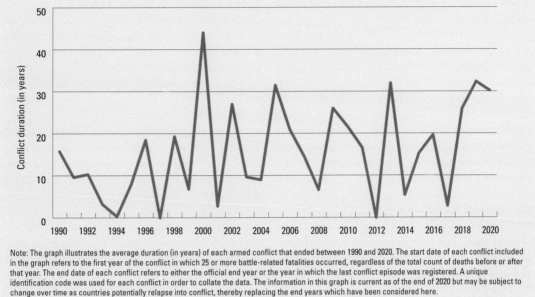

Note: The graph illustrates the average duration (in years) of each armed conflict that ended between 1990 and 2020. The start date of each conflict included in the graph refers to the first year of the conflict in which 25 or more battle-related fatalities occurred, regardless of the total count of deaths before or after that year. The end date of each conflict refers to either the official end year or the year in which the last conflict episode was registered. A unique identification code was used for each conflict in order to collate the data. The information in this graph is current as of the end of 2020 but may be subject to change over time as countries potentially relapse into conflict, thereby replacing the end years which have been considered here.

Sources: IISS calculation based on UCDP/PRIO Armed Conflict Dataset version 21.1; Nils Petter Gleditsch et al., 'Armed Conflict 1946–2001: A New Dataset', *Journal of Peace Research*, vol. 39, no. 5, September 2002, pp. 615–37; and Thérése Pettersson et al., 'Organized Violence 1989–2020, with a Special Emphasis on Syria', *Journal of Peace Research*, vol. 58, no. 4, July 2021, pp. 809–25.

Figure 2: Average duration of armed conflict worldwide, 1990–2020

the ensuing spread of conflicts involving the Islamic State, also known as ISIS or ISIL (see Figure 1). 2020 witnessed the highest number of conflicts since 1945. The conflict landscape also evolved: intra-state confrontations became even more predominant after 2010, especially those featuring third-party interventions, which have tripled in the last ten years.[2] On the other hand, inter-state conflicts have remained very limited since the end of the Cold War.

Today's conflict glut is caused not only by the spike in new conflicts since 2010 and their protractedness (e.g., Libya, the Sahel, Syria, Yemen), but also by the minimal progress made in resolving old ones (Afghanistan, Africa's Great Lakes Region, Iraq, Pakistan, Somalia and Sudan, among others). The time horizon of armed conflicts has also increased, with conflicts becoming more prolonged starting from the early 1970s and particularly after the Cold War. Conflict duration nearly doubled in the space of three decades: while the average duration of conflicts that ended in 1990 was approximately 16 years, in 2020 it was over 30 years (see Figure 2). In turn, the aftermath of conflict has become more protracted as the active phases of conflicts have themselves extended.

The conflict to post-conflict continuum

The intersection between conflict and post-conflict – and their seeming overlap – is primarily explained by increasing conflict recurrence. Of the conflicts that have broken out since the 1990s, a greater share have been recurrent conflicts instead of new conflicts arising in previously peaceful countries. Between 1989 and 2018, nearly half of all conflicts recurred. More than 90% of recurring conflicts concern the same or similar grievances, highlighting the failure of peacebuilding efforts to address root causes. Conflict recurrence is also explained by the fact that since the end of the Cold War negotiated settlements have become the main modality to end conflict, rather than military victory of one of the warring parties.[3] Although the former have been a positive development in terms of reducing human suffering and economic hardship, they seem to have been less effective in preventing conflict relapse.

Nevertheless, conflict recurrence is not a mere repetition of past conflicts. While grievances may be the same or similar, it may be more accurate to say that armed conflicts transition rather than statically recur. If war is the continuation of politics by other means, then conflicts may manifest either violently or non-violently, and war and peace are interacting manifestations of conflict dynamics.

In this vein, the conflict to post-conflict sequence is part of a non-linear transition between war and peace, where the two may either coexist or alternate. The trajectory of armed conflicts is dotted with frequent overlaps between the pre-, during- and post-conflict phases, which are all part of the conflict cycle. While analytically useful, a division of conflict into phases should be accompanied by the concept of war-to-peace transition, if policy responses and interventions are to be well-crafted.[4]

Overlapping war-making and reconstruction efforts

The non-linear transition between war and peace, including the intersection between war-making and post-conflict measures, is typified by the armed conflicts in Afghanistan and Colombia. Civil wars of a differing nature engulfed the two countries for several decades, and both implemented peace-building and stabilisation measures in parallel (see Box 1). While in Afghanistan the reconstruction has been supported and largely financed by the international community to promote state legitimacy, good governance and development in the country, Colombia represented a laboratory for innovative security and development policy (e.g., disarmament, demobilisation and reintegration (DDR), and urban violence reduction) and legislation (e.g., post-conflict transitional justice) during active conflict.

As in Afghanistan and Colombia, most of the conflicts featured in *The Armed Conflict Survey 2021*

Box 1: Post-conflict interventions during war in Afghanistan and Colombia

Over the past several decades, Afghanistan and Colombia have experienced protracted armed conflicts with varying levels of violence, alternating with non-linear transitions from war to peace, as well as conflict relapse. To different degrees, the post-conflict interventions have undoubtedly achieved some positive outcomes in both countries, although persistent war and violence has frustrated durable peacebuilding efforts over the years.

In post-9/11 Afghanistan, the United States-led military intervention that overthrew the Taliban was followed by protracted insurgencies opposing the Western-backed government for the following two decades. The deployment of a UN peacekeeping force – the International Security Assistance Force in Afghanistan (ISAF), which later became a NATO combat mission – and the US troop surge under the Obama administration did not quell the Taliban insurgency. Neither did negotiation attempts between the Afghan government and the Taliban over the years. An agreement between the Taliban and the US in February 2020 provided for the withdrawal of the latter's forces from the country during the course of 2021, opening the way for the Taliban to make strides in achieving control of Afghanistan.

The trajectory of the war in Afghanistan in the last two decades was accompanied by a parallel post-conflict reconstruction process resulting in one of the largest official development assistance (ODA) expenditures to date: over US$77 billion between 2001 and 2019.[5] The most significant and largest post-conflict development programme in the country, the National Solidarity Programme (NSP), ran between 2003 and 2016 and consisted of over US$1.6bn to establish legitimate governance mechanisms and invest in community-driven development initiatives and infrastructure projects, aimed at generating positive economic and social impacts for rural communities. The Provincial Reconstruction Teams (PRTs), which were civilian–military teams initially set up by the US in 2002 and later taken over by NATO, brought an innovative approach to security governance and reconstruction, promoting local development and good governance with a mix of defence, diplomacy and development. The PRTs' presence at the local level and their emphasis on flexibility was proven to have a critical, if variable, impact on local dynamics.[6] The overall effectiveness of the PRT approach depended on security conditions, on the PRTs' ability to engage with the local population, and on the contributing states' approach and level of funding.[7] While in United Kingdom-controlled provinces civilian-led missions were oriented to support local governance, the US-led PRTs, mostly located in highly unstable areas, saw a predominant military component involved in both combat and reconstruction operations. In Herat province, under the control of the Italian forces, PRT activities were almost exclusively aimed at reconstruction and socio-economic development.

The conflict in Colombia exemplifies an endemic civil war with a largely domestically driven post-conflict

display some post-conflict interventions aimed at reconstruction, a fact that reinforces the evidence for the tight interactions between the active phase of conflict and its aftermath.

The aftermath of war has also become politicised and contentious, as conflict parties instrumentalise the prospect of aid and support. Reconstruction often entails competing visions of how to implement peacebuilding and how to allocate resources. Incumbent governments may use post-conflict efforts as a tool to reinforce their power and legitimacy – something that typically can fuel further violence. In addition, in many cases in sub-Saharan Africa, the nature of the state is far removed from the Westphalian model promoted by Western-sponsored reconstruction efforts: therefore, it is more a case of 'state-building'.

The trajectory of post-conflict intervention

The current use of the label 'post-conflict' and its practical application derive from a particular period in history after the end of the Cold War. The end of the systemic confrontation between the US and the Soviet Union unlocked the resolution of a series of armed conflicts around the globe. Angola, Cambodia, El Salvador, Ethiopia, Mozambique and Namibia are examples of internal armed conflicts that were inextricably tied to the bipolar international order and that, to different degrees, achieved permanent resolution after 1991.[12] This new era of UN Security Council activism also led to novel, but then standardised, approaches to rebuilding countries after war.[13]

and peacebuilding process. Violence peaked in the early 2000s with the Marxist guerrilla Fuerzas Armadas Revolucionarias de Colombia (FARC) on the brink of taking over numerous regions of the country. By then, the country was mired in historical neglect of rural areas, a dramatic surge in coca cultivation and cocaine production, and territorial disputes between guerrillas and paramilitaries. The Colombian state decided to reverse this trend by pursuing a dual strategy: uproot and defeat the FARC and, together with civil society, invest heavily in post-conflict development and transitional-justice initiatives.

The US-supported *Plan Colombia*, which consisted of US transfers of over US$9.6bn in 2000–15, applied high military pressure against the guerrillas. While the bulk of *Plan Colombia*'s budget was allocated to combat narco-trafficking and to counter-insurgency efforts, almost one-third was earmarked to improve socio-economic conditions and deliver humanitarian assistance.[8] Various domestically driven peacebuilding efforts with security and development components were established, aimed at recovering areas under non-state armed groups' (NSAGs) control and reducing violence in urban and rural settings. For instance, since 1995 and for more than a decade, local-level Peace and Development Programmes have been implemented in several regions to reduce violence and build community institutions. Furthermore, in 2007–16, the policy of Territorial Consolidation included recovery, transition and stabilisation of conflict-affected areas through combined civil–

military initiatives in which counter-insurgency goals were complemented by and articulated with socio-economic development and governance.[9]

DDR in Colombia traditionally played a critical role in pacifying certain regions and/or achieving separate peace agreements with specific NSAGs. Since the 2000s, emphasis was placed on reintegration to ensure ex-combatants' progress toward successful reinsertion in society. In 2003–06, over 31,000 paramilitary members from the Autodefensas Unidas de Colombia (AUC) demobilised. In parallel with waging war on the FARC, since the early 2000s the Colombian government also implemented a DDR programme for FARC combatants who decided to desert. By the time a final peace agreement was reached with the group in 2016, the programme had incentivised approximately 19,000 FARC members to abandon the group.

Finally, while still in conflict, Colombia invested in a transitional-justice process to bring justice for victims, hold perpetrators to account and advance reparation and reconciliation. The Justice and Peace Law (2005) was established to guarantee the right to truth, justice and remedy for more than 238,000 war events committed by the AUC – even though few paramilitaries were sentenced.[10] In 2011, the landmark Victims' Law 1448 mandated the legal responsibility of the Colombian state for the recognition, attention and remedy of war victims since 1985. Under this law, over nine million victims have been identified, 88% of which were internally displaced persons (IDPs).[11]

The post-Cold War emergence of peacebuilding (led by multilateral institutions) resulted in an overarching policy focus on addressing the physical and human consequences of conflict. This focus targeted the immediate phase after violence halted, which policymakers labelled 'post-conflict'. The term 'reconstruction' was added to signal the set of actions to be prioritised during this phase. 'Post-conflict reconstruction'[14] was then adopted as an overall formula for economic, social, institutional and security activities to be implemented with the support of international actors.[15] While politics was purposefully left out of this equation – out of respect for sovereignty concerns – the post-conflict reconstruction approach implied that technocratic solutions and the successful execution of programmes in key areas would translate into successful and durable outcomes. The presumption that reconstruction could move forward successfully without considering the dynamics of the concluded war (and the political implications of the aftermath of war) has proven overly optimistic.

A fundamental disconnection took hold between international (i.e., Western) peacebuilding proponents and national elites in recipient conflict-affected countries, especially in Africa. While the former perceive reconstruction efforts as a new social contract, local elites see reconstruction as a discrete phase of war politics. Conflict-affected countries lack the capacity to implement peacebuilding policies and tend to perceive them as disconnected from the country's social and political systems. Furthermore, local elites in countries with endemic state fragility (i.e., where the post-colonial state is perceived as alien and sovereignty is anchored in pre-existing and pre-colonial institutions) may see peacebuilding as just another opportunity for resource extraction and maximisation of political power.[16] Notably, this has been the case for sub-Saharan African elites in conflict-affected countries, who would maintain an interest in preserving some level of state fragility or armed conflict.[17]

The 9/11 attacks on the US marked an inflection point. The ubiquity of transnational terrorism led to the adoption by state actors of a security paradigm anchored on counter-terrorism strategies, to which international institutions also adapted. For over a decade, the fight against al-Qaeda was the prism through which the US and its allies viewed many internal conflicts. With its emphasis on security, the war on terror overran reconstruction and development goals, grossly simplifying them with dangerous consequences. The post-conflict debacle in Iraq that followed the 2003 US–UK invasion was the tipping point of a post-conflict 'fantasy'[18] in which many post-conflict countries pursued the sudden but unrealistic establishment of pro-market-liberalisation institutions and multi-party democracy.

At the same time, multilateral actors (such as the UN and the World Bank) dedicated increasing attention to the sources of state fragility and the scope of post-conflict interventions. The progressive expansion of UN peacekeeping operations to include more robust security mandates and capacity-building functions, among others, is the clearest evidence of this trend. Other actors (including donors, development banks and civil society) spearheaded approaches to address war through integrated diplomatic, security and development efforts. While many of these initiatives are nascent, interventions to address conflict and post-conflict have become more intertwined than ever. Standard approaches that may have been considered 'best practice' were shown to be inadequate in particular cases, while the blurring of the line between conflict and post-conflict also challenged the putative impartiality of international actors in implementing peacebuilding programmes. As a result, expectations are now at a historic low regarding what can be achieved by external actors to address the ravages of war where it has become endemic.

Whither post-conflict?

The last decade witnessed an upward trend in the number and lethality of internal armed conflicts, reaching a record high in 2020. Therefore, there is urgent need to reappraise the different types of interventions that take place in the aftermath of conflict, as well as the timing of these interventions. The current international system is characterised by US–China global competition and there are tensions in several regional theatres: the recent trend of third-party intervention in internal armed conflicts by state actors includes Russia, the US, Turkey, Israel, Iran, Saudi Arabia and the United Arab Emirates, among others. While internal conflicts become more complex, the post-war phase too is characterised by a proliferation of state actors with their own interests.

The overlapping international and domestic dimensions of civil wars – exemplified by Colombia and Afghanistan – invite further reflection on the scope of post-conflict interventions and highlight the need for a conceptual and operational clarification of the 'post-conflict' label. The expansion in scope and mandates of peacekeeping operations has also seen them endure for far longer periods,[19] itself an indicator that the approach to peacekeeping needs to be adapted if it is to offer a proper solution to conflict.

Four factors in particular need to be considered more carefully. Firstly, timing: a prolonged and unstable conflict aftermath can be disaggregated into a short-term or immediate post-conflict phase (for example, following a peace settlement or a military victory), and a more long-term and protracted post-conflict. The policy and operational implications are different for each moment, and the short- versus long-term distinction should be a guiding principle when interventions are conceived. Secondly, a taxonomy of post-conflict typologies may be based on if and how the conflict ended and what is needed next. Conflict and post-conflict phases are often simultaneous, while some conflicts have seen post-conflict interventions take place only once violence

definitively ceased. Thirdly, the way a conflict ends (i.e., either by military victory or by peace agreement) has profound implications for the politics of the post-conflict phase. Finally, the type of investments needed during post-conflict is a key variable for which different strategies must be implemented. For example, the geographic scope of post-conflict may be limited to specific regions or areas, or peacebuilding may need to be implemented at the national level.

Post-conflict is commonly considered a discrete phase – separate from war – in which reconstruction occurs in the absence of violence. Yet contemporary conflicts feature frequent overlap between active conflicts and post-conflict. In turn, the quest for sound policy solutions to stabilise countries and regions and promote development depends on a reassessment of the boundaries and tenets of what post-conflict is and implies. The long aftermath of war requires its own special study that does not borrow too heavily from the classic understanding of peacekeeping and reconstruction policies but instead appreciates that 'peace', like 'war', has its grey areas.

Notes

[1]   See, for example, United Nations and World Bank, *Pathways for Peace: Inclusive Approaches to Preventing Violent Conflict* (Washington DC: World Bank, 2018); Lise Morjé Howard and Alexandra Stark, 'Why Civil Wars Are Lasting Longer', *Foreign Affairs*, 27 February 2018; and Julie Jarland et al., 'How Should We Understand Patterns of Recurring Conflict?', Conflict Trends, Peace Research Institute Oslo, 27 May 2020.

[2]   See 'Interventions in Armed Conflicts: Waning Western Dominance', in IISS, *The Armed Conflict Survey 2021* (Abingdon: Routledge for the International Institute for Strategic Studies, 2021), pp. 16–21.

[3]   Adam Day and David Passarelli, 'Governing Uncertainty', UN University Centre for Policy Research, March 2021, p. 37. See also Sebastian Von Einsiedel, 'Civil War Trends and the Changing Nature of Armed Conflict', Occasional Paper 10, United Nations University Centre for Policy Research, March 2017; Jarland et al., 'How Should We Understand Patterns of Recurring Conflict?'; Paul D. Williams, 'Continuity and Change in War and Conflict in Africa', *Prism*, vol. 6, no. 4, 16 May 2017, pp. 33–45; and Barbara F. Walter, 'Why Bad Governance Leads to Repeat Civil War', *Journal of Conflict Resolution*, vol. 59, no. 7, 31 March 2014, pp. 1242–72.

[4]   See Philippe Bourgois, 'The Continuum of Violence in War and Peace: Post-Cold War Lessons from El Salvador', in Nancy Scheper-Hughes and Philippe Bourgois (eds), *Violence in War and Peace: An Anthology* (Oxford: Blackwell, 2004); Mark Duffield, *Global Governance and the New Wars: The Merging of Development and Security* (London: Zed Books, 2014); Robert Muggah (ed.), *Security and Post-Conflict Reconstruction: Dealing with Fighters in the Aftermath of War* (New York: Routledge, 2009); and Michael Pugh (ed.), *Regeneration of War-torn Societies* (London: Macmillan Press, 2000).

[5]   World Bank, 'Net Official Development Assistance and Official Aid Received (Current US$) – Colombia, Afghanistan'.

[6]   See US Department of State, US Agency for International Development and US Department of Defense, 'Provincial Reconstruction Teams in Afghanistan: An Interagency Assessment', PN-ADG-252, June 2006.

[7]   William Maley, 'Provincial Reconstruction Teams in Afghanistan – How They Arrived and Where They Are Going', NATO Review, Autumn 2007.

[8]   Colombia, National Planning Department, SINERGIA, '15 Años del Plan Colombia' [15 Years of Plan Colombia], 4 January 2016.

[9]   Juan Carlos Palou et al., 'Balance de la Política Nacional de Consolidación Territorial' [Stocktaking of National Policy of Territorial Consolidation], Ideas for Peace Foundation (FIP), Report Series no. 14, September 2011.

[10]   Juan David López Morales, 'Las deudas y aciertos de Justicia y Paz, a 15 años de su creación' [Failure and Success of the Justice and Peace Law, 15 Years After Its Adoption], Tiempo, 28 July 2020.

[11]   Government of Colombia, Unidad Para Las Victimas, 'Registro Único de Víctimas' [Registry of Victims]; See also Colombia,

Ministry of Justice and Ministry of The Interior, 'Ley de Víctimas Y Restitución de Tierras', [Victims' Law and Land Restitution], 2011.

12 The end of the Cold War did not result in these internal conflicts concluding at once or in a similar manner. While some were permanently settled (e.g., Cambodia, Mozambique, Namibia, Nicaragua), some relapsed almost immediately (e.g., Afghanistan, Angola) and others morphed, taking on different dynamics (e.g., El Salvador, Guatemala, the Great Lakes Region, Somalia) and/or entering new phases (e.g., Colombia, Indonesia, Peru, Sudan). Finally, a series of conflicts unraveled in former Soviet territories or spheres of influence (e.g., the Balkans, Chechnya, Nagorno-Karabakh, Tajikistan).

13 The RAND Corporation was among the first proponents of standard approaches to post-conflict reconstruction. See James Dobbins et al, *America's Role in Nation-Building: from Germany to Iraq* (Santa Monica, CA: RAND Corporation, 2003).

14 The term 'reconstruction' as associated with the aftermath of war traces back to the American Civil War. Subsequently, it was embedded in the post-1945 international order through the establishment of the International Bank for Reconstruction and Development (World Bank). However, it is only after the Cold War that 'reconstruction' became a 'hegemonic strategy'. See Colin Flint and Scott Kirsch, 'Introduction: Reconstruction and the Worlds that War Makes', in Colin Flint and Scott Kirsch (eds), *Reconstructing Conflict: Integrating War and Post-War Geographies* (Burlngton, VT: Ashgate, 2011).

15 Barnett et al compile a list of the all the terms coined and adopted by different donors and multilateral organisations to define their engagement to sustain peace. See Michael Barnett et al, 'Peacebuilding: What Is in a Name?' Global Governance, vol. 13, no. 1, January–March 2007, pp. 38–41.

16 It is indicative that Cambodia and Mozambique – both reputedly good examples of practices of transition to peace – have high levels of corruption and impunity, a trend that shows the power of elites in capturing state resources. See Christopher Cramer, *Civil War Is Not a Stupid Thing: Accounting for Violence in Developing Countries* (London: Hurst & Company, 2006).

17 See Jean-Francois Bayart, 'Africa in the World: A History of Extraversion', African Affairs, vol. 99, no. 395, April 2000, pp. 217–67; and Pierre Englebert and Denis M. Tull, 'Postconflict Reconstruction in Africa: Flawed Ideas About Failed States', *International Security*, vol. 32, no. 4, pp. 106–39.

18 Cramer, *Civil War Is Not a Stupid Thing: Accounting for Violence in Developing Countries*, pp. 245–78

19 Von Einsiedel, 'Civil War Trends and the Changing Nature of Armed Conflict', p. 4.

Economic Migration, Forced Displacement and Armed Conflict in a COVID-19 World

Before the onset of the coronavirus pandemic, the world was facing unprecedented numbers of people on the move through voluntary economic migration (orderly and irregular) and forced displacement (refugees, asylum seekers and internally displaced persons (IDPs)). While globalisation, interconnectedness, livelihood inequalities and economic-activity trends have driven economic migration numbers upward, conflicts, violence and recurrent environmental crises have forced greater numbers to flee their homes over the last two decades. Most South–North migrants are in high-income countries, while an even higher proportion of forcibly displaced people are in the Global South. As economic migration has diminished considerably due to coronavirus-related restrictions, forced displacement has continued to increase. The impact of COVID-19 will likely exacerbate current drivers of migration and conflict, and effective global governance will be required to address interlinkages between these drivers and the root causes of people movement in the Global South.

The nexus of armed conflict and people movement

Economic migrants seek to improve their livelihoods by making a voluntary choice to move to another location to match their opportunities with their skills. Forcibly displaced people seek personal safety and leave their places of residence due to conflict, violence or persecution, moving either within their own country to seek safety or crossing borders to seek asylum. Some forced and economic movement may be attributable to climate-related resource depletion, which in turn can trigger armed conflict. For instance, a major drought in Syria in 2009–10 led to massive crop failure and loss of livelihoods that, together with anti-government sentiment and a lack of government response, was among the factors leading to armed conflict and large-scale forced displacement.

As forced displacement and economic migration are governed by different frameworks, distinguishing between them is essential but complicated. Overlap, confusion and complications emerge when irregular economic migrants[1] and refugees move along the same routes (notably within and from Africa towards Europe, and from Central America towards the United States), and when these movements are mixed with climate-induced voluntary or forced movements. Another problem is the difficulties receiving countries face in understanding the difference between economically driven migration and conflict-induced forced displacement, and the fundamental differences between the terms refugee and migrant. This confusion has influenced the articulation of public discourse and ideas regarding how to reconcile the conventional rights of people on the move with national policies and priorities. Often this discourse has contributed to destination countries' defensive and restrictive policy responses, which have involved externalising core aspects of migration management and asylum processing as part of a closed-border approach, combined with support to developing countries receiving displaced people.

Forced displacement and armed conflict are intrinsically linked. All armed conflicts generate some level of forced displacement while all refugee movements and some protracted internal-displacement situations can be traced back to armed conflict. Therefore, solving some of the most intractable conflicts would go a long way towards ending some of the worst displacement crises. A few major conflicts (in Afghanistan, Somalia, Sudan/South Sudan, Syria and Yemen) have produced the majority of the world's forcibly displaced population, most of whom are hosted internally or in neighbouring countries.[2]

Dynamics and governance structures pre-COVID-19

The total number of people on the move by the end of 2019 was estimated at 327 million, of which 82m were forcibly displaced (34m refugees and asylum seekers and 48m IDPs (see Figure 1)).[3] The remaining 245m were economic migrants of whom approximately 180m were of working age, with the remaining balance being children and elderly family members.[4] Forcibly displaced populations have a smaller working-age proportion. In addition, irregular movements of economic migrants are estimated at several million, but exact numbers are difficult to document.

While most economic-migrant workers (111.2m or 67.9%) are employed in high-income countries, recent years have seen an increasing proportion of economic migrants working in middle-income countries as compared to high-income host countries. An Organisation for Economic Co-operation and Development (OECD)–International Labour Organization (ILO) study has suggested that this change could be attributed to economic development in middle- and low-income countries, particularly those bordering countries that produce migrant workers, together with migration policies in high-income countries.[5]

The dynamics of orderly and irregular migration largely follow economic developments in both the origin and host countries, and until the coronavirus pandemic both forms of migration were on the rise amid widening inequality and record-high youth-unemployment levels in most origin countries. However, rising xenophobia and isolationist nationalistic policies in host countries, which show increasing disregard for human rights, have made irregular economic migration more difficult. This is in stark contrast to a concomitant trend to facilitate migration at regional levels (for example via the abolition of visa requirements[6] and expansion of free movement of persons through mechanisms such as the African Union's 2018 free-movement protocol and the new Intergovernmental Authority on Development Free Movement Protocol). Some African governments point to the fact that they have opened their borders and expanded rights while the West has done the opposite. On a more positive note, the European Union and individual member countries have begun providing development resources in support of these genuinely inclusive refugee policies in some African countries as a first step to contain and mitigate the impact of people movement within Africa.

Most European countries continue to close their borders to refugees and economic migrants, even when foreign labour could have a positive impact on domestic economies. Similar trends have been seen in the US. In the face of these dynamics, there has been growing international recognition of the need for better management of economic migration, leading to the 2018 Global Compact for Migration (GCM).

Since 1951, forced displacement has been governed by international instruments. In the years following the adoption of the Refugee Convention, many conflicts were resolved and displaced people found solutions to their plight. However, in the last three decades new armed conflicts have emerged that have not been resolved, including the long-running conflicts in Afghanistan, the Caucasus region, eastern Congo, Myanmar, South Sudan, Sudan, Syria and Yemen. This has led to the numbers of forcibly displaced persons increasing. As there are no eminent solutions, they face long-term livelihood challenges and are often hampered by exclusive and restrictive policy environments in asylum countries, leading to costly humanitarian dependency as opposed to enhanced self-sufficiency. A combination of nationalistic policies, dwindling official development assistance (ODA) resources and institutional and organisational resistance to change has meant that mitigation efforts have been insufficient, highlighting that the system is unsustainable and lacks global institutional mechanisms linking forced-displacement issues with conflict resolution.[7] Some of these challenges began to be addressed from 2015, notably spurred by the magnitude of the Syrian crisis.

The Global Compact on Migration (GCM) and the Global Compact on Refugees (GCR)

The GCM provides the first global framework for migration with the main objective to support international cooperation to address migration challenges. Its non-binding nature, and the fact that not all countries have signed up, has been a challenge to its implementation. The GCR in turn has a comprehensive and development-oriented vision, introducing a focus on preparedness, prevention and localisation. It is seen by many of the signature countries as an important step towards real change. Despite its non-binding nature, implementation is advancing, with real breakthroughs hampered by a lack of progress in achieving the central goal of agreement on burden and responsibility sharing.

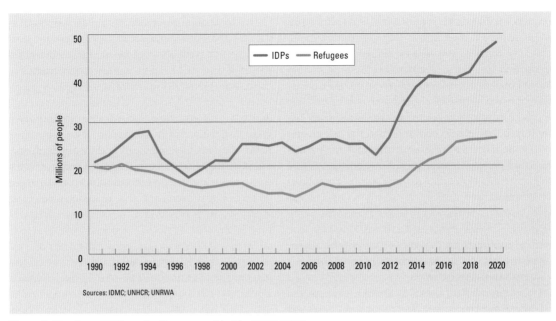

Sources: IDMC; UNHCR; UNRWA

Figure 1: Number of IDPs and refugees worldwide, 1990–2020

Substantial development efforts by the World Bank and the EU were combined with a growing understanding of the need to broaden the governance mechanism towards a new approach, culminating in the 2018 Global Compact on Refugees (GCR).

COVID-19's impact on human mobility and armed conflict: Rethinking global governance and solutions

For people on the move, the coronavirus pandemic has created disproportionate health, economic and safety challenges by exacerbating pre-existing problems and stifling economic opportunities. The pandemic has also had a direct impact on national and international ability to provide health services, with particular impact on low-income countries that are affected by conflict and with weak capacity. The pandemic has also caused an unprecedented global economic recession, leaving 115m people in extreme poverty – the worst setback in a generation[8] – and hampering livelihood opportunities across the globe, particularly in low- and middle-income countries and for the most vulnerable economic migrants and forcibly displaced people. In this way, COVID-19 further widened pre-existing inequality gaps. This is likely to expand mobility pressure and drive people to migrate at a greater risk, despite restrictions on movement and, at least in the short term, declining demand for migrant work. The pandemic

has provided governments with a convenient reason to close borders to refugees and migrants, which has also restricted opportunities for people to seek asylum.

Regarding the pandemic's long-term impact on economic migration, economic considerations may carry the day: irregular migration may pick up again as travel restrictions are gradually lifted. The socio-economic consequences of the pandemic have been severe in many developing countries, so it can be assumed that increasing numbers of people will seek to move. As vaccination coverage progresses (albeit with slower progress in the Global South) and the pressure from conflicts and unresolved inequality between the Global North and South persists, both forced and economic movements will increase again, likely with even higher risks. It is evident that COVID-19's impact on conflict, violence and war will continue to be significant; so too will be the impact of conflict on forced displacement and economic migration.

The coronavirus pandemic has impacted global efforts to govern people movements, leading to reduced demand for legal migrants amid declining economic activity. As mentioned above, the demand is likely to increase in the future with calls to stimulate economic recovery. This context will emphasise the need for operationalising the GCM. The pandemic has had a negative impact on GCR implementation, with reduced political focus on its implementation and fewer ODA resources available for burden and responsibility sharing. The pandemic has shown that drastic measures to close borders, societies and economies can be taken, albeit on a temporary basis. It should then also be possible to make drastic changes in approaches to mobility, in order to effectively operationalise the full visions of the GCR and GCM, even if this calls for permanent and controversial change. An important feature of such change would be a much stronger emphasis on localisation.

A localisation approach to aid is proposed as part of the 2030 Sustainable Development Goals (SDGs), the New Way of Working,[11] and indeed the GCR and GCM. There is growing international consensus – reflected in reforms to UN peace architecture – that ODA should be implemented through and by local structures.[12] A localisation approach would improve aid efficiency by supporting national ownership and local capacities and improving sustainability and protection of human rights while reducing the pressure on forced and irregular economic movements. This approach would cost

The vicious cycle of people movement, socio-economic trends, armed conflict and the coronavirus pandemic

To understand fully how the pandemic has impacted upon people movement, socio-economic trends and armed conflict, it is important to look at how these issues influence each other. Figure 2 provides an illustration of this. It highlights how the pandemic reinforces and multiplies these elements and which mitigation measures are required. The listed fragility and conflict triggers represent socio-economic and developmental trends, and are therefore impacted upon by international-aid architecture. The figure emphasises the importance of the interconnectedness of each of the individual parts and the need for forward-looking trend analysis.

The most important COVID-19-induced dynamic related to the movement of people is that while economic migration has reduced, forced displacement continues to increase as old conflicts linger and new ones emerge. This stimulates the vicious cycle by which an economic slump in the Global South generates more conflict; conflicts produce more forced displacement; and the economic slump increases the propensity for economic migration, which is stifled by border-crossing restrictions. All these factors add pressure on people movement.

Poor governance, inequality, poverty, exclusion, human-rights abuses and the slow and sudden onset of climate-related disasters are threat multipliers, key conflict drivers and root causes of forced displacement and sometimes economic migration.[9] People movement can be both a result of conflict drivers and a trigger for more conflict. The coronavirus pandemic exacerbates conflicts by increasing social and economic vulnerability, which in turn impacts upon these conflict

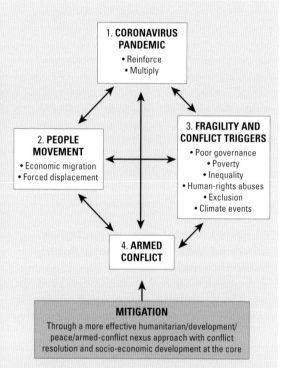

Figure 2: Impact implication matrix

drivers, leading to increases in forced displacement. The pandemic-induced economic slump further incites people to migrate for economic reasons. Therefore COVID-19 also has an indirect impact on community tension and migration. The pandemic has led to a reduction in economic-migrant remittances, thereby increasing poverty in middle- and low-income countries and indirectly impacting conflict propensity. These developments risk leading to further exclusion, with forcibly displaced people facing deeper poverty (adding to grievances and tension) and conflict propensity.[10]

less than mitigation efforts implemented in developing countries by external agencies. It could also reduce conflict drivers in some affected regions. The national and international response to COVID-19 has made it clear that localisation is crucial to achieving results. However, it has also further highlighted that international-aid architecture is incredibly resistant to such change. Localisation is indirectly linked to conflict dynamics and peacebuilding. The UN peace architecture continues to focus on armed-conflict resolution while the impact of the pandemic has inspired further emphasis on preventive efforts. These new efforts focus on national ownership and leadership, a theme that links to the SDGs given the role of inequality and exclusion as drivers of conflicts; political buy-in from member states and links to the World Bank's new 'fragility, conflict and violence' approach; and conflict sensitivity in response to COVID-19's seismic secondary impacts.[13]

The historic shock of the Second World War led to the UN Charter and other frameworks to secure global peace. The COVID-19 shock could similarly be inspiration for a new charter with a smarter multilateral approach to securing greater equality and climate solutions, preventing armed conflicts and addressing challenges faced by people on the move.

Conclusion

The main concerns for the future are how and to what extent the coronavirus pandemic will continue to exacerbate armed conflict and related forced displacement, as well as influence South–North and South–South irregular economic migration. This analysis has highlighted two interrelated narratives that are central to the future trends of people movement and armed conflict. One concerns economic development and people-movement policies in the Global North. The other concerns the need to build a new impetus for poverty alleviation and conflict prevention and resolution in the Global South.

Regarding the pandemic's long-term impact on people movement and armed conflict, it is reasonable to conclude that COVID-19 is here to stay in one form or another, and its impact level will stabilise over the coming years. The global economy will also have to adjust to the new normal. Wealthy countries will potentially need a larger migrant workforce to regenerate their economies. While this was the case before the pandemic, it will be even more important as part of the coming economic rebound. However, this need is at odds with nationalistic-driven restrictions in the Global North. In the long term it is likely that economic considerations will take priority. The likely result is differentiated and selective economic migration along geographic and cultural-historical proximity lines, which would increase fragility, frustration and economic-migration pressure in the Global South. Countries in the Global South will need external support to mitigate the impact of the pandemic on poverty and inequality, which in turn would contribute to the prevention of new armed conflicts and to solutions for ongoing struggles.

COVID-19 is an entirely new entity as well as a multiplier of existing weaknesses and drivers, presenting new opportunities and challenges. It exposes existing economic inequalities and system deficiencies to an extent that has not been seen before, and highlights the need for fundamental corrective action, including through localisation approaches.

The centre of gravity for mitigation efforts may need to be pursued in the Global South, which is home to most armed conflicts and most of the world's forcibly displaced people, as well as a growing destination for migrant workers. Minimising conflict-induced forced displacement and reducing the propensity for irregular economic migration will require building political will for an agreement on burden- and responsibility-sharing that addresses both forced-displacement and economic-migration challenges and opportunities. It will require a redoubling of efforts to combat inequality between the Global South and Global North. A state-led, global-systems change that improves approaches to humanitarian development, peace and armed conflict – including conflict prevention and resolution and the full implementation of global frameworks for refugees and migration – would have a positive impact on such efforts. This change is of geopolitical importance: if support to the Global South is not provided, the lasting effects of COVID-19 will lead to further conflict and war, generating additional forced displacement and irregular economic migration that will increase instability at the global, regional and national levels.

Notes

1   For this essay, defined as movement that 'takes place outside the laws, regulations, or international agreements governing the entry into or exit from the State of origin, transit or destination'. See International Organization for Migration, 'Key Migration Terms', 2011. It is important to note that the phenomenon of irregular migration refers to both the movement of people in an undocumented fashion, and irregular migration flows.

2   World Bank, *Forcibly Displaced: Toward a Development Approach Supporting Refugees, the Internally Displaced and Their Hosts* (Washington DC: World Bank, 2017), p. 88.

3   IDPs estimates vary across sources. According to the Internal Displacement Monitoring Centre (IDMC), there were more than 50.9m IDPs in 2019, considering conflict and environment displacements. See IDMC, '2020 Internal Displacement', Global Internal Displacement Database.

4   See Migration Data Portal, 'Types of Migration: Irregular Migration', 2020; Tijan L. Bah et al., 'How Has COVID-19 Affected the Intention to Migrate via the Backway to Europe', Policy Research Working Paper WPS9658, World Bank Group, 12 May 2021; and UN High Commissioner for Refugees (UNHCR), 'Global Trends in Forced Displacement – 2020', UNHCR Flagship Reports, 18 June 2021.

5   OECD and ILO, How Immigrants Contribute to Developing Countries' Economies (Paris: OECD Publishing, 2018).

6   European Migration Network, 'Impact of Visa Liberalisation on Countries of Destination: Synthesis Report for the EMN Study', March 2019.

7   Niels V. S. Harild, 'Keeping the Promise: The Role of Bilateral Development Partners in Responding to Forced Displacement', Evaluation, Learning and Quality Department, Ministry of Foreign Affairs, Denmark, May 2020; and UNHCR, 'Outcomes of the Global Refugee Forum 2019', Global Refugee Forum 2019.

8   Tara Vishwanat, Arthur Alik-Lagrange and Leila Aghabarari, 'Highly Vulnerable Yet Largely Invisible: Forcibly Displaced in the COVID-19-induced Recession', Joint Data Center on Forced Displacement, 20 November 2020; and European Migration Network, 'Impact of Visa Liberalisation on Countries of Destination: Synthesis Report for the EMN Study', European Commission, March 2019.

9   Hartwig Schafer, 'The Drivers of Conflict: Where Climate, Gender and Infrastructure Intersect', World Bank Blogs, 5 March 2018.

10 Dilip Ratha et al., 'Migration and Development Brief 34: Resilience: COVID-19 Crisis through a Migration Lens', (Washington DC: KONMAD-World Bank), 2021); and Maha Kattaa, Tewodros Aragie Kebede and Swein Erik Stave, 'Impact of COVID-19 on Syrian Refugees and Host Communities in Jordan and Lebanon', International Labour Organization, 2020.

11 UN Office for the Coordination of Humanitarian Affairs, 'The New Way of Working', 10 April 2017.

12 See, for example, Global Taskforce of Local and Regional Governments, UN Development Programme and UN-Habitat, 'Roadmap for Localizing the SDGs: Implementation and Monitoring at the Subnational Level', June 2016; UNHCR, 'The Sustainable Development Goals and the Global Compact on Refugees'; and International Organization for Migration, 'Global Compact for Migration'.

13 Paige Arthur, Céline Monnier and Leah Zamore, 'The New Secretary-General Report on Peacebuilding and Sustaining Peace: Prevention Back on the Agenda', Centre on International Cooperation, New York University, 10 September 2020.

CONFLICT REPORTS

An Afar Special Forces fighter among the debris of houses damaged in the village of Bisober, Tigray Region, Ethiopia

1 Americas

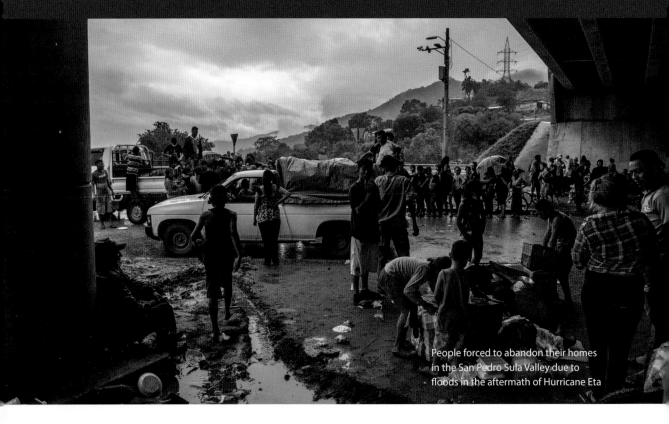

People forced to abandon their homes in the San Pedro Sula Valley due to floods in the aftermath of Hurricane Eta

Overview

The Americas' conflict landscape is characterised by grey zones between organised crime and political violence. Multiple criminal groups fight each other and the government, largely driven by competition over lucrative illicit economies, while increasingly challenging the state's territorial control and monopoly on the use of force. They try, and often succeed, to infiltrate state institutions and influence politics, using intimidation and violence but also electoral votes they control as bargaining chips. In some cases, they also play a quasi-state role, providing goods and services and ensuring basic governance in their areas of control. This was in full display during the coronavirus pandemic, with gangs across the region enforcing (or imposing) lockdown measures, distributing essential goods and personal protective equipment, and fixing prices of critical goods. In sum, although the main motivations of conflict are not ideological (with the exception of Colombia and to a lesser extent Brazil), violence is often used for political purposes and to fundamentally undermine public security and ultimately the state's authority.[1]

Conflict is particularly ripe along the transnational drugs routes that stretches from Colombia, South America's coca cultivation and production powerhouse, to the main markets in the United States (through Central America and Mexico), Brazil and (through the latter) Europe. This means that policies in destination markets (especially in the US) directly influence the evolution of conflict. In particular, hardline drug policies promoted by the US

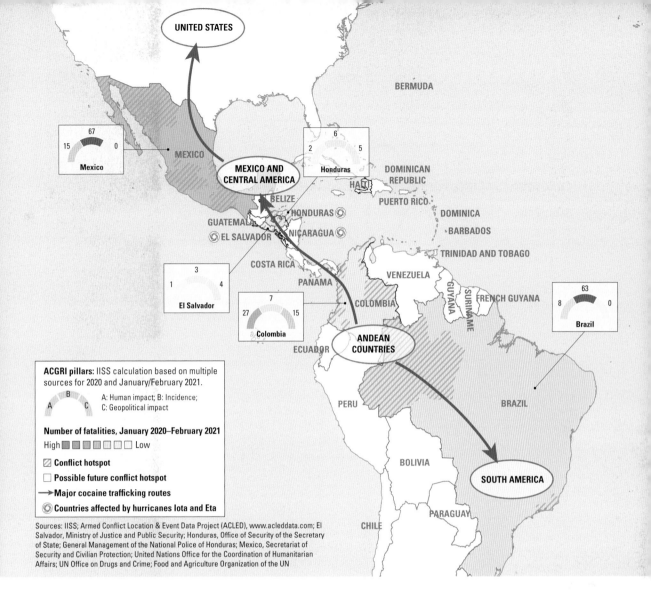

UNITED STATES

BERMUDA

| 67 |
| 15 | 0 |
| **Mexico** |

MEXICO

MEXICO AND
CENTRAL AMERICA

| 6 |
| 2 | 5 |
| **Honduras** |

DOMINICAN
REPUBLIC

HAITI

PUERTO RICO

DOMINICA

BELIZE

HONDURAS Ⓖ

BARBADOS

GUATEMALA

Ⓖ EL SALVADOR

NICARAGUA Ⓖ

TRINIDAD AND TOBAGO

| 3 |
| 1 | 4 |
| **El Salvador** |

COSTA RICA

PANAMA

VENEZUELA

GUYANA

SURINAME

FRENCH GUYANA

| 63 |
| 8 | 0 |
| **Brazil** |

| 7 |
| 27 | 15 |
| Ⓖ **Colombia** |

COLOMBIA

ANDEAN
COUNTRIES

ECUADOR

PERU

BRAZIL

ACGRI pillars: IISS calculation based on multiple
sources for 2020 and January/February 2021.

A: Human impact; B: Incidence;
C: Geopolitical impact

Number of fatalities, January 2020–February 2021
High ▣▣▣▣▣▢▢ Low

▨ **Conflict hotspot**

▢ **Possible future conflict hotspot**

→ **Major cocaine trafficking routes**

Ⓖ **Countries affected by hurricanes Iota and Eta**

BOLIVIA

SOUTH AMERICA

PARAGUAY

CHILE

Sources: IISS; Armed Conflict Location & Event Data Project (ACLED), www.acleddata.com; El
Salvador, Ministry of Justice and Public Security; Honduras, Office of Security of the Secretary
of State; General Management of the National Police of Honduras; Mexico, Secretariat of
Security and Civilian Protection; United Nations Office for the Coordination of Humanitarian
Affairs; UN Office on Drugs and Crime; Food and Agriculture Organization of the UN

and espoused by most Latin American countries
have failed to curb illicit-drugs economies, thereby
perpetuating violence.[2] The nexus between violence, migration and regional instability also raises
the global importance of Latin American conflicts
despite their inherently internal nature, without any
formal intervention by external powers.

Root causes of conflict include the many inequalities (of income, land ownership, access to basic
services, race, geography to name a few) that perme-
ate the region's societies and development models,
compounded by institutional fragilities and governance flaws. The coronavirus pandemic's devastating
health, human and economic toll on the region
simultaneously exacerbated social tensions and
socio-economic inequalities while reinforcing gangs'
legitimacy and further weakening government

effectiveness.[3] This is likely to aggravate violence
and instability in the medium term.

Regional Trends

Continued violence

Conflict continued unabated in 2020 and early 2021,
despite some initial coronavirus-related disruptions
to the activities of criminal gangs.[4] Homicide rates
decreased notably in El Salvador, and to a lesser
extent in Honduras, Colombia, Mexico and Brazil,
but this was likely linked to pandemic-related
mobility restrictions and other factors – including
data-collection flaws as well as arrangements/truces
with gangs – and not indicative of an improvement
in violence trends.[5] Indeed, the decline in homicides
was concomitant to spikes of violence in areas of

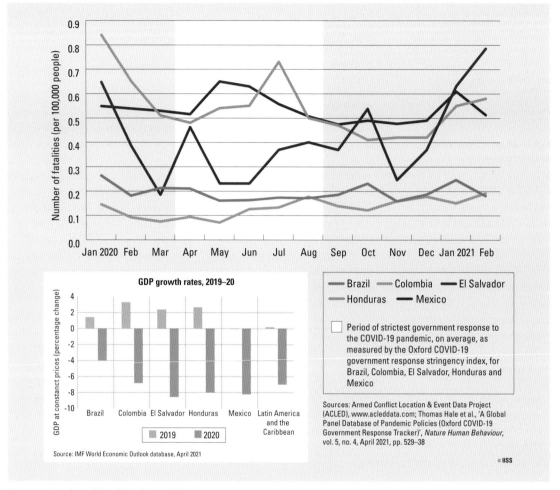

Figure 1: Number of fatalities from violent events per 100,000 people, January 2020–February 2021

contestation and increases in massacres and killings by security forces across the region.

Economic and social upheaval

The pandemic, coupled with hurricanes Eta and Iota which brought havoc in Central America in November 2020, substantially aggravated underlying root causes of violence in the region.[6] Despite most Latin American countries adopting emergency cash transfers to the most vulnerable segments of their populations, poverty rates are estimated to have increased from 30.5% of the regional population to 33.7% in 2019–20, with an additional 22 million people falling into poverty, the worst levels since 2008 (or since 2009 in the case of extreme poverty).[7] This further undid progress to reduce inequalities, as shown by an estimated 3% increase of the regional Gini index.[8] Employment indicators also

worsened, both in terms of unemployment numbers and quality of jobs. Informal workers (including migrants) and youth were among the most affected, boosting the size of the recruitment pool for criminal organisations. Border closures between countries in the region (and with the US) temporarily halted migration, removing a traditional escape valve for countries (notably in Central America) in times of economic hardship.

State inefficiency and growing politicisation of criminal groups

Governments, whose resources and efficiency were significantly stretched by the multiple emergencies, proved increasingly incapable of performing their basic functions. Criminal groups skilfully leveraged the resulting governance gaps to expand and reinforce their territorial control while gaining legitimacy with local populations by providing basic services and essential goods during lockdowns. This reinforced pre-existing trends of politicisation of criminal groups, whose goals to infiltrate or even replace the state became more prominent.

Regional Drivers

Political and institutional

State fragility:

Widespread governance flaws and rampant corruption in the region have historically created a conducive environment for impunity, crime and violence to thrive. The Economist Intelligence Unit's Democracy Index 2020 classified most countries in the region as either flawed democracies (including Brazil, Colombia and Mexico) or hybrid regimes (including El Salvador and Honduras).[9] Institutional limitations have also allowed criminal groups to operate freely and impose their rule in large portions of national territories. In deprived neighbourhoods in Brazil, El Salvador and Honduras, where state governance is poor, criminal gangs impose their own social rules, security measures and illegal taxation schemes. In Mexico, cartels use bribery and violence against public officials to extract favours or impunity. Meanwhile, impenetrable territories in the forest of Colombia create safe havens for coca cultivation and insurgent groups far from the state's reach.

Economic and social

Socio-economic divides:

Violence has marked the modern history of Latin America. Land disputes embedded in strong socio-economic divides between rural and urban areas bolstered insurgency in the 1960s. Peace agreements were eventually reached in Nicaragua (1987), El Salvador (1992), Guatemala (1996) and Colombia (early 1990s and 2016) and guerrillas demobilised, but violence soon re-ignited amid continued economic stagnation. Similar pressing social and economic issues also triggered a surge in criminality in countries hitherto unaffected by armed conflict, including Brazil and Mexico, as many in need turned to illicit economies as a source of income. Despite improvement in the last two decades, poverty levels and inequality remain very high in Latin America. By the 2010s, rapid urbanisation,[10] in a context of inequality and economic deprivation, further catalysed violence.[11] Around 25% of the urban population in

Latin America and the Caribbean is poor, and widespread informality and unemployment (especially for youth) provide the perfect terrain for criminal gangs and illicit activities to thrive.[12]

Drug-trafficking routes and territorial control:

In the late 1990s, drug production and trafficking established itself as a key root of conflict, with certain countries as well as national and transnational criminal groups playing specific roles in the drugs supply chain, further embedding violence in the region. In South America, most notably Colombia, coca cultivation rose dramatically as guerrillas and paramilitaries expanded their territorial control across the country. Honduras, and later El Salvador, increased their role in the transportation of cocaine between South and North America, progressively consolidating their position as transit countries.[13] Mexican cartels assumed control of the final narcotics delivery into the US after the dismantling of the largest Colombian cartels. In Brazil, the second-largest market for cocaine after the US, urban gangs consolidated control over the domestic trade of imported cocaine, mostly from Colombia.[14] As Brazilian gangs grew in strength and connections, they diversified their activities into cocaine trafficking to Europe, Africa and Asia.

Security

War on drugs:

The adoption of repressive drugs policies across the region, predominantly based on increased militarisation and eradication of illicit crops (including controversial aerial fumigation practices) has also fuelled conflict between state forces and criminal groups, while augmenting alienation among parts of the population (notably farmers and the rural poor). Repressive drugs policies also had the unintended consequence of reinforcing the territorial control and economic power of criminal groups by inducing higher retaliation capacity to confront state forces. The so-called war on gangs declared in El Salvador and Honduras in 2003 increased the defensive and offensive capacity of criminal groups, boosting their ability to hold territory and economic power. In Mexico, under the war on drugs declared by President Felipe Calderón in 2006, drug cartels morphed from a relatively contained business with limited geographical scope and low intensity of violence to a fragmented but organised network of criminal groups. This paved the way for increased violent confrontations and ter-ritorial disputes between cartels and against state forces. In Colombia, the implementation of the Plan Colombia in 2000 quickly escalated clashes between the army and guerrillas.[15]

Regional Outlook

Prospects for peace

The complex nature of conflict in the region, where the line between organised crime and political violence is blurred, will continue to weigh down prospects for durable peace.

Peace achieved through negotiation with non-state armed groups will remain unlikely in 2021 given the difficulty of engaging myriad actors with different agendas and loyalties, often in conflict with one another, and the legal constraints of negotiat-ing with criminal actors. In El Salvador, the Bukele administration's continued erosion of checks and balances could enable further negotiations with the Mara Salvatrucha (MS-13) gang, after an alleged truce was brokered in 2020. Even under this sce-nario, however, an escalation of violence in the short term cannot be ruled out as the two sides try to boost their bargaining power.

A continuation of iron-fist approaches to tackl-ing organised crime is likely in Brazil and Colombia amid increased popular concerns about security in the run-up to general elections in 2022 in both countries. Peace in Mexico will remain elusive amid shifting balances of power and areas of contestation among criminal groups.

Escalation potential and spillover risks

The social and economic damage from the coronavi-rus pandemic and hurricanes Eta and Iota in Central America, coupled with an unprecedented political and economic crisis in Venezuela and increasing political instability in the region, point to a worsen-ing conflict landscape and highlight some additional areas of fragility to watch. Climate change, which is particularly impacting the Dry Corridor in Central America, will be another multiplier of conflict in the medium to long term.

Deteriorating socio-economic conditions and increasingly limited fiscal space to provide support for vulnerable populations will drive greater numbers towards criminal groups or migration, in turn creating new business opportunities for illicit actors and threatening domestic and regional sta-bility across Central America, the US border with Mexico, and the border regions between Colombia and Venezuela.[16] Venezuela and Haiti, both mired in deepening political crisis, spiralling crime and collapsing institutions, represent other potential sources of conflict, with important regional spill-overs in terms of migration and violence.

The delayed roll-out of COVID-19 vaccinations in the region underscores the likelihood of additional lockdowns in the year ahead. This will add to exist-ing socio-economic strains and further weaken state legitimacy to the benefit of criminal groups. Likely strong demand for drugs – especially for cocaine in the US and Europe – will continue to drive illegal economies in the region and competition among criminal organisations for territorial control, which will sustain violence.

Geopolitical changes

Developments in the US, Colombia and Venezuela will continue to determine conflict trends in the region. US policies on drugs, access to firearms and migration will remain the main geopolitical influencer. In early 2021, the administration of Joe Biden pledged a US$4 billion four-year aid package to address root causes of migration in the Northern Triangle (El Salvador, Guatemala and Honduras), namely poverty, lack of economic opportunities, cor-ruption and climate-related issues. While this could improve these countries' outlook and governance in the medium to long term, it is unlikely to substan-tially curb migration flows in the short term; in fact, expectations of a more favourable migration policy will probably attract more migrants in the short term. Moreover, the Biden administration's focus on corruption will complicate cooperation with Central American governments given the deterioration in the rule of law across the region in recent years. It is also unlikely that the US will deviate substantially from its traditional repressive drugs policies, as sug-gested by Biden's support for Colombia's decision to restart its aerial coca-eradication programme in early March 2021.

Colombia's role as a global supplier of cocaine makes its security policy another key determinant of the regional violence outlook. While general elec-tions in 2022 may herald some changes in this realm, the incumbent government is almost certain to con-tinue its iron-fist security policy and discourse while it remains in office to retain the support of its core constituency. Lastly, the crisis in Venezuela, with its migrant outflows, its rampant illicit economies and the protection it affords to various Colombian non-state armed groups, will continue to affect dynamics of regional stability. Moreover, the country forms the main theatre for great-power competition in the region, featuring different forms of involvement from China, the European Union, Iran, Russia, Turkey and the US. Substantive progress towards breaking the political impasse and the organisation of free and fair elections seems doubtful in the short term amid irreconcilable negotiation positions from President Nicolás Maduro and acting president Juan Guaidó, a fragmented opposition and low appetite from Biden to use his domestic political capital to push for a negotiated solution. His Venezuela policy will likely resemble his predecessor's, based on sanctions for the Maduro regime and full support for Guaidó.

Notes

1   Armed Conflict Location & Event Data Project, 'Gang Violence: Concepts, Benchmarks and Coding Rules'.

2   Liberal policies on arms possession in the US have been another driver of violence, providing criminal organisations across the border in Mexico easy access to weapons. See Parker Asmann, 'Lack of US Gun Control Provokes Record Bloodshed in Mexico', InSight Crime, 31 August 2019.

3   Latin America has been the region worst affected by the pandemic, against a backdrop of high levels of urbanisation and informality (60%), underdeveloped social-security nets, and fragmented and underfunded healthcare systems. Although home to only around 8% of the global population, it accounted for almost 20% and 30% respectively of total active cases and deaths in the world as of the end of 2020, with Brazil and Mexico ranking second and fourth globally for fatalities. According to the IMF, Latin American GDP contracted by 7% in 2020, the worst performance across the world's regions. See Antonio David, Samuel Pienknagura and Jorge Roldos, 'Latin America's Informal Economy Dilemma', Diálogo a Fondo; Economic Commission for Latin America and the Caribbean, 'Social Panorama of Latin America 2020', March 2021, p. 13; World Health Organization, 'WHO Coronavirus (COVID-19) Dashboard'; International Monetary Fund, 'World Economic Outlook Database', April 2021.

4   When the strongest lockdown measures were in force in El Salvador, Honduras and Colombia (between April and August 2020) and Mexico (in December 2020 and January 2021), significant monthly spikes in conflict-related fatalities (namely battles, explosions/remote violence and violence against civilians, according to ACLED) were reported, signalling the rapid reactional and operational capacity of criminal groups to challenge state authority.

5   A truce was widely alleged to explain the substantial dip observed in El Salvador, where the murder rate halved year on year to 19.7 per 100,000. See Parker Asmann and Katie Jones, 'InSight Crime's 2020 Homicide Round-Up', 29 January 2021.

6   Duncan Tucker and Encarni Pindado, 'When it Rains it Pours: The Devastating Impact of Hurricanes Eta and Iota in Honduras', Amnesty International, 13 December 2020.

7   Economic Commission for Latin America and the Caribbean, 'Social Panorama of Latin America 2020', Graphic 1, p. 15.

8   Ibid, p. 28.

9   Only three countries in the region were considered 'full democracies', while a further three were classed as 'authoritarian regimes'. See Economist Intelligence Unit, 'Democracy Index 2020: In Sickness and in Health'.

10   With 81% of its population living in cities, Latin America is currently the most urbanised region in the world. See Economic Commission for Latin America and the Caribbean, 'Social Panorama of Latin America 2020', p. 16.

11   In 2013, for example, 84% of the 50 most violent cities (including the top 16) in the world were in Latin America and the Caribbean. World Bank, 'Stopping Crime and Violence in Latin America: A Look at Prevention from Cradle to Adulthood', Results Briefs, 17 May 2018.

12   Natalie Alvarado and Robert Muggah, 'Crime and Violence: Obstacles to Development in Latin America and Caribbean Cities', Inter-American Development Bank, November 2018, p. 2.

13   In 2010, Honduras was classified as a major drug-transit country by the United States government, followed by El Salvador in 2011. According to the US Department of State, by 2015, 90% of cocaine on the US market had first transited through the Central America–Mexico corridor. See US Department of State, Bureau for International Narcotics and Law Enforcement Affairs, 'International Narcotics Control Strategy Report, Volume I: Drug and Chemical Control', March 2016, p. 161.

14   Alongside cocaine and marijuana, more recently synthetic drugs have also been part of drug-trafficking operations.

15   Plan Colombia, adopted in 2000, primarily aimed to end the conflict in Colombia by supporting the Colombian armed forces (through funding and training) to eradicate drug trafficking.

16   All seven of Colombia's departments bordering Venezuela have seen the presence of multiple criminal groups. Some of them move across extensive areas on both sides of the border, including Revolutionary Armed Forces of Colombia (FARC) dissident units such as the Second Marquetalia. At least 70% of the National Liberation Army's forces are located in the borderlands. While clashes between dissidents from the FARC, the National Liberation Army (ELN) and the Venezuelan army in Venezuela's border regions and sporadic incursions of the latter into Colombian territory will continue in the year ahead, it is unlikely that political tensions between Colombia and Venezuela will result in a full-fledged military confrontation. See International Crisis Group, 'Disorder on the Border: Keeping the Peace between Colombia and Venezuela', Report No. 84, 14 December 2020.

MEXICO

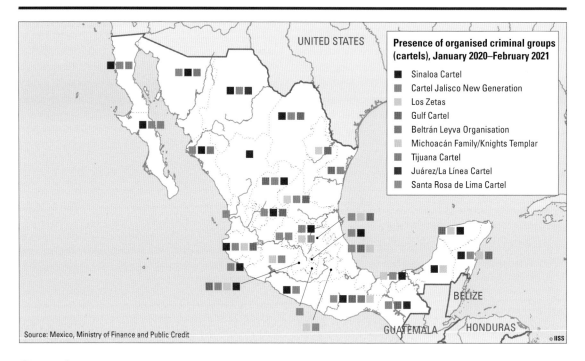

Presence of organised criminal groups (cartels), January 2020–February 2021

- Sinaloa Cartel
- Cartel Jalisco New Generation
- Los Zetas
- Gulf Cartel
- Beltrán Leyva Organisation
- Michoacán Family/Knights Templar
- Tijuana Cartel
- Juárez/La Línea Cartel
- Santa Rosa de Lima Cartel

UNITED STATES

BELIZE

GUATEMALA   HONDURAS

Source: Mexico, Ministry of Finance and Public Credit

© IISS

Overview

Mexican drug-trafficking organisations (DTOs) originated in the 1970s, serving as intermediaries trafficking cocaine from South America to the United States, in addition to producing drugs (primarily marijuana) locally. At the time, operations were largely controlled by the Guadalajara Cartel led by Miguel Ángel Félix Gallardo. After his arrest in 1989 – following the murder of a Drug Enforcement Administration (DEA) agent in Mexico – the territory it had controlled was split between four major DTOs run by Félix Gallardo's closest associates, namely the Sinaloa, Juarez, Tijuana and Sonora cartels, an arrangement that largely persisted for the next 15 years. Drug-related violence began escalating following the 2000 electoral defeat of the Institutional Revolutionary Party (PRI), after seven decades of continuous rule, which undid many existing unofficial agreements between the DTOs and the government. Numerous high-profile acts of violence led President Felipe Calderón (2006–12) to launch the war on drugs in December 2006, triggering a full-scale (ongoing) confrontation between state security forces and the DTOs. Of the 19 DTOs identified by the government, 11 operate in more than one state and two – the Sinaloa Cartel and the Cartel Jalisco New Generation (CJNG) – have a presence in every state of Mexico as well as strong international operations.

Despite restrictions caused by the coronavirus pandemic in 2020, violence showed little respite, with 35,484 intentional homicides recorded (or a homicide rate of 22.6 per 100,000). This represented a modest decrease of 0.4% compared to 2019's record number of absolute and relative homicides in Mexico.[1] Although the decrease reversed the continuous annual increases witnessed since 2014, it cannot yet be established whether it represented the beginning of a structural downward trend akin to the 2011–14 period.

During 2020, the government reinforced its existing strategy of combatting DTOs through the National Guard (GN), a gendarmerie-style force created in 2019 specifically to deal with cartel violence and fulfil a campaign promise by current President Andrés Manuel López Obrador to demilitarise the war against DTOs. The GN was involved in virtually every major operation against DTOs

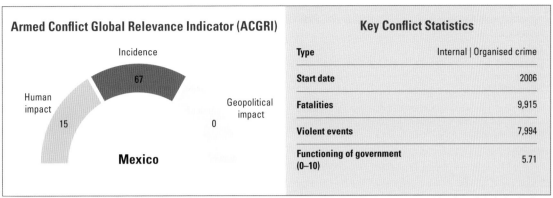

Armed Conflict Global Relevance Indicator (ACGRI)

Incidence
67

Human impact
15

Geopolitical impact
0

Mexico

Key Conflict Statistics

Type	Internal | Organised crime
Start date	2006
Fatalities	9,915
Violent events	7,994
Functioning of government (0–10)	5.71

ACGRI pillars: IISS calculation based on multiple sources for 2020 and January/February 2021 (scale: 0–100). See Notes on Methodology and Data Appendix for further details on Key Conflict Statistics.

in 2020 and by the end of the year had become the second-largest security force in the country.

However, the lack of substantive security advances translated into relatively high public disapproval levels for López Obrador's security policy, which throughout 2020 was among the most consistently poorly rated policy areas.

Conflict Parties

Secretariat of National Defence (SEDENA) – (Army and Air Force)

Strength: 165,500.

Areas of operation: Across the whole country but concentrates its forces in the north and the Pacific region: in Baja California, Chihuahua Coahuila, Jalisco, Guerrero, Michoacán, Sonora and Tamaulipas.

Leadership: General Luis Crecencio Sandoval (head of SEDENA); General Manuel de Jesús Hernández González (head of the air force).

Structure: SEDENA forms one branch of Mexico's two defence ministries. The army is divided into 12 military regions and 46 military zones. The air force is divided into four air regions. The General Staff of National Defence is divided into eight sections, of which the second section (intelligence) and the seventh section (combatting drug trafficking) focus on DTOs.

History: The Ministry of War and the Navy was created in 1821 to supervise the army, navy and air force. In 1939 it was divided to create SEDENA and the Secretariat of the Navy (SEMAR).

Objectives: Provide internal security and fight drug trafficking.

Opponents: DTOs.

Affiliates/allies: SEMAR, GN and special-forces combat group GAIN (Drug Trafficking Information Analysis Group), which is in charge of capturing DTO leaders. Also supported by the National Intelligence Centre (CNI) and the Attorney General's Office, as well as foreign governments through cooperation programmes (e.g. the Mérida Initiative with the US).

Resources/capabilities: Infantry, armoured vehicles and combat helicopters. 2020 budget: US$5.5 billion (approximately MXN 118bn).[2]

Secretariat of the Navy (SEMAR)

Strength: 50,500.

Areas of operation: The country's coasts, divided into the Pacific and Gulf of Mexico–Caribbean zones.

Leadership: Admiral José Rafael Ojeda Durán.

Structure: Divided into General (70%) and Naval Infantry Corps (marines; 30%), which operate in eight naval regions and 18 naval zones (12 in the Pacific and six in the Gulf and Caribbean). The marines' special forces also combat criminal groups in the country's interior.

History: Created in 1821. SEMAR separated from SEDENA in 1939.

Objectives: Defend Mexico's coasts, strategic infrastructure (mainly oil platforms in the Gulf of Mexico) and the environment at sea, and fight piracy.

Opponents: DTOs, particularly those that traffic people through the coasts, from South and Central America, and those that transport drugs via sea from Colombia and Venezuela.

Affiliates/allies: SEDENA, GN and CNI. Cooperates with US Coast Guard at the border.

Resources/capabilities: Fast vessels for interception, exploration and intelligence; supported by naval aviation. 2020 budget: US$1.63bn (approximately MXN 35bn).

National Guard (GN)

Strength: 92,100.

Areas of operation: Across the whole country. The states of Guanajuato, Jalisco, Mexico, Michoacán, Oaxaca and Sinaloa had the highest number of operational coordination regions at the end of 2020.

Leadership: Alfonso Durazo (secretary of public security and citizen protection (SSPC)); General (Retd) Luis Rodríguez Bucio (commander).

Structure: A total of 266 coordination regions expected to be operational by the end of 2021. 200 of these were operational as of 31 December 2020.

History: Began operating in May 2019, by presidential order. The law gave GN personnel the authority to stop suspected criminals on the streets.

Objectives: Reduce the level of violence in the country and combat DTOs.

Opponents: DTOs and medium-sized criminal organisations.

Affiliates/allies: SEDENA, SEMAR, and local and municipal police.

Resources/capabilities: Acquired resources from the defunct Federal Police, including their helicopter teams and equipment such as assault rifles. Relies on intelligence from SEDENA, SEMAR and the CNI.

Sinaloa Cartel (CPS)

Strength: Unknown.

Areas of operation: Headquartered in Culiacán, Sinaloa, but with a presence in all 32 states of Mexico. Outside Mexico, active in Asia, Canada, Central America and Europe. In the US, it has an important presence in California, Colorado, Texas and New York.

Leadership: Historical leader since the mid-1990s, Joaquín 'El Chapo' Guzmán was captured in 2016 and imprisoned for life in the US in 2019. His number two, Ismael 'El Mayo' Zambada García, is in a leadership struggle with El Chapo's sons, Ovidio and Iván Archibaldo.

Structure: Hierarchical organisation, with three sub-divisions: finance/business, logistics for drug transportation and military structures.

History: Preceded by the Guadalajara Cartel, co-founded in the late 1970s by leader Rafael Caro Quintero. In the 1990s, following the peace processes in Central America, the large-scale ground transit of cocaine began. In the mid-1990s, El Chapo became leader of the Sinaloa Cartel, opened routes from Guatemala to Mexico and the Tijuana route, and forged

alliances with the Medellín Cartel in Colombia. Focused for 20 years on cocaine, but now diversifying into heroin, methamphetamine and fentanyl.

Objectives: Control all drugs markets (for cocaine and methamphetamine in particular), including production networks in Colombia, distribution in Central America and Mexico and consumption in the United States.

Opponents: Other DTOs, including the Gulf Cartel, the Tijuana Cartel and the Juarez Cartel. SEMAR, SEDENA's intelligence section and special forces. The US DEA and Defense Intelligence Agency (DIA).

Affiliates/allies: Many subordinate medium-sized and small DTOs, at the regional level, including cocaine-producing partners in Colombia. Partners with many corrupt Mexican government officials. A large number of Sinaloa governors are suspected of supporting the cartel.

Resources/capabilities: High-powered weapons, such as the Barrett M107 sniper rifle and anti-aircraft missiles, and a large fleet of drug-transport planes.

Cartel Jalisco New Generation (CJNG)

Strength: Unknown.

Areas of operation: Headquartered in the state of Jalisco, with a presence in most states, particularly Colima, Guanajuato, Guerrero, Jalisco, Michoacán and Nayarit. It also controls the Pacific ports of Manzanillo and Lazaro Cardenas, where chemicals from China enter Mexico. It has rapidly expanded in the US, where it is thought to have a presence in 35 states and in Puerto Rico.

Leadership: The main leader is Nemesio Oseguera Cervantes, commonly known as 'El Mencho'.

Structure: El Mencho successfully co-opted all regional leaders of the Michoacán Family and the Knights Templar to control the laboratories in the Michoacán mountains.

History: Formed in 2011 in Guadalajara, Jalisco, CJNG initially produced methamphetamine in rural laboratories in Jalisco and Michoacán. In 2012–13, it expanded to Veracruz. Since 2015–16 its influence has grown throughout the country,

thanks in part to gaps left after the government successfully targeted other DTOs (such as the Michoacán Family, the Knights Templar, Los Zetas and the Sinaloa Cartel).

Objectives: Fully replace the Sinaloa Cartel at the helm of Mexico's criminal networks.

Opponents: Sinaloa Cartel, Los Zetas, the special forces of SEMAR and SEDENA.

Affiliates/allies: Demobilised members of the Michoacán Family and the Knights Templar, as well as large numbers of collaborating peasants.

Resources/capabilities: Estimated capital of US$1bn from the sale of methamphetamine and fentanyl as well as the extortion of merchants and money-laundering activities in Guadalajara.

Los Zetas

Strength: Unknown. Hit hard by the government between 2012 and 2016.

Areas of operation: Tamaulipas State, mainly along the border with Texas, as well as Coahuila, Nuevo León, Veracruz, Tabasco and the area along the border with Guatemala.

Leadership: Founded by Heriberto Lazcano, former member of the Mexican army. Since 2013, 33 of its main leaders (including Lazcano) have been arrested or killed in combat by military forces.

Structure: Horizontal, decentralised structure that works as a large business with multiple criminal activities. Unsuccessful at drug trafficking, its cells carry out extortions and kidnappings, collect criminal taxes from merchants and traffic migrants from Central America to Texas.

History: Originally the armed wing of the Gulf Cartel, drawing most of its members from the Mexican and Guatemalan armies. Notorious for perpetrating mass violence against the civilian population and migrants. Between 2010 and 2012, a major SEMAR offensive to dismantle the 'Gulf Corridor' weakened the group significantly. It is the DTO against which the Mexican government has been most successful.

Objectives: Control criminal activity in the Gulf of Mexico states.

Opponents: CJNG, Gulf Cartel and the special forces of SEMAR.

Affiliates/allies: Criminal networks in Tamaulipas State.

Resources/capabilities: Migrant smuggling and criminal taxes on merchants.

Gulf Cartel

Strength: Unknown.

Areas of operation: Operates and controls territories in Tamaulipas State, particularly the border area with Texas, including strategic border cities, such as Nuevo Laredo, Reynosa and Matamoros.

Leadership: The current leader is Homero Cárdenas Guillén. Many former leaders have been killed in combat or detained and extradited to the US.

Structure: Unstable, with fragmented leadership.

History: The second-oldest DTO in the country, smuggling alcohol, weapons and drugs across the US border since the 1940s. After forging a partnership with the Colombian Cali Cartel in the 1990s, the group focused on introducing cocaine to the US market. Los Zetas violently separated from the group in 2010.

Objectives: Smuggle drugs on the Texas–Tamaulipas border and control drug trafficking in northeast US.

Opponents: Los Zetas, CJNG and the special forces of SEMAR and SEDENA.

Affiliates/allies: Closely linked to Tamaulipas State's governors (three former governors have been charged in Texas) and criminal networks.

Resources/capabilities: Many Tamaulipas businessmen support the cartel in laundering money.

Beltrán Leyva Organisation

Strength: Unknown.

Areas of operation: Mainly in the states of Guerrero and Morelos, and the Mexico City–Acapulco highway. The group controls poppy production and the export of heroin from Iguala (Guerrero) to Chicago, IL.

Leadership: Founded by brothers Arturo, Alfredo, Carlos and Héctor Leyva – Arturo was killed in 2009 and the other three were imprisoned, with Héctor dying in 2018.

Structure: Based around vertically organised cells. After the death or imprisonment of the four brothers, seven local criminal groups emerged in Guerrero State: the Ardillos, the Granados, the Independent Cartel of Acapulco (CIDA), the Mazatecos, the Rojos, the Ruelas Torres and the United Warrios (GU).

History: A breakaway group of the Sinaloa Cartel formed in 2008 in Sinaloa before moving to the South Pacific–Acapulco (Guerrero State), Morelos and Mexico State.

Objectives: Control heroin trafficking in the South Pacific and from Mexico to Chicago.

Opponents: Sinaloa Cartel, CJNG and the special forces of SEDENA.

Affiliates/allies: An estimated 100,000 peasants who grow poppies in Guerrero.

Resources/capabilities: Profits from the sale of heroin in the US and from criminal activities such as extortion and kidnapping in Mexico.

Michoacán Family/Knights Templar

Strength: Unknown.

Areas of operation: The surviving criminal cells moved to Guanajuato, Guerrero and Mexico State.

Leadership: Fragmented following the 2015 arrest of Servando Gómez Martínez.

Structure: Organised into independent cells.

History: Gained power by producing methamphetamines, importing chemical precursors from China. Founded by Nazario Moreno Gonzalez in 2005, the organisation's initial recruitment was based on a religious discourse. Between 2006 and 2012, the group built a broad network of collaborators among the population, gained control of a large number of local politicians on the Pacific coast of Michoacán and ran methamphetamine labs in the mountains. However, it was practically dismantled by Mexican government forces between 2013 and 2016. Following the capture of its first leaders, the Michoacán Family became the Knights Templar in 2013–14, under the leadership of Servando Gomez.

Objectives: Control mining and agricultural production (of avocados for export to the US) in Michoacán State; control the port of Lazaro Cardenas (for smuggling the chemical base for producing methamphetamine); and steal fuel in Guanajuato State.

Opponents: Sinaloa Cartel, CJNG, Los Zetas and the special forces of SEDENA.

Affiliates/allies: A large number of collaborating peasants.

Resources/capabilities: The revenue from criminal taxes on many economic activities.

Tijuana Cartel (also known as Arellano Felix Family Organisation)

Strength: Exact numbers unknown, but thought to have regained some strength since 2018.

Areas of operation: A bi-national, cross-border organisation operating between Tijuana, Baja California and San Diego, CA; Los Angeles, CA.

Leadership: Fragmented as Benjamin Arellano Felix and his brothers Ramón, Eduardo, Luis Fernando, Francisco, Carlos and Javier are all imprisoned in California jails.

Structure: Groups of young people either become gunmen or cocaine exporters (middle-class youth who have visas to cross the border). Their leaders are family members.

History: During the 1980s and 1990s, the Arellano Felix brothers controlled the north of the country and transported drugs across the border through tunnels, migrants and people moving on foot or by car.

Objectives: Control drug trafficking from Baja California to California, US.

Opponents: Sinaloa Cartel, the special forces of SEDENA and US intelligence services cooperating with Mexican authorities at the border.

Affiliates/allies: Many people cross the border daily with small amounts of drugs.

Resources/capabilities: Revenue from the cross-border cocaine trade.

Juarez Cartel/La Línea

Strength: Unknown.

Areas of operation: A bi-national, cross-border organisation active in North Chihuahua and North Sonora in Mexico and Southwest Texas; Las Cruces and Albuquerque, NM, and Tucson, AZ, in the US.

Leadership: Founded by Amado Carrillo Fuentes in the 1990s. His brother Vicente Carrillo Fuentes directs it from prison.

Structure: Three local cartels in Ciudad Juárez: La Línea, Los Artistas Asesinos and Los Aztecas, which clash over cocaine shipments to be exported to El Paso, TX.

History: Amado Carrillo Fuentes, the 'Lord of the Skies', orchestrated the smuggling of drugs in small planes at low altitude, which went undetected by radars. In 2009 it began to fight with the Sinaloa Cartel for control of the Central Mexican and the US-highway trafficking routes.

Objectives: Control drugs crossing from Ciudad Juárez to El Paso, and into New Mexico and Arizona, and drug trafficking to northeast US.

Opponents: Los Zetas, CJNG, the special forces of SEDENA and the DEA.

Affiliates/allies: Groups of young people either become gunmen or drugs-exporters (middle-class youth who have visas to cross the border).

Resources/capabilities: The proceeds from drug trafficking.

Santa Rosa de Lima Cartel (CSRL)

Strength: Exact numbers unknown but experienced large-scale arrests in 2019–20.

Areas of operation: Guanajuato; minor operations in neighbouring states including Queretaro and Hidalgo.

Leadership: Founded by David Rogel Figueroa 'El Güero' in 2014 and from 2017 led by José Antonio Yépez Ortiz 'El Marro'. Unclear leadership structure following El Marro's arrest on 2 August 2020 though the organisation is highly family oriented.

Structure: Organised into numerous regional cells. One cell known as the Shadow Group was previously associated with the Gulf Cartel. Many high-level operatives (including financial operatives) are relatives of El Marro.

History: Formed in 2014 as a *huachicolero* (fuel theft) gang in the state of Guanajuato and grew to a fully fledged DTO after 2017 when El Marro assumed leadership, expanding its operations to include drug trafficking, retail drug trade,

kidnapping and extortion. Significantly weakened since 2019 because of the government's campaign against fuel theft as well as conflict with the CJNG, which has contested its dominance in the state.

Objectives: Control the fuel-theft market in the Bermuda Triangle area of Guanajuato as well as supplementary resources through drug trafficking (mainly cocaine) and other illegal activities in that area.

Opponents: CJNG, GN, other SEDENA and SEMAR forces.

Affiliates/allies: Local fuel-theft gangs.

Resources/capabilities: The proceeds from fuel theft and other drug-trafficking revenues. Fuel-theft income has fallen significantly since 2019 and it is believed the group is severely weakened, having possibly lost around 40% of its manpower.[3]

Americas

Conflict Drivers

Political

Institutional corruption and impunity:
Mexico has traditionally suffered from high levels of corruption and impunity, enabled by a permissive political culture as well as lax law enforcement. Mexico ranked 124th worldwide and second worst (only above Venezuela) among Latin America's seven biggest economies in the 2020 Transparency International's Corruption Perceptions Index.[4] Against this backdrop, DTOs have found it easy to bribe or intimidate public officials, particularly targeting municipal-level officials given the lack of protection offered to them and the underfunding and underarming of municipal police forces. An estimated 264 mayors, mayoral candidates and former mayors were murdered by DTOs between 2002 and 2019.[5] Higher-profile officials have also been targeted, including, for example, a district-court judge, Uriel Villegas Ortiz, in June 2020, the first killing of a federal judge since 2016, and the former governor of Jalisco, Aristóteles Sandovla, in December 2020, the highest-ranking public official killed since the drug war began.

Economic and social

Poverty and precarity:
Widespread poverty and precarious labour conditions among Mexico's youth (around a quarter of the population) contributes a constant supply of manpower for DTOs. An estimated 48.8% of Mexico's

population (61.1m people) lived under the national poverty line in 2018,[6] a figure that has not improved significantly since the 1990s and which highlights the poor future prospects for many young people as social mobility is also limited. This bleak economic picture increases the appeal of joining a DTO, as the potential income far outstrips that offered by most legal employment, despite the risk of death or imprisonment. Informal employment is high at 55.8% of the labour force,[7] facilitating money laundering and other financial crimes driven by DTOs.

It is also estimated that around 35–45,000 Mexican children may be involved to some degree with DTOs, usually as lookouts but even as hitmen, while girls are frequently coerced into the sex trade.[8]

Geography:
Mexico's location, situated between the main source of cocaine production (South America) and the main consumption market for all drugs (the US), triggered its emergence as a major drug-trafficking centre. Mexico is also a major drugs producer in its own right, being the largest producer of opium in the Western Hemisphere with an estimated 6% of the global supply (only behind Afghanistan and Myanmar) as well as the second-largest marijuana producer in the world (behind Afghanistan).[9] Mexico is also a major producer of synthetic drugs such as methamphetamine, and a transit route for fentanyl from China, where most of it is produced, into the US.

The so-called Golden Triangle region which encompasses the states of Sinaloa, Chihuahua and Durango is estimated to account for as much as three-quarters of Mexico's cultivated drug production. Jalisco and Michoacán are in turn the primary centres of synthetic-drugs production, leveraging precursor chemicals illegally imported from Asia through the ports of Lázaro Cárdenas and Manzanillo.

International

US drug demand and policy:
The market conditions driving the prevalence of DTOs in Mexico stem from the US demand for illegal drugs (estimated by some sources to be nearly US$150bn annually). DTOs are also able to easily obtain assault rifles and other weapons in the US and smuggle them across the border to Mexico, usually in small but steady quantities which are difficult to detect, in so-called 'ant trafficking'. US drug policy has largely supported the military strategies adopted by successive Mexican governments to combat DTOs. This, in turn, has precluded discussion of potential alternative approaches such as more widespread legalisation of drugs (including some hard drugs), or negotiations between government and the DTOs.

Political and Military Developments

The fight against financial crime

The López Obrador administration considerably strengthened the scope of operations of the Financial Intelligence Unit (UIF) of the secretariat of finance tasked with investigating money laundering and terrorist financing. During 2020, the UIF froze a total of 19,970 financial accounts related to organised crime, compared to 800 in 2018.[10] These accounts amounted to a total of US$372.3m (MXN $8bn) in assets, compared to US$244.2m (MXN $4.7bn) frozen in 2019 and dwarfing the US$3.6m (MXN $69.7m) in 2018. This rise in overall asset seizures suggests a stronger commitment to attacking DTO finances than previous administrations.

Arrest and exoneration of General Cienfuegos

On 15 October 2020, Mexico's former secretary of defence, General Salvador Cienfuegos, was arrested in the US on drug-trafficking and money-laundering charges. The López Obrador government, which had not been informed of the investigations, reacted strongly and managed to negotiate Cienfuegos's extradition to Mexico. In an unprecedented move, announced as a measure to strengthen bilateral security cooperation, all charges were dropped in November so that Cienfuegos could be transferred to Mexican custody. In January 2021, Cienfuegos was exonerated by Mexico's attorney general's office amid allegations of government interference in the investigation. However, the DEA's evidence against Cienfuegos was found to be riddled with translation errors which undermined their case.

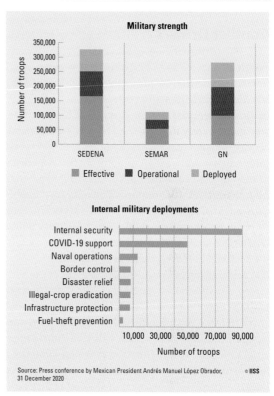

Figure 1: Mexican military strength and deployments (as of 31 December 2020)

New proposed regulation of foreign security officials

At the end of 2020, in what was widely seen as a response to Cienfuegos's arrest, a reform was proposed to the National Security Law to regulate foreign law-enforcement officials operating in

Mexico. The law would remove diplomatic immunity for foreign agents operating in Mexico and force them to share all information regarding ongoing investigations with their Mexican counterparts and would force Mexican officials to report all communications with foreign agents to the government. The reform was fast-tracked in the Senate on 9 December and in the Chamber of Deputies on 17 December, however López Obrador eventually had the law watered down before its final approval on 14 January 2021 to exclude the sharing of confidential information and to remove restrictions to electronic communications.

Continued militarisation of the fight against crime

A presidential decree signed in May 2020 allowed the armed forces to continue participating in public-security duties, as a complement to the GN, until 2024, in a further manifestation of the higher prominence of the military in public life under López Obrador compared to previous administrations. In July, the military was also tasked with administering Mexico's ports and customs, many of which have been significantly infiltrated by organised crime.

Focus on Guanajuato

José Antonio Yépez Ortiz, the leader of the CSRL, was captured in August 2020 in a combined operation involving federal and state police forces and the GN. The most important arrest of a major DTO leader in 2020, it highlighted the growing importance of Guanajuato State in Mexico's drugs war. Once one of Mexico's safest states and a major manufacturing hub, since 2018 it had become one of the most violent: in 2020 its homicide rate was the second-highest nationwide (72.1 per 100,00).[11] The biggest mass killing of 2020 occurred in Guanajuato in July when CSRL gunmen stormed a drug rehabilitation centre in Irapuato, killing 27 people.

Attack against Omar García Harfuch

In June 2020, CJNG gunmen ambushed a vehicle carrying Mexico City's secretary of public security, Omar García Harfuch, in broad daylight in one of the capital's most upscale neighbourhoods. Despite being shot several times, García Harfuch survived the attack. A dozen CJNG members were arrested for participating in the attack. Notably, the attackers were carrying military-grade weaponry including a .50-calibre sniper rifle.

Key Events in 2020–21

POLITICAL EVENTS

9 March 2020

'Day Without Women' march takes place in response to López Obrador's lack of attention towards feminicides and gender violence.

23 March

The government imposes social-distancing measures and closes non-essential activities to curb the coronavirus pandemic.

29 March

López Obrador visits Sinaloa and shakes hands with El Chapo's mother.

April

Large DTOs are seen distributing food and other pandemic-related aid in the absence of government support.

11 May

López Obrador signs a decree enabling the armed forces to continue internal public-security duties until March 2024.

MILITARY/VIOLENT EVENTS

16 June 2020

A district-court judge, Uriel Villegas Ortiz, and his wife are murdered in Colima State.

1 June

A new system of state-level pandemic alerts is introduced, allowing states with falling case levels to gradually begin reopening.

1–2 June

The UIF undertakes 'Operation Agave Azul', freezing the assets of nearly 2,000 people and companies related to the CJNG.

17 July

López Obrador announces a plan to hand over control of ports and customs to the military to reduce corruption.

15 October

Former secretary of defence Gen. Salvador Cienfuegos is arrested in the US on drug-trafficking and money-laundering charges.

17 November

US drops charges against Cienfuegos ahead of his return to Mexico to face investigation.

19 November

Senate approves marijuana-legalisation bill (following approval in the lower house, Senate will need to vote again).

15 December

Chamber of Deputies approves controversial reform to National Security Law.

18 December

Mexico City and the neighbouring state of Mexico are placed on the highest coronavirus alert level due to rising cases of COVID-19 from a second wave.

14 January 2021

Cienfuegos is cleared of all charges in Mexico. Watered-down version of National Security Law is approved.

26 June

Omar García Harfuch, Mexico City secretary of public security, is targeted in an assassination attempt by CJNG.

1 July

27 people in a drug rehabilitation centre in Irapuato, Guanajuato State, are murdered by hitmen of the CSRL.

2 August

'El Marro', leader of the CSRL, is arrested.

18 December

Aristóteles Sandoval, former governor of Jalisco, is murdered.

Impact

Human rights and humanitarian

Despite López Obrador pledging that it would not, one year after its creation, the GN appeared to have inherited many of the same complaints regarding human-rights abuses levelled at the armed forces and the now defunct Federal Police. Over the course of 2020, the National Commission for Human Rights (CNDH) received 350 human-rights complaints relating to the GN, almost equalling the 359 it received about SEDENA.[12] These complaints came from all but one state and involved arbitrary detentions, excessive use of force, intimidation, prevention of access to justice, cruel and degrading acts, torture and forced disappearances. Part of the problem lies in the fact that around half of the GN are former members of the Federal Police and armed forces, with low levels (20% of its members and just 0.3% of new recruits) of vetting on human-rights records and successful completion of police training.[13]

Many DTOs have branched out into migrant kidnapping, preying on Central Americans attempting to reach the Mexican border and cross over to the US. The 2019 US 'Remain in Mexico' policy kept asylum seekers in Mexico while their cases were reviewed by US authorities, which made them a target for DTOs: it was estimated that around 80% of migrants and asylum seekers sent to Mexico to wait for US court hearings were victims of violence in the first nine months of 2019.[14]

Political stability

The impact of drug-related violence on national domestic political stability was less severe than often perceived by the public or the media, however lower levels of government and certain regions were worse affected. Drug-related violence did not impede the functioning of government and state institutions at a federal level nor cause any interruption to democratic order. Likewise, DTOs rarely targeted high-level federal officials (with some exceptions, like a small number of federal judges). In contrast, state- and municipal-level institutions and officials suffered greatly from DTO threats, bribery and killings, especially in a small number of particularly violent states. Overall, however, the risk of severe political instability caused by DTO-related violence was low, with DTOs seemingly avoiding challenging the state directly.

Economic and social

The impact of DTO violence on economic stability was also relatively minor, given its limited negative effects on productive activity, public services and the functioning of markets. This is despite the considerable overall cost of violence in Mexico, with one estimate putting it as high as 21.3% of GDP, although this included indirect costs such as lost future income from homicides as well as opportunity costs from security spending (direct costs of violence accounted for only about one-fifth of the total).[15]

The López Obrador administration has recognised the economic factors driving the drug trade, arguing in favour of social development as a long-term solution to crime. In its two years in office, it has already implemented various youth-focused social-assistance schemes and raised the country's minimum wage considerably more than its predecessors, yet the pandemic-related recession will offset many of these actions, with poverty and labour precarity expected to persist and continue to drive crime.

Conflict Outlook

Political scenarios

Mexico will hold midterm elections on 6 June 2021 which will see the entire Chamber of Deputies up for election, as well as numerous other state and local positions. According to most polls, the ruling party, Morena, remained on course to retain its legislative majority, although it could lose the supermajority that has allowed it to reform the constitution at will. Regardless, there appeared to be few prospects of a change in security policy and most changes that would have required constitutional amendments have already been undertaken. López Obrador did not signal any willingness to change security policy, which will continue to prioritise the GN as the main force to combat the DTOs, despite few major successes to date.

Despite the expansion of the military's duties into civilian and economic life, it is unlikely that it will make inroads into Mexican politics, given the lack of modern historical precedence and the likelihood of strong public repudiation should the military step out of the bounds set by the executive.

Mexico's efforts against the DTOs will continue to rely heavily on US assistance, particularly in terms of information sharing: US intelligence has contributed significantly to the capture of major DTO leaders in the last 20 years. However, the controversial reform of the National Security Law and strong US opposition to it will threaten prospects for continued close cooperation.

Escalation potential and conflict-related risks

The dynamics of the drug war in Mexico make it difficult to estimate whether the conflict will intensify during any given year, as much depends on the balance of power between different DTOs, as well as arrests or killings of major DTO leaders causing power vacuums or escalations in violence. One trend that could impact DTOs' financial power (and therefore their capacity for violence) is the growing importance of the synthetic-drug trade, particularly fentanyl, which benefits from easy production and transportation, and high profit margins. The government has responded by intensifying seizures of these drugs. Fentanyl seizures in 2020 totalled 1,301 kg, which represented a 486% increase compared to the 222 kg seized in 2019. Additionally, a total of 175 clandestine laboratories producing synthetic drugs of all types were dismantled, nearly twice as many as in 2019.[16] Despite the increase in fentanyl seizures, the drug will continue to pose a challenge due to the ease of its illegal and legal importation into Mexico and the widespread use of its chemical precursors in the medical industry, ruling out the possibility of a total ban.

A more positive trend is the potential legalisation of marijuana, already decriminalised by a 2018 Supreme Court ruling. In November 2020, the Senate approved a bill which decriminalised the possession of up to 28 grams of marijuana, allowed individuals to grow as many as six plants and established a regulatory framework for the production and sale of cannabis products. Should the bill be signed into law in 2021, Mexico would become the fourth country in the world to legalise marijuana for recreational use. However, the drug's importance as a source of financing to DTOs has been vastly curtailed in recent years due to the shift towards synthetic drugs and reduced demand from the US.

Prospects for peace

The persistence of widespread poverty and lack of economic opportunities for large segments of the Mexican population, combined with the inability of successive governments to establish a security policy that demonstrably reduces violence, suggests that the conflict against DTOs will not end any time soon. At best, the consolidation of a few large DTOs (namely the Sinaloa Cartel and the CJNG) could reduce competition between them and thereby reduce violence. The impact of government efforts at combatting financial crime and synthetic drugs on DTO finances could either reduce their capacity for violence, or alternatively lead them to expand their reach into other criminal, or even some non-criminal, activity.

Strategic implications and global influences

Cooperation with the US on security matters will remain an important pillar of the strategic relationship between the two countries. Despite the Biden administration's focus on domestic issues in early 2021, migration was one aspect given immediate priority due to surging numbers of Central American migrants in the first months of the year. While Mexico largely cooperated with the Trump administration on migration, it will be tempted to assume a more assertive stance with Biden if it perceives that major disagreements can be avoided, such as occurred in mid-2019 and resulted in the threat of a trade war. This assertiveness could also further complicate cooperation on security matters, already strained by Cienfuegos's arrest and Mexico's reform of the National Security Law, which was ultimately watered down due to pressure. Mexico's dependency on US intelligence and, to a lesser extent, resources, including for its weapons procurement, means that changes to existing cooperation arrangements are likely to be marginal, and little more than posturing.

Notes

[1] Arturo Angel, 'En México Asesinaron a Más de 35 Mil Personas en 2020, Solo un 0.4% Menos que un Año Antes' [In Mexico, More than 35 Thousand People Were Murdered in 2020, Only 0.4% Less than a Year Before], Animal Politico, 21 January 2021; and Government of Mexico, Secretariat of Security and Civilian Protection, 'Cifras de Delitos y Víctimas por Cada 100 Mil Habitantes 2015–2021' [Crime and Victim Figures per 100 Thousand Inhabitants 2015–2021], 20 June 2021.

[2] Government of Mexico, Ministry of Finance, 'Informes sobre la Situación Económica, las Finanzas Públicas y la Deuda Pública' [Report on the Economic Situation, Public Finance and Public Debt], Fourth Trimestre, 2020, p. 38.

[3] Ilse Becerril, 'El Cártel de Santa Rosa de Lima Tras la Captura del Marro: Pactó con el CJNG y Ahora Opera con Solo el 60% de Sus Sicarios' [The Santa Rosa de Lima Cartel After the Capture of Marro: It Made a Pact with the CJNG and Now Operates with Only 60% of Its Hitmen], infobae, 9 September 2020.

[4] Transparency International, 'Corruption Perceptions Index', 2020.

[5] Justice in Mexico, 'Organized Crime and Violence in Mexico 2020 Special Report', 30 July 2020.

[6] Coneval, 'Medición de la Pobreza – Pobreza en México: Resultados de la Pobreza en México 2018 a Nivel Nacional y Por Entidades Federativas' [Measurement of Poverty – Poverty in Mexico: Results of Poverty in Mexico 2018 at the National Level and by Federal Entities], 2018.

[7] Inegi, 'Principales Resultados de la Encuesta Nacional de Ocupación y Empleo (nueva edición) (ENOEN) de Diciembre de 2020' [Main Results of the National Survey on Occupation and Employment (new edition) (ENOEN) December 2020], December 2020.

[8] 'Menores en la Delincuencia Organizada de México: a los 14 años Roban, Secuestran y Venden Droga' [Minors in Organised Crime in Mexico: At Age 14 They Steal, Kidnap and Sell Drugs], Forbes, 24 September 2020.

9   United Nations Office on Drugs and Crime, 'World Drug Report 2021, Chapter 3: Drug Market Trends: Cannabis, Opioids', June 2021, p. 88.

10   Mexican Government, 'Informe Anual de Seguridad 2020' [Annual Security Report 2020].

11   Government of Mexico, Secretariat of Security and Civilian Protection, 'Cifras de Delitos y Víctimas por Cada 100 Mil Habitants 2015–2021' [Crime and Victim Figures per 100 Thousand Inhabitants 2015–2021], 20 June 2021.

12   'Ejército y Guardia Nacional, a la par con quejas en CNDH' [Army and National Guard, On Par with Complaints to CNDH], *El Universal,* 8 February 2021.

13   Duncan Tucker, 'La Nueva Guardia Nacional de México Está Rompiendo Su Juramento de Respetar Los Derechos Humanos' [Mexico's New National Guard Is Breaking Its Oath to Respect Human Rights], Amnesty International, 8 November 2020.

14   'The Devastating Toll of "Remain in Mexico" One Year Later', Doctors Without Borders, 29 January 2020.

15   Institute for Economics & Peace, 'Mexico Peace Index 2020: Identifying and Measuring the Factors that Drive Peace', April 2020, p. 48.

16   'Informe 2020 del Gabinete de Seguridad. Conferencia Presidente AMLO' [2020 Security Cabinet Report. President AMLO Conference], Andrés Manuel López Obrador, YouTube, 31 December 2020.

Americas

COLOMBIA

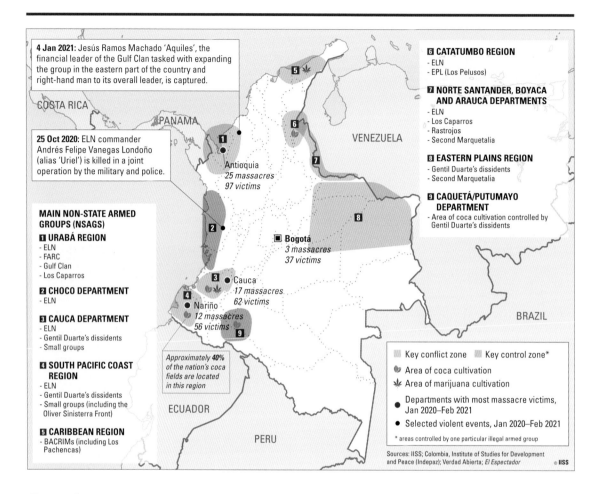

4 Jan 2021: Jesús Ramos Machado 'Aquiles', the financial leader of the Gulf Clan tasked with expanding the group in the eastern part of the country and right-hand man to its overall leader, is captured.

25 Oct 2020: ELN commander Andrés Felipe Vanegas Londoño (alias 'Uriel') is killed in a joint operation by the military and police.

MAIN NON-STATE ARMED GROUPS (NSAGS)

1 URABÁ REGION
- ELN
- FARC
- Gulf Clan
- Los Caparros

2 CHOCO DEPARTMENT
- ELN

3 CAUCA DEPARTMENT
- ELN
- Gentil Duarte's dissidents
- Small groups

4 SOUTH PACIFIC COAST REGION
- ELN
- Gentil Duarte's dissidents
- Small groups (including the Oliver Sinisterra Front)

5 CARIBBEAN REGION
- BACRIMs (including Los Pachencas)

6 CATATUMBO REGION
- ELN
- EPL (Los Pelusos)

7 NORTE SANTANDER, BOYACA AND ARAUCA DEPARTMENTS
- ELN
- Los Caparros
- Rastrojos
- Second Marquetalia

8 EASTERN PLAINS REGION
- Gentil Duarte's dissidents
- Second Marquetalia

9 CAQUETÁ/PUTUMAYO DEPARTMENT
- Area of coca cultivation controlled by Gentil Duarte's dissidents

COSTA RICA
PANAMA
VENEZUELA
BRAZIL
ECUADOR
PERU

Antioquia
25 massacres
97 victims

Bogotá
3 massacres
37 victims

Cauca
17 massacres
62 victims

Nariño
12 massacres
56 victims

*Approximately **40%** of the nation's coca fields are located in this region*

■ Key conflict zone   ■ Key control zone*
🍁 Area of coca cultivation
🌿 Area of marijuana cultivation
● Departments with most massacre victims, Jan 2020–Feb 2021
● Selected violent events, Jan 2020–Feb 2021
* areas controlled by one particular illegal armed group

Sources: IISS; Colombia, Institute of Studies for Development and Peace (Indepaz); Verdad Abierta; *El Espectador*   © IISS

Overview

Colombia has been ravaged by violence since it became a republic in 1810. A low-intensity civil war between political parties in the 1950s (La Violencia) evolved in the 1960s to include multiple Marxist guerrillas fighting the state. In response to these guerrillas, paramilitary groups emerged in the 1980s, supported by state authorities and private actors. Since the early 2000s, the conflict has moved away from political goals and increasingly towards economic incentives, especially as drug trafficking became the most important funding source for illicit groups, both fuelling violence and making it more protracted.

Illegal economies boosted insurgent and paramilitary capabilities amid a slow and weak state response, which resulted in the Revolutionary Armed Forces of Colombia (FARC) guerrilla group controlling 40% of Colombia's territory by 2000.[1] A stronger reaction by successive governments – along with support from the United States under Plan Colombia[2] – facilitated negotiation processes with FARC and the United Self-Defence Forces of Colombia (AUC) paramilitary group. By 2006, most paramilitary combatants had demobilised and in 2016 FARC signed a peace agreement with the government and began transitioning into a political party.[3] Yet deficiencies in the implementation of the demobilisation and reintegration of combatants from both the AUC and FARC contributed to the emergence of *bandas criminales* or BACRIMs (criminal gangs) and FARC dissident divisions. These groups, along with the National Liberation Army (ELN) and the Popular Liberation Army (EPL), also

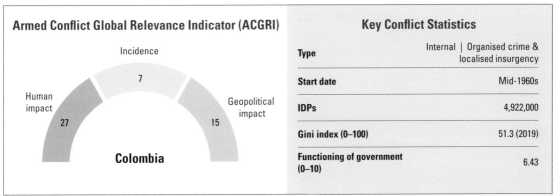

ACGRI pillars: IISS calculation based on multiple sources for 2020 and January/February 2021 (scale: 0–100). See Notes on Methodology and Data Appendix for further details on Key Conflict Statistics.

known as the Pelusos, have reshaped the armed conflict in recent years.

In 2020, the ELN remained the non-state armed group (NSAG) with the strongest territorial presence and most significant military capabilities. However, FARC dissident groups grew and became better organised, with a single commander, Miguel Botache Santillana, also known as 'Gentil Duarte', bringing together six FARC dissident fronts in over half the country.

Competition over former FARC-controlled areas, coca cultivation, cocaine production and distribution corridors, illegal mining and extortion continued to underpin ongoing dynamics of violence. In 2020, 91 massacres were registered, a steep escalation from the eight registered in 2015.[4] In 2020, the police registered a total of 368 terrorist attacks, representing a dramatic 98% and 204% increase compared to 2019 and 2018 levels respectively.[5] Between October 2019 and September 2020, there were 193 direct confrontations between NSAGs and the Colombian armed forces, and 61 confrontations solely between NSAGs.[6]

Conflict Parties

Colombian armed forces

Strength: 293,200 across the army, air force and navy. The national police has 189,000 police officers.

Areas of operation: Across the country but limited presence in some rural areas such as the Catatumbo, Urabá and Pacific coast regions.

Leadership: President Iván Duque (commander-in-chief); Diego Molano (minister of defence); Luis Fernando Navarro Jiménez (general commander).

Structure: Army, navy and air force. The National Police (PONAL) is in charge of public and civil security. Though not formally part of the military forces, PONAL has been controlled and administered by the Ministry of National Defence and has had a militarised structure since 1953.

History: Originated in the late 18th century as the Liberating Army of the independence movement against the Spanish Empire. The military forces were formally created with the 1821 Cúcuta Constitution.

Objectives: Defend national sovereignty, consolidate the state against NSAGs and maintain rule and order.

Opponents: ELN, FARC dissidents, BACRIMs including the Gulf Clan, EPL and other criminal organisations.

Affiliates/allies: National Police.

Resources/capabilities: 2020 defence budget of US$9.69 billion and US$10.69bn for 2021. Overall capabilities have improved in recent decades. The army is planning to modernise its armoured fighting vehicles, while the navy has improved its offshore-patrol capacities in recent years. The ground-attack capabilities of the air force remain limited.

Gentil Duarte's FARC dissidents

Strength: Approximately 3,000 members.[7]

Areas of operation: Presence in at least 12 of Colombia's 32 departments, mainly in Antioquia, Caquetá, Cauca, Guaviare, Meta, Nariño, Putumayo and Vaupes.[8]

Leadership: Miguel Botache Santillana, alias 'Gentil Duarte' (commander). 1st and 7th Fronts: Néstor Gregorio Vera Fernández, alias 'Iván Mordisco'; 33rd Front: Jhon Milicias; Western Coordinating Command: Gerson Antonio Pérez Delgado, alias 'Caín', and Euclides España Caicedo, alias 'Jonier'.

Structure: Replicates the former FARC operational structure with 'fronts' for each region. However, it did not retain FARC's hierarchal system across regional groups. The fronts therefore enjoy greater freedom to make decisions and manage their finances at the local level.

History: The group brought together multiple FARC units that rejected the 2016 peace agreement. Most remained in hiding until 2018–19, before beginning to conduct activities while claiming to be the 'true' FARC.

Objectives: Overthrow the government and establish a socialist state.

Opponents: Colombian armed forces, the Gulf Clan, the Second Marquetalia and other smaller local criminal groups such the EPL.

Affiliates/allies: ELN Western War Front in the Chocó region. Mexican drug-trafficking organisations (DTOs), mainly the Sinaloa Cartel and the Cartel Jalisco New Generation (CJNG).

Resources/capabilities: Inherited FARC's former economic structures and rent-seeking activities (including extortion, kidnapping, ransom and illegal mining). Drug trafficking or tax collection on drug distribution in its areas of influence. Possesses long- and short-range weapons, obtained from conflict zones in Central America, former Soviet bloc countries and illegal suppliers in the US.

Second Marquetalia (FARC dissidents)

Strength: Between 300 and 800 members.[9]

Areas of operation: Border areas with Venezuela, mainly in the departments of Guainía, Norte de Santander and Vichada, and others such as Antioquia, Cauca and Casanare.

Leadership: The main commanders include Luciano Marín Arango, alias 'Iván Márquez'; Hernán Darío Velásquez, alias 'El Paisa'; Seuxis Pausias Hernández Solarte, alias 'Jesús Santrich' (killed in May 2021); Henry Castellanos Garzón, alias 'Romaña'; and Olivio Iván Merchán Gómez, alias 'Loco Iván' (killed in combat in November 2020).

Structure: Sought to incorporate other groups under the unified coordination of its four main commanders. Its organisational structure remains unknown, but it likely replicates the old FARC structure.

History: Created in 2019 when a group of senior FARC commanders – who were signatories of the 2016 peace agreement – abandoned the reincorporation process and resumed fighting.

Objectives: Overthrow the government and create a socialist state. Recreate the original FARC.

Opponents: Colombian armed forces, Gentil Duarte's dissidents and the Gulf Clan.

Affiliates/allies: Non-aggression pact in Casanare with the ELN Eastern War Front and alliances with ELN fronts in Antioquia and Cauca. Allied with Los Caparros in Bajo Cauca where the Gulf Clan is present.

Resources/capabilities: Its sources of financing include former undeclared assets of FARC, the illegal transport of migrants, drug trafficking and smuggling. Renewed weaponry with more modern rifles such as the IWI *Tavor* X95.

National Liberation Army (ELN)

Strength: Approximately 4,000 members.[10]

Areas of operation: Operates in at least 16 of Colombia's 32 departments and capital cities, including Bogotá.[11] Retains a particularly strong presence along the border with Venezuela, especially in the departments of Arauca, Norte de Santander and Vichada, but also in the departments of Cauca, Chocó, Nariño and Valle del Cauca – where it has inherited FARC territories. Has also expanded rapidly in Venezuela.

Leadership: Nicolás Rodríguez Bautista, alias 'Gabino' (commander).

Structure: The Central Command (COCE) directs strategy and is composed of five commanders and divisions that operate independently. The ELN has seven war fronts, including the Camilo Torres Restrepo National Urban War Front which has a presence in multiple capital cities. Maintains a horizontal military structure with a high level of independence given to each front. Many FARC dissidents have joined the ELN in recent years.

History: Founded in 1964 by a group of Catholic priests, left-wing intellectuals and students embracing liberation theology and trying to emulate the 1959 Cuban Revolution.

Objectives: Overthrow the Colombian government and create a socialist state.

National Liberation Army (ELN)

Opponents: Colombian armed forces, the EPL in the Catatumbo region and the Gulf Clan in Arauca, Antioquia and Chocó.

Affiliates/allies: The Second Marquetalia and other FARC dissidents in regions such as Chocó and Catatumbo; Los Caparros in Antioquia.

Resources/capabilities: Extortion, illegal mining and gasoline black market. Controls the illegal trafficking of timber and cocaine in various departments. Weapons come mainly from illegal foreign trade, including remnants of Soviet arms.

The Gulf Clan (also known as Gaitanistas Self-Defence Forces of Colombia (AGC) or The Urabeños)

Strength: Approximately 3,000 members, though estimates vary.[12]

Areas of operation: Presence in at least 17 departments in Colombia, as well as abroad.[13] Based in the Gulf of Urabá (on the Atlantic coast, close to Panama). Also has an extensive presence in the city of Medellín and departments such as Antioquia, La Guajira, Norte de Santander, Santander and Valle del Cauca.

Leadership: Dario Antonio Úsuga David, alias 'Otoniel'.

Structure: About a third of the local cells are directly commanded by the leadership in Urabá, while the others are loosely affiliated with local criminal organisations, who use the name Gulf Clan and are expected to provide services or follow strategic orders when requested.

History: Emerged from the demobilisation of AUC paramilitaries in 2006. Some of its leaders and members are former EPL combatants and drug traffickers from groups that have since disbanded, such as the Popular Revolutionary Anti-Terrorist Army of Colombia (ERPAC).

Objectives: Drug trafficking. Using the name Gaitanistas Self-Defence Forces is a way of legitimising itself as a counter-insurgent group.

Opponents: Colombian armed forces, ELN, the Caparros, the EPL, Gentil Duarte's dissidents and the Second Marquetalia (except in Córdoba and Antioquia).

Affiliates/allies: Works with the Second Marquetalia in Córdoba and Antioquia.

Resources/capabilities: Financing comes from transnational drug trafficking, providing services for independent drug traffickers. Multiple group members, including leaders, run their own international trafficking routes. Also involved in illegal prostitution, human trafficking to Panama and extortion.

Los Caparros

Strength: 400 members.[14]

Areas of operation: Lower Cauca area of Antioquia. After the peace agreement, they extended their influence in places such as Briceño, El Bagre, Nechí, Valdivia, Yarumales, Valdivia in Antioquia and Puerto Libertador and San José de Uré in Córdoba.

Leadership: Robinson Gil Tapias, alias 'Flechas'.

Structure: Divided into three fronts: the Elmer Ordoñez Beltrán Front, the Carlos Mario Tabares Front and the Norberto Olivares Front.

History: Emerged from the demobilisation of the AUC in 2006 as one of the groups from the Gulf Clan. With the FARC demobilisation and the assassination of Danilo Chiquito, one of the main leaders decided to start his own group.

Objectives: Control drug trafficking in Córdoba, Antioquia, especially in the mountain range of the Paramillo Massif.

Opponents: The Gulf Clan and the Colombian armed forces.

Affiliates/allies: The Second Marquetalia and the ELN, in Córdoba, Sucre and the Urabá Gulf.

Resources/capabilities: Involved in all stages of drug trafficking (coca cultivation, cocaine production and international shipment) in the departments of Córdoba and Antioquia. Also engaged in illegal mining.

Conflict Drivers

Political

Slow implementation of the peace agreement:
President Iván Duque was elected in 2018 on a platform of scepticism around the 2016 peace agreement. While his government allocated around US$684 million for the Development Programmes with a Territorial Approach (PDETs), multiple voices have denounced the slow pace and low political will to produce tangible results.[15] For example, the construction of public works stipulated as part of the agreement has slowed down dramatically: whereas 544 construction projects began in 2019, only 53 started in 2020. Moreover, 38% of the required legal adjustments for implementation were still pending.[16]

As a result, NSAGs have reoccupied many areas of the country, with their presence reported in 30 out of 32 departments.[17] Meanwhile, demobilised FARC combatants faced increased insecurity, with homicides increasing sharply from 32 in 2017 to 73 in 2020.[18]

Economic and social

Socio-economic inequalities and institutional flaws:
Widespread inequalities, in land ownership and other areas, have historically fuelled the conflict. Colombia is Latin America's second-most unequal country, with a 27%[19] monetary poverty rate and a Gini index of 51.3.[20] This inequality is exacerbated by the state's inability to provide justice and resolve land disputes, as well as widespread corruption. Colombia also consistently ranks in the lower half of Transparency International's Corruption Perceptions Index.[21]

Illegal economies and coca eradication:
Coca crops and cocaine production remain important drivers of violence, as the most important revenue source for illicit criminal and terrorist groups, as well as an income source for marginalised rural communities. The latter's relationship with national authorities is therefore strained by efforts to forcefully reduce cultivation. Legal restrictions on aerial fumigations enforced by the Constitutional Court since 2017 have undermined government eradication efforts, necessitating the use of manual methods instead, making the process longer and more labour-intensive.

International

Venezuela:
Venezuela continues to play a significant role in the Colombian armed conflict, acting as a safe haven for Colombian NSAGs such as the ELN and some FARC dissidents. As of May 2019, around 50% of ELN members were thought to have taken refuge in Venezuela.[22] Ongoing socio-economic and political turmoil in Venezuela has also triggered a major regional migration crisis, causing approximately 5m people to flee, with most settling in neighbouring countries, including 1.8m in Colombia.[23] Over 50% of these migrants were deemed to have an irregular status,[24] and almost 30% settled in neighbouring departments such as Norte de Santander and La Guajira, areas with a strong military presence of diverse illegal armed groups.[25] This migrant crisis has further stretched the Colombian government's limited capacity to address diverse pressing economic and social problems in the country.

Political and Military Developments

JEP moves forward

Despite the controversy surrounding the Special Justice for the Peace (JEP) created by the peace agreement, the tribunal continued its investigations into the seven macro cases that have been opened. More than 300,000 victims have registered under the JEP and over 12,000 individuals have submitted themselves to its jurisdiction, including 9,806 former FARC combatants and 3,007 members of the military and police.[26]

The open cases cover accusations against both FARC members and state agents, for illegal retention – also known as kidnapping – and for illegitimate deaths presented by the military as casualties – also known as false positives. In January 2021, the tribunal formally charged eight former members of the FARC secretariat for the kidnapping of 21,396 victims, but no arrests or formal sanctions have yet been implemented.[27] Investigations continued in the case on civilian deaths presented as legitimate casualties by military forces. While charges have not been officially presented for the 6,402 homicides committed between 2002 and 2008, a former army commander and multiple former generals agreed to submit themselves and testify before the JEP.[28]

Creation of Comunes

As part of a new electoral strategy for the upcoming 2022 elections, the FARC political party – established in 2017 using the same acronym but with the name Common Alternative Revolutionary Force – changed its name to Comunes, in order to distance the party from the group's guerrilla history.

Social unrest and police violence

2020 saw a continuation of social unrest against the Duque government that had started in late 2019. Before the coronavirus outbreak in April 2020, protests centred on the murder of social leaders and human-rights defenders, and several wire-tapping scandals surrounding the military forces. In November 2020, protests re-ignited around the issues of unemployment, education, pension grievances and in defence of the 2016 peace agreement. Some protests escalated into looting and vandalism, while others also featured serious brutality against peaceful protesters, particularly by the Mobile Anti-Disturbances Squadron (ESMAD) of the police. Despite public outcry and international condemnation, Duque failed to clearly condemn this disproportionate use of force in a timely way.

Consolidation of FARC dissidents

Violence by the two main FARC dissident groups (Gentil Duarte's followers and the Second Marquetalia) increased following a military strategy to gain territorial control and national visibility,

expanding their respective presence to the south-western departments of Cauca, Caquetá and Nariño, among others, and to the border area with Venezuela. The Second Marquetalia was also affected by the killing of its commander, Olivio Iván Merchán Gómez or 'Loco Iván', by the Venezuelan army in November 2020. This event also confirmed the importance of the Venezuelan border as the group's headquarters.

ELN ceasefire and curfew enforcement

As a national lockdown was imposed to curb COVID-19 infections in March 2020, the ELN announced a suspension of armed action to encourage compliance with public-health measures in its areas of influence. Although the national government rejected this proposal, the ELN imposed lockdown measures in the Catatumbo region and the Cauca department, including restrictions on the movement of vehicles and people.

Key Events in 2020–21

POLITICAL EVENTS

21 January 2020

Social protests flare up in multiple cities against the government's socio-economic policies and voicing concern for increased violence against social leaders.

20 March

Duque announces the first Mandatory Preventive Isolation period in response to the pandemic. Colombian borders are officially closed.

7 July

An executive order is issued that offers legal benefits for individual members of organised armed groups who surrender. The president calls on the Gulf Clan, the EPL and Los Caparros to surrender immediately.

7 October

Carlos Antonio Lozada, former FARC commander and current senator, confirms the group's involvement in the 1995 assassination of the presidential candidate Álvaro Gómez Hurtado, sparking controversy around the ongoing transitional-justice process.

18 October

Several indigenous groups arrive in Bogotá after crossing the country from the southwest region, demanding better protection against the assassination of their leaders and control of their territories by armed groups.

MILITARY/VIOLENT EVENTS

12 February 2020

The ELN and EPL declare a month-long curfew in the Catatumbo region, prohibiting the movement of people and vehicles.

1 May

Pablo Beltrán, member of the ELN central command, declares a ceasefire to facilitate control of the coronavirus pandemic and enforces containment measures in its areas of influence.

16 June

The police kill Deimer Patiño Giraldo, also known as '80', who had assumed the leadership of the criminal organisation the Pachencas, one of the fastest-growing BACRIMs in the Caribbean region.

15 August

In an area controlled by the ELN, eight young people are murdered in the so-called Samaniego massacre. This event generates alarm due to the repeated use of massacres as a consolidation mechanism by the BACRIMs.

9 September

Javier Ordoñez dies after being arrested by the police and taken to a station for supposed violation of coronavirus restrictions. Footage showing brutal treatment is revealed on social media and results in major protests in Bogotá.

27 October

Following controversy around the alleged meddling of Colombian right-wing lawmakers in the US presidential race, the US Ambassador to Colombia publicly urges all Colombian politicians to remain uninvolved.

15 November

In an *El Espectador* interview, Euclides España Caicedo 'Jonier', a commander with Gentil Duarte's dissidents, emphasises the group's intention to pursue the original FARC project and recover its previous military strength.

21 November

New protests against the national government take place across the country.

26 November

A political-control debate is held in Congress against the Attorney General's Office for an alleged incrimination plot against 'Jesus Santrich', commander of the Second Marquetalia who returned to arms after being arrested in that same case.

16 December

The Constitutional Court establishes the conditions to resume aerial spraying of illicit crops. The government indicates that this strategy will be resumed in 2021.

11 January 2021

US President Donald Trump adds Cuba to the list of state sponsors of terrorism for hosting the ELN leaders in the country.

13 January

Iván Márquez, commander of the Second Marquetalia, appears in a video publicly supporting any political action that seeks to oust Duque.

24 September

Commander Andrés Felipe Vanegas Londoño, also known as 'Uriel', publicly confirms that the ELN had participated in protests earlier in September in which seven civilians were killed, 148 injured and 53 police stations destroyed. On 25 October 2020, the army kills 'Uriel' in the jungles of Chocó.

21 October

In a coordinated operation between the police, the army and the prosecutor's office, Richar Arley Díaz Garay, alias 'Cóndor', former head of the EPL, is captured, leading the group to lose control over the Catatumbo region.

18 November

The Venezuelan army kills 'Loco Iván', commander of the Second Marquetalia.

4 January 2021

Jesús Ramos Machado 'Aquiles', the financial leader of the Gulf Clan tasked with expanding the group in the eastern part of the country and right-hand man to its overall leader, is captured.

Impact

Human rights and humanitarian

With 310 cases in 2020, the assassination of social leaders and human-rights defenders remained a pressing concern as authorities failed to regain control in previously guerrilla territory.[29] During 2020 there were 171 victims of anti-personnel mines, further evidence of the insufficient implementation of the peace agreement which had stipulated the elimination of such weapons.[30]

The new power competition between the ELN, FARC dissidents and multiple BACRIMs increased displacement of and violence against civilians. In 2020 there were 90 forced-displacement events, an increase of 30 from 2019, while the number of victims of the armed conflict jumped from 25,100 to 28,509.[31]

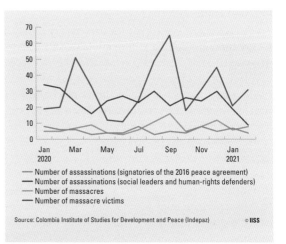

— Number of assassinations (signatories of the 2016 peace agreement)
— Number of assassinations (social leaders and human-rights defenders)
— Number of massacres
— Number of massacre victims

Source: Colombia Institute of Studies for Development and Peace (Indepaz)   © IISS

Figure 1: Number of assassinations and massacres in Colombia, January 2020–February 2021

Political stability

Threats to political figures by NSAGs re-emerged as a means of exerting control and intimidation. For example, in October 2020, Senator Feliciano Valencia was targeted by an assassination attempt in his electoral stronghold in the department of Cauca. The mayor of Medellín and several opposition congressmen also received threats from BACRIM gangs.

The murder of former FARC combatants has undermined the implementation of the peace agreement, causing the government to lose legitimacy with local and international audiences that demand action and FARC political leaders losing support from the group's rank-and-file members, who demand protection.

Recurring social mobilisation in urban centres also added a new dimension to local and national governance, as citizens forcefully rejected government policies, drawing attention to ongoing violence and denouncing the disproportionate use of force by the police and military.

Economic and social

Colombia's GDP contracted by 6.8% in 2020 as the result of the pandemic, with unemployment increasing significantly from 10.5% in 2019 to 16.1%.[32] The worsening economic situation simultaneously fuelled social protests across the country while constraining the government's fiscal ability to address social grievances.

Violence by NSAGs caused sustained economic losses as a result of disruptions to trade and cargo transporters, the burning of trucks and the imposition of tolls in regions under armed ELN curfews in the middle of the pandemic. Attacks against energy and oil infrastructure – a characteristic of the conflict – also persisted, with 52 attacks against pipelines registered during 2020.[33]

Relations with neighbouring and international partners and geopolitical implications

The growing transnational dynamics of the conflict continued to strain relations with Venezuela, especially given accusations against the government of President Nicolás Maduro of protecting multiple NSAGs and failing to contain the exodus of migrants. Recriminations escalated to the point of Duque accusing Maduro of committing crimes against humanity at the United Nations General Assembly in September 2020.

The election of Joe Biden as US president sparked hopes for an acceleration in the implementation of the peace agreement and for concrete violence-reduction measures, particularly in relation to the assassination of social leaders and former FARC combatants. Renewed US attention on the implementation of the 2016 agreement will add to existing international pressure, particularly from the European Union, to deliver results.

Conflict Outlook

Political scenarios

The government's track record on security and the socio-economic agenda will likely take centre stage in 2021 ahead of the 2022 general elections. As security and criminality have re-emerged as the main concern for Colombians, the political discourse will shift to effective solutions to curb violence, prompting the government to resume aerial spraying of coca crops to curtail the economic power of BACRIMs, as well as possibly considering other alternative strategies, such as the reduction of penalties for voluntary surrenders.

Meanwhile, rising poverty and inequality post-pandemic will continue to fuel public discontent and political polarisation, with candidates expected to promise higher levels of social spending and unorthodox solutions for economic recovery. The

Venezuelan crisis will also remain at the centre of political discussions both nationally and regionally, especially in border regions.

For the first time, the 2022 parliamentary elections will include candidates of the Comunes party who will need to demonstrate that they represent the rank and file of the former FARC to remain politically active amidst internal power disputes.

Escalation potential and conflict-related risks

The Gentil Duarte dissidents, through the Western Coordinating Command and the old 30th Front, will continue their efforts to become the dominant armed group in southwestern Colombia. Thus, higher levels of violence can be expected in the coastal municipality of Tumaco and other rural areas in the department of Cauca, where the ELN, the Gulf Clan and other marginal armed groups are also present.

Near the Venezuelan border and in the Llanos Orientales region, the conflict will likely intensify between Gentil Duarte's group and the Second Marquetalia, particularly its José Maria Córdova Front. In the Catatumbo area, fighting is likely to continue between the ELN's Northeastern War Front and the remaining groups of the defunct EPL. The 33rd Front of Gentil Duarte's dissidents and the Second Marquetalia's Danilo Garcia Command will also probably attempt to establish a presence in this region.

In rural areas of the country, such as Urabá, the armed conflict will likely continue between the Gulf Clan and the Caparros, and with the Second Marquetalia, which has already conducted exploratory actions in this region. Urban violence and criminality will also increase as an area of concern given Colombia's deteriorating socio-economic indicators and rising unemployment, even if not directly related to the existing dynamics of armed conflict.

Prospects for peace

The shortcomings in implementing the 2016 peace agreement remain the most serious obstacles towards a sustainable peace. The agreement included multiple avenues to directly address the root causes of the violence, particularly for safeguarding political-opposition activities and bridging the urban/rural gap.

The government has committed to accelerating programmes allowing tax benefits for private companies to develop public works, to reinforcing government-provided security measures for former FARC combatants and to conducting the rural cadaster.

However, the Duque administration has sent mixed messages around resuming a dialogue with the ELN in Cuba. The group's federal structure makes any potential negotiation challenging: the lack of hierarchy across regions means no single individual has the authority to negotiate on behalf of its diverse constituents. In the run-up to the 2022 elections, negotiating with the ELN could also be politically counterproductive for the government vis-à-vis its mostly right-wing electorate.

Strategic implications and global influences

In the absence of political relations with the Maduro government in Venezuela, the ELN and the Second Marquetalia could accelerate their expansion across the border, which could bring these guerrillas into violent confrontations with other BACRIMs such as the Rastrojos in the states of Zulia and Táchira. One of the most important impacts of this lack of cooperation and diplomatic channels between the two countries is that the Colombian government is unable to extradite Colombian citizens arrested in Venezuela for prosecution.[34]

The Biden administration's plan for the region will be an important driver of Colombia's local policies. US support for aerial spraying to reduce coca crops and thereby limit the inflow of cocaine to the US could provide the necessary impetus for Duque's strategy to decimate BACRIM revenues. However, the environmental and health consequences of aerial spraying could increase public backlash and further erode the government's already low popularity.

The two governments are likely to join together in efforts against Maduro, as solving the border crisis will be crucial for domestic and regional stability. Cooperation on other issues might be more complicated, as the Biden administration – as well as the UN and other international actors – might push for greater action to reduce violence against demobilised FARC combatants, social leaders and human-rights defenders.

Notes

1   Barcelona Centre for International Affairs, 'Conflicto en Colombia: Antecedentes Históricos y Actores' [Conflict in Colombia: Historical Background and Actors], 1 January 2014.

2   Plan Colombia, adopted in 2000, primarily aimed to support the Colombian armed forces (through funding and training) to reduce drug trafficking and terrorism. In 2016, it entered a new chapter of bilateral cooperation: Peace Colombia.

3   In November 2016, after four years of formal negotiations in Cuba and a failed attempt to obtain popular support through a referendum, the Colombian government signed a revised peace agreement with FARC (following an initial agreement in August 2016). The deal included chapters on rural reform, political participation of former combatants, conflict termination, illicit drugs, the creation a transitional truth and justice system and the implementation of the agreement.

4   Indepaz, 'Informe de Masacres en Colombia Durante el 2020 y 2021' [Report of Massacres in Colombia During 2020 and 2021], 28 June 2021; and Indepaz, 'Posacuerdo Traumático: Coletazos en la Transición Desde el Acuerdo de Paz al Posconflicto' [Post-agreement Trauma: The Transition from the Peace Agreement to Post-Conflict], 2020. Other sources may provide different estimates.

5   Colombian National Police, 'Estadística Delictiva – Terrorismo 2020/2019/2018' [Crime Statistics – Terrorism 2020/2019/2018].

6   Juan Carlos Garzón Vergara, '13 Gráficos para Entender La Violencia Organizada en El Post-Acuerdo de Paz' [13 Graphics to Understand Organized Violence Post-peace Agreement], Fundación Ideas para la Paz (FIP), 30 November 2020.

7   Eduardo Carrillo, '"Gentil Duarte", Disidente de las FARC, Comanda 3.000 Hombres' ['Gentil Duarte', Dissident of the FARC, Commands 3,000 men], El Nuevo Siglo, 11 October 2020.

8   'Mueren en un Bombardeo Militar Diez Disidentes de las FARC' [Ten FARC Dissidents Are Killed in a Military Bombing], DW, 3 March 2021.

9   'Disidencias de las FARC Duplican Su Número de Hombres en Solo 12 Meses' [FARC Dissidents Double Their Number of Men in Just 12 Months], El Tiempo, 31 May 2020; and Adriaan Alsema, 'FARC dissident "Ivan Marquez" Reemerges After Failed Rearmament Attempt', Colombia Reports, 29 September 2020.

10 InSight Crime, 'Ejército de Liberación Nacional (ELN)' [National Liberation Army (ELN)], 27 October 2020.

11 Ibid.

12 'Actúa en 124 municipios con más de 3 mil integrantes: así opera el "Clan del Golfo", el grupo criminal más grande de Colombia' [In 124 Municipalities with More Than 3,000 Members: This Is How the 'Clan del Golfo', the Largest Criminal Group in Colombia, Operates], infobae, 28 February 2021.

13 InSight Crime, 'The Urabeños', 14 March 2021.

14 'En Combate Con Ejército Murió "Caín", Máximo Jefe de "Los Caparros"' [In Combat with the Army, 'Caín', the Top Leader of 'Los Caparros', Died], El Tiempo, 17 November 2020.

15 PDETs are a rural planning instrument for subregional transformation born from the 2016 peace agreement. They seek to facilitate rural development in those territories most affected by armed conflict, poverty, illegal economies and institutional weakness. For criticism, see 'Alerta en Municipios Más Pobres por Parálisis de Proyectos', El Tiempo, 17 March 2021.

16 'Sexto Informe de Seguimiento a la Implementación del Acuerdo de Paz' [Sixth Follow-up Report on the Implementation of the Peace Agreement], http://www.juanitaenelcongreso.com, 18 February 2021.

17 Indepaz, 'Informe Sobre Presencia de Grupos Armados en Colombia' [Report on the Presence of Armed Groups in Colombia], August 2020.

18 United Nations Verification Mission in Colombia, 'Infographic Report of the Secretary General: 26 September to 28 December 2020', S/2020/1301, 15 January 2021.

19 Julián Alberto Gutiérrez, Nicolás Cortés Wilches and Carlos Javier Montaña Londoño, 'Multidimensional Poverty and its Relationship with Space: Case Study for Colombia', 25 April 2020.

20 World Bank, 'Gini Index – Colombia', 2019.

21 Transparency International, 'Corruption Perceptions Index 2020'.

22 'El 45 % de Los Combatientes del ELN Estarían en Venezuela: Fuerzas Militares' [45% of ELN Fighters Would Be in Venezuela: Military Forces], El Espectador, 8 May 2019; and Poly Martínez, 'La Nueva Marquetalia, La Razón Detrás de La Lucha Entre Las Disidencias de las FARC en La Frontera Venezolana' [The New Marquetalia: The Reason Behind FARC Dissident Disputes on the Venezuela Border], ABC España, 29 March 2021.

23 International Organization for Migration, 'Venezuelan Refugee and Migrant Crisis', March 2020.

24 Migración Colombia, 'After 6 Months, the Number of Venezuelans Living in Colombia Increases Again', 18 December 2020.

25 Government of Colombia, Ministry of Foreign Affairs, 'Distribución de Venezolanos en Colombia – Corte 31 de Enero de 2021' [Distribution of Venezuelans in Colombia – January 31, 2021], 3 March 2021.

26 Jurisdicción Especial para la Paz, 'Principales estadísticas' [Main Statistics], 25 June 2021.

27 'Colombia FARC: Former Rebels Charged with War Crimes', BBC News, 29 January 2021.

28 Jurisdicción Especial para la Paz, 'La JEP Hace Pública la Estrategia de Priorización Dentro del Caso 03, Conocido como el de Falsos Positivos' [The JEP Publishes its Prioritization Strategy within Case 03, Known as that of False Positives], Communication 019 of 2021.

29 José Ospina-Valencia, 'Asesinatos de Líderes Sociales: Colombia Mata a quienes Practican la Democracia en las Regiones' [Assassinations of Social Leaders: Colombia Kills Those Who Practice Democracy in the Regions], DW, 14 January 2021.

30 Office of the High Commissioner for Peace, 'Estadísticas de Asistencia Integral a las Víctimas de MAP y MUSE' [Statistics of Comprehensive Assistance to the Victims of Anti-personnel Mines and Unexploded Ordnance], 31 May 2021.

31 Didier Chica, 'En 2020 Creció el Desplazamiento Forzado en Colombia' [In 2020 Forced Displacement Increased in Colombia], Canal 1, 7 February 2021.

32 IMF, 'World Economic Outlook Database', April 2021.

33 Juan Carlos Echeverry, 'ELN y Actores Ilegales Siguen Volando Oleoductos' [ELN and Illegal Actors Continue to Blow Up Oil Pipelines], Caracol Radio, 28 January 2021.

34 See José González Bell, 'Extradición de la excongresista Aída Merlano abre nueva discusión binacional' [Extradition of Former Congresswoman Aída Merlano Opens New Binational Discussion], Asuntos Legales, 29 January 2020.

BRAZIL

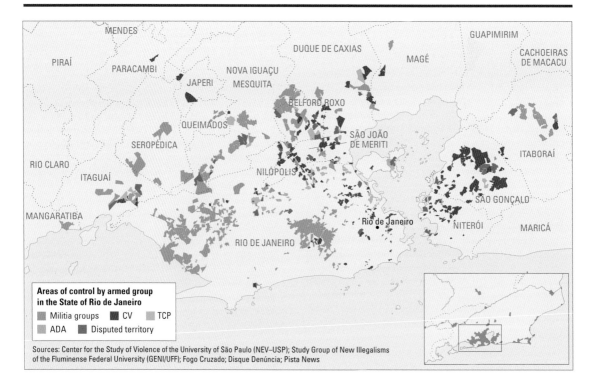

Areas of control by armed group in the State of Rio de Janeiro
Militia groups ▪ CV ▪ TCP
ADA ▪ Disputed territory

Sources: Center for the Study of Violence of the University of São Paulo (NEV–USP); Study Group of New Illegalisms of the Fluminense Federal University (GENI/UFF); Fogo Cruzado; Disque Denúncia; Pista News

Overview

Brazil has suffered armed violence for many years and in many forms. Although far from a failed state, criminal gangs contest large swathes of territory, offering goods and services to those who live under their control and challenging the state's presence.

One of Brazil's oldest criminal groups, the Red Command (CV), began in 1979 in the Candido Mendes prison on Rio de Janeiro's Ilha Grande. Its main rival, the São Paulo-based First Capital Command (PCC), began in the early 1990s in Taubaté prison. Both groups espouse a leftist political ideology that positions them against the Brazilian state and purports to fight for better prison conditions and the rights of the downtrodden and marginalised. Contesting the power of these two main gangs are militia groups, comprised of former police officers and other members of the security services, which control territory, extort local businesses and occasionally recruit members of defeated criminal organisations. Competition for territory and market share for drug trafficking has long driven the violence between these rival actors.

In 2020, violence among criminal groups continued in Rio de Janeiro with 3,536 homicides, a slight drop from the 4,004 in 2019.[1] However, a major cause for concern was the continued rise of police-inflicted killings driven by the hardline security policies adopted by the governor of Rio de Janeiro State, Wilson Witzel, an ally of President Jair Bolsonaro. Corruption in the police and militia recruitment from its ranks has pushed this trend upward.

Three major trends stood out in Brazil's armed conflict in 2020 and early 2021. Firstly, the coronavirus pandemic allowed gangs to showcase their capacity for criminal governance. By providing goods and social services, fixing prices of critical goods, distributing personal protective equipment and enforcing pandemic curfews, the gangs scored a major public-relations victory, demonstrating a more serious commitment to tackling the virus than Bolsonaro. On early evidence it also seemed as if gangs' criminal enterprises were not unduly slowed by the pandemic.[2]

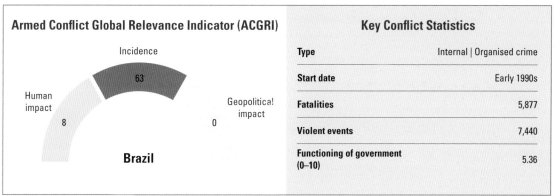

ACGRI pillars: IISS calculation based on multiple sources for 2020 and January/February 2021 (scale: 0–100). See Notes on Methodology and Data Appendix for further details on Key Conflict Statistics.

Secondly, in 2020, Amazonas State (and, to a lesser extent, Acre State) grew in strategic significance as a major point of criminal contestation in the country due to its vast river network and shared borders with major coca-producing countries, such as Bolivia, Colombia and Peru. The highly porous nature of these borders and the poor governance in these regions make them areas of heavy cross-border trafficking flows.

Thirdly, according to a much-discussed study, the territorial control of Rio de Janeiro's militia groups surpassed that of the city's drug-trafficking gangs. Armed groups control 96 of 163 neighbourhoods in Rio. Of these, militia groups were estimated to control about 33% of the city's population, or 2.1 million people. By comparison, 18% of the city, or 1.1m people, lived in areas under the control of the CV.[3]

Conflict Parties

Military Police of Rio de Janeiro (PMERJ/PM)

Strength: 41,024 members.[4]

Areas of operation: Rio de Janeiro State.

Leadership: Colonel Rogério Figueiredo de Lacerda (commander-in-chief).

Structure: Accountable to the Rio state government. Its hierarchy resembles that of the army and its members are reserves for the armed forces.

History: Created in May 1809. Current structure introduced in July 1975.

Objectives: Fight organised criminal groups.

Opponents: Organised-crime groups and militias.

Affiliates/allies: Unofficially, some militias and gangs, such as the Pure Third Command (TCP).

Resources/capabilities: Weapons currently used include the IMBEL *ParaFAL* 7.62mm battle rifle and the IMBEL IA2 assault rifle.

Red Command (CV)

Strength: 5,000 members in Rio de Janeiro State, and an estimated 30,000 associates in Amazonas State (and some in Acre State).[5]

Areas of operation: Rio de Janeiro, Acre, Amapá, Alagoas, Ceará, Federal District, Pará, Rio Grande do Norte, Rondônia, Roraima, Mato Grosso and Tocantins. Traditionally headquartered in the Alemão *favela* complex in the northern zone of Rio de Janeiro. Also present in Bolivia, Colombia and Paraguay.

Leadership: Márcio Santos Nepomuceno, alias 'Marcinho VP', and Elias Pereira da Silva, alias 'Elias Maluco', lead the group from jail. Gelson Lima Carnaúba, alias 'Gê', one of the founders of the Family of the North (FDN), switched sides in 2018 and now leads CV in Amazonas.

Structure: Decentralised structure with 'area leaders' in charge of neighbourhoods and *favelas*, 'managers' responsible for drug-dealing spots, which are secured by 'soldiers' who fend off threats by other dealers or the police. 'Scouts' keep watch for potential risks and warn 'soldiers'.

Red Command (CV)

History: The oldest and largest gang in Rio de Janeiro, which formed around 1979 in a maximum-security prison in Ilha Grande, off the southern coast of Rio de Janeiro. Involved in transnational drug trafficking since the 1980s, importing cocaine from Colombia and exporting it to Europe. Its activity declined after a police pacification programme in the Alemão *favela* complex in November 2010, but has since regained prominence and spread throughout Brazil and beyond.

Objectives: Maintain and enlarge its operating area to other neighbourhoods in Rio de Janeiro and other Brazilian states to expand its drug-trafficking market and extortion practices.

Opponents: In Rio de Janeiro: PMERJ, TCP, Friends of Friends (ADA), militia groups, PCC.
In Brazil: 13 Tram (B13), Guardians of the State (GDE), Crime Syndicate (SDC), Tocantins Mafia (MF), Class A Command (CCA), 30 Tram (B30), Northern Union (UDN), PCC.

Affiliates/allies: In Rio de Janeiro: None.
In Brazil: First Group of Santa Catarina.

Resources/capabilities: Revenue sources include drug trafficking, extortion of small businesses, kidnapping for ransom and weapons smuggling. Members are equipped with large numbers of handguns, AK-47s, bazookas and grenades.

First Capital Command (PCC)

Strength: Approximately 30,000.[6]

Areas of operation: Based in São Paulo State but maintains operations throughout much of Brazil, except the states of Goiás, Maranhão and Paraná. Also in Argentina, Bolivia, Colombia, the Netherlands, Mozambique, Paraguay, Peru, Portugal, South Africa and Venezuela.

Leadership: Marcos Willians Herbas Camacho, alias 'Marcola', took over the leadership in 2002, although he has been imprisoned since 1999.

Structure: Highly organised, with a CEO and strategic Deliberative Council (13 members); Board of Directors (three members), Administrative Board; Legal Board; State Board; Economic Board; Institutional Relations Board; and HR. These groupings are referred to as 'sintonias'. The structure on the street is comprised of 'managers', 'soldiers', 'scouts' and 'killers'.

History: Created by eight inmates on 31 August 1993 in a prison in Taubaté. In May 2006, after Marcola and 760 other prisoners were transferred to another prison, inmates rebelled in 74 state prisons and there were coordinated attacks on police officers, vehicles, jails and public buildings. More than 500 people were killed within a week.

Objectives: Deepen and entrench its position of power in Brazil and beyond.

Opponents: In Rio de Janeiro: PMERJ, TCP, ADA, CV.
In Amazonas State: CV, FDN.

Affiliates/allies: In Rio de Janeiro: TCP, ADA.

Resources/capabilities: Revenue sources include drug trafficking, bank and cargo robbery, money laundering, illegal gambling and kidnapping for ransom. The average revenue of the PCC is US$100m per year.[7] The gang uses pistols, rifles, bazookas and grenades.

Pure Third Command (TCP)

Strength: Unknown.

Areas of operation: Rio de Janeiro.

Leadership: Fernando Gomes de Freitas, Alvaro Malaquias Santa Rosa, alias 'Peixão'.

Structure: Decentralised structure with 'area leaders' in charge of neighbourhoods and *favelas*, 'managers' responsible for drug-dealing spots, which are secured by 'soldiers' who fend off threats by other dealers or the police. 'Scouts' keep watch for potential risks and warn 'soldiers'.

History: Created from the 2002 union of dissidents from ADA and the now-defunct Third Command (formed in the 1980s) after the death of Uê (who had been expelled from the CV for treason) and the arrest of Celsinho da Vila Vintém (head of ADA). Acquired partial control over several *favelas* since 2016, establishing itself as the second-most powerful criminal

organisation in Rio after the CV (excluding the vigilante militias). During 2017 and 2018, the rapid decline of ADA led many of its members to switch their allegiance to the TCP. The TCP's evangelical Christian members have been known to attack and expel followers of Afro-Brazilian religions from their areas.

Objectives: Maintain areas currently under its control and expand its operating area to other neighbourhoods in Rio de Janeiro and other states.

Opponents: CV, ADA, militias, PMERJ.

Affiliates/allies: PCC.

Resources/capabilities: Revenue sources include drug trafficking and extortion. Weapons include pistols, rifles, bazookas and grenades.

Friends of Friends (ADA)

Strength: Unknown, however, numbers have been waning for several years.

Areas of operation: Rio de Janeiro.

Leadership: Celso Luis Rodrigues, alias 'Celsinho da Vila Vintém', one of the gang's founders.

Structure: Decentralised structure with 'area leaders' in charge of neighbourhoods and *favelas*, 'managers' responsible for drug-dealing spots, which are secured by 'soldiers' who fend off threats by other dealers or the police. 'Scouts' keep watch for potential risks and warn 'soldiers'.

History: Created in 1998, in recent years ADA has suffered heavy losses in clashes with the CV and, to a lesser extent, the TCP.

Objectives: Maintain its few areas of control in Rio de Janeiro city and expand operations to other neighbourhoods, especially outside the Rio metropolitan area where there is less competition.

Opponents: CV, TCP, militias, PMERJ.

Affiliates/allies: PCC.

Resources/capabilities: Main revenue source is drug trafficking. Weapons include guns, pistols, rifles, bazookas and grenades.

Militias (various)

Strength: Unknown.

Areas of operation: 96 of 163 neighbourhoods around Rio de Janeiro city, particularly in the western neighbourhoods of Campo Grande, Paciência and Santa Cruz, as well as areas to the north of the city, such as Seropédica and Nova Iguaçu in Baixada Fluminense.

Leadership: The Justice League, the largest and most organised of the Rio militias, is led by Wellington da Silva Braga, also known as 'Ecko'. Brothers Jerominho and Natalino Guimarães, the League's founders, remain influential. The leadership of other smaller militia groups is unclear.

Structure: Similar structure to gangs, with area leaders, managers and soldiers, although at a different scale. Leaders control more than one neighbourhood or region and managers are responsible for a region or neighbourhood. Unlike in drug groups, soldiers operate from privileged positions (such as police stations). 'Killers' are responsible for executions.

History: Expanded rapidly during the 2000s. Comprised of former or current police officers (mostly from the PMERJ), firefighters and prison guards. The militias claim to provide security, but also traffic drugs, and extort, abduct and kill locals.

Objectives: Expand control over licit and illicit business and gain political influence, including by directly holding public offices in municipalities.

Opponents: ADA, CV, occasionally the PMERJ.

Affiliates/allies: TCP.

Resources/capabilities: Revenue sources include both licit and illicit business, such as drug trafficking, extortion, murder-for-hire operations, oil theft and sale, money laundering, real-estate transactions, and internet and TV services. Since militia members are often law-enforcement agents, they have access to the same weapons as those agencies, especially .40-calibre pistols and various types of rifles.

Family of the North (FDN)

Strength: Possibly the second-largest criminal group in the country with as many as 13,000 members.[8]

Areas of operation: Amazonas, Acre and Ceará states.

Leadership: José Roberto Barbosa, alias 'Zé Roberto da Compensa', and his son Luciano da Silva Barbosa, alias 'L7'.

Structure: Decentralised structure with 'area leaders' in charge of neighbourhoods and *favelas*, 'managers' responsible for drug-dealing spots, which are secured by 'soldiers' who fend off threats by other dealers or the police. 'Scouts' keep watch for potential risks and warn 'soldiers'.

History: Created by Carnaúba and Barbosa between 2006 and 2007, it became widely known after prison massacres in Manaus in 2015. That year, the FDN, together with the CV, carried out murders of PCC leaders; efforts by the state to broker a truce failed. The FDN competes for the treasured 'Solimões route', used to transport cocaine produced in Colombia and Peru through rivers in the Amazon region.

Objectives: Expand and consolidate control of drug-trafficking routes in the Amazon region; survive the onslaught from the CV in Amazonas.

Opponents: PCC, ADA, GDE, Primeiro Grupo Catarinense, CV.

Affiliates/allies: Okaida.

Resources/capabilities: Revenue sources include drug trafficking and money laundering. Members use pistols, rifles, bazookas and grenades.

Family of the North–Pure (FDN–P)

Strength: Unknown.

Areas of operation: Amazonas State.

Leadership: João Pinto Carioca, alias 'João Branco'.

Structure: Decentralised structure with 'area leaders' in charge of neighbourhoods and *favelas*, 'managers' responsible for drug-dealing spots, which are secured by 'soldiers' who fend off threats by other dealers or the police. 'Scouts' keep watch for potential risks and warn 'soldiers'.

History: Created in 2019 by João Branco, a former senior member of FDN, dissatisfied with the group's waning influence inside prisons, decreasing drug sales following the end of its alliance with CV. From a federal prison in Paraná,

João Branco gathered FDN members loyal to him in Amazonas to eliminate FDN leadership inside the prisons. This command leaked, sparking a war between FDN and FDN–P that led to the deaths of over 55 prisoners.[9]

Objectives: Eliminate FDN.

Opponents: FDN.

Affiliates/allies: Unknown.

Resources/capabilities: Revenue sources include drug trafficking and money laundering. Members use uses pistols, rifles, bazookas and grenades.

Other conflict parties

Several other relevant criminal groups were also active in the state of Acre, which borders Amazonas, namely, the 13 Tram (B13) and Ifara. These groups have demonstrated a nascent capacity to project power into Amazonas State, and more importantly have replicated the rivalries of larger Brazilian groups in Acre State, by offering themselves as proxies to the PCC in its battle against the CV. While information on these groups was limited, B13 was founded in Acre's prisons by

PCC members dissatisfied with that group's bureaucratic governance and rules. B13 itself splintered when some members formed the nascent group Ifara. To compete with the CV effectively, however, B13 still works closely with the PCC and with Ifara. Both groups thus likely share the PCC's broader aim of rolling back the CV's gains in Amazonas and Acre states.

Conflict Drivers

Political

Weakness of state institutions:
Neighbourhoods far from city centres and rural regions, such as in Amazonas State, receive reduced investment and public services, forcing residents to rely on criminal groups for the provision of internet and cable TV connections, trash collection and public transportation. Gangs therefore have an additional form of income to drug trafficking, as well as an opportunity to enhance their social legitimacy with the population.

Widespread corruption:
Brazil suffers from endemic corruption at all levels of government. The country ranked 94th in Transparency International's 2020 Corruption Perceptions Index, placing it in the bottom half.[10] Since 1998, every governor of Rio de Janeiro State has been arrested on corruption charges, with the trend continuing in 2020 with governor Witzel's suspension. Other high-profile figures have also been incarcerated in recent years and a legal inquiry was launched in 2020 investigating alleged corruption by President Bolsonaro's son.[11]

Economic and social

Intensifying competition in the illicit-drug trade:
One of the main drivers of armed conflict in Brazil is the desire to expand drug-trafficking routes and to consolidate territory in turf wars. Illicit drugs, such as cocaine, are trafficked to Brazil for domestic consumption as well as international export. In Rio de Janeiro, the large potential revenues and the proximity of *favelas* (slums) to wealthy enclaves in the city's South Zone sparked the proliferation of criminal drug-trafficking organisations (DTOs). The need to take and control territory in an environment characterised by fickle and constantly shifting alliances has generated intense clashes between rival factions. For this reason, Brazilian DTOs have sought to expand their operations internationally for several years, which helps explain the growing competition over Amazonas State as a principal node through which drugs pass on their way to Africa and eventually to Europe.

Increasing returns in Europe's cocaine market:
Europe has become the top destination for drugs transiting through Brazil, as DTOs have increasingly realized that it offers a more lucrative (and less

competitive) market than the United States.[12] One kilogram of cocaine in the US is worth US$28,000 wholesale, as compared to between US$40,000 and US$80,000 in Europe.[13]

Social and racial inequality:
Socio-economic and racial inequality is another major structural driver of armed violence in Brazil. Poverty disproportionately affects northern and northeastern states in Brazil and those of the population identifying as Black or Brown, as confirmed by the Brazilian Institute of Geography and Statistics (IBGE). Brazil's criminal groups deftly exploit social and racial inequality, espousing ideologies that purport to defend the downtrodden, uphold human rights in Brazil's inhumane prisons and hold police accountable for acts of impunity.

Political and Military Developments

The end of Witzel and Rio's police raids
Wilson Witzel began his second year in office as governor of Rio de Janeiro in 2020 and signalled that he intended to continue an iron-fist approach to security. As such, police raids into the *favelas* in Rio continued in the first half of 2020 and police-inflicted deaths mounted. In June, the Brazilian Supreme Federal Court prohibited police operations in Rio's slums until the end of the pandemic except in 'absolutely exceptional' cases.[14] As a result, the number of people killed by the police fell by 76% in June and July 2020 compared to the previous year.[15] However, this suspension of raids was short-lived; by October 2020, the number of police operations classified as 'exceptional cases' increased, contributing to the deaths of 125 people in that month alone.[16]

On 28 August 2020, the Superior Court of Justice suspended Wilson pending the outcome of a trial into corruption related to coronavirus supplies.

Access to firearms
In 2020 and early 2021 Bolsonaro continued fulfilling his campaign promise of facilitating greater access to firearms. In February 2021, his administration increased the previous limit on the number of guns and ammunition individuals could acquire, liberalised civilian access to certain types of firearms formerly restricted to law-enforcement agents and suspended the requirement to demonstrate an 'effective need' for a weapon as a precondition for purchase.[17]

Drug interdiction
Increased domestic demands for drugs amid coronavirus restrictions resulted in greater drug interdiction in 2020. Vehicle inspections at the Brazilian border also increased, as a result of reduced vehicle traffic on the roads and the expansion of activities under the National Border and Border-Security Programme (VIGIA) in April 2020.[18] In Amazonas State specifically, VIGIA inaugurated a floating base in August 2020 in the Solimões River to disrupt the major drug-trafficking route, supplemented by communications towers and water vehicles. However, the pandemic reduced the scope of joint Brazilian–Paraguayan marijuana-extermination operations, increasing the volume of the drug available in the regional marketplace.

Money laundering
Seized criminal-organisation assets in federal money-laundering operations nearly doubled in 2020. Property previously owned by Brazil's gangs – totalling over R$1 billion (around US$200m) and including mansions, farms, vehicles, aircraft and jewels – was sold in auctions, a process that had

Figure 1: Intentional homicide rates, January 2016–February 2021

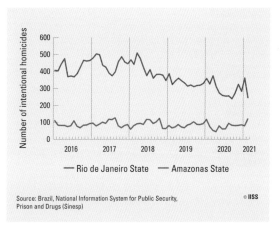

Source: Brazil, National Information System for Public Security, Prison and Drugs (Sinesp)   © IISS

been simplified by the Bolsonaro administration. The proceeds were invested back into the federal anti-drug organisation's coffers.[19]

Increasing violence in Amazonas

In January 2020, there were 106 murders in Manaus, the capital of Amazonas State, 54% more than in the same period the previous year according to official figures.[20] The CV led a major wave of violence in Manaus, capturing 80% of the FDN's territory and leaving the FDN – its erstwhile ally – reeling.[21] Other groups, such as the B13, itself a splinter from the PCC, also moved into this region to contest territory and act as a PCC proxy.

Key Events in 2020–21

POLITICAL EVENTS

1 January 2020
President Jair Bolsonaro and then-governor of Rio de Janeiro Wilson Witzel both mark one year in office.

10 February
Amazonas State opens a 'crisis office' in Manaus to analyse a spate of killings and the wider battle between FDN and CV.

24 April
Sérgio Moro, the high-profile lead prosecutor of the *Operation Car Wash* corruption probe, resigns his post as Bolsonaro's minister of justice and public security.

26 April
Brazil announces the release of around 30,000 prisoners on the grounds of personal health and safety as per coronavirus guidelines.

5 June
Brazil's Supreme Federal Court suspends police raids in Rio de Janeiro's *favelas* during the coronavirus pandemic.

10 June
In Rio, an impeachment process is opened against governor Witzel on corruption charges related to the misappropriation of coronavirus funds.

28 August
Brazil's Superior Court of Justice suspends Witzel from his duties due to the ongoing corruption investigation.

30 September
In one of the largest raids of the year, *Operation King of Crime* uncovers a money-laundering ring and seizes millions of dollars-worth of assets thought to belong to the PCC.

2 January 2021
Brazil's main COVID-19 variant (so-called P.1) is discovered.

5 January
Manaus, the capital of Amazonas State, declares a state of emergency after a surge of COVID-19 cases.

15 February
Bolsonaro issues four new decrees making gun ownership easier, following a similar set of decrees in 2019.

MILITARY/VIOLENT ATTACKS

13 February 2020
FDN loses several key neighbourhoods in Manaus as a result of the CV's campaign to take control of Amazonas State.

16 March
Hundreds of prisoners escape from four prisons in São Paulo State in protest over poor conditions related to the pandemic.

2 May
Inmates take seven prison guards hostage in a Manaus prison, rebelling over poor conditions related to the pandemic.

19 May
Police kill 13 people in an operation in the Alemão *favela* complex in Rio de Janeiro.

26 August
Heavily armed CV members engage in a shoot-out with police in Rio de Janeiro, taking hostages and killing an innocent passer-by.

12 September
In Rio Branco, Mailton da Silva Teixeira, leader of the B13, is found dead in his prison cell.

Impact

Human rights and humanitarian

The emphasis on 'confrontation' in Bolsonaro's security approach has had severe consequences for human rights. Rio's police killed nearly 800 people between June 2020 and the end of March 2021, despite the Supreme Federal Court ban on *favela* raids.[22] In the last decade, Rio's police force has killed nearly 9,000 people.[23] This translates to approximately three people per day on average. Brazilian government policies continued to focus on short-term tactical operations while neglecting long-standing drivers of violence, which would be better solved by creating viable political and social institutions, ensuring better access to, and provision of, basic services, and offering stable governance in peripheral communities.

Economic and social

As of the end of February 2021 Brazil had suffered the second-highest number of COVID-19 deaths globally, behind only the US, exacerbated by a surge in cases at the end of 2020 following the discovery of the more transmissible and deadly P.1 variant of the virus.[24] With much of the state's effort directed at fighting the pandemic, criminal groups had ample space to expand with little meaningful pushback.

The pandemic particularly affected Brazil's huge prison system, worsening the notoriously precarious conditions of mismanagement, violence, overcrowding and insufficient health services.[25]

Despite these alarming numbers, significant mitigation efforts were made to reduce the spread of COVID-19. Following voluntary guidelines set by the National Council of Justice as early as April 2020, judges throughout the country allowed tens of thousands of inmates, especially older and low-level offenders, to leave prisons under special conditions. Those who remained incarcerated, however, felt the government response to protect the prison population had been unsatisfactory.

Relations with neighbouring and international partners and geopolitical implications

Security shortcomings in Brazil have long been blamed on lax enforcement in neighbouring Bolivia and Paraguay. The conflict dynamics in 2020 ensured not only that the PCC in particular – the most internationalised criminal group in Brazil – could continue to operate internationally, but that it could do so without significant pushback, as demonstrated by its successful international recruitment in Bolivia and Paraguay. For example, in Paraguay, the PCC's membership quintupled between the end of 2018 and June 2019, successfully recruiting Spanish- and Guaraní-speaking Paraguayans rather than Brazilians.[26]

Conflict Outlook

Political scenarios

The political outlook in Brazil remains filled with uncertainty. Witzel's suspension from office raises serious questions about the future direction of Rio de Janeiro's security policies. The uptick in police raids since October 2020, despite the Brazilian Supreme Federal Court ban, suggests that these could be fully reinstated after the coronavirus pandemic subsides, unless Rio can be persuaded by the preliminary evidence gathered during the police-raid moratorium to commit to a different long-term strategy.

Witzel may be at risk of losing an ally in Bolsonaro at the federal level. The overturning of Luiz Inácio 'Lula' da Silva's conviction for corruption in March 2021 makes him eligible to run for president in 2022, all but guaranteeing a divisive second-round run-off between himself and Bolsonaro. As in the 2018 presidential campaign, such a scenario could prompt polarising rhetoric on security issues.

Escalation potential and conflict-related risks

Despite the expansion of militia-controlled territory in 2020, these spaces appeared to be a major blind spot for police, with only 6.5% of police operations conducted in Rio's militia-held territory, compared to 48% conducted in territory held by the CV, TCP and ADA.[27] There could be major potential for an escalation in violence if Rio's police prove unable to execute a strategic paradigm shift in thinking about criminal organisations, to include a stronger focus on deadly militia groups.

Violence in Amazonas State (and bordering Acre State) is also likely to intensify as ongoing conflicts continue between rival factions to retake territory, including the CV, FDN and FDN–P. To more effectively rebuff the 2020 territorial gains made by the CV in Manaus, in October 2020, Zé Roberto da Compensa, the leader of the FDN, proposed an alliance with the PCC. The historical rivalry between the two groups purportedly divided the PCC's leadership, but any potential agreement would require the FDN to remove the leaders involved in the 2017 Compaj prison massacre of PCC members. If an alliance did come to fruition, it could presage a major uptick in violence in 2021.

Prospects for peace
Given the status of flux in which Witzel's suspension has left Rio de Janeiro, there is little prospect of a shift away from the crime-fighting strategy based on 'confrontation', making peace unlikely. More generally, some of the biggest drivers of Brazil's violence remain unaddressed. Persistent inequality not only remains but has potentially been exacerbated by the pandemic's deep toll on the Brazilian economy. Meanwhile, Bolsonaro's loosening of gun-ownership regulations ensures that a ready supply of arms will remain available on the black market.

Strategic implications and global influences
Brazilian criminal groups will continue their strong internationalisation campaign. With a footprint in just about every country in South America, groups such as the PCC are more globally minded than ever before. The CV also maintains strong international links and sees transnational expansion as crucial to its survival.

Notes

1   Ben Oakley, 'Rio de Janeiro Has the Lowest Homicide Rate in 30 Years Due to the Pandemic', Globe Live Media, 28 January 2021.

2   For instance, drug seizures in South American ports bound for Europe, the major export destination for Brazilian groups, were up 20% in 2020. See Francesco Guarascio, 'Europe Flooded with Cocaine Despite Coronavirus Trade Disruptions', Reuters, 30 April 2020.

3   Nicolás Satriano, 'Rio Tem 3.7 Milhões de Habitantes em Areas Dominadas pelo Crime Organizado; Milícia Controla 57% da Area da Cidade, Diz Estudo' [Rio Has 3.7 Million Inhabitants in Areas Dominated by Organised Crime; Militia Controls 57% of the City's Area, Says Study], G1, 19 October 2020.

4   'Sem Concurso, PMERJ Tem 30 Mil Soldados a Menos que Previsto em Lei' [Without Contest, PMERJ Has 30 Thousand Soldiers Less than Provided in Lei], Folha Dirigida, 7 October 2019.

5   Robson Bonin, 'Comando Vermelho Vira Preocupação do Governo Bolsonaro – Entenda' [Comando Vermelho Becomes the Concern of the Bolsonaro Government – Understand], Veja, 22 August 2020.

6   'PCC', Americas Quarterly; and InSight Crime and American University's Center for Latin American & Latino Studies, 'The Rise of the PCC: How South America's Most Powerful Prison Gang Is Spreading in Brazil and Beyond', CLALS Working Paper Series, No. 30, 6 December 2020, p. 23.

7   Angelika Albaladejo, 'PCC Files Document Gang's Explosive Growth in Brazil and Beyond', InSight Crime, 5 June 2018.

8   'The Rise of the PCC', p. 52.

9   'FDN x FDN Pura: Conflito Entre João Branco e Zé Roberto Motivou mortes' [Family of the North vs Family of the North–Pure: Conflict Between João Branco and Zé Roberto Motivated Deaths], acrítica.com, 28 May 2019; and Chris Dalby, 'Brazil Prisons Become Battlegrounds for Familia do Norte Civil War', InSight Crime, 29 May 2019.

10 Transparency International, '2020 Corruption Perceptions Index'.

11 The architect of Rio's pacification and security strategy, former governor Sérgio Cabral, was sentenced to 14 years in prison in 2017. At the national level, in 2018 former president Luiz Inácio 'Lula' da Silva was convicted of money laundering and corruption and sentenced to nearly ten years in prison. In 2019, former president Michel Temer was arrested on charges of corruption too.

12 Ryan C. Berg and Andrea Varsori, 'COVID-19 Is Increasing the Power of Brazil's Criminal Groups', London School of Economics Latin America and the Caribbean blog, 28 May 2020.

13 Jeremy McDermott et al., 'The Cocaine Pipeline to Europe', Global Initiative against Transnational Organized Crime, February 2021, p. 1.

14 Gabriel Barreira, 'Ministro do STF Proíbe Operações em Favelas do Rio Durante a Pandemia' [STF Minister Prohibits Operations in Rio's Favelas During the Pandemic], G1, 5 June 2020.

15 Felipe Grandin and Matheus Rodrigues, 'RJ Tem Queda de 76% nas Mortes Cometidas por Policiais Após STF Restringir Operações nas Favelas' [RJ Has 76% Drop in Police Deaths after STF Restricts Operations in Favelas], G1, 25 August 2020.

16 Terrence McCoy, 'Rio Police Were Ordered to Limit Favela Raids During the Pandemic. They're Still Killing Hundreds of People', Washington Post, 20 May 2021.

17 The first two years of Bolsonaro's administration have seen a 183% increase in gun registrations. See Mariana Schreiber, 'Com Acesso Facilitado, Brasil Fecha 2020 com Recorde de 180 Mil Novas Armas de Fogo Registradas na PF, um Aumento de 91%' [With Easier Access, Brazil Closes 2020 with a Record

180,000 New Firearms Registered with the Federal Police, an Increase of 91%], BBC News Brasil, 8 January 2021.

[18] The VIGIA programme is an initiative launched by the Ministry of Justice and Public Security in 2019 to tackle illicit business activities on Brazil's borders by increasing collaboration between federal and state law-enforcement agencies. In its initial capacity, the government implemented VIGIA as a pilot programme in seven states bordering other South American countries and at the state border between Goiás and Tocantins. In its first year, VIGIA interdicted more than 125 tonnes of drugs, as well as other illicit products, totalling over R$750 million (over US$140m). Based on this initial success, the Brazilian government started to extend the programme to all 11 border states in April 2020.

[19] Mariana Schreiber, 'Por Que a Apreensão de Drogas é Recorde em 2020 — e o que Isso Significa' [Why Record Drug Seizures Happened in 2020 — and What It Means], BBC News Brasil, 22 December 2020.

[20] Fabiano Maisonnave, 'Comando Vermelho Toma Manaus em Meio a Onda de Assassinatos' [Red Command Takes Manaus in the Midst of a Wave of Murders], GZH Geral, 13 February 2020.

[21] Chris Dalby, 'Family of the North Likely Close to Its End in Manaus, Brazil', InSight Crime, 25 February 2020.

[22] Flávia Milhorance, 'Police Kill Hundreds in Rio de Janeiro Despite Court Ban on Favela Raids', *Guardian*, 18 April 2021.

[23] Institute of Public Safety, 'Dados: Visualização' [Data Visualization].

[24] World Health Organization, 'WHO Coronavirus (COVID-19) Dashboard', 28 February 2021.

[25] Brazil has the third-highest prison population in the world, with over 750,000 prisoners. See Institute for Crime and Justice Policy Research, 'World Prison Brief Database: Highest to Lowest – Prison Population Total', accessed 18 March 2021.

[26] Renan Nucci, 'Número de Membros de Facções Brasileiras Quintuplica na Fronteira, Diz Polícia' [Number of Brazilian Faction Members Quintuples on the Border, Says Police], *Midiamax*, 24 January 2020.

[27] Leandro Resende, 'Apenas 6.5% das Operações Policiais no Rio Foram em Área de Milícia, Diz Estudo' [Only 6.5% of Police Operations in Rio Were in the Militia Area, Says Study'], CNN Brazil, 30 October 2020.

Americas

EL SALVADOR

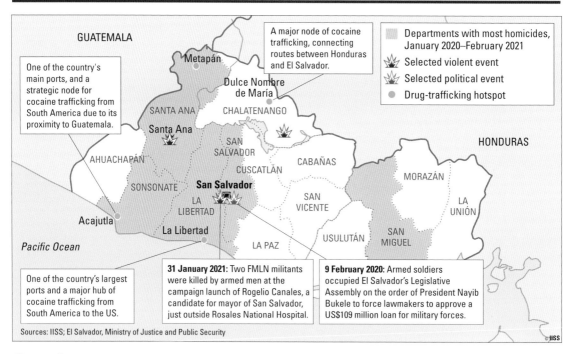

One of the country's main ports, and a strategic node for cocaine trafficking from South America due to its proximity to Guatemala.

A major node of cocaine trafficking, connecting routes between Honduras and El Salvador.

Departments with most homicides, January 2020–February 2021
Selected violent event
Selected political event
Drug-trafficking hotspot

GUATEMALA
Metapán
Dulce Nombre de María
SANTA ANA   CHALATENANGO
Santa Ana
SAN SALVADOR
AHUACHAPÁN   CABAÑAS   HONDURAS
CUSCATLÁN
SONSONATE   MORAZÁN
San Salvador
LA LIBERTAD   SAN VICENTE   LA UNIÓN
Acajutla
La Libertad   USULUTÁN   SAN MIGUEL
Pacific Ocean   LA PAZ

One of the country's largest ports and a major hub of cocaine trafficking from South America to the US.

31 January 2021: Two FMLN militants were killed by armed men at the campaign launch of Rogelio Canales, a candidate for mayor of San Salvador, just outside Rosales National Hospital.

9 February 2020: Armed soldiers occupied El Salvador's Legislative Assembly on the order of President Nayib Bukele to force lawmakers to approve a US$109 million loan for military forces.

Sources: IISS; El Salvador, Ministry of Justice and Public Security

Overview

The conflict involving the Mara Salvatrucha (MS-13) gang has been a multi-phased battle for territorial control, political legitimacy and economic resources. Established in the mid-1990s by members deported from California, mainly Los Angeles, by the early 2000s the MS-13 had evolved into a military force that challenged the state, thriving in the weak economic and legal structures of post-civil-war El Salvador. Over time it consolidated territorial control across the country and developed revenue streams from extortion, kidnapping, assassinations and the sale of marijuana, crack cocaine and cocaine. As it became entrenched in local communities, the MS-13 attracted new members with combat experience from El Salvador's civil war (1979–92). Despite attempts by successive administrations, repressive strategies failed to stem the gang's expansion. By 2012, the MS-13 counted over 12,000 members and its main rival, the Barrio 18 gang, had over 8,000 members.[1] El Salvador's homicide rate was also among the highest in the world. This situation prompted the government to engage the gangs in the first formal negotiations, resulting in the 'truce', where gangs reduced visible homicides in exchange for government concessions and payments. However, the pact collapsed in 2014 and meanwhile the gangs had learned the true scope of their political leverage. Since then, the MS-13 has consolidated its territorial control and grown its military capabilities, using spikes in violence as negotiating leverage with the government, while the Barrio 18 has suffered from internal divides and lost territory.

2020 saw a reduction in armed confrontation as the conflict shifted towards more sophisticated forms of political dialogue between the gang and the government. Numerous published accounts suggested that the MS-13 may have engaged in secret negotiations with the administration of President Nayib Bukele – something the latter denies – as it sought legal protection and limited incorporation into the country's formal political structure, in exchange for reducing the homicide rate and for delivering hundreds of thousands of votes in its areas of broad territorial control for the president's party in the February 2021 mid-term elections.[2]

Bukele's New Ideas party ultimately secured an absolute majority in the elections and won control

Armed Conflict Global Relevance Indicator (ACGRI)	Key Conflict Statistics	
Incidence	**Type**	Internal | Organised crime
3	**Start date**	2003
Human impact Geopolitical impact	**Gini index (0–100)**	38.8 (2019)
1 4	**GDP per capita, PPP (current international \$)**	8421.5
El Salvador	**Functioning of government (0–10)**	4.29

ACGRI pillars: IISS calculation based on multiple sources for 2020 and January/February 2021 (scale: 0–100). See Notes on Methodology and Data Appendix for further details on Key Conflict Statistics.

of over two-thirds of the nation's municipal governments, enabling it to name new Supreme Court justices, choose the attorney general, and further criminalise the opposition and media. This absolute majority also gave the government the power to enact legislative changes and constitutional reforms independently, including its strategy for managing the gangs.

The ongoing relationship between the MS-13 and the Bukele administration, described variously as a 'fragile informal understanding' or 'negotiation', fundamentally shifted the nature of the conflict away from its historic characterisation of fighting between the two main gangs and both gangs fighting against the state.[3] 2020 positioned the MS-13 and the government as protagonists, with violence spiking during communication breakdowns or shows of strength. Against this backdrop, the homicide rate dropped substantially from 2,398 in 2019 to 1,322 in 2020, a historic low of 19.7 per 100,000.[4] Disputing the truce narrative, the government attributed this decline to the success of its Territorial Control Plan, which had involved the deployment of over 5,000 police and soldiers to gang strongholds in 2019. Moreover, the official homicide statistics should be considered incomplete, since they do not include the high number

(1,225, as of November 2020) of 'disappeared', or certain types of violent deaths.[5]

The coronavirus pandemic drastically reduced migration from El Salvador to the Mexico–United States border, cutting the gang's revenue from human-smuggling routes. However, the MS-13 seized the opportunity to reinforce its territorial control by playing a quasi-state role, imposing curfews to curb the spread of COVID-19 – and beating violators with baseball bats – and providing rudimentary but effective neighbourhood food and water assistance and neighbourhood security. In March 2020, when Bukele decreed strict nationwide quarantine measures and punishments for their violation, the MS-13 took on the role of enforcing them in many neighbourhoods where the state was absent, enhancing its legitimacy as a semi-political actor.

The MS-13 continued to employ several tactics to assert its dominance – including executions, public beatings, extortion and forced displacement – which prevented economic growth and disrupted community cohesion. Although the pandemic limited some of their activities, the group pursued a multi-pronged strategy to expand its power while transporting cocaine, upgrading its weapons and diversifying its financial holdings.

Conflict Parties

El Salvador armed forces

Strength: 24,500 active military (20,500 army, 2,000 air force, 2,000 navy).

Areas of operation: Throughout El Salvador.

Leadership and structure: René Francis Merino Monroy (minister of defence).
Six brigades across the country; three infantry battalions; one special military-security brigade with two military-police and two border-security battalions; one artillery brigade; one mechanised cavalry regiment; special-forces command with one special-operations group and an anti-terrorist command.

Objectives: Responsible for defence against external threats. Works with the police for internal-security purposes, including fighting the MS-13. Plays a primary role in counter-narcotics operations and continues to play a law-enforcement role

(despite this being ruled unconstitutional by the Supreme Court).

Opponents and affiliates/allies:
Opponents: The MS-13, Barrio 18, cocaine-transport groups and other smaller criminal groups in El Salvador.
Allies: The National Civil Police (PNC) and some civilian paramilitary groups.

Resources/capabilities: Special-operations command, high-mobility multi-purpose wheeled vehicles (HMMWVs), light armoured vehicles, M113 armoured personnel carriers (APCs) and multiple other armoured vehicles, eight UH-1H helicopters, two UH-1M helicopters and assorted other helicopters.

The National Civil Police (PNC)

Strength: Approximately 23,000 members.[6] Proposed increase was prevented by the coronavirus pandemic and the ensuing budget crisis.

Areas of operation: Throughout El Salvador.

Leadership and structure: Mauricio Antonio Arriaza Chicas (director general).
The security force tasked with countering the MS-13 is comprised of three anti-gang units of approximately 600 special-forces troops and 400 PNC officers.[7] This is separate from the counter-narcotics and organised-crime units.

Objectives: Primarily responsible for internal threats, including combatting gangs, organised crime and drug trafficking. Anti-gang units are tasked with targeting the non-incarcerated MS-13 leadership and restricting the communications capabilities of the prison leadership.

Opponents and affiliates/allies:
Opponents: The MS-13, Barrio 18, cocaine-transport groups and other smaller criminal groups in El Salvador.
Allies: El Salvador's armed forces, especially since June 2019.

Resources/capabilities: Specialised units combine the use of helicopters, armoured vehicles and assault rifles, partially offsetting the PNC's lack of heavy weapons.

Mara Salvatrucha (MS-13)

Strength: Estimates range from 17,000 to 60,000.[8]

Areas of operation: Estimated to operate in around 93% of the country's municipalities (247 of 262), where each member is part of a network of at least six people.[9]

Leadership and structure: Run by *la ranfla histórica* (national leadership), which sets the overall policies and strategies from prisons throughout El Salvador. Faced with internal fissures, the *ranfla histórica* has devolved some decision-making power to the *ranfla libre* (the gang leadership not in prison).
Below them are the *palabreros* (those who delegate orders), *programas* (groups of *clicas* (highly compartmentalised street-level units)), with semi-autonomous leadership across multiple neighbourhoods and the *clicas*.

Objectives: The MS-13's primary objectives are twofold: control territory in which the gang is free to exercise its own laws and authority autonomously (without overthrowing the government on a national level), while displacing traditional, entrenched cocaine-transport groups (such as the Cartel de Texis, Los Perrones and others) for financial gain. However, as the gang has achieved more official political legitimacy,

this strategy may be shifting to embedding members within the state structure while learning how to extort the system rather than individuals.

Opponents and affiliates/allies:
Opponents: The Barrio 18 gang.
Allies: MS-13 structures in Honduras and Guatemala, parts of the Sinaloa Cartel and the Cartel Jalisco New Generation (CJNG) in Mexico.
Perception of state-security forces fluctuates between being considered the enemy and occasionally a tactical partner.

Resources/capabilities: Financial resources derived from extortion, protecting cocaine loads, kidnapping, murder-for-hire and money laundering. These are not evenly distributed among the gang's *clicas*. Those groups that control key cocaine-trafficking routes or beach areas for sea-transported loads are better off than those not involved with cocaine routes. Some centralised redistribution exists but inequality among groups on the ground is a constant source of tension. Armoury features a growing number of new weapons, including Dragunov sniper rifles, Uzis, rocket-propelled grenades (RPGs) and a small number of light anti-tank weapons.

Conflict Drivers

Political

State illegitimacy and entrenched governance flaws:

The state's perceived illegitimacy has been a primary driver of the conflict, due to widespread corruption, institutional weakness and its lack of a monopoly on the use of force. In the most recent comprehensive poll, only 12% of respondents felt the government ran the country, with 42% instead believing power rested with the gangs.[10]

Frustration with traditional political parties gave Bukele, who ran as an anti-corruption candidate, a handsome victory in the 2019 elections, albeit with the second-highest abstention rate since the end of the civil war (around 50%).[11] However, while Bukele's increasingly authoritarian tactics (including egregious episodes such as sending armed soldiers to occupy the Legislative Assembly to pressure members to approve a loan in February 2020) have prompted widespread international criticism and concern, they have not tarnished the president's enduring popularity.

Economic and social

Socio-economic challenges:

Despite significant economic reforms that were part of the 1992 peace agreement, deep economic inequality and high unemployment persist, especially among young people (15 to 24 years old). With 12% of young people unemployed, 50% underemployed and 24.8% neither studying nor working, there are limited viable alternatives to MS-13 recruitment, which continues to fuel the conflict.[12]

In 2020, the coronavirus pandemic and two major tropical storms (which caused billions of dollars of damage) exacerbated an already dire socio-economic situation, which resulted in an 8.6% GDP contraction.[13] Concurrently, the Trump administration worked to stem migration – a traditional safety valve in times of economic hardship – while increasing deportations to El Salvador. The Trump administration also asked that El Salvador spend scarce resources to act as a 'safe third country' where would-be immigrants could theoretically wait for asylum petitions to be processed.

Security

Increasing militarisation:

The MS-13 continued to present itself as having a legitimacy equal to that of the state, driving a conflict where the gang 'extort[s] residents throughout the country … Gangs kill, disappear, rape those who resist.'[14] In response, state-security forces, publicly encouraged by Bukele, were deployed in public-security operations – despite the 1992 peace accord stipulation against this tactic – resulting in a sharp rise in human-rights abuses committed by the state.

Key Events in 2020–21

POLITICAL EVENTS

12 March 2020

President Bukele announces national quarantine due to coronavirus pandemic, including stringent lockdown-enforcement measures that continue despite being declared illegal by the Supreme Court.

MILITARY/VIOLENT EVENTS

9 February 2020

Armed soldiers and law-enforcement officials occupy El Salvador's Legislative Assembly to force lawmakers to sign a US$109 million loan proposed by Bukele to fight violent gangs.

3 September

The El Faro news portal publishes first extensive report on negotiations between the Bukele administration and the MS-13 gang, including alleged illegal, clandestine meetings between senior cabinet officials and gang leaders.

24 September

Bukele counters the El Faro news portal with public (unsubstantiated) allegations of money laundering and initiates multiple audits of their accounts, drawing widespread criticism from human-rights groups and freedom-of-information organisations.

9 December

Héctor Gustavo Villatoro, head of El Salvador's Financial System Superintendence, releases a memo stating banks cannot terminate commercial relations with alleged financial criminals, drawing sharp international condemnation and allegations of Bukele's ties to transnational criminal organisations.

11 December

The Millennium Challenge Corporation, a prestigious US assistance programme that generates employment, is not renewed, on the basis of El Salvador's insufficient progress to curb corruption.

15 December

Attorney General Raúl Melara charges municipal mayor Roel Werner Martínez Romero and two other public officials with the homicide of two councillors in 2018 and 2019. All three are arrested as part of a massive operation against MS-13 members and collaborators in the country's eastern departments.

15 December

The Office of the Attorney General opens a criminal investigation against Mauricio Arriaza Chicas, the director general of the PNC, for failing to comply with his duties in the investigations against Health Minister Francisco Alabí and Minister of Finance Alejandro Zelaya.

28 February 2021

Bukele's New Ideas party sweeps legislative and municipal elections, winning an absolute majority in the unicameral Legislative Assembly.

April

A killing spree attributed to the MS-13 takes place over five days, leaving 85 dead despite a sharp decline in the national homicide rate.

25 April

Bukele imposes a 24-hour prison lockdown after 22 homicides are reported in one day, the highest since he took office in June 2019.

31 January 2021

Two militants of the Farabundo Martí National Liberation Front (FMLN) party are killed by security forces assigned to the finance ministry in an armed attack at the campaign launch of Rogelio Canales, a mayoral candidate for San Salvador.

Conflict Outlook

Political scenarios

Four likely political scenarios between the MS-13 and the government existed as of February 2021. The most extreme would involve talks between the two sides to produce a more formal understanding, whereby the MS-13 would gain access to government resources and formalise political control in municipalities under its de facto control, in exchange for de-escalating the armed conflict with state actors such as the PNC and continuing to reduce civilian killings. The second scenario would involve the two sides following historic precedent and breaking off communications, leading to an escalation of violence that would ultimately drive them back to informal or formal discussions around the homicide rate. A third scenario would maintain the status quo of informal discussions while the MS-13 moves more aggressively into cocaine trafficking and migrant smuggling with little resistance from the government. This would keep violence levels low, while economically empowering the MS-13 and allowing the state to crack down if politically expedient. The fourth scenario would involve the government's continued concentration of institutional power, undermining the country's checks and balances, including the use of force. The government would then adopt an iron-fist approach to fight criminal gangs, exacerbating violence. All four scenarios would likely increase the ongoing exodus of migrants from El Salvador to the US and strain the already tense relationship between the two countries. If the Biden administration were to follow through on its threat to revoke US visas and impose financial sanctions on senior Bukele administration officials for corruption charges, the Bukele administration may be more likely to enter formal negotiations and accept greater concessions.

Strategic implications and global influences

The Biden administration has vocalised its intent to enact comprehensive anti-corruption measures to address the root causes of instability, violence and migration in Central America and has already revoked the visa of the former minister of agriculture.

However, the administration's desire to work primarily through non-governmental organisations rather than the Salvadoran state will complicate such anti-corruption measures. Although it has pledged funds to tackle the drivers of migration (including poverty, unemployment and inequality), its anti-government stance, and the public allegations of corruption made against senior government officials, has infuriated the Bukele administration, which in turn has threatened to suspend all measures to reduce migration and joint counter-narcotics efforts. This stand-off could lead to further waves of emigration – potentially destabilising Guatemala and Mexico as well as the Mexico–US border – and could stall fundamental reforms in El Salvador while further reducing cocaine-interdiction efforts.

Notes

1   United Nations Office on Drugs and Crime, 'Transnational Organized Crime in Central America and the Caribbean', September 2012, p. 27.

2   While the negotiations were well known in Salvadoran political and law-enforcement circles, the September 2020 publication by the investigative website El Faro of the details of the negotiations infuriated the government. See Carlos Martínez et al., 'Gobierno de Bukele Lleva Un Año Negociando con la MS-13 Reducción de Homicidios y Apoyo Electoral' [Bukele Government Negotiating with MS-13 for a Year on Reducing Homicides and Electoral Support], El Faro, 3 September 2020. See also Bryan Avelar, 'El Salvador's MS13: "We Trust in God and in Bukele"', InSight Crime, 7 June 2019; and Héctor Silva Ávalos, 'MS13 Prison Releases Reinforce Potential Pact in El Salvador', InSight Crime, 20 January 2021.

3   International Crisis Group, 'Miracle or Mirage? Gangs and Plunging Violence in El Salvador', Report No. 81, 8 July 2020; and Martínez et al., 'Gobierno de Bukele Lleva Un Año Negociando con la MS-13 Reducción de Homicidios y Apoyo Electoral' [Bukele Government Negotiating with MS-13 for a Year on Reducing Homicides and Electoral Support].

4   Government of El Salvador, 'Gobierno Redujo los Delitos de Alto Impacto en 2020 con el Plan Control Territorial' [Government Reduced High Impact Crimes in 2020 under the Territorial Control Plan], 2 February 2021; and United Nations Development Programme, 'La Seguridad Ciudadana en El Salvador' [Citizen Security in El Salvador].

5   'El Salvador Registra Más de 1,200 Desaparecidos en 2020' [El Salvador Registers More than 1,200 Disappeared in 2020], DW, 20 November 2020.

6   National Civil Police, 'La Nueva Promoción Está Formada con Enfasis en Policía Comunitaria' [The New Promotion Is Formed with an Emphasis on Community Police].

7   Jeannette Aguilar, 'Las Políticas de Seguridad Pública en El Salvador 2003–2018' [Public Security Policies in El Salvador 2003–2018], p. 61.

8   Interviews conducted by IBI Consultants with National Police anti-gang-unit members and MS-13 members, January to October 2018. The lower estimates include only *hommies* (full-fledged members), who are less than one-third of the overall gang affiliates. Higher estimates include members who served as paid lookouts, messengers and retail crack and cocaine vendors.

9   Human Rights Watch, 'World Report 2020', 2020, p. 187.

10 Parker Asmann, 'El Salvador Citizens Say Gangs, not Government "Rule" the Country', InSight Crime, 8 November 2017.

11 Karla Arévalo, 'Cuál ha sido la elección presidencial con menos participación de votantes?' [What was the Presidential Election with the Lowest Voter Turnout?], elsalvador.com, 7 February 2019.

12 Organisation for Economic Co-operation and Development (OECD), 'Key Issues Affecting Youth in El Salvador'.

13 International Monetary Fund, 'World Economic Outlook Database', April 2021.

14 Human Rights Watch, 'World Report 2021: El Salvador', 2021.

Americas

HONDURAS

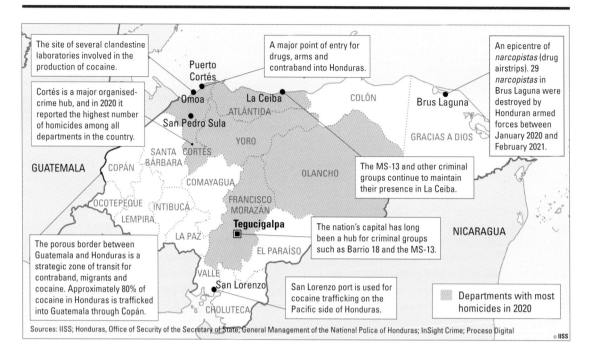

The site of several clandestine laboratories involved in the production of cocaine.

Cortés is a major organised-crime hub, and in 2020 it reported the highest number of homicides among all departments in the country.

A major point of entry for drugs, arms and contraband into Honduras.

An epicentre of *narcopistas* (drug airstrips). 29 *narcopistas* in Brus Laguna were destroyed by Honduran armed forces between January 2020 and February 2021.

The MS-13 and other criminal groups continue to maintain their presence in La Ceiba.

The porous border between Guatemala and Honduras is a strategic zone of transit for contraband, migrants and cocaine. Approximately 80% of cocaine in Honduras is trafficked into Guatemala through Copán.

The nation's capital has long been a hub for criminal groups such as Barrio 18 and the MS-13.

San Lorenzo port is used for cocaine trafficking on the Pacific side of Honduras.

Departments with most homicides in 2020

Sources: IISS; Honduras, Office of Security of the Secretary of State; General Management of the National Police of Honduras; InSight Crime; Proceso Digital

Overview

The conflict in Honduras centres on the Mara Salvatrucha (MS-13) gang as it seeks to expand its robust drug-trafficking structure, pitting it against parts of the state and other criminal elements that it seeks to displace. As in El Salvador and Guatemala, the MS-13 grew largely from gang members deported from the United States in the late 1990s. In Honduras the gang established itself as a major player in the cocaine-transportation and production business, and expanded into other drugs, while continuing to hold a near-monopoly on the internal drug market of cocaine, crack, marijuana and *krispy*.[1] More recently, lucrative drug income, particularly from *krispy*, allowed the gang to stop extorting local businesses in its areas of control, gaining significant political goodwill with the exhausted population. This community support allowed the MS-13 to operate freely in the drug trade and deal directly with Mexican drug-trafficking organisations as an independent partner, rather than limiting it to the protection of cocaine loads owned by other groups.[2]

In 2020 and early 2021, the MS-13 continued to expand its cocaine-trafficking activities, its ties to Mexican drug cartels, its territorial control and its political influence. Notably, it gained control of large cocaine laboratories, experimented with cultivating coca in the hills around San Pedro Sula and expanded its territorial control in the areas of Puerto Cortés-Omoa beach on the Atlantic coast and the Copán sector of the informal land crossings to Guatemala. These expanded operations led to tension and violence among different drug-trafficking groups, corrupt government security forces and smaller gangs.

However, the lockdown restrictions and border closures implemented to tackle the coronavirus pandemic curtailed the gang's expansion into migrant smuggling (through Mexico to the southern US border). At the same time, the pandemic did provide the MS-13 with an opportunity to further enhance its legitimacy among the population, by assuming a quasi-state role in imposing curfews to curb the spread of COVID-19 and punishing violators, as well as in providing rudimentary neighbourhood food and water assistance in impoverished areas and neighbourhood security.

The MS-13 continued its complex relationship with the current administration of President

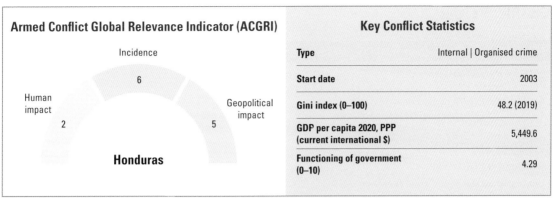

Armed Conflict Global Relevance Indicator (ACGRI)		Key Conflict Statistics	
		Type	Internal | Organised crime
		Start date	2003
		Gini index (0–100)	48.2 (2019)
		GDP per capita 2020, PPP (current international $)	5,449.6
		Functioning of government (0–10)	4.29

Incidence — 6
Human impact — 2
Geopolitical impact — 5
Honduras

Americas

ACGRI pillars: IISS calculation based on multiple sources for 2020 and January/February 2021 (scale: 0–100). See Notes on Methodology and Data Appendix for further details on Key Conflict Statistics.

Juan Orlando Hernández and the security forces he controls, alternating between fighting against and occasionally allying with the latter. Despite the expulsion of 5,775 police members – including senior commanders – for corruption and human-rights abuses between 2016 and 2019, many in the police corps remained connected to drug trafficking, aligning themselves with the MS-13 when mutually beneficial.[3]

Following the November 2019 conviction of President Hernández's brother, and close adviser, Juan Antonio 'Tony' Hernández for large-scale cocaine trafficking, in December 2020 US prosecutors also alleged in court that the president himself had taken bribes from Mexican drug cartels and had used the armed forces to protect laboratories and cocaine shipments to the US.[4] The president denied these charges (and his brother's guilt), but these legal cases clouded his relationship with key allies, including the US administration of Joe Biden, Central American governments and the European Union. Another example of the country's institutional weakness came as police assisted in violently freeing the MS-13's national leader Alexander Mendoza (also known as El Porky) from custody in February 2020. Footage of the escape caused upheaval on Honduran social-media networks.

The MS-13 also expanded the geographical scope of its criminal, political and economic operations in 2020, with increased collaboration with Mexican transnational criminal organisations such as the Sinaloa Cartel and the Cartel Jalisco New Generation (CJNG) to ship cocaine from Colombia and Venezuela to Mexico and by conducting processing steps in Honduran laboratories. The group also increased its digital and technological skilfulness, using encrypted apps for communications, the dark web and cyber currency for financial transactions, and drones for reconnaissance.

In 2020, COVID-19, hurricanes Eta and Iota and a slowdown in migration caused compounded crises of violence, food insecurity and massive unemployment. The government and the country's economic and political elites seemed unable or unwilling to adopt comprehensive recovery strategies, as the economy contracted by 8% in 2020, with a 2021 forecast of 4.5%, with GDP per capita at purchasing power parity not expected to go back to the pre-pandemic level until 2022.[5]

Although the reported homicide rate dropped from 44.5 to 37.6 homicides per 100,000 habitants year on year, it remained the third highest in the hemisphere.[6] Moreover, this drop may have reflected MS-13's military victory in its areas of control rather than an actual improvement in the security situation across the country. Violence remained high in prisons with targeted killings, massacres and riots. 55 homicides were reported between November 2019 and August 2020, including six MS-13 members killed in May in the country's largest women's prison.[7]

Conflict Parties

Military Police of Public Order (PMOP) and National Anti-Gang Force (FNAMP)

Strength: The PMOP has around 4,300 members.[8] The FNAMP has 500 members.[9]

Areas of operation: Throughout Honduras, with a focus on areas with high gang and drug-trafficking presences, usually major urban centres or locations with formal or informal border crossings such as Tegucigalpa, San Pedro Sula, Palmerola and the Guatemala–Honduras border centered in Copán.

Leadership and structure: Colonel Willy Oseguera Rodas (PMOP leader). Lieutenant-Colonel Amílcar Hernández (FNAMP leader).
PMOP has eight combat battalions and one canine battalion and reports to the Ministry of Defence. The FNAMP reports to the police but has not publicly defined its operational structure.

Objectives: Retake territory from the MS-13 and decapitate its operational structures while combatting transnational organised crime and drug trafficking.

Opponents and affiliates/allies:
Opponents include the MS-13 transnational gang, other smaller gangs and local drug-trafficking organisations. Allies include the national police, the TIGRES special-forces unit of the police, the military and US military/police trainers.

Resources/capabilities: Total military budget: US$344 million.[10] Line items of budgets have not been published publicly.

Mara Salvatrucha (MS-13)

Strength: The gang has 9,000–15,000 full members and around 40,000 recruits in training, lookouts and messengers waiting to be formally initiated into the gang. These figures do not include long waiting lists of would-be recruits.

Areas of operation: Throughout Honduras, with concentrated territorial control in the cities of San Pedro Sula, Puerto Cortes and Omoa and in the department of Copán along the border with Guatemala.

Leadership and structure: Senior MS-13 leadership in Honduras remain largely in prison, though few are identified. The group's national leader Alexander Mendoza escaped in February 2020 and remains at large. Carlos Alberto Álvarez (also known as Cholo Houston) and Dimas Aguilar (also known as Taca el Oso) are considered key leaders. Compartmentalised leadership structure with numerous *clicas* (highly compartmentalised units at the street level), forming *programas* (groups of *clicas*), which in turn report to the *ranfla* (prison-based senior leadership).

Objectives: Diversify its criminal portfolio by controlling key cocaine-trafficking nodes and migrant-smuggling routes.

Opponents and affiliates/allies:
Opponents: Sectors of the state security forces not involved in corruption practices, smaller gangs (such as Barrio or Calle 18, the Chirizos and Ponce) and extra-judicial paramilitary groups, rival cocaine groups.
Allies: The MS-13 structures in El Salvador and Guatemala; the Sinaloa Cartel and the Cartel Jalisco New Generation (CJNG) in Mexico; Venezuelan and Colombian cocaine suppliers.

Resources/capabilities: Proceeds from cocaine trans-shipment, migrant smuggling and controlling local drug markets provide the group with a yearly income of tens of millions of US dollars. Other localised revenue sources include investments in motels, car lots, private security firms, buses and public transportation. Advanced tunnelling techniques, cocaine-laboratory operation and expanding territorial control have allowed the gang to protect its operations, store product and increase revenues.

Conflict Drivers

Political

Corruption and impunity:
High levels of corruption and impunity – Honduras was ranked a dismal (joint) 157th in 2020 by Transparency International – allow criminal organisations to expand and grow stronger, ultimately fuelling conflict.[11] In January 2020, the Honduran government failed to renew the contract for the Mission to Support the Fight against Corruption and Impunity in Honduras (MACCIH) backed by the Organization of American States (OAS), clearly indicating the lack of political will to address corruption, in addition to the criminal allegations made by the US against President Hernández.

Economic and social

Poverty and inequality:

Prevalent poverty and inequality in Honduras have been caused by unequitable wealth distribution, low income and education and high unemployment. Although poverty levels have decreased in the past two decades, 48% of the population continued to live below the poverty line, including 60% of rural communities.[12] Despite the country's growing industrial base and the government's efforts to diversify exports, unemployment remained high in Honduras and investment low amid widespread violence and corruption. The MS-13 and smaller groups – often acting with the Honduran state's complicity – reinforce structural poverty and weak institutions by extorting business, recruiting from schools, bribing public officials and executing enemies, including civilians.

Natural disasters and the coronavirus pandemic:

The pandemic compounded the country's pre-existing environmental, social and political drivers of conflict. Widespread governance flaws undermined the response to the crisis: for instance, a Honduran agency charged with procuring emergency medical supplies wasted tens of millions of dollars in overpriced contracts.[13] Meanwhile, in November 2020, hurricanes Eta and Iota affected more than 4m Hondurans and damaged 85,000 homes.[14] As of February 2021, at least 2.9m people were expected to face severe hunger, with numbers expected to rise to more than a third of the population as the situation seemed set to worsen.[15]

Security

Criminal infighting:

Constant armed fighting for territorial control between multiple groups, exacerbated by shifting alliances and battle lines in contested areas for drug production and transport, reinforces the conflict, driving mass migration to the Mexico–US border and internal displacement and undermining state legitimacy. As of December 2020, an estimated 247,000 Hondurans were internally displaced due to violence, and at least one migrant caravan left the country in January 2021 with over 4,000 migrants.[16]

Key Events in 2020–21

POLITICAL EVENTS

16 March 2020

A COVID-19 state of emergency is declared in Honduras, and all borders are shut for a week.

6 May

A published report links Mauricio Olivia Herrera, the president of the National Congress, to the acquisition of properties in Tegucigalpa from Inversiones Acrópolis, a company connected to the Honduran drug-trafficking cartel Los Cachiros.

8 June

The state of emergency is lifted in most of the country and the economy begins to reopen.

MILITARY/VIOLENT EVENTS

16 May 2020

Former congressman Hugo Pinto Aguilar, who was allegedly part of the Los Pinto clan, is killed in the border town of El Paraiso near Copán.

23 May

A group of Barrio 18 members stab and kill six other inmates at the National Women's Penitentiary for Social Adaptation (PNFAS), suspected to be members of the rival MS-13.

11 June

An alleged member of MS-13's rival, Barrio 18, is strangled by her cellmates at PNFAS.

29 June

After a year-long stalemate, the National Congress passes a new criminal code that lowers the sentences for corruption and drug-trafficking cases, allowing many of those convicted to avoid jail time.

26 October

A government investigation accuses the mayor of Tegucigalpa, Nasry 'Tito' Asfura, of embezzling more than one million dollars in city funds, after he had announced in September that he would run for president in the 2021 elections.

14 January 2021

First migrant caravan of 2021 departs from San Pedro Sula with up to 4,000 migrants en route for Mexico and the US. Most are returned to their home countries before reaching their intended destination.

5 February

US prosecutors name Honduran President Juan Orlando Hernández as a target in a major cocaine-trafficking investigation. Hernández denies the charges.

6 August

Three suspected Barrio 18 members are found strangled in La Tolva prison, east of the capital Tegucigalpa.

13 February 2021

MS-13 leader Alexander Mendoza is freed from police custody after 20 gunmen storm a court building in El Progreso and kill three police officers.

Conflict Outlook

Political scenarios

With elections scheduled for November 2021, the MS-13 will likely increase its attempts to influence the outcome, especially as multiple unconfirmed reports suggest that Hernández will seek an additional term.

Food insecurity and critical-infrastructure damage will remain a high risk for a country very much exposed to climate change and regularly affected by tropical storms, floods, droughts and landslides. Ongoing and future disasters will increasingly strain the government's effectiveness in supporting populations at risk and in need.

Violence, economic hardship and sub-par post-hurricane humanitarian assistance will continue to push Hondurans to flee the country, which may empower the MS-13 to take control of migrant routes and further delegitimise the Honduran state.

Escalation potential and conflict-related risks

Additional risks are posed by the MS-13's diversified revenue streams in 2020, its expanded transnational operations with Colombian producers and its position as direct wholesale supplier for Mexican transnational criminal organisations. The suggested shift in the gang's operations from transit to cultivation and production (with vertically integrated capabilities) will also expand the gang's political power, enhance its military strength and further undermine anti-corruption efforts.

Strategic implications and global influences

The less draconian approach to deterring Central American migration taken by the US administration under Biden may increase migration flows and create instability in Guatemala, Mexico and along the Mexico–US border. While the Biden administration intends to combat the root causes of migration, a reluctance to fund a government led by a president publicly accused of cocaine trafficking and corruption will likely reduce collaboration between the two countries.

The US must also consider its strategic forward-basing position operated by the Joint Task Force–Bravo on the Palmerola base, which is important to the US Southern Command. Hernández has signalled an intent to play the US against China, stating that any lost US aid could be replaced by recognising Beijing. This web of interests likely means that Honduras will continue to drive regional instability.

Notes

1. *Krispy* is a marijuana derivative sold in blocks and laced with chemicals. In interviews the drug was described as much more powerful than marijuana and is favoured by criminal groups because of its addictiveness and the fact it can be sold at much higher prices.

2. For a broader look at this evolution, see Douglas Farah and Kathryn Babineau, 'The Rapid Evolution of the MS13 in El Salvador and Honduras from Gang to Tier-One Threat to Central America and US Security Interests', Perry Center Occasional Paper, William J. Perry Center for Hemispheric Defense Studies, National Defense University, March 2018.

3. Cat Rainsford, 'Honduras Police Purge May Be Derailed by Alternative Agenda', InSight Crime, 26 July 2019.

4. 'Honduras President Took Bribes from Drug Traffickers, US Prosecutors Say', *Guardian*, 9 January 2021.

5. International Monetary Fund, 'World Economic Outlook Database', April 2021.

6. United Nations Development Programme, 'La Seguridad Ciudadana en Honduras' [Citizen Security in Honduras]; and Parker Asmann and Katie Jones, 'InSight Crime's 2020 Homicide Round-up', InSight Crime, 29 January 2021.

7. Victoria Dittmar, 'Honduras Unable to Curb Rising Violence Inside Prisons', InSight Crime, 20 August 2020; and Victoria Dittmar, 'Gang Violence Increasingly Spreading to Women's Prisons in Honduras', InSight Crime, 17 June 2020.

8. Government of Honduras, 'Se Integran Nuevos Policias Militares del Orden Publico al Servicio de la Poblacion' [New Military Police Troops Join to Serve the Community], 26 November 2020.

9. Washington Office on Latin America, 'El Papel de las Fuerzas Armadas en la Seguridad Pública en Honduras' [The Role of the Armed Forces in Public Security in Honduras], August 2020; and Iris Amador, 'Honduras Transforms Unit to Counter Maras and Gangs', Diálogo, 20 September 2018.

10. 'Honduras Aumenta en Casi 40% la Inversión Para Equipos Militares en 2020' [Honduras Increases Investment for Military Equipment by Almost 40% in 2020], Infodefensa, 20 December 2019.

11. Transparency International, 'Corruption Perceptions Index 2020'.

12. The World Bank, 'The World Bank in Honduras: Overview – Context'.

13. Zachary Goodwin, 'Massively Overpriced Contracts Hamper Honduras' Pandemic Response', InSight Crime, 17 July 2020.

14. 'Honduras: After the Storms …', United Nations Sustainable Development Group, 16 December 2020.

15. 'Honduras: Nearly One Third of the Population Faces Hunger', CARE, 22 February 2021.

16. Internal Displacement Monitoring Centre, 'Honduras Country Information'; and 'IOM Responds to Humanitarian Needs of Migrant Caravan in Guatemala', International Organization for Migration, 24 January 2021.

Americas

An Azerbaijani soldier near the ruins of a destroyed military recruitment office

Overview

The flashpoints in eastern Ukraine and Nagorno-Karabakh continued to dominate the conflict landscape in Europe and Eurasia. The former saw a build-up of Russian forces along the Ukraine–Russia border in early 2021 that, coupled with an increase in the frequency and intensity of skirmishes and artillery fire, de facto nullified the Minsk ceasefire agreement that entered into force in July 2020.[1] Nagorno-Karabakh made international headlines in September 2020 when an outbreak of hostilities between Armenia and Azerbaijan escalated into a six-week military conflict. As a result, Azerbaijan made significant territorial gains in areas lost to Armenia in previous outbreaks of the conflict.

Both conflicts unfolded along Eurasian geopolitical fault lines, sharing a combination of domestic drivers and regional accelerators. These factors were further compounded by external actors' influence. While the war in Ukraine is not simply a 'war in Europe' but also 'a war about European security',[2] the Nagorno-Karabakh conflict has shown how quickly so-called 'frozen conflicts' can reignite, escalate and create long-term consequences.[3]

Combined, events that took place on these two front lines paint a picture of growing restlessness and geopolitical competition. They also show how escalating crises to de-escalate them has an inherent strategic value, as ultimately does freezing a conflict – as long as military pressure can be maintained. Turkey's involvement in the Nagorno-Karabakh war and its deployment of advanced technology helped

ACGRI pillars: The scores are displayed for Ukraine and the Nagorno-Karabakh conflict. IISS calculation based on multiple sources for 2020 and January/February 2021.

A: Human impact; B: Incidence;
C: Geopolitical impact

Conflict hotspot

Source: IISS

Azerbaijan to escalate and win the military confrontation with Armenia, but also highlighted Ankara's eagerness to assume a more prominent role at the negotiating table. Russia's enduring presence in and around eastern Ukraine, coupled with the escalation in military activities of early 2021, highlighted the 2020 Minsk ceasefire's fragility, and how Moscow can threaten military escalation to stall Kyiv's attempts to align more firmly with its European and Western partners.

Regional Trends

Interplay of state and non-state actors
Despite new factors that add further layers of complexity to the two conflicts – elements of hybrid and proxy warfare,[4] the strategic advantage provided by armed drones and other emerging technologies,[5] and the utility of plausible deniability[6] – at their core they remain inter-state confrontations for territorial control. In both cases, states are the primary actors. However, this does not mean that non-state actors have not played a role. This is particularly apparent in Ukraine, where both the Ukrainian and pro-Russian fronts have progressively blended state military capabilities, non-state militias and paramilitary forces.[7] Recent trends demonstrated how Russia's diminishing appetite for all-out annexation of the Donetsk and Luhansk 'people's republics' has fragmented separatist entities into 'a proxy leadership dependent on Moscow'; irredentist militias still fighting to obtain independence or annexation; and the local population, which feels increasingly marginalised by both Ukraine and Russia.[8] Against this

backdrop, Russia's military movements in early 2021 may be interpreted as an attempt to restore hopes of independence, or as sabre-rattling aimed at disrupting the ongoing peace talks.[9]

The 2020 Nagorno-Karabakh conflict displayed slightly different characteristics: with the Armenian and Azerbaijani armed forces as the two main belligerents, non-state and quasi-state actors only had a secondary role. The Armenian military is supported by the Artsakh Defence Army (also known as the Nagorno-Karabakh Defence Army, NKDA), the 18,000–20,000-strong, conscript-based military organisation of the (internationally unrecognised) Republic of Artsakh/Nagorno-Karabakh Republic, which suffered significant losses from the Azerbaijani offensive in 2020.

New technologies and actors, old objectives

Azerbaijan reaped the benefits of the massive strategic advantage brought by Turkey's military support, mainly in the form of armed drones, whose advanced technology could not be matched by Armenian air-defence capabilities.[10] In addition, reports have emerged that suggest Turkey brought in Syrian mercenaries to carry out combat and support tasks in Nagorno-Karabakh.[11]

The conflict hotspots in Europe and Eurasia display some important commonalities: while advanced technology and non-state actors are part of the politico-military equation, at their core these conflicts remain inter-state business, where territorial control is the ultimate goal and the possibility of conventional military escalation is ever present.

Regional Drivers

Political and institutional

Self-determination:
The conflicts in Europe and Eurasia demonstrated the extent to which self-determination remains a key driver – particularly in the post-Soviet world. To a certain degree, events in eastern Ukraine have displayed commonalities with the Georgian–Russian struggle over South Ossetia and Abkhazia in 2008,[12] highlighting once more the ambiguities and legal grey areas of international law when it comes to the implications of the right to self-determination. In Nagorno-Karabakh, Yerevan's military adventurism achieved the exact opposite of what Prime Minister Nikol Pashinyan had hoped: instead of rallying the

Armenian people around the flag of an existential threat to their self-determination, ultimately the consequences stemming from the defeat damaged the government's legitimacy and worsened political divisions, besides costing Armenia the control of large swathes of Nagorno-Karabakh.[13]

Pursuit of marginal political gains:
In both conflicts, the pursuit of marginal political gains – rather than long-term strategic objectives – has become a driver in and of itself. The sharp drop in ceasefire violations in eastern Ukraine in 2020 might have signalled that the armed conflict had reached a stalemate, and that progress through military action was perceived as too costly or risky. Alternatively, it may have been a consequence of Russia refocusing on hybrid and non-military activities to achieve marginal political gains without triggering a military escalation. (Its use of soft power and political and civil disruption to stall Ukraine's progress towards closer alignment with European partners is an achievement in itself.[14]) While the *Novorossiya* grand project of annexing eastern Ukraine might have been shelved for now,[15] lingering military and political tensions between pro-Russian separatists and the Ukrainian government mean that every decision about the future of the region (and the country as a whole) will require Moscow's approval. Short-termism has also dictated the pace and evolution of the Nagorno-Karabakh war. Pashinyan's short-sighted and erratic foreign-policy posturing aimed at drumming up domestic support for his government, coupled with his overconfidence in Armenia's military strength, were key factors in starting the chain reaction that led to the 2020 war.[16] For Azerbaijan, the military escalation provided a unique opportunity to quickly regain control of territories in Nagorno-Karabakh, while also deflecting most of the international pressure to de-escalate the conflict on Armenia.[17]

Conflict dynamics in the region therefore appear to be driven by an opportunistic rationale. In this sense, the de facto stalemate in the Donbas and the new chapter in the war between Armenia and Azerbaijan are two sides of the same coin. Under certain circumstances, as was the case in Nagorno-Karabakh, armed conflict is likely to re-ignite. Furthermore, the absence of major military operations does not necessarily imply progress towards a resolution, as the situation in eastern Ukraine has demonstrated. Sporadic clashes and skirmishes have punctuated parallel non-military initiatives: Russian artillery strikes have caused growing concerns within Ukraine's leadership over a possible escalation,[18] while Armenia's deadly attacks against Azerbaijani border outposts in July 2020 were pivotal in fuelling Azeri public support for military retribution, and in pushing Turkish President Recep Tayyip Erdogan even closer to Azerbaijan's President Ilham Aliyev.

Geopolitical

Traditional alliances and geopolitical drivers continued to play an important role in the conflicts. In September 2020, Ukrainian President Volodymyr Zelensky approved the country's new National Security Strategy, centred around reinforcing Ukraine's partnership with NATO, with membership as the ultimate goal – a major source of concern for Moscow.[19] The growing tensions between Azerbaijan and Armenia (that eventually led to the 2020 war) pushed Baku and Ankara closer together, with the latter playing a central role in providing military support to Azeri operations in Nagorno-Karabakh, against the backdrop of a military partnership that goes back decades.[20]

Regional Outlook

Prospects for peace

As the conflicts in Nagorno-Karabakh and Ukraine can be described as frozen,[21] the distinction between a lack of armed clashes and peace needs to be at the forefront of any meaningful consideration of the prospects for their resolution. Ceasefires are a temporary expedience, and, as the 2020 Nagorno-Karabakh war demonstrated, years of relative quiet can be followed by a sudden military escalation. Russian armed forces' deployment as peacekeepers in Nagorno-Karabakh since the November 2020 ceasefire and the agreement signed with Turkey for the creation of a joint observation centre are likely to prevent possible flare-ups in hostilities;[22] in addition, from Aliyev's perspective, the ceasefire is enough to seal Azerbaijan's successful campaign in Nagorno-Karabakh and avoid opening further negotiations.[23] However, the dispute is far from resolved. In eastern Ukraine, aware that any major military offensive may prove counterproductive, both sides rely on the Minsk agreements' terms that attempt to facilitate a

political solution. However, as long as the Luhansk and Donetsk people's republics exist as semi-autonomous political entities, any progress is highly unlikely, as political authority will remain contested between Kyiv and secessionist entities.[24]

International organisations – the Organization for Security and Co-operation in Europe (OSCE) above all – are well positioned to contribute to resolution efforts in both conflicts: The OSCE's Special Monitoring Mission (SMM) to Ukraine has access to the Luhansk and Donetsk people's republics, although its tasks mainly include monitoring and reporting ceasefire violations. However, its status and effectiveness are undermined by Russia's involvement (with Russian OSCE observers monitoring Russian military units), which creates frictions and potential conflicts of interest.[25]

In Nagorno-Karabakh, the OSCE is present through the Minsk Group, which is co-chaired by France, Russia and the United States. It aims to facilitate conflict resolution between Armenia and Azerbaijan. A pivotal entity since its creation in 1992, the Minsk Group now faces strong criticism not only from Armenian leaders, but also from Aliyev and Erdogan, who claim Azerbaijan and Turkey are being sidelined in the ongoing negotiations.[26] Promoting Turkey to the status of co-chair, the two leaders claim, would rebalance the group and give new impetus to the negotiations.[27] With Yerevan pulling in the opposite direction, it seems unlikely the Minsk Group will survive in its current form.

Escalation potential and spillover risks

The risk of escalation remains moderate in both conflicts. Reports of Russia delivering 650,000 Russian passports to eastern Ukrainians since 2019 have raised concerns in Kyiv and European capitals about a possible escalation of Russian military involvement in the region under the guise of a peacekeeping mission to protect Russian citizens that would de facto consign the Donbas to Russia.[28] There is also concern in Baltic countries and within NATO more broadly that Russian influence activities targeting Russian-speaking minorities in other regional states could create new crises.[29]

Geopolitical changes

The presidency of Joe Biden in the US has the potential to make waves in both conflicts. Zelensky optimistically saluted his election as the catalyst that would 'help settle the war in Donbas, and end the occupation',[30] while Biden's April 2021 decision to honour the 2019 US Congress resolution recognising the Armenian genocide – and formally declaring it as such – alienated Turkey.[31] Aliyev declared Biden's remarks 'unacceptable', continuing that the United States' stance would 'seriously damage cooperation in the region'.[32] Both crises are also affected by the dramatic shift in US–Russia relations triggered by Donald Trump's departure from the White House, as Biden is unlikely to allow Putin the same geopolitical leeway granted by his predecessor.[33]

Notes

1   Andrew E. Kramer, 'Fighting Escalates in Eastern Ukraine, Signaling the End to Another Cease-fire', *New York Times*, 30 April 2021.

2   International Crisis Group (ICG), 'Peace in Ukraine I: A European War', Europe Report no. 256, 28 April 2020, p. i.

3   See, for example, Svante E. Cornell (ed.), *The International Politics of the Armenian–Azerbaijani Conflict: the Original 'Frozen Conflict' and European Security* (New York: Palgrave Macmillan, 2017).

4   Mark Galeotti, 'Hybrid, Ambiguous, and Non-linear? How New Is Russia's "New Way of War"?', *Small Wars & Insurgencies*, vol. 27, no. 2, 21 March 2016, pp. 282–301.

5   Zachary Kallenborn, 'Drones Are Proving to Have a Destabilizing Effect, Which Is Why Counter-Drone Systems Should Be a Key Part of US Military Aid to Partners', West Point Modern War Institute, 9 December 2020.

6   Adam Lammon, 'Nagorno-Karabakh: Why Turkey Is Sending Syrian Mercenaries to War in Azerbaijan', *National Interest*, 29 September 2020.

7   On Russia, see Galeotti, 'Hybrid, Ambiguous, and Non-linear? How New Is Russia's "New Way of War"?'; on Ukraine, see Andreas Umland, 'Irregular Militias and Radical Nationalism in Post-Euromaydan Ukraine: The Prehistory and Emergence of the "Azov" Battalion in 2014', *Terrorism and Political Violence*, vol. 31, no. 1, 26 February 2019, pp. 105–31.

8   ICG, 'Rebels Without a Cause: Russia's Proxies in Eastern Ukraine', Europe Report no. 254, 16 July 2019, p. 11.

9   Olena Prokopenko, 'Ukraine's Fragile Reform Prospects amid Ongoing Russian Aggression', German Marshall Fund of the United States (GMF), 28 May 2021.

10   Michael Kofman and Leonid Nersisyan, 'The Second Nagorno-Karabakh War, Two Weeks in', *War on the Rocks*, 14 October 2020.

11   Liz Cookman, 'Syrians Make Up Turkey's Proxy Army in Nagorno-Karabakh', *Foreign Policy*, 5 October 2020.

12   For context, see ICG, 'Georgia and Russia: Why and How to Save Normalisation', Crisis Group Europe Briefing, no. 90, 27 October 2020.

13   Laure Delcour, 'The Future of Democracy and State Building in Post-conflict Armenia', Carnegie Endowment for International Peace, 19 January 2021.

14   See, for example, Kateryna Zarembo and Sergiy Solodkyy, 'The Evolution of Russian Hybrid Warfare: Ukraine', Center for European Policy Analysis, 29 January 2021.

15   ICG, 'Rebels Without a Cause: Russia's Proxies in Eastern Ukraine', p. 8.

16   Michael A. Reynolds, 'Confidence and Catastrophe: Armenia and the Second Nagorno-Karabah War', *War on the Rocks*, 11 January 2021.

17   Philip Remler et al., 'OSCE Minsk Group: Lessons from the Past and Tasks for the Future', OSCE Insights, 29 December 2020, p. 6.

18   Kramer, 'Fighting Escalates in Eastern Ukraine, Signaling the End to Another Cease-fire'.

19   Taras Kuzio, 'The Long and Arduous Road: Ukraine Updates Its National Security Strategy', *Commentary*, Royal United Services Institute, 16 October 2020.

20   Haldun Yalçınkaya, 'Turkey's Overlooked Role in the Second Nagorno-Karabakh War', GMF, 21 January 2021.

21   Tom Mutch, 'Nagorno-Karabakh Is Moscow's Latest Frozen Conflict', *Foreign Policy*, 20 May 2021.

22   'Turkey, Russia Sign Joint Observation Center Agreement for Nagorno-Karabakh', *Daily Sabah*, 1 December 2020.

23   Philip Remler et al., 'OSCE Minsk Group: Lessons from the Past and Tasks for the Future', p. 9.

24   Thomas de Waal and Nikolaus von Twickel, 'Scenarios for the Future of Eastern Europe's Unresolved Conflicts', in Michael Emerson (ed.), *Beyond Frozen Conflict: Scenarios for the Separatist Disputes of Eastern Europe* (London: Rowman and Littlefield International, 2020), pp. 31–2.

25   Paul Niland, 'Russia Has No Place in the OSCE Special Monitoring Mission in Ukraine', Atlantic Council, 23 July 2018.

26   ICG, 'Improving Prospects for Peace after the Nagorno-Karabakh War', Crisis Group Europe Briefing, no. 91, 22 December 2020.

27   'Azerbaijan Wants Turkey to Co-chair Minsk Group', TWTWorld, 12 October 2020.

28   Peter Dickinson, 'Russian Passports: Putin's Secret Weapon in the War Against Ukraine', Atlantic Council, 13 April 2021.

29   Josh Rubin, 'NATO Fears That This Town Will Be the Epicenter of Conflict with Russia', *Atlantic*, 24 January 2019.

30   Steven Pifer, 'The Biden Presidency and Ukraine', Brookings Institution, 28 January 2021.

31   Thomas De Waal, 'What Next After the US Recognition of the Armenian Genocide?', Carnegie Endowment for International Peace, 30 April 2021.

32   Andalou Agency, 'Biden's Remarks Unacceptable, Historical Mistake: Azerbaijan's Aliyev', *Daily Sabah*, 24 April 2021.

33   Robert Kagan, 'The United States and Russia Aren't Allies. But Trump and Putin Are', Brookings Institution, 24 July 2018.

UKRAINE

KHARIV
Severodonetsk
Kramatorsk
Zolote
Popasna
Luhansk
Svitlodarsk
City
Debaltseve
Donetsk
Horlivka
International
Donetsk
Airport
Petrivske
DONETSK
Mariupol
Line of Contact

RUSSIA
CHERNIHIV
SUMY
Kyiv
Kharkiv
KYIV
POLTAVA
KHARKIV
CHERKASY
LUHANSK
KIROVOHRAD
DNIPROPETROVSK
DONETSK
MYKOLAIV
ODESSA
ZAPORIZHZHIA
Odessa
KHERSON

Armed
insurgency
Controlled
by Russia

CRIMEA
ROMANIA
Sevastopol
©IISS
Source: IISS

Overview

2020 represented the seventh year of the conflict in Ukraine, following its outbreak in 2014, when Russia's armed forces intervened to annex Crimea and to support the separatist armed groups of the Donetsk People's Republic (DPR) and the Luhansk People's Republic (LPR). In the first year of the war the battlefield was dynamic, with territory forcibly changing hands between the Ukrainian armed forces and Russian-backed separatists. In subsequent years, the war has settled into a pattern of ongoing hostilities that wax and wane in intensity, and that unfold across an increasingly static Line of Contact. The conflict continues to fuel tensions between Russia on one side, and European states and the United States on the other.

In parallel to the fighting has been the Minsk peace process, which is based on the Minsk Protocol (5 September 2014) and a supplementary package of measures known as 'Minsk II' (12 February 2015). Progress has been made in implementing some of its provisions such as on prisoner exchanges. However, an enduring end to the hostilities remains elusive. One complication faced by the Minsk accords is that they name the LPR and DPR as conflict parties but

not Russia, despite the latter's vital role in supporting the separatist groups. Russia's role has instead been enshrined as one of the 'Normandy Four' alongside France, Germany and Ukraine at the highest level of conflict-resolution diplomacy. To break the impasse around implementing the Minsk accords, the 'Steinmeier formula' was proposed in 2016 to suggest steps to grant Donetsk and Luhansk some autonomy. This was accepted by Ukrainian President Volodymyr Zelensky in 2019 on the condition that other aspects of the Minsk accords would first be implemented. The matter of sequencing these steps has been mired in conflicting interpretations by Russia and Ukraine.

Intermittent fighting and inconclusive negotiations continued in 2020 and early 2021. A ceasefire came into effect on 27 July 2020 and largely held for several months, before beginning to break down towards the end of 2020. The working-level forum for talks on de-escalation continued to be the Trilateral Contact Group (TCG), chaired by the Organization for Security and Co-operation in Europe (OSCE), with representatives from Ukraine and Russia, plus the DPR and LPR. The TCG met

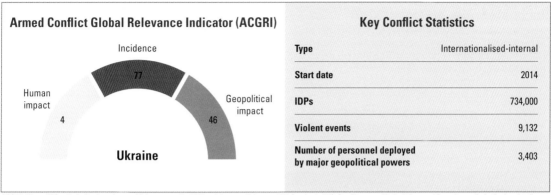

Armed Conflict Global Relevance Indicator (ACGRI)

Incidence

77

Human impact

4

Geopolitical impact

46

Ukraine

Key Conflict Statistics

Type	Internationalised-internal
Start date	2014
IDPs	734,000
Violent events	9,132
Number of personnel deployed by major geopolitical powers	3,403

ACGRI pillars: IISS calculation based on multiple sources for 2020 and January/February 2021 (scale: 0–100). See Notes on Methodology and Data Appendix for further details on Key Conflict Statistics.

regularly during this period, but its work remained inconclusive.

The conflict was overshadowed by a Russian military build-up in March and April 2021, in which large amounts of military personnel and equipment were moved into Crimea and near the Russia–Ukraine border. While Moscow said that it had massed these personnel for a snap military exercise, the event was widely interpreted as a coercive gambit intended to signal Russia's ability to ratchet up the level of tension surrounding the conflict in Ukraine. By late April, the fear of a Russian escalation had diminished as the additional forces were withdrawn.

Conflict Parties

Ukrainian armed forces

Strength: 209,000 active military personnel including 145,000 in the army, 45,000 in the air force and 11,000 in the navy.

Areas of operation: Along the 500-kilometre Line of Contact in the Donbas region of Ukraine.

Leadership: In March 2020, President Zelensky divided the posts of commander-in-chief and chief of the general staff to bring Ukraine in line with NATO principles. The commander-in-chief is the professional head of the armed forces and is Lieutenant-General Ruslan Khomchak. The chief of the general staff is Lieutenant-General Serhiy Korniychuk. General Volodymyr Kravchenko is commander of the Joint Forces in Donbas.

Structure: Divided into four regional HQs. In 2020, the Ukrainian government announced a range of ongoing reforms to defence structures, including a division of responsibilities to relieve pressure on the General Staff by establishing four new commands: Joint Forces Command; Communication and Cyber Security Forces Command; Support Forces Command; and Medical Forces Command.

History: Severely unprepared at the start of the war, a significant modernisation process has taken place since 2014, mobilising a large army with advanced equipment.

Objectives: In 2020, holding the current front line has been more of a priority than the previous strategy of slowly regaining territory along the Line of Contact, as seen in 2018 and 2019.

Opponents: DPR, LPR.

Affiliates/allies: US, European Union, Poland and NATO (as of 2020).

Resources/capabilities: In 2020, Ukraine's defence budget was US$4.35 billion, an increase from US$3.97bn in 2019, and approaching double the amount before the start of the war in 2013 when it was US$1.88bn. The Ukrainian air force fields an estimated 188 fixed-wing aircraft including 71 fourth-generation fighters (Su 27s and MiG 29s). The Ukrainian army fields 1,820 artillery pieces and 3,246 armoured fighting vehicles including 858 main battle tanks.

Donetsk People's Republic (DPR)

Strength: The number of active-duty personnel is unknown.

Areas of operation: Across the Line of Contact in the Donetsk region.

Leadership: Led by Denis Pushilin since November 2018.

Structure: Since 2014, the multiple militias operating across Donetsk have been integrated into the main DPR force. The DPR has sought to demonstrate that it can perform governmental functions in the occupied territories, and originally formed 16 specialised committees tasked with

Europe and Eurasia

Donetsk People's Republic (DPR)

working on bills. It has a parliamentary body, the People's Council, as well as localised governmental bodies, such as city administrators and 'local soviets'. The DPR has drawn up a constitution, issued its own vehicle number plates, changed the currency to the Russian rouble from the Ukrainian hryvnia and instituted Russian as the official regional language.

History: Formed by the protesters and volunteers of the Maidan Revolution protests across Donetsk in 2014, who proclaimed the DPR in June 2014 after seizing government buildings and assets.

Objectives: The DPR has changed its strategy throughout the conflict but hopes to achieve autonomy for the Donetsk region by breaking away from Kyiv and becoming either a province of Russia or an independent state.

Opponents: Ukrainian armed forces.

Affiliates/allies: LPR, Russia.

Resources/capabilities: Difficult to ascertain, though much equipment was captured from Ukrainian forces and shipped from Russia.

Luhansk People's Republic (LPR)

Strength: The number of active-duty personnel is unknown.

Areas of operation: Across the Line of Contact, particularly in the Luhansk region.

Leadership: Leonid Pasechnik since November 2017.

Structure: Appears less centralised than the DPR, with several armed groups retaining power in various parts of the occupied Luhansk territory.

History: Emerged from the same events that resulted in the formation of the DPR.

Objectives: Similar to the DPR but aimed at the Luhansk region.

Opponents: Ukrainian armed forces.

Affiliates/allies: DPR, Russia.

Resources/capabilities: Difficult to ascertain, though much equipment was captured from Ukrainian forces and shipped from Russia.

Pro-Kyiv paramilitaries

Strength: Disparate groups including Azov, Dnipro and Donbas battalions. Their strength is unknown, and some battalions have been integrated into the Ukrainian armed forces.

Areas of operation: Azov battalion active in Zolote.

Leadership: A complex relationship exists between the paramilitary battalions and the Ukrainian armed forces. Some battalions have been fully integrated into the Ukrainian armed forces and Ministry of Internal Affairs. Others have retained more independence, such as the Dnipro battalion which has been funded by the oligarch Igor Kolomoisky.

Structure: Variable between the battalions, with some having used more formalised hierarchical structures and others structured in a more ad hoc way.

History: Volunteer battalions were formed following the Maidan Revolution to mobilise against pro-Russian separatists in the east.

Objectives: Fight back against the DPR, LPR and Russian forces in Ukraine. Different pro-Kyiv paramilitary battalions have had more specific territorial and ideological objectives that reflect where they have operated, their sources of funding, and their levels of internal discipline.

Opponents: DPR, LPR.

Affiliates/allies: Ukrainian armed forces.

Resources/capabilities: Unknown.

Russian armed forces and Russian private military contractors

Strength: The number of Russian armed forces operating in the Donbas is unknown. Also unknown is the balance between regular armed-forces personnel, special-forces and military-intelligence personnel, and private military contractors.

Areas of operation: Likely to either be fully embedded in DPR and LPR forces or fighting independently in the same areas of operation as the DPR and LPR.

Leadership: Unknown.

Structure: Unknown.

History: Since 2014 investigative reports have highlighted the presence of Russian armed-forces personnel fighting in Ukraine. Moreover, numerous Russian armed-forces personnel have been captured as prisoners of war by the Ukrainian authorities. Moscow continues to deny the involvement of its soldiers in the conflict.

Objectives: In accordance with an undeclared Russian government policy, to occupy and wage war in parts of Ukrainian territory as part of a low-intensity armed conflict that has the wider aim of disrupting Ukrainian sovereignty.

Opponents: Ukrainian armed forces.

Affiliates/allies: DPR, LPR.

Resources/capabilities: Unknown.

Conflict Drivers

Political

The Maidan Revolution:

Popular protests began in Ukraine at the end of 2013 after Russian pressure led then-president Viktor Yanukovych to reverse his plans to sign an association and free-trade agreement with the EU. The protesters, wanting greater integration between Ukraine and the EU, perceived the Yanukovych presidency as having pivoted towards Russia. Known as the Maidan Revolution ('Revolution of Dignity'), the protests were also fuelled by longer-term drivers of discontent such as opposition to corruption and political nepotism. Yanukovych was deposed in February 2014 and subsequently fled the country. A coalition of opposition parties, Batkivshchyna (Fatherland) and the far-right Svoboda, formed the post-Maidan government. The Maidan Revolution was centred around Kyiv and was supported in other parts of Ukraine, notably in western cities like Lviv. However, it exacerbated some regional divisions within the country and sparked counter-protests elsewhere in Ukraine.

In the eastern Donbas region (including Donetsk and Luhansk), an initial seizure of government buildings coalesced into a separatist movement supported by Russia. Anger at the way in which Yanukovych had been deposed was one factor, but the separatist movement was also fuelled by longer-term discontent, specifically the poor economic outlook of the region due to the increasing unprofitability of the heavy industry it relied on, and by the underlying tensions and misperceptions between Donbas residents and other parts of Ukraine.

Economic and social

Intra-Ukrainian tensions:

A degree of alienation had developed between Donbas inhabitants and Kyiv after independence. Periodic tensions arose around the coexistence of the Ukrainian and Russian languages for instance, with some Donbas residents perceiving that Ukrainian nationalism had marginalised their Russian-leaning heritage. Economic tensions focused on the distribution of wealth by successive governments in Kyiv and the industrial Donbas region. Once a thriving heavy-industry heartland during the Soviet era, the local economy of the Donbas had been reduced to a rust-belt territory in the years leading up to the conflict. Its coalmines, fertiliser plants and other industrial facilities had become less profitable due to corruption, mismanagement and the obsolescence of production methods.

Security

Crimea accession to Russia and conflicting narratives:

The Ukrainian government mobilised its army, augmented by nationalist volunteer battalions from the Maidan Revolution, to counter the rising threat from pro-Russian separatists. The blockade of the Donbas territories by the Ukrainian government, and escalating fighting, caused significant loss of life and displacement around the areas where the pro-Russian separatists had proclaimed the Donetsk and Luhansk 'people's republics' (DPR/LPR). Concurrently, Russian troops without insignia were deployed at strategic points in the Ukrainian Crimean Peninsula on 27 February 2014. The Crimean parliament held a referendum on 16 March that allegedly demonstrated overwhelming support for Russian accession by the Crimean people, though the conduct of the referendum was criticised by foreign governments. Russia formally claimed sovereignty over Crimea on 18 March 2014. Ukraine has depicted the war as an attempt to defend its territory from Russian aggression, while the pro-Russian separatists have argued that they are protecting their citizens from 'fascists' in Kyiv.

International

Regional influences:

While intra-Ukrainian tensions were unlikely themselves to degenerate into war, the intervention by Russia provided the decisive spark. Russia had various motivations for intervening. Domestically, in 2014, the outbreak of war and the seizure of Crimea boosted President Vladimir Putin's popularity. Geopolitically, Ukraine became a battleground in Russia's attempts to assert its regional power, as it seeks to avert Ukraine's hypothetical future memberships in the EU and NATO.

Europe and Eurasia

Political and Military Developments

Change of negotiators

In January 2020, during Putin's cabinet reshuffle, Vladislav Surkov was replaced as Russia's chief political-military adviser and representative on the Ukraine conflict by Dmitry Kozak, who in 2003 had tried to broker a deal between Moldova and Transnistria. The Ukrainian government also changed its key appointments to the talks, with former president Leonid Kuchma replaced in the TCG by another former president, Leonid Kravchuk. Oleksii Reznikov also became Ukraine's Minister for the Reintegration of Temporarily Occupied Territories.

Continued fighting

The first half of 2020 saw intermittent fighting around several hotspots, notably three areas in the Donetsk region (around Donetsk airport; east of Mariupol; around Svitlodarsk) and one area in the Luhansk region (between Popasna, Zolote and Pervomaisk). Some signs suggested a slowing down in fighting, yet military activity persisted along the Line of Contact, including the continued deployment of heavier weapons – in violation of the Minsk Protocol – especially in non-government-controlled areas of the Donbas.

Ceasefire brokered

The coronavirus pandemic precluded some in-person talks, resulting in a virtual meeting of the Normandy Four in April 2020, before an in-person meeting in Berlin on 3 July. A virtual meeting of the TCG on 22 July yielded an agreement over the implementation of a comprehensive ceasefire, containing 'measures to strengthen the ceasefire' and a 'coordination mechanism' to report violations. In November, the TCG agreed to four new disengagement zones: in Luhansk's villages of Petrivka, Slovyanoserbsk and Nyzhnoteple, and near Hryhorivka in Donetsk.

Fluctuating ceasefire violations

The ceasefire that came into effect on 27 July initially seemed effective, with ceasefire violations progressively and significantly decreasing: from 60,188 in the first quarter, to 56,879 in the second, 13,977 in the third and 3,723 in the fourth quarter. The daily average of ceasefire violations fell almost 20-fold after July 27 (623 to 33 respectively).[1] However, by the end of 2020 the ceasefire had come under strain as the OSCE reported over 200 ceasefire violations in the Donetsk region on three separate days (11, 19 and 29 December). In the first quarter of 2021, a total of 8,676 ceasefire violations were recorded by the OSCE, indicating a return to regular hostilities along the Line of Contact.[2]

Local council elections

Local council elections were held on 25 October 2020, except in the areas controlled by the Russian-backed separatists due to the prevailing political and security conditions. Other parts of Donetsk and Luhansk under Ukrainian-government control were also excluded from voting under the advice of civil–military administrators.

Russia's military build-up

In late March 2021, Russia moved a large amount of its military personnel, weapons systems and equipment into Crimea and into its western regions bordering Ukraine, notably Rostov and Voronezh. The total number of Russian military personnel massed close to Ukraine was estimated at 100,000, supposedly for a snap military exercise, as explained by Russian Defence Minister Sergey Shoygu.[3] However, the Ukrainian government, the EU and NATO interpreted these actions as Russia either flexing its military muscle in a show of strength or preparing for a military incursion. Tension and uncertainty around Russia's intentions remained high until late April, when Russia declared the end of its exercise and began to withdraw the additional forces.

Key Events in 2020–21

POLITICAL EVENTS

29 January 2020
Dmitry Kozak replaces Vladislav Surkov as Moscow's lead negotiator on Ukraine.

11 February
Andriy Yeramak replaces Andriy Bohdan as Kyiv's Head of Presidential Office.

16 March
Amid the spread of COVID-19, all entry–exit checkpoints along the Line of Contact close.

30 April
A virtual meeting of the Normandy Four is held.

13 May
Kozak visits Berlin to discuss next steps on conflict resolution with German officials.

12 June
NATO makes Ukraine an Enhanced Opportunities Partner on inter-operability issues.

30 July
Leonid Kravchuk replaces Leonid Kuchma as Ukraine's chief envoy to the Minsk talks.

4 August
Kravchuk suggests 'special status of administration' for DPR/LPR, who reject this.

25 October
Local elections held nationwide, excluding parts of Donetsk and Luhansk.

27 October
Ukraine's Constitutional Court outlaws the National Agency for Prevention of Corruption (NACP).

11 November
Russia rejects Ukraine's 'joint steps' proposal to demilitarise the conflict zone.

29 December
Zelensky suspends Constitutional Court head Oleksandr Tupytskyy.

28 January 2021
'Russia Donbas Forum' held in Donetsk city.

3 February
Zelensky bans three pro-Russian TV channels and extends Tupytskyy's suspension.

MILITARY/VIOLENT EVENTS

18 February 2020
Spike in fighting near Zolote disengagement area in Luhansk.

22 April
The TCG meets as fighting continues unabated by the coronavirus pandemic.

8 May
The United Nations appeals for de-escalation as fighting continues to claim lives.

27 July
'Full and comprehensive ceasefire' comes into effect at 00:01.

12 August
Although hostilities substantially decrease, one Ukrainian soldier is killed.

28 August
The ceasefire broadly holds, but two Russian-backed separatist fighters are killed.

6 September
Ceasefire still broadly holding, but one Ukrainian soldier killed in Luhansk.

29 December
Ceasefire under pressure in a third day of escalating hostilities in this month.

31 January 2021
Further fighting in Donetsk hotspots during the month as the ceasefire wanes.

19 February
The OSCE reports a particularly high tally of 594 ceasefire violations in Donetsk.

Europe and Eurasia

Impact

Human rights and humanitarian

The war claimed 24 lives and injured 105 people in 2020. Half of these deaths and injuries were inflicted by mines and unexploded ordnance, with the rest inflicted by shelling or small arms and light weapons.[4]

There were 734,000 internally displaced persons (IDPs) in Ukraine as of February 2021.[5] Housing, employing and integrating these IDPs in their host communities remained an ongoing process. The coronavirus pandemic exacerbated the privations already suffered by many IDPs and by people who live near the war zone as quarantine restrictions and travel limitations were introduced and the five crossing points along the Line of Contact were closed.

In a prisoner swap ahead of Orthodox Easter, 20 Ukrainians were returned to Kyiv from detention by the Russian-backed separatists, who in turn received 14 people held by the Ukrainian authorities. Ukrainian prisoners in the DPR and LPR remained an agenda item for the Normandy Four, with discussions on potential access to these prisoners being given to the International Committee of the Red Cross. The Office of the UN High Commissioner for Human Rights (OHCHR) reported that while its staff had unimpeded access to official places of detention in government-controlled territory, such access was denied in the DPR and LPR territories.

Political stability

The war caused some disenfranchisement in the October 2020 local council elections. Ukraine's Central Election Commission announced in August that voting would not be held in ten communities in the Donetsk region and eight in the Luhansk region, on the government-controlled side of the Line of Contact, based on the advice of the civil–military administration of these areas. Nationwide turnout for the election was 36.88%, with Zelensky's party, Servant of the People, securing 15.05% of local deputies. Second place went to Fatherland with 10.63%, and third place to the Opposition Platform – For Life with 9.91% (the latter party being broadly sympathetic towards Russia).[6] The low turnout, and the fragmentary outcome, reflected the enduring hold of local allegiances, as well as the relative success of decentralisation reforms since 2014.

President Zelensky, in his second year in office, faced challenges in implementing two of his major campaign pledges: ending the war and fighting corruption. In October, the Constitutional Court curbed the powers of the National Agency for Prevention of Corruption, which had been created after the Maidan Revolution. This prompted criticism from the US Embassy in Kyiv, which expressed concern on behalf of Ukraine's international partners and donors. The Court reinstated the agency's powers, but tensions persisted between Zelensky and the head of the court, Oleksandr Tupytskyy, who was suspended and later dismissed by Zelensky in 2021.

Economic and social

The conflict has had a catastrophic impact on Ukraine's economy, resulting in rising inflation and poverty rates as well as years of macroeconomic contraction. The coronavirus pandemic added further pressure on Ukraine's economy, which shrank by 4.2% in 2020.[7] Consumer inflation was forecast by the National Bank of Ukraine to reach 7% as of year-end 2021.[8]

In November 2020, the World Bank approved a US$100 million project to support 'Ukraine's efforts to promote socio-economic recovery and development of Eastern Ukraine with these funds earmarked for the government-controlled areas in the Luhansk region'.[9] The region's heavy industry remained mainly located in separatist-controlled areas, and the conflict had prevented those in government-controlled areas who might have previously travelled across the region for work to access these jobs. Many residents of the Donbas fled once the war began, with some from the separatist-controlled areas moving to Russia, while others were displaced internally within Ukraine. On both sides of the Line of Contact, some of the Donbas residents who remained in their homes have become dependent on economic opportunities from the mixture of legal and illicit trade across the front line. The economy of the separatist-controlled areas has suffered, with the properties in Luhansk city losing around half their value since the war began.

Relations with neighbouring and international partners and geopolitical implications

Ukraine–Russia relations remained in a dire condition due to Russia's role in the war. Russia's past use of military contractors in Ukraine resulted in a well-publicised incident in neighbouring Belarus, as authorities in Minsk arrested 33 contractors on 29 July 2020 reportedly from the Russian private military company the Wagner Group. President Zelensky demanded that Ukraine take custody of 28 of these contractors, including nine who had Ukrainian passports, while the Ukrainian Prosecutor General's office cited the Wagner Group's past role in the Donbas war. However, all but one of those arrested were sent back to Russia (the remaining individual held Belarusian citizenship). Although it is not possible to estimate the scale of past Russian military-contractor involvement in the Ukraine war, their utility to the Russian government is clear, given the close links between private military companies like Wagner and the Russian state, and the benefits of deniability that military contractors offer to Russia instead of deploying its regular soldiers abroad.[10] Ukraine also remained concerned by signs of Russia extending its security presence in the region, as it sought to deepen its defence ties to Belarus, including through joint military drills and by exploring the possibility of basing Russian troops in Belarus.

Conflict Outlook

Political scenarios

Although the 27 July ceasefire demonstrated that a significant de-escalation in the fighting could be achieved, the peace process remained blocked by persistent disagreements over the ultimate status and level of political autonomy of the DPR- and LPR-controlled areas. On this matter there is little sign of an immediate breakthrough in the respective positions of Russia and Ukraine. Moscow still accuses Kyiv of a reluctance to fully implement the Minsk accords; conversely, Kyiv remains politically constrained, given the domestic criticism that this would attract. The likely outlook is of a continuing peace process stymied on the core issues that could end the conflict.

An indication of Russia's sentiments regarding the Donbas came on 28 January 2021, at the 'Russia Donbas Forum' held in DPR-controlled Donetsk city attended by Russian senator Kazbek Taysaev, DPR leader Denis Pushilin and LPR leader Leonid Pasechnik. Margarita Simonyan, chief executive of the RT news channel, made a direct emotional appeal, declaring: 'Mother Russia, take Donbas home'.[11] However, Putin's press secretary later distanced the Kremlin from the event, saying that integrating the Donbas into Russia was not a policy worth pursuing. Nevertheless, the event conveyed a public doubling-down of Russia's material and ideological hold over the region and reflected a Russian line of thinking against returning the LPR and DPR to Ukrainian government control. Ukraine's former president Kravchuk promised in February 2021 to raise the Russia Donbas Forum in the TCG negotiations.

Escalation potential and conflict-related risks

The possibility of escalation cannot be precluded, especially after the concern raised by Russia's massing of its armed forces near its border with Ukraine in March–April 2021. The eventual withdrawal of these forces rather than their deployment into Ukraine suggests that Russia's intention in this instance was to intimidate Ukraine rather than to seek additional military gains. One possibility is that Russia wants to step up measures to integrate the separatist-controlled Donbas areas, which have been in place for years – for example the DPR and LPR adopted Moscow's time zone in 2014 – *without* escalating its existing military involvement.

Prospects for peace

The conflict defies straightforward characterisation as either an invasion, a proxy war, an insurgency or a civil war – featuring some constituent properties of each, even if the parties to the conflict may prefer to use only one of these terms. The mix of local, regional and international drivers, and Russia's incentives around the war, present continuing obstacles to conflict resolution.

The OSCE has monitored the ceasefire since 2014 from its patrol hubs, vehicle patrols, uninhabited aerial vehicles and cameras. As a monitoring mission, its leverage over the conflict parties is low, and it can only offer an off-ramp from the war if the

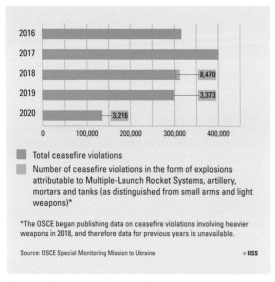

Total ceasefire violations

Number of ceasefire violations in the form of explosions attributable to Multiple-Launch Rocket Systems, artillery, mortars and tanks (as distinguished from small arms and light weapons)*

*The OSCE began publishing data on ceasefire violations involving heavier weapons in 2018, and therefore data for previous years is unavailable.

Source: OSCE Special Monitoring Mission to Ukraine   © IISS

Figure 1: Number of ceasefire violations recorded in Ukraine, 2016–20

parties come to an agreement. The OSCE's reporting provides an order-of-magnitude overview of the war. The 134,767 ceasefire violations it reported in 2020 were a steep decline from recent years.[12] It remains to be seen whether the overall number of ceasefire violations recorded in 2021 will continue this annual downward trajectory.

Strategic implications and global influences

Several regional and international developments have been of consequence to the conflict. On 12 June 2020, NATO recognised Ukraine as an Enhanced Opportunities Partner, reflecting the past contribution made by Ukrainian troops in NATO missions in Kosovo and Afghanistan. This status granted

Ukraine access to inter-operability exercises and equipment programmes, although it did not confer a commitment to future Ukrainian membership of NATO. In parallel, Ukraine set out several reforms to its military apparatus. In March 2020 Zelensky announced the separation of the armed forces leadership roles of chief of the general staff and commander of the armed forces, in line with NATO principles. Other changes to Ukraine's military training, leadership structures and equipment procurement were also announced.[13]

The US diplomatic line with Russia became tougher since President Biden's administration came to power in January 2021. An early step was the announcement of a US$125m military aid package comprising training, equipment and advisory assistance, including 'defensive lethal weapons' to improve the Ukrainian military's ability to defend against 'Russian aggression'.[14]

Tensions around the Nord Stream 2 gas pipeline project in 2020–21 had some bearing on Ukraine's regional position. The first Nord Stream pipeline already connects Russia's gas supplies to Europe via the Baltic Sea, and Nord Stream 2 would greatly increase Russia's capacity to bypass Ukraine when exporting its gas. Ukraine perceives the German-backed Nord Stream 2 as an anti-Kyiv project, intended by Russia to deprive it of future revenue from the transit of gas and to make it more vulnerable to Russia. With the Biden administration's criticism of Nord Stream 2, Germany came under pressure to recalibrate its support for the project and mooted an idea by which it would agree to shut off Nord Stream 2 if Russia used it to put pressure on Ukraine.

Notes

[1] Organization for Security and Co-operation in Europe, Special Monitoring Mission to Ukraine, 'January – March 2020 Trends and Observations'; 'April – June 2020 Trends and Observations'; 'July – September 2020 Trends and Observations', 28 January 2021.

[2] Organization for Security and Co-operation in Europe, Special Monitoring Mission to Ukraine, 'January – March 2021 Trends and Observations', 5 May 2021.

[3] 'Russia: Speech by High Representative/Vice President Josep Borrell at the EP Debate', European Union External Action Service, 28 April 2021.

[4] Organization for Security and Co-operation in Europe, Special Monitoring Mission to Ukraine, '2020 Trends and Observations', 28 January 2021.

[5] United Nations High Commissioner for Refugees, 'Ukraine: Country Fact Sheet', February 2021.

[6] Organization for Security and Co-operation in Europe, 'Ukraine, Local Elections, 25 October 2020: ODIHP Limited Election Observation Mission Final Report', 29 January 2021, pp. 33, 36, 42.

[7] International Monetary Fund, 'World Economic Outlook Database', April 2021.

8   National Bank of Ukraine, 'Speech by NBU Governor Kyrylo Shevchenko at a Press Briefing on Monetary Policy', 21 January 2021.

9   World Bank, 'New World Bank Project to Help with Economic Recovery and Development of Eastern Ukraine', 6 November 2020.

10 See 'Russia's use of its private military companies', IISS *Strategic Comments*, vol. 26, no. 39, December 2020.

11 Alvydas Medalinskas, 'Kremlin TV Chief: Russia Must Annex East Ukraine', Atlantic Council, 9 February 2021.

12 Organization for Security and Co-operation in Europe, Special Monitoring Mission to Ukraine, '2020 Trends and Observations'. There are distinctions in ceasefire violations, and the OSCE specified that of the 134,767 violations in 2020, 3,216 involved 'explosions attributable to MLRS (Multiple Launch Rocket Systems), artillery, mortars and tanks', as distinguished from small arms and light weapons.

13 Government of Ukraine, 'National Defence'.

14 United States Department of Defense, 'Defense Department Announces $125M for Ukraine', 1 March 2021.

Europe and Eurasia

NAGORNO-KARABAKH

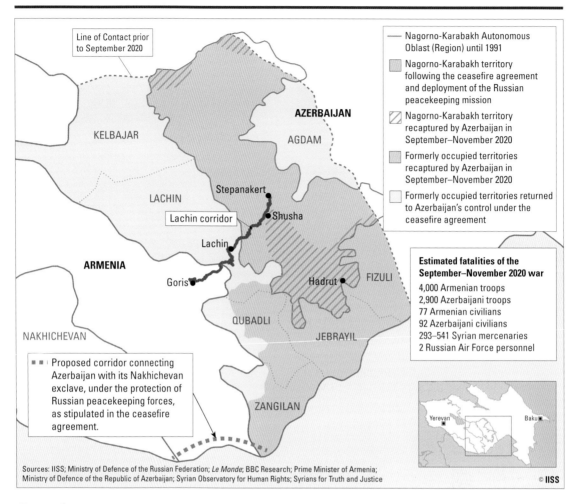

Line of Contact prior to September 2020

— Nagorno-Karabakh Autonomous Oblast (Region) until 1991

Nagorno-Karabakh territory following the ceasefire agreement and deployment of the Russian peacekeeping mission

Nagorno-Karabakh territory recaptured by Azerbaijan in September–November 2020

Formerly occupied territories recaptured by Azerbaijan in September–November 2020

Formerly occupied territories returned to Azerbaijan's control under the ceasefire agreement

AZERBAIJAN

KELBAJAR

AGDAM

LACHIN

Stepanakert

Lachin corridor

Shusha

Lachin

ARMENIA

Goris

Hadrut

FIZULI

Estimated fatalities of the September–November 2020 war

4,000 Armenian troops
2,900 Azerbaijani troops
77 Armenian civilians
92 Azerbaijani civilians
293–541 Syrian mercenaries
2 Russian Air Force personnel

QUBADLI

JEBRAYIL

NAKHICHEVAN

■ ■ ┆ Proposed corridor connecting Azerbaijan with its Nakhichevan exclave, under the protection of Russian peacekeeping forces, as stipulated in the ceasefire agreement.

ZANGILAN

Yerevan

Baku

Sources: IISS; Ministry of Defence of the Russian Federation; *Le Monde*; BBC Research; Prime Minister of Armenia; Ministry of Defence of the Republic of Azerbaijan; Syrian Observatory for Human Rights; Syrians for Truth and Justice

© IISS

Overview

The Nagorno-Karabakh conflict is a dispute over a mountainous area of some 4,400 square kilometres that formed part of Soviet Azerbaijan, but which has a majority ethnic Armenian population. The conflict is one of several in the former Soviet Union frequently depicted in terms of clashing principles of self-determination and territorial integrity, and featuring an unrecognised, secessionist entity or 'de facto state', in this case the Nagorno-Karabakh Republic (NKR), also known as the Republic of Artsakh, which remains unrecognised by any United Nations member, including Armenia.

In 1987 Nagorno-Karabakh's Armenian population began a campaign to separate from Azerbaijan and unify with Armenia. With the collapse of the Soviet Union in 1991 and the subsequent power vacuum, an ongoing low-level conflict escalated into a full-scale war between Azerbaijan and Armenia-supported Nagorno-Karabakh, which ended in 1994 with a decisive Armenian military victory and a Russian-brokered ceasefire agreement. Armenian forces took control of almost all of Nagorno-Karabakh itself while occupying several surrounding regions not originally part of the dispute, and an approximately 200-km Line of Contact was established between the two forces. The Minsk Group, which was created by the Conference on (later the Organization for) Security and Co-operation in Europe (CSCE/OSCE), has been mediating Armenian–Azerbaijani negotiations since 1992.

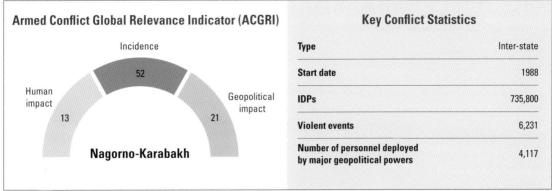

ACGRI pillars: IISS calculation based on multiple sources for 2020 and January/February 2021 (scale: 0–100). Variables represent the sum of the raw-data values for the countries involved in the conflict. See Notes on Methodology and Data Appendix for further details on Key Conflict Statistics.

Since the mid-2010s, low-intensity violence has continued, punctuated by occasional major escalations such as the April 2016 'four-day war'. In 2020, another major escalation took place, with clashes in July along the Armenia–Azerbaijan border to the north of Nagorno-Karabakh, followed by the September onset of a full-scale 44-day war along the Line of Contact. This time Azerbaijan prevailed – with significant Turkish support – restoring control over most of the territories it had lost to Armenian forces in the early 1990s, including approximately one-third of the territory originally under dispute in Nagorno-Karabakh itself.

A Russian-mediated ceasefire brought the war to an end on 10 November 2020. The agreement included the deployment of a peacekeeping force, provided by Russian Ground Forces, for a minimum of five years to those parts of Nagorno-Karabakh not recaptured by Azerbaijan and the Lachin corridor linking Armenia and Nagorno-Karabakh. Also agreed was the Armenian withdrawal from occupied territories surrounding Nagorno-Karabakh, the exchange of prisoners between all parties and an Armenian safety guarantee for transit across southern Armenia between mainland Azerbaijan and the Azerbaijani exclave of Nakhichevan.

Conflict Parties

Azerbaijani armed forces

Strength: 66,950 active-service personnel in Azerbaijan's conscript-based armed forces and an estimated 300,000 reservists. Military service lasting 18 months (12 months for university graduates) is mandatory for able-bodied males aged 18–35.

Areas of operation: Prior to, and during, the 2020 war, the bulk of Azerbaijani forces were deployed along the Line of Contact. Troops were also deployed to Azerbaijan's Nakhichevan exclave.

Leadership: President Ilham Aliyev (commander-in-chief); Colonel-General Zakir Hasanov (minister of defence).

Structure: The majority of troops serve in Azerbaijan's land and air forces. A small navy comprising some 2,200 service personnel is based on the Caspian Sea.

History: Independent Azerbaijan's armed forces were established in 1991–92 from Soviet army units and Azerbaijani militias. The army's slow and disorderly formation contributed to its defeat at the hands of Armenian forces in the First Nagorno-Karabakh War. Significant military expenditures have substantially upgraded capabilities since then.

Objectives: In 2020, defend and restore Azerbaijan's territorial integrity.

Opponents: Armenian armed forces; Nagorno-Karabakh Defence Army (NKDA).

Affiliates/allies: Azerbaijan and Turkey have cooperated closely on defence and security since the early 1990s and Turkish support was key to Azerbaijan's military success in 2020.

Resources/capabilities: Azerbaijan has modernised its military through supplies from Israel, Russia and Turkey, among others. In 2020, Azerbaijan's defence budget was US$2.27 billion (approximately 5.32% of GDP), a significant increase from the US$1.79bn in 2019. Azerbaijan has supremacy over Armenia in most areas, particularly uninhabited aerial vehicles (UAVs). Turkish *Bayraktar* TB2 drones delivered in summer 2020 played a major role in the subsequent war.

Armenian armed forces

Strength: 45,000 service personnel, around half of whom are conscripts. Reservists currently stand at 210,000 members. Military service lasting 24 months is mandatory for males aged 18–27, including dual nationals residing abroad. Although exact figures are unavailable, several units composed of reservists served with the Armenian army during the 2020 war.

Areas of operation: Mainly deployed along the international border with Azerbaijan.

Leadership: Prime Minister Nikol Pashinyan (commander-in-chief); Vagharshak Harutyunyan (minister of defence).

Structure: Armenia's armed forces – comprising five army corps, air and air-defence forces – have close ties to the NKDA, although a separate command structure is maintained.

History: Ex-Soviet Army corps and volunteer paramilitary units fighting in Nagorno-Karabakh formed the basis for the Armenian armed forces, officially established in 1991 following the collapse of the Soviet Union.

Objectives: Before the 2020 war, to provide extended deterrence to the de facto jurisdiction of the NKR. After the 2020 war, to protect the country's territorial integrity.

Opponents: Azerbaijani armed forces; Turkish armed forces.

Affiliates/allies: Armenia is a founding member of the Russia-led Collective Security Treaty Organisation. It is also covered by extended deterrence through bilateral agreements with Russia, which has a military base with an estimated 3,300–5,000 troops in Gyumri, near the Turkish border.

Resources/capabilities: In 2020 Armenia's defence budget was US$613 million (approximately 4.97% of GDP), registering a decline relative to 2019's US$644m. Russia is Armenia's main arms supplier; Soviet-era stock in some items was still in use in 2020.

Nagorno-Karabakh Defence Army (NKDA)

Strength: Until 2020, an estimated 18,000–20,000 personnel served in the armed forces of the unrecognised NKR. Over half the troops are thought to have been Armenian citizens.[1]

Areas of operation: Prior to the 2020 war, the NKDA was deployed along the heavily fortified Line of Contact. Troops were also deployed to the occupied territories surrounding Nagorno-Karabakh proper. During the 2020 war they were deployed along the Line of Contact and the main battle areas in Fizuli, Jebrayil, Zangilan, Lachin and Nagorno-Karabakh.

Leadership: Arayik Harutyunyan, Nagorno-Karabakh's de facto president since March 2020, is commander-in-chief. Lieutenant-General Jalal Harutyunyan was defence minister from 24 February until he was wounded on 27 October 2020. He was replaced by Lieutenant-General Mikael Arzumanyan. Decisions on defence and security are taken by the Artsakh Security Council; Vitaly Balasanyan, a 1990s war veteran, general and former presidential candidate, is its secretary.

Structure: The majority of personnel serve in the NKDA's ground forces.

History: Established in 1992 from local paramilitary units engaged in small-scale fighting with Soviet and Azerbaijani forces in the early 1990s.

Objectives: The primary objective before the 2020 war was to defend Nagorno-Karabakh and the surrounding occupied territories against Azerbaijani attack.

Opponents: Azerbaijani armed forces and their affiliates.

Affiliates/allies: Closely integrated with the Armenian armed forces although they maintain a separate chain of command.

Resources/capabilities: The NKR receives financial subsidies from Armenia, although the proportion of this dedicated to military spending is unknown. Armenia has also supported the NKDA through military training and education.

Russian Armed Forces

Strength: 1,960 peacekeepers.[2]

Areas of operation: The bulk of Russian peacekeepers are deployed along the Lachin corridor and the eastern and southern areas of Nagorno-Karabakh not recaptured by Azerbaijan in 2020. Russia also maintains a military presence including several bases in Armenia. In the aftermath of the 2020 war, Russian border guards established several outposts in southern Armenia near the border with Azerbaijan.

Leadership: President Vladimir Putin (supreme commander-in-chief); Sergey Shoygu (minister of defence).

Structure: Most peacekeeping units currently stationed in Nagorno-Karabakh belong to the 15th Separate Motor Rifle Brigade of the Central Military District (Russian Ground Forces). Border guards operating under Federal Security Service (FSB) command are currently deployed in both Armenia and Nagorno-Karabakh.

History: Deployed to Nagorno-Karabakh following the ceasefire signed on 10 November 2020.

Objectives: Ceasefire monitoring in Nagorno-Karabakh for a minimum of five years, subject to renewal if neither Armenia nor Azerbaijan states their intention to terminate the agreement. FSB border guards have been instructed to guarantee transport links between Azerbaijan and its Nakhichevan exclave as set out in the ceasefire agreement.

Opponents: n/a.

Affiliates/allies: Russia and Armenia are founding members of the Collective Security Treaty Organisation. Obligations include extended deterrence, although guarantees do not extend to Nagorno-Karabakh.

Resources/capabilities: Russian peacekeepers in Nagorno-Karabakh have light weapons and at least 90 armoured personnel carriers and 380 units of special equipment including vehicles at their disposal. Russia's military presence in Armenia is accompanied by advanced-weapons systems; since 2020, this likely includes several *Iskander* short-range ballistic missiles.[3]

Turkish Armed Forces (TSK)/ Turkish-backed Syrian private military contractors	
Strength: Strong evidence suggests that Turkey deployed 1,500–2,500 Syrian private military contractors (PMCs) to fight for Azerbaijan in the 2020 Nagorno-Karabakh War, although both countries have denied this.[4] It has been alleged that Turkish personnel participated directly in the Azerbaijani campaign, including as operators of some of the Turkish-made drones deployed by Baku.[5] One Turkish general and approximately 40 servicemen have operated a joint Russian–Turkish ceasefire monitoring facility since January 2020 in the Agdam region of Azerbaijan.[6]	PMCs were mainly recruited through the Syrian National Army, a Turkish-backed force opposed to President Bashar al-Assad.
	History: Turkish-backed PMCs were reportedly dispatched to Nagorno-Karabakh in late September 2020 in waves, before or just after the start of the war. Several hundred Turkish military personnel allegedly remained in Azerbaijan following joint military exercises in July–August 2020 and were, according to some reports, later involved in the operation in Karabakh.
Areas of operation: Syrian fighters were reportedly deployed to the front line during the 2020 war, in particular to the southern flank of the Azerbaijani offensive.	**Objectives:** Support Azerbaijan's military campaign.
	Opponents: NKDA, Armenian armed forces.
Leadership: President Recep Tayyip Erdogan (commander-in-chief); General (retd.) Hulusi Akar (minister of national defence); General Yasar Guler (chief of general staff).	**Affiliates/allies:** Azerbaijan.
	Resources/capabilities: Turkish-backed Syrian PMCs fighting in Nagorno-Karabakh were thought to have been extremely poorly equipped.
Structure: The command structure for Syrian units deployed to Nagorno-Karabakh is unclear. Sources suggest Syrian	

Conflict Drivers

Political
Unresolved legacies of the First Nagorno-Karabakh War:
The First Nagorno-Karabakh War of 1992–94 left significant legacies that remained prominent in the domestic politics of both Armenia and Azerbaijan. In the case of Azerbaijan, the occupation of significant swathes of territory and the seemingly permanent forced displacement of internally displaced persons remained consistent sources of grievance. For Armenia, the establishment of an unrecognised republic, or 'de facto state', in Nagorno-Karabakh was perceived as the only alternative to the loss of the territory's Armenian identity in the absence of any credible commitments to self-governance for its Armenian population within Azerbaijan.

Security
Militarisation:
Conflicting Armenian and Azerbaijani commitments to, respectively, retaining or restoring control over Nagorno-Karabakh increasingly intersected with rising militarisation. Bolstered by oil revenues, from the mid-2000s Azerbaijan engaged in a comprehensive overhaul of its military involving substantial arms purchases from a variety of suppliers, notably Israel, Russia and Turkey. Armenia reciprocated through embedding itself within a Russian extended deterrent, hosting a Russian base in its second-largest city Gyumri and other Russian military installations.

Yet while Russia's extended deterrence covered the territory of the Republic of Armenia, it has never been framed as including the contested territory in Nagorno-Karabakh – creating a grey zone in Armenia's own deterrent and reducing the costs for Azerbaijan of military action. After 2014, regular escalations and skirmishes became common along both the Line of Contact and the internationally recognised border between Armenia and Azerbaijan to the north.

International
Declining multilateralism:
Growing securitisation of the Line of Contact narrowed the space for the negotiations mediated by the OSCE's Minsk Group. After a significant escalation along the Line of Contact in April 2016, Armenia and Azerbaijan agreed to a number of measures to strengthen the ceasefire and move to more substantive talks; none were implemented. Within the Minsk Group, France and the United States effectively defaulted to de facto Russian leadership of the process. Perceiving the risks of a major war testing its deterrent capacity, from 2015 Russia unsuccessfully sought the conflict parties' agreement to a peace-plan variant – sometimes referred to as the 'Lavrov plan' after Russian Foreign Minister Sergey Lavrov – involving the deployment of a Russian peacekeeping mission to Nagorno-Karabakh. In 2020 the OSCE experienced a leadership crisis, as the 57-member

organisation failed to agree on mandates for the heads of its Office for Democratic Institutions and Human Rights, High Commissioner on National Minorities and the Representative on Freedom of the Media (RFoM), leaving these posts unfilled for several months. Azerbaijan was one of the states that objected to the candidacy of Harlem Desir in the role of RFoM.

Rising multipolarity:
The decline of multilateral diplomacy left a vacuum increasingly filled by rising regional powers. In the South Caucasus neighbourhood, Russia and Turkey have increasingly projected power into the Middle East, North Africa and the eastern Mediterranean. While indirectly confronting each other through local actors in Syria and Libya, and occasionally coming to direct blows, Russia and Turkey are also aligned in advancing their respective capacities for structural and strategic autonomy from Euro-Atlantic powers and the associated liberal international order. In the Armenian–Azerbaijani context, Russia is deeply embedded with both countries in a variety of roles, including as an arms provider, trading partner and mediator. Turkey has traditionally provided moral support to Azerbaijan, with which it has close ethnolinguistic ties; conversely, Turkey has a highly conflicted history and no diplomatic relations with Armenia. These factors inhibited Turkish diplomacy vis-à-vis the Nagorno-Karabakh conflict, leaving the option of a more militarised strategy of the kind seen in 2020.

International distraction:
In 2020 global distraction due to the coronavirus pandemic combined with a number of other events to divert international attention, which offered a window of opportunity for military action. Protests in Belarus that began in May and escalated in August served to distract Russian attention from the South Caucasus and, at least at their onset, to illustrate the fragility of authoritarian rule in the region. The US was also distracted by presidential elections, which in turn presented regional actors with the prospect of a new president less sympathetic to Russia and Turkey.

Political and Military Developments

Instability in domestic politics
In February 2020 snap parliamentary elections in Azerbaijan – seemingly intended to counter unfavourable comparisons with Armenia's 2018 democratic breakthrough – did not result in the changes that many observers expected. In Armenia, controversy surrounded Prime Minister Pashinyan's efforts to indict figures associated with the previous regime under the Republic Party of Armenia (RPA), notably former president Robert Kocharian, on charges associated with civil disorder in March 2008. Kocharian's trial was the first of a former incumbent in the post-Soviet space, becoming a point of tension in Pashinyan's already tense relationship with Vladimir Putin.

Tensions and symbolic politics
Bilateral relations between Armenia and Azerbaijan had already deteriorated early in 2020. This signalled the definitive end to a perceived opening in 2019 following an announcement by the Minsk Group that both countries' foreign ministers had agreed, after a meeting in Paris in January, on the necessity of 'preparing populations for peace'. This rhetoric was already faltering by summer 2019 as no breakthrough materialised. A tense public meeting between President Aliyev and Prime Minister Pashinyan at the Munich Security Conference in February 2020 ended in familiar historical claim and counter-claim. In May, the inauguration of de facto Karabakh leader Harutyunyan in Shusha (spelled Shushi by Armenians), a crucial symbolic site for Azerbaijanis, and announcements suggesting that Shusha could become the territory's political capital, sparked offense in Azerbaijan. This was compounded in June when approval was given for a third road across the occupied territories connecting southern Armenia and southern Karabakh, casting further doubt on the likelihood of these territories ever passing back to Azerbaijani jurisdiction.

Clashes along the international Armenia–Azerbaijan border
On 12 July 2020, cross-border clashes broke out along the international Armenia–Azerbaijan border in the Tavush/Tovuz area, killing 17 – mostly Azerbaijanis

– over the following days. Protests calling for war began near Baku after 12 July, and escalated after two high-ranking officers, Major-General Polad Hashimov and Colonel Ilgar Mirzayev, were killed. Reactions to these deaths resulted in an unprecedented, spontaneous street protest in Baku on 14 July demanding more muscular military action against Armenia. Azerbaijani foreign minister Elmar Mammadyarov was dismissed following severe public criticism from President Aliyev of the OSCE-mediated negotiations process. Mammadyarov was replaced by education minister Jeyhun Bayramov.

Increased Turkish–Azerbaijani cooperation

Increased Turkish support for Azerbaijan was evident in the aftermath of the July clashes, with Azerbaijani and Turkish defence officials meeting repeatedly and visibly, and senior Turkish officials, including Minister of Defence Hulusi Akar, publicly issuing threats to Armenia.[7] The full extent of Turkish military support to Azerbaijan in 2020 remains unknown and contested. Following joint military exercises with the Azerbaijani armed forces in July, substantial materiel and hundreds of servicemen and military advisers reportedly remained in the country in readiness for subsequent deployment.[8] Some of these may have operated newly delivered *Bayraktar* TB2 drones during the subsequent war, which were used to significant tactical effect. While Ankara and Baku deny having employed Syrian foreign fighters in Nagorno-Karabakh, their presence in the region was widely reported in international media, and the Syrian Observatory of Human Rights claimed that over 540 Syrian mercenaries died in hostilities between September and November.[9]

War breaks out

Azerbaijan launched large-scale offensive operations along the Line of Contact on 27 September 2020, focused on the Armenians' more vulnerable southern flank, striking population centres and spurring intense fighting. By mid-October Azerbaijan had made substantial territorial gains, wresting control of a number of Armenian-controlled districts surrounding Nagorno-Karabakh, bringing the town of Hadrut in Nagorno-Karabakh proper under its control, and advancing along the Azerbaijani–Iranian border. On 8 November, Azerbaijan cemented its victory by taking the symbolically and strategically important town of Shusha. After several failed attempts at a ceasefire, the fighting was finally ended by a Russian-brokered trilateral agreement on 10 November after 44 days of war. This agreement was enforced by a Russian peacekeeping mission rapidly deployed to Nagorno-Karabakh.[10]

Key Events in 2020–21

POLITICAL EVENTS

15 February 2020
Armenian Prime Minister Nikol Pashinyan and Azerbaijani President Ilham Aliyev meet in a tense live debate at the Munich Security Conference.

28 February
First case of COVID-19 is reported in Azerbaijan.

1 March
First case of COVID-19 is reported in Armenia.

31 March
Elections in the unrecognised NKR proceed despite the onset of the coronavirus pandemic; incumbent Arayik Harutyunyan is re-elected.

21 May
In Nagorno-Karabakh, de facto leader Arayik Harutyunyan's inauguration takes place in Shusha, a city of symbolic importance to Azerbaijanis.

MILITARY/VIOLENT EVENTS

12 July 2020
Cross-border clashes break out along the international Armenia–Azerbaijan border in the Tavush/Tovuz area, killing 17 over the following days, including a popular Azerbaijani general.

21 July
Armenian and Azerbaijani demonstrators clash at a rally in Los Angeles.

23 July
Armenian–Azerbaijani street fighting in Moscow leads to up to 30 arrests.

27 September
Azerbaijan launches offensive operations along the Line of Contact, with missile and artillery strikes on several population points in Nagorno-Karabakh continuing over the following weeks. Intense fighting ensues.

14 July

Unprecedented popular protest in the Azerbaijani capital Baku, calling for military action against Armenia.

3 September

Deputy chairman of the Azerbaijani opposition Musavat party, Tofig Yaqublu, is sentenced to four years' imprisonment for 'hooliganism' after an altercation he claimed was staged.

10 October

Russian Foreign Minister Sergey Lavrov announces a humanitarian ceasefire, which fails almost immediately.

17 October

A second ceasefire, negotiated by France under the auspices of the OSCE's Minsk Group, is announced and fails.

25 October

A third ceasefire, negotiated by the US under the auspices of the OSCE's Minsk Group, is announced and fails.

20 November

The formerly occupied (and uninhabited) Azerbaijani city of Agdam returns to Azerbaijani jurisdiction, followed by the region of Kelbajar on 25 November and the region of Lachin on 1 December; the French Senate votes to recognise the NKR.

11 January 2021

At a meeting with President Vladimir Putin in Moscow, Aliyev and Pashinyan agree to the establishment of a working group that will select infrastructure and border-opening projects for presentation by March 2021.

4 October

The Azerbaijani city of Ganja is hit by ballistic missiles, in the first of four missile strikes that claim 26 lives in total.

5 October

Use of cluster munitions to bombard Nagorno-Karabakh's capital Stepanakert is documented; use by both sides is later documented.

9 October

After making significant territorial gains over preceding days, Azerbaijan captures the town of Hadrut in Nagorno-Karabakh on or around this date.

18 October

Azerbaijani armed forces advance as far as the Khudaferin bridge on the Azerbaijan–Iran border.

27–28 October

The Azerbaijani city of Barda is hit by ballistic missiles, in the first of three missile strikes that claim 27 lives in total.

8 November

Azerbaijani forces take the town of Shusha after intense fighting.

10 November

A Russian–Armenian–Azerbaijani ceasefire declaration ends the war, as a Russian peacekeeping mission is rapidly deployed to Nagorno-Karabakh.

11 December

Clashes break out in a cluster of villages near Hadrut that had remained under Armenian control despite encirclement. The villages later passed to Azerbaijani control.

Impact

Human rights and humanitarian

The 2020 war, though short, wrought a devastating humanitarian impact. There were some 6,000 confirmed fatalities among Armenian and Azerbaijani combatants at the time of writing, while the total is most likely higher than 7,000, with more than 10,000 wounded, in addition to some 170 fatalities among civilians.[11] Approximately 130,000 people were displaced, some 90,000 of them Armenians from Nagorno-Karabakh.[12] Numerous reports of human-rights violations against civilians and war crimes were recorded. Hundreds of prisoners were taken during and just after the fighting, with many Armenian prisoners still unaccounted for as of the time of writing. Indiscriminate attacks hitting hospitals, schools, religious sites and other civilian infrastructure were also recorded on each side of the conflict, as well as the use of cluster munitions, which pose long-term risks to local populations of being maimed or killed by explosive remnants. With civilians crowding into basements and temporary accommodation to escape the fighting, the war coincided with an eightfold increase in COVID-19 cases in Armenia.[13] Meanwhile, the return of Azerbaijanis displaced by the First Nagorno-Karabakh War to former front-line areas now under Azerbaijani control was constrained by extensive destruction in these areas and the presence of a substantial number of mines and unexploded ordnance.

Political stability

In Armenia, the defeat created an enduring political crisis. Pashinyan's signing of the agreement which saw Armenia turn over significant swathes of territory on top of that already lost militarily to Azerbaijan was met with fury from large segments of the population. His continued presence in post sparked months of protest and even the prospect of civil–military tensions as senior army officers openly called for his resignation, until he conceded to holding snap elections, scheduled for June 2021. By contrast, military victory further strengthened the position of Aliyev in Azerbaijan, despite escalating restrictions on civil liberties during the coronavirus pandemic.

Economic and social

The war further radicalised already polarised societies. In both Armenia and Azerbaijan, pro-peace voices were silenced through harassment and targeting by the authorities. Real-time coverage of events on the front line and videos showing summary killings and beatings circulated across social media, generating public outrage. The war had devastating economic impacts on all parties involved, and particularly on the local economy in Nagorno-Karabakh itself, which had a small but reportedly vibrant economy estimated to be worth $713m in 2019.[14] The fighting caused heavy damage to infrastructure, including the loss of road links to Armenia on which the territory formerly depended, which will heavily constrain Armenia's ability to provide needed resources and have long-term impacts on Nagorno-Karabakh's viability as an economic entity.

Relations with neighbouring and international partners and geopolitical implications

The 2020 war established significant new geopolitical dynamics in the South Caucasus as the Nagorno-Karabakh conflict became yet another theatre where Russia and Turkey are actively engaged. Russia now shares responsibility with Turkey for managing the ceasefire monitoring centre, located in Azerbaijan's Agdam district to the east of Nagorno-Karabakh. This Russian–Turkish duopoly represents a new 'regionalisation' of the Nagorno-Karabakh conflict, with Moscow and Ankara working together in a symbiotic relationship to marginalise Euro-Atlantic actors and other international organisations in general and the OSCE in particular.

Turkey's penetration of the South Caucasus reciprocates Russia's own entry into the conflicts in Libya and Syria. It also represents an assertive challenge to Russia's presumed hegemony in the former-Soviet sphere. While playing only a secondary role in monitoring the ceasefire, Turkey nevertheless stands to benefit strategically from the new guarantee of transit across southern Armenia

that will connect it to Azerbaijan and Central Asia – assuming that sufficient momentum is sustained for the corridor to be constructed.

If no longer the sole outside player, Russia remains the dominant one. The war's outcome permitted a new military presence in the South Caucasus, and substantially increased Russian leverage over both Azerbaijan and Armenia, while excluding Euro-Atlantic powers. Russia's responses demonstrated significant tactical flexibility and successfully averted outcomes less favourable to Moscow. Yet Russia's insertion into the context both represented a substantial escalation of its commitments and posed new challenges for its bilateral relationship with each of the parties. Russia will likely face countervailing pressures regarding its presence, with Azerbaijan wishing to limit its duration and Armenia to extend it.

Other neighbouring states struggled to contain overspill from the conflict and maintain friendly relations with both Armenia and Azerbaijan. Georgia's offer to broker peace talks was not accepted, and the country was later accused in Armenian media reports of facilitating the transit of Azerbaijani military supplies.[15] Renewed Armenian–Azerbaijani conflict also threatened radicalisation among Georgia's own Armenian and Azerbaijani national-minority populations. The strengthening of Russia's presence in the South Caucasus is seen in Georgia through the lens of Tbilisi's own territorial conflicts in Abkhazia and South Ossetia/Tskhinvali district, which are recognised by the vast majority in the international community as parts of Georgia but by Russia and a handful of aligned states as independent from Georgia. The prospect of an alternative corridor running through Armenia also threatens the monopoly that Georgia has held on east–west transit since the 1990s.

Iran also offered good offices for Armenian–Azerbaijani negotiations to no avail. Iran's own ethnically Azerbaijani population – located in the northwest of the country just south of the conflict zone – increasingly voiced support for Azerbaijan in the 2020 war. While Iran's political leadership responded to pro-Azerbaijani protests in Tabriz and other cities with rhetorical support for Azerbaijan's territorial integrity, increased Turkish presence in the South Caucasus and the significant role played by Israeli weaponry in Azerbaijan's military victory were not welcomed in Tehran.

Conflict Outlook

Political scenarios

The political outlook remained extremely uncertain. The 10 November 2020 ceasefire declaration resolved only some of the issues previously under negotiation in the OSCE-mediated Minsk Group process. Official rhetoric suggests that Azerbaijan considers the conflict resolved as it focuses on the rehabilitation of the de-occupied territories. However, the absence from the ceasefire declaration of the core issue that drives the conflict, the status of Nagorno-Karabakh, and the marginalisation of the OSCE Minsk Group negotiations, drive Armenian concerns over whether and how this issue can be reopened. Neither Armenia nor Azerbaijan abandoned belligerent postures. The post-war situation continued to be inflamed by several issues, notably Azerbaijan's detention of dozens of prisoners amid reports of their deaths and torture;[16] Azerbaijani fatalities owing to landmines in de-occupied areas; and the alteration and destruction of Armenian cultural and community heritage in areas restored to Azerbaijani control.

Escalation potential and conflict-related risks

While the ceasefire largely held, the new status quo brought various security risks. The mandate of the Russian peacekeeping mission in Nagorno-Karabakh remained to be defined, and while renewable if neither Armenia nor Azerbaijan objects, it had a formal five-year lifespan. Further ambiguities surrounded the Armenian armed forces in the territory: while all its units were required to withdraw in the 10 November 2020 declaration, the status of Karabakh-Armenian armed units of the NKDA remained unclear. The 2020 war and its outcome dissolved the previous context of long-distance segregation of Armenians and Azerbaijanis. In a variety of theatres from Nagorno-Karabakh itself to southern areas on either side of the international Armenia–Azerbaijan border, representatives of each nationality were brought into closer proximity than at any time since the early 1990s.

Prospects for peace

Prospects for a negotiated peace remain dim, with Armenia and Azerbaijan continuing to hold opposite views and the stalling of the formal negotiations

Figure 1: Distribution of Russian peacekeeping forces in Nagorno-Karabakh (as of 27 January 2021)

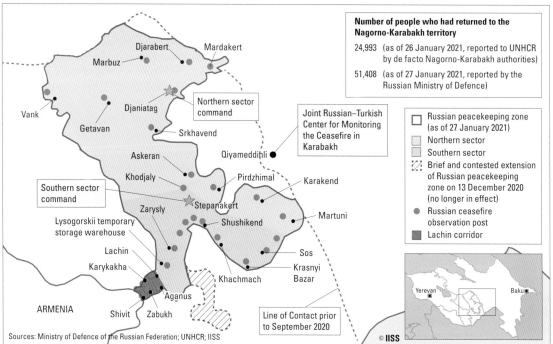

Sources: Ministry of Defence of the Russian Federation; UNHCR; IISS

© IISS

process mediated by the OSCE's Minsk Group. In the absence of a multilateral peace process, Russia continues to pursue a trilateral format aimed at implementing the measures foreseen in the 10 November 2020 declaration, including a working group tasked with identifying new infrastructure and communications projects.

Strategic implications and global influences

The 2020 war marked a significant inflection point in the history of the conflict by resituating it as a theatre of contestation by regional powers Russia and Turkey, rather than a theatre of mediation and conflict resolution by an international coalition. Regionalisation was demonstrated in the post-war period by Russia's leading role in negotiations with Armenia and Azerbaijan, overseeing the implementation of the 10 November 2020 agreement. It remained unclear whether, under what conditions, and with what agenda the OSCE Minsk Group talks might resume.

Notes

[1] Sergey Minasyan, *Sderzhivanie v Karabakhskom Konflikte* [Deterrence in the Karabakh Conflict] (Yerevan: Caucasus Institute, 2016), pp. 266–9.

[2] 'Russia Sends Nearly 2,000 Peacekeepers to Nagorno-Karabakh, Defense Ministry Says', TASS, 10 November 2020. The International Crisis Group subsequently reported a total of 'some 4,000 Russian soldiers and emergency services staff'. See International Crisis Group, 'Post-war Prospects for Nagorno-Karabakh', Report no. 264, 9 June 2021, p. i.

[3] In 2019, Russian officials announced plans to double the combat potential of the 102nd Russian military base in Gyumri without increasing the number of personnel.

[4] 'After Azerbaijani Government's Refusal of Their Settlement, Over 900 Turkish-backed Mercenaries Return to Syria', Syrian Observatory for Human Rights, 2 December 2020; and Ed Butler, 'The Syrian Mercenaries Used as "Cannon Fodder" in Nagorno-Karabakh', BBC News, 10 December 2020.

[5] Elena Chernenko, 'Prinuzhdenie k konfliktu' [Compelled into Conflict], *Kommersant*, 16 October 2020.

[6] 'Turkish–Russian Center Begins Monitoring Nagorno-Karabakh Truce', Radio Free Europe/Radio Liberty, 30 January 2021.

[7] Amberin Zaman, 'Turkish Defense Minister Vows to "Avenge" Azerbaijanis Killed in Armenian Attacks', Al-Monitor, 16 July 2020.

[8] Chernenko, 'Prinuzhdenie k konfliktu'.

[9] Syrian Observatory for Human Rights, 'Death Toll of Mercenaries in Azerbaijan Is Higher Than That in Libya, While Syrian Fighters Given Varying Payments', 3 December 2020. See also Butler, 'The Syrian Mercenaries Used as "Cannon Fodder" in Nagorno-Karabakh'; and Syrians for Truth and Justice, 'Government Policies Contributing to Growing Incidence of Using Syrians as Mercenary Fighters', 2 November 2020.

[10] 'Zayavlenie Prezidenta Azerbaydzhanskoy Respubliki, Prem'er-ministra Respubliki Armenii, i Prezidenta Rossiyskoy Federatsii' [Statement by the President of the Azerbaijani Republic, Prime Minister of Armenia and President of the Russian Federation], 10 November 2020.

[11] For the civilian and lower combatant figure, see International Crisis Group, 'The Nagorno-Karabakh Conflict: A Visual Explainer', 7 May 2021; the Armed Conflict Location & Event Data Project (ACLED) identifies 6,706 fatalities for Armenia and Azerbaijan in 2020 as a whole. The latest official data as of this writing suggests that 2,895 Azerbaijanis were killed in action (including deaths from landmines after the ceasefire). Estimates of Armenians killed in action have been more variable, with 4,000 cited by officials as a likely approximate total. See 'Azerbaijan Updates Death Toll in Karabakh', Caucasian Knot, 9 May 2021; and 'Pashinyan Says About 4,000 Armenian Troops Killed in Nagorno-Karabakh', TASS, 14 April 2021.

[12] United Nations Office of the High Commissioner for Human Rights, 'Nagorno-Karabakh Conflict: Bachelet Warns of Possible War Crimes as Attacks Continue in Populated Areas', 2 November 2020.

[13] Comment, 'War in the Time of COVID-19: Humanitarian Catastrophe in Nagorno-Karabakh and Armenia', *The Lancet*, vol. 9, no. 3, 1 March 2021, E243–E244.

[14] 'Nagorno-Karabakh's Record Growth in Ruins Amid Conflict and Pandemic', DW, 12 October 2020.

[15] 'Arms Transit Reports to Azerbaijan "Disinformation," Georgia Says', civil.ge, 5 October 2020.

[16] 'Azerbaijan: Armenian POWs Abused in Custody', Human Rights Watch, 19 March 2021.

3 Middle East and North Africa

A joint Russian–Turkish military patrol near Syria's border with Turkey

Overview

Ten years after the start of the Arab uprisings, the landscape in the Middle East and North Africa (MENA) continued to undergo major transformations. The collapse of the regional order paved the way for major inroads and intervention by third parties and assertive regional powers, which took advantage of the gradual disengagement of the United States. Driven by renewed geopolitical and geo-economic ambitions, 'adversarial collaboration' between Russia and Turkey became increasingly central in the region throughout 2020 and early 2021, with important reverberations in other theatres such as the Caucasus.[1] Foreign meddling increased the intractability of conflicts in MENA, especially in contexts where state authority and central institutions had visibly fragmented or collapsed. The coronavirus pandemic further strained these war-torn countries, whose health services had already been crippled by intense fighting.

The escalation of fighting in Libya in 2020 was a direct consequence of the internationalisation of the conflict, increasing its regional and international relevance. However, in Yemen, political and military fragmentation made the fighting more local, exacerbating the conflict's immense humanitarian cost. Syria remained a source of instability, as a decade of civil war has caused significant infrastructure damage, food insecurity, famine and the highest number of internally displaced persons (IDPs) in the world.[2] The conflict's potential for destabilisation mainly resided in power competition and external state interventions that edged dangerously

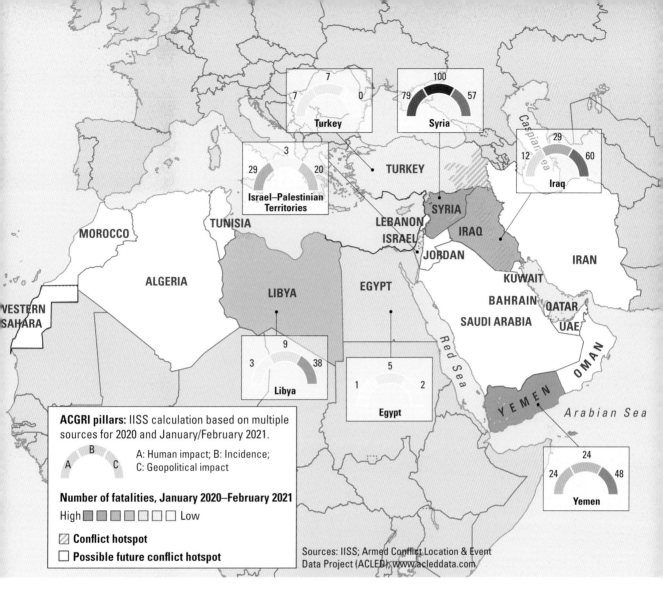

ACGRI pillars: IISS calculation based on multiple sources for 2020 and January/February 2021.

A: Human impact; B: Incidence;
C: Geopolitical impact

Number of fatalities, January 2020–February 2021

High ▣▣▣▣▢▢▢ Low

▨ Conflict hotspot
▢ Possible future conflict hotspot

Sources: IISS; Armed Conflict Location & Event
Data Project (ACLED), www.acleddata.com

Map labels: Turkey 7, 7, 0 | Syria 100, 79, 57 | Iraq 29, 12, 60 | Israel–Palestinian Territories 3, 29, 20 | Libya 9, 3, 38 | Egypt 5, 1, 2 | Yemen 24, 24, 48

close to an all-out war, while the resilience of terrorist organisations posed another major risk. In Iraq, jihadist groups remained active though severely weakened and diminished after successful counter-terrorism operations. However, Baghdad continued to suffer structural deficiencies, such as the fragmentation of its security sector and an economic crisis exacerbated by the pandemic and falling global oil prices, which will likely fuel ongoing discontent. In Libya, competition between Ankara and Moscow was on the brink of becoming a major confrontation, but fatigue and Egypt's threat of a direct military intervention produced a stalemate that allowed the United Nations to relaunch the peace process.

Sitting on the major fault line between Sunni and Shia powers, Iraq remains conflict-prone and vulnerable to tensions between Iran and the US, and violent escalation similar to that which preceded and followed the January 2020 assassination of Qasem Soleimani seems likely. Another area of concern is the northern Syrian province of Idlib, the last rebel stronghold outside Damascus's control, as Russia and Turkey struggle to find a durable accommodation that satisfies their own interests and provides for the needs of millions of IDPs without resorting to further violence.

Regional Trends

Civil wars and third-party state interventions

For much of the 20th century, the Israel–Palestinian Territories conflict had represented the major source of instability in the Middle East.[3] However,

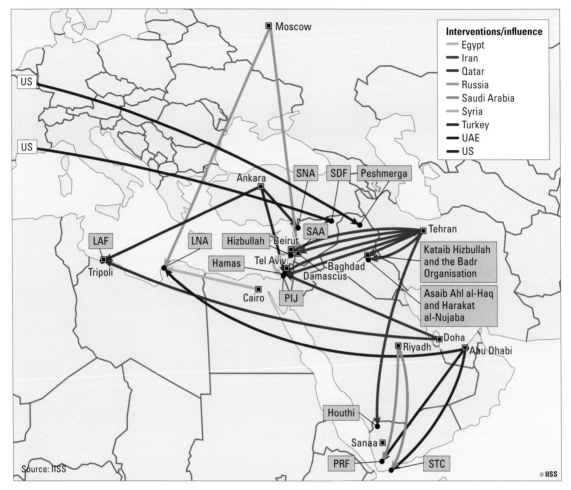

Figure 1: Civil wars with third parties' interventions

the fast pace of events in the Arab world since the 2003 Iraq War and the 2011 uprisings paved the way for multiple civil wars with immediate international implications. Apart from the localised insurgency in Egypt's Sinai Peninsula, where the Islamic State (also known as ISIS or ISIL) tapped into unaddressed local grievances, and the low-intensity conflict between Turkey and the Kurdistan Workers' Party (PKK) which has spilled over into Iraq and Syria, most of the conflicts in the region can be described as internal armed conflicts with third-party interventions, commonly featuring a regional confrontation between two competing geopolitical blocs.[4]

In this context, the Yemeni case is particularly telling. The fight between the Iran-supported Houthi rebels and the Saudi-led coalition – established to restore the internationally recognised government in Sanaa – highlighted the divide in the Gulf region. The intersection between foreign interventions and the fragmentation of Yemeni state authority significantly increased the type and level of violence, accompanied by repeated violations of international human rights and humanitarian law.[5] In Yemen, just as in Iraq and Syria before it, state interventions reinforced sectarian narratives: in each case, geopolitical rivalries relied on and fuelled the proliferation of non-state militias. The Popular Mobilisation Units (PMU) in Iraq represented this phenomenon well. This collection of mostly Shia militias with deep ideological and security ties to Iran obtained formal recognition and resources from the Iraqi government for its role in defeating ISIS but remained outside Baghdad's control, with clear negative humanitarian implications.[6]

The rise of non-Arab powers

The sectarian divide also exacerbated the Syrian conflict, where the Alawite-controlled regime, backed by Iran and its regional proxies, confronted a largely Sunni opposition supported for a time by Sunni regional powers. The Russia–Turkey entanglement added a further layer of complexity to the Syrian conflict. As historic rivals with strategic differences, they each cultivated local Syrian proxies to hold territory and exert influence, but also to project power in other theatres. Indeed, Russia and Turkey deployed Syrian military contractors in Libya alongside their respective forces. Their presence, numbering thousands, recruited by Russia and Turkey to support the Libyan National Army or the Libyan Armed Forces respectively, not only complicated the prospects for the Libyan peace process, but also highlighted the privatisation of war as an emerging trend in MENA conflicts.

Regional Drivers

Political and institutional

Polarisation has increased, as the idea of a clash between revolutionary and counter-revolutionary forces stemming from the Arab uprisings has reinforced perceptions that most conflicts pit Islamists against secularists. An oversimplification of complex realities, this narrative further reduced an already shrinking political space and drove extremism on both sides of the political spectrum, as actors viewed as illegitimate turned to greater levels of authoritarianism and radicalisation. This polarisation has deepened societal divides and benefitted hardliners who brand political opponents as illegitimate. This dynamic has undermined post-2011 democratic transitions across the region, with the exception of Morocco and Tunisia, where the legitimacy of Islamist parties has been accepted, albeit with some reservations. It has also influenced Western thinking, as rule by strongmen is increasingly seen as a viable option to end a decade of chaos and contain the Islamist threat. The case of Egypt is particularly noteworthy: President Abdel Fattah Al-Sisi represents a model that many aspiring strongmen with a similar military background (such as Libya's Field Marshal Khalifa Haftar) have tried to emulate.

Economic and social

Socio-economic grievances remained a source of instability, building on the second wave of Arab uprisings in 2018–19 that tested the resilience of the Algerian regime and brought down Omar al-Bashir in Sudan. Anti-government demonstrations in Lebanon and Iraq also highlighted the perennial issue of weak governance, exacerbated by the economic crisis caused by the twin shocks of the coronavirus pandemic and the oil plunge in 2020.[7] As most conflict-affected countries in MENA also produce oil, their reliance on patronage-based systems has incentivised corruption. While the redistribution of wealth from an abundance of oil revenues had previously ensured social peace, it also left important segments of society under-represented and marginalised. The pandemic and the oil plunge pushed these structural deficiencies to breaking point, while eroding foreign-exchange reserves.[8] As the economy unravelled, the subsidy-based systems on which most oil-producing countries relied became increasingly unsustainable, putting additional pressure on outdated social contracts.

Security

The 2011 Arab uprisings aggravated state fragility and weaknesses and shook the legitimacy of many governments in the region. Several regimes faced myriad armed groups representing different tribal, regional or sectarian identities and using rallying calls of socio-economic grievances or ideological and political affinities that threatened the unity and the very existence of the state. Faltering regimes weakened by sustained insurgency turned to foreign patrons, who have also used local armed groups as vectors for regional proxy wars. The fragmentation of the security sector characterised contemporary conflicts in the region. In Libya, central authorities failed to rein in militias that thrived post-Gadhafi; in Yemen, the erosion of central authority triggered a multiplication of competing 'militiadoms'.[9] More generally, the proliferation and hybrid nature of militias in Iraq, Libya, Syria and Yemen provided a breeding ground for proxy interventions, which gave foreign meddlers considerable leverage vis-à-vis the conflict parties.[10]

Geopolitical

The confrontation between two regional blocs brought to the fore multiple geopolitical rivalries, which, in turn, were powerful drivers of conflict in the region. As the US progressively disengaged from the region, the quest for regional hegemony between Iran and Saudi Arabia intensified, leading to proxy-war dynamics in conflict zones. Adding to the regional divide between Sunni and Shia powers, which fomented sectarianism and fractured social fabrics, the rivalry between Turkey and the United Arab Emirates (UAE) also reinforced the Islamist/secularist narrative lying at the intersection of domestic and foreign policy. Similarly, the 2017 Gulf crisis had magnified this regional polarisation, highlighting the intra-Sunni split between Qatar and other members of the Gulf Cooperation Council. The intra-Gulf rift allowed counter-revolutionary powers to present an illusory trade-off between security and democracy, which, to some extent, garnered support in Donald Trump's US administration and European Union member states. At the same time, the containment of Qatar brought Turkey's role to the fore, with an assertive foreign policy featuring several interventions in regional theatres, including in Iraq, Libya and Syria. In light of Iran's and Russia's perceived expansionism, non-Arab states positioned themselves in an increasingly central role to shape a new security architecture in the MENA region according to their own interests.

Regional Outlook

Prospects for peace

In early 2021 President Joe Biden adopted a more multilateralist foreign-policy approach, particularly towards Gulf monarchies, than the transactionalism of his predecessor. Anticipating this change, Gulf states had already agreed to a detente over the Qatar crisis at the al-Ula summit in January 2021. The US review of arms sales to the UAE and the recalibration of its relations with Saudi Arabia were other clear indications of a reversal of Trump's policies. Despite significant challenges, such as the controversy around the sequencing between sanctions and compliance, a US return to the Joint Comprehensive Plan of Action (JCPOA) with Iran also seems likely. This could have important ramifications in Iraq, reducing tensions and paving the way for a new government after general elections scheduled for October 2021.

Elections are also expected to be held by the end of 2021 in Libya, where brinkmanship policies led to a military stalemate that proved beneficial to the UN-led peace process. The February 2021 establishment of a new executive authority offered Libya a serious opportunity to end its decade-old conflict. However, disgruntled spoilers could still derail the transition, and much will also depend on the intentions of Russia and Turkey as their military presence poses the risk of a frozen conflict scenario along the Sirte–Jufra front line. Turning the page on the so-called 'Deal of the Century', Biden's administration is also likely to craft a new balancing act between Israel and the Palestinian Territories, where elections will be crucial in determining the way forward.[11]

Geopolitical changes

The Western Sahara risks becoming a new hotspot to watch in 2021, as a frozen conflict reaches its melting point. Signs of escalation were visible in late 2020, as the Polisario Front declared the end of the 1991 ceasefire and resumed its armed struggle for independence from Morocco. Military operations coincided with a diplomatic push from Gulf states, including Bahrain and the UAE, that pushed Rabat to accept normalising ties with Israel in exchange for US recognition of Moroccan sovereignty over the disputed Western Sahara.

This normalisation process stemmed from the September 2020 signing of the Abraham Accords, which is expected to generate a warm peace between its signatories, Bahrain, Israel and the UAE (followed by Sudan in October 2020), in contrast to Israel's cold peace with Egypt and Jordan. A Saudi Arabian decision to join too would be transformational. Meanwhile, the process has already led to the emergence of a normalisation front, including Gulf monarchies and counter-revolutionary powers, that is challenged by a revisionist front, led by Iran and, to a lesser extent, Turkey and Qatar. The spillover of this confrontation was particularly visible in the eastern Mediterranean Sea, where Turkey's ambitions were opposed by its regional rivals.[12] In the medium to long term, an escalation in the eastern Mediterranean cannot be ruled out, also due to the uncertain fate of Cyprus, where Turkish President Recep Tayyip Erdogan has called for a two-state solution following his visit to the Turkish Republic of Northern Cyprus in November 2020.

Socio-economic challenges placed additional pressures on Iraq and Lebanon: although popular uprisings in 2019 fizzled out in 2020, more unrest is likely given the negative economic outlook. Prospects for peace also remain particularly dim for Syria, where the humanitarian catastrophe and the economic collapse could seed future conflict.[13] Presidential elections in 2021 are expected to cement President Bashar al-Assad's stay in power, despite concerns over the lack of transparency that had emerged in the 2020 parliamentary elections. Furthermore, a decisive battle for Idlib looks set to still be fought, while volatility in northeast Syria represents a source of constant tension between Russia,

Turkey and the Syrian Democratic Forces (SDF). Similarly, competition among several power centres in conflict-torn Yemen has resulted in fragmentation beyond repair.[14] Despite Saudi Arabia's de-escalation and the new US administration's decision to end all support for offensive military operations in February 2021, local sources of violence continued to prevail over the international dimension of the conflict. The multiplication of front lines and fiefdoms contributed to the intractability of the conflict, preventing any meaningful attempt to rebuild state institutions.

Notes

[1] Guney Yildiz, 'Turkish–Russian Adversarial Collaboration in Syria, Libya and Nagorno-Karabakh', *SWP Comment*, 2021/C, 22 March 2021.

[2] According to the Internal Displacement Monitoring Centre (IDMC), there were approximately 6.6 million IDPs in Syria as of the end of 2020, with more than 1.8m of these being new displacements that occurred in 2020. See Internal Displacement Monitoring Centre (IDMC), '2020 Internal Displacement', Global Internal Displacement Database.

[3] The sustained fighting that broke out in April 2021 and the subsequent ceasefire signed in May are not covered in detail in this report as they fall outside the scope of the reporting period for *The Armed Conflict Survey 2021*.

[4] See John Raine, 'Washington Returns to a Reordered Middle East', IISS blog, 31 March 2021.

[5] See UN Human Rights Council, 'Situation of Human Rights in Yemen, Including Violations and Abuses Since September 2014', A/HRC/45/CRP.7, 28 September 2020.

[6] See Renad Mansour, 'Networks of Power: The Popular Mobilization Forces and the State in Iraq', Chatham House, 25 February 2021. See also Human Rights Watch, 'Iraq: Human Rights Watch Submission to the Working Group on Enforced or Involuntary Disappearances', 121st session, 17 May 2020, HRW.

[7] Lebanon experienced an unprecedented economic downturn, described by the World Bank as the country's 'largest peace-time financial crisis', with its GDP contracting by 20.3% in 2020.

See 'Lebanon's Economic Update – April 2021', World Bank, 2 April 2021.

[8] Facing the progressive erosion of its foreign-exchange reserves, in December 2020 the Central Bank of Iraq was forced to devalue the dinar by more than 20%. See Chloe Cornish, 'Iraq Devalues Currency by a Fifth as Oil-price Collapse Hits', *Financial Times*, 20 December 2020.

[9] Eleonora Ardemagni, 'Beyond Yemen's Militiadoms: Restarting From Local Agency', EUISS *Conflict Series*, no. 8, 21 April 2020.

[10] See Frederic Wehrey, 'Armies, Militias and (Re)-integration in Fractured States', Italian Institute for International Political Studies, 30 October 2018.

[11] Presented on 28 January 2020 with the official name of 'Peace to prosperity: a vision to improve the lives of the Palestinian and Israeli people', the US peace plan was strongly criticised as biased in favour of Israel and immediately rejected by the Palestinian leadership, who did not participate in the negotiations. The sustained fighting that broke out in April 2021 and the subsequent ceasefire signed in May are not covered in detail in this report as they fall outside the scope of the reporting period for *The Armed Conflict Survey 2021*.

[12] See Emile Hokayem, 'Libya: A Cauldron for Mediterranean Power Politics', IISS blog, 6 July 2020.

[13] See Oz Katerji, 'Assad's Violence Started a Conflict That Will Burn for Decades', *Foreign Policy*, 19 March 2021.

[14] See Gregory D. Johnsen, 'The End of Yemen', Brookings Institution blog – Order from Chaos, 25 March 2021.

TURKEY

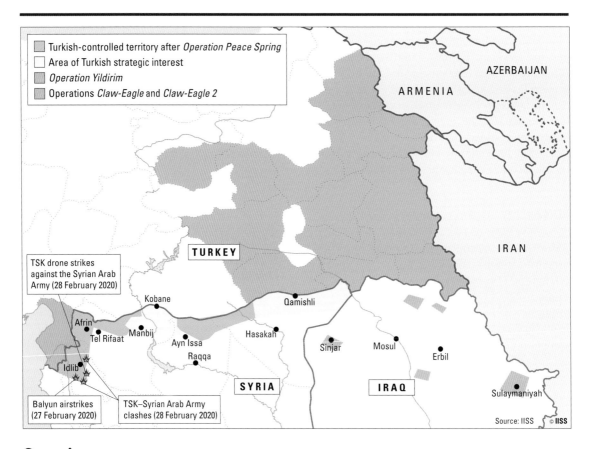

Legend:
- Turkish-controlled territory after *Operation Peace Spring*
- Area of Turkish strategic interest
- *Operation Yildirim*
- Operations *Claw-Eagle* and *Claw-Eagle 2*

AZERBAIJAN

ARMENIA

TURKEY

IRAN

TSK drone strikes against the Syrian Arab Army (28 February 2020)

Kobane

Qamishli

Afrin

Manbij

Tel Rifaat

Ayn Issa

Hasakah

Sinjar

Mosul

Erbil

Raqqa

Idlib

SYRIA

IRAQ

Sulaymaniyah

Balyun airstrikes (27 February 2020)

TSK–Syrian Arab Army clashes (28 February 2020)

Source: IISS   © IISS

Overview

Since it began in the mid-1980s, the conflict between Turkey and the Kurdistan Workers' Party (PKK) has remained a constant feature of national politics, with the PKK seeking political and social recognition for the Kurdish minority in the country. The conflict has ebbed and flowed over time, and the PKK has progressively shifted away from violent actions that target civilians to acts striking Turkish armed and security forces.

The Turkish government views the organisation as a terrorist group whose only aim is dismantling national unity. While the European Union and the United States have also previously viewed the PKK as a terrorist organisation, this stance has become increasingly ambivalent, chiefly due to Turkey's uncompromising categorisation of even peaceful pro-Kurdish activities as 'terrorist acts', Western countries' growing ties with PKK affiliates in Iraq and Syria, and more broadly due to the renewed international visibility the Kurdish plea for recognition, autonomy and independence has attracted.

In 2020, the Turkey–PKK conflict continued to unfold on three front lines: in southeast Turkey, where Turkish armed and security forces were actively engaged against the PKK itself; in northern Syria, where there is significant overlap between the PKK and the People's Protection Units (YPG) – the main combat component of the Syrian Democratic Forces (SDF); and in northwestern Iraq, where PKK/YPG presence had grown.

Throughout the year, Turkish armed and security forces carried out a string of military operations against the PKK in the southeast of the country; meanwhile, arrests of politicians belonging to the centre-left liberal and pro-Kurdish rights Peoples' Democratic Party (HDP) continued, while prosecutors also tried to ban the party from the political arena for alleged ties to terrorist acts.

Armed Conflict Global Relevance Indicator (ACGRI)

Incidence

7

Human
impact

7

Geopolitical
impact

0

Turkey

Key Conflict Statistics

Type	Internal | Localised insurgency
Start date	1984
IDPs	1,099,000
Gini index (0–100)	41.9 (2019)
Functioning of government (0–10)	5.36

ACGRI pillars: IISS calculation based on multiple sources for 2020 and January/February 2021 (scale: 0–100). See Notes on Methodology and Data Appendix for further details on Key Conflict Statistics.

In Syria, the Turkish military consolidated its presence but faced an enduring insurgent challenge. Since 2017, the Turkish Armed Forces (TSK) have established control over a large swathe of northern and northwestern Syria with the support of the Turkey-backed Syrian National Army (SNA), mostly within territories previously controlled by the SDF. While clashes between the TSK and SDF continued throughout 2020 and into 2021, there was no major breakthrough, partly due to the fact that Turkish forces were also engaged in a major confrontation against pro-Assad groups (supported by Russian forces) around the Idlib governorate.

Airstrikes targeting locations in northern Iraq grew significantly throughout 2020 and into 2021, culminating with a major military operation in Gara in February 2021. PKK spokespeople and Turkish authorities traded accusations on the responsibility for the resulting deaths of 13 Turkish hostages the PKK had been holding in the targeted location. This incident paved the way for an escalation in Turkey's concerns over actual control of strategic areas in northern and northwestern Iraq.[1] This increase in Turkey's military activities in Iraq generated significant tensions with the PKK, Iraqi authorities and the international community.

Conflict Parties

Turkish Armed Forces (TSK)

Strength: 512,000 total (355,200 active military, 156,800 active paramilitary). 30,000 (estimate) deployed in southeast Turkey and northern Iraq, 22,000 (estimate) deployed in Syria.

Areas of operation: Southeast Turkey, northern and northwestern Iraq, northern and northwestern Syria.

Leadership: President Recep Tayyip Erdogan (commander-in-chief); General (retd) Hulusi Akar (minister of national defence); General Yasar Guler (chief of general staff).

Structure: Turkish army units operating under the Turkish Land Forces Command and squadrons carrying out airstrikes operating under the Air Force Command are subordinate to the chief of general staff. Gendarmerie units reporting to the Gendarmerie Command are subordinate to the Ministry of Interior.

History: Rebuilt after the collapse of the Ottoman Empire in 1922. Significantly restructured after the country joined NATO in 1951, to become NATO's second-largest armed force.

Objectives: Eradicate the PKK and preserve national unity.

Opponents: The PKK and its affiliate organisations, particularly the YPG/SDF in Syria.

Affiliates/allies: Relies extensively on the SNA as a support force in northern Syria.

Resources/capabilities: Turkey's defence budget for 2020 is US$10.88 billion. Its military capabilities include air attack and intelligence, surveillance and reconnaissance (ISR) assets such as the F-16 and the *Bayraktar* TB2 uninhabited aerial vehicle (UAV), armoured tanks and special-forces units.

Kurdistan Workers' Party (PKK)

Strength: 30,000 (estimate).

Areas of operation: Southeast Turkey, northern Iraq.

Leadership: Abdullah Ocalan (ideological leader, despite his imprisonment since 1999); Murat Karayilan (acting leader on the ground since Ocalan's capture); Bahoz Erdal (military commander).

Middle East and
North Africa

Kurdistan Workers' Party (PKK)

Structure: While operating under the same command and leadership, the PKK's armed wing is divided into the People's Defence Forces (HPG) and the Free Women's Unit (YJA STAR).

History: Founded by Ocalan in 1978. Engaged in an insurgency campaign against Turkish armed forces since 1984.

Objectives: Political and cultural recognition of the Kurdish minority in Turkey; adoption of a Democratic Federalist system of governance.

Opponents: TSK, Arab rebel groups (SNA) and Syrian government forces.

Affiliates/allies: SDF/YPG in Syria.

Resources/capabilities: Relies on money-laundering activities and drug trafficking to generate revenues, in addition to donations from the Kurdish community and diaspora and left-wing international supporters. The PKK relies on highly mobile units, using guerrilla tactics against Turkish military targets.

(Turkey-sponsored) Syrian National Army (SNA)

Strength: 70,000–90,000 (estimate).[2]

Areas of operation: Northern Syria.

Leadership: SNA units are currently deployed alongside Turkish military forces, and therefore operate under Turkish leadership.

Structure: A conglomerate of dozens of different militias, ranging vastly in size, affiliation and ideology, composed of Syrian militants, who are trained and equipped by Turkey. Divided into seven main legions, each composed of a wide array of divisions and brigades.

History: Created as a splinter group of the Turkey-backed Free Syrian Army. Trained and equipped by the Turkish government since 2016. In 2019, the Idlib-based and Turkey-sponsored National Front for Liberation was merged into the SNA.

Objectives: Take control of northern Syria.

Opponents: YPG/SDF, Syrian government forces.

Affiliates/allies: Turkey.

Resources/capabilities: While a handful of formations have received US-sponsored training and equipment, the SNA has been fully reliant on Turkey's support since its creation. Turkey has provided small arms as well as infantry vehicles, and SNA military operations have benefitted from the Turkish army's fire support via artillery and airstrikes.

People's Protection Units (YPG)/Syrian Democratic Forces (SDF)

Strength: Around 100,000.[3]

Areas of operation: Northern Syria.

Leadership: Mazloum Kobani Abdi, also known as Sahin Cilo (military commander). Abdi is a former senior PKK member.

Structure: Organised mainly along ethnic and territorial lines. Syrian Kurds lead the People's Protection Units (YPG) and the Women's Protection Units (YPJ); both include a small component of international volunteers grouped into an international battalion. Other ethnic groups are organised under various military formations within the SDF, mainly as military councils.

History: Created in 2015 as a direct response to the advance of the Islamic State (also known as ISIS or ISIL) into northern Syria, building on various pre-existing alliances. Since then, it has fought against ISIS and the Turkish military.

Objectives: Control northern Syria.

Opponents: Turkey, SNA, Syrian government forces.

Affiliates/allies: PKK, Russia, US.

Resources/capabilities: While it built upon the experience of its militias, since its formal creation the SDF has been equipped, trained and advised by the US. SDF units are equipped with small arms and some infantry vehicles.

Conflict Drivers

Political

The self-determination quest and Kurdish marginalisation:

The conflict is rooted in the incompatibility between the PKK's own pursuit of political autonomy, amid a wider Kurdish quest for self-determination, and Turkey's wholesale opposition to recognising the minority rights of its Kurdish population. Turkey sees any expansion of Kurdish political influence in Turkey's regional neighbourhood as a potential threat to national security and, ultimately, to the unity of the country. While the PKK represents only one, albeit prominent, faction advocating for the Kurdish cause, the Turkish government tends to conflate most forms of Kurdish political activism into PKK- or terrorism-related activities, further compounding tensions between the two sides.

The fate of pro-Kurdish political parties in Turkey provides one of the most prominent examples of this dynamic. Since the 1990s, all Kurdish parties that have run for parliamentary elections have been disbanded by the Constitutional Court for alleged ties with the PKK. Turkey's current pro-Kurdish party, the HDP, focuses in its present form on a wide social-democratic political agenda, in which the Kurdish issue is one of many issues, rather than being its defining element. Nonetheless, since its main electoral success in the 2019 elections, HDP leaders and many of its members of parliament and mayors have been imprisoned or removed from office by the Ministry of Interior. In early 2021, public prosecutors attempted to have the HDP banned for allegedly actively providing personnel to the PKK and aiming to destroy the country's unity, only to see their case rejected by the Constitutional Court.

International
Kurdish progress in the region:
The Kurds live as a divided minority across national boundaries between Iran, Iraq, Turkey and Syria. Iraqi Kurds reached a breakthrough achievement towards self-determination in 2005 with the constitutional recognition of the Kurdistan Regional Government (KRG) as an autonomous government in northern Iraq. Despite deep political divisions, both among Iraqi Kurds and between them and the rest of the Kurdish political world, for many Kurds this was still a milestone development towards the creation of a Kurdish state. In 2017, however, Kurdish independence aspirations in Iraq suffered a setback after regional powers and the Iraqi central government responded forcefully to a referendum and seized significant portions of Iraqi territory held by Kurdish factions since 2003.

Nevertheless, the political progress of Iraqi Kurds, coupled with the turmoil caused by the 2003 US-led invasion of Iraq, bolstered the PKK's ambitions for Kurds in Turkey, leading to a resumption of hostilities after a five-year-long ceasefire (1999–2003). The PKK launched a continuous stream of attacks against Turkish forces from strongholds based in the Qandil Mountains of northern Iraq, and Turkish security forces retaliated with counter-insurgency operations in both Turkey and northern Iraq. The 2011 outbreak of civil war in Syria and particularly the 2013–14 advance of ISIS in that country further aggravated the Turkey–PKK conflict, adding a cross-border front in northern Syria to the long-established domestic front in southeastern Turkey. While the March 2019 territorial defeat of the Islamic State caliphate fostered a brief period of relative stability in SDF-controlled northern Syria, the sudden withdrawal of US forces the following October paved the way for a new Turkish military campaign against the SDF, dragging the region back into conflict.

Political and Military Developments

Continued crackdown against the HDP and PKK
In Turkey, the crackdown on the HDP and military operations against the PKK continued unabated in 2020 and early 2021. The Turkish government itself remained adamant in its intentions to see the HDP eventually banned, with the right-wing Nationalist Movement Party (MHP) leader Devlet Bahceli declaring it a crucial priority for national security.

Meanwhile, Turkish security forces launched a string of coordinated operations across southeastern Turkey: the first wave, called *Operation Kapan* – with its multiple component phases denoted by numerical suffixes – began with *Kapan-1* in the Mardin province in January 2020 and ended with *Kapan-9* in the Bingol province in March. The operation largely aimed at disrupting the PKK's supply lines, by locating weapons caches and shelter areas. A second wave, called *Operation Yildirim*, attempted to further weaken the PKK's presence in the region. According to Turkish government figures, security forces killed around 150 PKK members through 17 discrete operations launched between July and December 2020.[4]

PKK legitimacy recognised by Belgium
A watershed decision by Belgian courts in January 2020 recognised the Turkey–PKK conflict as a non-international armed conflict, following lengthy deliberations including escalation to the top level of the country's judiciary hierarchy. This verdict recognised the PKK as a legitimate armed actor, instead of labelling it a terrorist organisation. While the decision only applies to Belgium – and was contradicted by the Belgian government, which reiterated the categorisation of the PKK as a terrorist organisation – it reflected a potential shift in narrative among European countries (and international organisations), many of whom are increasingly at odds with Ankara's stance on the Kurdish issue, the PKK's

legal status and, more importantly, the SDF's role in Syria and Iraq.

Turkey targeting the Sinjar Alliance in Iraq

A similar conundrum in Turkey–NATO relations arose over the role of SDF-linked militias in north-western Iraq. The growing influence of the Sinjar Alliance – an SDF-trained and PKK-aligned Yazidi armed group formed in 2015 to counter the advance of ISIS – in and around Sinjar and the broader Nineva governorate, at the expense of the Kurdish paramili-tary Peshmerga forces linked to the KRG and its Kurdistan Democratic Party (KDP), made it a target for large-scale joint Turkish military operations from mid-2020. However, Turkey's plans – to eradicate the Sinjar Alliance from, and boost the chances of a KDP return to, the area – are at odds with both the Iraqi government's goals and NATO's expanded role in the country under the new February 2021 mandate for NATO Mission Iraq.[5] The Turkish oper-ations, *Claw-Eagle* (between June and September 2020) and *Claw-Eagle 2* (February 2021), targeted alleged PKK camps and facilities across northern Iraq, from Sinjar to Sulaymaniyah, culminating with the February 2021 operation in Gara.

Focus on northwest Syria

In Syria, 2020 did not lead to any major territorial breakthrough in the conflict between the Turkish-sponsored SNA and the SDF. On the other hand, the fighting between Turkish forces and pro-Assad units around Idlib temporarily moved Turkey's focus to northwest Syria. This pivot was accelerated by the February 2020 Balyun airstrike, in which the Syrian and Russian air forces hit a Turkish military convoy, killing around 34 soldiers.[6] Turkey responded by launching *Operation Spring Shield* to stop the Syrian–Russian advance into the Idlib governorate. This triggered a temporary cooling in relations between Turkey and Russia and a downscaling in military activities against the SDF.

In November 2020 the TSK and SNA launched an offensive to take control of Ayn Issa (in Syria's Raqqa governorate) and push SDF forces out. From Turkey's perspective, taking control of Ayn Issa would significantly limit the SDF's ability to resup-ply and move in and out of the cities of Manbij and Kobane, which it currently controls; the potential capture of the two cities would give Turkey unin-terrupted military control over the vast majority of Syria's northern border.[7]

Key Events in 2020–21

POLITICAL EVENTS

29 January 2020
Belgian courts refuse to put 36 alleged PKK members on trial for terrorism, arguing the organisation's activities are part of an armed conflict rather than acts of terrorism.

6 February
Turkey strongly criticises the European Parliament for hosting a conference on the EU, Turkey, the Middle East and the Kurds, claiming it provided a propaganda platform for the PKK.

23 March
Five HDP mayors in southeastern Turkey are detained for alleged ties to the PKK.

7 April
Diyarbakir's former HDP mayor is sentenced to nine years in prison for ties to the PKK.

4 June
Two HDP members of parliament are stripped of their immunity and arrested for alleged ties to the PKK.

29 June
Turkey criticises the Austrian government for allowing a pro-PKK rally to take place in Vienna.

MILITARY/VIOLENT EVENTS

8 January 2020
Four Turkish soldiers are killed in a YPG attack in northern Syria.

3 February
After clashes between Turkish and Russia-backed Syrian regime forces in Idlib, a joint Turkey–Russia patrol in northern Syria is cancelled.

30 March
Turkey claims Nazife Bilen, a high-ranking PKK member, is killed in a military operation.

19 May
Three Turkish soldiers are killed in attacks carried out by the PKK.

23 May
Turkish defence minister Hulusi Akar inspects military outposts along the Syrian border.

11 August
The Iraqi military accuses Turkey of killing two of its high-ranking officers in a drone strike in the KRG.

5 July
Turkey's foreign ministry defends its military operations in northern Iraq claiming they are carried out in self-defence.

16 July
A Turkey correspondent for the German newspaper *Die Welt* is sentenced to two years and nine months *in absentia* for allegedly spreading propaganda for the PKK.

6 September
Turkey slams France over the existence of a high-school textbook containing supposed propaganda around the Kurdish issue.

25 September
Turkey issues arrest warrants for 82 individuals over pro-Kurdish rallies that took place in 2014.

19 November
Turkish Interior Minister Suleyman Soylu states the PKK will be eliminated within one year.

27 November
In a rare interview with the *Jerusalem Post*, PKK field commander Murat Karayilan discusses the PKK's vision and its relations with Turkey and other countries.

11 December
MHP leader Devlet Bahceli strongly condemns more than 800 academics who signed a petition calling for an amnesty for individuals arrested on terrorism charges.

24 February 2021
Turkey's presidential spokesperson Ibrahim Kalin criticises the EU for its alleged inaction against the PKK.

12 August
Over 1,000 security personnel are deployed in the Hatay province for a major operation against the PKK.

7 October
The Turkish parliament ratifies a motion extending authorisation for the TSK to carry out military operations in northern Iraq and Syria.

28 October
President Erdogan threatens a new offensive in northern Syria if the SDF does not withdraw from the Turkey–Syria border.

6 December
Turkey supports the Sinjar deal between the Iraqi government and the KRG, through which Iraqi federal forces will patrol Sinjar.

18 January 2021
Akar visits Iraq and stresses the Turkish military are ready to deploy alongside Iraqi forces in Sinjar.

26 January
Two Turkish civilians are killed by an improvised explosive device (IED) in northern Syria.

14 February
13 Turkish citizens held captive in a cave complex in Gara (northern Iraq) are allegedly killed by the PKK.

23 February
Two SNA soldiers are killed in an SDF attack in Tal Abyad.

Impact

Human rights and humanitarian

The Turkey–PKK conflict continued to have a significant impact on human rights in Turkey, as well as in northern Iraq and northern Syria. In Turkey, the crackdown on the pro-Kurdish HDP led to the detention of 16,000 individuals alleged to have connections with the PKK, including politicians, journalists and grassroots activists.[8] In northern Syria, Turkish airstrikes caused civilian fatalities and displacement. In northern Iraq, recurring airstrikes around the Sinjar area exacerbated long-standing issues related to internally displaced persons (IDPs), with roughly 90,000 Yazidis who had fled in the midst of the ISIS advance still struggling to return and a new wave of IDPs leaving Sinjar due to the deteriorating security conditions.[9]

The conflict also continued to curtail freedom of expression. In two separate instances, Halk TV, a popular TV channel, was ordered by the court to cease broadcasting for several days, after its criticism of ongoing military operations was deemed an action 'against the independence of the State'; a third occurrence within the next year would mean it would lose its licence to operate in Turkey.[10] In a similar vein, an anti-terrorism law passed in December 2020 gave the Ministry of Interior extensive powers over non-governmental organisations operating in Turkey, allowing it to establish annual inspections and giving it the authority to suspend individuals who are subject to open investigation.

Political stability

At the domestic level, Turkey was fairly insulated from the repercussions of the PKK's presence and activities. The continued crackdown against the HDP in 2020 resulted in the removal from office of 60 out of 65 HDP mayors and their replacement by governmental officials.[11] The coalition government formed by President Erdogan's Justice and Development Party (AKP) and the right-wing MHP thrived as a result of the 'rally around the flag' effect engendered by the prevalent anti-terrorism narrative.

Economic and social

While up-to-date data on the economic impact of the conflict was not available, Turkey's increased domestic and international military activism significantly and consistently increased the country's defence budget. After the 2019 deployment of Turkish armed forces in northern Iraq (*Operation Claw*) and in northern Syria (*Operation Peace Spring*) had pushed Turkey's defence spending to US$10.88bn, 2020 deployments in Iraq, Syria and elsewhere drove Minister of National Defence Hulusi Akar to request a further year-on-year increase, which was approved for the 2021 defence budget.

Relations with neighbouring and international partners and geopolitical implications

While Turkey has long handled the domestic instability resulting from the fight against the PKK, from a diplomatic standpoint, the international ramifications of the events of 2020 and early 2021 further isolated Ankara. Its treatment of the PKK as a terrorist organisation was increasingly viewed within Europe and NATO as a dogmatic choice rather than one validated by actual events. Ankara's growing presence in Iraq, and particularly Sinjar, also put it on a collision course with Baghdad and NATO, while its relations with Russia, previously on a net positive trend, suffered significant strain, mainly due to the countries' divergent visions on the future of the Assad regime generally and the political situation of northern Syria specifically, with regard to the future role of the SDF and Syrian Kurds, and the status of Idlib.

Conflict Outlook

Political scenarios

The political stalemate between Turkey and the PKK is likely to continue. While the Turkish government still believes that it is possible to eradicate the group by force alone, almost 40 years of conflict point to the opposite. Without any attempt to de-escalate the anti-terrorism narrative and mend political relations with the HDP, the Kurdish issue and the PKK's existence will continue to be wrongfully merged into a single policy item. And as the stability of Erdogan's government depends upon keeping the MHP on board as the coalition's 'junior' partner, an escalation in rhetoric and in actions against both the HDP and the PKK remains the most likely scenario. With Turkey having to deal with a potentially dire economic downturn in 2021, a scaling up of the nationalist narrative is highly probable, under the guise of fostering unity against perceived 'enemies of the nation'. Turkey's narrative is also likely to include inflammatory rhetoric against the EU and the US, as a continued rebuttal to external criticism. This leaves no margin for any steps towards negotiations for a ceasefire, let alone towards a wider political solution to the PKK issue.

Escalation potential and conflict-related risks

The potential for conflict escalation applies mainly to Syria and northern Iraq. As front lines in Syria become more stable, the SDF's role in northern Syria will become a major point of contention regionally. With Turkey still holding a distant objective of a security zone along its border with Syria, negotiations between Ankara, Damascus, Moscow, Tehran and, indirectly, Washington will be critical to determine the future of northern Syria, which in turn will have repercussions for Syria as a whole, and for the region too. A similar pathway seems to be emerging in parts of the KRG in Iraq. The growing influence of both the PKK itself and PKK-linked groups in the strategic hub of Sinjar and from their safe haven in the Qandil Mountains is likely to make major Turkish military operations such as *Claw-Eagle* and *Claw-Eagle 2* a recurrent feature in the region.

Strategic implications and global influences

The strategic implications emerging from the course of the Turkey–PKK conflict in 2020 will affect Turkey's relations with its allies and partners, both in the region and globally. As relations with the EU worsen further, the issue of Kurdish identity is likely to remain a major irritant: attempts to separate the matter from the security angle were met

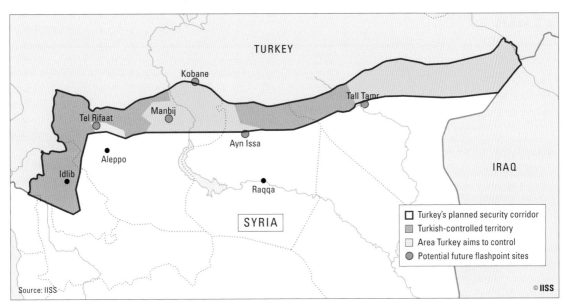

Figure 1: Turkey's strategic buffer zone in northern Syria

Middle East and North Africa

by Turkey with systematic criticism and accusations that EU institutions were favouring the PKK. Relations with NATO also look problematic, with further strains potentially arising from growing tensions between Turkey and the KRG/KDP over how to deal with the PKK and between Turkey and the Iraqi government over violations of Iraqi sovereignty. Finally, the ongoing Astana peace talks on Syria, involving Iran, Russia and Turkey, will continue to feature a trade-off between Russia's concerns over the use of Idlib as a safe haven by hostile armed groups and Turkey's ambition to push the SDF further away from its southern border. As such, the leverage vis-à-vis Russia that Turkey has obtained through its involvement in the conflicts in Libya and in Nagorno-Karabakh will also need to be factored in, as they are likely to be concurrent issues for discussion.

Notes

1   Carlotta Gill, 'Deaths of Soldiers and Policemen Held by Kurdish Guerrillas Roil Turkish Politics', *New York Times*, 15 February 2021.

2   Omer Ozkizilcik, 'Uniting the Syrian Opposition: The Components of the National Army and the Implications of the Unification', SETA, October 2019, p. 10.

3   Based on 'Operation Inherent Resolve: Lead Inspector General Report to the United States Congress April 1 2019 – June 30 2019', p. 30.

4   'Yıldırım-16-Sehi Ormanları Operasyonu Başladı!' [Operation Yildirim 16 Sehi Forests has begun!], Turkish Gendarmerie, 7 December 2020.

5   Following a request by the Iraqi government, NATO Mission Iraq may expand its activities to locations other than Baghdad and include a broader variety of Iraqi security institutions. See NATO, 'NATO Mission Iraq (NMI) Factsheet', May 2021.

6   'Syria War: Alarm After 33 Turkish Soldiers Killed in Attack in Idlib', BBC News, 28 February 2020.

7   Despite continuing and escalating into March 2021, the Ayn Issa offensive failed to achieve its objectives, partly due to the deterring presence of Syrian and Russian units in the area. Occasional tensions between YPG militias and Syrian/Russian units, however, signalled that the SDF remained wary of a looming agreement between Turkey and Russia, which could pave the way for a major offensive against their positions.

8   Bethan McKernan, 'Turkey: The Rise and Fall of the Kurdish Party that Threatened Erdogan', *Guardian*, 27 December 2020.

9   ACAPS, 'Iraq: The Return to Sinjar', Briefing Note, 20 November 2020.

10   'Halk TV beş gün karartılıyor!' [Halk TV will be obscured for 5 days!], HalkTV, 25 September 2020.

11   McKernan, 'Turkey: The Rise and Fall of the Kurdish Party that Threatened Erdogan'.

SYRIA

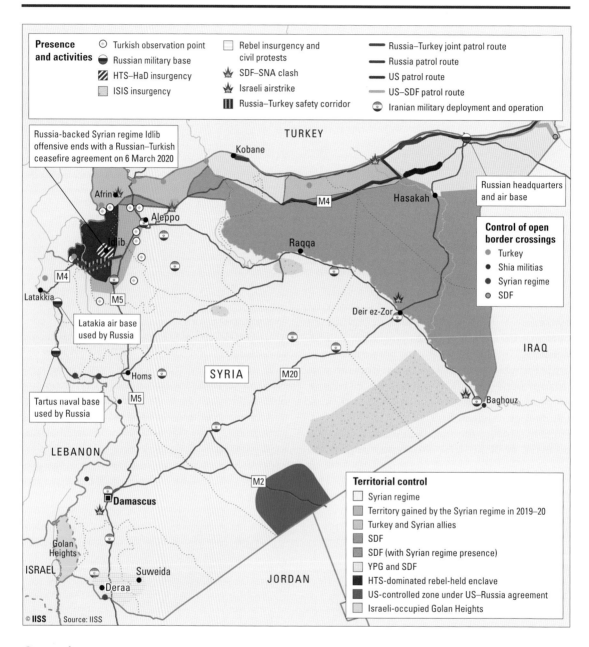

Presence and activities

- ⊙ Turkish observation point
- ◐ Russian military base
- ▨ HTS–HaD insurgency
- ▢ ISIS insurgency
- ▢ Rebel insurgency and civil protests
- ⚔ SDF–SNA clash
- ⚔ Israeli airstrike
- ▮▮▮ Russia–Turkey safety corridor
- ━━ Russia–Turkey joint patrol route
- ━━ Russia patrol route
- ━━ US patrol route
- ━━ US–SDF patrol route
- ◑ Iranian military deployment and operation

Russia-backed Syrian regime Idlib offensive ends with a Russian–Turkish ceasefire agreement on 6 March 2020

TURKEY

Kobane

Afrin

Aleppo

Idlib

M4

Hasakah

Russian headquarters and air base

Raqqa

Control of open border crossings
- ● Turkey
- ● Shia militias
- ● Syrian regime
- ◐ SDF

Latakkia

M4

M5

Latakia air base used by Russia

Deir ez-Zor

IRAQ

Tartus naval base used by Russia

Homs

M5

SYRIA

M20

Baghouz

LEBANON

M2

Damascus

Territorial control
- ▢ Syrian regime
- ▨ Territory gained by the Syrian regime in 2019–20
- ▨ Turkey and Syrian allies
- ▨ SDF
- ▨ SDF (with Syrian regime presence)
- ▢ YPG and SDF
- ■ HTS-dominated rebel-held enclave
- ▨ US-controlled zone under US–Russia agreement
- ▢ Israeli-occupied Golan Heights

Golan Heights

ISRAEL

Suweida

JORDAN

Deraa

© IISS   Source: IISS

Overview

The Syrian popular uprising in 2011, born from political and social grievances against the authoritarian and sectarian rule of President Bashar al-Assad, morphed over time into a complex set of intractable conflicts that have pulled in regional and international powers. By 2012 a full-fledged civil war had broken out between rebel forces, backed by their foreign patrons Turkey, Saudi Arabia, Qatar and the United States, and the Assad regime, supported by Iran, the Lebanese Hizbullah and Russia.

The conflict was further complicated by thorny ethno-sectarian dynamics between Shias and Sunnis

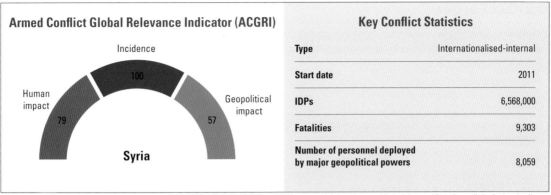

Armed Conflict Global Relevance Indicator (ACGRI)	**Key Conflict Statistics**	
Incidence — 100	**Type**	Internationalised-internal
Human impact — 79	**Start date**	2011
Geopolitical impact — 57	**IDPs**	6,568,000
Syria	**Fatalities**	9,303
	Number of personnel deployed by major geopolitical powers	8,059

ACGRI pillars: IISS calculation based on multiple sources for 2020 and January/February 2021 (scale: 0–100). See Notes on Methodology and Data Appendix for further details on Key Conflict Statistics.

in Syria, transnational violent extremism and regional rivalries between the Arab Gulf states, Iran, Israel and Turkey. In particular, the collapse of the state made Syria a fertile ground for the development of a range of Islamist as well as al-Qaeda-affiliated insurgent groups, including the Islamic State (also known as ISIS or ISIL) in 2013. A combined joint task force, led by the US, *Operation Inherent Resolve* was launched in October 2014 to uproot ISIS. By March 2019, its last remaining enclave, Baghouz, fell, but ISIS remained active as an organisation, adopting insurgent warfare tactics across eastern and southern Syria.

A decade after the war began, Syria remains in tatters. Not only have the initial demands of the Syrian population for political and economic reform gone unaddressed, but the conflict has taken an almost unprecedented humanitarian and economic toll. Assad, with the support of his foreign patrons, had largely defeated the fractured armed opposition and regained control over nearly 70% of the country, although power remained highly fragmented amidst an abundance of pro-government militias, warlords and racketeers.[1]

Domestic and geopolitical competition over Syria continued in 2020 and the year started with regime and pro-regime troops attacking the last stronghold of the Syrian opposition in Idlib, with Russian support. A Turkish counter-operation followed, leading to a Russia–Turkey ceasefire on 6 March. Turkey and its rebel allies suffered territorial and human losses, but the counter-operation stopped the regime's advance and exacted a heavy toll on government forces. Despite recurring violations on both sides, the ceasefire continued to hold, as of February 2021.

With the ceasefire in northwestern Syria, armed confrontation shifted to southern and eastern Syria, with increasing kinetic activity by ISIS, which tried to exploit the security vacuum to (re-) gain footholds through intense and geographically widespread attacks.

The southwestern province of Deraa, nominally held by the regime under a shaky Russian-brokered agreement, continued to be a hotbed for civil and armed unrest throughout 2020 and early 2021, which was met with violence by regime and pro-regime forces. Against this backdrop, parliamentary elections in regime-held areas on 19 July 2020 were predictably won by the ruling National Progressive Front (NPF) coalition, led by the Ba'ath Party.

In northeastern Syria, external competing powers maintained the status quo, with an uneasy and volatile coexistence and military entanglements by Syrian government and militia forces, the Syrian Democratic Forces (SDF), as well as Russia, Turkey and the US. At the local level, unrest caused by governance and ethnic tensions between the SDF leadership and Arab tribes continued, mainly in Deir ez-Zor, as did SDF attempts to co-opt tribes in Hasakah, Manbij and Raqqa.

Middle East and North Africa

Conflict Parties

Syrian Armed Forces (SAF)/ The Syrian Arab Army (SAA)

Strength: Unknown.

Areas of operation: Coastal, central, northern and southwestern Syria with areas of shared presence with SDF in northeastern Syria.

Leadership: President Bashar al-Assad (commander-in-chief), Lieutenant-General Salim Harba (chief of staff). Key elite units of the Syrian Arab Army (SAA), such as the Republican Guard and the 4th Division, fall under the command of Maher al-Assad, the president's brother. Other units, such as the Tiger Force or the 5th Corps, respond to either Russian or Iranian commanders.

Structure: Consists of the army, navy, air force, intelligence services and the National Defence Forces. The SAA is the main actor involved in the conflict and adopts a hybrid military structure that compensates for its shrinking military personnel with paramilitary militias and pro-regime fighters. Since 2017, with Russian support, efforts have focused on integrating or dissolving these militias and reorganising and equipping the command-and-control structure. The SAA is divided into regional commands, elite units and strike forces.

History: Since its establishment in 1945, the SAA has played a key role in Syrian politics. Involved in bringing Hafez al-Assad and the Ba'athist-Alawite dynasty to power in 1970. The high percentage of Alawites in key positions in the SAA, installed by Hafez al-Assad, and left as a result of Sunni defections, exacerbated sectarianism after the 2011 outbreak of war. By the summer of 2015, the Syrian armed forces were completely exhausted and demoralised in command and control, resulting in Russia's military involvement.

Objectives: Regain military control over the entire Syrian territory.

Opponents: Israeli forces, Turkish forces, US forces, SDF/People's Protection Units (YPG), ISIS and al-Qaeda affiliates, Syrian National Army (SNA).

Affiliates/allies: Iranian and Iranian-backed forces, Russian and Russian-backed forces, Lebanese Hizbullah and other Shiite militias.

Resources/capabilities: Benefits from significant Russian air, artillery and missile support and intelligence capabilities. Russian military equipment improved the Syrian army's light motorised infantry capabilities to better fight mobile forces in the desert setting.

Hayat Tahrir al-Sham (HTS)

Strength: 12,000–15,000 (estimate).[2]

Areas of operation: Idlib province, northwestern Syria, where it controls the last stronghold of the Syrian opposition and competes with other rebel groups for governance.

Leadership: Abu Mohamed al-Golani.

Structure: Maintains a joint military-operations room with other local rebels. The HTS-linked Syrian Salvation Government focuses on territorial control and on the provision of public services via a centralised governance system and quasi-formal service-provision institutions.

History: Originally an extension of al-Qaeda in Iraq and known as Jabhat Fatah al-Sham (JFS), in 2017 it merged with several other factions, split from al-Qaeda and rebranded itself as HTS.

Objectives: Overthrow the Assad regime, defeat ISIS and al-Qaeda and their affiliates in Idlib.

Opponents: SAF, Iranian and Iranian-backed forces, ISIS, al-Qaeda and affiliates.

Affiliates/allies: Turkish forces around the mutual objective of unrooting radical groups affiliated to al-Qaeda, such as Hurras al-Din (HaD).

Resources/capabilities: Light weaponry, rocket launchers, anti-tank guided missiles as well as a small number of mechanised vehicles. It has seized weaponry from other rebel groups, including those equipped by Turkey and Western governments. Has used vehicle-borne improvised explosive devices (VBIEDs) and suicide bombings. Finances itself primarily through taxation in Idlib province by controlling border crossings with Turkey.

Hurras al-Din (HaD)

Strength: 1,500–2,000 (estimate).[3]

Areas of operation: Idlib province, northwestern Syria.

Leadership: Unknown after Khaled al-Aruri (also known as Abu al-Qasim al-Urduni) was killed in a car-bomb attack in mid-2020.

Structure: Led and guided by several key figures, and made up of at least 16 factions, with half of the fighters being foreigners. Operates through different alliances and operations rooms with partners ranging from small pro-al-Qaeda groups to major local factions like HTS. Operates at least four military-training camps in the greater Idlib area.

History: In February 2018 seven hardline factions united to form HaD as an explicitly pro-al-Qaeda militant faction in Syria under the command of Samir Hijazi. Ten more minor rebel factions joined the group later, all with a history of ideological and leadership ties to al-Qaeda. HaD claims to have carried out over 200 attacks in Syria's Aleppo, Hama, Idlib and Latakia provinces, often in conjunction with other Syrian rebel factions such as HTS. The two groups have worked together to carry out combat operations against the Syrian regime, though HaD's increasing presence in Idlib province has fuelled rivalry between itself and HTS. In 2020, HTS began cracking down on HaD and arresting many of its leaders.

Hurras al-Din (HaD)

Objectives: Cement its local power base, attract followers for al-Qaeda ideology.

Opponents: Syrian forces, Turkish forces, ISIS, HTS.

Affiliates/allies: Al-Qaeda-affiliated groups.

Resources/capabilities: Uses small arms and light weapons such as mortars and technicals. Finances itself through online campaigns and is supported by HTS in food and ammunition.

(Turkey-sponsored) Syrian National Army (SNA)

Strength: 70,000–90,000 (estimate).[4]

Areas of operation: Northern and northwestern Syria, Idlib province.

Leadership: Deployed alongside Turkish military forces, and therefore operates under Turkish leadership.

Structure: A conglomerate of dozens of different militias, ranging vastly in size, affiliation and ideology, composed of Syrian militants, who are trained and equipped by Turkey. Divided along seven main legions, each composed of a wide array of divisions and brigades. The National Front for Liberation (NLF), a coalition of more than ten rebel militias, forms a core element within the SNA.

History: Created as a splinter group of the Turkey-backed Free Syrian Army. Trained and equipped by the Turkish government since 2017. In 2019, the Idlib-based and Turkey-sponsored NLF was merged into the SNA.

Objectives: Take control of northern Syria.

Opponents: Syrian forces, Iranian and Iranian-backed forces, SDF/YPG, ISIS.

Affiliates/allies: Turkish forces.

Resources/capabilities: Excepting a handful of formations that have received US-sponsored training and equipment, fully reliant on Turkey's support. Turkey has provided small arms as well as infantry vehicles, and SNA military operations have benefitted from Turkish fire support via artillery and airstrikes.

Syrian Democratic Forces (SDF)/People's Protection Units (YPG)

Strength: 100,000 (estimate).[5]

Areas of operation: Northern Syria.

Leadership: Mazloum Kobani Abdi, also known as Sahin Cilo (military commander). Abdi is a former senior member of the Kurdistan Workers' Party (PKK).

Structure: Organised mainly along ethnic and territorial lines. Syrian Kurds lead the YPG and the Women's Protection Units (YPJ); both include a small component of international volunteers grouped into an international battalion. Other ethnic groups are organised under various military formations within the SDF, mainly as military councils.

History: Created in 2015 as a direct response to the advance of the Islamic State into northern Syria, building on various pre-existing alliances. Since then, it has fought against ISIS and the Turkish military.

Objectives: Control northern Syria.

Opponents: Turkish forces, SNA, ISIS, al-Qaeda and affiliates.

Affiliates/allies: US forces, Russian forces.

Resources/capabilities: Equipped, trained and advised by the US, building upon the experience of its militias. Equipped with small arms and some infantry vehicles.

Islamic State, also known as ISIS or ISIL

Strength: 10,000 in Iraq and Syria (estimate).[6]

Areas of operation: Across eastern Syria, notably along the Euphrates River and the Badiya desert as well as in the governorate of Homs in central Syria and along the M20 highway that runs between Palmyra and Deir ez-Zor.

Leadership: Abu Ibrahim al-Hashimi al-Qurashi (caliph and leader of ISIS).

Structure: ISIS's presence in Syria changed considerably since the 2017 loss of Raqqa and its gradual territorial defeat. Its central command remains in place, but greater autonomy is granted to local cells across the country to facilitate an insurgent campaign. Since 2019, ISIS has been restructuring internally to reinforce its capacities and attract recruits.

History: After seizing the northeastern third of Syria in 2014, ISIS established a 'caliphate' across Syria and Iraq. A US-led international coalition, in partnership with the SDF and local Arab forces, successfully defeated ISIS territorially in 2019. The same year al-Baghdadi was assassinated by US airstrikes in northern Syria, ending the era of ISIS's caliphate.

Objectives: Regain territorial hold in Syria and Iraq.

Opponents: SAF, SNA, HTS, Russian, Turkish and US armed forces, Iranian and Iranian-backed and commanded militias, SDF/YPG.

Affiliates/allies: ISIS branches, fighters and global affiliates.

Resources/capabilities: Relies on guerrilla warfare, hit-and-run tactics and conventional asymmetrical operations, using light and small weaponry and deploying insurgent tactics including suicide bombings.

Russian armed forces

Strength: 4,000 (estimate) troops in Syria.

Areas of operation: Across Syria.

Leadership: Lieutenant-General Alexander Chayko (commander of Russian forces in Syria).

Structure: The Russian mission in Syria combines ground forces, special forces, attack aircraft and bombers, an air-defence component and military intelligence. Russian private military contractors operate in front-line roles alongside conventional units.

History: Since first intervening in 2015, Russia has shaped the Syrian battlefield, playing a crucial strategic and operational role to shore up and reorganise Syrian government forces and help the Assad regime capture key areas.

Objectives: Reform the Syrian army, integrate irregular and rebel groups into the SAA and support capacity-building.

Opponents: US forces, SNA, HTS, ISIS, al-Qaeda and affiliates.

Affiliates/allies: SAF, 5th Corps of SAA, Tiger Force.

Resources/capabilities: Has deployed significant air, artillery, missile, missile-defence and intelligence capabilities in Syria, testing new weapons and tactics.

Turkish Armed Forces (TSK)

Strength: 10,000–15,000 in Syria.[7]

Areas of operation: Northwestern and northern Syria along the Syria–Turkey border.

Leadership: President Recep Tayyip Erdogan (commander-in-chief); General (retd.) Hulusi Akar (minister of national defence); General Yasar Guler (chief of general staff).

Structure: In Syria, the TSK is present with ground forces, special forces, military intelligence and reconnaissance.

History: Involved in Syria since the conflict started in 2011. Between 2011 and 2016, mainly provided training and equipment to the Syrian armed opposition and humanitarian aid. Military operations have since increased amid growing ISIS terrorist attacks in Turkey and the YPG's territorial gains.

Objectives: Eradicate the PKK and its Syrian offshoot YPG, unite the Syrian armed opposition under one umbrella military formation, preserve Syrian territorial integrity and border security, limit refugee influx to Turkey.

Opponents: SAF, Iranian and Iranian-backed and commanded militias, Russian Armed Forces, YPG, ISIS, al-Qaeda and affiliates.

Affiliates/allies: Relies extensively on the SNA as a local actor and support force in northern Syria.

Resources/capabilities: Trains, equips and arms the SNA and deploys its own military mechanised infantry battalions on the ground in Syria, as well as F-16 fighter jets and ANKA-S uninhabited aerial vehicles (UAVs). Its military capabilities include air attack and intelligence, surveillance and reconnaissance (ISR) assets such as the F-16 and the *Bayraktar* TB2 UAV, armoured tanks and special-forces units.

Iranian armed forces

Strength: 3,000 in Syria (estimate).

Areas of operation: Predominantly southeastern and southwestern Syria.

Leadership: Brigadier-General Esmail Ghaani (military leader of the Quds Force (QF)).

Structure: Iran operates militarily in Syria through various military organisations, as well as local and regional Shia militias. Iran's military operations in Syria are orchestrated by the QF, the ground forces of the Islamic Revolutionary Guard Corps (IRGC), and a smaller group of units from the regular Iranian army, Artesh, that began arriving in Syria in early 2016. The QF conducts external military operations in Syria, training and equipping pro-Iranian and regime militias from Afghanistan, Iraq, Lebanon, Pakistan and Syria. Specific brigades within the SAA were created, such as the Local Defence Forces (LDF) operating mainly in Deir ez-Zor, and private security companies were also established in Syria.

History: Active in Syria since 2011. In the early stages of the conflict Iran provided the Assad regime with financial aid, arms shipments and communication-jamming equipment. With the gradual intensification of fighting, Iran dispatched a few hundred senior QF and Hizbullah operatives as military advisers and planners, with significant escalation in mid-2014 after the rise of ISIS and the subsequent weakening of the Assad regime. Iran sent thousands of fighters from various military organisations to fight in Syria under Iranian leadership and deploys Iranian manpower mainly as battlefield commanders in key positions. Iranian and pro-Iranian forces fought leading battles in Homs (2012–14), Aleppo (2015–16), Deir ez-Zor (2017) and Deraa (2018).

Objectives: Preserve the Assad regime, shore up militia partners, build a military infrastructure inside Syria, contain Russian and Turkish influence, deter Israel, maintain 'Shia Crescent'.

Opponents: Israeli forces (airstrikes), SDF/YPG, ISIS and al-Qaeda affiliates, SNA.

Affiliates/allies: SAF, Russian forces, Hizbullah and other Shia militias in Syria, Iraq, Lebanon, Afghanistan and Pakistan.

Resources/capabilities: Operates several military bases and camps inside Syria with entrenched strategic infrastructure throughout the country. Provides an array of weaponry to its allies, including anti-tank guided missiles and UAVs, but its main contribution is command and control.

Combined Joint Task Force–*Operation Inherent Resolve* (CJTF–OIR)	
Strength: The exact number of coalition forces (including advisers, special forces, etc.) in Syria is unknown.	The developing partnership between the US and the SDF/YPG became a main conflict factor between the US and its NATO ally, Turkey. In late 2019, upon Turkish pressure, and by unilateral decision of then-president Donald Trump, the US contingency withdrew most of its 2,000 military personnel from Syria.
Areas of operation: Northeastern Syria, areas under control of the SDF/YPG and southern Syria in al-Tanf garrison, near the Iraqi and Jordanian borders.	
Leadership: General Kenneth 'Frank' McKenzie (US Central Command).	**Objectives:** Protect oil infrastructure and conduct counter-insurgency operations against ISIS.
Structure: The US leads the CJTF–OIR, which brings together over 20 coalition partners.	**Opponents:** ISIS, al-Qaeda and affiliates.
	Affiliates/allies: SDF/YPG.
History: Established in October 2014 when the US Department of Defense formalised ongoing military operations against ISIS. In late 2015, the first US ground troops entered Syria to recruit, organise and advise Syrian Kurdish and Arab opposition fighters in the fight against ISIS.	**Resources/capabilities:** Airstrikes targeting ISIS and air support to Israeli airstrikes (targeting Iranian and Iranian-backed forces). Armoured vehicles protect oilfields in northeastern Syria.

Conflict Drivers

Economic and social

Sectarian governance and socio-economic inequalities:
Long-standing sectarian governance by the minority Alawite (Shia) ruling elite had marginalised large segments of the population, denying them equal access to political, social and economic opportunities and fuelling unrest. Even though Syria's average annual GDP growth rate and macroeconomic fundamentals had been fairly solid in 2011 and 2012, the benefits did not reach the majority of the population, as evidenced by a decline in private real expenditures and a rise in poverty rates. Subsidised but inefficient social services, including healthcare, education and basic goods, could not offset crony capitalism, poor productivity and the negative effects of a large informal sector. By mid-2020, 80% of the Syrian population lived below the international poverty line of US$1.90 per day and was increasingly dependent on foreign aid.[8]

Environmental pressures:
Unprecedented drought between 2005 and 2010 massively disrupted agricultural production, leading to rising inflation of food items and food riots and the collapse of the country's agricultural centre in the northeast. Mismanagement and inadequate agricultural policies exacerbated the devastating impact of the drought, causing massive crop failures and livestock mortality. The drought crisis led to large numbers of internally displaced persons (IDPs), who moved from rural areas to urban areas, which already suffering from rapidly growing population density, illegal settlement, weak infrastructure, high unemployment rates and crime, became the birthplace of social unrest in 2011.

International

Regional interests:
Syria's geographic location makes it a geostrategic hotspot for several regional and international players. At the regional level, competition exists between three axes of interest and ideological outlook, enacted through local allies on the ground: the resistance axis of Assad–Iran–Iraq–Lebanese Hizbullah, the pro-Islamist axis of Qatar–Turkey and the conservative axis of Saudi Arabia, Egypt and the United Arab Emirates (UAE). Israel is another important regional player.

For Iran, preserving the status quo in Syria remains essential to maintain its role as a regional power, to maintain land access to Lebanon and to uphold the anti-Israeli front in the Middle East. Israel, in turn, sees Iran as the major existential threat to its national security, leading it to intervene in Syria since 2013 to prevent the establishment of Iranian military infrastructure and the opening of a new front in the Golan Heights. The Gulf axis entered the Syrian fray to counter Iranian influence by backing anti-Assad rebel forces, but later focused on containing Turkish and Islamist influence.

For Turkey, the 2011 outbreak of unrest in Syria represented a window of opportunity for regime change to support affiliated Islamists seeking political power, as happened in Tunisia and Egypt

Middle East and North Africa

following the Arab Spring. However, after 2014, as the YPG gained a foothold in northeast Syria, Turkey's main objective shifted to containing Kurdish expansion and maintaining Syria's territorial integrity in order to protect its own territorial integrity, particularly along the Syrian border and around Ras al-Ayn, Manbij, Kobane, Afrin and the northeastern city of Qamishli, where Syrian Kurds have historically been present, and where many have an affiliation with the PKK.

Figure 1: Number of violent events, January 2020–February 2021

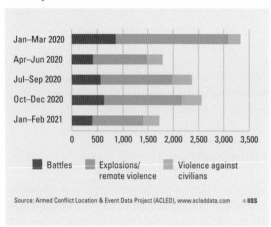

Source: Armed Conflict Location & Event Data Project (ACLED), www.acleddata.com © IISS

Violent extremism and transnational Islamic terrorism: As al-Qaeda and its affiliates filled the political vacuum left by the Arab Spring to expand and establish jihadi governance, Jabhat al-Nusra (now HTS) and ISIS emerged as its branches in Syria and Iraq respectively, with the latter attracting foreign fighters in greater numbers than Afghanistan in the 1980s and Iraq and Afghanistan in the 2000s. In 2014, ISIS's territorial hold and power in Iraq and Syria peaked, with the formation of a caliphate in June that occupied almost a third of Syria and almost 40% of Iraq.[9] To counter global terrorism, the US-led coalition launched its military campaign against ISIS with *Operation Inherent Resolve* in October 2014.

The geopolitical game: Russia intervened in September 2015 to prevent the collapse of the Assad regime, which would have had far-reaching negative geopolitical implications for its own national-security strategy. It also aimed to contain ISIS's transnational extremism from spreading to its domestic separatist Chechen Muslim minority, and to prevent the legitimisation of a Western-imposed regime change in one of its traditional spheres of influence. US intervention in Syria was aimed at defeating ISIS, and later at containing Iran and its affiliates.

Political and Military Developments

Flawed parliamentary elections

Following the regime's territorial recovery with Russian and Iranian military support, parliamentary elections were held in July 2020 and were won by Assad's Ba'ath party and the NPF, which secured 177 seats out of 250. Despite compulsory voting for the military, police and government employees, turnout was very low (33% according to official sources) and there were no mechanisms in place to ensure transparency and fairness.[10]

Stalled progress on internationally led peace processes

The Iran–Russia–Turkey tripartite forum within the Astana framework met in April 2020, six weeks after the Idlib ceasefire agreement between Russia and Turkey.[11] However, the forum's second meeting in July was overshadowed by the recent military escalation between Turkish and rebel forces and

regime and Russian troops in Idlib, which led to a loss of confidence between Russia and Turkey, and effectively to a temporary suspension of the Astana process by Turkish President Erdogan. Russia has increasingly dominated the Astana process, while Turkey considered that its priorities, such as border security and refugee-flow management, had gone unaddressed.

In Geneva, three meetings in 2020 achieved little for the Small Body tasked with drafting a new constitution by the United Nations-initiated Syrian Constitutional Committee (SCC). Since its formation in 2019 the regime has continued to obstruct the SCC's work and it remained highly doubtful that the political initiative of UN Special Envoy to Syria Geir Pedersen would be able to bridge the gap between the diametrically opposed stances of the regime and the opposition. While Assad cannot risk being formally excluded from the UN initiative and upsetting

Moscow by resisting a UN-mandated process, he showed no real interest in making the concessions necessary for genuine reconciliation within the framework of the SCC.

Idlib – *Operation Spring Shield*

A spiral of violence started with a Syrian–Russian military offensive on Idlib on 19 December 2019 causing heavy casualties on both sides. On 27 February 2020 Turkey officially launched its fourth cross-border military campaign in Syria since 2015 – *Operation Spring Shield* – in retaliation for the SAF's and Russia's continued violation of the 2018 Idlib de-militarisation agreement between Russia and Turkey. A new ceasefire agreement on 6 March between Russia and Turkey brought an end to this intense confrontation.

The confrontation had effectively advanced Russia's presence further north into Idlib and consolidated Assad's power, while Turkey managed to retain its foothold in the province and avert a new influx of refugees. Despite its fragility amid recurrent violations, the March ceasefire agreement held throughout the rest of 2020 and was extended in February 2021. However, Turkey continued to reposition its forces in the greater Idlib province to deter a pro-regime offensive, suggesting that a decisive battle could yet take place.

Insurgency in southwestern Syria

The declining economic situation and living standards, amid tighter international sanctions, fuelled escalating civil protests in Deraa province that peaked in mid-2020. The harsh regime response escalated the situation from protests to a series of insurgent attacks involving the seizure of checkpoints, raids, the establishment of roadblocks and coordinated assassinations of pro-Assad militiamen.

By the end of 2020, Russian-backed military and security structures had consolidated power in southern Syria and established a Joint National Committee in the south to govern the provinces of Deraa, Qunaytrah and Sweida. Russia's presence also complicated Iranian-backed operations in southern Syria. Yet local actors unsatisfied with Russia's perceived inability to enforce the 2019 reconciliation agreement further inflamed tensions. The Syrian government gradually increased its presence and control in Deraa, with substantial reinforcements and the establishment of new checkpoints, bringing it into greater competition with Russian-backed and Iranian-backed militias.

ISIS resurrection

ISIS capitalised on ongoing fighting between the regime and protesters in southern Syria to consolidate its attack capabilities by expanding its area of operations in northern, central and southern Syria. It targeted critical infrastructure, regime convoys on supply routes and transport lines, and assassinated prominent regime and Russian-backed figures. In December 2020 it claimed responsibility for an IED attack in Afrin, in the first such attack since Turkish forces had taken control of the area.

Middle East and North Africa

Key Events in 2020–21

POLITICAL EVENTS

17 February 2020
Turkish delegation arrives in Moscow to discuss Russian-backed regime advance in northern Syria.

22 April
Foreign ministers of Iran, Russia and Turkey hold virtual meeting of the Astana process.

17 June
US sanctions enter into force, as part of the Caesar Syria Civilian Protection Act.

MILITARY/VIOLENT EVENTS

11 February 2020
Pro-regime forces seize control of key M5 highway for first time since 2012.

16–17 February
Pro-regime forces make large territorial gains in western Aleppo province, take control of a cluster of towns and villages west of Aleppo city and reportedly advance toward the Turkish observation post in western Aleppo province.

24–28 February
Russian airstrikes kill dozens of Turkish troops in Idlib province.

6 March
Russia and Turkey reach ceasefire agreement.

1 July

Iran, Russia and Turkey hold another round of Astana talks.

19 July

After being delayed twice, parliamentary elections are held in Syria.

17 August

Iranian delegation meets with Assad in Damascus to discuss the UN political process and the normalisation of relations between Israel and the UAE.

29 August

Small Body of the SCC resumes third round of talks in Geneva.

1 September

Representatives of Kurdish Syrian Democratic Council (political wing of the SDF) and the People's Will Party reach agreement with Russia in Moscow that the SDF will be included in the political process.

30 November–4 December

Small Body of the SCC holds fourth round of peace talks in Geneva.

25–29 January 2021

The SCC meets for the fifth time in Geneva, ahead of the Syrian presidential elections scheduled to take place between 13 April and 13 May.

16–17 February

15th official Astana peace process meeting takes place in Sochi, Russia, with the participation of the UN.

26 April

Kinetic escalation between al-Qaeda-affiliated group and Turkish forces in greater Idlib province.

14–20 June

Three US drone strikes target al-Qaeda-affiliated leaders and a key ISIS figure.

22 July

Increased security measures enable the first successful Russian–Turkish joint patrol of the entire M4 highway.

25 August

Russian vehicles collide with US patrol as Russia seeks to pressure US ground-supply routes in northern Hasakah.

16 December–7 January 2021

Turkey shells villages in SDF-controlled territory across Aleppo, Hasakah and Raqqa provinces; Russia reinforces positions in support of the SDF.

20 December

ISIS claims first attack in Afrin province since 2017; uptick in IED attacks in Turkish-controlled areas.

31 January–15 February

Al-Qaeda affiliates carry out attacks on Turkish and Russian forces in Idlib province with Russian and SAA casualties, leading to Russian and regime counter-attacks and targeted assassinations by HTS against Islamist hardliners to preserve the Idlib ceasefire.

9 February

Russian and Turkish forces exchange fire in Aleppo province in response to SDF forces' shelling of Turkish local allies.

Impact

Human rights and humanitarian

The human-rights situation in Syria remained dire throughout 2020. Major human-rights abuses were recorded, particularly during the Idlib offensive and the regime's suppression of civil unrest in southern Syria, with repeated accusations levelled at regime and Russian forces of deliberately targeting IDPs, civilians and civilian infrastructure.[12] In Idlib, the Russian-backed SAF alone created about one million new IDPs between December 2019 and February 2020, taking the total number of IDPs in the country to an estimated 6.7m.[13]

Around 11.1m Syrians were estimated to need humanitarian aid, with a record 12.4m counted as food insecure by the end of 2020.[14] The Syrian government severely restricted the delivery of humanitarian aid, with selective approval used as a mechanism to punish civilians in anti-government-held areas. The Russian and Chinese veto in December 2019 against UN Security Council Resolution (UNSCR) 2165 had prevented the UN from providing cross-border delivery of humanitarian aid to Syria in 2020. However, in July the passing of UNSCR 2533 with a narrower remit finally legalised the provision of some humanitarian aid through the Bab al-Hawa crossing at the Syria–Turkey border, however its scope did not extend to the northwest of the country.

Economic and social

The Lebanese economic and financial crisis that started in 2019 compounded Syria's economic misery. Lebanon had served as the banking and trading hub for both the legal and illegal Syrian economy, with Lebanese banks holding billions of dollars in Syrian assets. The domino effect was brutal, with the Syria lira sinking in parallel with the Lebanese pound, and the drop in Lebanese imports affecting Syria's own. The July 2020 US Caesar Syria Civilian Protection Act, which criminalised economic activity with the Syrian regime and was intended as an instrument of pressure on the latter and its allies, further exacerbated the existing woes of the Syrian civilian population.

The economic cost of a decade of war in Syria was estimated to be over US$1.2 trillion.[15] An already crumbling economy was further hit in 2020 by the coronavirus pandemic. According to official data published by the parties controlling Syria's three main territories, at the end of January 2021 there were 44,132 cases of COVID-19 and 1,661 deaths.[16] However, actual infection figures were likely to be much higher given Syria's low testing capacity. Economic losses due to the March and April 2020 government-imposed lockdown measures alone were estimated at 2trn Syrian pounds (around US$1bn a month), disproportionately affecting the most vulnerable, such as IDPs, children, single parents and the elderly.[17]

Relations with neighbouring and international partners and geopolitical implications

Syria remained an arena for competition among global and regional powers. Russia secured strategic victories – allowing the Assad regime to consolidate its territorial control – and gained geopolitical clout in the country. Meanwhile, relations with Turkey remained tense in 2020 due to the Turkish human and territorial losses suffered in Idlib.

Having upgraded diplomatic relations with Syria in 2019, the UAE and Bahrain moved even closer to Assad in 2020 out of hope that doing so would help curb Iranian and Turkish inroads in the country and the region.

The US continued its dual objectives in Syria of containing Iran and defeating ISIS. However, following the October 2019 withdrawal of US troops from northern Syria, in 2020 US forces on the ground were kept to the minimum required to deny Assad and Russia an overall victory while securing and exploiting oil resources in northern Syria. The United States' enduring partnership with the SDF continued to be a source of conflict and mistrust in its relations with its NATO ally, Turkey.

Conflict Outlook

Political scenarios

Assad will seek to use presidential elections scheduled for 26 May 2021 to further consolidate his grip on power and legitimacy, building on the outcome of the disputed 2020 parliamentary elections. Despite rising dissatisfaction with the regime – even in traditionally and to date pro-regime areas such as Damascus, part of Deraa, Latakia, Tartus – Assad's re-election appears certain, especially as legal requirements prevent opposition figures in exile from running and oblige candidates to secure the favour of Assad's Ba'ath party.

Russia had hoped that the legitimacy of the polls would be recognised, leading to the international reintegration and reconstruction of Syria through the restoration of diplomatic ties and financial aid from Arab and European countries. However, in October 2020, signatory states of the Small Group on Syria, which include the US and several European and Arab Gulf countries, rejected any presidential elections that did not comply with the UNSCR 2254's framework, making Syria's continued international isolation seem certain.[18]

Escalation potential and conflict-related risks

Risks of renewed military confrontation between the SNA and the SDF and between the SNA and regime forces remained strong, particularly in Turkish-controlled areas in the provinces of Idlib, Raqqa, Hasakah and Aleppo.

In Idlib signs indicated that all parties were preparing for another military confrontation, with both Turkey and the Syrian government expanding their military presence following the March 2020 ceasefire. A protocol added to the Sochi agreement after the March 2020 ceasefire agreement called for the establishment of a security corridor and joint Russia–Turkey patrols around the M4 highway, an area that saw increased IED attacks in 2020 by al-Qaeda-affiliated splinter groups, particularly HaD.[19] As indicated by Russian and regime military preparations in Idlib, Russia will likely attempt to gain control of the southern part of this security corridor, by expelling HTS and HaD radicals from the area, either directly or by using the Syrian regime. To pre-empt such a Russian assault, increased urgency lies with Turkey to eliminate these factions before Russia does.[20]

The provinces of Raqqa and Hasakah are also potential hotspots for violence, as Turkey and its local allies prepare to engage militarily with ISIS and YPG forces in the face of increased IED attacks. To prevent an impending Turkish offensive against the SDF, Russia increased military materiel and personnel deployed along the Turkish–SDF line of confrontation, with large contingents of Russian-backed regime forces moved from Idlib front lines to Manbij, Aleppo province, in February 2021.

In the northeast, the power struggle between local tribes and the SDF over autonomy and local administrative control remains a highly likely source for continued local conflict. In the southwest and Deraa, competition among various administrative and security organs of the Syrian government risks violent escalation, in the absence of a coherent Russian strategy to handle the complex social environment and multiple players.

The increasing severity and geographic scale of ISIS attacks in 2020 showed its expanding freedom of action in Syria. As ISIS militants and family members continue to be released by the SDF, the organisation will be able to further expand its operation.

Prospects for peace

The failure of the fifth meeting of the SCC on 25–29 January and the 15th meeting of the Astana trio in Sochi on 16–17 February 2021 showed the dysfunctionality of current peacebuilding mechanisms.

Assad, in a position of strengthened territorial control and facing upcoming presidential elections, will not make any political concessions. A Russian agreement with the SDF would ignite Turkey's fears that anti-Turkish Kurdish forces would be included in the political process and thus legitimised, increasing the need to use Idlib as a diplomatic counterweight in negotiations. Iran's increasing exclusion from the Astana process will ensure it continues to undermine Russian and Turkish efforts.

A formal political settlement to the conflict might take years. Until that time, an informal 'non-deal'

agreement maintaining the status quo could be possible. US clarification of its endgame in Syria – especially concerning the future status of the SDF and anti-Turkish Kurdish elements within it – could create a new dynamic accelerating a political settlement. Turkey might accept a decentralised northeast within an inclusive system of governance and with more Arab representation to prevent domination by anti-Turkish YPG elements.

Strategic implications and global influences

Syria is likely to remain a source of regional and global instability, given the conflict-fuelling geo-strategic interests of the main external actors. Two prospective developments will strategically affect Syria's outlook and global/regional security and stability.

Firstly, US airstrikes on 25 February 2021 against Syrian facilities used by an Iranian-backed militia responsible for attacking US positions in Iraq gave an early glimpse of President Joe Biden's policy on Syria. The most likely scenario would be a continuation of the traditional US–Israeli intelligence-sharing and military cooperation to weaken Iran's influence in Syria and beyond. In terms of the US–Russia confrontation playing out in Syria, the US will continue to internationally isolate and domestically weaken the Assad regime by obstructing its access to oil exploitation and financial reconstruction support, while continuing to impose sanctions.

Meanwhile, a US priority will be to secure a foothold in northern Syria to prevent Iran, Russia or Turkey filling the power vacuum there. For this reason, the US will need to balance the conflicting interests of Turkey and the SDF, particularly around the Turkish military operation in northeastern Syria. However, the appointment of officials within the US administration critical of Turkey suggests that disagreements may continue and prevent a united NATO front against Russia.

Secondly, Turkey alone would not and could not manage the large influx of refugees that renewed high-intensity military confrontations in Idlib would likely trigger. Such a scenario would result in a repeat of the 2015 Syrian refugee crisis, entailing massive political, security, social and economic challenges for Europe.

Notes

1   Etana, 'Military Control Across Syria – March-2021', 1st March 2021.

2   United Nations Security Council, 'Twenty-fourth Report of the Analytical Support and Sanctions Monitoring Team Submitted Pursuant to Resolution 2368 (2017) Concerning ISIL (Da'esh), Al-Qaida and Associated Individuals and Entities', S/2019/570, 30 August 2019.

3   *Ibid.*

4   Omer Ozkizilcik, 'Uniting the Syrian Opposition: The Components of the National Army and the Implications of the Unification', SETA, October 2019.

5   Based on 'Operation Inherent Resolve: Lead Inspector General Report to the United States Congress April 1 2019 – June 30 2019', p. 30.

6   Edith M. Lederer, 'UN: Over 10,000 Islamic State Fighters Active in Iraq, Syria', *Washington Post*, 24 August 2020.

7   'Turkey Has Evacuated Seven Syrian Military Posts', Reuters, 18 December 2020.

8   'Syria: Economic Crisis Compounds Conflict Misery as Millions Face Deeper Poverty, Hunger', International Committee of the Red Cross, 28 June 2020.

9   'Timeline: The Rise, Spread, and Fall of the Islamic State', Wilson Center, 28 October 2019.

10 'Syria: Assad's Baath Party Wins Majority in Parliamentary Polls', Al-Jazeera, 22 July 2020.

11 The Astana peace process was launched in 2017 as a counterweight to the political failure of the Western powers to end the fighting in Syria.

12 See Syrian Network for Human Rights (SNHR), 'Tenth Annual Report: The Most Notable Human Rights Violations in Syria in 2020: The Bleeding Decade', 26 January 2021.

13 'White Helmets Appeal For Help From World Powers in Syria's Idlib', BBC News, 26 February 2020; and United Nations Office for the Coordination of Humanitarian Affairs, 'Syrian Arab Republic – 2021 Needs and Response Summary', February 2021.

14 See Humanitarian Programme Cycle, 'Humanitarian Response Plan – Syrian Arab Republic', December 2020, p. 8; and 'Food Insecurity in Syria Reaches Record Levels: WFP', UN News, 17 February 2021.

15 See World Vision and Frontier Economics, 'Too High a Price to Pay: The Cost of Conflict for Syria's Children', 4 March 2021, p. 3.

16 'COVID-19 Update: China to Donate 150,000 Vaccines to Syrian Government', The Syria Report, 10 February 2021.

17 Salam Said, 'COVID-19 and the Syrian Economy: Implications for Social Justice', Friedrich-Ebert Stiftung, July 2020.

18 United Nations Security Council Resolution 2254 requires the SCC to approve a draft constitution, followed by a public referendum, to trigger UN-monitored and approved presidential elections. As such, the May 2021 presidential elections will not qualify.

19 The 2018 Sochi agreement between Russia and Turkey obliged the latter to withdraw heavy weapons and remove radical militants from an agreed upon de-escalation zone in Idlib. Turkey's failure to do so was one major factor for the Russian and regime assault on Idlib.

20 Such a scenario would further weaken Turkey's position east of the Euphrates. One possible rationale for Turkey would be to bargain with Russia, giving it and the Syrian regime parts of Idlib south of the security corridor in exchange for expanding the Turkish security zone in eastern Syria. However, such a compromise would involve the US in negotiations as it controls airspace in eastern Syria. Against this complex backdrop and its potentially unpredictable outcomes, Turkey accelerated efforts to expel radical elements by enlisting more moderate and cooperative HTS members to meet its requirements under the Sochi agreement.

IRAQ

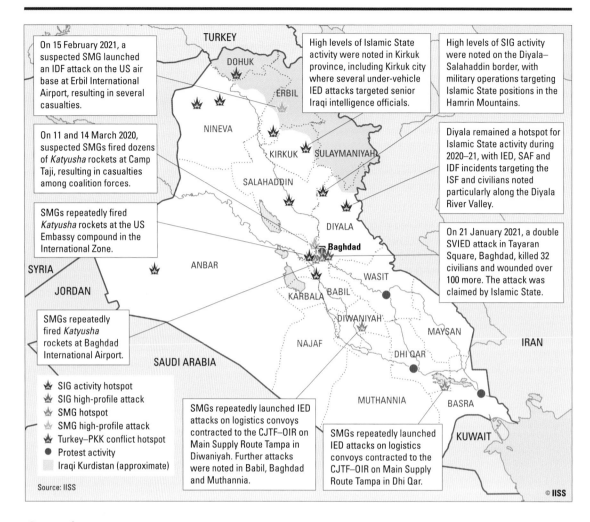

On 15 February 2021, a suspected SMG launched an IDF attack on the US air base at Erbil International Airport, resulting in several casualties.

On 11 and 14 March 2020, suspected SMGs fired dozens of *Katyusha* rockets at Camp Taji, resulting in casualties among coalition forces.

SMGs repeatedly fired *Katyusha* rockets at the US Embassy compound in the International Zone.

SMGs repeatedly fired *Katyusha* rockets at Baghdad International Airport.

High levels of Islamic State activity were noted in Kirkuk province, including Kirkuk city where several under-vehicle IED attacks targeted senior Iraqi intelligence officials.

High levels of SIG activity were noted on the Diyala–Salahaddin border, with military operations targeting Islamic State positions in the Hamrin Mountains.

Diyala remained a hotspot for Islamic State activity during 2020–21, with IED, SAF and IDF incidents targeting the ISF and civilians noted particularly along the Diyala River Valley.

On 21 January 2021, a double SVIED attack in Tayaran Square, Baghdad, killed 32 civilians and wounded over 100 more. The attack was claimed by Islamic State.

SMGs repeatedly launched IED attacks on logistics convoys contracted to the CJTF–OIR on Main Supply Route Tampa in Diwaniyah. Further attacks were noted in Babil, Baghdad and Muthannia.

SMGs repeatedly launched IED attacks on logistics convoys contracted to the CJTF–OIR on Main Supply Route Tampa in Dhi Qar.

⚜ SIG activity hotspot
⚜ SIG high-profile attack
⚜ SMG hotspot
⚜ SMG high-profile attack
⚜ Turkey–PKK conflict hotspot
● Protest activity
　 Iraqi Kurdistan (approximate)

Source: IISS

© IISS

Overview

The main conflict in Iraq remains the ongoing struggle against the Islamic State, also known as ISIS or ISIL. Since the group seized control of the key Sunni cities of Fallujah, Ramadi and Mosul in 2014 until its territorial defeat in December 2017, it has been combatted by a combination of Iraqi Security Forces (ISF), Popular Mobilisation Units (PMU), Kurdish Peshmerga and the United States-led Combined Joint Task Force–*Operation Inherent Resolve* (CJTF–OIR). Since December 2017, the Iraqi government has faced insurgent attacks from ISIS networks concentrated mainly in central and northern provinces and, to a lesser extent, in Anbar in the west. The rate

of ISIS attacks increased markedly in 2020, culminating in a high-profile attack (HPA) on 21 January 2021 in Baghdad's Tayaran Square. The coronavirus pandemic, the first wave of which hit Iraq in February 2020, exacerbated existing drivers of conflict, particularly on the economic front, creating new strategic opportunities which ISIS sought to exploit.

Tensions also increased along other dimensions of conflict during the year. Of note, the Iran–United States confrontation in Iraq escalated following the assassination by the US of Islamic Revolutionary Guard Corps (IRGC) Quds Force commander Qasem Soleimani in January 2020. In response, Iran-aligned

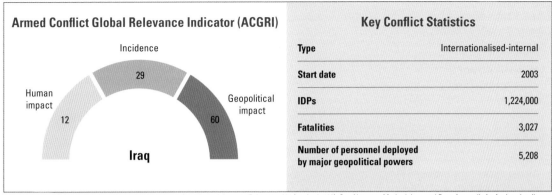

ACGRI pillars: IISS calculation based on multiple sources for 2020 and January/February 2021 (scale: 0–100). See Notes on Methodology and Data Appendix for further details on Key Conflict Statistics.

Shia militia groups (SMGs) escalated a campaign of indirect fire (IDF) and improvised-explosive-device (IED) attacks on US and CJTF–OIR targets, leading the US to threaten an immediate withdrawal of its Baghdad embassy in late September 2020. A unilateral and conditional ceasefire by SMGs followed. However, attacks picked up following the victory of Joe Biden in the November 2020 US elections as brinkmanship began over returning to the Joint Comprehensive Plan of Action's (JCPOA) nuclear agreement with Iran.

In northern Iraq, Turkish air and artillery strikes against Kurdistan Workers' Party (PKK) positions, mainly in Dohuk, also increased in 2020. Meanwhile, PMU leadership continued to criticise the Sinjar agreement between the Kurdistan regional government and the government of Iraq which had been signed on 9 October 2020.[1] Part of the agreement was intended to deal with the contentious presence of PKK militants in the strategic western sector of Nineva province. The issue has become

a further point of contention between Turkey and Iran: Turkey seeks to eliminate PKK forces and suspects Iran and its PMU allies of cooperating with the PKK in the sector to preserve Iran's land bridge to Syria. On 13 February 2021, local media reported that an additional three PMU brigades had been deployed to Sinjar following an announcement by Hadi al-Ameri, the leader of Fatah and the Badr Organisation (and therefore one of the most prominent Iran-aligned Shia Islamist figures in Iraq) that PMU forces would resist what he described as an imminent Turkish military incursion into the area.[2]

Finally, in central and southern Iraq, SMGs and the ISF used considerable violence to confront activists connected to a protest movement that had emerged in October 2019. Several HPAs on demonstrators resulted in mass casualties, while sporadic kidnap, assassination and intimidatory IED and small-arms-fire (SAF) attacks targeting activists persisted throughout the year, particularly in protest hotspots such as Baghdad, Dhi Qar and Basra.

Conflict Parties

Iraqi Security Forces (ISF)

Strength: 193,000.

Areas of operation: All areas of Iraq excluding the Kurdistan Region of Iraq (KRI).

Leadership: Prime Minister Mustafa al-Kadhimi (commander-in-chief); Abdul Amir Rashid Yarallah (army chief of staff); Jummah Enaad al-Jibori (minister of defence); Othman al-Ghanmi (minister of interior).

Structure: The Iraqi armed forces consist of the army, air force and navy. In the fight against ISIS, the army has cooperated with the Federal Police and the Ministry of Interior (MoI) intelligence (the Federal Investigation and Intelligence Agency, Falcons Cell), the Counter-Terrorism Service (CTS), PMU, and other intelligence organs. The army reports to the Ministry of Defence, the Federal Police to the MoI and the CTS to the Prime Minister's Office (PMO).

Iraqi Security Forces (ISF)

History: The capture of Tikrit and Mosul by ISIS in 2014 led to the partial disintegration of Iraqi forces. The forces have been rebuilt with the assistance of the US-led coalition but remain insufficiently equipped for counter-insurgency tasks.

Objectives: Defeat ISIS and ensure security across the country. Since the territorial defeat of ISIS, Iraqi forces have focused on eliminating remaining cells in rural areas. The armed forces also play a role in providing security in the provinces to tackle tribal fighting, protest-related violence and criminality.

Opponents: ISIS.

Affiliates/allies: Kurdish Peshmerga, CJTF–OIR, PMU, CTS.

Resources/capabilities: A range of conventional land, air and naval capabilities including armoured fighting vehicles, anti-tank missile systems, artillery and fixed- and rotary-wing aircraft.

Popular Mobilisation Units (PMU)

Strength: Approximately 100,000.

Areas of operation: Areas previously held by ISIS including Anbar, Nineva, Diyala and Salahaddin provinces, and areas of southern Iraq, particularly Jurf al-Sakhar in Babil province, and shrine cities of Najaf, Karbala and Samarra (north of Baghdad).

Leadership: The PMU has a distinct chain of command from the rest of the ISF. Formally under the PMO and technically directly answerable to the prime minister, de facto leadership of the organisation had resided with the PMU Commission's chief of staff (formerly Abu Mahdi al-Muhandis). The latter's assassination in 2020 triggered a leadership struggle. Kataib Hizbullah (KH) commander Abdul-Aziz al-Muhammadawi (also known as Abu Fadak) was elevated to lead the organisation, although power is thought to operate more via a committee of senior figures. However, some PMU brigades loyal to Najaf-based Grand Ayatollah Ali al-Sistani split from the PMU Commission altogether and re-formed as a separate entity answerable to the PMO. Moreover, various groups within the PMU have a high degree of operational autonomy, such as the Sadrists, Saraya al-Salam, the Badr Organisation and Asaib Ahl al-Haq.

Structure: Approximately 40–60 paramilitary units under the umbrella organisation. Formally, the PMU are a branch of the Iraqi security apparatus, but each unit is organised around an internal leader, influential figures and fighters.

History: Formed in 2014 when Grand Ayatollah Ali al-Sistani called upon the Iraqis to protect their homeland against ISIS, the PMU brought together new and pre-existing groups. In 2016, the units were formally recognised as a branch of the Iraqi security apparatus.

Objectives: Initially, to fight ISIS. Some units have evolved into hybrid entities seeking political power. Also functions as an effective counter-protest force and seeks to use violence and coercion to intimidate political rivals. All groups are committed, at least nominally, to expelling US and foreign forces from Iraq. Rising tensions with Turkey have also been noted, with a rocket attack on the Turkish military base near Mosul (Zilkan) in April 2021 attributed to PMF groups.

Opponents: ISIS, US and allied forces, Turkey.

Affiliates/allies: ISF, IRGC.

Resources/capabilities: Capabilities differ between units. Those supported by Iran receive arms and training from the IRGC, including heavy weapons and small arms.

Islamic State, also known as ISIS or ISIL

Strength: Approximately 10,000 in Iraq and Syria, including members and fighters.[3]

Areas of operation: Active predominantly in Iraq's northern and central provinces in mountainous and desert areas. Most attacks in 2020–21 occurred in the governorates of Anbar, Baghdad, Diyala, Kirkuk, Nineva, Salahaddin and Babil.

Leadership: Abu Ibrahim al-Hashimi al-Qurashi (caliph and leader of ISIS). Jabbar Salman Ali Farhan al-Issawi, also known as Abu Yasser al-Isawi (deputy caliph and senior commander in Iraq), was killed by an airstrike in January 2021.

Structure: ISIS operates as a covert terrorist network across Iraq, using a largely autonomous sleeper-cell structure. The organisation continues to have meticulous bureaucratic structures, internal discipline and robust online presence and financial systems.

History: Originated in Iraq around 2003 but proclaimed itself a separate group from al-Qaeda in Iraq, fighting to create a caliphate during the Syrian civil war. Between 2014 and 2017, ISIS controlled extensive territories and governed more than eight million people in Syria and Iraq. It has now lost all its territory, since 2017 in Iraq and since March 2019 in Syria.

Objectives: ISIS continues to fight and project ideological influence globally. In Iraq it operates through decentralised, guerrilla-style insurgent tactics, with hit-and-run attacks, kidnappings and killing of civilians, and local tribal and political leaders, as well as targeted assassinations of members of the ISF.

Opponents: ISF, Kurdish Peshmerga, PMU, CJTF–OIR.

Affiliates/allies: ISIS fighters in other countries.

Resources/capabilities: Carries out attacks through shootings and explosions, using small arms, cars, IEDs, suicide vest improvised explosive devices (SVIEDs), suicide-vehicle-borne improvised explosive devices (SVBIEDs) and mortar bombs.

Kurdish Peshmerga

Strength: Approximately 150,000 personnel.

Areas of operation: KRI.

Leadership: Nechirvan Barzani (commander-in-chief), Shoresh Ismail Abdulla (minister of Peshmerga affairs), Lt-Gen. Jamal Mohammad (Peshmerga chief of staff).

Structure: A Kurdish paramilitary force, acting as the military of the Kurdistan regional government and Iraqi Kurdistan. While remaining independent, operates officially as part of the Kurdish military system. Split between political factions, the dominant ones being the Kurdistan Democratic Party and the Patriotic Union of Kurdistan.

History: Began as a Kurdish nationalist movement in the 1920s and soon developed into a security organisation. Following the ISIS advance, the Peshmerga took disputed territories in June 2014 – including Kirkuk – which were retaken by the ISF in October 2017.

Objectives: Ensure security in the KRI, including fighting ISIS.

Opponents: ISIS, PKK.

Affiliates/allies: CJTF–OIR, ISF.

Resources/capabilities: Poorly equipped, lacking heavy weapons, armed vehicles and facilities. The US has provided some financial assistance and light weapons such as rifles and machine guns.

Turkish Armed Forces (TSK)

Strength: 1,000 personnel unilaterally deployed in Iraq (+ 30 under the aegis of NATO Mission Iraq (NMI)).

Areas of operation: Northern Iraq, especially Dohuk and Nineva plains. Currently engaged in *Operation Claw-Tiger* against the PKK in the Haftanin region. Maintains Zilkan base in Nineva.

Leadership: President Recep Tayyip Erdogan (commander-in-chief); General (retd) Hulusi Akar (minister of national defence); General Yasar Guler (chief of general staff).

Structure: Turkish army units operating under the Turkish Land Forces Command and squadrons carrying out airstrikes operating under the Air Force Command are subordinate to the chief of general staff; gendarmerie units reporting to the Gendarmerie Command are subordinate to the Ministry of Interior.

History: Rebuilt after the collapse of the Ottoman Empire in 1922. Significantly restructured after the country joined NATO in 1951, to become NATO's second-largest armed force.

Objectives: Combat the PKK and their allied forces and prevent them from establishing safe havens and mobility corridors in northern Iraq; prevent PMU from overrunning Sinjar and establishing a land corridor to Syria for Iran.

Opponents: PKK, Sinjar Alliance, PMU.

Affiliates/allies: Miscellaneous local militias, such as those connected to the Iraqi Turkmen Front who received training from Turkish special forces from 2015.

Resources/capabilities: Turkey's defence budget for 2020 was US$10.88 billion. Its military capabilities include air attack and intelligence, surveillance and reconnaissance (ISR) assets such as the F-16 and the *Bayraktar* TB2 uninhabited aerial vehicle (UAV), armoured tanks and special-forces units.

Kurdistan Workers' Party (PKK)

Strength: 30,000 (estimate) in Turkey and Iraq.

Areas of operation: Sinjar, northern Iraq.

Leadership: Abdullah Ocalan (ideological leader, despite his imprisonment since 1999); Murat Karayilan (acting leader on the ground since Ocalan's capture); Bahoz Erdal (military commander).

Structure: While operating under the same command and leadership, the PKK's armed wing is divided into the People's Defence Forces (HPG) and the Free Women's Unit (YJA STAR).

History: Founded by Ocalan in 1978. Engaged in an insurgency campaign against the TSK since 1984.

Objectives: Preserve its operational autonomy and capacity with a base of operation in Iraq to support its broader agenda in Turkey.

Opponents: TSK.

Affiliates/allies: Sinjar Alliance in Iraq.

Resources/capabilities: Relies on money-laundering activities and drug trafficking to generate revenues, in addition to donations from the Kurdish community and diaspora and left-wing international supporters. The PKK relies on highly mobile units, using guerrilla tactics against Turkish military targets.

Middle East and North Africa

Combined Joint Task Force–*Operation Inherent Resolve* (CJTF–OIR)

Strength: The exact number of coalition forces (including advisers, special forces, etc.) in Iraq is unknown, but the US, the largest component of the coalition, has been repositioning its forces, handing over Iraqi bases to the Iraqi government, and drawing down its overall force commitment. However, the new Biden administration announced that it was reviewing the previous administration's decisions to withdraw forces from Iraq.

Areas of operation: Working in tandem with the ISF in areas previously held by ISIS, including Anbar, Diyala, Nineva and Salahaddin.

Leadership: Marine Gen. Kenneth 'Frank' McKenzie (US Central Command).

Structure: The US leads the CJTF–OIR, which brings together over 20 coalition partners.

History: Established in October 2014 when the US Department of Defense formalised ongoing military operations against ISIS.

Objectives: Fight ISIS in Iraq and Syria, through airstrikes in support of Iraqi and Kurdish forces. Ground forces are deployed as trainers and advisers.

Opponents: ISIS, PMU.

Affiliates/allies: ISF, Kurdish Peshmerga.

Resources/capabilities: Air support (airstrikes complementing military operations by Iraqi armed forces) and artillery.

Other conflict parties

A number of other conflict parties active in the country should also be mentioned. The Sinjar Alliance, affiliated with the PKK, was created in 2015 after the 2014 Sinjar massacre and aims at establishing an autonomous Yazidi region in Iraqi Kurdistan.

The NATO Mission Iraq (NMI) was established in 2018 and currently comprises around 500 staff officers, advisers and support staff (to be incrementally increased to 4,000 following a request by the Iraqi government approved by NATO in February 2021).[4] It focuses solely on training and logistical support to the ISF to combat ISIS. NMI supports and supplements the CJTF–OIR training in Iraq.

Iran maintains a significant role in the command-and-control structure of the PMU. Its military presence in Iraq is primarily covert: senior officers of the Islamic Revolutionary Guard Corps Quds Force (IRGC-QF) have served as advisers to the ISF as well as PMU commanders, and Iran has deployed niche military capabilities during the fight against ISIS. The IRGC-QF maintains a privileged relationship with several PMU militias, notably Kataib Hizbullah, Asaib Ahl al-Haq, the Badr Organisation, Harakat Hizbullah al-Nujaba and their splinter groups. These factions have conducted operations against Iraqi and Western targets at Iran's behest.

Conflict Drivers

Political

Patronage, corruption and sectarianism:
Iraq has a patronage-based system of government built on oil revenues. The political elite uses oil rents to reward allies and pursue personal projects, as opposed to funding public goods and services. Coveted jobs in the public sector are awarded based on party connections or in response to public discontent that has manifested in protests. Consequently, the legitimacy of central government has been eroded while resources have been diverted from the reconstruction and development of Sunni areas affected by the ISIS campaign. This has further fuelled militia recruitment, while degrading the competence and fighting efficacy of the ISF. The patronage system also encourages sect-based mobilisation as most parties are organised along Shia, Sunni or Kurdish lines. More recently, the treatment of Sunni internally displaced persons (IDPs), the flawed justice of Iraq's anti-terrorism legislation and legal processes, and human-rights abuses

by victorious Shia militants, have all contributed to Sunni discontent and driven recruitment for ISIS.

Economic and social

Fiscal pressures:
A fiscal budget crisis triggered by the coronavirus pandemic and falling global oil prices exacerbated the structural factors just outlined. The pandemic also disrupted non-oil-based economic activity, particularly for informal workers in contact-intensive sectors. As a result, despite a modest recovery of oil prices in early 2021, Iraq's economic outlook remains negative. According to the IMF, GDP contracted by 10.9% in 2020, with growth in 2021 forecast at only 1.1%.[5]

The Central Bank of Iraq (CBI) undertook a controlled currency devaluation in late December 2020 – a measure that had not been adopted for decades. Devaluation led to rising inflation almost overnight in a country that relies heavily on imports of basic goods. When combined with unemployment,

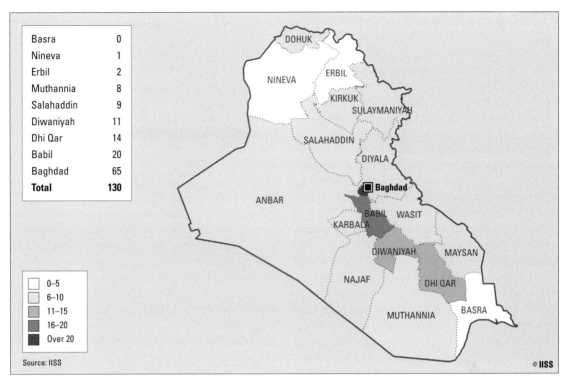

Basra	0
Nineva	1
Erbil	2
Muthannia	8
Salahaddin	9
Diwaniyah	11
Dhi Qar	14
Babil	20
Baghdad	65
Total	**130**

0–5
6–10
11–15
16–20
Over 20

Source: IISS

Figure 1: Number of attacks by SMGs on US and CJTF–OIR military and diplomatic targets, January 2020–February 2021

delayed infrastructure projects and reduced investment in public services, this is likely to drive both violent anti-government demonstrations and insurgent activity. Moreover, the short-term tactic pursued by previous Iraqi governments of circumventing protests by offering public-sector jobs had built up further structural rigidities in Iraq's finances. However, the current Iraqi government will have less recourse to such a strategy, due in part to the additional fiscal pressures created by the coronavirus pandemic.

International

Geopolitical rivalries:

Geopolitical rivalries have eroded Iraq's capacity to build a coherent, unified state and security apparatus. The Iran–US and regional rivalries have contributed to the proliferation of non-state paramilitaries that challenge the government's monopoly over the legitimate use of force in its territory. Iran and the US vie for influence over Iraq's political institutions and security forces, even running competing networks within the MoI. This fragmentation of the Iraqi state erodes its capacity to confront

challenges posed by both insurgents and SMGs and to enact political reforms.

Iran–US tensions continued to drive conflict in Iraq during 2020. The Trump administration's so-called 'maximum pressure' strategy against Tehran sought to isolate Iran, while the Abraham Accords in September 2020 (between Israel and Bahrain and the United Arab Emirates) were intended to facilitate cooperation between Iran's main regional rivals. As a result, Iraq became increasingly important to Iran as an economic outlet, for access to dollars and for sanction-busting oil exports. At the same time, Iran, and its Iraqi allies, sought to retaliate against the US by politically and militarily targeting its military and diplomatic presence in Iraq, and to intimidate those – including the new Iraqi Prime Minister Mustafa al-Kadhimi – considered too close to the US.

Elsewhere, Turkish–Iranian rivalries increasingly played out in northern Iraq and the Sinjar area, with Iran criticising Turkey's military presence in both Syria and Iraq, viewing its campaign against PKK militants and the struggle for influence in Nineva as threats to its own influence in the area and its land bridge to Syria.

Political and Military Developments

A new prime minister

On 6 May 2020, Mustafa al-Kadhimi was appointed Iraq's new prime minister. Kadhimi, formerly the head of the Iraqi National Intelligence Service (a Western-aligned intelligence agency) and widely regarded as espousing a fairly pro-US viewpoint, came to office promising to respond to the demands of the October 2019 protesters, such as holding early elections in June 2021. He also sought to rebalance Western and Iranian influence in Iraq, particularly by reshuffling senior security posts in the MoI along with other intelligence agencies and Iraqi Army commands at the provincial level. Kadhimi also engaged in a Strategic Dialogue with the US, which was heralded as an opportunity to 'reset' Iraq–US relations, deepen economic and cultural ties, and place the US military presence in the country on a firmer legal and practical footing. However, these talks sparked a backlash from Iran-aligned elements, with a series of assassinations, including Kadhimi's friend and adviser Hisham al-Hashimi in July 2020 and against activists in Basra during August 2020.

ISIS insurgency

The reporting period saw a modest resurgence in ISIS activity in Iraq, culminating in the 21 January 2021 twin SVIED attack on a clothing market in Baghdad's Tayaran Square, resulting in several casualties in the first significant breach of the city's security perimeter by ISIS since 2018. Shortly after, ISIS militants clashed with the PMU in the vicinity of al-Ayth, Salahaddin.

However, aside from these HPAs, Sunni-insurgent-group (SIG) activity remained largely constrained to sabotage, asymmetric hit-and-run SAF and IED attacks on the ISF, and assassinations and kidnappings to raise funds and prevent cooperation between local populations and the Iraqi government. These activities were largely confined to remote desert regions, and difficult-to-secure spaces such as the Hamrin Mountains, the Makhoul Mountains, the Diyala–Salahaddin border, southern Nineva and western Anbar province. ISIS also continued to exploit disputed territories and mixed-sect areas such as Diyala and Kirkuk. Meanwhile, ISIS activity in southern Iraq was constrained to infrequent probing hit-and-run SAF and IED attacks on PMU positions in Jurf al-Sakhar.

On 22 January 2021, Iraq's CTS responded to the Baghdad attack by launching *Operation Revenge of the Martyrs*. Of note, an airstrike in Zaidan, Abu Ghraib, killed four insurgents including the ISIS 'Emir of southern Iraq', Abu Hassan al-Gharibawi. Meanwhile, a further airstrike killed the leader of the Islamic State in Iraq, Jabbar Salman Ali Farhan al-Issawi, in the vicinity of Kirkuk.

Iran–US conflict

An escalating military campaign against CJTF–OIR interests in Iraq followed Soleimani's assassination in January 2020. Of note, two IDF incidents on Camp Taji (north of Baghdad), on 11 and 14 March, resulted in fatalities and injuries to coalition forces. In response, the US launched airstrikes against KH facilities in Babil, Karbala and south of Baghdad. Nevertheless, Western interests in Iraq continued to face hostile IDF from SMGs, focused mainly on the US Embassy compound in the International Zone. An escalating campaign of IED attacks also targeted logistics convoys contracted to the CJTF–OIR on the main supply routes through Dhi Qar, Diwaniyah, Babil and Baghdad.

In response, the US threatened to close its embassy in Baghdad in late September 2020, leading to panic among the Iraqi political class and the declaration of a unilateral ceasefire by SMGs. However, hostilities escalated again after the victory of Joe Biden in the November 2020 US elections as Iran and its Iraqi proxies sought to pressure the US administration to return to the JCPOA without preconditions or caveats. This culminated in the 15 February 2021 IDF attack on the US military base at Erbil International Airport, claimed by an SMG. The Biden administration opted for a restrained response, launching airstrikes against KH targets in Al-Bukamal, Syria, and leaving open a possible pathway to JCPOA compliance.

Splintering within the PMU

In April 2020, several factions of the PMU loyal to Najaf-based Grand Ayatollah Ali al-Sistani split from the PMU Commission. The brigades – Kataib Imam Ali, Ali al-Akbar, Abbas and Ansar al-Marjaiya – henceforth reported directly to the PMO. The move reflected discontent within the PMU at the efforts to install a KH commander, Abu Fadak, as de facto PMU chief following the assassination of Abu Mahdi al-Muhandis. Overall, the move by the so-called 'shrine' militias reflected broader fragmentation within the PMU/SMG structure following the removal of its central pillars (Soleimani/Muhandis). Soleimani's replacement, Esmael Qaani, focused on building his own support base within Iraq's SMGs, sponsoring the proliferation of new 'splinter' groups that broke off from more established factions and organised around the KH network. These new splinter groups have claimed responsibility for the majority of IED and IDF attacks on US and CJTF–OIR targets in Iraq between February 2020 and February 2021.

Regional competition in northern Iraq

Turkey continued to pursue PKK militants in northern Iraq, launching dozens of raids, airstrikes and artillery strikes. Most of this activity was concentrated in the mountainous regions of Dohuk, although operations were also noted in the northern sectors of Erbil, Sulaymaniyah and Nineva. Iran and Turkey also clashed over the Sinjar agreement, with Turkey suspecting that the Iran-aligned PMU were cooperating with PKK elements in Sinjar to preserve Iran's land bridge to Syria through the territory. In early February 2021, it was reported that PMU units had been moved to the area after receiving intelligence pointing to an imminent Turkish military operation against Sinjar.

Key Events in 2020–21

POLITICAL EVENTS

MILITARY/VIOLENT EVENTS

3 January 2020

Soleimani and Muhandis are assassinated by the US in a Baghdad airstrike.

24 January

Sadrist protesters in Baghdad condemn the killing of Soleimani and Muhandis and demand the withdrawal of the US presence in Iraq.

5 February

Sadrist paramilitaries begin attacking protesters in Najaf and Karbala following the announcement that Muqtada al-Sadr was withdrawing his forces from the October 2019 protest movement.

15 February

Iraq begins imposing strict COVID-19 mitigation measures including curfews and restrictions on public gatherings as case numbers rise.

April 2020

Several factions of the PMU loyal to Najaf-based Grand Ayatollah Ali al-Sistani split from the PMU Commission.

6 May

Kadhimi becomes Iraqi prime minister, succeeding Adil Abdul-Mahdi who resigned in November 2019 in response to the October protest movement.

6 July

Prominent Iraqi security analyst and friend and adviser to Kadhimi, Hisham al-Hashimi, is assassinated in Baghdad by a suspected SMG.

August

Kadhimi visits Washington DC to conclude the Strategic Dialogue talks with the US.

September

In response to escalating attacks on its diplomatic and military interests, the US threatens to close its embassy in Baghdad.

October

Activists attempt to rejuvenate the nationwide protest movement that had erupted in October 2019 on the one-year anniversary of the protests.

21 January 2021

A twin SVIED attack on a clothes market in Tayaran Square, Baghdad, kills dozens and injures over 100.

Middle East and North Africa

28 October

The Economic Contact Group (composed of the G7 countries, the IMF and the World Bank) holds its first session in the United Kingdom. The group intends to coordinate financial and technical support for Iraq to help the country respond to the coronavirus pandemic, economic crisis and ongoing war against ISIS.

20 December

The CBI undertakes a controlled (almost 20%) devaluation of the Iraqi dinar against the US dollar, prompting some limited protest activity.

18 February

NATO announces an expansion of its security training mission in Iraq, from circa 500 to 4,000 troops, on the back of a partial drawdown of US forces in January (from 3,000 to 2,500).

25 February

US launches strikes against Iranian militias in Syria, who were responsible for attacks on US troops in Erbil.

Impact

Human rights and humanitarian

The ISIS insurgency continues to feed on the marginalisation of Iraq's Sunni community, particularly in areas affected by displacement or where local populations suffer abuses by Shia armed groups. There is also widespread belief in these areas that corruption has delayed reconstruction projects or siphoned off their funding. Other specific forms of discrimination, such as punitive counter-terrorism legislation and inadequate due process in terrorism-related trials, all pose a risk of future radicalisation.

Attacks on humanitarian workers in Iraq are relatively rare as most combatants (excluding the Islamic State) have an interest in seeing international-development and aid projects continue for political and financial reasons. However, intimidation, assaults and arrests against aid workers have been documented in Sunni IDP camps and in areas previously under ISIS control, along with accusations that aid workers are supporting ISIS. Elsewhere, a small number of incidents involving attacks on international aid workers were attributed to SMGs.

According to the United Nations High Commissioner for Refugees, more than 3m Iraqis have been displaced across the country since the war with ISIS escalated in 2014.[6] This group has faced multiple humanitarian challenges including extreme poverty, mass executions, systematic rape and other human-rights abuses.[7] As of late 2020, the Norwegian Refugee Council estimated that there remained at least 240,000 IDPs inside Iraq. In October 2020 the Iraqi government moved to shut down IDP camps, fearing that they may become institutionalised and function as a haven of militants and insurgent recruitment, and resettle or relocate IDPs. However, aid agencies warned that rushing to move IDPs to other camps or to communities that lacked the infrastructure and support networks to reintegrate displaced persons risked harming IDPs further.[8]

Political stability

Political and economic stability continues to be undermined by the country's fragmented politics, which makes addressing many of the structural drivers of conflict more difficult. Compounding this, Kadhimi lacks his own political bloc in parliament, meaning he is forced to cut deals and balance between the various political factions to advance his policy agenda. Kadhimi proposed a plan for public-sector cutbacks designed to secure IMF budgetary assistance in a so-called 'White Paper' on economic reform.[9] However, Iraq's political class has repeatedly refused to countenance salary or pension cuts for public-sector employees. With an eye on forthcoming elections in 2021, politicians are reluctant to take ownership of unpopular austerity measures, especially at a time of rising inflation. Moreover, the Iraqi parliament, the Council of Representatives (CoR), has effectively had limitless power to rewrite the budget-proposal draft submitted by the government. Whereas the Federal Supreme Court had previously ruled as unconstitutional amendments made by members of parliament to Iraq's federal budget law because they diverged too radically from the original text submitted by the Council of Ministers (CoM), it cannot currently mount such a challenge as it lacks a quorum. As a result, the CoM's agenda for economic reforms was largely dismantled in the CoR by February 2021.

Relations with neighbouring and international partners and geopolitical implications

Kadhimi has sought to rebalance Iraq's relations with its neighbours and between Iran and the US. This has involved reshuffling senior security posts in the MoI, army, CTS and various Iraqi intelligence agencies. In part, these moves were designed to reassure the US of the seriousness of the Iraqi government's intent to reduce Iranian influence in the country's security apparatus. Kadhimi's outreach to the US during the Strategic Dialogue and his refusal to act upon the CoR's January 2020 vote to expel US forces provoked opposition from both powerful Shia Islamist factions in Iraq and Iran, who are keen to see Kadhimi replaced by a less antagonistic figure.

On the economic front, the government has been keen to build bridges with Iraq's Sunni neighbours, signing economic agreements with Kuwait and Saudi Arabia, and making progress on a plan to connect the Iraqi and Saudi electrical grids. Nevertheless, Iraq remains highly dependent on energy exports from Iran and Kadhimi has repeatedly been forced to back down from significant confrontations with Iran-backed groups who have directly challenged his authority.

Conflict Outlook

Political scenarios

Various obstacles forced Kadhimi to postpone the early elections – initially scheduled for June 2021 – until October 2021, although many observers and Iraqi politicians expressed doubt over whether this postponed date will be met. The main obstacles to early elections include the lack of a quorum on the Federal Supreme Court, funding for the Iraqi Higher Electoral Commission, the registration and distribution of biometric data (particularly difficult for areas impacted by ISIS and high levels of displacement), and the resurgence of the coronavirus pandemic in early 2021. Should elections go ahead, the new electoral law (initially ratified in December 2019 but still subject to debate), which radically alters how elections in Iraq are conducted, is widely expected to be of most benefit to the Sadrist movement given its unique powers of local mobilisation.

Various new parties have emerged to represent the October 2019 protest movement. Of note, Imtidad, led by prominent Dhi Qar activist Alaa al-Rikabi, has attempted to mobilise the Iraqi youth as an untapped electoral demographic. However, it is unlikely that they will make significant electoral gains, given the fragmented nature of protest politics, voter apathy and the ability of the existing elite to shore up its position through violence and economic patronage.

Since the fall of Nouri al-Maliki in 2014, Iraq's political class has preferred to keep power dispersed, dividing up the state and its resources in such a way that has prevented intra-elite conflicts escalating into violence. This tends to preclude the emergence of a dominant power centre that could drive political or economic change: this mode of politics is highly likely to persist following the elections. Thus, the Sadrists' increased political influence will probably be somewhat offset by bandwagoning amongst other factions. In any event, the prime ministership, ministerial positions and directors general (senior civil-service positions) will continue to be divided among the main political blocs via backroom post-elections negotiations. The outcome will most likely be agreement on another compromise candidate for prime minister with little autonomous power who will not threaten the core interests of the main political factions. As a result, there is little prospect of the Iraqi government pushing through meaningful political or economic reforms, particularly if these require approval by the CoR. Instead, Iraq's political class will likely hope to hold the state together until oil prices rebound.

However, even in this scenario, given the fiscal overextension of the state, spending on investment in services, development, reconstruction and humanitarian programmes will probably have to fall. Meanwhile, the state's capacity to absorb increasing numbers of unemployed youth into the public sector will also be more constrained. This scenario is likely to drive localised and national discontent across Kurdish, Sunni and Shia provinces, fuelling insurgent activity and protests alike.

Escalation potential and conflict-related risks

ISIS networks are likely to continue to expand their operations in remote and difficult-to-secure regions of Iraq, taking advantage of political inertia at the heart of the Iraqi political system, and the discontent in Sunni communities over corruption and human-rights abuses. Nevertheless, HPAs in highly populated locales are unlikely, provided cooperation continues between key Iraqi security organs (primarily the CTS and the MoI's Falcons Cell) and the CJTF–OIR, along with supportive airpower. The late February 2021 news that NATO was significantly expanding its advisory mission to Iraq indicates that the new US administration and its allies remain somewhat committed to cooperating to contain an ISIS resurgence, despite Washington also wanting to reduce its exposure in Iraq.

As seen in recent years, the Iraqi state and its parastatal armed factions have also become increasingly adept at deploying violence to quell protesters. However, such violence carries the risk of escalation, particularly if local (heavily armed) tribes engage on one side or another of the confrontation between protesters, the ISF and militias. A potential for violent escalation and a multidimensional – albeit localised – conflict involving these different parties cannot be discounted, particularly in hotspots for violent protest dynamics, most notably in Dhi Qar.

Strategic implications and global influences

The US–Iran conflict in 2021 will revolve around attempts to choreograph a return to the JCPOA, which is the stated objective of both sides. However, while the US and its allies continue to demand that Iran comply with the agreement before any lifting of sanctions, and to threaten to impose new conditions relating to Iran's missile programme and regional proxy wars, Iran is unlikely to de-escalate its attacks on US and allied targets in Iraq. Moreover, Iraq's so-called 'resistance factions' (the main SMGs) are unlikely to intrinsically link US military and diplomatic presence in Iraq to the JCPOA and will seek to maintain a level of hostility against the US and the CJTF–OIR irrespective of progress on the Iran nuclear agreement. Added to this, the Biden administration's reduced appetite to undertake retaliatory military strikes in Iraq, or other high-risk actions – such as the Soleimani assassination – will likely embolden SMGs to intensify IED and IDF attacks on US-linked targets. This said, agreement on reciprocal confidence-building measures between Iran and the US is likely during 2021, with a return to the JCPOA the most likely scenario by the end of the year. While this may reduce tensions in Iraq, Iran and its Iraqi allies will probably continue to pursue US withdrawal from Iraq via a more gradual war of attrition on US and allied interests in the country.

Notes

[1] The Sinjar agreement seeks to remove all armed groups from the Sinjar area except for armed forces of Federal Iraq, while the Kurdistan regional government was accorded powers to influence local political appointments and to coordinate reconstruction efforts.

[2] See, for example, Tahsin Qasim, 'Three PMF Brigades Deployed to Shingal to Counter Turkish Threats', RUDAW, 13 February 2021; and 'Al-Amiri Says Turkey Intends to Attack Sinjar Mountains in Iraq', Iran Press, 14 February 2021.

[3] 'Iraq Bombing: IS Says It Was Behind Deadly Suicide Attacks in Baghdad', BBC News, 22 January 2021.

[4] Hiwa Shilani, 'NATO Announces Eight-fold Increase in Number of Forces in Iraq', Kurdistan24, 18 February 2021.

[5] International Monetary Fund, 'World Economic Outlook Database', April 2021.

[6] IDPs estimates vary across sources. According to the Internal Displacement Monitoring Centre (IDMC) the total number of conflict IDPs amounts to 5.6m since 2014. See IDMC, '2020 Internal Displacement', Global Internal Displacement Database.

[7] United Nations High Commissioner for Refugees, 'Iraq Emergency', 31 March 2021.

[8] 'Iraq's Decision to Shut Down IDP Camps Too Hasty, NGOs Say', Al-Jazeera, 16 November 2020.

[9] Government of Iraq, 'White Paper for Economic Reform', 22 October 2020.

Middle East and North Africa

ISRAEL–PALESTINIAN TERRITORIES

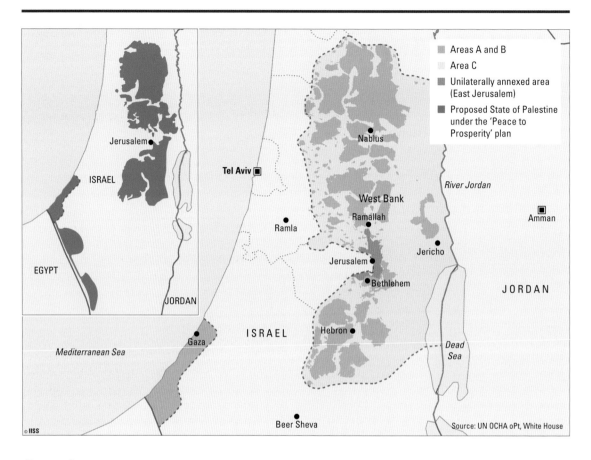

Areas A and B
Area C
Unilaterally annexed area (East Jerusalem)
Proposed State of Palestine under the 'Peace to Prosperity' plan

Source: UN OCHA oPt, White House

Overview

The Israeli–Palestinian conflict began with the outbreak of a civil war between Jews and Palestinian Arabs in British Mandate Palestine on 30 November 1947, a day after the United Nations adopted the partition plan that called for the creation of a Jewish state alongside a Palestinian one. Following the formal ending of the British Mandate in 1948, the conflict was transformed into a multi-state war: after Israel declared its independence on 14 May, the armies of Egypt, Iraq, Syria and Transjordan and contingents from other Arab countries attacked the newly founded state. The 1948 Arab–Israeli War resulted in the displacement – including through force – of between 650,000 and one million Palestinians from their homes inside what became the 1948 borders. A further 30,000–40,000 Palestinians were internally displaced within the territory of Israel. As in the case of the Palestinian refugees who were displaced/

expelled beyond the borders of the new state, Israel refused to allow internally displaced Palestinians to return to their homes and villages and designated them 'present absentees'.[1]

The 1948 Arab–Israeli War did not end the regional and domestic conflict. In two successive wars (the 1967 Six-Day War and the 1973 Yom Kippur War), Israel defeated a coalition of Arab states led by Egypt and Syria. During the Six-Day War, Israel captured East Jerusalem, the Gaza Strip, the Golan Heights, the Sinai Peninsula and the West Bank. The dire socio-economic effects of Israel's military occupation subsequently led to the outbreak of two Palestinian uprisings – known as Intifadas – in the territories (1987–93 and 2000–05), three Israeli military operations in Gaza (2008–09, 2012 and 2014), and intermittent waves of violence and terrorist attacks.[2] Despite the initial buoyancy of the 1993

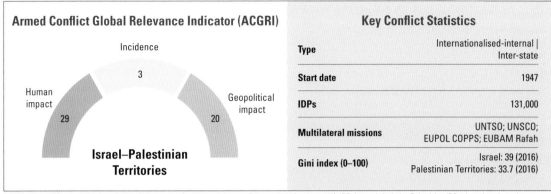

ACGRI pillars: IISS calculation based on multiple sources for 2020 and January/February 2021 (scale: 0–100). IDP data only includes Palestinian IDPs since there is no data available for Israel. See Notes on Methodology and Data Appendix for further details on Key Conflict Statistics.

Oslo Accords, final-status negotiations, as set out in the Declarations of Principals encapsulated in Oslo I, have failed to materialise so far.

The conflict saw no signs of abating in 2020. Israeli–Palestinian political and security coordination was halted mid-year amid threats of an impending unilateral Israeli annexation of West Bank territory but was re-established following the signing of the Abraham Accords, which staved off an official Israeli annexation. Brokered by the United States' administration, these accords led Israel to establish official, open diplomatic and economic relations with Bahrain and the United Arab Emirates (UAE) – followed by Morocco and Sudan.[3] However, Israel's de facto annexation did not end, as existing settlements were expanded and units that had been built without permits were legalised.

The state of ongoing conflict was compounded by an economic and health crisis resulting from the coronavirus pandemic. Conflict-related inequalities in access to healthcare and diverging financial situations, however, led to disparities in governmental responses. In December 2020, Israel moved quickly to roll out its newly approved coronavirus vaccine, achieving higher inoculation levels than any other country, reportedly receiving an acquisition edge by paying almost twice as much per double-shot dose as the European Union and the US.[4] The vaccination programme, as of February 2021, did not fully extend to the Palestinian population in the West Bank and Gaza, as Israel claimed that the cash-strapped Palestinian Authority (PA) was responsible for its citizens' healthcare, pursuant to the 1993 Oslo Accords.[5]

Conflict Parties

Israel Defense Forces (IDF)

Strength: As of 2020, the IDF had a standing strength of about 170,000 personnel, with a further 465,000 in reserve.

Areas of operation: Gaza Strip, Iraq, Lebanon, Syria and West Bank.

Leadership: Aviv Kochavi has been chief of staff since 2019.

Structure: The IDF is divided into three service branches: ground forces, navy and air.

History: The IDF was founded in 1948 from the paramilitary organisation Haganah, which fought during the 1948 Arab–Israeli War.

Objectives: Israel's defence policy prioritises homeland defence, but its anti-Iran strategy became increasingly overt in 2020, with strikes targeting Iranian positions in Syria and, allegedly, Iraq, to curb Iranian weapons transfers and military build-ups.

Opponents: Hamas, Hizbullah, Iran and Iran-backed groups.

Affiliates/allies: The IDF maintains close military relations with the US. In 2016, the two governments signed a new ten-year Memorandum of Understanding (MoU), covering fiscal years 2019–28, under which the US pledged to provide US$38 billion in military aid to Israel.[6]

Resources/capabilities: The IDF relies on sophisticated equipment and training. It has a highly capable and modern defence industry, including aerospace; intelligence, surveillance and reconnaissance (ISR), and counter-rocket systems. It is also believed to have an operational nuclear-weapons capability, though estimates of the size of such arsenal vary. The IDF can operate simultaneously in West Bank, Gaza, Lebanon, Syria and Iraq – usually favouring a clandestine, incursive nature when operating outside the Palestinian Territories.

Middle East and North Africa

Hamas

Strength: Hamas's military wing, the Izz al-Din al-Qassam Brigades (IDQ), is estimated to comprise around 15,000–20,000 fighters trained in urban warfare.

Areas of operation: Gaza Strip, Israel and West Bank.

Leadership: Since 2017, Yahya Sinwar has been head of Hamas; Ismail Haniyeh is chief of the central Political Bureau.

Structure: Hamas's internal political leadership exercises ultimate authority; other wings and branches, including the IDQ, follow the strategy and guidelines set by Hamas's Shura Council and Political Bureau, or Politburo.

History: Founded in 1987 by members of the Muslim Brotherhood in the Palestinian Territories, Hamas is the largest Palestinian militant Islamist group. It has been designated a terrorist group by the European Union and the US, but many Palestinians view it as a legitimate popular resistance group.

Objectives: Hamas's original charter called for the obliteration or dissolution of Israel, but Haniyeh stated in 2008 that Hamas would accept a Palestinian state within the 1967 borders. This position was confirmed in a new charter in 2017, which stated that Hamas's struggle was with the 'Zionist project'.

Opponents: Fatah-led PA, Israel, Palestinian Islamic Jihad (PIJ) (periodically) and Salafi jihadi groups.

Affiliates/allies: Hamas relies on financial support and arms and technology transfers from its main regional backer, Iran. A 2019 report found that Iran had agreed to increase its funding to Hamas by US$24m a month (to the total tune of US$30m) in exchange for intelligence on Israeli missile stockpiles.[7]

Resources/capabilities: The IDQ's capabilities include artillery rockets, mortars and anti-tank systems. Israel's military actions have periodically degraded the command and the physical infrastructure of Hamas but seemingly have had little effect on the long-term ability of the IDQ to import and produce rockets and other weapons.

Palestinian Islamic Jihad (PIJ)

Strength: The al-Quds Brigades, the armed wing of the PIJ, consists of approximately 6,000 combatants.

Areas of operation: Gaza Strip.

Leadership: Since September 2018, Ziad al-Nakhalah has been in charge of the PIJ.

Structure: The PIJ is governed by a 15-member leadership council. In 2018, in the first elections since 1980, the PIJ elected nine new members to the council, who represent its members in the West Bank, the Gaza Strip, Israeli prisons and abroad.

History: The PIJ was established in 1979 by Fathi Shaqaqi and Abd al-Aziz Awda, who were members of the Egyptian Muslim Brotherhood until the late 1970s. Among the Gaza-based militant groups, PIJ poses the greatest challenge to Hamas's authority in the Strip and has derailed unofficial ceasefire agreements between Hamas and Israel.

Objectives: To establish a sovereign, Islamic Palestinian state within the borders of pre-1948 Palestine. Since the late 1980s, the PIJ has carried out suicide-bombing attacks and, in the past decade, fired rockets into Israeli territory, at times in coordination with Hamas. The PIJ refuses to negotiate with Israel and does not seek political representation within the PA.

Opponents: Israel and, periodically, Hamas.

Affiliates/allies: The PIJ's primary sponsor is Iran, which has provided the group with millions of dollars of funding in addition to training and weapons. Since the leadership's relocation to Damascus in 1989, the Syrian regime has also offered military aid and sanctuary to the PIJ.

Resources/capabilities: The PIJ has increased the size of its weapons cache by producing its own rockets. Nakhalah has stated that the PIJ would have the ability to fire more than 1,000 rockets daily for a month in the event of a new war. Analysts, however, estimate that the PIJ has some 8,000 rockets in its stockpile.[8]

Conflict Drivers

Political

Settlements:

The occupation of the West Bank in 1967 heralded the beginning of Israel's settlement policy. The Allon Plan (named after the then Israeli minister of labour Yigal Allon) was based on the doctrine that sovereignty over large swathes of Israeli-occupied territory was necessary for Israel's defence, creating a so-called 'Iron Wall', and became the framework for the settlement policies implemented by successive Israeli leaders. Since then, more than 140 Israeli settlements have been established across the West Bank and East Jerusalem (with circa 640,000 people), despite the fact that settlements are illegal under international law, violating Article 49 of the Fourth Geneva Convention of 1949.

The PA sees the settlements as proof of Israel's lack of commitment to a two-state solution, a view reinforced by the fact that settlements continue to proliferate. Some Israeli administrations have attempted to restrict or reverse the movement of settlers: for example, then-prime minister Ariel Sharon forcibly evacuated some 8,800 settlers from the Gaza Strip in 2005.[9] However, although the Israeli government stopped approving new settlements in the West Bank in the mid-1990s, dozens of unauthorised outposts have since been established. Constant settlement growth has fragmented and dramatically reduced the territory foreseen for an independent Palestinian state as part of the 1993 Oslo Accords. The two-state solution based on pre-1967 borders has therefore become increasingly difficult to realise.

International

Foreign involvement:

The Israel–Palestinian Territories conflict is by no means a one-dimensional crisis; from its very beginning, foreign actors have been drawn into the conflict, both as mediators and as participants. For instance, in the 1948 Arab–Israeli War, similarly to the Six-Day War, Israel faced coalitions of Arab states acting on varying motivations and with divergent objectives. As a result, to this day, Arab- and Muslim-majority nations claim a commitment – if somewhat cursory – to the Palestinian cause and quest for independent nationhood. The Arab Peace Initiative, which was endorsed by the Arab League's 22 members at the 2002 Beirut Summit, accordingly conditioned Arab normalisation with Israel upon a set of prerequisites: full withdrawal by Israel from the occupied territories; a 'just settlement' of the Palestinian refugee problem based on the 1948 UN Resolution 194; and the establishment of a Palestinian state, with East Jerusalem as its capital. Nevertheless, in 2020, in an apparent departure from this premise, Bahrain, Morocco, Sudan and the UAE moved to normalise relations with Israel despite a lack of advancement in the peace process.

Multilateral mediation has long been considered key to achieving a solution to the Israel–Palestinian Territories conflict. The Madrid Conference of 1991 and the resulting 1993 Oslo Accords, which were premised on conducting future discussions on key 'final status' issues, have often been used as a framework for subsequent peace negotiations. The 1993 Oslo Accords also cemented the mediatory role played by outside actors, especially the US, which has traditionally acted as the key broker, often resulting in strengthened or secured Israeli interests. US dominance as a third-party mediator has equally complicated other actors' formative involvement in peace negotiations, including that of the EU.[10] Emblematic of Israel's ongoing reproval of European foreign-policy heads, the EU has typically been referred to as a 'payer' but not a 'player' in the aftermath of the 1993 Oslo Accords – regardless of its long-standing commitment to the two-state solution and its continued monetary support for the PA.[11]

Political and Military Developments

Failed peace negotiations

The 2020 Peace to Prosperity peace agreement drawn up by the Trump administration in January offered a political vision for Israeli–Palestinian peace. In defiance of international law, the political element of this so-called 'Deal of the Century' supported Israeli sovereignty over parts of the West Bank, including the Jordan Valley.[12] Constructed without Palestinian input or interest, the plan proved a non-starter and, instead, cemented Palestinians' perception of the Trump administration as an unfit mediator. Future negotiations will be further complicated by the persistent inter-Palestinian political rivalry between Gaza-based Hamas and the West Bank-based PA, in spite of multiple attempts at political reconciliation. Increased diplomatic ties between Israel and the Arab- and Muslim-majority states, meanwhile, challenge Arab claims of support for the Palestinian cause, as laid out in the 2002 Arab Peace initiative, and have heightened Palestinian feelings of international alienation and disenfranchisement. Emblematic of this geopolitical shift, Palestinian leaders were not informed in advance of the 2020 Abraham Accords, and after the news broke the PA 'accused the UAE of selling them out'.[13]

No end to Israel's settlements

In late 2020, 441,600 settlers were living in the West Bank across 132 settlements and 135 outposts, constituting approximately 14% of the entire West Bank population.[14] In addition, over 220,000 Jews live in East Jerusalem across 13 Israeli neighbourhoods.[15] In 2020, settlement expansion and creation continued. In February, the Higher Planning Council of the Civil Administration approved 1,737 housing units in

Figure 1: Timeline of previous peacemaking initiatives

Peace Talks and Official Accords	Date	Negotiators/Mediators	Achievements
Madrid Conference	1991	Co-sponsored by the US and Soviet Union. Hosted by Spain. Participation of Israeli and Palestinian–Jordanian delegations.	Palestinians were part of a joint Palestinian–Jordanian delegation. Direct and multilateral negotiations followed the conference.
Oslo Accords	1993–95	Israeli prime minister Yitzhak Rabin and chairman of the Palestine Liberation Organization (PLO) Yasser Arafat. Mediation of US president Bill Clinton and the Norwegian Ministry of Foreign Affairs.	Declaration of Principles on Interim Self-Government Arrangements (Oslo I) signed in Washington DC on 13 September 1993. Interim Agreement on the West Bank and the Gaza Strip (Oslo II) was signed in Taba, Egypt, on 24 September 1995 and then in Washington DC on 28 September 1995. Mutual recognition of the State of Israel and the PLO. The Palestinian Authority (PA) was created and tasked with limited self-governance over the West Bank and the Gaza Strip.
Wye River Memorandum	1998	Israeli Prime Minister Benjamin Netanyahu and PLO chairman and PA president Arafat. Mediation of US president Clinton.	Negotiations held in Maryland, US, from 15–23 October 1998, were aimed at resuming the implementation of the 1995 Oslo II Accord. The agreement was signed in Washington DC on 23 October 1998.
Sharm el-Sheikh Memorandum	1999	Israeli Prime Minister Netanyahu and PLO chairman and PA president Arafat. Overseen by US secretary of state Madeleine Albright. Witnessed and co-signed by Egyptian president Hosni Mubarak and King Abdullah II of Jordan.	The Sharm el-Sheikh Memorandum on Implementation Timeline of Outstanding Commitments of Agreements Signed and the Resumption of Permanent Status Negotiations was signed on 4 September 1999.
Camp David Summit	2000	Israeli prime minister Ehud Barak and PLO chairman and PA president Arafat. Peace meetings brokered by US president Clinton.	No solution was reached that could satisfy both Israeli and Palestinian demands. Talks ended without an agreement.
Taba Summit	2001	Israeli minister of foreign affairs Shlomo Ben-Ami and Palestinian diplomat Saeb Erekat. Mediation of US president Clinton.	Held in Taba, Egypt on 21–27 January, following the collapse of the Camp David Summit talks. US president proposed 'The Clinton Parameters' (including the 'Land Swap' principle). Talks ended without an agreement.
Roadmap for Peace	2002	Proposed by the Quartet on the Middle East (EU, Russia, the UN and the US). Discussed between PA prime minister Mahmoud Abbas and Israeli prime minister Ariel Sharon. Mediation of US president George W. Bush.	The Quartet outlined the principles of a Roadmap for Peace, including an independent Palestinian state. The final text of the Roadmap, mainly drafted by the US administration, was released on 30 April 2003. The process reached a deadlock and the plan was never implemented.
Sharm el-Sheikh Summit	2005	Israeli prime minister Sharon, PA President Mahmoud Abbas, Egyptian president Mubarak and King Abdullah II of Jordan.	After a series of meetings, the Israeli and Palestinian participants reaffirmed their commitment to the 2002 Roadmap.
Annapolis Conference	2007	Organised and hosted by US president Bush. Israeli prime minister Ehud Olmert and PA President Abbas. Foreign delegations included the Arab League, China, the EU and Russia.	Held on 27 November at the US Naval Academy of Annapolis, Maryland, to revive the peace process and implement the 2002 Roadmap for Peace. Negotiations continued after the conference but ended in September 2008 without an agreement.
Bilateral talks	2010	Israeli Prime Minister Netanyahu and PA President Abbas. Mediation of US president Barack Obama, represented by US secretary of state Hillary Clinton.	Talks were held in Washington DC and Sharm el-Sheikh to revive the peace process. They ended in September 2010 when the partial Israeli moratorium on settlement construction in the West Bank expired and the Palestinian leadership refused to continue the negotiations.
Bilateral talks/ The Kerry Initiative	2013–14	Israeli minister of justice Tzipi Livni and Palestinian diplomat Erekat. Mediation of US secretary of state John Kerry and US special envoy Martin Indyk.	Held in Washington DC, Jerusalem and Hebron. The parties were given nine months to reach a final-status agreement. On the day of the deadline, 29 April 2014, negotiations collapsed.
Manama Summit	2019	US-sponsored workshop hosted in Manama, Bahrain. Both Israeli and Palestinian government representatives were absent.	The US presented its 'Peace to Prosperity' plan, a vision for economic investment in the West Bank and Gaza based on a US$50 billion investment fund, but repeated delays in the US publication of its peace plan meant that the required political framework to implement the plan was lacking by the time of the conference. No economic pledges were made by key participants, including Gulf Arab states, to offer the required funding for the plan.
Peace to Prosperity	2020	Israeli Prime Minister Netanyahu. The plan's conception was led by Jared Kushner, chief negotiator Jason Greenblatt, ambassador David Friedman and adviser Avi Berkowitz.	The White House published the political portion of its 'Peace to Prosperity' peace plan. The plan, which was drawn up without Palestinian engagement, envisioned a truncated Palestinian state and Israel gaining sovereignty over its West Bank settlements. The plan is a non-starter for the Palestinians, and no follow-up negotiations were held on its basis.

West Bank settlements. This announcement followed the unveiling of the political portion of the Trump administration's peace plan. The Peace to Prosperity plan, unveiled in late January 2020, offered endorsement for a de facto Israeli annexation of parts of the West Bank, backing a 2019 election pledge by Israeli Prime Minister Benjamin Netanyahu. Netanyahu, however, ultimately shelved these plans as part of the Abraham Accords.

While the Abraham Accords might have temporarily halted a unilateral Israeli annexation of West Bank territory, de facto Israeli annexation practices continued in 2020, in part to bolster Netanyahu's support among the right wing amid his legal woes and alleged mishandling of the coronavirus pandemic. Peace Now, which began recording statistics in 2012, reported that Israel approved or forwarded construction of over 12,000 settlements in 2020, the highest annual number on record.[16] Meanwhile, data compiled by Israeli human-rights group B'Tselem showed that between January and September 2020 at least 741 Palestinian homes were demolished by Israeli authorities on the grounds of lacking building permits – the highest statistics since 2016.[17] In early January 2021, on the eve of Joe Biden's assumption of the US presidency, Netanyahu approved the construction of 800 new housing units in Jewish settlements in the West Bank. This move set the stage for further tension between the Israeli prime minister and the new US president, as Biden is expected to reverse course from his predecessor and adopt the traditional American stance of opposing settlement constructions.

Daily violence and military clashes

Violent clashes between Israelis and Palestinians occurred – if mostly on a limited, small scale – both in the West Bank and Gaza. In August 2020, in a reported attempt to pressure Israel to ease its economic blockage of Gaza, Hamas fired rockets towards Israel, which responded with airstrikes on the Strip. A Qatari-mediated ceasefire agreement, reached in late August 2020, came to an end in December when Israeli air raids targeted Hamas positions in Gaza. A UN report found that between January and October 2020, Israeli forces carried out 42 incursions in Gaza, causing damage to agricultural land and vegetation.[18] The Gaza Ministry of Agriculture reported that damages exceeded US$32,000.[19]

In the West Bank, Palestinians and Israelis were embroiled in repeated confrontations. 2020 witnessed a surge in settler and Jewish extremist violence targeting Palestinians, reportedly spiking by 78% between 17 and 30 March compared to the same period in 2019.[20] Settler violence also claimed Israeli victims. A January 2021 *Haaretz* article documented an increase in settler attacks aimed at Israeli soldiers and police officers in the West Bank; 2020 saw 42 instances of such attacks compared to 29 in 2018.[21] Israeli forces and Palestinian civilians also frequently engaged in violent confrontations. In October, IDF troops clashed with Palestinians at al-Amari refugee camp, leaving 53 Palestinians injured, according to reports by the Red Crescent.[22] B'Tselem found that Israeli security forces were responsible for the deaths of 23 Palestinians over the course of 2020 in the West Bank, including six children.[23]

Middle East and North Africa

Key Events in 2020–21

POLITICAL EVENTS

28 January 2020

The Trump administration releases the Peace to Prosperity plan that strongly favours Israel. It proves a non-starter.

22 March

Gaza confirms two cases of COVID-19, raising fears about how the besieged territory's overstretched health system will cope. The PA imposes a curfew in the West Bank to curb the spread of the coronavirus.

20 April

Netanyahu and his political rival, Benny Gantz, sign an agreement to form an emergency unity government to tackle the pandemic.

MILITARY/VIOLENT EVENTS

31 January 2020

Israeli soldiers and Palestinians clash in the West Bank, with 48 Palestinians and one IDF soldier injured during protests over the newly released Peace to Prosperity plan.

2 February

Israeli military jets and helicopters strike Gaza in retaliation for projectiles fired from the Strip.

6 February

A Palestinian driver rams a car into a group of Israeli soldiers, injuring 14 people.

19 May

Palestinian President Mahmoud Abbas announces that Palestinians will no longer abide by security agreements with Israel and the US in response to Israel's impending threats of annexation of the West Bank.

23 May

Netanyahu, the longest-serving prime minister in Israel's history, becomes the first serving Israeli prime minister to go on trial. He is charged with bribery, fraud and breach of trust.

September

Israel normalises relations with Bahrain and the UAE, in an accord brokered by the Trump administration.

23 October

Sudan agrees to normalise relations with Israel as part of a deal to be taken off a US State Department list of state sponsors of terrorism.

17 November

The PA, encouraged by Biden's victory, announces the resumption of security and civil ties with Israel.

10 December

Morocco agrees to establish diplomatic relations with Israel in return for US recognition of the kingdom's sovereignty over the disputed Western Sahara territory.

22 December

Israel's unity government crumbles after the coalition fails to pass a budget; elections are announced for around March 2021.

1 January 2021

Israel establishes itself as a coronavirus-vaccine powerhouse, giving a first dose of the coronavirus vaccine to more than 10% of its population since vaccination began in late December. At the time, the vaccination plan does not extend to the Palestinian population in the West Bank and Gaza.

January 26

Biden's administration announces the restoration of relations with the Palestinians and renews aid to Palestinian refugees.

February 5

The Pre-Trial Chamber of the International Criminal Court (ICC) rules that the court has jurisdiction to investigate suspected war crimes in Palestinian territories occupied by Israel. Israel rejects the ruling, claiming, in part, that Israel is not a party to the ICC and has not consented to its jurisdiction.

1–22 April

B'Tselem records 23 settler attacks against Palestinians in the first three weeks of April, in spite of coronavirus-related movement restrictions.

12 May

An Israeli soldier is killed during clashes in the West Bank.

3 July

Dozens of Palestinians are injured during clashes in the West Bank with the Israeli army.

August

Hamas and Israel engage in frequent violent exchanges; Israel launches repeated strikes in response to firebombs and incendiary balloons launched by unidentified Palestinians into southern Israel.

1 September

Hamas announces that it has reached an agreement to cease hostilities with Israel, yet attacks continue.

22 November

The Israeli military conducts a series of air raids on Gaza, causing widespread damage to property.

4 December

During stone-throwing clashes in the West Bank, an Israeli soldier fatally shoots a 13-year-old Palestinian child.

7 December

Clashes in the West Bank village of Qalandia injure six Israeli underground border police and four Palestinians.

26 December

Hamas claims that strikes by the IDF – in response to rocket fire from Gaza – damaged a children's hospital; Israel denies the charges.

Impact

Human rights and humanitarian

Israel continued to enforce severe and discriminatory measures against Palestinians, including restrictions on the right of movement within the West Bank and travel between the Gaza Strip and the West Bank, into East Jerusalem, Israel and abroad. Daily life in the West Bank was further complicated by Israeli road closures, which constitute a method of collective punishment. In January and February 2020, B'Tselem documented the blocking of entrances to five West Bank villages, partly in response to locals throwing rocks at Route 505. These blocks preceded limitations on movement that were imposed on all West Bank residents (by both the Israeli military and the PA) in an attempt to control the spread of the pandemic.[24] Restrictions on press freedom and the application of a carrot-and-stick policy by the PA have also sought to curtail Palestinian journalists from exposing societal flaws. Human-rights groups have repeatedly shed light on extra-judicial arrests and the persecution of journalists who are suspected of opposing Fatah-led government policies.[25] Egyptian and Israeli restrictions on movement out of Gaza harm the civilian population to an equal extent. These restrictions include limiting approval of permit applications from Palestinians seeking medical treatment outside of Gaza to 'exceptional humanitarian cases'.

Regular outbreaks of violence between Gaza's Islamist rulers and Israel, together with infighting among Palestinian factions, have affected public facilities and worsened an already precarious humanitarian situation. Considering the deteriorating health system in Israeli-occupied territory and the ongoing spread of COVID-19, in December 2020 and January 2021 international aid groups called on Israel to 'maintain health services' and, in accordance with the Fourth Geneva Convention, provide vaccines to the approximately five million Palestinians in these areas.[26] While Israel rejected any legal responsibility, in early February Israeli officials agreed to give a total of 5,000 doses of the COVID-19 vaccine for the inoculation of front-line Palestinian medical workers, claiming the move was 'a clear necessity' for Israel's battle with the pandemic.[27] Anxious about delays in access to the World Health Organization's COVID-19 Vaccines Global Access (COVAX) initiative, the PA approved emergency usage of the Russian Sputnik V vaccine in January 2021 – offering a soft-power win for Russia and increasing the potential for Russian expansion in the Middle East.[28] Nevertheless, financial limitations, in addition to uncertainties regarding vaccine delivery and medical storage capabilities, will continue to challenge the vaccine roll-out. At the same time, it remained unclear to what extent the PA would share its vaccines with Gazan inhabitants and how Israeli-imposed delays would complicate future shipments.[29]

Economic and social

Failed peace negotiations have hampered any viable Palestinian economic development. Restrictive import and export policies, in addition to the territories' reliance on foreign aid and Israeli management of Palestinian taxes and import duties, have had a devastating effect on the Palestinian economy. Since 2007, Egypt and Israel have imposed a crippling economic blockade on the Gaza Strip, resulting in a shortage of basic products, including food, medical supplies, fuel and construction materials. A 2020 UN report found that Gaza had suffered losses amounting to US\$16.7bn due to the ongoing occupation and economic siege, resulting in serious water and electricity shortages, and endemic poverty and unemployment.[30] Gisha, a human-rights organisation, reported that the unemployment rate in Gaza reached 49.1% in the second quarter of 2020, an increase of two percentage points compared to 2019, in part due to the outbreak of COVID-19 and the resulting contraction in economic activities.[31] At the same time, the World Bank reported that the share of 'poor households' increased to 64% in Gaza, compared to 30% in the West Bank.[32] In January 2021, Qatar pledged to continue its funding to the Strip by providing US\$360m in an effort to reduce tensions between Israel and Hamas and provide relief to the local economy.[33]

A reduction in Israeli–Palestinian cooperation resulting from impending threats of Israeli annexation had dire effects on Palestinian fiscal stability in 2020. The UN found that the fiscal crisis derived primarily from a collapse in domestic tax revenues during the coronavirus emergency, but also from the Palestinian government's refusal in early June to receive *maqasa* (tax revenues) from Israel.[34] Under the 1994 Paris Protocol, which governs Israeli–Palestinian economic relations, Israel is supposed to collect value-added tax, import duties and other taxes on the PA's behalf and transfer them on a monthly basis. The PA is highly dependent on these tax revenues; they account for approximately 60% of its budget. As a result of this decision, hundreds of thousands of Palestinian civil servants – some 15–20% of the PA's economy, according to an assessment by the World Bank – did not receive their salaries. In November 2020, the PA announced that it would return to accepting the monthly transfers of taxes. According to Palestinian Prime Minister Mohammad Shtayyeh, the decision to resume contacts with Israel was based in part on confronting the ongoing health crisis.

Conflict Outlook

Prospects for peace

The Israel–Palestinian Territories peace process remains mired in a hazardous stalemate. The ongoing political instability in both Israel and the Palestinian Territories has been compounded by the coronavirus health crisis. At the same time, the ongoing governmental and economic crisis in Israel has pushed the conflict down the order of urgency. Indeed, after the December 2020 collapse of the coalition government between the Blue and White party and Likud over the failure to agree on a national budget in December, new national elections were called for March 2021 – the fourth to take place in just two years. The legally embattled Netanyahu is likely to stress Israel's vaccine success and recent normalisation with Arab-majority nations to secure his political survival.

The inter-Palestinian political struggle has equally hampered the possibility of any effective mediation. The Fatah–Hamas division, despite repeated brokering attempts by Egypt and other actors, enables Israel and its allies to invoke the 'no partner for peace' narrative to justify the absence of mediation. Despite their public, unified opposition against Israeli annexation, a new initiative in 2019 that aimed at ending the Fatah–Hamas split failed to make significant progress in 2020. A democratic solution might resolve the impasse with parliamentary elections scheduled for 2021, along with the first presidential elections in 15 years to be held in July, as announced by Abbas at the start of the year. Recent polls suggest a tight contest. In December 2020, the Palestinian Center for Policy and Survey Research found that 38% would vote for Fatah in parliamentary elections, against 34% for Hamas. The centre also predicted that Hamas would have the edge in a presidential vote, with 50% preferring the Hamas leader Ismail Haniyeh and 43% preferring Abbas. Nevertheless, it remains unclear whether the various parties, in addition to the international community, will enable a fair electoral process and accept the election results.[35] Indeed, in early 2021, it was reported that the PA and Hamas were both targeting each other's supporters in an effort to foil their upcoming election participation.[36]

Strategic implications and global influences

Faced with an ongoing global health crisis and a focus on near-peer competitors, Israeli–Palestinian peacemaking will not top the international community's foreign-policy agenda in 2021. Significant challenges will likely prevent the EU from becoming a key player in the conflict in 2021, such as the continuing pandemic, a far-right political surge and its dogged commitment to an 'illusory status quo ante'.[37] Nevertheless, bolstered by a new occupant in the White House and a new EU foreign-policy head, the European bloc is likely to deepen its 'differentiation policy' of excluding Israeli settlements from bilateral relations with Israel while pushing for a unified Palestinian engagement.

Bilateral relations between the US, the key Middle East interlocutor, and Israel/the Palestinian Territories are bound to change with the new Biden administration. While the new president is unlikely to prioritise Israel or a new Israeli–Palestinian peace effort, he is expected to return a modicum of credibility and objectivity to US mediation of the Israeli–Palestinian negotiations, following four years of Donald Trump's unabashedly pro-Israeli policies. An early telling sign, just six days after taking office, was the decision to restore aid to the Palestinians and reinstate contributions to the United Nations Relief and Works Agency for Palestine Refugees, the UN agency that provides aid to the Palestinians. Israel's fractured government, conversely, will need to adapt to a new, downgraded ranking on the list of US foreign-policy priorities. Israelis are bracing for what they believe will be a downturn in relations with Washington; a post-election poll showed that 74% of Israelis believe that the new US administration will be less friendly. This perception, however, does not augur well for renewed peace negations; only 2% of Israelis polled in July 2020, while Trump was still in power, believed that a peace deal would be 'Very likely' by 2025.[38] With several key US foreign-policy officials signalling an intent to re-enter the Iran nuclear deal, Israel is expected to capitalise on recent normalisation deals with the Arab world in an effort to solidify its anti-Iran campaign while consolidating a domestic status quo.

Notes

1   Nihad Boqa'i, 'Palestinian Internally Displaced Persons Inside Israel: Challenging the Solid Structures', *Palestine–Israel Journal of Politics, Economics and Culture*, vols 15–16, no. 3, 2008.

2   'Gaza Crisis: Toll of Operations in Gaza', BBC, 1 September 2014.

3   'Sudan Quietly Signs Abraham Accords Weeks After Israel Deal', Reuters, 7 January 2021.

4   Stuart Winer, 'Israel Will Reportedly Pay Much More Than US, EU for Pfizer Coronavirus Vaccine', *Times of Israel*, 16 November 2020.

5   The sustained fighting that broke out in April 2021 and the subsequent ceasefire signed in May are not covered in detail in this report as they fall outside the scope of the reporting period for *The Armed Conflict Survey 2021*.

6   This MoU replaced a previous US$30bn ten-year agreement, which ran until the financial year of 2018. Matt Spetalnick, 'U.S., Israel Sign $38 Billion Military Aid Package', Reuters, 14 September 2016.

7   Anna Ahronheim, 'Iran Increases Hamas Funding in Exchange for Intel on Israel', *Jerusalem Post*, 8 August 2019.

8   Shlomi Eldar, 'Behind Egypt's Gift to Islamic Jihad', Al-Monitor, 21 October 2019.

9   Martin Gilbert, *The Routledge Atlas of the Arab–Israeli Conflict*, (Routledge: Oxford, 2012), p. 170.

10 This stance is reflected in various surveys; for example, in the 2018 Israeli Foreign Policy Index of the Mitvim Institute, 55% of the Israeli participants said that the EU is currently more of a foe, compared to 18% who saw it as a friend. An EU poll asked Israelis to describe their country's relations with the EU, and only 45% responded that they were good. A majority of Israelis also think Brussels is not a neutral actor and the EU is not a strong defender of Israel's right to exist. See Muriel Asseburg, 'Political Paralysis: The Impact of Divisions among EU Member States on the European Role in the Israeli–Palestinian Conflict', in Muriel Asseburg and Nimrod Goren (eds), *Divided and Divisive: Europeans, Israel and Israeli–Palestinian Peacemaking* (Israel: Mitvim, 2019), p. 22.

11 Herb Keinon, 'Top EU Foreign Policy Nominee Has Record of Slamming Israel, Praising Iran', *Jerusalem Post*, 5 July 2019; Asseburg and Goren, *Divided and Divisive: Europeans, Israel and Israeli-Palestinian Peacemaking*, p. 37; and Anders Persson, 'Introduction: The Occupation at 50: EU–Israel/Palestine Relations Since 1967', *Middle East Critique*, vol. 27, no. 4, October 2018, pp. 317–20.

12 Jeremy Bowen, 'Trump's Middle East Peace Plan: "Deal of the Century" Is Huge Gamble', BBC, 29 January 2020.

13 Anne Gearan and Souad Mekhennet, 'Israel–UAE Deal Shows How the Very Notion of Middle East Peace Has Shifted Under Trump', *Washington Post*, 16 August 2020.

14 See 'Settlements Data', Peace Now, 2021.

15 *Ibid*.

16 Josef Federman, 'Israel OKs Hundreds of Settlement Homes in Last-Minute Push', ABC News, 17 January 2021.

17 'Number of Palestinians Made Homeless by Israeli Demolitions Hits Four-year High Despite Pandemic', *Independent*, 30 October 2020.

18 Gisha, 'Human Rights Groups Demand Israeli Military End Incursions into Gaza's Farmlands, Compensate Farmers for Damages', 11 November 2020.

19 *Ibid*.

20 Tovah Lazaroff, 'UN: Settler Violence Against Palestinians Has Increased During COVID-19', *Jerusalem Post*, 4 April 2010.

21 Yaniv Kubovich, 'Israeli Defense Officials Alarmed by Rise in Settler Violence Against Police, Soldiers', *Haaretz*, 10 January 2021.

22 'Dozens of Palestinians Injured in West Bank Clashes With IDF: Report', i24News, 11 October 2020.

23 United Nations Human Rights Office of the High Commissioner, 'UN Experts Alarmed by Sixth Palestinian Child Killing by Israeli Forces in 2020, Call for Accountability', 17 December 2020.

24 B'Tselem, 'Jan.–Feb. 2020: Military Blocks Five West Bank Villages as Collective Punishment', 9 April 2020.

25 Omar Shakir, 'Palestinian Authority Jails Journalist Again Over Facebook Post', Human Rights Watch, 25 June 2020.

26 'Israel: Ensure Equal COVID-19 Vaccine Access to Palestinians – UN Independent Experts', UN News, 14 January 2021.

27 Adam Rasgon, 'Israel's Vaccine Success Unleashes a Debate on Palestinian Inequities', *New York Times*, 4 February 2021.

28 In early February the PA received 10,000 doses of the Russian vaccine; see *ibid*.

29 Fares Akram and Joseph Krauss, 'After Delay, Israel Allows Vaccines into Hamas-run Gaza', *Washington Post*, 17 February 2021.

30 'UN Report Finds Gaza Suffered $16.7 Billion Loss from Siege and Occupation', UN News, 25 November 2020.

31 Gisha, 'Gaza Unemployment Rate in the Second Quarter of 2020: 49.1%', 21 September 2020.

32 World Bank, 'Palestinian Economy Struggles as Coronavirus Inflicts Losses', 1 June 2020.

33 'Qatar Pledges $360 Million in Aid to Hamas-ruled Gaza', Associated Press, 31 January 2021.

34 'Coronavirus "Feeds Off Instability", Disrupting Israel–Palestine Peace Efforts', UN News, 26 October 2020.

35 'Mahmoud Abbas Announces First Palestinian Elections in 15 Years', *Guardian*, 15 January 2021.

36 Khaled Abu Toameh, 'PA Arrests Hamas Supporters Ahead of Elections', *Jerusalem Post*, 31 January 2021.

37 Hugh Lovatt, 'The End of Oslo: A New European Strategy on Israel–Palestine', European Council on Foreign Relations, 9 December 2020.

38 See 'Israeli Public Opinion Polls: Regarding Peace With the Palestinians 1978–2020', poll by Zogby Research Services, 4 December 2016.

YEMEN

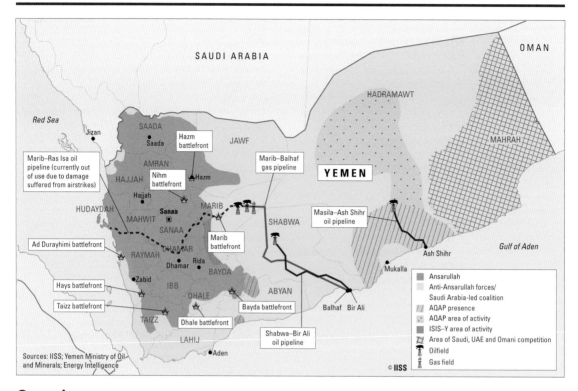

Overview

The conflict in Yemen is the outcome of the contested evolution of the 2011 popular uprising against Ali Abdullah Saleh, as well as continued unaddressed grievances from Yemen's post-1990 unification. Despite a power-sharing government and the efforts of the National Dialogue Conference to redraw the constitution and introduce a federal state between 2012 and 2014, conflict prevailed over compromise. The externally brokered transition in 2012 that replaced Saleh with Abdu Rabbu Mansour Hadi proved fraught and led to the gradual emergence of three political-military poles with competing external backing: a loose alliance supporting president Hadi, backed by Saudi Arabia and the Saudi-led coalition; the Houthi movement, also known as Ansarullah ('Partisans of God'), which receives military support from Iran; and the secessionist Southern Transitional Council (STC), informally supported by the United Arab Emirates (UAE).

In January 2015, the Houthis – informally allied with the power bloc that remained loyal to former president Saleh (1990–2011) – completed the takeover of the capital Sanaa, which began in September 2014. The Houthis seized the presidential palace, putting transitional president Hadi under house arrest: in a de facto coup, they released a constitutional declaration and appointed a revolutionary committee. In March 2015, a Saudi-led coalition – including Bahrain, Egypt, Jordan, Kuwait, Morocco, Qatar, Sudan and the UAE, and receiving logistical and intelligence support from the United States – launched a military operation to restore the internationally recognised government of Yemen and received a United Nations mandate under Resolution 2216 (April 2015).

After years of stalemate, in 2020 the conflict in Yemen intensified with new front lines, while Saudi Arabia sought to reduce its involvement. The Houthis, who run a de facto authority in the northwestern area of the country,[1] seized strategic territories in the internationally recognised government's strongholds of Jawf and Marib, and launched a ground offensive against Marib City and neighbouring oilfields (east of the governorate). Trying

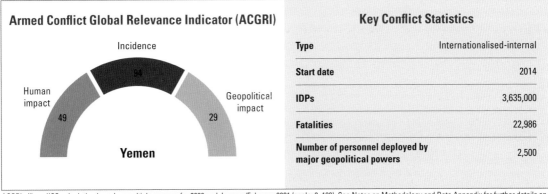

Armed Conflict Global Relevance Indicator (ACGRI)

Incidence 94

Human impact 49

Geopolitical impact 29

Yemen

Key Conflict Statistics

Type	Internationalised-internal
Start date	2014
IDPs	3,635,000
Fatalities	22,986
Number of personnel deployed by major geopolitical powers	2,500

ACGRI pillars: IISS calculation based on multiple sources for 2020 and January/February 2021 (scale: 0–100). See Notes on Methodology and Data Appendix for further details on Key Conflict Statistics.

to build leverage ahead of UN-mediated talks, they also escalated attacks against Saudi Arabia and targets in the Red Sea with repeated ballistic-missile and uninhabited-aerial-vehicle (UAV) attacks, risking potential conflict spillover at a regional level. The Hadi government and the STC secessionists, deeply distrustful of each other despite the November 2019 Riyadh Agreement and the formation of a unity government in Aden in December 2020, failed to reorganise the security sector.

As Yemen fractures into sub-national fiefdoms (with implications at institutional, political, economic and security levels), the legitimacy and power of central institutions continues to wane, resulting in blurred boundaries between formal and informal actors.[2] In this context, diplomatic efforts towards conflict resolution face a complex and fluid reality featuring myriad local players who, in many cases, rely on external support but also on a war economy.

Conflict Parties

The Houthi movement (Ansarullah)

Strength: Around 200,000 fighters.[3]

Areas of operation: Principally northern Yemen, including in Amran, Hajjah, Hudaydah, Ibb, Jawf, Mahwit, Saada, Sanaa and Taizz provinces, with clashes in Bayda and Marib. Also operates along the border of Saudi Arabia, into Jizan province.

Leadership: Abdul Malik al-Houthi.

Structure: Includes former military personnel loyal to Saleh but largely depends on fighters from the Zaydi Shia region in the north of the country and its constituent tribes.

History: Emerged in opposition to Saleh in the 1990s under the leadership of former parliamentarian Hussein Badr al-Din al-Houthi. Abdul Malik al-Houthi became leader after the founder's assassination in 2004 (in the first of the six Saada wars). In mid-2013, the movement informally allied with Saleh's power bloc against Hadi's interim institutions.

Objectives: Meaningful inclusion in Yemen's political system and expulsion of the Saudi-led coalition.

Opponents: Saudi-led coalition, the Islamic State in Yemen (ISIS–Y), al-Qaeda in the Arabian Peninsula (AQAP), Al-Islah, the STC and the Hadi government.

Affiliates/allies: Iran and Hizbullah.

Resources/capabilities: Small arms and light weapons, intelligence, surveillance and reconnaissance (ISR) and armed UAVs, missiles.

Popular Resistance Forces

Strength: Around 170,000.[4]

Areas of operation: Aden, Bayda, Hadramawt (particularly Mukalla), Hudaydah, Marib and Taizz provinces.

Leadership: Divided between Hadi, Saudi Arabia, the UAE, Tareq Saleh (Ali Abdullah Saleh's nephew) and local commanders.

Middle East and North Africa

Popular Resistance Forces

Structure: Decentralised with different levels of cohesion among various groups.

History: The Popular Resistance Forces comprise mostly former Yemeni army members, Hadi loyalists and local Salafi fighters from the south, who were the first to take up arms against the Houthis in 2015. Between mid-2015 and 2016, they were joined by a series of local Yemeni-based militias organised by the UAE such as the Hadhrami and Shabwani Elite Forces, and the Security Belt Forces (SBF) (operating in Aden, Lahij, Abyan and Dhale). Although institutionalised within the Yemeni regular security sector they still act autonomously. In 2019 remnants of the Republican Guard led by Tareq Saleh, the Tihama Resistance Forces and the Giants Brigades active in Mokha and the Bab el-Mandeb Strait were integrated as the 'West Coast Forces' under the umbrella of the Joint Forces Command, which supports the anti-Houthi fight but remains outside of the formal security sector.

Objectives: Militarily defeat the Houthis, in line with the Saudi-led coalition's goals but without seeking to restore Hadi's legitimacy. Security governance in southern regions.

Opponents: The Houthis, ISIS–Y and AQAP.

Affiliates/allies: Al-Islah (only in the fight against the Houthis), Saudi Arabia, the STC and the UAE.

Resources/capabilities: ISR UAVs, small arms and light weapons, vehicles and tanks. Receives operational assistance and logistical support from Hadi's government and the Saudi-led coalition.

Southern Transitional Council (STC)

Strength: Around 90,000 (rough estimate).[5]

Areas of operation: Abyan, Aden, Dhale, Hadramawt, Lahij, Shabwa and Socotra.

Leadership: Aidarous al-Zubaidi, Hani bin Brek.

Structure: Political organisation with several affiliated armed groups operating within the Popular Resistance Forces. Supported by a significant part of the Southern Movement (al Hiraak al Janubi), the STC presents itself as the most organised representative of the southern cause.

History: The Southern Movement emerged after the 1990 unification process, when the vice-president of South Yemen Ali Salem al-Beidh protested Ali Abdullah Saleh's power-sharing agreement. The movement was formally established in 2007 after peaceful demonstrations in Aden by southern military veterans. Founded in 2017, the STC is the movement's most organised political body, and operates as an umbrella organisation of secessionists in the south.

Objectives: Secession of south Yemen from the north. The movement has expressed willingness to share power, as a temporary measure, on the condition of fair representation in any future government.

Opponents: Al-Islah, AQAP, the Houthis, ISIS–Y.

Affiliates/allies: Saudi Arabia, Popular Resistance Forces, the UAE.

Resources/capabilities: The UAE has provided small arms and light weapons, and light infantry vehicles. It also provided financial and military support, including training and equipment for affiliated armed groups. These strong patronage ties persist despite the UAE's consistent military withdrawal from Yemen since 2019.

Al-Islah

Strength: Unknown.

Areas of operation: Marib and Taizz, by supporting tribal fighters.

Leadership: Mohammed bin Abdullah al-Yadumi.

Structure: Political organisation comprising a general secretariat and executive offices and supported by militia forces. The political party is composed of the local Muslim Brotherhood branch alongside tribal and conservative groups, businessmen and part of the Salafi community. The participation of tribal groups has provided the party with mobilisation power.

History: The Yemeni Congregation for Reform (Al-Islah) was established in 1990 following unification. Although claiming to be a member of the General People's Congress (GPC), General Ali Mohsin al Ahmar (Yemen's vice-president and deputy commander of the armed forces since 2016) is close to the Muslim Brotherhood component of Al-Islah.

These ties helped raise armed fighters, most notably in the early 2000s against the Houthis. While the party has received backing from both Qatar and Saudi Arabia, both Saudi Arabia and the UAE designated its Muslim Brotherhood component as a terrorist organisation. Despite the UAE militarily targeting Al-Islah and its affiliates, Saudi Arabia maintains a positive political relationship with it due to its support for Hadi.

Objectives: Restore Hadi's internationally recognised institutions and oppose both Houthi control of northern Yemen and the southern secessionist movement.

Opponents: The Houthis, the STC and the UAE.

Affiliates/allies: Hadi, Saudi Arabia.

Resources/capabilities: No military resources/capabilities. However, tribes who supported Al-Islah in the past have fought in support of the party in armed clashes.

Al-Qaeda in the Arabian Peninsula (AQAP)

Strength: Around 6,000–8,000.[6]

Areas of operation: Abyan, Bayda, Shabwa, and to a lesser extent Hadramawt and Taizz.

Leadership: Khalid Batarfi.

Structure: Decentralised with allegiances cemented through marriages.

History: Created in 2009 through the merging of the al-Qaeda franchises in Saudi Arabia and Yemen. The organisation rebranded locally in Abyan to be known as Ansar al-Sharia in 2011 and as Abna Hadramawt in Mukalla in 2015. It created seven proto-emirates in Abyan in 2011 and gained control of the strategically important southern city of Mukalla in 2015. It was defeated after government counter-terrorism operations in Abyan in 2012 and by the UAE in Mukalla in 2016, with further hotbeds suppressed in 2017–18 in Abyan, Hadramawt and Shabwa. In all these cases, the role of local militias was decisive.

Objectives: Retain territorial control, oppose Saudi Arabia, the Houthis and the Popular Resistance Forces, and win over local tribes.

Opponents: Al-Islah, the Houthis, ISIS–Y, the Popular Resistance Forces, the Saudi-led coalition and the STC.

Affiliates/allies: Local tribes.

Resources/capabilities: Small arms and light weapons, and improvised explosive devices (IEDs). AQAP competes with the Popular Resistance Forces and ISIS–Y for recruitment of combatants.

Islamic State in Yemen (ISIS–Y)

Strength: Estimated 250–500.[7]

Areas of operation: Mostly in Bayda.

Leadership: Abu Ibrahim al-Hashimi al-Qurashi.

Structure: Decentralised.

History: Formed in November 2014 and rejected by AQAP on ideological grounds, it seeks to recruit from the same demographics. ISIS–Y competes directly with AQAP for influence in Bayda (Qayfa district). The group has exploited sectarianism towards the Zaydi Shia population in northern Yemen as a means of gathering support for anti-Houthi and anti-Zaydi attacks.

Objectives: Prevail over AQAP for regional influence and, in line with the Islamic State (also known as ISIS or ISIL), attack Zaydi Shia groups/communities, which it considers out of the fold of Islam.

Opponents: AQAP, Al-Islah, the Houthis, the Popular Resistance Forces, the Saudi-led coalition and the STC.

Affiliates/allies: ISIS (all franchises).

Resources/capabilities: Relies heavily on IEDs, small arms and light weapons.

Saudi-led coalition

Strength: Initial 2015 force strength of around 150,000–200,000 (air, land and naval personnel).[8]

Areas of operation: Aden, Bayda, Hadramawt, Hudaydah, Lahij, Mahrah, Marib, Shabwa and Taizz provinces, as well as Saudi Arabia's Jizan province.

Leadership: Muhammad bin Salman Al Saud (Saudi Arabia's crown prince and minister of defence).

Structure: Conventional hierarchical command-and-control structure. The coalition, which mostly comprises troops from Saudi Arabia and the UAE, combines ground forces and locally trained Yemeni militias. To a lesser extent, it is supplemented by Yemeni fighters and contractors answering to Saudi Arabia who are deployed on the Yemeni–Saudi border, as well as mercenaries from South Sudan and Latin America.

History: Following the Houthi takeover of large swathes of Yemen, including Aden, in 2015, Saudi Arabia formed a coalition to restore Hadi to power and roll back Houthi territorial control.

Objectives: For Saudi Arabia, defeat the Houthis militarily and reinstate the Hadi presidency. For the UAE, conduct counter-terrorism operations against AQAP and ISIS–Y.

Opponents: AQAP, the Houthis and ISIS–Y.

Affiliates/allies: Al-Islah, Popular Resistance Forces.

Resources/capabilities: ISR assets (UAVs and satellites), fighter jets, air defences, small arms and light weapons, and tanks.

Other conflict parties

In addition to the conflict parties above, since 2015, the United States (through the US Central Command) has supported the Saudi-led coalition in Yemen by providing logistical and intelligence support – including target data on Houthi positions – and military assistance and training to Saudi military forces operating airstrikes. Until November 2018, it also provided air refuelling to coalition warplanes. With regard to counter-terrorism, the US has operated drone strikes against jihadi groups in Yemen, primarily AQAP, since 2002. In 2016 it also confirmed the deployment of a small force to Yemen to offer advice and intelligence support for UAE efforts against AQAP, especially around the area of Mukalla.

Middle East and North Africa

Other conflict parties

In February 2021, President Joe Biden announced, without elaboration, that US offensive operations in Yemen would cease, although defensive ones countering jihadi groups would continue. General Kenneth McKenzie, the head of US Central Command, stressed that the US was 'not a party to Yemen's civil war', with national interest in the country limited to counter-terrorism.[9]

After withdrawing the bulk of its forces in 2019, the UAE had a limited military presence in the country, mainly in Aden, Balhaf, Mokha, Riyan and Socotra. It continues to be involved in counter-terrorism operations against jihadi groups and in providing air support to the Saudi-led coalition against the Houthis in defence of Marib city. Despite its reduced control over STC-affiliated military forces, the UAE remains an influential player among military forces in the country's south.

Since the conflict began, Iran has provided political and military support to the Houthis, including supplying weapons and military advice on weapons-manufacturing technology.

Conflict Drivers

Political
Struggle between old and new elites:
The struggle between Saleh's old oligarchy and those who rallied around Hadi during the 2011–12 presidential transition has shaped the conflict in Yemen. Between mid-2013 and 2017, the military, tribal, political and economic power bloc still loyal to the deposed Saleh allied with the Houthis against interim president Hadi and Al-Islah, a leading tribal-Islamist political actor. The Houthis managed to absorb much of Saleh's power network but his party, the GPC, fractured between those who supported Hadi's interim institutions and those loyal to Saleh. The Houthis successfully captured much of Yemen's power infrastructure in the north, killing Saleh in December 2017 after the former president was found to be in talks with Saudi Arabia to stop the military intervention.

Centre vs periphery dynamics:
Another domestic driver is the opposition between the players in the country's peripheries (the Houthis, the STC, other local tribes) and the Sanaa-based power centre. No group has ever successfully secured the monopoly of force in contemporary Yemen, nor have state institutions ever represented the complex mosaic of geographic and confessional identities in the country. However, since Yemen's 1990 unification, centrifugal dynamics have worsened. Saleh's northern-driven system of power marginalised southerners from the government, the public and security sectors and land ownership (leading to a short conflict in 1994), and discontent manifested in the form of strikes and protests. Similarly, the Houthi insurgency in the underdeveloped upper north region waged six Saada wars between 2004 and 2010 against government security forces and pro-government tribal and Salafi militias. Both these phenomena paved the way for the 2014 conflict.

Alliance-making and local fragmentation:
Intra-Yemeni alliances typically fluctuate and are driven by politics and pragmatism, rather than by ideology or religious loyalties. For instance, the Sunni-vs-Shia divide – in and of itself not a powerful driver of conflict – has been exploited for political purposes by some fighting parties, such as the Houthis, AQAP and ISIS–Y.

The conflict also revitalised simmering fault lines. As of 2020, the state has devolved into a series of local, informal 'militiadoms'. These are geographically adjacent, often competing micro-powers that have evolved from hybrid military structures. Their existence reflects the fractured nature of Yemeni society, intense local competition and, often, external interference.[10]

International
External variables reshaping domestic balances:
Though not triggered by it, the conflict has become interwoven in the post-2011 competition between Saudi Arabia and Iran in the Middle East. Saudi Arabia's goal in countering the Houthis is to contain the expansion of Iran-aligned players at its border. Indeed, Iran responded to the launch of Saudi-led coalition operations in 2015 by providing weapons and expertise to the Houthis, thus integrating Yemen into its 'Axis of Resistance'. In southern regions, the UAE has built military, commercial and maritime influence by controlling port cities (such as Aden

and Mukalla) and energy infrastructure, and by training and organising local Yemeni forces to fight

the Houthis and AQAP and provide security governance at a local level.

Political and Military Developments

UN diplomatic efforts

In April 2020, the United Nations Special Envoy for Yemen Martin Griffiths began diplomatic efforts between warring parties, leading to a proposal for a joint declaration between the Hadi government and the Houthis. The proposed declaration focused on achieving a national ceasefire, the creation of a power-sharing government and the economic revival of the country, but agreement on the final text remained elusive. This comprehensive approach to the conflict was intended to overcome the limitations of diplomacy focused on local de-escalation, as was the case of the December 2018 UN-brokered Stockholm Agreement. This agreement had committed the recognised government and the Houthis to an immediate ceasefire in the port city of Hudaydah (plus Saleef port and Ras Isa Marine Terminal) and to the creation of a joint committee to address the situation of the sieged city of Taizz. Though it succeeded in averting fighting in this crucial port city, the deal was only partially implemented, generating distrust and concern that a localised approach would undermine a broader settlement.

Unsuccessful COVID-19 ceasefire

In April 2020, Saudi Arabia declared a two-week unilateral ceasefire in Yemen to allow the country to cope with its first registered cases of COVID-19. However, this quickly broke down: the Houthis rejected the truce and the different factions remained focused on achieving military gains or containing rivals on the ground. Conversely, the coronavirus pandemic offered the Houthis an opportunity to tighten repression and information flows, thus further centralising their model of security governance.[11]

Progress towards the Riyadh Agreement

In the areas under the formal control of the Hadi government, alliances remained fluid and political breakdowns often led to violence. The Saudi-brokered Riyadh Agreement, signed in November 2019 between the Hadi government and the STC, had outlined the formation of a government with an equal proportion of northern and southern ministers as well as the reorganisation of the security apparatus and the redeployment of military forces to the positions held before August 2019 clashes. However, on 25 April 2020, the STC declared that it would 'self-govern', effectively abandoning the Riyadh Agreement. The declaration statement was rejected by most southern governors (including those in Abyan, Hadramawt, Lahij, Mahrah, Shabwa and Socotra[12]), achieving a consensus only in Aden and Dhale, the geographical backbone of the STC's leadership. Successive Saudi-led de-escalation efforts in Abyan led the STC to withdraw its self-government declaration in June and to accept an implementation mechanism. In December 2020, the formation of a power-sharing government represented a successful, if still partial, implementation of the Riyadh Agreement.

Geopolitical competition between Gulf monarchies in southern Yemen

Saudi Arabia has gradually replaced the UAE as the main power broker with the STC. The Riyadh Agreement gave the kingdom direct supervision of the SBF and other elements of the Popular Resistance Forces until their incorporation within the Yemeni Ministry of Defence.[13] However, despite reducing its military involvement from 2019, the UAE maintained strong connections with southern pro-secessionist groups. In Mahrah, Saudi Arabia used local alliances, military units and outposts to carve out an area of influence, but it continued to compete with Oman and the UAE. In July 2020, pro-STC and pro-UAE local forces seized the island of Socotra – a geostrategic linchpin for military, commercial and maritime routes through the Gulf, Africa and Asia – replacing its governor, a Hadi loyalist, and assuming control of government sites.

New Houthi ground offensives

In 2020, with the Houthis sensing Saudi fatigue and disarray in the Hadi camp, conflict intensified in Abyan, Bayda, Hudaydah, Jawf, Marib, Nihm and Taizz. According to the United Nations Office for

Middle East and North Africa

the Coordination of Humanitarian Affairs (OCHA), Yemeni front lines increased from 33 to 47, after a long period of military stalemate.[14] The Houthis seized the city of Hazm in Jawf and made advances in Marib province towards Marib City, the stronghold of the Hadi government and army. No humanitarian progress was made in breaking the siege of Taizz city, which has been besieged by the Houthis since 2015, making it the theatre of the longest ground battle in this phase of the conflict. Local fighting during 2020 also prevented the implementation of the Stockholm Agreement. In response to a shooting incident in Hudaydah, the Hadi government withdrew in March from the UN-chaired Redeployment and Coordination Committee that had been tasked with overseeing a ceasefire and the redeployment of forces in the city under the Stockholm Agreement.

Houthi missile and UAV attacks

The conflict continued to spill over Yemen's boundaries in 2020, with increased Houthi attacks against civilian – notably economic and infrastructural – targets in Saudi Arabia. The Houthis also combined ballistic missiles and UAVs with waterborne improvised explosive devices (WBIEDs) launched in the Red Sea waters against civilian vessels. The group increased its level of coordination with Iran-affiliated armed groups in the Middle East, and Iranian individuals and entities provided significant supplies of weapons and other components.[15]

Key Events in 2020–21

POLITICAL EVENTS

8 April 2020

Saudi Arabia announces a unilateral two-week ceasefire in Yemen in response to the UN call for a COVID-19 global ceasefire.

25 April

The STC issues a self-government declaration to be implemented in its territories, such as Aden.

20 June

The STC takes political and military control of the strategic island of Socotra.

29 July

Saudi Arabia announces that Yemeni parties have agreed upon an implementation mechanism for the Riyadh Agreement. The STC withdraws its self-government declaration.

16 October

The Houthis and the Hadi government agree upon the biggest prisoner exchange since 2015, mediated by the UN and overseen by the International Committee of the Red Cross.

18 December

Hadi and STC leaders announce the formation of a power-sharing government.

30 December

The new power-sharing government returns to Aden from Riyadh.

19 January 2021

The US State Department (Trump administration) lists Ansarullah as a foreign terrorist organisation (FTO).

MILITARY/VIOLENT EVENTS

18 January 2020

A missile attack against the mosque of a military camp in Marib, attributed to the Houthis, kills approximately 70 soldiers of the Presidential Guard who were to be deployed in Aden.

25 January

A US drone strike kills the leader of AQAP, Qasim al Raymi, in Yakla, Bayda.

7 February

A Houthi sea mine kills three Egyptian fishermen in the southern Red Sea.

15 February

A Saudi retaliatory airstrike in Jawf kills 31 civilians after a Saudi *Tornado* aircraft supporting pro-government forces was reportedly downed by Houthi rebels.

2 June

A Yemeni journalist who supported independence for the south, Nabil Hasan al Quaety, is shot dead in his car in Aden by unidentified men.

11 November

A Houthi WBIED attack targets a Saudi Aramco floating platform at the oil terminal of Jizan.

23 November

A Houthi missile strikes a Saudi Aramco distribution station in Jeddah.

14 December

A Houthi WBIED attack targets a Singapore-flagged oil tanker anchored at the fuel terminal of Jeddah.

16 February

The US State Department (Biden administration) delists Ansarullah as an FTO, confirming sanctions for top Houthi leaders.

4 February

President Biden announces the end of US support for offensive operations in Yemen (excluding those against jihadi organisations) and asks the Houthis to stop asymmetric attacks against Saudi Arabia.

23 December

The Houthis burn the historic library at Sunnah mosque in Hajjah city, destroying old manuscripts and books.

30 December

A double missile and drone attack at Aden International Airport kills at least 26 people, as a plane carrying the new power-sharing government and the STC lands in the provisional capital.

Impact

Human rights and humanitarian

At the time of writing, the conflict had already caused 233,000 deaths, including 131,000 from indirect causes such as lack of food, poor health services and damaged infrastructure.[16] About 24 million Yemenis (out of a total population of 31m) required humanitarian assistance and 5m were on the brink of famine.[17] In 2020, natural disasters such as floods and locust swarms exacerbated the humanitarian situation. At least 172,000 people were displaced in 2020, 82% of which was due to the conflict, with 1m internally displaced persons (IDPs) camped in Marib governorate.[18] In 2020, the UN cut about 75% of its programmes in Yemen due to decreased US funding and systematic obstruction in Houthi-held areas (and sporadically Aden).[19] The Houthis continued to use landmines and child recruitment, while arbitrary detentions and repression of journalists occurred throughout the country.

Political stability

The formation of a power-sharing government in December did not end disagreements and violence. The anti-Houthi camp has been plagued by fragmentation and mistrust due to competition over power and resources, as well as clashing political agendas, notably between secessionists and Hadi loyalists and between Al-Islah and the STC.

Economic and social

Economic profiteering by all warring factions has devastated the Yemeni economy. In 2020, fuel shortages at gas stations particularly hit Houthi-held areas. Using its de facto authority, the Houthis introduced an Iranian-style *khums* (one-fifth) law in June, which, when applied, would allow them to collect 20% of the value of public resources and

private assets to be redistributed to the Hashemite class, to which the Houthi leadership belongs, but not the majority of Yemenis who instead have tribal lineage.

An ongoing currency crisis – which began in 2017 with the central bank's decision to float the riyal – also worsened.[20] The currency depreciation led to high food prices mostly in southern governorates. Coupled with lacking or delayed payments of public salaries – including those in the security and health sectors – and the fact that 90% of Yemen's food supply depends on imports, this further deteriorated the humanitarian outlook.[21] COVID-19 restrictions (mostly lifted by October 2020) also affected Yemenis' work and income, as most of the population survives on temporal jobs.

The Yemeni economy also experienced a fall in remittances caused by the drop in global oil prices, the impact of the COVID-19 pandemic and the implementation of labour-nationalisation policies introduced by the Gulf Cooperation Council states where most Yemeni migrants live and work.

Relations with neighbouring and international partners and geopolitical implications

External actors continued to play a significant role in the conflict, on a formal (Saudi Arabia) and informal (Iran, the UAE) level. Oman's traditional neutrality on Yemen was threatened by the military build-up of Saudi forces on its border with Yemen's Mahrah province and the permeability of coastal and border crossings where weapons smuggling occurs. The United Nations Security Council (UNSC) documented the transhipment of Iranian arms and equipment to smaller boats (dhows) in Omani waters, ultimately destined for the Houthis.[22] At the time of writing, no strong evidence supported claims of leverage in Yemen by actors such as Qatar or Turkey. The signing of the Abraham Accords in 2020 was met with contrasting reactions from Yemeni groups: the Houthis condemned them while the STC remained open to possible relations with Israel.

Conflict Outlook

Political scenarios

Yemen's ongoing political-military fragmentation is likely to continue. Stability in the de facto Houthi quasi-state will primarily depend on two dynamics. Firstly, the evolving relationship between the *saada* elite (Houthi leadership) and the tribal population: tribal resistance to Houthi rule has risen as Houthi repression of unarmed populations continues unabated, especially in Hajjah, Ibb and Bayda.[23] The *khums* tax issue is a case in point, as people living in Houthi-controlled areas will be taxed by the Houthi authorities despite economic collapse and lack of services. Secondly, intra-Houthi leadership competition has become more apparent with the development of competing security and intelligence structures and business interests.

From a political-military-economic perspective, the survival of the internationally recognised government depends on controlling the 'oil and gas triangle' of Marib, Shabwa and Wadi Hadramawt.[24] If the Riyadh Agreement is gradually if tentatively implemented, tensions within the secessionist movement could reflect shifting foreign patronage, with Saudi Arabia supplanting the UAE. In STC-held areas, armed groups are proliferating: Salafi factions (such as the SBF, the Facilities Protection Force, the Support and Reinforcement Brigades and the Asifah Brigade) are active, particularly in Aden and Lahij governorates, prompting violent skirmishes for territorial control.

In the south, AQAP is trying to regroup under the new leadership of Khalid Batarfi, a Saudi-born militant with Hadhrami origins. Having suffered operational setbacks, AQAP is likely to continue prioritising sectarian attacks against the Houthis over the fight against ISIS–Y for control of the Yemeni jihadi landscape. If renewed large-scale fighting occurs in the south, the most extremist Salafi wing of the STC could coalesce with AQAP and local offshoots against northern groups.

Escalation potential and conflict-related risks

On the strategic Red Sea coast, the West Coast Forces led by Tareq Saleh remain excluded from UN- and Saudi-brokered agreements according to the April 2015 UNSC Resolution 2216, which remains the legal basis for negotiations. These anti-Houthi forces, courting Emirati and Saudi patronage, may pursue their territorial ambitions, especially in Mokha and the Bab el-Mandeb Strait. The floating oil-storage and offloading tanker, *Safer*, carrying more than a million barrels of crude oil, that is moored off Yemen's western coast also risks generating severe damage to the environment and fishing in the Red Sea as negotiations with the Houthis over access to the tanker and the sale of its oil continue to suffer delays.

The increasing presence of ballistic missiles in Yemen, combined with strengthened Houthi–Iranian coordination, also increases the risk of miscalculation and potential border crises, particularly on the west coast of Saudi Arabia (targeting its energy infrastructure, airports and ports) and in Red Sea waters (with sea mines and WBIEDs targeting commercial vessels). Houthi missile and UAV attacks against Saudi Arabia are increasingly perceived as not just a bilateral problem but a regional

Figure 1: Perceptions of the Yemeni public on who ensures the provision of security in their local areas

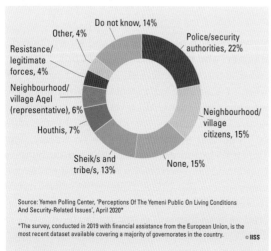

Do not know, 14%

Other, 4%

Resistance/ legitimate forces, 4%

Neighbourhood/ village Aqel (representative), 6%

Houthis, 7%

Sheik/s and tribe/s, 13%

Police/security authorities, 22%

Neighbourhood/ village citizens, 15%

None, 15%

Source: Yemen Polling Center, 'Perceptions Of The Yemeni Public On Living Conditions And Security-Related Issues', April 2020*

*The survey, conducted in 2019 with financial assistance from the European Union, is the most recent dataset available covering a majority of governorates in the country.   © IISS

issue by the US and the European 'E3' group (France, Germany, United Kingdom). Escalating attacks and intensifying Houthi anti-Israeli rhetoric have also triggered defensive moves by Israel, including the deployment of *Iron Dome* and *Patriot* missile-defence batteries around Eilat.

Prospects for peace

Yemen's stabilisation would require the containment and resolution of several micro-battles on the ground. De-escalation at the local level and increased coordination between central and local authorities is crucial for political and economic reconstruction. Such progress remains geographically limited. For example, in the oil-rich regions of Hadramawt, Marib and Shabwa, governors retain 20% of energy revenues for local development programmes, in coordination with the Hadi government.[25] In the Outcome Document of the Comprehensive National Dialogue Conference (2013–14), Yemeni parties had already agreed upon the principle of federal government, but this would require strong and legitimised central institutions to work effectively in practice.

Strategic implications and global influences

The Biden administration, which reversed the previous designation of Ansarullah as a terrorist organisation, is working to regain political leverage over Yemen's warring parties – for instance with selected sanctions on Houthi leaders – and on Saudi Arabia – by ending US offensive operations in Yemen and arms sales to Riyadh. While this might restart the diplomatic process, the prospects of a durable national agreement for conflict resolution remain poor.

Regional energy and maritime security could be threatened by Yemen's ongoing violence. Its coasts and waters are critical for freedom of navigation in the Red Sea–Bab el-Mandeb Strait–Indian Ocean triangle, especially given the competition between major states in the Horn of Africa and the western Indian Ocean such as China, India, Iran, Qatar, Russia, Saudi Arabia, Turkey, the UAE and the US. However, the presence of sea mines in Red Sea waters and the weakness and fragmentation of Yemeni maritime forces complicate multilateral efforts to protect the freedom of navigation in the area. In relatively stable areas, Yemeni oil production and export is likely to continue. Oil export from Yemen restarted in 2019, with around 40% more barrels per day exported compared to 2018 and destined for Asian markets.[26] Beyond Hadramawt's fields, Marib also resumed extraction and export in 2020. In the case of a full-scale ground attack by the Houthis against the area, the oil industry could be affected.

Middle East and North Africa

Notes

[1]   See ACAPS, 'Yemen: The Houthi Supervisory System', 17 June 2020.

[2]   Eleonora Ardemagni, 'Yemen's Defence Structure: Hybridity and Patronage after the State', *Journal of Arabian Studies*, vol. 10, no. 15, February 2021, pp. 72–89.

[3]   Naif Al-Qodasi and Adnan Al-Jabrani, 'Parallel Militaries: Anatomy of the Armed Forces Fighting Yemen's War', Almasdar Online, 3 January 2021.

[4]   This rough estimation is based on combined data regarding STC-affiliated forces, armed groups known as West Coast forces and the Abu al-Abbas Brigade of Taiz. For example, see Mustafa Naji and Ibrahim Jalal, 'Building Peace by Restricting Arms in Yemen', MEI@75, 25 January 2021; Al-Qodasi and Al-Jabrani, 'Parallel Militaries: Anatomy of the Armed Forces Fighting Yemen's War', pp. 8–9; and Nicholas A. Heras, 'Securing Southern Yemen for the UAE: Abu al-Abbas and the Battle for Taiz', *Militant Leadership Monitor*, vol. 9, no. 5, 6 June 2018.

[5]   Precise estimates on STC forces strength are not available. Refer also to note 4.

[6]   United Nations Security Council, 'Letter Dated 16 July 2020 from the Chair of the Security Council Committee Pursuant to Resolutions 1267 (1999), 1989 (2011) and 2253 (2015) Concerning Islamic State in Iraq and the Levant (Da'esh), Al-Qaida and Associated Individuals, Groups, Undertakings and Entities Addressed to the President of the Security Council', S/2020/717, 23 July 2020, p. 8.

[7]   United Nations, 'Seventh Report of the Secretary-General on the Threat Posed by ISIL (Da'esh) to International Peace and Security and the Range of United Nations Efforts in Support of Member States in Countering the Threat', S/2018/770, 16 August 2018.

[8]   Jon Gambrell, 'Here Are the Members of the Saudi-led Coalition in Yemen and What They're Contributing', Insider, 30 March 2015.

[9]   Jared Szuba, 'US to Continue Defensive Intelligence Support to Saudi Arabia on Yemen', Al-Monitor, 8 February 2021.

[10]   See Eleonora Ardemagni, 'Beyond Yemen's Militiadoms: Restarting from Local Agency', EUISS *Conflict Series*, no. 8, 21 April 2020.

[11]   See ACAPS, 'Yemen: The Houthi Supervisory System'.

[12]   See 'STC Declaration of Self-administration Rejected by Majority of Southern Governorates', Almasdar Online, 26 April 2020; and 'Yemeni Governorates Reject STC Autonomy Announcement', Debriefer, 27 April 2020.

[13]   United Nations Security Council, 'Final Report of the Panel of Experts on Yemen', S/2021/79, 25 January 2021, p. 69.

[14]   United Nations Office for the Coordination of Humanitarian Affairs, 'Global Humanitarian Overview 2021: Inter-agency Coordinated Appeals – Yemen', 1 December 2020.

[15]   United Nations Security Council, 'Final Report of the Panel of Experts on Yemen', p. 2.

[16]   United Nations Office for the Coordination of Humanitarian Affairs, 'Global Humanitarian Overview 2021: Inter-agency Coordinated Appeals – Yemen'.

[17]   United Nations High Commissioner for Refugees, 'Global Focus: Yemen, 2021 Planning Summary', 29 December 2020.

[18]   Internal Displacement Monitoring Centre (IDMC), '2020 Internal Displacement', Global Internal Displacement Database; United Nations High Commissioner for Refugees, 'Yemen: UNHCR Operational Update', 7 January 2021; and United Nations Security Council, 'As Conflict, Humanitarian Crisis Grows, Yemen "Speeding towards Massive Famine", Under-Secretary-General Warns, in Briefing to Security Council', SC/14470, 16 March 2021.

[19]   Maggie Michael and Maggie Hide, 'UN Forced to Cut Aid to Yemen, Even as Virus Increases Need', Associated Press, 1 June 2020; and Human Rights Watch, 'Deadly Consequences: Obstruction of Aid in Yemen during COVID-19', 14 September 2020.

[20]   See, for example, World Food Programme, 'Yemen Teeters on the Brink as Conflict and Economic Crises Grind On', 23 September 2020.

[21]   Oxfam, 'Missiles and Food: Yemen's Man-made Food Security Crisis', Oxfam Briefing Note, December 2017, p. 6.

[22]   United Nations Security Council, 'Final Report of the Panel of Experts on Yemen', pp. 3, 13.

[23]   Andrea Carboni, 'The Myth of Stability: Infighting and Repression in Houthi-controlled Territories', The Armed Conflict Location & Event Data Project (ACLED), 9 February 2021.

[24]   See, for example, Ammar Al Aulaqi, 'The Yemeni Government's Triangle of Power', in *Hostage on the Red Sea – The Yemen Review Summer Edition, July–August 2020* (Sanaa: Sanaa Center for Strategic Studies, 2020), pp. 13–16.

[25]   See 'Crude Oil Exports Resumed from Hadramout Province in Eastern Yemen', Debriefer, 1 October 2019; Casey Coombs and Ali Al-Sakani, 'Marib: A Yemeni Government Stronghold Increasingly Vulnerable to Houthi Advances', Sana'a Center for Strategic Studies, 22 October 2020; and Omar Saleh Yaslm BaHamid, 'Wartime Challenges Facing Local Authorities in Shabwa', Sana'a Center for Strategic Studies, 10 October 2020.

[26]   Herman Wang, 'Promising Signs for Yemen's Oil Industry, but Civil War Rages', S&P Global, 23 January 2020.

LIBYA

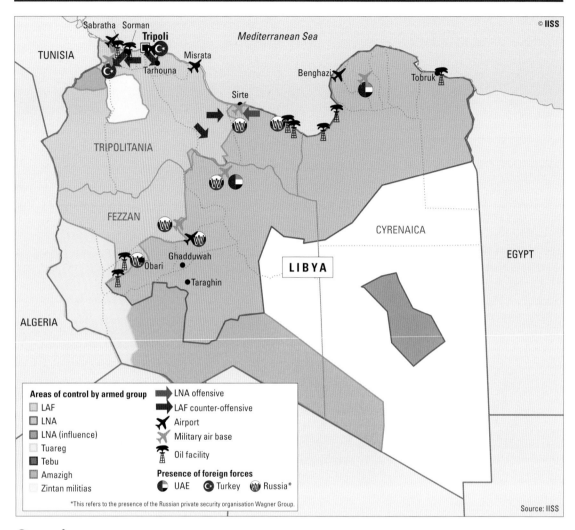

Source: IISS

Overview

In 2011, mass protests and an international intervention precipitated a regime change in Libya that ousted Muammar Gadhafi after 42 years in power. Revolutionary forces prevailed but increasing insecurity and proliferating armed groups exposed the weakness of transitional institutions.

A new civil war erupted in 2014, polarising the country, accelerating its fragmentation and creating a breeding ground for terrorist organisations. This second phase of the conflict deepened the rift between counter-revolutionary forces that were part of *Operation Dignity* on the one hand – whose aim was to restore order and fight Islamist and

terrorist groups – and revolutionary and Islamist-leaning forces that had regrouped under *Operation Libya Dawn* on the other. Since then, Tripoli and the western region have been under the control of revolutionary groups and militias from the capital and the cities of Misrata and Zintan. In the east and the south, the Libyan National Army (LNA), under the command of field marshal Khalifa Haftar, gradually imposed its control across Cyrenaica and Fezzan.

In 2019, Haftar's decision to launch *Operation Flood of Dignity* against the Government of National Accord (GNA) in Tripoli – the internationally recognised national unity government established in 2015

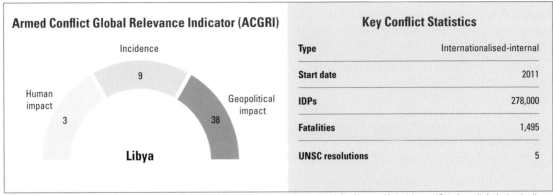

ACGRI pillars: IISS calculation based on multiple sources for 2020 and January/February 2021 (scale: 0–100). See Notes on Methodology and Data Appendix for further details on Key Conflict Statistics.

– represented a watershed moment that escalated the conflict from low-intensity fighting into a major confrontation. As foreign powers, including Russia and Turkey, significantly increased diplomatic, economic and military support to their local allies, this third phase of the civil war exposed the full extent of external interference in Libyan affairs.

The conflict, which continued unabated by the coronavirus pandemic despite the United Nations Secretary-General António Guterres' call for a global ceasefire, became even more internationalised in 2020. After a high-level international conference in Berlin at the start of the year failed to prevent a conspicuous military build-up on both sides, between May and June the LNA lost ground to the Turkish-backed Libyan Armed Forces (LAF), which supported the GNA. This forced Haftar to withdraw his troops from Tripolitania and abandon his plan to take the capital. Faced with the LAF's successful counter-offensive and the prospect of a rapid LNA collapse, Egypt – which had backed Haftar's campaign to remove Islamist groups in Libya – declared the front line between Sirte and Jufra a 'red line' and threatened a direct military intervention.[1]

The risk of Libya transforming from a civil war with third-party intervention into the theatre of direct military confrontation between rival powers reinvigorated efforts to advance the peace process. In October 2020, the UN Support Mission in Libya (UNSMIL) brokered a ceasefire agreement and a month later facilitated the first meeting of the Libyan Political Dialogue Forum (LPDF). In February 2021, the appointment of a new executive authority to lead the country towards elections in December 2021 raised reasonable hopes of ending Libya's chaotic transition ten years after the revolution.

Conflict Parties

Libyan Armed Forces (LAF)

Strength: It is impossible to determine the exact strength of the LAF, as an undisclosed number of armed groups and militias affiliated to the GNA in Tripoli have been considered part of the LAF, though the relationship between them and the central command is unclear.

Areas of operation: In early 2020 the LAF was still mainly deployed along the front line in southern Tripoli, near the disused international airport, and in the nearby districts of Ain Zara, Aziziya, Qasr Ben Ghasir, Sawani and Tajoura. The 2020 counter-offensive extended the LAF's areas of operation to Sabratha, Sorman, Tarhouna and the Watiya air base, and eventually reached the outskirts of Sirte and Jufra.

Leadership: As head of the Presidency Council (PC), Mohammed al-Menfi is supreme commander of the LAF, while Major-General Mohammed al-Haddad is chief of staff. There are seven military zones in Libya and the commanders of the active zones include Haddad (Central zone), Maj.-Gen. Abdel Basset Marwan (Tripoli zone), Maj.-Gen. Osama al-Juwaili (Western zone) and General Ali Kanna (Southern zone).

Structure: The Tripoli Protection Force represents the backbone of the LAF, consisting of militias in the capital (including the Abu Salim Brigade, the Bab al-Tajoura Brigade, the Nawasi Brigade and the Tripoli Revolutionaries Brigade), and other militias from Misrata, Zawiya and Zintan. The Misrata militias are considered the most powerful in Libya (it is estimated that there are more than 200 militias in Misrata, with a total of 18,000 fighters).[2]

Libyan Armed Forces (LAF)

History: In response to Haftar's 2019 attack on Tripoli the GNA launched a counter-offensive codenamed *Operation Volcano of Rage*. Most of the armed groups and militias in the city and western Libya rallied to this call and were integrated into the LAF, in an effort to establish an army.

Objectives: Initially, repel the LNA's offensive on the capital and thwart Haftar's plan to take control. Having routed Haftar's forces, launch a successful counter-offensive, with the aim of reasserting its control in Tripolitania and moving eastward towards Sirte.

Opponents: The LNA and its allies; terrorist groups such as the Islamic State (also known as ISIS or ISIL) in Libya (ISIS–Libya) and al-Qaeda in the Islamic Maghreb (AQIM).

Affiliates/allies: Armed groups opposing the LNA's offensive in western and southern Libya, including Tebu militiamen of the South Protection Force; Turkey, which deployed thousands of mercenaries from the Syrian National Army (SNA) to halt Haftar's offensive on Tripoli; and Qatar.[3] Some Chadian rebel forces active in Libya have also backed the LAF in the past.

Resources/capabilities: Soviet-era military equipment and weapons, such as the T-54/T-55, as well as infantry fighting vehicles and anti-aircraft guns, artillery pieces and mortars. Pick-up trucks and sport utility vehicles (SUVs) are provided by the different militias. Already depleted and in need of a revamp, the LAF's air force suffered significant losses in recent years, partially offset by Turkey's military intervention. Ankara provided military training to the LAF, including at the Omar al-Mukhtar Training Centre in Tajoura, southeast of Tripoli.

Libyan National Army (LNA) or the Libyan Arab Armed Forces

Strength: Around 25,000 total fighters, but some 7,000 regular troops.[4] The 106th Brigade is the largest unit, exceeding 5,000 fighters.[5] About 18,000 fighters are considered auxiliary forces, including tribal militias mainly in eastern Libya (the Awaqir tribe in Cyrenaica) but also in Tripolitania (approximately 2,500 fighters in Zintan) and Fezzan (the al-Ahly and the Awlad Suleiman).[6]

Areas of operation: In early 2020 the LNA took Sirte in a surprise move. However, after losing Sabratha, Sorman and the Watiya air base in May, it also withdrew from Tarhouna.

Leadership: Officially Agila Saleh is supreme commander, as president of the House of Representatives (HoR), the parliament in Benghazi. However, real power rests with Haftar, who was appointed field marshal in 2016. Maj.-Gen. Abdul Razzaq al-Nazhuri is the chief of staff and Oun al-Furjani is chief of staff of Haftar's office.

Structure: The LNA includes the Al-Saiqa Special Forces, the 106th Brigade, the 166th Brigade, the 101st Brigade and other groups such as the Awliya al-Dam (Blood Avengers). The LNA also relies on co-opting local armed groups where the opportunity presents itself.

History: In 2014, against a backdrop of deteriorating security, Haftar launched *Operation Dignity* against Islamist factions in Benghazi. In 2015, the HoR gave legitimacy to *Operation Dignity*, leading to the establishment of the LNA. However, it is not recognised as the legitimate Libyan military by Haftar's opponents.

Objectives: Originally established to fight Islamist and terrorist groups, the LNA gradually became instrumental in Haftar's project to seek absolute power and circumvent civilian oversight. Given its strong anti-Islamist background, the LNA has often been considered a secularist force in Libya. Nevertheless, some groups inside the LNA have a Salafist orientation and the influence of the Madkhali doctrine has grown.

Opponents: Islamist groups and terrorist organisations, such as AQIM, the Benghazi Defence Brigades, ISIS–Libya and the Muslim Brotherhood; revolutionary groups such as the militias in Misrata, Tripoli and Zintan; Tebu armed groups and Chadian rebel forces.

Affiliates/allies: In Kufra, the Subol al-Salam Brigade since 2015; Madkhalist and Salafist armed groups like the Tariq Ibn Ziyad Brigade and the al-Tawhid Brigade; the eastern and central branches of the Petroleum Facilities Guard; Sudanese rebel forces and paramilitaries; mercenaries from Chad and Syria, the latter reportedly recruited by Russia and mostly coming from the ranks of the pro-Assad militias and paramilitary organisations affiliated with the Syrian army. Private military companies (PMCs) such as the Russian Wagner Group. Foreign backers such as Egypt and the United Arab Emirates (UAE).

Resources/capabilities: LNA aerial capability has increased, as shown by the use of Chinese-made *Wing Loong* II drones allegedly provided by the UAE and armed with *Blue Arrow* (BY7) air-to-surface missiles. The UAE has also deployed military personnel and transferred at least five types of military equipment into Libya, including armoured personnel carriers, patrol vehicles and French Dassault *Mirage* 2000-9 fighters.

ISIS–Libya

Strength: Recent UN estimates suggest that there are only 'a few hundred fighters in Libya' as of August 2020.[7]

Areas of operation: After the fall of Sirte in 2016, ISIS–Libya remnants moved to desert areas in southern Libya to regroup. ISIS–Libya still maintains a presence in Ghadduwah, Obari and Taraghin and also operates sleeper cells in coastal areas, including Sabratha and Tripoli. Bani Walid offers a safe haven for different terrorist groups. ISIS–Libya militants frequently move across Libya's porous southern borders with Chad, Niger and Sudan.

Leadership: Multiple counter-terrorism operations have severely weakened ISIS–Libya's leadership in Libya. Former emir Abu Moaz al-Tikrit, also known as Abdul Qader al Najdi, was killed by the LNA in September 2020 in Sabha.

Structure: Since 2014, there have been three *wilayat* (provinces) in Libya: Wilayah al-Barqa in Cyrenaica, Wilayah al-Fizzan in Fezzan and Wilayah al-Tarablus in Tripolitania. Despite some distinction between the three branches, as confirmed by separate claims of responsibility (for instance, Wilayah Tarablus claimed the January 2015 Corinthia hotel attack in Tripoli), ISIS maintained a centralised structure in Libya.

History: ISIS–Libya gained an initial foothold in Libya in 2014, in the eastern city of Derna, but was eventually forced to withdraw. It found more fertile ground in Sirte in 2015, taking advantage of the marginalisation of the city by Libyan authorities. ISIS–Libya also seized neighbouring towns such as Nawfaliya and Harawa, took control of the Ghardabiya air base and threatened Misrata. In May 2016 the GNA launched *Operation Solid Structure* against Sirte and took control of the group's stronghold in December 2016 with the crucial support of US AFRICOM. The 2019 resumption of hostilities provided favourable conditions for the resurgence of ISIS–Libya.

Objectives: Re-establish its presence in Libya by increasing attacks, particularly in remote areas of central and southern Libya.

Opponents: The GNA and affiliated militias; the LNA and its local allies; the Muslim Brotherhood and other moderate Islamist groups (including Sufi followers); third parties engaged in the fight against terrorism (the US in particular).

Affiliates/allies: The group has not historically allied with other terrorist organisations in Libya. However, since its 2016 defeat in Sirte, reports suggest that it has begun collaborating with other jihadist groups, including AQIM.

Resources/capabilities: ISIS–Libya militants have seized trucks carrying fuel and gained revenue from taxation of human traffickers and arms smugglers. The group has also resorted to kidnapping for ransom.

Turkish Armed Forces (TSK)

Strength: At least 100 military officers deployed to Libya.[8]

Areas of operation: Overlapping with the LAF in southern Tripoli, Sabratha, Sorman and Tarhouna, extending to the outskirts of Jufra and Sirte. Reported presence at the Mitiga airport in Tripoli and the Watiya air base, with speculation over the establishment of a Turkish naval base in Khoms or Misrata.

Leadership: President Recep Tayyip Erdogan (commander-in-chief); Gen. (retd.) Hulusi Akar (minister of national defence); Gen. Yasar Guler (chief of general staff).

Structure: Turkish army units (under the Turkish Land Forces Command) and squadrons carrying out airstrikes (under the Air Force Command) are subordinate to the chief of general staff.

History: In November 2019 Turkey signed a Memorandum of Understanding (MoU) with the GNA, which provided for military assistance and training to the LAF. Since the start of 2020, Turkey began to intervene militarily in support of the GNA, contributing significantly to repelling Haftar's offensive on Tripoli.

Objectives: Initially, prevent Haftar's forces from taking control of Tripoli. Following the collapse of the LNA's offensive, consolidate the GNA and extend its control over Libya.

Opponents: The LNA and its foreign backers.

Affiliates/allies: The GNA/LAF and Qatar.

Resources/capabilities: Turkey has sent weapons, advisers and military equipment, including TB-2 *Bayraktar* and ANKA S-1 drones, *Kirpi* armoured vehicles and air-defence systems, such as *Hawk* air-defence missile batteries and 3D Kalakan radar to the Libyan theatre. According to the UNSC Panel of Experts, Turkey also sent military hardware, including electronic-warfare systems, anti-tank guided missiles, self-propelled air-defence guns and artillery, surface-to-air missile systems, frigates and fighter-ground-attack aircraft. In March 2021, Turkey appeared to have supplied the LAF with US-made M60 tanks for training purposes.

Wagner Group

Strength: 3,000 personnel and 2,000 Syrian mercenaries on the ground in Libya, the largest Wagner deployment worldwide.[9]	**Objectives:** Initially provide training, hardware, non-kinetic security services and battlefield advice to the LNA, backing its offensive on Tripoli.
Areas of operation: Having been present along the front line in southern Tripoli, Wagner operatives were spotted in different air bases (Jufra, Brak al-Shati, Ghardabiya, Sabha and Waddan) and oilfields (Sharara and El Feel), having moved to secure facilities and provide support to LNA-affiliated local armed groups. Wagner members were also present at the Es Sider oil terminal.	Since September 2019, act as a force multiplier for the LNA, giving it tighter coordination, anti-drone capability, expert snipers and advanced equipment. After the collapse of the LNA's offensive, consolidate Haftar's position and reinforce his grip on critical infrastructures.
	Opponents: The GNA, TSK, the US.
Leadership: Dmitry Utkin (commander); Alexander Eermolaev (deputy commander); Andrei Troshev (chief of staff).	**Affiliates/allies:** The LNA and its foreign backers.
Structure: Unknown.	**Resources/capabilities:** Throughout 2020 Russian military cargo aircraft, including Il-76s, supplied the Wagner Group with military armoured vehicles, SA-22 air-defence systems, fuel, ammunition and other supplies. In May 2020, at least 14 MiG-29 and SU-24 jets were deployed from Russia to Libya through Syria, and were reportedly flown by Wagner pilots, who carried out several ground strikes and other missions in support of the LNA. The UAE reportedly provided financial assistance to the Wagner Group to deploy its mercenaries to Libya.
History: The Wagner Group is a Russian security organisation closely linked to the Kremlin and military intelligence. It is used by Russia to carry out a range of officially deniable military and intelligence operations, and commercial activities, abroad, including in the Middle East and Africa. Reports about the presence of the group in Libya first emerged in 2018, when Wagner operatives were spotted in eastern Libya.	

Other conflict parties

Despite not being formally part of the conflict in Libya, and with limited active involvement in the fighting in 2020, Egypt and the UAE were found responsible for repeated violations of the UN arms embargo and also provided air support to Haftar's forces on several occasions.

Conflict Drivers

Political

The fragmentation of state authority:
The lack of institutional architecture to navigate the transitional challenges after the fall of the former regime has pushed Libya to the brink of fragmentation. The power and rule-of-law vacuum has led to a resurgent tribalism, in which local grievances have frequently prevailed over centralisation efforts, undermining state-building.

Particularly since 2014, polarisation has created centrifugal forces that threaten national unity. The split between the east and the west of Libya has been epitomised by the proliferation of parallel institutions, in both the economic sphere – such as the Central Bank of Libya and the National Oil Corporation – and the political one, with the GNA based in Tripoli and an interim government headquartered in Bayda. The third phase of the civil war in 2019 further aggravated this division. Indeed, although the HoR had moved to Tobruk after the 2014 conflict emerged, in 2019 a splinter group of parliamentarians relocated to Tripoli, in protest against Haftar's attack on the capital.

Economic and social

Control of oil revenue:
The January 2020 closure of terminals and oilfields in the oil-crescent region highlighted the importance of oil as an economic driver of the conflict. Despite blame falling on local tribes, the blockade was Haftar's attempt to economically choke the GNA, depriving it of oil revenues in areas under the LNA's control. Wresting control of oil revenues would have been instrumental in Haftar's plans to sustain the war effort and dispense patronage among local allies, while also addressing redistribution claims common in federalist milieus in Cyrenaica.

At the same time, the move also aimed at creating friction in Tripoli, to destabilise the already rocky relationship between the GNA and the armed groups that support it. The pervasive control of economic and financial institutions by armed groups in the capital has frequently highlighted the asymmetric relation between the central authority and the militia cartel responsible for the predatory behaviour associated with the war economy.

International

The regional rift:

The deepening regional rift between rival fronts in the Middle East and North Africa played a crucial role in exacerbating the conflict in Libya, magnifying the internal polarisation between revolutionary and counter-revolutionary forces. External support to the rival factions broadly mirrored ongoing regional competition since the Arab uprisings of 2011. External intervention escalated during the latest round of fighting since 2019 with Egypt, Saudi Arabia and the UAE backing Haftar's political project and revolutionary powers such as Qatar and Turkey supporting the authorities in Tripoli.

Inquiries about a missile strike that killed 26 cadets at the Tripoli Military Academy on 4 January 2020 highlighted the extent of external interference in Libya. Evidence confirmed that the strike was carried out by a *Wing Loong* II drone provided by the UAE to the LNA.[10] On the other hand, Turkey opted for open military intervention in support of the GNA and its military support for the LAF significantly changed the conflict's dynamics.

Political and Military Developments

Changing military dynamics

Frustrated by the military stalemate along the front line in southern Tripoli, in early 2020 Haftar decided to advance elsewhere. In a surprise move on 6 January, the LNA took control of Sirte, opening a second front and threatening the nearby city of Misrata, the main revolutionary stronghold opposed to Haftar's political project. The advance was made possible by the about-face of the 604th Brigade, which switched allegiance to Haftar and left the GNA-affiliated Sirte Protection Force. This allowed Haftar's forces to take control of the strategic Ghardabiya air base.[11]

Despite the increased military support from his foreign sponsors, Haftar's success in Sirte remained sporadic and relied on co-optation. Moreover, territorial expansion exposed the LNA to the risk of overstretching. When Turkey started to double down on its local allies, gaining aerial supremacy

Figure 1: The hybrid war in Libya

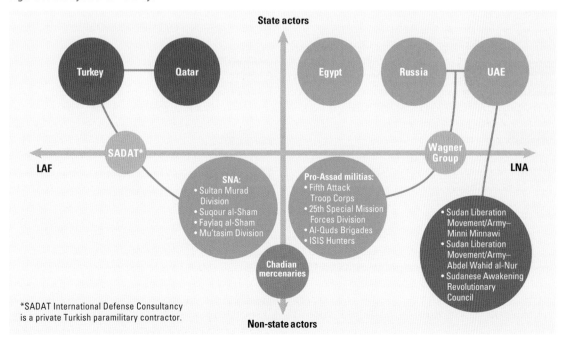

*SADAT International Defense Consultancy is a private Turkish paramilitary contractor.

in Tripolitania using both TB-2 *Bayraktar* and ANKA S-1 drones (highly effective in neutralising the Russian-made *Pantsir* S-1 air-defence systems supplied by the UAE), the LNA's offensive started to crumble. Launched in March 2020, the GNA's *Operation Peace Storm* drove out Haftar's forces from Sabratha and Sorman, relieving pressure west of Tripoli. The Watiya air base fell in May, in a prelude to the LNA's withdrawal from Tarhouna, which had been one of its main springboards for launching *Operation Flood of Dignity* in 2019.

After the fall of Tarhouna, Russian private contractors from the Wagner Group were redeployed to the Jufra air base, where Moscow had already moved several military aircraft in May, raising concerns about a Russian military presence on the southern flank of NATO. As a result of Russia's hybrid warfare and Egypt's threat of a direct military intervention, the Turkish-backed counter-offensive lost momentum. The conflict froze along the Sirte–Jufra 'red line', giving political negotiations a new chance.

International peace initiatives

Inconclusive peace talks in Moscow on 13 January 2020 gave the European Union, until then paralysed by the conflicting agendas of some of its member states, a chance to reaffirm its central role over the Libyan crisis. A conference held in Berlin on 19 January 2020 adopted a number of positive measures,

such as the International Follow Up Committee and the Joint Military Commission (JMC, also known as 5+5), which proved to be crucial in the de-escalation phase. However, it failed to end foreign intervention, as evident by the multiple and flagrant violations of the arms embargo, which eventually led to the resignation of the UN Special Representative of the Secretary-General (SRSG) Ghassan Salamé in March.

Following the LNA's withdrawal from Tarhouna, Egypt unsuccessfully launched a ceasefire initiative known as the Cairo Declaration, elevating Saleh as a political alternative to the discredited Haftar. On 21 August 2020 both Saleh and the GNA Prime Minister Fayez al-Sarraj issued separate statements calling for a ceasefire, providing an opening for the acting UN SRSG Stephanie Williams to relaunch the peace process.

On 23 October 2020, the warring parties signed a landmark ceasefire agreement in Geneva. UNSMIL began facilitating the intra-Libya dialogue through the newly established LPDF, which eventually resulted in the establishment of a new executive authority in February 2021. Despite the UN's leadership in bringing conflict parties closer, it is interesting to note the important role played by Russia and Turkey during the negotiation process. Indeed, the agreement to resume oil exports and production reached in September 2020 was negotiated in Sochi, Russia, a clear indication of Moscow's growing clout in Libya.

Key Events in 2020–21

POLITICAL EVENTS

13 January 2020
During a summit in Moscow, Haftar rejects a proposed ceasefire.

19 January
The Berlin Conference takes place.

2 March
UN SRSG Ghassan Salamé resigns.

6 June
Egypt proposes a new ceasefire (the Cairo Declaration) in Libya.

17 September
Agreement is reached to resume oil exports and production.

23 October
The JMC signs a ceasefire agreement brokered by UNSMIL.

MILITARY/VIOLENT EVENTS

4 January 2020
26 military cadets are killed in a drone strike on the Tripoli Military Academy.

6 January
The LNA takes control of Sirte and the Ghardabiya air base.

25 March
The GNA launches *Operation Peace Storm*.

13 April
The LAF takes control of several towns west of Tripoli, including Sabratha and Sorman.

18 May
The LAF takes control of the Watiya air base.

26 May
AFRICOM confirms that Russia has transferred several military aircraft to the Jufra air base, including MiG-29s and SU-24s.

7 November
The first round of the LPDF begins in Tunis.

18 January 2021
Ján Kubiš appointed new UN SRSG to Libya.

5 February
The LPDF appoints a new executive authority for Libya.

5 June
The LNA withdraws from Tarhouna.

5 July
Unknown aircraft target Turkish air-defence systems at the Watiya air base.

21 August
Sarraj and Saleh separately announce a ceasefire.

Impact

Human rights and humanitarian

Indiscriminate shelling and air and drone strikes caused frequent civilian casualties, while targeted assassinations against prominent human-rights activists prompted international outcry.[12] Evidence that private contractors and PMCs were responsible for several violations of international humanitarian law clearly emerged after the LNA withdrawal from Tripolitania.[13] Explosions caused by landmines and remnants of war also took place in the southern district of Tripoli (Ain Zara and Salahuddin) where the Wagner Group was present.[14] The difficulty of conducting clearing operations prevented the return of an estimated 392,000 internally displaced persons, as of January 2021.[15]

Local groups were also responsible for gross violations and war crimes. For example, 27 mass graves were discovered in Tarhouna after the LNA withdrawal, shedding light on the brutal rule of the Kani Brigade affiliated with Haftar's forces.[16] International organisations such as the International Criminal Court were investigating war crimes and crimes against humanity in Libya. However, significant hurdles remain, such as insufficient funding causing delays to the work of the Independent Fact-Finding Mission on Libya established by the UN Human Rights Council in 2020.

Economic and social

The new round of fighting in Libya further strained a health service already struggling after years of neglect and fragmented governance, as well as violence, with hospitals and medical staff frequently targeted by conflict parties. The above left it overexposed to the spread of the coronavirus pandemic. As of 28 February 2021, Libya had registered 132,458 confirmed cases of COVID-19 and 2,174 related deaths.[17] Government restrictions to combat COVID-19 worsened the economic crisis caused by the conflict, the oil blockade and plummeting global oil prices.[18] In war zones civilians were caught between lockdown and LNA airstrikes in densely populated areas. Government-imposed restrictions also had a huge impact on the living conditions of migrants and refugees, resulting in the loss of livelihoods, food insecurity and reduced healthcare access, as well as affecting voluntary returns and resettlement programmes.[19]

Relations with neighbouring and international partners and geopolitical implications

The 2019 MoU between the GNA and Turkey had offered the latter the opportunity to expand its military footprint in Libya as well as advance territorial claims in the eastern Mediterranean Sea based on the *mavi vatan* (blue homeland) doctrine. However, escalating tensions in the region led to the emergence of an anti-Turkey axis, highlighted by the establishment in September 2020 of the East Mediterranean Gas Forum that included Ankara's main regional rivals.

The revamp of the EU Naval Force Mediterranean (EUNAVFOR MED) also proved controversial for Turkey, as *Operation Irini* was established to enforce the arms embargo in Libya at the end of March 2020. The new mission deepened fissures between Ankara and Brussels, while creating rifts inside NATO. Naval incidents between European and Turkish vessels led to frequent protests by Ankara and Tripoli, which deemed *Operation Irini* too focused on the maritime dimension of the arms embargo, with insufficient monitoring of the arms supply to the LNA via military-transport aircraft or across Libya's terrestrial border with Egypt.

Middle East and North Africa

Conflict Outlook

Political scenarios

The October 2020 ceasefire agreement represented a watershed moment in the Libyan transition process. Even if fighting had already diminished by the summer due to external and internal factors, the ceasefire gave new momentum to the UNSMIL-facilitated negotiations. The first round of the LPDF in Tunis in November 2020 followed widespread popular protests in August 2020 that clearly indicated the Libyan people's frustrations and expectations for change. Organised by the Libyan Hirak (movement), the protests put additional pressure on the leadership, forcing both Sarraj and the prime minister of the interim government, Abdullah al-Thinni, to announce their resignations, paving the way for a much-needed and long-awaited turnover in the Libyan political elite.

The LPDF's vote on 5 February 2021 to appoint an interim executive authority, including a new GNU led by the Misrata businessman Abdulhamid al-Dbeibah and a three-member PC led by Menfi and including Musa al-Koni and Abdullah al-Lafi, represents an important opportunity to reverse the political fragmentation since 2011. The new GNU is expected to shepherd the country to elections on 24 December 2021 and eventually to a referendum on the draft constitution. However, it will have to navigate a hostile environment in which frustrated and marginalised actors may try to spoil the political process.[20]

Escalation potential and conflict-related risks

Full implementation of the ceasefire agreement is required to complete Libya's transition to democratic and representative institutions. In this context, reports of a trench being constructed between Sirte and the Jufra air base by the Wagner Group threaten prospects of reconciliation, especially as the ceasefire agreement stipulated that all foreign forces and private contractors should leave Libya by 23 January 2021.

Reports about the continuing presence of 20,000 foreign fighters – including Turkish military forces, Russian private contractors and Syrian fighters, as well as Chadian non-state armed groups and Sudanese militias – further signal the privatisation of war and highlight Russia's and Turkey's growing sway on the ground, which makes any successful political solution contingent on their support. Without this, the prospect of a frozen conflict along the Sirte–Jufra 'red line' looms.

Strategic implications and global influences

The outcome of the 2020 US elections helped create fertile ground to relaunch political negotiations. The first foreign-policy moves of the Biden administration – including the review of arms sales to the UAE and the recalibration of US relations with Saudi Arabia – suggested a change of attitude towards the Gulf monarchies, which had seen Haftar as instrumental in containing revolutionary movements and political Islam in Libya.

Already aware of the LNA's limited military capabilities and sceptical of Haftar's chances in taking Tripoli, Egypt was particularly receptive to these changing regional dynamics. In trying to cultivate relations with authorities in Tripoli, Cairo effectively decoupled from the counter-revolutionary front to preserve its geostrategic gains in Libya. These included a buffer zone along its western border against Turkish-backed armed groups, secured to date by the LNA's control of Cyrenaica.

The Cairo Declaration and the Sirte–Jufra 'red line' were clear attempts by Egypt to reinforce its clout in a conflict that had been tending towards a Russian–Turkish military duopoly. Compared to Ankara's staunch commitment to the GNA, however, Moscow adopted an opportunistic approach, diversifying its strategy and cultivating relations with different stakeholders.[21] In the event of a resumption in hostilities, this could reinforce Moscow's central role, especially considering Russia's excellent relations with two major Libyan neighbours: Algeria and Egypt.

Notes

1   Samer al-Atrush, 'Egypt's Sisi Warns of Intervention in Libya Over Sirte', Bloomberg, 20 June 2020.

2   Jason Pack, 'Kingdom of Militias: Libya's Second War of Post-Qadhafi Succession', Italian Institute for International Political Studies, 31 May 2019.

3   In August 2020 the GNA, Qatar and Turkey signed a tripartite agreement for cooperation in training of the LAF. In October 2020, the GNA also signed an MoU on security cooperation with Qatar. The agreement provided for intelligence exchange between Doha and Tripoli to fight terrorism and organised crime.

4   Pack, 'Kingdom of Militias: Libya's Second War of Post-Qadhafi Succession'.

5   Jalel Harchaoui and Mohamed-Essaïd Lazib, 'Proxy War Dynamics in Libya', Virginia Tech School of Public and International Affairs in Association with Virginia Tech Publishing, 2019.

6   Arnaud Delalande, 'Forces on the Libyan Ground: Who Is Who', Italian Institute for International Political Studies, 28 May 2018.

7   United Nations Security Council, 'Eleventh Report of the Secretary-General on the Threat Posed by ISIL (Da'eash) to International Peace and Security and the Range of United Nations Effort in Support of Member States in Countering the Threat', S/2020/774, 4 August 2020.

8   International Crisis Group, 'Turkey Wades into Libya's Troubled Waters', Report no. 257, 30 April 2020.

9   Jared Szuba, 'Wagner Has Already Crashed Two Russian Fighter Jets in Libya, AFRICOM Says', Al-Monitor, 11 September 2020.

10 At that time Wing Loong IIs were only operating from the al-Khadim air base in eastern Libya, where the UAE maintains a military presence. See 'UAE Implicated in Lethal Drone Strike in Libya', BBC News, 28 August 2020. Egypt's role in allowing the UAE to use the Sidi Barrani and Siwa military air bases near the border with Libya also came under scrutiny, confirming Cairo's support for Haftar's attack on the capital.

11 Scenes of jubilation in Sirte in the aftermath of the LNA's advance highlighted the marriage of convenience between nostalgic Gadhafists and Haftar's forces, as well as indicating Haftar's clout over Salafist-Madkhalist followers, whose doctrine is common to both the 604th Brigade and many LNA units. See Umberto Profazio, 'Il piano inclinato della guerra in Libia' [The Inclined Plane of the Libyan War], The Institute for International Political Studies, 10 January 2020.

12 Between 1 January and 30 June 2020 UNSMIL documented at least 489 civilian casualties (including 170 deaths and 319 injuries). See United Nations Support Mission in Libya, 'Civilian Casualties Report from 1 January–31 March 2020', 30 April 2020; and 'Civilian Casualties Report from 1 April–30 June 2020', 29 July 2020. At the same time, the killing of Hana al-Barasi, a vocal opponent of Haftar, in Benghazi on 10 November 2020 was the latest incident in a long list of violence against female activists in Libya. It came after the disappearance of Siham Sergiwa in 2019 and the killing of Salwa Bughaighis and Fariha al-Barkawi in 2014. See Andrea Backhaus, 'Libya's Peace Process Doomed to Failure Without Its Women', Qantara, 23 December 2020.

13 Landmines, booby-traps and unexploded ordnances have caused at least 206 casualties (73 deaths and 133 injuries) since May 2020, of which 136 were civilians. See United Nations Office for the Coordination of Humanitarian Affairs, 'Libya December Humanitarian Bulletin', 22 January 2021.

14 The list of weapons found on the battlefield includes fragmentation-rocket warheads, Russian Kornet anti-tank missiles and Turkish MAM-L smart micro munition, possibly dropped by Turkish drones. See Daniel Hilton, 'Booby-trapped Bodies and Trip-wire Toys: The Perils of Clearing Tripoli of Mines', Middle East Eye, 2 December 2020.

15 United Nations Office for the Coordination of Humanitarian Affairs, 'Libya December Humanitarian Bulletin', 22 January 2021.

16 At least 338 residents have been reported missing since the militia, led by the Kani brothers, took control of the city in 2015. See Human Rights Watch, 'Libya: Militia Terrorized Town, Leaving Mass Graves', 7 January 2021.

17 World Health Organization, 'WHO Coronavirus (COVID-19) Dashboard – Libya', 28 February 2021.

18 According to IMF estimates, real GDP decreased by 59.7% in 2020. See International Monetary Fund, 'World Economic Outlook Database', April 2021.

19 As of December 2020, there were 571,464 migrants in Libya. See International Organization for Migration, 'Libya – Migrant Report Key Findings Round 34 (November–December 2020)', 17 February 2021.

20 At the same time, allegations of vote buying in the LPDF also undermined the new government, highlighting the need for transparency to be an integral part of any successful attempt to reform governance in Libya. See 'Le Dialogue Politique Entaché de Corruption, Selon des Experts de l'ONU' [Political Dialogue Tainted by Corruption, According to UN Experts], L'Orient Le Jour, 28 February 2021.

21 Despite the Wagner Group's support for the LNA clearly indicating Russia's preference for Haftar's camp, Moscow has been able to cultivate relations with both conflict parties in Libya and thereby expand its influence. See Jalel Harchaoui, 'The Pendulum: How Russia Sways Its Way to More Influence in Libya', War on the Rocks, 7 January 2021.

Middle East and North Africa

EGYPT

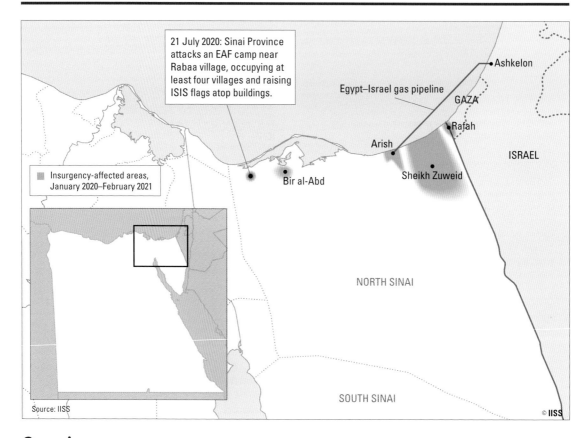

21 July 2020: Sinai Province attacks an EAF camp near Rabaa village, occupying at least four villages and raising ISIS flags atop buildings.

Egypt–Israel gas pipeline

Ashkelon

GAZA

Rafah

Arish

ISRAEL

Sheikh Zuweid

Bir al-Abd

■ Insurgency-affected areas, January 2020–February 2021

NORTH SINAI

SOUTH SINAI

Source: IISS

© IISS

Overview

The Sinai Peninsula has been a distinctly uncon-trolled area of Egyptian territory since the end of the Arab–Israeli wars in the 1960s and 1970s, and the return of territory from Israel with the signing of the Camp David Accords in 1978. As a result, armed groups have long existed in the area, albeit with a low impact on security. When the Arab Spring pro-tests began in Egypt in January 2011, creating a political vacuum in Cairo, armed groups in North Sinai governorate seized the opportunity to become more active and more visible. The largest militant group, Ansar Beit Al Maqdis (ABM), began targeting the Egypt–Israel gas pipeline, with at least a dozen attacks in 2011 alone, creating significant insecurity within the Sinai Peninsula. Egypt remained in a state of significant political flux during its brief demo-cratic experiment between 2011 and 2013.

In 2013 a popularly supported *coup d'état* reinstated military rule in Egypt by removing

the country's democratically elected president Mohamed Morsi. As a result, the Sinai Peninsula has been in a state of emergency since September 2013.[1] ABM took on a more political shape by reject-ing Morsi's ouster, targeting security personnel in response to the violent clearing of the protest centre at Rabaa in Cairo, in August 2013. ABM (and its suc-cessor, an offshoot of the Islamic State, also known as ISIS or ISIL, in the Sinai Peninsula) has aggressively targeted both military positions and state interests through successive terror attacks. Since then, the Egyptian Armed Forces (EAF) has sought to extin-guish the insurgency by establishing control over the area through military designated zones, where it has deployed significant numbers of troops – up to 75,000 during *Operation Sinai* in 2018. Following a pledge of allegiance to ISIS in November 2014, ABM morphed into Sinai Province and expanded its insurgency activities, initially focused on the eastern

Armed Conflict Global Relevance Indicator (ACGRI)	Key Conflict Statistics	
	Type	Internal | Localised insurgency
Incidence	**Start date**	2011
5	**Gini index (0–100)**	31.5 (2017)
Human impact 1 Geopolitical impact 2	**GDP per capita 2020, PPP (current international $)**	12,789.9
Egypt	**Functioning of government (0–10)**	3.21

ACGRI pillars: IISS calculation based on multiple sources for 2020 and January/February 2021 (scale: 0–100). The indicator's results and certain Key Conflict Statistics refer to the country as a whole rather than the specific conflict. See Notes on Methodology and Data Appendix for further details on Key Conflict Statistics.

areas of Arish, Rafah and Sheikh Zuweid in North Sinai, later moving to include the western city of Bir al-Abd. At its peak in July 2015, the insurgency battled the Egyptian army for control of Sheikh Zuweid city. The connection to ISIS has drawn in Egypt's allies (namely Israel and the United States, who have provided reconnaissance and intelligence-gathering support) in the ongoing low-level insurgency, although the number and impact of insurgent attacks have diminished significantly in recent years.

In 2020, violence levels seemingly decreased, as the insurgency remained contained, meaning it was little affected by the coronavirus pandemic. However, small signs suggested attempts by Sinai Province to regroup in different parts of the peninsula. In July 2020, the militant group took control of a small portion of territory in the Bir al-Abd area, further west in the North Sinai governorate, raising ISIS flags atop buildings in four neighbouring villages. Furthermore, in early 2021 attacks focused on forces based in central parts of North Sinai, highlighting the continued inability of the EAF to eliminate the insurgency.

Despite the apparent reduction in violence, less potent attacks occurred frequently across the governorate, centred on the areas of Arish, Rafah and Sheikh Zuweid, while infrequent though higher-impact attacks took place in Bir al-Abd.[2] In addition to targeted attacks on security installations and personnel, Sinai Province continued terrorising local communities. A number of civilian kidnappings took place during 2020, as well as the execution of a Coptic man alleged to be a spy.

An attack on the Egypt–Israel pipeline in February 2020, claimed by Sinai Province (the first recorded attack since 2014), and an additional lower-impact attack in November suggested a possible change of focus by the militants towards strategic installations as opposed to purely military/security checkpoints or personnel. Historic attacks on the pipeline had sought to undermine the long-standing peace between Egypt and Israel, by undermining an agreement through which gas from the former was exported to the latter. However, given changes to Egypt's gas diplomacy and energy policy in recent years – with Israeli gas now imported to Egypt for liquification and further export – these attacks are now more reasonably viewed as direct attacks against the Egyptian state as they threaten a large and needed source of revenue and income for the country.

Conflict Parties

Egyptian Armed Forces (EAF)

Strength: 438,500 active armed personnel, with 479,000 in reserve (310,000 active army officers).

Areas of operation: North Sinai governorate, militarised triangle (Halayeb/Shalateen), Western Desert and Salloum border (the western border with Libya).

Leadership and structure: Supreme Council of the Armed Forces, led by Major-General Mohamed Zaki (defence minister). The EAF consists of the army, air force and navy; paramilitary forces are formed under the Ministry of Interior.

Middle East and North Africa

Egyptian Armed Forces (EAF)

Objectives: Control border security, and all national-security threats originating abroad. Since 2013 it has remilitarised the Sinai Peninsula, notably in North Sinai.

Opponents and affiliates/allies: Opposes Sinai Province, ABM, the Muslim Brotherhood.
Allies include US, Israel, United Kingdom, France, Germany, the United Arab Emirates (UAE) and Russia.

Resources/capabilities: The EAF does not publicise its defence budget. 2020 estimates placed the budget at US$4.11 billion, or 1.13% of GDP. It also receives around US$1.3bn in Foreign Military Financing annually from the US.

Directorate of Military Intelligence (DMI)

Strength: Unknown, although the ascension of Abdel Fattah Al-Sisi to Egypt's presidency in 2014 strengthened the DMI within the armed forces. Sisi was director of the DMI between 2010 and 2012.

Areas of operation: North Sinai governorate.

Leadership and structure: Major-General Khaled Megawer, December 2018–present.

Objectives: Protect the state, DMI and Sisi from any attack; monitor foreign threats towards Egypt (alongside the General Intelligence Services).

Opponents and affiliates/allies: Opposes Sinai Province. Allies include the EAF, General Intelligence Services.

Resources/capabilities: Unknown.

Sinai Province

Strength: Estimated 1,000–1,300 militants. Since 2019 includes small numbers of Palestinian militants and ISIS foreign fighters displaced from conflict in Iraq/Syria.

Areas of operation: North Sinai.

Leadership and structure: As of June 2019, led by Abu Jafar al-Ansari (*nom de guerre*). Some evidence suggests training camps in Sinai and the Gaza Strip. Several jihadists are known to have travelled to Syria for training, suggesting that the ISIS leadership structure periodically plays a role in the Sinai insurgency.

Objectives: Establish an Islamic state.

Opponents and affiliates/allies: Opposes the EAF, wider Egyptian security forces, Israel, non-Sunni Muslims and non-Muslims.

Resources/capabilities: Anecdotal evidence suggests most income is received via economic smuggling between the Sinai Peninsula and Gaza via tunnels. The group also benefits from an active weapons-smuggling war economy bringing weapons from Libya into Sinai.

Conflict Drivers

Economic and social

Marginalisation:
Long-standing grievances of citizens in Sinai are the main driver of the conflict and extremism in the region. The region remains separated – physically and figuratively – from the Egyptian mainland, a continued after-effect of the Arab–Israeli wars in the 1960s and 1970s.

The peninsula is underdeveloped, with sub-par access to basic public services compared to the rest of the country. For several years, Sinai residents were unable to officially register their citizenship. Since Sinai Province was established, attitudes have changed somewhat, with an increasing number of communities supporting the military against the jihadists, however anger at the regime for the marginalisation of Sinai citizens continues.

Despite the Sinai development plan, launched by the EAF in 2019, little has been achieved.[3] Reconstruction of the largely destroyed infrastructure across North Sinai cities has not progressed, and the electrical grid across much of the region remained damaged. A strict state of emergency and curfew continued, preventing freedom of movement and access to fuel. Meanwhile, economic prosperity remained elusive, with few job opportunities and continuous interruptions to education owing to ongoing security threats. A continued domestic and international media blackout over activity in the Sinai Peninsula eliminated any visibility on the region.

International

Geopolitical and regional drivers:
The Sinai Peninsula remained vulnerable to continued smuggling between Egypt and the Gaza Strip, along the Rafah border, given the ongoing besiegement of the latter by the Israeli government. Sinai Province has benefitted from the conflict in Libya, through increased weapons smuggling across Libya's eastern border into the mainland and up into the peninsula, as well as the uncontrolled movement of militants across borders.

The same ideological drivers behind ISIS's expansion across the Middle East region were potent in North Sinai, yet the conflict did not reach the level of confrontation previously seen in parts of Iraq and Syria. Continued cycles of radicalisation have not been effectively tackled or tempered domestically, and Sinai residents remained disenfranchised and marginalised in Egypt. However, the conflict in Sinai stayed local, with conflict drivers and recruitment efforts focused on the domestic Egyptian context. This distances Sinai Province slightly from the broader ISIS regional organisation, despite occasional training and funding support.

While security concerns have prompted informal US and Israeli support in intelligence and reconnaissance, this effort remained an almost entirely Egyptian undertaking towards an inherently Egyptian conflict.

Key Events in 2020–21

POLITICAL EVENTS

11 August–9 September 2020
Elections for the Senate (upper house of parliament) are held. The Mostaqbal Watan (Future of Homeland) party – allied to the Sisi regime – wins the majority of seats.

24 October–December
Elections for the House of Representatives are held. The Mostaqbal Watan (Future of Homeland) party wins the majority of seats.

24 December
The outgoing US administration makes a portion (US$75 million of the total US$1.3bn) of foreign/military aid to Egypt conditional on the release of political prisoners. Another portion of US$225m is made conditional on human-rights measures (subject to the use of the national-security waiver by the US Department of State).

MILITARY/VIOLENT EVENTS

3 February 2020
Sinai Province claims responsibility for an attack on the Egypt–Israel pipeline.

21 July
Sinai Province attacks an EAF camp near Rabaa, 23 kilometres west of the town of Bir al-Abd, and occupies at least four villages. Unverified video appears online of the ISIS flag flying on top of buildings.

22 July
The EAF launches operations in Bir al-Abd and announces the killing of 18 militants.

19 November
Sinai Province claims another attack on the Egypt–Israel gas pipeline. There are no casualties.

19 February 2021
Sinai Province claims five attacks on forces in central areas of North Sinai, including on military convoys, part of the 'Awakening' forces.

Conflict Outlook

Political scenarios

While still an ongoing conflict, the impact and implications of the North Sinai insurgency have diminished as instability in the peninsula has been effectively contained by government travel restrictions and increased security at the Sinai–mainland border, alongside continued media control limiting reporting from and about the area. The North Sinai insurgency remains a source of insecurity, but one that is largely out of sight, with political energy directed more towards security priorities in Libya, where Egypt is an important actor, and the long-standing water-security issue along the River Nile, where Ethiopian dam construction threatens Egypt's water supply.

Escalation potential and conflict-related risks

Despite a comparatively quiet year, the July 2020 events around Bir al-Abd served as a reminder of the enduring conflict drivers in the region, and Sinai Province's ability to regroup. The Bir al-Abd attacks in February 2021 showed the insurgent group's continued ability to move with relative ease across the peninsula and create new targets and conflict areas. Alternatively, these attempts to regroup in more central parts of the North Sinai governorate could also demonstrate the relative efficacy of military containment in the insurgency's more traditional areas of Arish, Bir al-Abd, Rafah and Sheikh Zuweid.

Thus, the potential of a significant escalation in the Sinai Peninsula appears low. Rather, the insurgency will remain largely contained to existing spheres of Sinai Province influence, while continuing to disrupt services and daily life for citizens across the conflict areas and general freedom of movement within the peninsula. The security presence is unlikely to disappear, given EAF control over the funding and procurement for development of the area, which has effectively remilitarised the peninsula for the foreseeable future. Although a significant escalation is not likely, neither is a complete resolution of the conflict, given the EAF's continued inability to wholly eliminate militant activity in the area. 'Tit-for-tat' attacks and persistent recruitment

– even if in low or decreasing numbers – will allow the low-level insurgency to continue.

Strategic implications and global influences

Instability in North Sinai continues to impact Egypt's ability to project an independent foreign policy and affects both national and regional strategic objectives – notably the security of the Suez Canal and broader Red Sea security – through the continuous diversion of resources and personnel to the peninsula. Ongoing smuggling routes, the threat of instability and an active low-level insurgency on the border with Israel limit Egypt's capacity to frame or focus policy goals away from militancy and security challenges, despite an increasing need to shift attention towards strategic issues such as the conflict in Libya, and more urgent priorities along the Nile Basin.

Red Sea security remains a potent driver of geopolitical tensions, notably pitting Egypt, Saudi Arabia and the UAE against Qatar and Turkey. Despite the confidence-building arrangements agreed among actors to resolve the 2017 Gulf Crisis, an erratic transition in Sudan and growing instability in the Horn of Africa have increased the urgency of controlling access to and the resources of the Red Sea. Meanwhile the Abraham Accords signed in September 2020 heralded a more prominent Israeli role in the regional security architecture with Arab states and appeared to have isolated Egypt by reducing the role it had played since the Camp David treaty as the gatekeeper for engagement with Israel.

Notes

[1]   A nationwide state of emergency was invoked in 2014, although the North Sinai governorate has been under a separate state of emergency since 2013. Despite the 2014 Constitution essentially making a state of emergency renewable only once, and lasting a maximum period of six months, Sisi has managed to extend the full state of emergency by merely allowing it to lapse for a day, and then ordering parliament to approve a new state of emergency. In addition, he amended the emergency law to allow for strengthened powers to be devolved from institutions to the presidency, notably the nomination of courts and judges. Currently the judges of the Emergency State Security Courts, which oversee most criminal cases in Egypt, are directly appointed by the president and his delegated authority. These courts have historically overseen foreign espionage cases, in periods where the country is not under a state of emergency.

[2]   Since 2013, a pattern has emerged of a regular uptick in violence and attacks by militants during the summer months of June, July and August. While no concrete explanation has been offered, some analysts attribute this to the anniversaries of the 2013 coup (in July) and the 2013 Rabaa massacre (in August).

[3]   Announcements in 2019 included an ambitious US$315m investment for the Sinai Peninsula, an increase of 75% on previous years. No census data is available for the peninsula, a particularly neglected area during the Mubarak regime, despite a national census being conducted once a decade by the government's statistics agency, the Central Agency for Public Mobilization and Statistics. Investment is tied significantly to the military's own development plans. The port-development projects and other city developments that have been announced are concurrent with significant development of new air, land and sea bases, and all contractors are military partners.

4 Sub-Saharan Africa

IDPs who fled armed-insurgent violence in the northern part of Cabo Delgado, Mozambique, gather for a community meeting

Overview

Armed conflict and instability in sub-Saharan Africa, historically among the most conflict-prone regions in the world, increased significantly during 2020 and early 2021 – to a record high, according to some measures.[1] This trend was coupled with the problems created by the economic paralysis that resulted from measures taken to contain the coronavirus pandemic, which caused regional GDP to contract by 1.9%[2] and poverty rates to increase considerably (with an estimated 40 million people falling into extreme poverty).[3] Although infection and mortality rates on the African continent were generally lower than elsewhere, the pandemic's economic toll may act as a conflict enabler for years to come, especially considering lost development gains, rising poverty

and food insecurity, not to mention dwindling aid resources, reduced fiscal space and looming debt crises faced by many African countries.

Nine of the 11 armed conflicts in sub-Saharan Africa covered by *The Armed Conflict Survey 2021* are primarily based in one country, while two are regional conflicts. The escalation of the insurgency in Mozambique's Cabo Delgado province prompted its inclusion for the first time. 2020 and early 2021 continued many of the regional trends and dynamics that have unfolded in the last decade: the proliferation of non-state armed groups (NSAGs), the intersection of jihadist transnational ideology with local grievances, the systematic targeting of civilians, and a considerable uptick in third-party interventions in internal conflicts by African states and great powers.

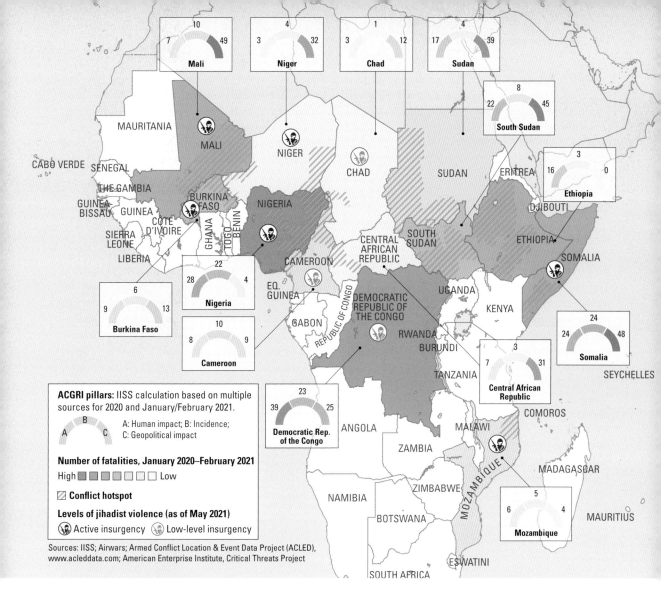

Sources: IISS; Airwars; Armed Conflict Location & Event Data Project (ACLED), www.acleddata.com; American Enterprise Institute, Critical Threats Project

Regional Trends

Proliferation of conflict

2020 marked a record high for state-based (28) and non-state-based (48) conflicts in sub-Saharan Africa since the end of the Second World War according to data by the Uppsala Conflict Data Program (UCDP), one of the leading quantitative sources on armed conflict globally.[4] Since 2010, conflicts in the region have skyrocketed: the number of conflicts between NSAGs in 2020 was more than three times the 2010 figure, while the number of internal armed conflicts (where the state is one of the conflict parties) also more than tripled. Furthermore, the number of countries (19) experiencing armed violence in 2020 was higher than any year since 1998. The number of conflict-affected countries has steadily grown but

at a slower pace than the number of conflicts, while fatality rates have declined overall, when accounting for population size.[5] The humanitarian needs of conflict-affected populations and forced displacement have also increased since 2010.[6] In sub-Saharan Africa in 2020, there were 6.8m internally displaced persons (IDPs), taking the total number to nearly 22m by the end of the year – the highest figure on record.[7] The region also hosted nearly 6.6m refugees by the end of 2020, including 250,000 new refugees.[8]

Increasing internationalisation

Internal conflicts have become strikingly internationalised. While 1991–2000 and 2001–10 respectively registered 23 and 19 internal conflicts with third-party intervention, in 2011–20 that number soared to 90. As inter-state wars have nearly disappeared,[9] competing interests and rivalries among African countries have increasingly manifested through transnational support for NSAGs by third-party states. Overt third-party interference has rendered many contemporary conflicts de facto regional wars – even if they are formally confined to a single state's boundaries (for example, the Central African Republic, CAR; the Democratic Republic of the Congo, DRC; and Somalia). The current geopolitical context further enables states to assert their interests more openly.[10]

Rise in jihadist violence

The trend of increasing jihadist violence was most clearly seen in West and Central Africa, as well as in Mozambique. In total, 11 countries in the region experienced jihadist violence in 2020.[11] Attacks by jihadist groups and other insurgencies dramatically escalated in several Western Sahel countries (Burkina Faso, Mali and Niger) and in the Lake Chad Basin (Nigeria, Chad and Cameroon). As a result, West and Central Africa is an extremely complex theatre of conflict with compounding security and humanitarian issues. In Cabo Delgado, Mozambique, a local

insurgency loosely and opaquely affiliated with the Islamic State, also known as ISIS or ISIL, escalated the conflict in 2020 and early 2021. Underestimated by the Mozambican authorities, the attacks caused high numbers of fatalities, displacement and economic disruption to an important offshore natural-gas project.

Regional Drivers

Sub-Saharan Africa's conflicts are characterised by intertwined drivers, which are grouped in the categories below. Weak governance and volatile political settlements remain central drivers of conflicts in the continent and underpin internal confrontations over power and/or territory. Perceptions of injustice, socio-economic marginalisation and inadequate service provision, including security, are among the grievances fuelling tensions in today's African countries. Additional drivers have also rendered some conflicts more intractable in recent years, including increasing illicit flows and rent-seeking resource extraction (i.e., logging, mining), climate-change-induced strains on resources and livelihoods, and

Figure 1: Conflict trends in sub-Saharan Africa, 1991–2020

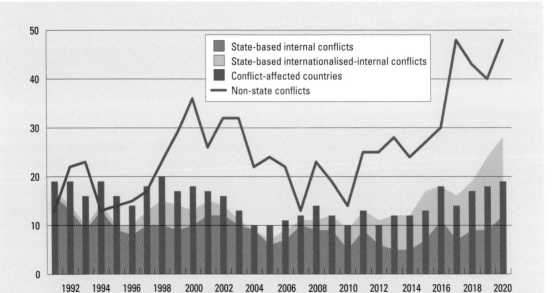

Sources: UCDP/PRIO Armed Conflict Dataset version 21.1; UCDP Non-State Conflict Dataset version 21.1; Nils Petter Gleditsch et al., 'Armed Conflict 1946–2001: A New Dataset', *Journal of Peace Research*, vol. 39, no. 5, September 2002, pp. 615–37; Ralph Sundberg, Kristine Eck and Joakim Kreutz, 'Introducing the UCDP Non-State Conflict Dataset', *Journal of Peace Research*, vol. 49, no. 2, March 2012, pp. 351–62; Therése Pettersson et al., 'Organized Violence 1989–2020, with a Special Emphasis on Syria', *Journal of Peace Research*, vol. 58, no. 4, July 2021, pp. 809–25.

the undermining of traditional customary institutions that play a role in dispute resolutions and in preventing violence from escalating.

Political and institutional

Weak governance and political settlements:
Weak political settlements, faltering governance and the exclusion of peripheral regions or groups have driven both ongoing protracted armed struggles (such as in the CAR, the DRC, Somalia, South Sudan and Sudan) and more recent conflicts (Ethiopia). For instance, Ethiopia's 2020 war in Tigray followed the 2018 power transition that ended nearly 30 years of rule by the Tigrayan minority. Contestation over the 1995 constitution's provision that sets borders between the ethnic states is at the core of Ethiopia's volatile political settlement: the contestation turned violent once power changed hands in 2018.

Dysfunctional electoral competition and active military participation in domestic politics are further manifestations of this driver, and they link to conflict. Presidential elections concern the control of state resources (i.e., donor aid and revenues from natural resources) and power over state institutions: as such, elections are a zero-sum game in which the runner-up(s) may face political marginalisation. Arguably, African democracies face increased risk of conflict when their rulers try to circumvent two-term limits: in 2021, more than two-thirds of conflict-affected African countries lacked effective two-term limits.[12] High economic stakes, weak legitimacy of institutions and low national cohesion reduces trust between contenders and increases the risk of violence. In turn, mobilising (ethnic) identity and manipulating grievances become critical tools for pursuing political and economic goals through violent or non-violent means.[13] Nevertheless, one notable success in 2020 was registered by Niger's first democratic transition of power (though this was not without electoral violence and fraud accusations) amid the Sahel's multiple conflicts. In contrast, the military takeover in Mali represented a political setback and underscored the fragility caused by expanding insurgencies and rising intercommunal violence across all Sahelian countries.

Economic and social

Centre–periphery dynamics:
Political and socio-economic marginalisation and neglect of peripheral regions by the centre and its elites fuel many sub-Saharan African conflicts, which commonly occur in the peripheries of countries and feature NSAGs fighting one another as well as state forces. However, the primary motivation is not power contestation or territorial gains but rather a combination of rent-seeking activities and competition over local sources of livelihoods (i.e., land, water, livestock). NSAGs may control territory and adopt alternative forms of governance in areas where the limited state presence is almost exclusively exercised through security forces. Abuses against civilians committed by these security forces often exacerbate local distrust of the centre. Moreover, the demise of traditional local institutions that previously played essential conflict-resolution functions, combined with an increasingly young population, appeared to accelerate conflict dynamics in diverse areas such as the Lake Chad Basin, the Sahel, Somalia and South Sudan.

Security

NSAGs and transnational jihadist extremism:
The proliferation of NSAGs – including Islamist extremist groups – is a further sign of deteriorating governance and of a broken social contract. With notable variations, armed groups have become more fragmented and incoherent and less willing to negotiate. They also engaged in indiscriminate violence against civilians. Transnational Islamist extremism has exploited and exacerbated local-level conflict dynamics (Mozambique, the Lake Chad Basin). By adapting different strategies and propaganda to local, national and international contexts and audiences, violent extremism has played out in multiple 'spaces'. The jihadist threat worsened in 2020 and early 2021, as groups such as Islamic State West Africa Province (ISWAP), al-Shabaab and Boko Haram (and their many affiliates) demonstrated their financial viability and capability of providing alternative governance structures and services, and conducted increasingly lethal attacks in all Lake Chad Basin countries, Mozambique and Somalia, among others.[14]

Regional Outlook

Prospects for peace

The prospects for conflict resolution in sub-Saharan Africa depend on the effectiveness of several multilateral, regional and bilateral initiatives that variously focus on peacekeeping, countering violent extremism (CVE), traditional peacemaking, security and development. In 2020, the United Nations (with missions in Abyei, CAR, DRC, Mali and South Sudan) and the African Union (AU) (through its mission in Somalia) remained active in peacekeeping operations that encompassed peace-enforcement goals and wider combat roles in addition to their traditional functions. December 2020 also saw the termination of the mandate of the UN–AU hybrid operation in Darfur. The European Union conducted three military training operations (in the CAR, Mali and Somalia) and a maritime operation to counter piracy off the Somali coast.

Sub-regional institutions have also increasingly acted as a forum for states to raise security concerns that have regional relevance. For instance, the Southern African Development Community (SADC) – a bloc of southern African nations – committed in principle to supporting Mozambique's security forces against the insurgency in Cabo Delgado, though concrete steps towards a regional military intervention remain to be determined.

In parallel, comprehensive approaches, including humanitarian, development and security components, have sought to address both active conflict situations and countries or areas at risk of violence. For instance, in 2020, the World Bank, which spearheaded some of these integrated approaches in the Sahel and the Lake Chad Basin, launched a strategy that enhances its mandate on addressing conflict globally, through dedicated resources to address fragility and conflict challenges in some of the most difficult environments.

Escalation potential and spillover risks

The escalation of conflict in 2020 and early 2021 has left various potential hotspots. Several countries in West Africa and the Sahel are already suffering from transnational regional wars that could spill into Côte d'Ivoire and Senegal. Similarly, the rising conflict in northern Mozambique threatens Tanzania's ability to contain the spillover from the insurgent threat. In the Horn of Africa, given Ethiopia's role as regional hegemon, the war in Tigray and the country's continuing insecurity could potentially destabilise the whole sub-region. Eritrea's military involvement in Tigray is already a concern. Parliamentary and presidential election results in Ethiopia and Somalia

respectively will also be watched to gauge regional trends.

Geopolitical changes

Regional and global trends point to a new phase of foreign intervention in Africa. On a global level, the post-Cold War era of cooperation on conflict resolution in Africa and elsewhere has given way to the return of great-power intervention. This may be pursued via economic means and security-focused initiatives – through diverse strategies including counter-terrorism and stabilisation operations – and through local actors (state and non-state alike). In particular, the shifting approaches of the United States and France could make 2021 an inflection point for the region.

The US military approach to addressing jihadist threats in Somalia, Mali and Niger has had limited success and extremism has spread elsewhere in the continent. The Biden administration has shown a renewed engagement with the continent, for example, through the appointment and swift deployment of Jeffrey Feltman as US Special Envoy for the Horn of Africa in early 2021. The implementation of the Global Fragility Act may also represent an opportunity to rebalance soft-power tools and military interventions through greater US engagement on development and governance issues in conflict-affected countries.

In early 2021, France announced a shift in the size and mandate of the 5,000-strong *Operation Barkhane* in the Sahel, which has provided military support to Burkina Faso, Chad, Mali, Mauritania and Niger since 2014. It would be easy to dismiss the operation as a failure, given the expansion of the jihadist threat.[15] The new French strategy will likely focus on securing development gains in the region and encouraging Sahelian countries to take more responsibility for their security. France is also likely to implement more targeted counter-terrorism operations with the support of European partners. Meanwhile, the EU's European Peace Facility provides almost US$6 billion for military support to African governments to combat extremism and protect civilians.

Other global powers have pursued their respective interests in the region through diverse strategies. China has focused on economic and infrastructure investments that come together with alternative governance structures, although some signs suggest that such investments are beginning to slow down.[16] Meanwhile, Russia's more direct engagement in some of the armed conflicts in the region, through heavy-handed security support and tightening political ties with client states, such as the CAR, seems likely to continue in the short term.

Notes

[1] See, for example, Therése Pettersson et al., 'Organized Violence 1989–2020, with a Special Emphasis on Syria', *Journal of Peace Research*, vol. 58, no. 4, July 2021, pp. 809–25; and Nils Petter Gleditsch et al., 'Armed Conflict 1946–2001: A New Dataset', *Journal of Peace Research*, vol. 39, no. 5, September 2002, pp. 615–37.

[2] International Monetary Fund (IMF), 'Regional Economic Outlook: Sub-Saharan Africa: Navigating a Long Pandemic', World Economic and Financial Surveys, April 2021.

[3] World Bank, 'World Bank's Response to COVID-19 (Coronavirus) in Africa', Factsheet, 8 April 2021.

[4] UCDP disaggregates between state-based (i.e., at least one conflict party is a state) and non-state-based armed conflicts (i.e., conflict parties are exclusively NSAGs), and defines an armed conflict as the 'use of armed force between two parties' that 'results in at least 25 battle-related deaths in one calendar year'. Conflict 'parties' can be either state- or non-state-based depending on the type of conflict under consideration. Based on this definition, each country can have several different ongoing conflicts per year. This methodology explains the larger number of conflicts accounted for by UCDP compared to the 11 conflicts covered in *The Armed Conflict Survey 2021*, which adopts the country as primary unit of analysis. See UCDP/PRIO Armed Conflict Dataset, version 21.1; and UCDP, 'UCDP Non-State Conflict Dataset version 21.1', UCDP Dataset Download Center. See also Gleditsch et al., 'Armed Conflict 1946–2001: A New Dataset'; Pettersson et al., 'Organized Violence 1989–2020, with a Special Emphasis on Syria'; and Ralph Sundberg, Kristine Eck and Joakim Kreutz, 'Introducing the UCDP Non-State Conflict Dataset', *Journal of Peace Research*, vol. 49, no. 2, April 2012, pp. 351–62.

[5] The six countries with the greatest fatality rate per capita during the last decade were CAR, DRC, Mali, Somalia, South Sudan and Sudan. See Jakkie Cilliers, *The Future of Africa: Challenges and Opportunities* (Cham, Switzerland: Palgrave Macmillan, 2021), pp. 282–5.

[6] Ongoing International Committee of the Red Cross (ICRC) research indicates that an estimated 70m people live in 'hard to reach places', particularly on the front lines of conflict, where they fall beyond effective control of governments and therefore have limited access to essential services. See ICRC, 'Enhancing Strategic Collaboration with Non-state Partners for "Last Mile Solutions" in Conflict-affected Situations', Draft Background Non-paper for IDA20, unpublished, 9 April 2021.

[7] Internal Displacement Monitoring Centre (IDMC), 'Global Report on Internal Displacement (2021): Internal displacement in a changing climate', 28 May 2021, p. 25.

[8] UN High Commissioner for Refugees, 'Global Trends: Forced Displacement in 2020', 11 June 2021.

[9] UCDP/PRIO recorded four different inter-state conflicts in sub-Saharan Africa since the end of the Cold War, cumulatively running for seven years: Cameroon–Nigeria (1996), Eritrea–Ethiopia (1998–2000, 2016), Djibouti–Eritrea (2008) and South Sudan–Sudan (2012).

[10] See Paul D. Williams, 'Continuity and Change in War and Conflict in Africa', *PRISM*, vol. 6, no. 4, May 2017, pp. 33–45; Alex de Waal, 'Africa's "Civil Wars" Are Regional Nightmares', *Foreign Policy*, 22 October 2019; and Noel Twagiramungu et al., 'Re-describing Transnational Conflict in Africa', *Journal of Modern African Studies*, vol. 57, no. 3, October 2019, pp. 377–91.

[11] Critical Threats Project, 'Figure 1. The Salafi-Jihadi Movement in Africa: May 2021', American Enterprise Institute, 12 May 2021.

[12] Joseph Siegle and Candace Cook, 'Circumvention of Term Limits Weakens Governance in Africa', Africa Center for Strategic Studies, 17 May 2021.

[13] For context, see Charles G. Thomas and Toyin Falola, *Secession and Separatist Conflicts in Post-colonial Africa* (Calgary, ON: University of Calgary Press, 2020).

[14] Critical Threats Project, 'Figure 1. The Salafi-Jihadi Movement in Africa: May 2021'.

[15] The five Sahelian countries are also part of a regional cooperation vehicle – the G5 Sahel Joint Force – to promote common development and security goals, as well as share military and intelligence capabilities in the fight against extremists.

[16] Zainab Usman, 'What Do We Know About Chinese Lending in Africa?', Carnegie Endowment for International Peace, 2 June 2021.

THE SAHEL

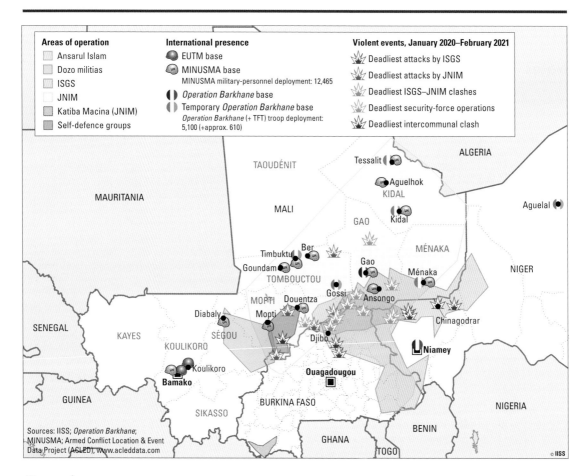

Areas of operation
- Ansarul Islam
- Dozo militias
- ISGS
- JNIM
- Katiba Macina (JNIM)
- Self-defence groups

International presence
- EUTM base
- MINUSMA base
  MINUSMA military-personnel deployment: 12,465
- *Operation Barkhane* base
- Temporary *Operation Barkhane* base
  Operation Barkhane (+ TFT) troop deployment:
  5,100 (+approx. 610)

Violent events, January 2020–February 2021
- Deadliest attacks by ISGS
- Deadliest attacks by JNIM
- Deadliest ISGS–JNIM clashes
- Deadliest security-force operations
- Deadliest intercommunal clash

Sources: IISS; *Operation Barkhane*; MINUSMA; Armed Conflict Location & Event Data Project (ACLED), www.acleddata.com

© IISS

Overview

Over the past decade, the Sahel has experienced unprecedented escalation in armed hostilities despite several multilateral military interventions, driven by myriad non-state armed groups (NSAGs), self-defence militias and intercommunal fighting.

The multifaceted and interrelated conflicts in the Sahel were triggered by the 2012 secessionist uprising by Tuareg and Islamist NSAGs in northern Mali. The insurgency saw a coalition of NSAGs oust the underfunded military and political administrations from Mali's northern and central regions, prompting the intervention of France, the United Nations and other international organisations such as the African Union (AU) and the Economic Community of West African States (ECOWAS). A popular uprising also brought down long-time Burkinabe president Blaise Compaoré in 2014, exacerbating the regional

security vacuum. The involvement of France and international organisations, and a subsequent 2015 peace agreement – the Algiers accord – halted the intense hostilities and managed to, momentarily, put the separatist and Islamist NSAGs on the back foot.

Nevertheless, Mali's militant groups – such as the Group to Support Islam and Muslims (JNIM) – managed to regroup, allying with al-Qaeda and later the Islamic State (also known as ISIS or ISIL), and clashes have expanded and intensified throughout the region since 2016. These groups have maintained and expanded their presence in northern, central and southern Mali and moved into neighbouring Burkina Faso and Niger, carrying out high-impact attacks in the capitals of Bamako and Ouagadougou. Political instability, government weakness, highly porous borders and long-established transport and

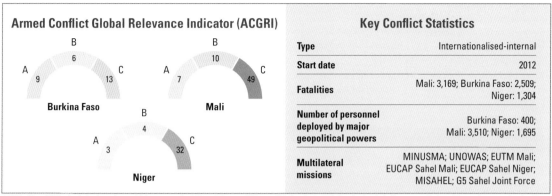

Key Conflict Statistics	
Type	Internationalised-internal
Start date	2012
Fatalities	Mali: 3,169; Burkina Faso: 2,509; Niger: 1,304
Number of personnel deployed by major geopolitical powers	Burkina Faso: 400; Mali: 3,510; Niger: 1,695
Multilateral missions	MINUSMA; UNOWAS; EUTM Mali; EUCAP Sahel Mali; EUCAP Sahel Niger; MISAHEL; G5 Sahel Joint Force

ACGRI pillars: IISS calculation based on multiple sources for 2020 and January/February 2021 (scale: 0–100). Results for the indicator are displayed for each country involved in the conflict. A: Human impact; B: Incidence; C: Geopolitical impact. See Notes on Methodology and Data Appendix for further details on Key Conflict Statistics.

communication routes have also allowed militants to conduct attacks in neighbouring littoral states, such as Côte d'Ivoire.

While the coronavirus pandemic slowed down international efforts to stabilise the wider region, it had a minimal impact on the Sahelian conflicts. 2020 and early 2021 saw an unprecedented 6,982 people killed across Burkina Faso, Mali and Niger.[1] The number of refugees and internally displaced persons (IDPs) across the region increased by more than one million.[2]

The intensity and sophistication of militant attacks also grew. After ISIS-affiliated militants conducted their hitherto deadliest attack on Nigerien soil, in the western town of Inates, in December 2019, fighters of the same group conducted an even deadlier assault on a military base in Chinagodrar at the beginning of January 2020.

The expanding insurgencies also undermined government stability, as highlighted by prolonged anti-government protests and a military coup in Mali in August 2020. Intercommunal fighting concomitantly caused an unprecedented number of fatalities and accounted for the vast majority of casualties and human-rights violations in the reporting period. Such violations were also increasingly carried out by state security forces, sometimes with impunity. In turn, this fuelled a vicious circle of inter-communal violence, anti-government sentiment and fertile recruiting ground for armed militants.

The launch of the Coalition for the Sahel (CFS) in January 2020 sought to bring a more holistic response to the crisis, including development assistance. As part of the CFS, European powers pledged increased deployment through the Task Force Takuba (TFT), a multilateral mission under the command of France's *Operation Barkhane*. Chad also significantly increased its military deployment to the Group of 5 Sahel Joint Force (FC-G5S).

Conflict Parties

Malian Armed Forces (FAMa)

Strength: 13,000 active military personnel and 7,800 paramilitary personnel (1,800 gendarmerie, 1,000 national police, 3,000 militia and 2,000 national guard).

Areas of operation: Northern and central Mali, particularly in the tri-border Liptako-Gourma area near Burkina Faso and Niger.

Leadership: General Oumar Diarra (chief of general staff), who replaced Abdoulaye Coulibaly following the August 2020 coup.

Structure: Consists of the army, the National Gendarmerie and the National Guard.

History: Created at independence in 1960. Following years of underinvestment, FAMa has been significantly strengthened over the past decade.

Objectives: Counter-terrorism and territorial security.

Opponents: Ansarul Islam, Islamic State in the Greater Sahara (ISGS), JNIM.

Affiliates/allies: Burkina Faso, ECOWAS, European Union, FC-G5S, France, Niger, UN Multidimensional Stabilization Mission in Mali (MINUSMA), United States.

Resources/capabilities: Mali's defence budget for 2020 was US$787m (4.46% of GDP), up from US$722m in 2019.

Sub-Saharan Africa

Niger Armed Forces (FAN)

Strength: 5,300 active military personnel (5,200 and 100 air force) and 5,400 paramilitary (1,400 gendarmerie, 2,500 republican guard and 1,500 national police).

Areas of operation: Regions of Tahoua and Tillabéri, western Niger, as well as the southeastern region of Diffa.

Leadership: Brigadier-General Salifou Modi, appointed in January 2020.

Structure: Composed of the army, the air force, the gendarmerie, the republican guard and the national police.

History: Founded in 1961 and initially officered by French Colonial Forces, it was reorganised following the 1974 military coup. In 2003, it integrated the Nigerien air force.

Objectives: Maintain internal and border security against Islamist NSAGs and protect territorial integrity.

Opponents: Ansarul Islam, ISGS, Islamic State West Africa Province (ISWAP), JNIM.

Affiliates/allies: Burkina Faso, FC-G5S, France, Mali, MINUSMA.

Resources/capabilities: Niger's defence budget for 2020 was US$211m (1.54% of GDP), up from US$172m in 2019.

Burkina Faso Armed Forces (FABF)

Strength: 11,200 active military personnel (6,400 army, 600 air force, 4,200 gendarmerie). There are also 45,000 personnel in the People's Militia (reserve military/conscripts) and 250 active paramilitary personnel.

Areas of operation: In 2019, northern and eastern Burkina Faso, particularly the border area with Mali. Also conducted a joint mission with Ivoirian forces along the shared border between April and May 2020.

Leadership: Brigadier-General Moïse Minoungou (chief of staff), since January 2019.

Structure: Comprised of the army, the air force, the gendarmerie and paramilitary forces.

History: Reached its current form in 1985 with the inauguration of the air force.

Objectives: Maintain national security and territorial integrity, and counter jihadist groups.

Opponents: Ansarul Islam, ISGS, JNIM.

Affiliates/allies: Benin, Côte d'Ivoire, FC-G5S, France, Ghana, Mali, MINUSMA, Niger.

Resources/capabilities: Burkina Faso's defence budget for 2020 was US$388m (2.34% of GDP).

Group to Support Islam and Muslims (JNIM)

Strength: 800–2,000 fighters.[3]

Areas of operation: Northern and central Mali, northern and eastern Burkina Faso, and, to a limited extent, western Niger and southern Mali and the rest of Burkina Faso.

Leadership: Iyad Ag Ghaly, a long-time Tuareg militant who is also the leader of Ansar Dine, one of the main groups constituting JNIM.

Structure: Created as an alliance of equals.

Objectives: Establish an Islamic state in the Sahel, replacing existing state structures and expelling foreign forces.

Opponents: FAMa, FC-G5S, ISGS, MINUSMA, *Operation Barkhane*, TFT.

Affiliates/allies: Al-Qaeda, al-Qaeda in the Islamic Maghreb–North Africa (AQIM–North Africa), Ansarul Islam, Katiba Serma.

Resources/capabilities: Heavy weaponry; improvised explosive devices (IEDs), including those that are vehicle borne and suicide-vehicle borne.

Islamic State in the Greater Sahara (ISGS)

Strength: 200–425 fighters.[4]

Areas of operation: Mali (Gao, Ménaka and Mopti), western Niger (Tahoua and Tillabéri regions) and Burkina Faso (Boucle du Mouhon, Cascades and East).

Leadership: Adnan Abu Walid al-Sahrawi.

Structure: Unclear.

History: ISGS split from al-Mourabitoun in 2015 and pledged allegiance to ISIS, but was only formally recognised as a *wilayat* (province) of the Islamic State in 2019 and was grouped together with ISWAP in ISIS claims thereafter.

Objectives: Establish an Islamic caliphate based on strict interpretation of the Koran and adherence to ISIS ideology.

Opponents: FABF, FAMa, FAN, JNIM, MINUSMA, *Operation Barkhane*.

Affiliates/allies: ISIS, ISWAP, Katiba Salaheddine, other smaller militias.

Resources/capabilities: IEDs and light weaponry.

Ansarul Islam

Strength: Very few estimates are available, but estimated to be about 200 fighters.[5]

Areas of operation: Northern and eastern parts of Burkina Faso, as well as parts of Mali (Timbuktu and Mopti regions).

Leadership: Jafar Dicko – brother of Malam Ibrahim Dicko, the founder who passed away in 2017.

Structure: No clear structure. While recruiting mostly among Fulani and Rimaibe communities, it does not pursue an identity-based insurgency.

History: Formed in 2016 as a local insurgency against provincial authorities and the prevailing social order in Soum, Burkina Faso. The group has become one of the most active groups in northern and eastern Burkina Faso.

Objectives: The founder, Malam Ibrahim Dicko, was a preacher of radical Islam who vowed to resurrect the ancient kingdom of Djeelgodji. Its main objective now is to challenge the social order in Burkina Faso.

Opponents: FABF, FAMa, FC-G5S, ISGS, *Operation Barkhane*.

Affiliates/allies: Regularly cooperates with JNIM, with some indications that it has also previously cooperated with ISGS. However, it is not formally affiliated with either of the alliances.

Resources/capabilities: IEDs and light weaponry.

Self-defence groups

Strength: Dozens of groups spread across the region, varying greatly in size and capabilities.

Areas of operation: Central and southern Mali, primarily in Mopti and Ségou; northern, western and southern Burkina Faso; Tillabéri, Niger.

Leadership: Most groups are community-led militias and structures may vary greatly. Dan Na Ambassagou, led by Youssouf Toloba, is the best-known militia, operating in central Mali and northern Burkina Faso.

Structure: Self-defence groups are usually community-based and organised along ethnic affiliations. These include Bambara, Dogon, Fulani, Fulsé, Mossi and Tuareg Imghad.

History: Self-defence militias proliferated following the 2012 Tuareg rebellion in Mali, with violence increasing and spreading across the region since then. Their presence is symptomatic of governments' inability to impose territorial control.

Objectives: Protect local communities from external threats and maintain law and order on behalf of state authorities.

Opponents: These depend on the ethnic affiliation of individual groups. There is growing antagonism between Fulani groups on one side, and Bambara and Dogon groups on the other, partly due to recruitment by Islamist NSAGs among Fulani communities.

Affiliates/allies: National authorities (FABF, FAMa, FAN).

Resources/capabilities: Light and often old weaponry.

Coordination of Azawad Movements (CMA)

Strength: Exact numbers are unclear. Prior to the 2015 Algiers accord they were estimated to be between 800 and 4,000.[6]

Areas of operation: Northern Mali, including the towns of Aguelhok, Diré, Gao, Kidal, Ménaka, Tessalit and Timbuktu.

Leadership: As a coalition between several NSAGs, the leadership rotates on a regular basis. The head of the Arab Movement of Azawad (MAA) Sidi Brahim Ould Sidati was also the president of CMA.

Structure: An umbrella organisation that includes the National Movement for the Liberation of Azawad (MNLA), the High Council for the Unity of Azawad (HCUA) and a CMA-affiliated faction of the MAA.

History: Historically dominated by Tuareg separatist militias fighting for the independence of Azawad, a claimed area in northern Mali. It was created to represent separatist views among combatants, as part of the 2015 Algiers accord.

Objectives: Self-determination. Independence is not an objective anymore but may become so again due to friction of the implementation of the Algiers accord.

Opponents: FAMa, ISGS, JNIM, Platform. Fighting occurs sporadically with all these forces.

Affiliates/allies: Formally cooperates with FAMa, MINUSMA and Platform, but has previously collaborated with Islamist NSAGs, with indications of continued relations since the signing of the 2015 peace agreement suggesting fluid allegiances.

Resources/capabilities: Small arms and light weaponry, remnants of the Libyan military arsenal left behind after the 2011 ousting of Muammar Gadhafi in Libya.

Sub-Saharan Africa

Platform

Strength: Not known.

Areas of operation: Northern Mali, including the towns of Bourem, Gao, Gossi, Gourma, Ménaka, Tilemsi and Timbuktu.

Leadership: A loose alliance of autonomous NSAGs and self-defence militias.

Structure: An umbrella organisation which includes the Imghad Tuareg Self-Defence Group and Allies (GATIA), the MAA–Platform faction (MAA–PF) and the Coordination for the Movements and Fronts of Patriotic Resistance (CMFPR-1).

History: The coalition formed in June 2014 during peace negotiations in a bid to represent the views of NSAGs that support Malian unity.

Objectives: Formed in support of Mali's territorial integrity. However, its members have widely differing agendas and interests, with some engaging in local disputes while others support the FAMa as security forces.

Opponents: CMA and Islamist NSAGs.

Affiliates/allies: FAMa, MINUSMA, *Operation Barkhane*. The MAA–PF has been accused of having close links with Islamist NSAGs.

Resources/capabilities: Small arms and light weaponry.

French armed forces (*Operation Barkhane* and Task Force Takuba (TFT))

Strength: *Operation Barkhane*: 5,100 French troops. TFT troops include around 60 from the Czech Republic, 105 from Denmark, 95 from Estonia, 200 committed by Italy, 150 from Sweden, with political support from the United Kingdom.[7]

Areas of operation: Burkina Faso, Chad, Mali, Mauritania and Niger, with a particular focus on the Liptako-Gourma tri-border area between Burkina Faso, Mali and Niger.

Leadership: General Marc Conruyt (commander of *Operation Barkhane*).

History: *Operation Barkhane* replaced *Operation Serval* in August 2014, expanding the French forces' mandate beyond Mali's borders across the wider Sahel. Following a summit in Pau, southern France, in January 2020, deployment increased to 5,100 troops. In addition, the force was further enhanced by Task Force Takuba, a contingent of special forces from individual EU member states, which is due to become fully operational in 2021.

Objectives: Enhance the capacities and capabilities of regional host states, support international forces, engage in direct combat against terrorist NSAGs and help improve governance including through medical aid.

Structure: *Operation Barkhane* has three permanent support bases in N'Djamena (Chad), Niamey (Niger) and Gao (Mali), in addition to six temporary support bases spread across the G5 Sahel countries. The operation includes ground combat forces, airland, and air elements, as well as intelligence capabilities. The TFT increases *Operation Barkhane*'s capacity.

Opponents: Ansarul Islam, ISGS, JNIM.

Affiliates/allies: Canada, Czech Republic, Denmark, Estonia, Germany, G5 Sahel countries, MINUSMA, Spain, Sweden, UK, US.

Resources/capabilities: Primarily composed of special forces, with access to sophisticated military equipment including uninhabited aerial vehicles (UAVs), infantry-combat vehicles and combat helicopters.

United Nations Multidimensional Stabilization Mission in Mali (MINUSMA)

Strength: The UN Security Council (UNSC) authorised a total of 13,289 military personnel for MINUSMA, with troops being contributed by 32 member states. As of February 2021, there were 12,465 military personnel deployed in-country.[8]

Areas of operation: Countrywide, with a concentration of forces in the central and northern regions.

Leadership: Lieutenant-General Dennis Gyllensporre (force commander).

History: Established in April 2013 by UNSC Resolution 2100 to support the Malian authorities and stabilise the country following the 2012 Tuareg rebellion. In the same year, ECOWAS's African-led International Support Mission in Mali (AFISMA) was incorporated under MINUSMA's command. Resolution 2531 extended its mandate to June 2021. MINUSMA has seen the largest number of casualties among UN peacekeeping operations. Alongside MINUSMA, there are a series of multilateral organisations and missions, including the European Union Training Mission (EUTM) in Mali and the African Union Mission for Mali and the Sahel (MISAHEL),

which support with capacity-building and peacebuilding activities, including delivering humanitarian aid.

Structure: As of February 2021, 12,465 military, 1,760 police and 3,384 civilians. The top three contributors of soldiers and police are Bangladesh, Senegal and Togo.

Objectives: Ensure the implementation of the 2015 Algiers accord, including the protection of civilians, the reduction of communal violence and the restoration of state presence in central and northern Mali.

Opponents: Ansarul Islam, ISGS, JNIM.

Affiliates/allies: FAMa, FC-G5S, *Operation Barkhane*.

Resources/capabilities: A US$1.3 billion budget for 2021, renewed on an annual basis. Military equipment is advanced, including armoured mine-resistant personnel carriers, and combat helicopters.

G5 Sahel Joint Force (FC-G5S)	
Strength: Approximately 6,100 troops provided by the five member countries Burkina Faso, Chad, Mali, Mauritania and Niger.[9]	**History:** While the G5 Sahel as an organisation was established in 2014, the joint force was created in February 2017 with the support of France and the UN, to address threats across the Sahel, including terrorism and transnational organised crime, such as smuggling of goods and human trafficking.
Areas of operation: Border areas of Burkina Faso, Chad, Mali, Mauritania and Niger.	
Leadership: Nigerien General Oumarou Namata Gazama replaced Mauritanian General Hanena Ould Sidi as commander of the FC-G5S in July 2019.	**Objectives:** Strengthen security along the borders of member states through intelligence sharing and the deployment of joint patrols.
Structure: A joint counter-terrorism task force, with troops across eight battalions in three sectors across all five countries.	**Opponents:** Ansarul Islam, ISGS, JNIM.
	Affiliates/allies: Foreign and regional armed forces, MINUSMA.
	Resources/capabilities: Suffers from endemic under-funding and unpredictable financing. Troop deployment is slow due to a lack of operating bases, capacity and equipment.

Conflict Drivers

Economic and social

Intercommunal violence and competition over resources:
Spiralling intercommunal violence since 2019, particularly in Burkina Faso and Mali, has weakened social cohesion and undermined development efforts. This is true too in parts of Niger, where communities outside the major urban areas have felt increasingly marginalised.

Furthermore, increasing competition for resources has also played a role in driving violence. On the one hand, organised criminal activity has flourished amid ineffective government control, providing NSAGs with significant financial and material resources to support their operations. Diversified finance streams include the collection of *zakat* (Islamic duties), extortion and the smuggling of goods, such as motorbikes, fuel and livestock. Often these activities have effectively created a double taxation system for local populations. On the other hand, large numbers of forcibly displaced people seeking jobs in the informal sector in their new host communities have increased competition for employment, which in turn has fuelled grievances and animosity between communities.

Security

Increasing number and sophistication of NSAGs:
The multiplication of violent actors in the Sahel is the main driver of violence. The eruption of armed hostilities in northern and central Mali in 2012 and the Burkinabe uprising of 2014 created a security vacuum that allowed NSAGs to establish a durable foothold from which to also expand into Niger. The number of NSAGs in the region has more than doubled since 2012, and two main alliances (JNIM and ISGS) have polarised groups along allegiances to either al-Qaeda or ISIS. Ansarul Islam is a third major force that also appears to be aligned with JNIM, although with some anecdotal evidence of cooperation with ISGS too.

These groups have conducted increasingly ambitious, sophisticated and deadly attacks against state security forces and local communities, competing for influence and territorial control. Their zones of operations have grown too: both ISGS and JNIM have moved southwards towards the northern borders of Benin, Côte d'Ivoire and Togo, and also westwards towards Senegal.

In response to this mounting insecurity, self-defence groups and local militias have proliferated, partly due to the breakdown in overall state security responses and in order to respond to alleged mutual targeting of local communities. For instance, JNIM allies have been perceived to be recruiting among Fulani communities, prompting Dogon self-defence militias to target such communities in central Mali and northern Burkina Faso. In 2020, these self-defence groups and local militias were at times responsible for the highest number of human-rights violations, accounting for 35–40% of incidents recorded by MINUSMA on a quarterly basis.[10]

Overlapping and ineffective state and international security responses:

The proliferation of self-defence groups is a result of failed state security responses and unsuccessful French and multilateral military interventions. It also reflects the failure to implement the 2015 Algiers accord – which had ended the Malian civil war and the 2012 northern uprising – as sporadic fighting continues between signatory parties. While security budgets have been growing over the past five years in all countries involved, they remain inadequate, which has undermined the effectiveness of security strategies.

Attempts to pool resources and strengthen capabilities through initiatives such as the FC-G5S, MINUSMA, *Operation Barkhane*, and more recently the TFT, have had little impact. Despite the wide array of actors present in the region, funding issues, limited troop numbers and a narrow focus on counter-terrorism measures by international partners has reduced their efficacy. Until 2020, France was the only non-Sahelian troop-contributing country deploying to all three affected states (Burkina Faso, Mali and Niger), while MINUSMA and the EUTM only operate in Mali. The US has provided material and reconnaissance support to *Operation Barkhane*, capabilities training to local forces, and conducted discrete combat missions. However, resistance to deployment has grown in both France and the US, with more than half of the French population opposed to *Operation Barkhane*'s continued deployment in the region, as of January 2021.[11]

Political and Military Developments

Coup in Mali

The primary political development in 2020 was the military coup in Mali in August. The coup was preceded by two months of widespread anti-government protests denouncing the ineffective implementation of the 2015 Algiers accord, growing insecurity and human-rights violations, election-fraud allegations and increasing resentment towards France.

A military junta took control of the government and in September pledged to launch a political transition and hold democratic elections. The National Transitional Council (CNT) – the transitional government, established in October – effectively launched an 18-month transitional period. However, many in civil society remained suspicious of the CNT, due to its unrepresentative make-up and continued military control. The CNT's action plan, presented in February 2021, did little to reduce these grievances. The highly ambitious plan, with over 200 objectives, echoes overtures made in February 2020 by then Malian president Ibrahim Boubacar Keïta (IBK) recommending negotiations with JNIM and the recalibration of the Algiers accord.

General elections in Burkina Faso and Niger

General elections in Burkina Faso in November 2020 saw President Roch Marc Christian Kaboré re-elected, but with fewer votes than in 2015. The results favoured the Congress for Democracy and Progress (CDP) party of ousted former president Blaise Compaoré. The party, banned from running in 2015, saw its presidential candidate obtain 15.54% of the vote in 2020.[12]

General elections were also held in Niger in December 2020. The incumbent president Mahamadou Issoufou did not seek re-election, and his anointed successor, Mohamed Bazoum, was declared winner in a run-off held in February 2021. Opposition protests in Niamey and other cities erupted in the weeks following the vote and Bazoum's rival, Mahamane Ousmane, made claims of electoral fraud, laying the basis for a protracted period of civil unrest and political instability.[13]

A new, 'holistic' approach to security

Following growing tensions between France and its FC-G5S partners, the CFS was announced at a security summit in January 2020. This four-pillar strategy seeks to combine humanitarian and development assistance with increased counter-terrorism efforts and a targeted military deployment to the tri-border area of Liptako-Gourma, with a particular focus on degrading ISGS's capabilities. It also attempts to reduce France's profile by involving special forces from other individual EU member countries and implementing a more holistic approach that links security, development and humanitarian concerns.

Symbolic victories and leadership changes

Operation Barkhane achieved several strategic and symbolic victories in the reporting period, notably the killing of hundreds of Islamist fighters including senior figures such as Abdelmalek Droukdel (*nom de guerre* Abu Musab Abdel Wadoud), the leader of AQIM–North Africa, which is allied to JNIM. While the loss of such experienced and battle-hardened leaders may undermine JNIM's strategic and kinetic capabilities, such killings also risk fuelling deadlier attacks and intensifying attempts to provoke intercommunal antagonism.

Expanding war-affected areas and intensifying Islamist attacks

Despite multilateral efforts to contain it, violence continued and spread, with increasingly sophisticated ISGS and JNIM attacks and deadlier intercommunal clashes. In January 2020, ISGS launched its deadliest attack to date through a complex assault on a Nigerien military base in Chinagodrar, just one month after the same group had staged its hitherto deadliest attack in Inates.

JNIM and ISGS-affiliated groups expanded to southern and southwestern Mali (Ségou and Kayes), as well as southern Burkina Faso. In June 2020, presumed JNIM militants attacked a joint gendarmerie and military outpost in Kafolo, northern Côte d'Ivoire, killing a dozen security-force personnel on the Burkinabe border, in the first Islamist attack on Ivoirian soil since 2016. Finally, ISGS militants also staged several attacks in southern Niger, including the killing of six French humanitarian workers in August 2020.

The ISGS's and JNIM's expansionary ambitions led to a series of battles during the first half of 2020 in northern and eastern Burkina Faso and northern Mali in areas where their presence had historically overlapped without violence, ending what had hitherto been called the 'Sahelian exception'.[14]

Key Events in 2020–21

POLITICAL EVENTS

12 January 2020
CMA and Platform formally agree to improve security in Ménaka city and region, stopping short of pledging to remove fighters, as requested by MINUSMA.

13 January
FC-G5S and France announce the launch of Coalition for the Sahel and Paris announces increased troop deployment.

10 February
Malian president IBK says the government is open to negotiations with JNIM.

8 March
JNIM leader Iyad Ag Ghaly says he is prepared to negotiate with the Malian government on the condition that foreign forces leave the country.

27 March
Launch of Task Force Takuba.

29 March
Legislative elections take place in Mali.

29 March
Burkina Faso orders lockdown of Ouagadougou and Bobo-Dioulasso over COVID-19.

MILITARY/VIOLENT EVENTS

6 January 2020
JNIM attack on security convoy in Alatona, Ségou region (Mali), kills five soldiers.

9 January
ISGS militants launch complex assault on military base in Chinagodrar, Tillabéri, killing at least 89 soldiers.

14 January
ISGS claims responsibility for Chinagodrar attack.

14 February
Dozo hunters (Dogon) stage attack against Peuhl community in the village of Ogossagou (Mali), killing 31 people.

23 May
Bukinabe and Ivoirian forces conduct first joint cross-border patrol as part of *Operation Comoé*.

3 June
France claims to have killed Abdelmalek Droukdel.

11 June
JNIM militants target a joint Burkinabe–Ivoirian outpost in Kafolo, northern Côte d'Ivoire, killing about a dozen Ivoirian soldiers and injuring seven more. This marks the first attack on Ivoirian soil since 2016.

June
ECOWAS calls for election rerun and formation of unity government in Mali; IBK's proposed unity government is rejected by the opposition.

June–August
Broad-based anti-government protests take place in Mali.

18–19 August
Coup d'état in Mali.

September
Interim authorities are appointed in Mali for 18-month transition.

22 November
General elections are held in Burkina Faso.

27 December
The first round of presidential elections is held in Niger.

24 February 2021
Mohamed Bazoum wins Niger's presidential election run-off.

18 June
AQIM confirms Droukdel's death.

25 June
At least ten Nigerien humanitarian workers are kidnapped in Tillabéri, about 5 km from the Burkinabe border.

9 August
ISGS conducts targeted killing of six French humanitarian workers and two Nigerien colleagues.

10 November
Operation Barkhane forces assassinate Bah ag Moussa, a senior JNIM commander.

22 November
AQIM announces Sheikh Mujahid Yazid Mubarak (also known as Abu Ubaida Yusuf al-Annabi) as its new leader.

3 January 2021
France allegedly targets civilians in an airstrike in Mali's Mopti region.

Impact

Human rights and humanitarian

Human-rights violations were widespread across the region. Islamist NSAGs, security forces and self-defence militias were all accused of extrajudicial killings, harassment and intimidation of local communities. Islamist NSAGs and security forces were also accused of war crimes, including the targeting of civilian communities and institutions, such as schools and hospitals. In 2021, French forces were also accused of committing war crimes, though Paris denied the claims.[15] The lack of legal redress for atrocities presents long-term challenges for the protection of human rights and breeds a continued culture of impunity. Many lawyers and judges have been displaced by violence, disrupting court processes.

The intensification of the Sahelian conflicts in 2020 exacerbated the existing humanitarian crisis. The number of fatalities and forced displacements reached unprecedented levels, accelerating a trend that began in 2017. The rise in IDPs was particularly marked in Burkina Faso, which accounts for more than half of all IDPs in the Sahel, while the largest proportion of refugees and asylum seekers are Malian.[16] While 2019 saw a sharp relative rise in the number of IDPs regionally, increasing by 130%, the absolute number of new IDPs in 2020 exceeded that of the previous year by 236,000.[17]

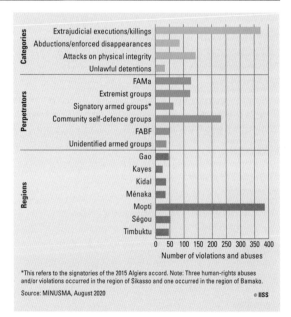

*This refers to the signatories of the 2015 Algiers accord. Note: Three human-rights abuses and/or violations occurred in the region of Sikasso and one occurred in the region of Bamako.
Source: MINUSMA, August 2020   © IISS

Figure 1: Human-rights violations and abuses in Mali, 1 April–30 June 2020

Food insecurity across Burkina Faso, Mali and Niger increased markedly, from 2.4m food-insecure people in September 2019 to 3.7m by November 2020.[18] In addition, the impacts of global warming, including desertification, drought and extreme weather events such as irregular and heavy rains and flooding, undermined regional food-production systems and resilience, making both IDPs and host communities increasingly reliant on food imports and humanitarian-relief efforts.

Political stability

Political stability continued to weaken in 2020. In Mali, the morphing operational zones of ISGS and JNIM, and the continued inability of security forces to reimpose control in the north, fuelled anti-government sentiment, particularly among urban elites. This was in full display during mass anti-government demonstrations in Bamako and other cities from June to August, which preceded the August coup.

In Burkina Faso, attacks by Ansarul Islam and ISGS undermined Kaboré's legitimacy, as insecurity disrupted the elections in several districts in the regions of East, Boucle du Mouhoun and Sahel. The election results themselves manifested voters' frustration with the government's inability to reimpose its authority, as the CDP made a strong comeback, becoming the second-largest parliamentary party.

Similar popular frustration with the government was apparent in Niger, where some Peuhl/Fulani communities expressed a growing sense of marginalisation amid the government's failure to improve security in the rural areas targeted most frequently by ISGS. The February 2021 presidential-election run-off was conducted largely peacefully, with the exception of the killing of seven electoral-commission workers in Tillabéri region.

Economic and social

The continued insurgencies in the Sahel hampered economic growth, deterred foreign investment and robbed communities of their livelihoods. At the local level, the large number of IDPs – many of whom no longer plan to return to their original homes – increased competition over arable land. Many engage in subsistence activity, such as informal mining, market hawking, home care or prostitution. In turn, worsening local economic conditions fuelled intercommunal antagonism and resentment.

Despite ongoing conflict, macroeconomic performances in the region have remained resilient over the decade due to the concentration of fighting in largely rural areas, removed from the countries' main productive centres. Nevertheless, the coronavirus pandemic slowed economic growth in all three countries in 2020, particularly in Mali, whose GDP contracted by 1.9% as compared to a 0.8% contraction in Burkina Faso and a slight 1.2% increase in Niger.[19]

Relations with neighbouring and international partners and geopolitical implications

The military coup and planned 18-month transition strained Mali's relations with the international community and its regional neighbours. ECOWAS pressured Mali to shorten the transition to one year, imposed an embargo and closed borders, while the EUTM temporarily suspended its training missions in the country. These relations are likely to remain tense throughout the transition period until new elections are held.

Relations with France have also likely been further strained due to allegations of French forces killing civilians in 2021. Thus far, opposition to French and foreign presence appears strongest in Mali, but such sentiments could also grow in Burkina Faso and Niger throughout 2021. However, the deployment of other European combat forces may reduce the focus on France as the former colonial, and current neocolonial, power in the region.

Conflict Outlook

Political scenarios

The potential for a comprehensive political deal in the short term remains bleak, especially as the coronavirus pandemic continues to undermine the ability of all three countries' governments to deal with the conflict situation.

While it is encouraging that broad development issues and security matters are covered in the CFS and the CNT's action plan, their objectives appear overly ambitious and potentially unrealistic within the given time frame. For instance, the Malian government's plan consists of 275 targets and 291 indicators to achieve in just 18 months.[20] This may drive further grievances in 2021.

Plans to engage in talks with Islamist and non-terrorist NSAGs may break a certain deadlock but are unlikely to lead to a durable peace. It is doubtful that the demands of the NSAGs and those of the Malian government – including accelerating the implementation of the Algiers accord and ensuring the return of state institutions to all northern towns and regions – could be combined in a negotiated agreement towards peace.

In Burkina Faso and Niger, post-electoral grievances may foster further anti-government sentiment in 2021, creating a new set of political and security issues for the new administrations there.

The significant increase in the number of IDPs and refugees will further strain national finances and capabilities and, without strengthened international support, will likely undermine their ability to address underlying grievances – such as weak governance – and reimpose sovereignty outside large urban areas.

Escalation potential and conflict-related risks

The regional security environment in the region will remain volatile amid continued political instability. Malian efforts to recalibrate the implementation of the Algiers accord are an encouraging step but could potentially upset the current balance of power in northern and central regions. While Iyad Ag Ghaly and other senior JNIM leaders have expressed an openness to negotiations, they remain vehemently opposed to the presence of French and other foreign forces. It is also unclear if such moves will be accepted by all militant groups in the JNIM alliance, which operate in different local contexts. Nor is it certain that the CMA will be willing to accept any changes to the terms of the Algiers accord.

France's continued engagement, and increased deployment by both European countries and Chad, indicates growing kinetic capacity for regional forces, which may improve morale and strengthen public trust in the fight against terrorist NSAGs. However, the increasing intercommunal fighting seen since 2018 remains unaddressed. In the absence of improved peacemaking efforts targeting these local conflicts, regional NSAGs will continue to instrumentalise them to increase their recruitment pool.

Prospects for peace

The growing deployment of troops to the region reduces the prospects for a serious de-escalation of the conflicts in 2021 and signals a recognition of the deteriorated security environment and growing capability needs.

At the same time, growing opposition in Western countries to foreign interventions and aid, including in France, the UK and the US, complicates efforts to further boost military- and development-personnel numbers. While intentions to negotiate with JNIM in Mali may provide a lull in attacks there, similar efforts would also be needed in Burkina Faso and Niger to meaningfully reduce the conflict, which appear unlikely at this stage.

Strategic implications and global influences

The risk of jihadist groups continuing to expand into neighbouring countries like Benin, Côte d'Ivoire and Senegal remains high, due to the NSAGs' proximity to those countries and their documented ability to move across borders, especially as the post-pandemic context will further constrain available funding for governments' intelligence and counter-insurgency operations.

Authorities in Benin claimed to have foiled two coup attempts by dissidents since 2019. However, as domestic anti-government protests continue in Burkina Faso, Mali and Niger, the capabilities of their national security forces to collect intelligence and monitor insurgent cross-border movements will remain stretched. Ghana's growing profile, with the secretariat of the African Continental Free Trade Area located in Accra, combined with the increasingly polarised political environment, makes the country an attractive target for high-impact attacks, posing additional security risks in the region.

In addition, disinformation campaigns by unidentified actors, believed to be tied to global geopolitical frictions between Western powers and Russia, are also likely to continue to undermine public trust in current military interventions and public institutions, and thereby to destabilise local contexts.

Notes

1   Armed Conflict Location & Event Data Project (ACLED), www.acleddata.com.

2   United Nations High Commissioner for Refugees, 'Coordination Platform for Forced Displacements in Sahel'.

3   Jason Warner and Charlotte Hulme, 'The Islamic State in Africa: Estimating Fighter Numbers in Cells Across the Continent', *CTC Sentinel*, vol. 11, no. 7, August 2018; and Danish Ministry of Immigration and Integration, 'Violent Extremism in West Africa', June 2020.

4   Warner and Hulme, 'The Islamic State in Africa: Estimating Fighter Numbers in Cells Across the Continent'.

5   Seidik Abba, 'Jafar Dicko, Le Nouveau Visage Du Djihadisme Au Burkina Faso' [Jafar Dicko, The New Face of Jihadism in Burkina Faso], *Le Monde*, 21 December 2017.

6   Baba Ahmed, 'Mali: Le Business du Cantonnement?' [Mali: The Cantonment Business?], *Jeune Afrique*, 26 April 2016; and Baba Ahmed and Christophe Boisbouvier, 'Nord-Mali: Guerre à Huis Clos' [North Mali: War behind Closed Doors], *Jeune Afrique*, 21 February 2012.

7   French Ministry of Foreign Affairs, 'France's Action in the Sahel', April 2020; Florence Parly (@florence_parly), tweet, 28 October 2020; 'Internationellt Möte om Takuba-insatsen i Mali' [International Meeting on the Takuba Operation in Mali], Regeringskansliet, 8 April 2021; Fergus Kelly, 'Estonia Parliament Approves Mali Troop Increase for Operation Barkhane', The Defense Post, 8 November 2019; Jeremy Binnie, 'Task Force Takuba Reaches IOC in Mali', Janes, 21 July 2020; and 'Mali (Task Force Takuba)', Swedish Armed Forces, 18 January 2021.

8   United Nations Peacekeeping, 'MINUSMA Fact Sheet'.

9   French Ministry of Foreign Affairs, 'France's Action in the Sahel'; and Madjiara Nako and Michel Rose, 'France Rules Out Immediate Troop Cuts in Sahel, Chad Deploys Reinforcements', Reuters, 16 February 2021.

10   United Nations Multidimensional Stabilization Mission in Mali, 'Note Sur Les Tendances Des Violations et Abus de Droits de l'Homme au Mali 1er Juillet – 30 Septembre 2020' [Brief on Trends of Human-Rights Violations and Abuses in Mali 1 July – 30 September 2020], 2 February 2021; 'Note Sur Les Tendances Des Violations et Abus de Droits de l'Homme 1er Avril – 30 Juin 2020' [Brief on Trends of Human-Rights Violations and Abuses in Mali 1 April – 30 June 2020], August 2020; and 'Note Sur Les Tendances Des Violations et Abus de Droits de l'Homme 1er Janvier – 28 Février 2020' [Brief on Trends of Human-Rights Violations and Abuses in Mali 1 January – 28 February 2020], April 2020.

11   'Sahel: La Moitié des Français Opposés à la Présence Française' [Half of French People Opposed to the French Presence], Le Point, 11 January 2021.

12   Burkina Faso, Constitutional Council, 'Extrait des minutes du Greffe du Conseil constitutionnel: Décision n° 2020-011/CC/EPF portant proclamation des résultats définitifs de l'élection du Président du Faso du 22 novembre 2020' [Extract of the Clerk of the Constitutional Council's minutes: Decision no. 2020-011/CC/EPF proclaiming the definitive results of Burkina Faso's 22 November 2020 presidential election], 18 December 2020.

13   See, for example, Kizzi Asala, 'Niger Election: Opposition Leader Ousmane Challenges Court Verdict', *Africanews*, 23 March 2021.

14   Héni Nsaibia and Caleb Weiss, 'The End of the Sahelian Anomaly: How the Global Conflict between the Islamic State and al-Qa`ida Finally Came to West Africa', *CTC Sentinel*, vol. 13, no. 7, July 2020.

15   'Mali: la France Accusée D'avoir Tué des Civils Lors d'une Frappe Contre des Djihadistes' [Mali: France Accused of Killing Civilians in a Strike Against Jihadists], Le Point, 5 January 2021.

16   United Nations High Commissioner for Refugees UK, 'Grim Milestone as Sahel Violence Displaces 2 Million Inside Their Countries', 22 January 2021.

17   United Nations High Commissioner for Refugees, 'R4 Sahel Coordination Platform for Displacements in the Sahel'. See 'IDP Population trend' and 'Refugee & Asylum Seekers Population trend' graphs.

18   United Nations World Food Programme, 'Central Sahel Emergency Dashboard', September 2019 and November 2020.

19   International Monetary Fund, 'World Economic Outlook Database (Burkina Faso, Mali and Niger)', April 2021.

20   'Transition: Le Plan d'Action du Gouvernement Approuvé par le CNT' [Transition: The Government Action Plan Approved by the CNT], Studio Tamani, 22 February 2021.

LAKE CHAD BASIN

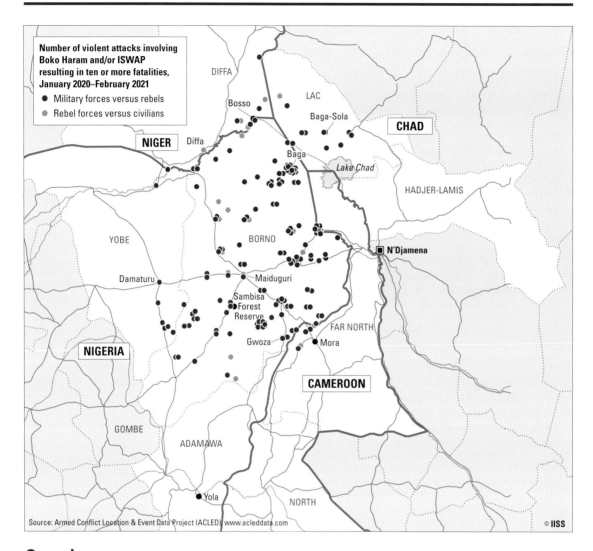

Number of violent attacks involving Boko Haram and/or ISWAP resulting in ten or more fatalities, January 2020–February 2021
- ● Military forces versus rebels
- ● Rebel forces versus civilians

Source: Armed Conflict Location & Event Data Project (ACLED) www.acleddata.com

© IISS

Overview

Over a decade since the start of the violent insurgency in northeastern Nigeria, the Lake Chad Basin area is the theatre of a complex regional crisis. In 2020, the two main factions of Boko Haram – Jama'atu Ahlis Sunna Lidda'awati wal-Jihad (JAS) and the Islamic State West Africa Province (ISWAP) – stepped up attacks against civilians, humanitarian workers and army troops in Nigeria's North East and across the border into neighbouring Cameroon, Chad and Niger. The Nigerian Army's 'Super Camps' strategy, which focused on defending large military bases at the expense of protecting villages and rural

areas, presumably contributed to this increased targeting of civilians. ISWAP also competed with JAS for influence within local communities in the North East and, increasingly, in the North West near the border with Niger.

Boko Haram was established in Nigeria's impoverished North East in early 2002 by the charismatic preacher Mohammed Yusuf. The goal of the militant group was to establish sharia law in Nigeria and dispense with Western-influenced institutions, including those underpinning the education system and democracy. After the Nigerian security forces

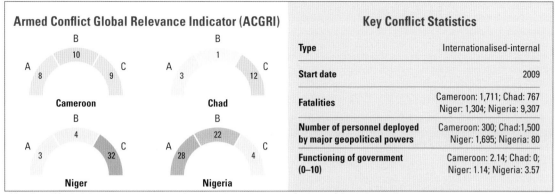

Armed Conflict Global Relevance Indicator (ACGRI)

Cameroon
- B: 10
- A: 8
- C: 9

Chad
- B: 1
- A: 3
- C: 12

Niger
- B: 4
- A: 3
- C: 32

Nigeria
- B: 22
- A: 28
- C: 4

Key Conflict Statistics

Type	Internationalised-internal
Start date	2009
Fatalities	Cameroon: 1,711; Chad: 767 Niger: 1,304; Nigeria: 9,307
Number of personnel deployed by major geopolitical powers	Cameroon: 300; Chad:1,500 Niger: 1,695; Nigeria: 80
Functioning of government (0–10)	Cameroon: 2.14; Chad: 0; Niger: 1.14; Nigeria: 3.57

ACGRI pillars: IISS calculation based on multiple sources for 2020 and January/February 2021 (scale: 0–100). Results for the indicator are displayed for each country involved in the conflict. A: Human impact; B: Incidence; C: Geopolitical impact. See Notes on Methodology and Data Appendix for further details on Key Conflict Statistics.

killed Yusuf in July 2009, the desire to avenge the founder's extrajudicial killing became a powerful rallying call for Boko Haram, which regrouped in 2010 under the leadership of former second-in-command Abubakar Shekau. This was a major turning point: the group escalated its violent insurgency and conducted high-profile attacks against security forces and civilians, broadening its influence and territorial control. From 2013, the insurgency developed into a regional crisis, extending into parts of Cameroon, Chad and Niger. The resultant widespread violence prompted the Nigerian government to launch the country's largest military deployment since the Nigerian–Biafran War of 1967–70. Despite its recurrent claims of victory, however, the violence did not diminish.

In 2015, Boko Haram pledged its allegiance to the emir of the Islamic State (also known as ISIS or ISIL) and adopted the new name ISWAP. Disputes between Shekau and senior commander Mamman Nur emerged over the leader's intransigent tactics, leading ISIS to appoint Abu Musab al-Barnawi, Yusuf's son, as the new ISWAP leader in August 2016. Shekau refused to recognise al-Barnawi and broke away from ISWAP, returning to the group's original name, JAS.

The escalation of the crisis led the governments of Benin, Cameroon, Chad, Niger and Nigeria to revive the Multinational Joint Task Force (MNJTF) in 2015, a joint military body supporting counter-terrorism operations. Large-scale operations conducted by the MNJTF since 2015 have achieved some success, making inroads into Boko Haram's core territory. Yet budget constraints and dwindling support from the contributing countries have often hampered the MNJTF's effectiveness.

Conflict Parties

Nigerian armed forces

Strength: 143,000 military personnel, including 100,000 army personnel. Paramilitary forces number approximately 80,000 troops. An estimated 30,000 troops are deployed in Nigeria's North East.

Areas of operation: North East of Nigeria (particularly Adamawa, Borno and Yobe states).

Leadership: Nigerian President Muhammadu Buhari (commander-in-chief of the armed forces), Major-General Ibrahim Attahiru (army chief of staff).

Structure: The Nigerian armed forces comprise the army, the air force and the navy. The army is organised into headquarters, divisions, brigades, battalions, companies, platoons and sections.

History: The Nigerian armed forces have been fighting Boko Haram since 2009. Their strategy has evolved drastically over time, including an expansion from five to eight divisions and the relocation of their headquarters in 2015 to Maiduguri, the capital of Borno State, closer to the epicentre of the insurgency.

Objectives: Secure Nigeria's territorial integrity and end the threat to the populations in the Lake Chad Basin.

Opponents: JAS and ISWAP.

Affiliates/allies: MNJTF, Civilian Joint Task Force (CJTF), Cameroon, Chad, Niger, international partners (United States, United Kingdom, France).

Sub-Saharan Africa

Nigerian armed forces

Resources/capabilities: Heavy and light weaponry in land, air, sea and cyber spheres. The Nigerian armed forces have significantly improved the resources and capabilities of the military (including the air force and the Cyber Warfare Command) over the past five years. However, poor equipment and training in the army remain areas of concern.

Jama'atu Ahlis Sunna Lidda'awati wal-Jihad (JAS)

Strength: Between 1,500 and 2,000 fighters.[1]

Areas of operation: Lake Chad Basin region spanning Cameroon, Chad, Niger and Nigeria. Core area of control in Sambisa Forest and Gwoza Hills, south of Maiduguri (Nigeria).

Leadership: Abubakar Shekau since 2010.

Structure: Highly decentralised structure with weak command chain, various offshoots and cells that can act independently.

History: Popularly known as Boko Haram, JAS was established in the early 2000s by Mohammed Yusuf. After he was killed in 2009, Shekau escalated the group's violent campaigns and broadened its influence and territorial control. JAS pledged allegiance to ISIS in 2015, operating under the name of ISWAP. In 2016, Shekau split from ISWAP and revived the group's original name, JAS.

Objectives: Establish an Islamic caliphate in the North East of Nigeria and in neighbouring regions.

Opponents: Nigerian armed forces, MNJTF, CJTF, Western institutions.

Affiliates/allies: ISIS and al-Qaeda.

Resources/capabilities: Stolen weaponry from military bases and acquisitions from the black market, including assault rifles, tanks, rocket-propelled grenades, improvised bombs, mortars and armoured personnel vehicles. It has a limited anti-aircraft capability and reportedly has been using uninhabited aerial vehicles (UAVs) since 2018.

Islamic State West Africa Province (ISWAP)

Strength: Between 3,500 and 5,000 fighters.[2]

Areas of operation: Lake Chad Basin region spanning Cameroon, Chad, Niger and Nigeria. Core area of territorial control on the islands of Lake Chad and the forests of northern Borno State and eastern Yobe State (Nigeria).

Leadership: Abu Abdullah al-Barnawi (also known as Ba Idrissa) replaced previous leader Abu Musab al-Barnawi in March 2019. Reports emerged in March 2020 that Ba Idrissa had been purged, and perhaps killed, in a new round of factional fighting within ISWAP.

Structure: ISWAP controls parts of northeastern Nigeria, erecting checkpoints and levying taxes on herders, fishermen and farmers.

History: Boko Haram began to be known as ISWAP after Shekau pledged allegiance to ISIS in 2015. Tensions between Shekau and former rival Mamman Nur surfaced in the following months, until ISIS recognised Nur-aligned Abu Musab al-Barnawi as the new ISWAP leader in August 2016.

Objectives: Establish an Islamic caliphate in the North East of Nigeria and in neighbouring regions.

Opponents: Nigerian armed forces, MNJTF, CJTF, Western institutions.

Affiliates/allies: ISIS.

Resources/capabilities: ISWAP has acquired much of its weaponry – including assault rifles, rocket-propelled grenades, mortars and armoured personnel vehicles – by raiding military bases and attacking troops. Financial assistance from ISIS was also used to acquire looted military equipment from its own fighters.[3]

Civilian Joint Task Force (CJTF)

Strength: Around 26,000 self-defence militants (most recent estimate).[4]

Areas of operation: North East of Nigeria (particularly Adamawa, Borno and Yobe states). The CJTF is based in Maiduguri, the capital of Borno State.

Leadership: No overarching leadership. There are local commanders who oversee different sectors.

Structure: The CJTF has a decentralised structure, with local groups and sectors modelled on the Nigerian military.

History: Formed in May 2013 as a response to Boko Haram's growing violence in Borno State, Nigeria. It began as a popular youth movement known as *yan gora* ('youth with sticks' in the Hausa language) to protect communities from violence. Its founder Baba Lawan Jafa was a trader from Maiduguri who gained notoriety after confronting a Boko Haram gunman with a stick.

Civilian Joint Task Force (CJTF)

Objectives: Assist the Nigerian armed forces in the fight against Boko Haram and ISWAP; protect local communities from attacks; and free villages and towns from insurgent control. The CJTF patrols the streets, establishes checkpoints and provides intelligence to the security forces.

Opponents: JAS and ISWAP.

Affiliates/allies: Nigerian armed forces and MNJTF.

Resources/capabilities: Bows and arrows, swords, machetes, axes, daggers, cutlasses, handmade muskets and sticks. Most fighters have never received formal military training.

Multinational Joint Task Force (MNJTF)

Strength: Approximately 10,000 troops from Benin, Cameroon, Chad, Niger and Nigeria.[5]

Areas of operation: Lake Chad Basin.

Leadership: Major-General Ibrahim Manu Yusuf (MNJTF force commander since November 2019).

Structure: Headquartered in N'Djamena (Chad), the MNJTF comprises four geographical sectors: Baga (Nigeria); Baga Sola (Chad); Diffa (Niger); and Mora (Cameroon). Each sector is led by a commander with wide autonomy while the MNJTF force commander has coordination powers.

History: First created in 1998 to tackle cross-border crimes and banditry affecting the Basin area. After years of inactivity, the Peace and Security Council of the African Union (AU) agreed to revive the MNJTF in 2015 to counter Boko Haram's growing activity.

Objectives: Coordinate the regional counter-insurgency efforts and restore security in the areas affected by JAS and ISWAP in the Lake Chad Basin. The force is also involved in supporting stabilisation programmes, humanitarian assistance and the return of those forcibly displaced.

Opponents: JAS and ISWAP.

Affiliates/allies: The national armies of Cameroon, Chad, Niger and Nigeria, as well as international partners (the AU, European Union, US, UK)

Resources/capabilities: The initial operational budget was estimated to be approximately US$700 million. The EU is the main contributor to the force, channelling its funds through the AU. Bureaucratic delays and lack of adequate resources have hampered the MNJTF's ability to fulfil its mandate.

Conflict Drivers

Political

Radical ideology:

JAS and ISWAP are Salafi-jihadi groups and radical ideologies still provide a strong motivation for the insurgency. One of the drivers of the conflict is the quest to create an Islamic caliphate based on sharia law and to erase 'Western' influence in the region. From its inception, Boko Haram has strived to present its radical version of Salafism as the antidote to societal 'evils' including Westernised, corrupted elites, inequality and poverty, and Islamic religious leaders who they perceive to have gone astray by adopting moderate positions. While the leadership of both groups believes in the ideology of radical Salafi jihadism, the rank-and-file members seem less ideologically driven and more motivated by opportunism or pragmatism.

Weak governance and ineffective government response:
The militarised response to the insurgency, along with widespread human-rights abuses committed by state security forces and paramilitaries, have alienated local communities. In the early stages of the insurgency, the government's violent crackdown

on Boko Haram fighters and the killing of Yusuf in police custody allowed a more radical leadership to emerge. Ever since, the Nigerian military and government-sponsored vigilante groups, including the CJTF, have engaged in arbitrary detentions, torture, extrajudicial killings and other illegal activities that aggravated the sense of civilian insecurity and eroded popular trust in the government.[6] Overall, the Nigerian government has persistently failed to restore security – and to curb a rise in criminality – for the populations of northeastern Nigeria.

Economic and social

Socio-economic grievances:
The ideological dimension is intertwined with socio-economic grievances. The regions surrounding the Lake Chad Basin have suffered from decades of marginalisation, exclusion and environmental degradation. Poverty, illiteracy and youth unemployment rates in Nigeria's North East and Cameroon's Far North regions are among the highest in their respective countries.[7] Climate change has also affected rainfall seasons and increasing unpredictability has eroded livelihoods and exacerbated competition

over scarce land and water. Chronic neglect and economic insecurity have therefore left the local youth more susceptible to recruitment into criminal activity or armed groups like Boko Haram, which offer them a mix of spiritual glorification and financial rewards.

International
Regionalisation of the insurgency:
Uneven governance, developmental challenges and environmental degradation are common across the regions bordering Lake Chad and have contributed to the extension of the insurgency into a regional threat. Despite operating largely in northeastern Nigeria, Boko Haram took advantage of its porous borders with Cameroon, Chad and Niger to conduct cross-border attacks, recruit fighters among similarly marginalised communities and occasionally establish safe havens in these neighbouring countries. A lack of coordination between the Lake Chad countries has often hampered a joint response to the insurgency.

Political and Military Developments

Rising insurgent attacks against civilians
2020 saw a sequence of deadly attacks against civilians across the Lake Chad Basin. Boko Haram's JAS faction and, increasingly, ISWAP targeted local communities and humanitarian workers in Borno State, with several large-scale killings. In June, ISWAP was responsible for the assassination of over 80 cattle herders in Felo, a remote community situated 80 km northwest of Borno State capital Maiduguri that had previously resisted the insurgents. For its part, JAS conducted its deadliest attack of the year on 28 November, killing an estimated 110 farmers in Kashoba village, also around Maiduguri. Insurgents continued to abduct civilians and use improvised explosive devices (IEDs) and suicide bombers in civilian-populated areas.

This surge in civilian-directed violence may be partially linked to the Nigerian Army's 2019 'Super Camps' strategy, which consisted of concentrating its troops in heavily protected strongholds. The new strategy was designed to boost the protection of the armed forces and to limit military casualties and the looting of weapons and equipment. However, withdrawing troops from local communities had the unintended consequence of allowing insurgents to move freely and set up checkpoints along several roads in Borno.

Regional response to the insurgency
By securing Nigerian military bases and preventing weaponry from falling into the hands of insurgents, the 'Super Camps' strategy arguably inflicted a major setback to both ISWAP and JAS. Yet they continued to launch deadly attacks against the military forces deployed across the Lake Chad Basin. On 23 March 2020, nearly 100 Chadian soldiers were killed in a seven-hour attack conducted by suspected Boko Haram fighters affiliated with Shekau on an army base in Boma peninsula. On the same day, ISWAP fired rocket-propelled grenades at a military truck in Borno, killing at least 70 Nigerian troops.

The Nigerian Army, along with the MNJTF, troops from neighbouring countries and the CJTF, spearheaded several counter-insurgency operations. Military officials regularly claimed that Nigerian Army troops and airstrikes had inflicted several losses to JAS and ISWAP in Borno, and especially in the insurgent stronghold of Sambisa Forest. Chadian President Idriss Déby Itno also claimed that 1,000 Boko Haram fighters were killed in April in a counter-offensive that drove insurgents out of his country. Yet these and other claims were disputed, with governments accused of regularly exaggerating their successes in the fight against the insurgents. Meanwhile, the February 2021 victory of ruling party candidate Mohamed Bazoum in Niger's presidential elections, and the holding of local elections in Borno State, Nigeria and Cameroon in November and December 2020, are unlikely to substantially change the course of the counter-insurgency.

Internal developments in the insurgent camp
Having become the leader of ISWAP in March 2019, Ba Idrissa, a relatively moderate figure, was purged 12 months later amid reports of factional infighting within the group.[8] It is unclear whether Ba Idrissa or his predecessor (Abu Musab al-Barnawi) is still alive. Observers noted that ISWAP's increased targeting of the civilian population could indicate that a more radical leadership had taken over the group.[9] Increasing competition was also reported between JAS, ISWAP and Ansaru, another splinter

of Boko Haram, over their projected expansion into northwestern Nigeria, where they seek the loyalty of local bandit groups. Throughout 2020, occasional internecine fighting between rival Boko Haram factions resulted in several casualties in both Niger and Nigeria.

Key Events in 2020–21

POLITICAL EVENTS

28 February 2020
Nigerian authorities report the first case of COVID-19 in sub-Saharan Africa.

18 April
Abba Kyari, the influential chief of staff of Nigerian President Buhari, dies of COVID-19.

13 May
Nigerian President Buhari names former diplomat Ibrahim Gambari as his new chief of staff.

28 November
Long-delayed local elections are held in Borno State, Nigeria amid rising insecurity.

6 December
Cameroon holds its first regional elections.

26 January 2021
Nigeria's four military chiefs resign and retire from service.

21 February
Ruling party candidate Mohamed Bazoum wins the second round of Niger's presidential elections.

MILITARY/VIOLENT EVENTS

4 January 2020
Chad announces the withdrawal of 1,200 troops from Borno State.

15 January
Internecine fighting between JAS and ISWAP leaves several dead in Borno State.

9 February
Suspected JAS gunmen kill 30 civilians near Auno, 15 km north-west of Borno State capital Maiduguri.

23 March
JAS and ISWAP launch attacks on Chadian and Nigerian troops, killing nearly 170 soldiers.

1 May
The Nigerian Army launches *Operation Kantana Jimlan* against insurgents in the North East.

9 June
Suspected ISWAP militants kill over 80 civilians in a cattle-herding village north of Maiduguri.

13 June
Boko Haram attacks two villages in Borno State, killing over 40 civilians.

22 July
ISWAP executes five aid workers who had been abducted in Borno in June.

28 November
JAS kills 110 farmers near Maiduguri, Borno State.

12 December
JAS kills 34 civilians in an attack on the Nigerien town of Toumour, near Diffa.

23 February 2021
A rocket attack on Maiduguri claimed by JAS leaves 16 dead, including nine children.

Sub-Saharan Africa

Impact

Human rights and humanitarian

The conflict continued to severely affect the humanitarian situation in the Lake Chad Basin in 2020. Across the region over 10m people are in need of emergency humanitarian assistance.[10] Protracted fighting has displaced more than 3m, including 2.9m internally displaced persons in northeastern Nigeria alone.[11] More than 6.2m are estimated to be food insecure during the 2021 lean season, a significant increase from the previous year.[12] Additionally, attacks against humanitarian actors, as well as restrictions introduced by the Nigerian authorities in 2019 under the pretext of safeguarding national security, increasingly undermined the ability to deliver life-saving assistance.

Many of the actors involved in the conflict – including Boko Haram, the CJTF and the Nigerian security forces – were responsible for widespread human-rights abuses in 2020. The Nigerian armed forces were accused of unlawfully detaining and torturing tens of thousands of people, including children, in the North East region.[13] JAS and ISWAP continued to target civilians, killing close to 1,000 civilians across Cameroon, Chad, Niger and Nigeria in the reporting period.[14] The Nigerian government failed to protect the civilian population, forcing Nigerian refugees to return from Cameroon despite safety concerns and rampant abductions.[15]

Political stability

Despite multiple pledges from Nigerian President Buhari to end insecurity, over ten years since the onset of the insurgency, and over five since he assumed the presidency, Boko Haram remains a significant security threat. In fact, attacks against the civilian population increased considerably in 2020. The persistence of the threat in the country's North East, and signs of its possible expansion to other northern regions, highlight the failure of the government's strategy. The military's lacklustre performance against Boko Haram, and its heavy response to protests in October 2020 against the Special Anti-Robbery Squad (SARS) of the police, eroded Buhari's trust in the country's military chiefs, leading to their eventual resignation in January 2021. Buhari also promised to increase resources for Nigeria's poorly equipped military. Separately, Niger's presidential elections, and local elections in Cameroon and Nigeria's Borno State, did little to alter the course of the insurgency.

Economic and social

The coronavirus pandemic aggravated Nigeria's economic predicament. Lockdowns shut down economic activity in most states, while remittances, which make up approximately 5% of GDP, are estimated to have fallen by 20% in 2020. With Nigeria's GDP shrinking by 6% year-on-year in the second quarter of 2020 (and by a projected 4% annually), the World Bank estimated that an additional 15–20m people would be driven into poverty by 2022.[16]

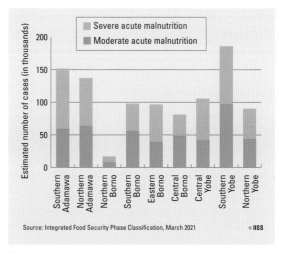

Source: Integrated Food Security Phase Classification, March 2021   © IISS

Figure 1: Estimated malnutrition levels among children under five years in North East Nigeria, September 2020–August 2021

There are concerns that the country's health-care system may struggle to cope with an increasing number of reported coronavirus cases. The pandemic has further exposed the country's socio-economic inequalities, with COVID-19 testing and treatment for the poor not universally available. This is particularly worrying in Nigeria's North East, which has witnessed outbreaks of severe malnutrition, malaria and other diseases in recent times, and where the scarcity of functioning health facilities limits the capacity to treat patients.

Relations with neighbouring and international partners and geopolitical implications

In 2020, the World Bank approved new programmes amounting to US$346m to strengthen livelihoods in the Lake Chad Basin, while the IMF and the African Development Bank pledged further financial contributions to fight the coronavirus pandemic and the Nigeria Humanitarian Fund of the UN Office for the Coordination of Humanitarian Affairs allocated an additional US$22.4m to address the combined humanitarian crisis caused by the conflict and the pandemic in northeastern Nigeria.[17] Regional security cooperation also continued in 2020 amidst a surge in violence and growing anxiety among the countries bordering the Lake Chad Basin. The Chadian government expressed its frustration over Nigeria's financial and military contribution to the war against Boko Haram. After an ISWAP attack resulted in the heaviest death toll ever suffered by its armed forces, Chadian President Déby announced on 9 April that no more troops would be deployed outside the country, having already withdrawn 1,200 troops from Nigeria in January.[18] However, N'Djamena withdrew the announcement days later after pressure from its European and US partners.

Conflict Outlook

Political scenarios

With just two more years left in power, Buhari radically reshuffled Nigeria's military establishment in early 2021. All four military chiefs – defence staff, army, navy and air force – were forced to resign amidst increasing pressure to deliver results. Buhari appointed Major-General Ibrahim Attahiru as the new army chief of staff, replacing Lieutenant-General Tukur Yusuf Buratai, who had faced criticism for his role in the repression of the #EndSARS protests. The new Chief of Defence Staff, Leo Irabor, had led *Operation Lafiya Dole*, a major offensive against Boko Haram, and also previously headed the MNJTF. Irabor, a southerner from Delta State, in contrast to the president's northern heritage, is widely seen as an effective military commander.

Nigeria's new military chiefs have been tasked with reviewing the 'Super Camps' strategy, enhancing the protection of civilians from increasing insurgent attacks and ending defence-procurement scams linked to the conflict economy that have thrived since the presidency of Goodluck Jonathan (2010–15). It is hoped that renewed pressure from regional partners and local authorities concerned by the escalating violence could eventually lead Buhari and the new military chiefs to better equip the armed forces, tackle defence-sector corruption and ultimately transform the fight against Boko Haram. Yet budget constraints and entrenched corporate interests linked to endemic military corruption remain obstacles.[19]

Escalation potential and conflict-related risks

Competition within the insurgent camp may contribute to an escalation of violence. In the northern area of Lake Chad, the presence of another Boko Haram faction led by 'Bakura' and aligned with JAS is likely to heighten competition and lead to clashes. Early signs of increasing tensions surfaced in Niger's Bosso and Diffa areas, where factional clashes between JAS and ISWAP were reported in January 2021. ISWAP – predominantly active in northern Borno and Yobe, southeastern Niger and southwestern Chad – and Shekau's JAS – the weaker faction largely operating across central and southern Borno – are also seeking to make inroads in north-central and northwestern Nigeria, where they compete with al-Qaeda-aligned Ansaru for the loyalty of local bandit groups. Both JAS and ISWAP could potentially set aside rivalries over conflicting affiliation to ISIS or al-Qaeda to defeat Ansaru and gain a foothold in the region. With Boko Haram's expansion into northwestern Nigeria, there are serious concerns over a possible linkage with insurgents from the Sahel region.

Prospects for peace

Without substantial changes to the 'Super Camps' strategy, which has allowed insurgents to take control of large swathes of territory left undefended by Nigerian troops, Boko Haram is likely to continue to wage attacks against the civilian population, humanitarian workers and military forces. ISWAP in particular has been successful in earning the support of local populations – more than JAS ever did – by providing state services and filling governance gaps in the North East. Outside northeastern Nigeria, Boko Haram has failed to establish a durable presence, opting for sporadic incursions to preserve its supply lines through looting and kidnappings. Hence, defeating the group in northeastern Nigeria will require a commitment to reconstructing state–society relations, restoring trust in the armed forces – often held responsible for extortion and corruption practices – and ensuring effective protection of the civilian population that are displaced or threatened by the ongoing violence. With the coronavirus pandemic hitting Nigeria's fragile economy hard, such plans are unlikely to materialise any time soon.

Strategic implications and global influences

The MNJTF remains a primary actor in the fight against Boko Haram, especially in its effort to gain trust among the civilian population. However, funding issues, limited coordination and irregular commitment have hindered its effectiveness. The appointment of former MNJTF commander Leo

Sub-Saharan Africa

Irabor at the head of the Nigerian Army, and the diplomatic experience of Buhari's new Chief of Staff Ibrahim Gambari, may eventually boost Nigeria's contribution to the MNJTF and especially reassure its regional partners, Chad above all. In late 2020, the EU, the MNJTF's main donor, pledged to provide additional support to the force. Yet further progress is needed to improve military planning and coordination, enhance the protection of human rights, and enable the MNJTF to cooperate with civilian actors to support service delivery and local governance programmes.

Notes

1   International Crisis Group, 'Facing the Challenge of the Islamic State in West Africa Province', Report no. 273, 16 May 2019.

2   *Ibid.*

3   Vincent Foucher, 'The Islamic State Franchises in Africa: Lessons from Lake Chad', International Crisis Group, 29 October 2020.

4   The figure is difficult to confirm due to the absence of centralised recruitment structures. See International Crisis Group, 'Watchmen of Lake Chad: Vigilante Groups Fighting Boko Haram', Report no. 244, 23 February 2017.

5   Camillo Casola, 'Multinational Joint Task Force: Security Cooperation in the Lake Chad Basin', Italian Institute for International Political Studies, 19 March 2020.

6   See Chitra Nagarajan, 'To Defend or Harm? Community Militias in Borno State, Nigeria', Center for Civilians in Conflict, 30 April 2020.

7   See United Nations Development Programme, 'Business Case Assessment for Accelerating Development Investments in Famine Response and Prevention: Case Study – North-East Nigeria', 2017; UNICEF, 'Nigeria: Education'; and World Bank, 'Lifting Cameroon's Most Vulnerable Out of Poverty: Building Resilience and Fostering Local Governance to Address the Root Causes of Fragility and Conflict in Northern Regions of Cameroon', 8 November 2019.

8   Jacob Zenn, 'Islamic State in West Africa Province's Factional Disputes and the Battle with Boko Haram', Jamestown Foundation, 20 March 2020.

9   Agence France-Presse, 'Nigeria Attacks Spark Fears of Bloodier Jihadist Strategy', 18 June 2020.

10   United Nations Office for the Coordination of Humanitarian Affairs, 'Ten Crises to Watch in 2021', 9 February 2021.

11   United Nations High Commissioner for Refugees, 'Nigeria Emergency', 31 December 2020. IDPs estimates vary across sources. According to the Internal Displacement Monitoring Centre (IDMC), the total number of conflict IDPs was approximately 2.7m in 2020. See IDMC, '2020 Internal Displacement', Global Internal Displacement Database.

12   European Commission, 'Lake Chad Basin Crisis', ECHO Crisis Report no. 19, 11 February 2021.

13   Amnesty International, 'Nigeria: "We Dried Our Tears": Addressing the Toll on Children of Northeast Nigeria's Conflict', 27 May 2020.

14   Armed Conflict Location & Event Data Project (ACLED), www.acleddata.com.

15   US Department of State, '2020 Trafficking in Persons Report: Nigeria', June 2020.

16   See Alexis Akwagyiram, 'UPDATE 2: Nigeria's Economy Shrinks 6% in Second Quarter on Oil Crash, Pandemic Double Whammy', Reuters, 24 August 2020; IMF Data Mapper: Country Data – Nigeria, October 2020; and Neil Munshi, 'Nigerian Economy at Risk of "Unravelling", Warns World Bank', *Financial Times*, 10 December 2020.

17   World Bank, 'World Bank Provides $346 Million to Strengthen Resilience and Livelihoods in the Lake Chad Region', 26 May 2020; and United Nations, 'Nigeria Humanitarian Fund Announces Record $22.4 Million Funding for Life-saving Activities and COVID-19 Response', 15 June 2020.

18   'Chad to Stop Participating in Regional Fight Against Armed Groups', Al-Jazeera, 10 April 2020.

19   'Generals on the Run', *Africa Confidential*, vol. 61, no. 4, 20 February 2020.

Sub-Saharan Africa

CENTRAL AFRICAN REPUBLIC

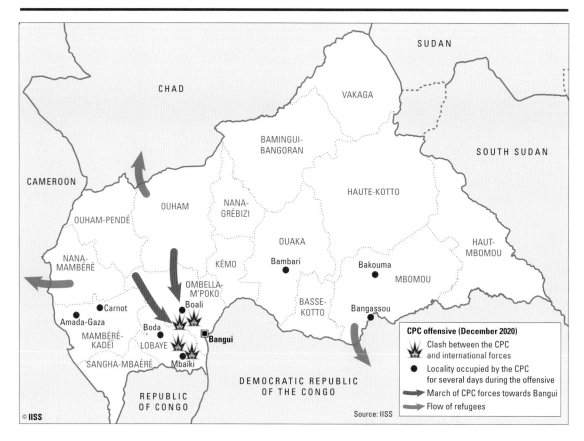

Overview

The conflict in the Central African Republic (CAR) broke out at the end of 2012 when armed groups in the Muslim-populated northern part of the country formed a coalition (Séléka) with the objective of ousting then-president François Bozizé. Following a failed peace deal mediated by the Economic Community of the Central African States (ECCAS), the Séléka rebel coalition marched into the capital Bangui and overthrew Bozizé in March 2013. However, the rebels proved unable to establish a functional government and the coalition collapsed in 2014, leaving a security vacuum in which armed groups proliferated. Since 2014, 11,000 United Nations peacekeepers have been deployed, elections were held in 2015–16, bringing Faustin-Archange Touadéra to power as president, and a peace agreement was signed in 2019 (the Khartoum agreement).[1] Despite this, most of the CAR territory remains under the control of armed groups without any meaningful political agenda and whose activities centre around extortion and banditry.

Towards the end of 2020, a security and political crisis triggered by general elections in December resulted in a new surge of violence. In response to the Constitutional Court's rejection of the candidacy of former president Bozizé – which had been supported by the newly formed Coalition of the Democratic Opposition (COD-2020) – Bozizé gathered together 3R (Return, Reclamation, Rehabilitation), the Popular Front for the Renaissance in the Central African Republic (FPRC), the Union for Peace in the Central African Republic (UPC), the Central African Patriotic Movement (MPC) and some 'anti-balaka' (self-defence) groups to form the armed Coalition of Patriots for Change (CPC). The CPC took up arms and marched on Bangui to disrupt the electoral process.

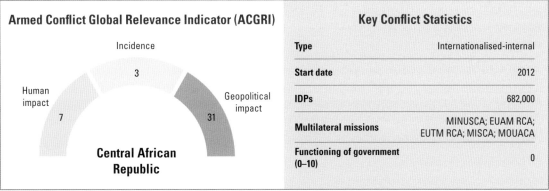

ACGRI pillars: IISS calculation based on multiple sources for 2020 and January/February 2021, (scale 0–100). See Notes on Methodology and Data Appendix for further details on Key Conflict Statistics.

This offensive was stopped by the UN Multidimensional Integrated Stabilization Mission in the Central African Republic (MINUSCA) with the help of the Rwandan army and the Russian private military company (PMC) Wagner. Elections went ahead as planned on 27 December, but armed groups disrupted the vote in 12 out of 16 provinces.[2] Touadéra was re-elected in the first round of the presidential election with 53.92% of the votes, but turnout was extremely low, reportedly only around 35%, and several irregularities were observed.[3] As of February 2021, the security situation appeared to be stabilising after international forces had pushed back the CPC. However, opposition parties have rejected the electoral results of the first round and have withdrawn from the second round of the legislative election.

Conflict Parties

Central African Armed Forces (FACA)

Strength: About 9,000.

Areas of operation: Main cities.

Leadership: Marie-Noelle Koyara (minister of defence), General Zéphirin Mamadou (chief of the army).

Structure: The army consists only of an infantry force (except for a river unit in charge of patrolling the Ubangi River), and the presidential guard is the best trained and equipped unit.

History: Experienced mutinies in 1996 and 1997, involved in many coups since independence, the army evaporated when the Séléka took power in 2013, with many soldiers joining the anti-balaka groups. The army reconstruction process began gradually in 2014, supported by the European Union, Russia and the UN.

Objectives: Protect the Touadéra regime.

Opponents: Armed groups.

Affiliates/allies: MINUSCA, Rwandan soldiers, Wagner private contractors.

Resources/capabilities: Lack of budget and mobility. Wages are often unpaid.

Union for Peace in the Central African Republic (UPC)

Strength: Unknown.

Areas of operation: Central and southeastern CAR (Ouaka, Kémo, Mbomou, Haut-Mbomou, Basse-Kotto and Haute-Kotto provinces), with militiamen deployed in seven out of 16 provinces.

Leadership: Ali Darassa, a long-standing Fulani rebel and bandit, formerly a commander of the Baba Laddé militia. The UPC leadership (*comzones*) is made up of professional bandits and regional mercenaries.

Structure: Unknown.

History: The first group to split from the Séléka coalition in 2014, the UPC has strategically enlarged its territory since then and is widely considered the most powerful armed group currently operating in the CAR.

Objectives: Officially, the UPC protects Fulani communities, but its main objective is to control natural resources and trade routes between the CAR and some of its neighbours.

Sub-Saharan Africa

Union for Peace in the Central African Republic (UPC)

Opponents: Government forces, some anti-balaka groups.

Affiliates/allies: 3R and possibly MPC. The UPC is a member of the CPC but has kept a low profile within the coalition. In some locations, the UPC has also been cooperating with the FPRC.

Resources/capabilities: Involved in the cattle and gold trade and weapons trafficking between Chad, the Democratic Republic of the Congo (DRC) and South Sudan.

Popular Front for the Renaissance in the Central African Republic (FPRC)

Strength: Unknown.

Areas of operation: Northeastern CAR: Vakaga, Haute-Kotto and Bamingui-Bangoran provinces.

Leadership: Abdoulaye Hissène (military leader) and Noureddine Adam (political leader).

Structure: Originally composed of Rounga, Goula, Chadian and Sudanese fighters, most of the Goula elements left the movement in 2017–18 and joined the Patriotic Rally for the Renewal of Central Africa.

History: Created after the fall of the Séléka coalition in 2014 by Séléka leaders Hissène and Adam to maintain their grip on northeastern CAR. In 2019, the FPRC fought unsuccessfully against the Movement of Central African Liberators for Justice (MLCJ) and were pushed out of Birao, the main city in Vakaga province.

Objectives: The FPRC's political agenda focuses on the protection of Muslim communities and the partition of the country. In 2015, Adam briefly proclaimed the creation of an independent state, the Logone Republic. Since 2015, Adam has unsuccessfully tried to reunite the former Séléka armed groups.

Opponents: MLCJ and government forces.

Affiliates/allies: Member of the CPC.

Resources/capabilities: Main revenue sources consist of weapons trafficking and the taxation of pastoralists and traders between Sudan, Chad and the CAR. Based in northeastern CAR, it is well connected to the Chadian and Sudanese security services, which send mercenaries and military equipment.

3R (Return, Reclamation, Rehabilitation)

Strength: Unknown.

Areas of operation: Ouham-Pendé and Nana-Mambéré provinces, with headquarters in De Gaulle town.

Leadership: Bidi Sidi Souleman, alias Sidiki Abass, a Fulani warlord. Abass was sanctioned by the UN in 2020. His death has been falsely reported several times, including in December 2020.

Structure: Unknown.

History: Emerged in late 2015 at the northwest border between the CAR and Cameroon and was mandated by Fulani cattle-owners based in Cameroon to protect their cattle during the transhumance. Its recruitment is Fulani-based.

Objectives: Protect Fulani cattle and economic predation.

Opponents: MINUSCA, government forces and anti-balaka groups.

Affiliates/allies: UPC, member of the CPC.

Resources/capabilities: Revenue mainly comes from the taxation of Fulani pastoralists and gold and weapons smuggling between Chad and Cameroon. Most of its military equipment comes from Chad.

Central African Patriotic Movement (MPC)

Strength: Unknown.

Areas of operation: Ouham and Nana-Gribizi provinces, with a stronghold in Kaga-Bandoro.

Leadership: Mahamat Al-Khatim, a Chadian whose family has settled in the CAR. He was appointed special adviser to the prime minister after the Khartoum agreement but resigned in August 2019. The *comzones* are all Chadian fighters.

Structure: Mostly composed of Chadian fighters from the Salamat region. The Salamat traditional leaders have a strong influence over Khatim.

History: The MPC was initially a splinter group of the FPRC, created by Khatim in mid-2015. The MPC is the strongest armed group in Ouham province. In July 2020, Khatim unsuccessfully attempted to form the 'Markounda coalition' under his leadership.

Objectives: Secure the interests of the Salamat communities in Ouham and Nana-Gribizi provinces (cattle migration, access to land and markets) and economic predation.

Opponents: Anti-balaka groups.

Affiliates/allies: Chadian security forces, member of the CPC.

Resources/capabilities: Revenue mainly comes from weapons smuggling between Chad and the CAR, the taxation of pastoralists from Chad and the taxation of trade and artisanal gold mining in the CAR provinces under its control.

Anti-balaka groups

Strength: Unknown.

Areas of operation: The anti-balaka militiamen are present in most of the CAR provinces (except for the Bamingui-Bangoran, Haut-Mbomou and Vakaga) but their activity was sporadic in 2020. Some of them have joined the CPC.

Leadership: No central leadership and chain of command but François Bozizé has some political influence over the movement. Two coordination branches (run by Maxime Mokom and by Sébastien Wenezoui and Patrice-Edouard Ngaissona, respectively) present themselves as interlocutors for the movement and have signed the Khartoum agreement. Suspected of war crimes, Ngaisonna was arrested in France in 2018 and handed over to the International Criminal Court (ICC). Mokom and Wenezoui were both part of the Touadéra government in 2019 but the former was dismissed in January 2021 after joining the CPC.

Structure: No structure.

History: A loose network of anti-Muslim local militias, which initially emerged as a self-defence movement against the Séléka in François Bozizé's ethnic stronghold and spread to western CAR in late 2013. They entered Bangui in December 2013 to drive out the Séléka coalition. In 2014 they became infamous for their retaliations against Muslim communities. In 2017, the movement's territorial reach was extended with the emergence of the so-called 'self-defence' groups in southeastern CAR. At present, the active anti-balaka groups focus on banditry and extortion.

Objectives: No clear agenda. The initial goal to drive Muslims out of the CAR quickly morphed into violent economic predation (looting and extortion). Despite their initial anti-Séléka motive, some have allied with Muslim armed groups. In December 2020, two anti-balaka factions close to François Bozizé (the Ndomaté and Mokom branches) joined the CPC.

Opponents: Muslim armed groups and other anti-balaka groups.

Affiliates/allies: Some anti-balaka groups are part of the CPC but not all.

Resources/capabilities: Artisanal weaponry, very few automatic weapons. No organised control of natural resources and trade routes.

United Nations Multidimensional Integrated Stabilization Mission in the Central African Republic (MINUSCA)

Strength: 14,921 personnel, as of January 2021.

Areas of operation: Throughout the CAR.

Leadership: Mankeur Ndiaye (head of MINUSCA), Lieutenant-General Balla Keita (force commander).

Structure: MINUSCA comprises 11,014 military personnel, 2,057 police, 1,162 civilians, 299 staff officers, 134 Experts on Mission and 255 volunteers. 3,700 additional peacekeepers were authorised by the UN Security Council in March 2021.

History: MINUSCA was authorised by the UN Security Council on 10 April 2014.

Objectives: MINUSCA's highest priority is the protection of civilians. Other tasks include supporting the transition process, facilitating humanitarian assistance, promoting and protecting human rights, supporting justice and the rule of law, and supporting disarmament, demobilisation, reintegration and repatriation processes.

Opponents: Various armed groups, including 3R.

Affiliates/allies: CAR government.

Resources/capabilities: Approved budget for mid-2020–mid-2021: US$1 billion.

Rwandan army

Strength: Unknown / infantry troops.

Areas of operation: Throughout the CAR.

Leadership: Rwandan Ministry of Defence.

Structure: Unknown.

History: On 21 December 2020, the Rwandan defence ministry confirmed it had deployed troops to the CAR under a bilateral security agreement with the CAR government. Rwandan forces participated in the protection of Bangui in December 2020 and in the counter-offensive led by Russian contractors and FACA against the CPC that started in January 2021.

Objectives: Secure the elections and protect the contingent of Rwandan troops within MINUSCA against targeting by CPC rebels.

Opponents: CPC forces.

Affiliates/allies: MINUSCA, FACA and Russian contractors (Wagner Group).

Resources/capabilities: Unknown.

Wagner Group

Strength: Unknown.

Areas of operation: Bangui and Lobaye in 2020 and central and eastern provinces in 2021.

Leadership: Dmitry Utkin (commander), Alexander Eermolaev (deputy commander), Andrei Troshev (chief of staff).

Structure: The company was established by businessman Yevgeny Prigozhin. It has particularly close ties with Russian military intelligence (GRU), the Ministry of Defence and President Vladimir Putin.

Sub-Saharan Africa

Wagner Group

History: The Wagner Group is a Russian security organisation closely linked to the Kremlin and military intelligence. It is used by Russia to carry out a range of officially deniable military and intelligence operations, and commercial activities abroad, including in the Middle East and Africa. Reports about the presence of the group in the CAR first emerged in 2018, when Russian instructors were sent to train the CAR army in the Berengo base.

Objectives: Initially, provide close protection for President Touadéra, training for the CAR army and set up two bases: Berengo for military training (Lobaye province) and Bria for medical facilities (Haute-Kotto province). Since December 2020 and the CPC attack, protect Bangui and organise a counter-offensive with the FACA and Rwandan troops.

Opponents: CPC forces.

Affiliates/allies: FACA and Rwandan troops.

Resources/capabilities: In December 2020, cargo aircraft supplied the Wagner Group with ammunition, vehicles and combat helicopters. At the end of January 2021, following discussion about the violation of the UN arms embargo, Russian diplomats announced the withdrawal of these helicopters but there was no confirmation on the ground. At the end of March 2021, another convoy of Wagner fighters entered the CAR from Sudan.

Conflict Drivers

Political

Deep-seated governance flaws and state ineffectiveness:
Since the early 1990s, deep-seated institutional corruption has undermined government effectiveness and its relations with international investors, who have often been arbitrarily taxed, and contributed to the state's collapse in 2013.[4] Despite donors' efforts to support reconstruction since 2016 (with budget support and technical assistance), governance has not improved under the Touadéra administration, as demonstrated by a series of corruption scandals.[5] The provision of basic services in most of the country remains subpar amid a low national budget (around US$515 million in 2020) and the diversion of aid money.[6]

Economic and social

Widespread competitive economic predation:
The gradual disintegration of the CAR state created a security vacuum in which an expanding range of armed groups competed for territory and resources. Most of the CAR territory is now controlled by non-state armed groups, of both domestic and foreign (Sudanese and Chadian) origin, whose revenue channels rely on violent predation on trade routes (through roadblocks) and natural resources (diamonds, gold, wildlife, marijuana and cattle), including the illegal taxation of the informal economy. Over time, they have built ties with important national and regional political and economic actors, and their activity has been increasingly integrated into the lucrative regional illicit economy (notably involving weapons, gold and cattle trafficking). Non-state armed groups occasionally agree on predatory cooperative arrangements.

Reversing the historic ethno-religious divide:
The Séléka power grab in March 2013 marked a fundamental reversal of the CAR's traditional political landscape. Since the country's independence in 1960, military officers drawn from savanna and riverside communities (central and southern CAR) had dominated the political system. The armed groups that ultimately formed the Séléka coalition in 2012 emerged in northern CAR, rebelling against the longstanding political and economic marginalisation of the Muslim northern provinces. For the first time in the CAR's post-independence history, a rebel force composed of Muslims from the north took power in a country where Muslims are a minority. Their emergence awoke the collective memory of historic Muslim slaving raids, which had depopulated entire regions between the sixteenth and nineteenth centuries. This has been leveraged by politicians to mobilise support against the Muslim 'invaders'.

International

The spillover effect:
Political and economic instability in neighbouring Chad and Sudan has historically impacted and fuelled conflicts in the CAR. Rising instability in both those countries amid increasing economic turmoil, governance flaws and political fragilities has expanded the recruitment pool for armed groups and bandits. Meanwhile, declining recruitment of

Sudanese and Chadian militiamen in Libya and Yemen has led to an increasing number of them moving into the CAR territory looking for looting and illicit business opportunities. Militiamen are also sometimes hired by CAR non-state armed groups who need additional forces.

Regional pastoralist conflicts:
Less visible than the movement of foreign fighters is that of pastoralist communities that have started to settle in northern CAR, driven by a deterioration of living conditions in Chad (notably from Ouaddai and Salamat provinces). They compete with local communities for resources and push out other pastoralist communities, such as the Fulani, who are gradually moving from the CAR to the DRC with their cattle.

Conflicting foreign interests:
The CAR government had signed security and training agreements in 2017 with the Wagner PMC, and in October 2019 with the Rwandan military. Russia's influence over the CAR has grown significantly since then, with the 2020 elections representing a key inflection point. Armoured vehicles were donated to the CAR army, expertise around online propaganda was provided prior to the elections, and additional military trainers were deployed to secure the elections and protect Touadéra's regime as the electoral crisis developed.[7] This deployment prompted a US call for transparency and respect of the UN arms embargo.[8]

The foreign actors supporting the peace process in the CAR (the African Union, ECCAS, the EU, France, Russia, the UN, the United States and the World Bank) formed a coordinating body called the G5 in 2014. However, this coordination effort has proven little more than a façade and the CAR has become a battleground for influence, particularly between France and the US, and Russia. The latter has been developing its military presence across Africa and was looking for a country in the region to host a Russian military base.[9] This international competition complicates conflict resolution as it divides the UN Security Council over the pathways to peace in the CAR and over the arms embargo. In addition, the motive behind the 2020 Rwandan military intervention remains unclear and raises concerns among countries neighbouring the CAR, who consider it an intrusion in their backyard.

Political and Military Developments

The failed elections
The first round of presidential and legislative elections scheduled for 27 December dominated the political backdrop in 2020. The run-up to the elections was characterised by various government ploys to skew the playing field – including, among others, a low registration rate, the withdrawal of refugees' voting rights and an attempt to prolong the mandate of the electoral commission's leadership – undermining trust and prompting most of the opposition parties to create the COD-2020 in February.[10] The coalition included Kwa na Kwa (KNK), the party of the former president François Bozizé, who had returned to the country in December 2019 despite an international warrant against him issued in 2013, and who was not arrested for fear of a popular uprising in the capital city. In mid-2020, Bozizé became KNK's presidential candidate and, later, the leader of the COD-2020.

In early December, the Constitutional Court ruled that the candidacy of Bozizé and those of several

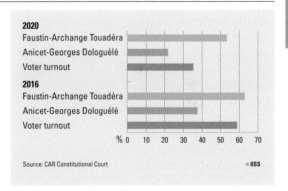

Figure 1: CAR presidential election results, 2016 and 2020

small warlords were invalid. Although Bozizé said he would respect the court's decision and endorsed Anicet-Georges Dologuélé as the replacement presidential candidate, he contacted the leaders of several armed groups behind the scenes. On 17 December, they formed a new armed-group coalition, the CPC, composed of 3R, FPRC, UPC, MPC and the Ndomaté and Mokom anti-balaka groups.

Sub-Saharan Africa

Despite the formation of the CPC, armed groups obstructing voting in many provinces and a COD-2020 request to postpone the vote, the government and the G5 pressed ahead with the first round of the elections as scheduled on 27 December. This prompted the CPC to occupy some cities and move towards Bangui to disrupt the electoral process. Their offensive was stopped by UN peacekeepers, the Rwandan military and Wagner paramilitaries close to the capital city. Touadéra was re-elected but with a low voter turnout and under dubious conditions (many irregularities were documented by the civil-society electoral observers).[11] Moreover, only 22 out of 140 MPs were elected as voting could only be completed in certain areas. The COD-2020 rejected the results of the presidential and legislative elections and withdrew from the second round of the legislative vote scheduled for 2021. Arbitrary arrests were made in opposition circles in January and February 2021.

The collapse of the Khartoum peace deal and the prospect of a new mediation

As several signatories of the Khartoum agreement are members of the CPC, the peace deal is effectively defunct. However, Angola has signalled a willingness to play a mediating role between the CPC and the government. In early February 2021, the Angolan chairperson of ECCAS, Gilberto Da Piedade Veríssimo, met with CPC representatives in southern Chad and with the leader of the FPRC, Noureddine Adam, in Sudan. This represented an initial step to revive the peace deal, although the stakeholders have yet to agree on the agenda of the negotiations in Angola.

Foreign-military deployments to support the government

The provision of Russian military equipment to Touadéra's government through the Wagner PMC increased ahead of the elections and turned into a direct military deployment during the electoral crisis as the CPC marched on Bangui. Responding to calls from the Touadéra regime, the Russian government sent over 300 'military instructors' and helicopters to help regular CAR government forces, and the Rwandan government deployed several hundred troops. MINUSCA was also reinforced with 300 additional Rwandan peacekeepers.[12] Both Russian and Rwandan fighters played a key role in pushing back the CPC in December 2020 and in launching a counter-offensive in late January 2021.

The deployment of additional Russian private contractors and Rwandan soldiers demonstrated the ineffectiveness of the national security forces. Various sources, including the head of MINUSCA, reported mass desertion by prison staff, soldiers and policemen as news spread about the CPC attacks.[13] Afterwards about 1,000 soldiers were dismissed by the government.[14]

Deteriorating security situation

Despite initially committing to the Khartoum agreement, 3R's Abass blocked its implementation in 2020, attacking MINUSCA peacekeepers several times, and was therefore put on the UN sanctions list in August 2020. The 3R played a major role in the CPC attack on Bangui in December. Since the elections, the CPC has targeted MINUSCA peacekeepers. Worried by the deterioration of the security situation, the head of MINUSCA, Mankeur Ndiaye, officially requested 3,000 additional peacekeepers in January 2021 and the CAR government asked the UN Security Council to lift the arms embargo.

Key Events in 2020–21

POLITICAL EVENTS

10 February 2020

16 opposition parties create the COD-2020.

5 June

The 3R announces its withdrawal from the Khartoum agreement.

17 June

The 3R and the UPC sign a cooperation agreement.

28 July

The KNK supports François Bozizé as its presidential candidate.

30 July

Touadéra meets with Ali Darassa, the UPC leader, to reach an agreement about the elections in the territory under his control.

2 September

Some armed groups criticise the Khartoum agreement in a press communiqué and call for the mediation of the Gabonese President, Ali Bongo.

Early September/13 October

The electoral commission registers voters for the December elections.

2 October

The government approves an election security plan.

3 December

The Constitutional Court rejects the candidacy of François Bozizé.

17 December

The CPC is created.

19 December

The COD-2020 suspends its electoral campaign due to insecurity.

26 December

The Constitutional Court rejects demands by opposition parties to postpone the elections.

27 December

The first rounds of legislative and presidential elections take place.

4 January 2021

The electoral commission announces the re-election of Touadéra as president.

4 January

An investigation is launched against François Bozizé on accusations of attempting a coup.

18 January

The Constitutional Court confirms the re-election of Touadéra.

19 January

The COD-2020 rejects the results of the elections.

21 January

The government declares a 15-day state of emergency.

1 February

The COD-2020 withdraws from the second round of legislative elections.

Early February

The Angolan chairperson of the ECCAS meets with CPC representatives.

MILITARY/VIOLENT EVENTS

15 June 2020

MINUSCA launches an operation against the 3R.

18–23 December

The CPC takes over several cities and blocks the supply road to Bangui.

21 December

Russian and Rwandan troops are deployed.

24 December

300 UN peacekeepers are deployed.

13 January 2021

The CPC attacks Bangui.

21 January

Government troops and allied forces launch a counter-offensive against the CPC.

Sub-Saharan Africa

Impact

Human rights and humanitarian

Human-rights violations increased in 2020 as the humanitarian situation worsened significantly. Violations of the Khartoum agreement (including violence or territorial extension by armed groups) rose and incidents directly affecting humanitarian workers or property increased by 39% compared to 2019.[15] The electoral crisis also led to an unknown number of casualties (including seven peacekeepers), extrajudicial executions, sexual abuses, arbitrary arrests, population displacement in the CAR (318,000) and a new outflow of refugees.[16] According to the United Nations High Commissioner for Refugees, in January 2021 more than 60,000 people had fled to Cameroon, Chad and the DRC.[17] The return of earlier refugees from Cameroon, which had started in the previous two years, was also stopped by the electoral violence in the western provinces (Ouham, Ouham-Pendé, Lobaye, Nana-Mambéré, Mambéré-Kadéi and Ombella-M'poko). The counter-offensive led by Russian and Rwandan troops caused civilian casualties, especially in Bambari.[18] Against this backdrop, the 2020 Humanitarian Response Plan (US$553m) was funded at 66%.[19] In 2021, 2.8m people – more than half of the CAR population – will need humanitarian assistance and 1.9m are food insecure.[20] To meet these urgent needs in 2021, humanitarian partners estimate that they will require US$444.7m.

Political stability

Fragility in the CAR increased significantly in 2020. Compared to the 2015–16 elections, the 2020 elections were a major setback, amid the upsurge of violence and insecurity and the collapse of the Khartoum agreement. In addition, the much lower voter turnout in 2020 and alleged electoral fraud undermined Touadéra's legitimacy. Moreover, most of the opposition parties withdrew from the legislative election and will not be represented in the new National Assembly.

Relations with neighbouring and international partners and geopolitical implications

The electoral crisis elevated the security partnerships between the CAR government and Rwanda and Russia respectively into military deployments and direct confrontations. The ineffectiveness of the national security forces increased the dependence of the CAR government on these partners. As these new security partnerships may also carry strategic and economic components (for instance the allocation of mining rights or the creation of a military base), they raised scrutiny from the CAR's neighbours, as well as from France and the US.[21] In addition, the actions of Russian troops, who may have committed human-rights abuses against civilians during the counter-offensive against the CPC, put the UN peacekeeping mission in a delicate position.[22]

Conflict Outlook

Political scenarios

The 2020 electoral crisis increased fragility in the CAR, and the outlook for 2021 is complicated by yet more uncertainties, including a president with a very weak mandate and the risk of a new military confrontation. The COD-2020's withdrawal from the second round of the electoral process will result in a victory for President Touadéra's party in the legislative election and give him a very strong majority in the National Assembly. But the complete marginalisation of opposition parties will undermine his legitimacy.

Moreover, if the CPC continues to oppose the re-elected president and launches new attacks, the government's and MINUSCA's control of territory outside the main cities will be threatened, with dire consequences for state-building efforts funded by donors.

Prospects for peace

Angola has expressed a willingness to mediate between the CPC and the government to break the stalemate, offering to organise peace talks in Luanda. Although Angolan President João Lourenço is viewed favourably by Touadéra and his allies in Rwanda and Russia, he is not trusted by Bozizé and the CPC.

The government and the UN hope that the Angolan mediation will revive the Khartoum agreement and convince the UPC, MPC and other armed groups to recommit to the very same peace deal that they have repeatedly violated. However, non-state armed groups may take this opportunity to renegotiate the original terms. The government and the UN will probably have to make concessions in order to end the conflict with the CPC and Bozizé.

The success of this strategy will depend on whether the CPC remains cohesive and whether its members prefer the status quo to military confrontation, particularly before the start of the rainy season in May 2021. Given the successful government–Rwandan–Russian counter-offensive, the CPC will need to seek reinforcement from Sudanese and Chadian armed groups to continue the fight.

Strategic implications and regional and global influences

The deployment of Russian private contractors and Rwandan soldiers changed the course of the conflict and saved the Touadéra regime. Given the ineffectiveness of the CAR security forces, it is very likely that these troops will remain in the country. Although Russian authorities – in response to the negative US reaction to their military intervention in the CAR – promised to withdraw their helicopters and troops, at the time of writing only the helicopters had been withdrawn.

Russia's decisive role in the run-up and aftermath of the elections will likely increase its influence in the CAR in 2021. However, Rwandan and Russian military interventions are negatively perceived by the CAR's neighbours, especially Chad and the Republic of Congo, who see the CAR as their backyard and view military deployments from non-regional actors with suspicion.

The inadequacy of the CAR armed forces highlighted the failure of the UN-sponsored security-sector reform over the last five years. International efforts to rebuild the CAR security and defence sectors will need to be rethought. However, coordinating these foreign actors and reaching agreement with the CAR government on a new strategy for security-sector reform will prove challenging.

Notes

[1] The main provisions of the Khartoum agreement are a framework for the inclusion of armed groups in the government, a disarmament, demobilisation and reintegration (DDR) programme, and the creation of mixed units of state-security personnel and militiamen.

[2] Phone interview conducted with a journalist, 29 December 2020.

[3] AFRICA24 (@AFRICA24TV), tweet, 4 January 2021.

[4] International Crisis Group, 'Central African Republic: Anatomy of a Phantom State', 13 December 2007.

[5] Nathalia Dukhan, 'State of Prey Proxies, Predators, and Profiteers in the Central African Republic', State of Prey, October 2020.

[6] The United Nations Office for the Coordination of Humanitarian Affairs reported that 2.8 million people will need assistance in 2021. See United Nations Office for the Coordination of Humanitarian Affairs, 'Central African Republic: Situation Report', 12 March 2021.

[7] 'Russia Sends 300 Military Instructors to Central African Republic', BBC News, 22 December 2020.

[8] 'US Calls for Transparency as Russians Enter Central Africa', EURACTIV, 24 December 2020.

[9] Andrew Roth, 'Central African Republic Considers Hosting Russian Military Base', *Guardian*, 25 October 2019.

[10] Eugenia Pandora and Thierry Vircoulon, 'Centrafrique: des Élections sans Témoin, sans Arbitre et peut-être sans le Peuple' [Central African Republic: Elections without Witnesses, without Referees and Perhaps without the People], Afrique Décryptages, 30 November 2020.

[11] Réseau Arc-en Ciel, 'Déclaration Préliminaire du Réseau Arc-en Ciel (RAC) sur les Élections Présidentielle et Législatives Couplées du 27 Décembre 2020 en République Centrafricaine' [Preliminary Statement by the Arc-en Ciel Network (RAC) on the Coupled Presidential and Legislative Elections of 27 December 2020 in the Central African Republic], 30 December 2020.

[12] 'Helping Hands: UNMISS Peacekeepers Support Sister UN Mission in Central African Republic', United Nations Peacekeeping, 11 January 2021.

[13] United Nations Security Council, 'Top Official Calls Upon Security Council to Deploy More Peacekeepers in Central African Republic, amid Post-election Surge in Violence', Press Release SC/14418, 21 January 2021.

[14] Achille Mbog Pibasso, 'Centrafrique: Près de 1000 Soldats Radiés de L'armée' [Central African Republic: Nearly 1,000 Soldiers Struck Off from the Army], Centrafrique Presse, 7 February 2021.

[15] United Nations Office for the Coordination of Humanitarian Affairs, 'Central African Republic: Situation Report', 3 February 2021.

[16] See Internal Displacement Monitoring Centre (IDMC), '2020 Internal Displacement', Global Internal Displacement Database. Adrienne Surprenant, '"Our Village Is Completely Destroyed"': Displaced Central Africans Recount Rapes and Disappearances', The New Humanitarian, 15 February 2021; and United Nations Office for the Coordination of Humanitarian Affairs, 'Central African Republic: Situation Report', 2 March 2021.

[17] Florence Morice, 'Crise Sécuritaire en Centrafrique: Plus de 60 000 Réfugiés Ont Déjà Fui Le Pays' [Security Crisis in the Central African Republic: Over 60,000 Refugees Have Already Fled the Country], RFI, 12 January 2021.

[18] Amnesty International, 'Central African Republic: Amnesty Investigation Reveals Full Horror of Conflict and Election Violence', 25 February 2021.

[19] United Nations Office for the Coordination of Humanitarian Affairs, 'Central African Republic: Situation Report', 12 March 2021.

[20] *Ibid.*

[21] Roth, 'Central African Republic Considers Hosting Russian Military Base'.

[22] Amnesty International, 'Central African Republic: Amnesty Investigation Reveals Full Horror of Conflict and Election Violence'; and Nacer Talel, '"UN Not Collaborating with Russian Forces in CAR"', Anadolu Agency, 3 February 2021.

Sub-Saharan Africa

SOUTH SUDAN

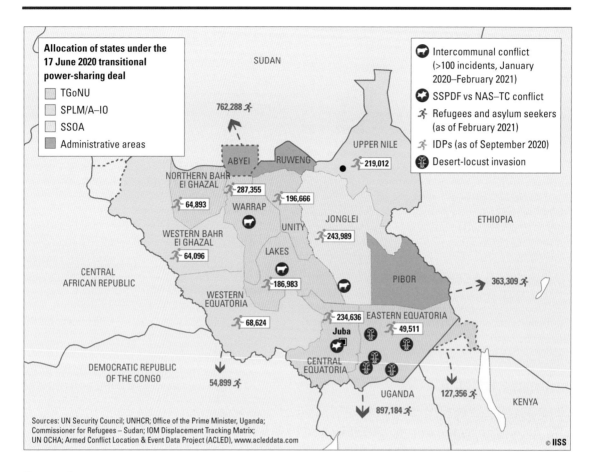

Allocation of states under the 17 June 2020 transitional power-sharing deal
- TGoNU
- SPLM/A–IO
- SSOA
- Administrative areas

- Intercommunal conflict (>100 incidents, January 2020–February 2021)
- SSPDF vs NAS–TC conflict
- Refugees and asylum seekers (as of February 2021)
- IDPs (as of September 2020)
- Desert-locust invasion

SUDAN

762,288

ABYEI   RUWENG   UPPER NILE

NORTHERN BAHR El GHAZAL   287,355

64,893

196,666

WARRAP

219,012

WESTERN BAHR El GHAZAL

UNITY

JONGLEI   243,989

ETHIOPIA

64,096

LAKES

CENTRAL AFRICAN REPUBLIC

186,983

PIBOR   363,309

WESTERN EQUATORIA

234,636   EASTERN EQUATORIA

68,624   Juba   49,511

DEMOCRATIC REPUBLIC OF THE CONGO

CENTRAL EQUATORIA

54,899

UGANDA   127,356   KENYA

897,184

Sources: UN Security Council; UNHCR; Office of the Prime Minister, Uganda; Commissioner for Refugees – Sudan; IOM Displacement Tracking Matrix; UN OCHA; Armed Conflict Location & Event Data Project (ACLED), www.acleddata.com

© IISS

Overview

Two years after gaining independence from Sudan in 2011, South Sudan was plunged into a civil war that stemmed from power struggles within the ruling Sudan People's Liberation Movement/Army (SPLM/A). After President Salva Kiir dismissed then vice-president Riek Machar, the SPLM/A split as Machar loyalists formed the SPLM/A–In Opposition (SPLM/A–IO). This started a spiral of violence that divided the country along ethnic lines. The Agreement on the Resolution of the Conflict in the Republic of South Sudan (ARCSS) was signed by the two main parties in August 2015, but quickly collapsed as fighting resumed between Kiir's and Machar's forces in 2016, triggering a second and more complex wave of conflict. Successive negotiations mediated by the regional bloc Intergovernmental Authority on Development (IGAD) culminated in

the signing of the Revitalised ARCSS (R-ARCSS) in September 2018, raising hope for peace in this brutal conflict which has killed almost 400,000 people[1] and displaced around four million.[2]

Fighting between the government and opposition groups has subsided after the R-ARCSS. In February 2020, a Transitional Government of National Unity (TGoNU) was formed after key concessions were made by both Kiir and Machar. However, obstacles to a durable peace settlement remained. Rebels in the Equatoria region continued to fight the government, demanding full implementation of federalism. Competition over scarce resources caused rising intercommunal clashes – involving the two country's main ethnic groups, Dinka and Nuer, but also subsections of these groups and other tribes, such as the Shilluk and Murle – which the government

Armed Conflict Global Relevance Indicator (ACGRI)

Incidence

8

Human impact

22

Geopolitical impact

45

South Sudan

Key Conflict Statistics

Type	Internal | Localised insurgency & intercommunal
Start date	2013
IDPs	1,436,000
Fatalities	2,640
Multilateral missions	UNMISS; CTSAMVM

ACGRI pillars: IISS calculation based on multiple sources for 2020 and January/February 2021 (scale 0–100). See Notes on Methodology and Data Appendix for further details on Key Conflict Statistics.

lacked mechanisms to solve. Meanwhile, the misappropriation of oil revenues and peace-deal funds undermined investments in South Sudan's post-war institutions.

In addition, the drop in global oil prices and disruption of commercial activities caused by the coronavirus pandemic dealt a serious blow to the South Sudanese economy, which in 2018–19 had just been starting to recover from a war-driven four-year contraction cycle, with improved oil revenues and stability after the 2018 R-ARCSS. The pandemic strained already dire humanitarian and food-security situations, worsening the effects of massive floods and locust invasions in 2020. Coronavirus restrictions also threatened peace and security by slowing an already lagging army-unification process, which could hamper the gains made on the political front.

Conflict Parties

Sub-Saharan Africa

Sudan People's Liberation Movement/Army (SPLM/A)/ Transitional Government of National Unity (TGoNU)/ South Sudan armed forces

Strength: The SSPDF has approximately 185,000 soldiers. Its precise size is unknown, after alliances shifted and various militias were integrated into it.

Areas of operation: Presence throughout the country, except for pockets in opposition areas (Central and Western Equatoria states).

Leadership: Salva Kiir.

Structure: Nine territorial divisions and three services (ground force, air force and defence, and navy). Hierarchical leadership including the commander-in-chief, the minister of defence and veteran affairs, the chief of defence force, the deputy chief of defence force and the inspector general.

History: The SPLM/A was founded in 1983 by generals who defected from the Sudanese army to fight for South Sudan's autonomy. In 2018, the SPLA was renamed the South Sudan People's Defence Force (SSPDF). In 2019, the party was reunified to include the Former Detainees (FD) group and the SPLM/A–IO splintered faction led by Taban Deng Gai.

Objectives: Govern South Sudan and defeat armed opposition groups.

Opponents: National Salvation Front–Thomas Cirillo (NAS–TC), South Sudan Opposition Movements Alliance (SSOMA).

Affiliates/allies: SPLM/A–IO (in Equatoria region against the NAS–TC). Tribal militias: Maban Defence Force, Mathiang Anyoor, Gelwent. Regional allies during the civil war: Uganda People's Defence Force, Justice and Equality Movement, SPLM–North.

Resources/capabilities: Equipped with heavy artillery, tanks, armoured fighting vehicles and attack helicopters. The 2020 defence budget was US$93.9m, or 2.25% of the country's GDP. However, security expenditures are opaque and official data is not reliable, with significant off-budget spending believed to occur. In 2020, the UN maintained and extended its arms embargo on South Sudan.

Sudan People's Liberation Movement/Army–In Opposition (SPLM/A–IO)

Strength: Unknown. After the signing of the 2018 R-ARCSS, increased recruitment was reported (but denied by Machar) ahead of the planned unification of the army.

Areas of operation: Cantonment across the country, fighting against the NAS–TC in the states of Central and Western Equatoria.

Sudan People's Liberation Movement/Army–In Opposition (SPLM/A–IO)

Leadership: Riek Machar.

Structure: Loose grouping of fragmented armed groups, low institutionalisation.

History: Founded in 2013 following the split between Kiir and then vice-president Machar. Ethnically dominated by the Nuer. In 2018, the SPLM/A–IO signed the R-ARCSS with the government and has since mostly respected the ceasefire but has also cooperated with the SSPDF against the NAS–TC. In 2020, the SPLM/A–IO was weakened by multiple defections caused by rising discontent over Machar's leadership.

Objectives: Prior to the R-ARCSS: remove Kiir from power and govern South Sudan. After the R-ARCSS: secure a favourable position in the new government and the new unified army.

Opponents: NAS–TC, SSOMA.

Affiliates/allies: The group cooperated with the SSPDF against the NAS–TC in 2020.

Resources/capabilities: Assault rifles, mortars, rockets, grenades, pistols and machine guns. Ammunition mostly from China and Sudan.

National Salvation Front–Thomas Cirillo (NAS–TC)

Strength: Unknown.

Areas of operation: Central and Western Equatoria states.

Leadership: Thomas Cirillo Swaka.

Structure: The NAS–TC mostly appeals to members of the Bari community in the Equatoria region. After its creation, the group was joined by some SPLM/A–IO officials, who accused Machar of disenfranchising non-Nuers.

History: Formed in March 2017 by General Thomas Cirillo Swaka, who defected from the SPLA in February 2017. After rejecting the R-ARCSS in 2018, the NAS–TC became the main armed opposition to the government.

Objectives: Call for greater federalism and inclusion of Equatorians' local demands, and overthrow Kiir.

Opponents: SSPDF, SPLM/A–IO.

Affiliates/allies: Cirillo is also chair of the SSOMA.

Resources/capabilities: The NAS–TC possesses equipment looted from the SSPDF, mainly during ambushes. Weapons include AK-47s and AKM general-purpose machine guns. The group has a small supply of uniforms and ammunition. It also takes part in forced recruitment and kidnappings.

South Sudan United Front/Army (SSUF/A)

Strength: Unknown.

Areas of operation: Western Bahr el-Ghazal (Raja town).

Leadership: Paul Malong Awan.

Structure: Unknown.

History: Created in April 2018 under the leadership of Paul Malong Awan, former chief of staff of the SPLA and former governor of Northern Bahr el-Ghazal State. Excluded from the 2018 R-ARCSS, Malong had expressed his willingness to join the peace process and later joined Cirillo's South Sudan National Democratic Alliance (SSNDA) rebel coalition along with Pagan Amum's Real Sudan People's Liberation Movement (R–SPLM) in August 2019 to form the SSOMA.

Objectives: 'Arrest the carnage' of the conflict and overthrow Kiir, whom Malong accuses of mismanaging the country and looting its resources. The SSUF also calls for greater federalism.

Opponents: SSPDF.

Affiliates/allies: SSNDA, R–SPLM.

Resources/capabilities: Exact supplies are unknown – the SSUF most likely possesses weapons formerly belonging to the SSPDF, including machine guns, assault rifles, pistols and ammunition.

South Sudan Opposition Movements Alliance (SSOMA)

Strength: Unknown.

Areas of operation: Western and Central Equatoria states.

Leadership: Thomas Cirillo Swaka.

Structure: The SSOMA is composed of the NAS–TC, the R–SPLM, the SSUF/A, the United Democratic Revolutionary Movement/Army, the National Democratic Movement–Patriotic Front (NDM–PF) and the South Sudan National Movement for Change.

History: The SSOMA was created in August 2019 out of the merger of the SSNDA with Malong's SSUF/A, and a new

party called the R–SPLM. The SSNDA was itself an offshoot of the SSOA, which joined the R-ARCSS in September 2018. In September 2020, the SSOMA split as Thomas Cirillo suspended the membership of Malong's SSUF/A, which Pagan Amum's R–SPLM rejected.

Objectives: Reject the R-ARCSS and obtain a renegotiation of the agreement to achieve 'fundamental Democratic Transformation change in South Sudan'.

Opponents: SSPDF and SPLM/A–IO.

Affiliates/allies: Unknown.

Resources/capabilities: Unknown.

United Nations Mission in the Republic of South Sudan (UNMISS)	
Strength: 19,078 total personnel (as of January 2021).	**Objectives:** After the civil war broke out in 2013, UNSC Resolution 2155 (2014) updated the UNMISS mandate to prioritise civilian protection and human-rights monitoring, as well as supporting the delivery of humanitarian aid and the ceasefire implementation. The UNSC also authorised the Regional Protection Force 'to use robust action to facilitate the conditions for safe and free movement' around Juba.[3]
Areas of operation: Presence across the country.	
Leadership: Special Representative David Shearer.	
Structure: As of January 2021, UNMISS was composed of 14,169 contingent troops, 214 Experts on Mission, 1,638 police personnel, 2,275 civilians (2018 data), 386 staff officers and 396 UN volunteers.	
	Opponents: n/a.
History: Established on 8 July 2011 by UN Security Council (UNSC) Resolution 1996 to consolidate peace and security and to help establish conditions for development. On 12 March 2020, the UNSC extended the mission's mandate until 15 March 2021.	**Affiliates/allies:** n/a.
	Resources/capabilities: Approved budget (July 2020–June 2021): US$1.26 billion.

The Conflict Parties table only features armed groups that were involved in state-linked fighting and negotiations in 2020 and not communal fighting. In 2018, some of South Sudan's main opposition groups renounced armed struggle to join the R-ARCSS, including the coalition of opposition groups called the South Sudan Opposition Alliance (SSOA), so it has not been included in the Conflict Parties table.

Conflict Drivers

Political

Centre–periphery dynamics:
The South Sudanese leadership has focused on state-building from the centre to the detriment of local institutions. Although the 2005 Interim Constitution had provided for a decentralised system, this was weakened by the 2011 Transitional Constitution and not applied in practice. In this context, the SPLM/A-led central government monopolised institutions at both national and local levels and based local appointments on patronage rather than competency, compromising local governance and fuelling local rebellions. Since the 2018 R-ARCSS, rebels in the states of Central and Western Equatoria led by Thomas Cirillo have continued to contest the centralisation of power, calling for the implementation of federalism to address local grievances and enact inclusive politics.

Elite power competition:
Infighting within the SPLM/A over leadership, resources and power is deeply rooted. Kiir, who enjoyed sweeping and largely unchecked constitutional powers after independence, made many unilateral decisions – including on oil production – that intensified SPLM/A rivalries. The group's 2013 split mobilised fighters who targeted communities along ethnic lines beyond the Dinka–Nuer dichotomy. Compounding these divisions, Kiir's decision to increase the number of states (from ten to 28 in 2015 and to 32 in 2017) in favour of Dinka communities caused national-level tensions and local rebellions, especially in Upper Nile, Central and Western Equatoria and Western Bahr el-Ghazal.

Economic and social

War economy:
Oil dependency, weak institutions, arbitrary regulatory management of natural resources (crude oil, gold, timber), misappropriation and diversion of public resources, and elite predatory behaviours are at the heart of the South Sudanese armed conflict. The resulting shortfalls have made licit and illicit economies interdependent. Rivalries over the control of oilfields have caused violent fighting and infrastructure destruction, especially in Upper Nile, and leaders' misappropriation of hydrocarbon revenues has perpetuated the war by financing and equipping militias, while also hampering the development of accountable institutions.[4] Not only has oil been integrated in the prevailing rent-seeking patronage system, but the 2012 oil-production halt was also a key conflict trigger in 2013.

Intercommunal resource competition:
Intercommunal fighting stems from herding practices that predate the civil war. However, political

elites have mobilised local communities for their own interests and, in combination with the proliferation of small weapons, thereby complexified and intensified intercommunal conflict. Climate change has also compounded violent competition over land and water by intensifying floods and droughts.

The coronavirus pandemic:
South Sudan's weak health system, sub-par sanitation standards and camp overcrowding made the population particularly vulnerable to COVID-19 transmission. As of 28 February 2021, South Sudan had recorded 7,349 total cases and 87 deaths, but the actual number of cases could have been higher, given limited testing and under-reporting due to stigma against COVID-19 patients.[5] Beyond the health impact of the pandemic, mobility restrictions to curb transmission obstructed peace in South Sudan by delaying political negotiations and army unification, slowing humanitarian aid and worsening the economic and food-security situation.

International
Involvement of third parties:
Neighbouring countries have fuelled the conflict by supporting rival factions in South Sudan. Uganda, a long-standing SPLM/A ally, has provided Kiir's army with troops and weapons, while Sudan backed rebel groups after South Sudan's independence amid unresolved bilateral territorial and oil-revenue disputes.[6] However, a rapprochement between Khartoum and Kampala, and their increasing interest in securing peace – Uganda hosts the largest South Sudanese refugee population, while Sudan needs to secure South Sudan's payments to its oil-export pipeline – has led them to become key R-ARCSS mediators.[7] In addition, South Sudan's porous borders have facilitated illegal trafficking in arms, drugs and wildlife, which has contributed to the continuation of the armed conflict. Wider international pressure has also influenced the conflict dynamics: after a relative diplomatic withdrawal, the United States' decision to sanction Vice-President Taban Deng Gai in January 2020 and threats of additional measures reportedly pressed Kiir and Machar to cooperate.[8]

Political and Military Developments

Unity government's slow progress
In February 2020, the R-ARCSS signatories formed a transitional government, ending a nine-month stalemate after significant concessions from the main rivals. Amid regional pressure, Kiir reinstated the pre-war number of ten states (with three administrative areas), while Machar agreed to return to Juba under the protection of Kiir's security. The new government then started negotiations to distribute both state- and local-level positions among formerly warring parties, but disagreements arose over strategic positions, especially the governorship of the oil-rich Upper Nile. From March 2020, the coronavirus pandemic slowed power-sharing talks, as face-to-face meetings were limited and many officials contracted the virus. Despite these difficulties, members of the unity government made progress on key power-sharing points and completed the appointment of state governors in January 2021.

Rome peace talks
In parallel, the government participated in talks with the SSOMA coalition (which comprises rebel groups who continue to reject the R-ARCSS) under the mediation of the Community of Sant'Egidio organisation in Rome, Italy. A ceasefire was agreed in January 2020, but with meetings halted by the pandemic from March, the agreement ultimately fell apart in April amid renewed clashes between NAS–TC (which dominates the SSOMA) and SSPDF and SPLM/A–IO troops in Central and Western Equatoria. Following the split of the SSOMA, the two splintered factions – one led by Cirillo and the other by SSUF/A leader Malong – separately resumed the Rome talks in October and agreed to another ceasefire with the government. The resumption of talks reduced fighting at the end of 2020 and led to agreement on some principles for future negotiations. However, the pandemic again slowed down talks in early 2021. Given the difficulty of holding talks in Rome amid pandemic restrictions, the Sant'Egidio mediators suggested moving the negotiations to Kenya. Malong's faction accepted such a move, pending Kenyan government approval, but Cirillo's camp rejected it, adding uncertainty over the future of these peace talks.

Continuing hostilities in the Equatoria region

The signatories of the 2018 R-ARCSS mostly refrained from fighting each other (despite occasional skirmishes between the SSPDF and SPLM/A–IO) in 2020–21.[9] However, the SSPDF and SPLM/A–IO forces continued joint operations against NAS–TC rebels, who had rejected the R-ARCSS on the grounds of demanding greater implementation of federalism. The aforementioned Rome talks represented an attempt to stem this violence in the states of Central and Western Equatoria, South Sudan's most active hotspots since 2018.[10]

The January 2020 ceasefire between the NAS–TC and the SSPDF (allied with the SPLM/A–IO) collapsed as fighting resumed with an NAS–TC attack on the SPLM/A–IO on 9 April, in supposed retaliation for a wave of SPLM/A–IO assaults against civilians.[11] The two sides regularly clashed afterwards amid government offensives to regain control over NAS–TC-held territories, which ousted rebels from strategic zones.

Intercommunal conflict

Intercommunal conflict soared in South Sudan in 2020. Fighting involved cattle raiding and disputes over land and boundaries, which triggered deadly retaliation cycles among rival tribes, especially in Jonglei, Lakes, Unity, Warrap and Western Bahr el-Ghazal states.[12] Warrap State alone recorded more than 1,000 fatalities between June and November 2020.[13] A wider range and quantity of available arms, in addition to the power vacuum left by vacant local-government positions, may have contributed to this alarming trend.[14] In response, Kiir announced the launch of a disarmament campaign across the country in July. However, this process was itself problematic, as it involved the killing, beating and detention of civilians unwilling to give up arms, which is likely to fuel further conflict.

Army unification

The implementation of the R-ARCSS's security provisions – including army unification and disarmament, demobilisation and reintegration (DDR) – was more limited than its political elements. In 2020, coronavirus measures undermined the unification of rival forces, as troop mobility was restricted and training was suspended in March. The lack of essential goods and flooding in cantonment sites also caused desertions, which risks discouraging cantonment registrations and hinders DDR.

Key Events in 2020–21

POLITICAL EVENTS

8 January 2020

The United States sanctions Vice-President Taban Teng Gai over allegedly arranging and directing the killings of opposition politician Aggrey Idri Ezibon and human-rights lawyer Dong Samuel Luak.

13 January

The government and SSOMA sign the Rome Declaration, agreeing to cease hostilities, discuss mechanisms to resolve differences and guarantee humanitarian access.

22 February

Salva Kiir and Riek Machar form a new coalition government scheduled to remain in power for a 36-month transitional period. Machar is sworn in as the first of five vice-presidents.

20 March

South Sudan imposes a series of partial lockdown measures and a curfew to prevent the spread of the coronavirus pandemic.

MILITARY/VIOLENT EVENTS

9 March 2020

A UN report accuses government and rebel forces of having used deliberate starvation during the war.

9 April

The January ceasefire breaks down between the government and SSOMA after the NAS–TC attacks Machar's SPLM/A–IO forces in Yei River county.

18 May

Machar and his wife Angelina Teny test positive for COVID-19, shortly followed by two other vice-presidents and all 15 members of South Sudan's COVID-19 task force, amid eased lockdown restrictions.

17 June

Kiir and Machar reach a transitional power-sharing deal over the control of states after three months of disagreement.

10 August

The unity government agrees on further power-sharing points but Kiir and Machar remain divided over the Upper Nile governorship candidate (Jonson Olony).

16 September

Reacting to budgetary losses in the context of a drop in global oil prices, Kiir dismisses the finance minister and the heads of the National Revenue Authority and the Nile Petroleum Corporation.

12 October

Resumed negotiations between the government and the sub-factions of SSOMA in Rome result in a renewed ceasefire agreement.

14 November

The SSOMA branch led by Tomas Cirillo agrees to join the R-ARCSS's ceasefire monitoring body (Ceasefire and Transitional Security Arrangements Monitoring and Verification Mechanism) in January 2021.

29 January 2021

Kiir appoints a new governor and deputy governor for Upper Nile State after months of disagreements with the SPLM/A–IO. The government agrees to set up the Hybrid Court for South Sudan (HCSS).

30 January

Negotiations in Rome between the two SSOMA factions are postponed as government delegates contract COVID-19.

4 February

The government imposes a new partial lockdown as COVID-19 cases surge.

16 May

A cycle of clashes between Murle and Lou Nuer communities kills hundreds of civilians in Jonglei.

29 May

The UNSC extends its arms embargo on the South Sudanese government and targeted individuals until May 2021.

8 July

Kiir vows to launch a nationwide disarmament programme and intercommunal mediations to tackle increasing intercommunal fighting.

11 August

A disarmament operation led by government troops in Tonj East county, Warrap, leads to clashes with Dinka civilians who refuse to give up arms, killing at least 148.

2 September

UNMISS sets up a temporary base in Lobonok, Central Equatoria State, after an alleged rise of NAS–TC attacks against civilians and humanitarian workers in the area.

17 November

The UN reports that intercommunal fighting killed more than 1,000 people in Warrap State in the previous six months.

December

Civilians in Kajo-Keji county, Central Equatoria State, are forced to flee to areas bordering Uganda after clashes between the SSPDF and former SPLM–IO forces loyal to Major General Moses Lokujo, who defected from the SSPDF in September.

19 February 2021

The UN reports that the scope and scale of localised violence documented in 2020 in South Sudan spread across three quarters of the country and 'far exceeds the violence between 2013 and 2019'.[15]

Impact

Human rights and humanitarian

Displacement:

Almost 4m South Sudanese people remained forcibly displaced as of January 2021 (including 2.18m outside the country and around 1.7m internally).[16] Intercommunal conflict and continued fighting between the state and rebels in the Equatoria region displaced tens of thousands during 2020, adding to at least 480,000 people displaced by heavy flooding throughout the country.[17] Fear of conflict resumption and pandemic-related mobility restrictions limited the voluntary return of internally displaced persons (IDPs) to their homes. In September 2020, IDPs in Juba, Bor and Bentiu protested against UNMISS's withdrawal from these Protection of Civilians sites (which have been redesignated as IDP camps), as they still needed protection from the ongoing conflict.

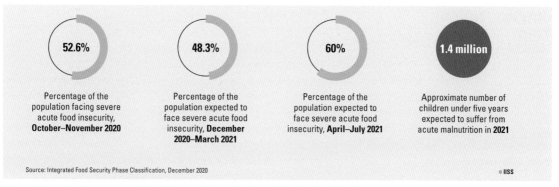

Figure 1: Levels of severe acute food insecurity and malnutrition in South Sudan

Human-rights violations:

Surging intercommunal violence caused the number of attacks on civilians to increase significantly compared to 2019. In Central Equatoria State, both rebels and government forces were involved in extrajudicial executions, abductions, torture, rape and destruction of civilian property.[18] The coronavirus pandemic worsened human-rights violations across the country as the authorities used arbitrary arrest and detention, ill-treatment and extortion to enforce lockdown measures. Lockdown restrictions and subsequent income losses also made women more vulnerable to sexual exploitation, abduction, trafficking and gender-based violence.[19]

Food insecurity:

As the livelihoods of the South Sudanese continued to bear the cumulative effect of the country's civil war, an alarming number of more than 7.2m people were projected to face severe food insecurity between April and July 2021: almost 1m more people than between October and November 2020. Child malnutrition reached its peak since 2013, with around 1.4m children under five years old projected to experience acute malnutrition in 2021.[20] Coronavirus lockdown measures disrupted food-supply chains and raised food prices, while school closures prevented children from receiving free school meals. Mass flooding and a desert-locust invasion that spanned east Africa also damaged crops, caused new displacement and worsened the disruption of escalating local conflicts on livelihoods and food insecurity.

Humanitarian aid:

Revised to account for the effects of the pandemic, the 2020 South Sudan Humanitarian Response Plan budget was unprecedented: almost US$2bn to provide relief to almost 7.5m people in need of humanitarian aid.[21] Adding to the strains caused by flooding, the pandemic delayed aid delivery due to movement restrictions, visa suspensions and entry denials for humanitarian workers. Aid workers continued to experience attacks and ambushes, leading some to relocate or suspend their activities.

Economic and social

Years of civil war have weakened South Sudan's productive capacity and hampered economic development, resulting in more than four out of five people living on less than US$1 per day.[22] In 2020, South Sudanese people still had limited access to services as government expenditures disproportionately focused on defence and security rather than service provision.[23] Worsening already dire living conditions, the coronavirus pandemic and subsequent drop in global oil prices severely hit the South Sudanese economy in 2020. This halted the fledgling recovery it had experienced in 2018–19 (+3.4%) – amid increased oil production and improved stability after the 2018 R-ARCSS – after a four-year war-driven contraction. The IMF estimated a 3.6% contraction for 2020–21, down from a 6.6% pre-pandemic growth projection.[24] The economic shock and rising inflation caused by the pandemic, as well as lockdown restrictions, took a particularly severe toll on the most vulnerable segments of the population, particularly informal workers (including women).

In response to this crisis, Kiir set up an economic-management committee and appointed a new finance minister in September 2020, but these measures were criticised as largely inadequate. To help mitigate the fiscal deficit caused by the pandemic, the IMF disbursed its first funding to South Sudan (US$52.3m) in November.[25]

Sub-Saharan Africa

Conflict Outlook

Political scenarios

The concessions between Kiir and Machar – although made under diplomatic pressure – suggested that the former rivals are more willing to cooperate than previously. Kiir's acceptance of ten states allowed Machar to join the government without betraying his supporters, for whom this was a key issue. Machar's return to Juba under Kiir's protection was also a major show of trust, as Kiir's troops had attacked Machar in Juba in 2013 and 2016. The overall respect for the ceasefire among R-ARCSS signatories and their eventual agreement on contested issues, such as the Upper Nile governorship, offers positive prospects for cooperation within the 36-month transitional period. After years of avoidance, in February 2021 the government also agreed to establish accountability institutions, including the African Union (AU) Hybrid Court for South Sudan (HCSS), which is a positive step towards more sustainable peace. However, given the government's past lobbying against the court's establishment, the AU will need to closely monitor the level of commitment to its operationalisation.[26]

While the above developments offered encouraging signs of collaboration in 2020, challenges to political stability remain. The delayed reconstitution of the legislative assembly prevents the passing of important laws and reduces oversight over the executive. Moreover, lagging local appointments foster local conflicts, and a continued failure to respect the 35% quota for women in transitional institutions, which was embedded in the R-ARCSS, undermines representation and hinders the prioritisation of gender-based violence. Even if these points were resolved, hostility could potentially resume ahead of presidential elections, which will pit Kiir against Machar at the end of the transitional period.

Escalation potential and conflict-related risks

Although the 2018 R-ARCSS offered a power-sharing solution to accommodate leaders in the medium term, it did not address the conflict's root causes. Equatorian rebels continued to contest their lack of political inclusion and are unlikely to renounce arms unless their grievances are accommodated. Kiir announced in January 2021 that the government would stop intervening in intercommunal fighting in key hotspots, even though creating mechanisms to address such conflicts will be necessary for long-term peace. The patronage and corruption practices that have fuelled war remain rife: for example, funds dedicated to the peace deal have been embezzled, preventing the timely development of institutions and increasing reluctance among international donors to finance further peace implementation.

One shortcoming from the 2015 ARCSS was the reliance on the logic of 'payroll peace': by providing material incentives to join an inflated unified army, armed groups were encouraged to accept peace, but this also incentivised leaders to recruit new soldiers to reap further financial and military benefits.[27] This allowed armed groups to strengthen their forces ahead of renewed conflict in 2016. As the 2018 R-ARCSS retained this logic, it has risked creating similar levels of mobilisation for potential renewed violence, especially given the trend of signatories inflating their troop numbers ahead of cantonment.[28] Given the problems faced in cantonment sites in 2020, however, disgruntled soldiers could also see holdout rebel groups as more rewarding than the army, which could breed new conflict.

As preventing armed groups from accessing new weapons is essential, especially since the UN arms embargo was repeatedly violated, the UN Security Council has accordingly extended its embargo until May 2021.

Strategic implications and influences

The involvement of IGAD members, especially Ugandan President Yoweri Museveni and Sudanese Prime Minister Abdalla Hamdok, was key to securing the transitional government. This makes sustained regional commitments essential to consolidate existing gains. As international donors' continued use of incentives and targeted sanctions will also be crucial to sustain peace, the administration of US President Joe Biden could use Kiir's desire for the withdrawal of US sanctions against South Sudan to press the government to accelerate negotiations with holdout groups and to support needed reforms.

Beyond the Horn of Africa, South Sudan intensified its relations with Egypt in 2020, which could be linked to Egypt's bid to secure allies in its Nile water dispute with Ethiopia. While the rapprochement is economically promising for South Sudan and could allow the country to reduce its reliance on rival neighbours, this could also affect future relations with Ethiopia, which could retaliate by offering its support to South Sudanese rebels.

Notes

1   Francesco Checchi et al, 'Estimates of Crisis-attributable Mortality in South Sudan, December 2013–April 2018 – A Statistical Analysis', London School of Hygiene and Tropical Medicine, September 2018.

2   United Nations High Commissioner for Refugees, 'Operational Portal: Refugees and Asylum-seekers from South Sudan – Total', 28 February 2021; and International Organization for Migration, 'Displacement Tracking Matrix: South Sudan – Baseline Assessment Round 9 – IDP and Returnee', 31 January 2021. IDPs estimates vary across sources. According to the Internal Displacement Monitoring Centre (IDMC), the total number of conflict IDPs was approximately 1.4m in 2020. See IDMC, '2020 Internal Displacement', Global Internal Displacement Database.

3   United Nations Security Council, 'Resolution 2459 (2019)', S/RES/2459 (2019), 15 March 2019.

4   Brian Adeba and the Enough Project Team, 'A Hijacked State: Violent Kleptocracy in South Sudan', Enough Project, February 2019.

5   World Health Organization, 'WHO Coronavirus (COVID-19) Dashboard – South Sudan', 28 February 2021.

6   Conflict Armament Research, *Weapon Supplies into South Sudan's Civil War: Regional Retransfers and International Intermediaries* (London: Conflict Armament Research Ltd, 2018).

7   United Nations High Commissioner for Refugees, 'Operational Portal: Refugees and Asylum-seekers from South Sudan – Total'.

8   Justin Lynch and Robbie Gramer, 'Diplomats Fear a Collapse of South Sudan's Latest Peace Deal', *Foreign Policy*, 5 March 2020.

9   H.E. Maj. Gen. (Retd.) Charles Tai Gituai, 'On the Status of the Implementation of the Revitalised Agreement on the Resolution of the Conflict in the Republic of South Sudan for the Period 1st July to 30th September 2020', Report no. 008/20, Reconstituted Joint Monitoring and Evaluation Commission, October 2020.

10 International Crisis Group, 'Toward a Viable Future for South Sudan', Report no. 300, 10 February 2021.

11 'SPLA–IO, NAS Accuse Each Other of Attacks in Mugwo', Radio Tamazuj, 14 April 2020.

12 Armed Conflict Location & Event Data Project (ACLED), www.acleddata.com.

13 'Violence, Insecurity Continues to Plague South Sudan Communities', UN News, 18 November 2020.

14 'Renewed Violence and Delayed Implementation of the Peace Agreement Severely Threaten Peace and Stability in South Sudan, UN Experts Note', United Nations Office of the High Commissioner for Human Rights, 14 August 2020.

15 United Nations Human Rights Council, 'Despite Renewed Political Commitment, Staggering Levels of Violence Continued Across South Sudan for the Second Successive Year, UN Experts Note', 19 February 2021.

16 United Nations High Commissioner for Refugees, 'Operational Portal: Refugees and Asylum-seekers from South Sudan – Total'; and International Organization for Migration, 'IOM Displacement Tracking Matrix: – South Sudan – Baseline Assessment Round 9 – IDP and Returnee'.

17 Armed Conflict Location & Event Data Project (ACLED), www.acleddata.com; and United Nations Office for the Coordination of Humanitarian Affairs, 'South Sudan: Flooding Situation Report', 18 November 2020.

18 Amnesty International, 'South Sudan: United Nations Arms Embargo Must Remain in Place after Surge in Violence against Civilians in 2020', AFR 65/3383/2020, 30 November 2020.

19 See United Nations Human Rights Council, 'Statement by Yasmin Sooka, Chair of the UN Commission on Human Rights in South Sudan to the Human Rights Council', 23 September 2020.

20 Integrated Food Security Phase Classification, 'South Sudan: IPC Acute Food Insecurity and Acute Malnutrition Analysis, October 2020–July 2021', 18 December 2020.

21 United Nations Office for the Coordination of Humanitarian Affairs, 'South Sudan Humanitarian Response Plan, COVID-19 Addendum', June 2020, pp. 6–7.

22 The World Bank, 'The World Bank in South Sudan'.

23 Security accounted for 9.90% of the government's budget for 2019–20, against 8.46% for health, education and social and humanitarian affairs combined. See Ministry of Finance and Planning, Government of the Republic of South Sudan, with UNICEF South Sudan, 'National Budget Brief – South Sudan 2019/20', November 2020, Figure 4, p. 13.

24 The fiscal years used for these estimates run from July to June. See IMF African Department, 'Republic of South Sudan: Request for Disbursement under the Rapid Credit Facility', Country Report no. 2020/301, International Monetary Fund, 16 November 2021.

25 *Ibid.*

26 See Ayen Bior, 'South Sudan Pays Millions to Block Establishment of Hybrid Crimes Court', Voice of America, 29 April 2019.

27 Alan Boswell and Alex de Waal, 'South Sudan: The Perils of Payroll Peace', London School of Economics, 4 March 2019.

28 See Joshua Craze, 'The Politics of Numbers: On Security Sector Reform in South Sudan, 2005–2020', Centre for Public Authority and International Development, July 2020.

Sub-Saharan Africa

ETHIOPIA

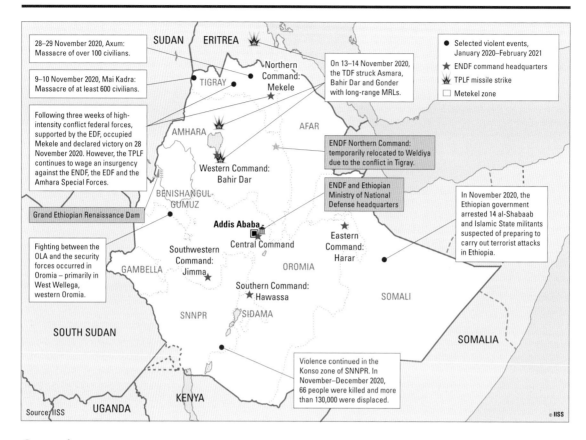

28–29 November 2020, Axum: Massacre of over 100 civilians.

9–10 November 2020, Mai Kadra: Massacre of at least 600 civilians.

Following three weeks of high-intensity conflict federal forces, supported by the EDF, occupied Mekele and declared victory on 28 November 2020. However, the TPLF continues to wage an insurgency against the ENDF, the EDF and the Amhara Special Forces.

Grand Ethiopian Renaissance Dam

Fighting between the OLA and the security forces occurred in Oromia – primarily in West Wellega, western Oromia.

On 13–14 November 2020, the TDF struck Asmara, Bahir Dar and Gonder with long-range MRLs.

● Selected violent events, January 2020–February 2021
★ ENDF command headquarters
✦ TPLF missile strike
☐ Metekel zone

ENDF Northern Command: temporarily relocated to Weldiya due to the conflict in Tigray.

ENDF and Ethiopian Ministry of National Defense headquarters

In November 2020, the Ethiopian government arrested 14 al-Shabaab and Islamic State militants suspected of preparing to carry out terrorist attacks in Ethiopia.

Violence continued in the Konso zone of SNNPR. In November–December 2020, 66 people were killed and more than 130,000 were displaced.

SUDAN, ERITREA, Northern Command: Mekele, TIGRAY, AMHARA, AFAR, Western Command: Bahir Dar, BENISHANGUL-GUMUZ, Addis Ababa, Central Command, Eastern Command: Harar, Southwestern Command: Jimma, OROMIA, Southern Command: Hawassa, SNNPR, SIDAMA, SOMALI, SOUTH SUDAN, SOMALIA, KENYA, UGANDA

Source: IISS   © IISS

Overview

Conflict in Ethiopia is not a new phenomenon and has been a constant feature in the last 50 years throughout its troubled transition from empire to nation-state.

With the fall of the emperor in 1974, the Provisional Military Government of Socialist Ethiopia (the Derg) initiated a system of repressive rule, which was eventually brought down in 1991 after an uprising by the Ethiopian People's Revolutionary Democratic Front (EPRDF), a coalition of resistance groups. In 1995, Ethiopia became a federation of nine regions created along ethnic lines with the EPRDF in power, and the Tigray People's Liberation Front (TPLF) one of its main constituents. The federal state began consolidating its power while the autonomy of the regions diminished.

A series of protests directed at the political establishment (in 2015, mid-2016 and February 2018) and reactive states of emergency (from October 2016 to August 2017 and February to June 2018) eventually led to the resignation of then-prime minister Hailemariam Desalegn Boshe. His successor, Abiy Ahmed – the EPRDF's first ethnic Oromo leader – enacted sweeping reforms to liberalise the economy and increase political freedom in the country. He also successfully negotiated a solution to the long territorial stalemate between Eritrea and Ethiopia following the 1998–2000 war, signing a peace agreement in 2018.

In November 2019, Abiy dissolved the EPRDF and formed the Prosperity Party by amalgamating the ruling parties of the Ethiopian regions. However, the TPLF, which had dominated Ethiopian political life since 1991, refused to join, isolating Tigray as the only region whose ruling party was not a member of the national governing party.

Rising tensions between the federal government in Addis Ababa and the TPLF-led Tigray

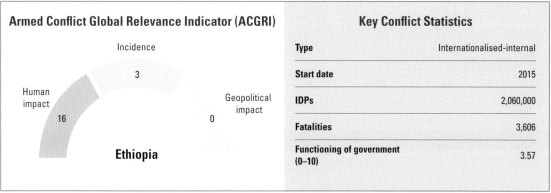

Armed Conflict Global Relevance Indicator (ACGRI)

Incidence
3

Human impact
16

Geopolitical impact
0

Ethiopia

Key Conflict Statistics

Type	Internationalised-internal
Start date	2015
IDPs	2,060,000
Fatalities	3,606
Functioning of government (0–10)	3.57

ACGRI pillars: IISS calculation based on multiple sources for 2020 and January/February 2021 (scale 0–100). See Notes on Methodology and Data Appendix for further details on Key Conflict Statistics.

regional administration turned into armed conflict on 3–4 November 2020. Following three weeks of high-intensity conflict, federal government troops occupied Mekele, the capital of Tigray, and declared victory on 28 November. By the end of 2020, the TPLF and its armed forces, the Tigray Defence Force (TDF), had lost ground and most of its heavy equipment, and turned instead to guerrilla warfare as fighting continued in early 2021 to deny freedom of movement to federal forces and their allies.

In 2020, Ethiopia also continued to experience violence among ethnic groups and between these groups and the federal government in several hotspots around the country. In Oromia, fighting occurred between the Oromo Liberation Army (OLA) and the security forces, mainly in West Wellega in the western part of the region. The 29 June 2020 killing of Oromo singer Hachalu Hundessa, allegedly on the orders of the TPLF and reportedly carried out by OLA members, sparked protests across Oromia and in Addis Ababa, in which at least 123 were killed and 500 injured.[1] Elsewhere, a massacre in mid-September in the Metekel zone of the Benishangul-Gumuz region prompted a state of emergency in the area from January 2021. Ethiopia also experienced new tension with Sudan as the latter attempted to exploit the Tigray crisis to reopen a long-standing border dispute.

Politically, a tenth region, Sidama, was formed on 18 June 2020 following a 98.52% favourable result in the November 2019 referendum.

Conflict Parties

Ethiopian National Defence Force (ENDF)

Strength: 138,000 active all-volunteer military personnel (army: 135,000, air force: 3,000).

Areas of operation: Across all regions of Ethiopia.

Leadership: Prime Minister Abiy Ahmed (commander-in-chief), General Berhanu Jula (chief of staff – appointed in November 2020).

Structure: The ENDF is designed to conduct both conventional war (using infantry, armoured vehicles and artillery) and counter-insurgency missions (both inside Ethiopia and across borders). It is organised in commands, each of which has several allocated mechanised and infantry divisions. In October 2020, two new headquarters were formed at Bahir Dar and Addis Ababa, in addition to those at Harar, Hawassa, Mekele and Nekemte, reflecting the increasing internal focus and activities of the ENDF.

The composition of the ENDF reflects the ethnic percentages of the overall Ethiopian population for ranks up to major. However, until October 2020 a disproportionate number of ENDF generals were ethnic Tigrayan.

History: The ENDF grew out of a coalition of former guerrilla armies, mainly the TPLF and EPRDF. Since the EPRDF took power in 1991, the ENDF has been an all-volunteer force. Over the past two decades it has undergone a continuing defence-transformation process, making it one of the major military powers in Africa. Until July 2020, the ENDF had been the top troop contributor to United Nations peacekeeping missions (principally to those in South Sudan, Abyei and Darfur), while also supplying troops to the African Union (AU) mission in Somalia.

Objectives: Maintain Ethiopia's territorial integrity and fight armed opposition/secessionist movements inside the country.

Sub-Saharan Africa

Ethiopian National Defence Force (ENDF)

Opponents: Regional rivals and secessionist movements in Ethiopia.

Affiliates/allies: Eritrea, France, Israel, United States.

Resources/capabilities: Prior to the prolonged conflict in Tigray, the ENDF was the most powerful army in the region, with a defence budget of US$472 million in 2020. The effect of the conflict on the strength, equipment and morale of the ENDF has yet to be assessed. The ENDF has excellent support capabilities (logistics, training, maintenance) but efficiency fluctuates greatly between units. The conflict in Tigray revealed the previously unreported holdings of long-range multiple rocket launchers (MRLs) and uninhabited aerial vehicles (UAVs).

TPLF armed forces (also known as the Tigray Defence Force (TDF))

Strength: The total number likely exceeded 200,000 individuals at the start of the Tigray conflict. Of these only about 20,000–30,000 were formed in paramilitary units, with the remainder composed of village-level militias.[2]

Areas of operation: Tigray region.

Leadership: The former president of Tigray, Debretsion Gebremichael.

Structure: The TDF combines all forces in Tigray that came under the command of the Tigrayan government at the outset of the Tigray conflict, including:
Special Police/Special Force: Organised into paramilitary groupings equivalent to platoons, companies and battalions.
Regional militia (village-level uniformed and armed defence/security responders): Organised into groups of 30–50 at village level under locally elected leadership.
ENDF elements: A few organised elements of the ENDF appeared to have sided with the TPLF at the start of the Tigray conflict.

History: Following the TPLF's refusal to join the newly created Prosperity Party, it began to form regional forces for the defence of Tigray. Following the outbreak of armed conflict on 3/4 November 2020, it fought several battles against the ENDF, the Eritrean Defence Forces (EDF) and the Amhara Special Forces. After the ENDF recapture of Mekele, the TDF withdrew to the countryside and continued a heavily armed insurgency/guerrilla war.

Objectives: Defend Tigray's territorial integrity.

Opponents: Ethiopian federal forces (the ENDF and the Federal Police), the Amhara Special Forces, the EDF.

Affiliates/allies: Seeking Sudanese and other international support. Established an office in Khartoum, Sudan by the end of February 2021.

Resources/capabilities: In early November 2020, the TDF seized significant amounts of ENDF equipment including tanks, artillery and long-range rockets.

Regional Special Police – also referred to as 'Special Force'

Strength: Addis Ababa (numbers unknown. Formed in late 2019), Afar (2–3,000), Amhara (5,000), Benishangul-Gumuz (3–4,000), Dire Dawa (2–3,000), Gambella (2–3,000), Oromia (9–10,000), Somali (15,000), Southern Nations, Nationalities, and People's (SNNPR) (4–5,000), Sidama (numbers unknown), Tigray (27–28,000).[3]

Areas of operation: All regions of Ethiopia.

Leadership: Under regional police commissioners. Answerable to regional presidents.

Structure: Formed into paramilitary units.

History: Somali became the first region to form a special police force in 2008–09. By 2014, all regions had small special police forces. In the 2016–19 period, force numbers increased in areas experiencing civil unrest (Amhara, Oromia and SNNPR). In 2019–20, force numbers increased further in areas where neighbouring regions posed a threat (Amhara, Oromia, Tigray).

Objectives: Preserve public order and peace within the region, as constitutionally mandated.

Opponents: Armed political opposition, local *shifta* (armed bandits), neighbouring regional Special Police and militia.

Affiliates/allies: N/A.

Resources/capabilities: Funded from regional police budgets.

Oromo Liberation Army (OLA), previously the Oromo Liberation Front (OLF)

Strength: Over 2,000 estimated OLA fighters in 2020.[4]

Areas of operation: Oromia region.

Leadership: The OLA no longer comes under Dawud Ibsa's political leadership and has split into at least four armed factions under local leadership.

Structure: Locally organised into loose groupings of fighters.

History: The OLF was established in 1973 by Oromo nationalists. In mid-2018, the OLF agreed with the central government to lay down its arms and return 1,200 fighters from Eritrea. The OLA officially split from the political OLF party in April 2019 as part of the negotiation process to allow the OLF to become a registered political party. However, various OLA factions have continued to operate under the Oromo traditional leadership, predominantly in western and southern Oromia.

Oromo Liberation Army (OLA), previously the Oromo Liberation Front (OLF)

Objectives: Self-determination for the Oromo people against what they see as Amhara colonial rule.

Opponents: The federal government.

Affiliates/allies: Until 2018, Eritrea. Following the rapprochement between Eritrea and Ethiopia, this support ceased and the OLA in Oromia survived on local support and resources. In 2020, the TPLF were accused of providing clandestine support including finances and weapons.

Resources/capabilities: The OLF acts clandestinely and is weak in military terms.

Eritrean Defence Forces (EDF)

Strength: 201,750 estimated active military personnel (army: 200,000, navy: 1,400, air force: 350).

Areas of operation: Across all regions of Eritrea, and since November 2020, throughout the Tigray region of Ethiopia.

Leadership: President Isaias Afwerki (commander-in-chief), Major-General Filipos Weldeyohanes (chief of staff).

Structure: The EDF comprise mostly conscripts, with only a small cadre of regular troops. National service is universal for Eritrean men and women between the ages of 18 and 40. In 2016, Eritreans between the ages of 40 and 65 were ordered to reservist duty to support the formation of local security militias under the army's intelligence structure. A further call-up of reservists was announced by President Isaias in late November 2020. The army is made up of approximately 41 divisions and is divided between five military zones, largely covering the border with Ethiopia. Up to 20 EDF divisions were reported to be in Tigray as of February 2021.

History: The EDF was officially formed after Eritrea's separation from Ethiopia in 1993 but it has its roots in the former Eritrean People's Liberation Front (EPLF) armed opposition to the Derg communist regime in Ethiopia. The

army has continued to engage in low-level border conflicts with Ethiopia and several other neighbours, including Djibouti, Sudan and Yemen, most notably in the Ethiopian–Eritrean War from 1998 until 2000. From 2000 to 2018, the army was predominantly deployed on the border with Ethiopia.

Objectives: Maintain Eritrea's territorial integrity and fight armed opposition/secessionist movements inside the country.

Opponents: Regional rivals, including Ethiopia until 2018, secessionist movements in Eritrea.

Affiliates/allies: Ethiopia, Saudi Arabia, Somalia, United Arab Emirates (UAE).

Resources/capabilities: The scale of the Eritrean defence budget is unknown. Due to prolonged UN sanctions (lifted in November 2018), much of Eritrea's military equipment still comprises outdated Soviet-era systems and will have resulted in serviceability issues. However, Russia has since agreed to supply Eritrea with light multipurpose helicopters. The navy remains capable of only limited coastal-patrol and interception operations. There is some equipment-maintenance capability, but no defence-manufacturing sector.

Sub-Saharan Africa

Conflict Drivers

Political

Lack of independent institutions:

The division of political control between Ethiopia's regional states and federal government has long stoked tensions. In addition, weak political and security institutions at both local and federal-government levels and the uncertainties created by Abiy's envisaged political transition that was being enacted have facilitated violence.

State fragility is compounded by the lack of legitimacy and rise in corruption in public administration at all levels caused by the cancellation of local elections – originally scheduled for May 2018 then postponed until August 2020 but now slated for June 2021 – which would have put 3.6m local administrators up for re-election.

Abiy's political reforms in the context of existing ethnic divisions:

The historical divisions between Ethiopia's different ethnic communities have long fuelled violence in the country. For example, the dominance of the Tigrayan ethnic minority within Ethiopia's political and security elites and national discourse from 1991, the political marginalisation of the Oromo until Abiy's appointment in 2018 and the disenfranchisement of the Amhara elite, have all stoked ethnic rivalry.[5]

Abiy's unprecedented reforms since 2018 proved divisive as they lacked dialogue and consultation at national and regional levels. Allowing various opposition parties to return from exile without effectively integrating them into the political sphere stoked ethnic frustrations and led to calls for greater regional autonomy. This in turn served to reignite old tensions between ethnic groups and to stoke dissent from those who had benefitted from the previous EPRDF regime, sparking a rise in 'ethnic nationalism'. Some elements of the former armed opposition returned to arms to fight for political equality, encouraged in many cases by local elites threatened by the reforms.

Economic and social
Environmental change:
Environmental change, particularly drought, has driven conflict between pastoralist communities and between pastoralists and settled farmers in the Afar and Somali regions, and between these two and neighbouring Amhara, Oromia and Tigray. The 2020 locust invasion further damaged crops and negatively impacted community livelihoods in affected regions across the Horn of Africa.

Security
Continuing militarisation and security fragmentation:
As disputes over regional boundaries became more violent, all Ethiopian regions developed paramilitary regional special police forces. The continuing militarisation of these police forces throughout 2020, particularly in Amhara, Oromia and Tigray, established rival and competitive regional 'armies' within the country. Thousands of additional paramilitary forces were trained and publicly paraded in all three regional states to illustrate their strength and effective preparation for conflict against neighbouring regions.[6] For example, in August 2020, TPLF parades showcased their readiness to defend the region against any armed aggression.[7] These armed and camouflage-uniformed forces usurped the ENDF's position as the sole legitimate army in Ethiopia and enabled regional politics, particularly in Amhara, to become more expansionist and aggressive.

The militarisation of the regional special police forces coincided with increased importation of illegal arms into a vibrant private-weapons market, fed by growing civilian insecurity. Widespread and almost instantaneous attacks on ethnic minorities in Oromia in the wake of the killing of the singer Hachalu Hundessa in late June 2020 further encouraged the self-defence-weapons market and the organisation of local self-protection militias.

International
Regional dynamics:
Following Abiy's peace initiative, Eritrea played a nebulous role in the war on Tigray. Enmity between President Isaias and the TPLF drove Eritrean support for, and ultimately the success of, Abiy's political and military campaigns in Tigray.

Internal conflicts of differing natures and scales within neighbouring countries, such as Somalia, South Sudan and Sudan, added further strains and instability on Ethiopia's borders. For example, al-Shabaab not only posed a continued threat to Ethiopian troops in Somalia but also attacked Ethiopia itself. These conflicts continued to drive very large numbers of refugees into Ethiopia, altering the ethnic composition in its border regions (primarily Gambella) and creating tensions within and between communities over crime, trafficking, resources, land and security. In this light, Abiy's active stance on regional affairs and conflict resolution in neighbouring countries can be seen as an attempt to stabilise Ethiopia by stabilising its neighbours.

However, the separate security dynamic of the contentious Grand Ethiopian Renaissance Dam (GERD) proved a continued source of tension in Ethiopia's relationship with Egypt and Sudan, in the absence of agreed mechanisms for the ownership and management of the Nile waters.

Political and Military Developments

Delayed national elections and regional elections in Tigray
The March 2020 decision to postpone the scheduled 29 August national elections amid a lack of preparation by the National Election Board of Ethiopia (NEBE) and the coronavirus emergency left many political questions unaddressed, leading to accusations of power-grabbing by Abiy and the Prosperity Party. Uncertainties around the new election date persisted well into the autumn following a second postponement decision in June. The elections were eventually scheduled for June 2021 – with political campaigning to start in February – for all regions of Ethiopia except Tigray.[8]

In defiance of the federal government, the TPLF decided to hold regional elections in Tigray on 9 September 2020, triggering an institutional conflict. Despite a federal-government announcement on 7 September that it would not recognise any election held in Tigray, elections went ahead on 9 September, with Tigray officials warning that any federal-government intervention would amount to a 'declaration of war'.[9]

War in Tigray

The September regional election in Tigray increased tensions between the federal and regional governments. On the night of 3–4 November, the TDF, under orders of the TPLF, carried out a 'pre-emptive strike' on the headquarters of the ENDF Northern Command and on several key units including air defences and MRL batteries. Some ENDF units withdrew across the borders into Amhara region or neighbouring Eritrea, while some individuals of Tigrayan ethnicity defected to the TDF, taking their equipment with them.

The ENDF regrouped and responded with a three-week campaign, which captured all the major population centres and key routes in Tigray, supported by Amhara special forces and the EDF.[10] The technological sophistication of the conflict, including the use of armed drones, possibly of Emirati origin, and the use of long-range MRLs between African countries, surprised even expert observers.[11]

The federal government declared victory in late November and the conflict entered a new phase of insurgency and guerrilla warfare. As of February 2021, the TPLF/TDF had lost most of its heavy equipment and withdrawn to the mountainous rural areas of eastern and central Tigray but retained support from at least some of the Tigrayan population. The Amhara regional government exploited the institutional weakness in Tigray to establish new administrations in parts of western and southern Tigray in a de facto expansion of its territory.

Inter-ethnic violence

Inter-ethnic tensions that had escalated in 2017–18 in Ethiopia continued throughout 2020, with no resolution of the internal border disputes between the regional states and bouts of inter-ethnic violence in the regions of Amhara, Benishangul-Gumuz, Gambella, Oromia and Somali. The extreme and fast-spreading violence against non-Oromos in Oromia following the killing of the Oromo singer Hachalu Hundessa in June 2020 displaced thousands and killed over 100, and resulted in the arrest of the popular Oromo activist, media figure and politician Jawar Mohammed. Inter-ethnic violence also broke out in the Metekel zone of Benishangul-Gumuz in western Ethiopia before and after the conflict in Tigray. Violence continued in the Konso zone of SNNPR, killing 66 and displacing more than 130,000 in November–December 2020.[12]

Al-Shabaab in Ethiopia

In November 2020, the Ethiopian government arrested 14 al-Shabaab and Islamic State (also known as ISIS or ISIL) militants suspected of planning terrorist attacks in Ethiopia.[13] This was the latest in a long-running series of attempts to attack Ethiopia by al-Shabaab and ISIS. Ethiopia's continued support to the government of Somalia and active military operations in the country, and the location of AU, European Union and UN offices in Addis Ababa, make Ethiopia a highly prized target for al-Shabaab.

Redeployment of ENDF commands

The increasing commitment of ENDF troops to internal security in Ethiopia, in support of the Federal Police Commission and regional special police, prompted a reorganisation of commands with headquarters in Harar, Hawassa, Mekele – relocated to Weldiya during the Tigray conflict – and Nekemte, and the establishment of two new commands in October 2020 to strengthen counter-insurgency operations, headquartered in Addis Ababa and Bahir Dar.

Key Events in 2020–21

POLITICAL EVENTS

January 2020
Ethiopia adopts amended anti-terrorism and firearms legislation in response to increased arms trafficking.

February
Ethiopia rejects a US-brokered deal on the GERD. Egypt says it will use 'all means' to defend its interests in the Nile.[14]

March
The first case of COVID-19 is recorded in Ethiopia. The NEBE cancels the 29 August national elections due to the pandemic.

8 April
A COVID-19 national state of emergency is declared for five months.

18 June
The Sidama region is formed by decision of the SNNPR council.

July
First filling of the GERD is completed.

September
The federal government declares upcoming Tigrayan local elections will be deemed illegal, but the elections proceed on 9 September. The TPLF wins all seats.

7 October
The Ethiopian parliament withholds budgetary support for the TPLF administration in Tigray.

November
Following the outbreak of hostilities, the Ethiopian parliament creates an interim administration for Tigray and declares a state of emergency in the region.

16 December
The EU withholds €90m (over US$100m) in direct budget support pending full humanitarian access to Tigray.

25 December
The NEBE announces national elections will be held on 5 June 2021.

February 2021
Revelations begin to circulate of atrocities during the war in Tigray, including an alleged massacre perpetrated by the EDF.

MILITARY/VIOLENT EVENTS

29 June 2020
Oromo singer Hachalu Hundessa is killed, sparking three days of widespread protests across Oromia and in Addis Adaba.

Mid-September
ENDF and Amhara special forces move to southern and eastern Tigray borders. At least 140 people are massacred in the Metekel zone in Benishangul-Gumuz.

3–4 November
Armed conflict breaks out between the federal government and the TPLF.

8 November
The ENDF chief of staff Adem Mohammed is replaced by his deputy, Berhanu Jula.

9–28 November
Active military operations against the TDF are conducted by the ENDF, with support from the Amhara special forces and the EDF, including a massacre of 600 civilians at Mai Kadra and 60,000 reported Tigrayan refugees in Sudan.[15] The TDF fires long-range MRL at Asmara, Bahir Dar and Gonder. The UN calls for the creation of humanitarian corridors.

28 November
The ENDF captures Mekele and the federal government declares victory.

November–December
The EDF massacres hundreds of civilians in Axum.

12 December
The first humanitarian-aid convoy reaches Mekele.

15–26 December
Sudanese and Ethiopian forces clash in Sudan. Sudanese forces reinforce the Sudan–Ethiopia border. The Sudanese army claims to have occupied 60% of the land in Sudan previously held by Ethiopian security forces.[16]

29–31 December
Ethiopia warns Sudan of a possible counter-attack by Ethiopian forces. Sudan and Ethiopia claim to be seeking a peaceful solution.

January–February 2021
Conflict continues in Tigray as the ENDF and its allies fight the TPLF in a heavily armed insurgency.

Impact

Human rights and humanitarian

In response to the conflict in 2020, the international community demanded humanitarian access to Tigray to support all populations in need in the region, including almost 1.7m internally displaced persons (IDPs) and the nearly 100,000 Eritrean refugees living in four camps and in the community in Tigray.[17] Delays in granting full, unhindered access prompted the EU to suspend nearly €90m (over US$100m) in budgetary aid to Ethiopia in December.[18] The UN High Commissioner for Refugees (UNHCR) stressed the urgent need for an objective, independent assessment of the facts on the ground in the Tigray region given the persistent reports of serious human-rights violations and abuses. The Ethiopian Human Rights Commission actively followed and investigated reports of massacres in Tigray and elsewhere in the country, producing evidence of over 100 people killed in a massacre at Axum alone.[19]

The UNHCR assessed that 2.3m IDPs would require assistance across Ethiopia in 2021, however this number is likely to rise as the Tigray conflict continues.[20] The Food and Agriculture Organization of the UN (FAO) projected that across the country 12.9m people would face high acute food insecurity, 1.8m would be displaced internally, 1.1m would be affected by flooding and 1.3m hectares of crops and pasture would be damaged by locusts.[21]

Although the quality and number of TV and radio stations and print journals has improved, the Ethiopian government continued to regularly restrict internet access, with blocks put in place in the immediate aftermath of the killing of Hachalu Hundessa in June and again at the start of the conflict in Tigray.

The anti-terrorism amendment in January 2020 and the approval of a new media proclamation in December improved legislation in these two important areas.[22] However, detentions of both politicians and journalists continued.

Economic and social

Continuing conflict in multiple regions of the country, the new active conflict in Tigray and uncertainty for investors caused by expectations of violence around the upcoming 2021 national elections combined to both reduce domestic GDP and deter foreign direct investment. Figures for the cost of the war in Tigray were not released but the Federal Police Commission estimated losses of ETB 2.9 billion (US$73m) due to damage to infrastructure and interruption of services, with an additional loss of nearly ETB 2bn (US$50.4m) in domestic taxes from November 2020 to January 2021.[23] To this must be added the cost of losses of livelihoods, property and crops, and the financial costs of waging the conflict.

The coronavirus pandemic and its containment measures compounded Ethiopia's economic difficulties, resulting in an estimated loss of up to 2.4m jobs.[24] Foreign-exchange reserves saw a notable drop amid an African Development Bank estimate of a 10% reduction in remittances to 5.3% of GDP from the Ethiopian diaspora in countries hit by COVID-19, and foreign direct investment also declined by 20% to 2.2% of GDP.[25] Meanwhile the IMF estimated GDP growth declining from 9.0% in 2019 to 6.1% in 2020 and 2.0% for 2021.[26]

In September 2020, a five-year, US$7.1bn UN Sustainable Development Cooperation Framework agreement was unveiled to support the Ethiopian national priorities that had been outlined in June in a ten-year economic-development plan.[27]

Relations with neighbouring and international partners and geopolitical implications

Despite its internal problems, Ethiopia continued to play a major role in the region in 2020. In GERD negotiations, Ethiopia proved itself strong enough to resist US pressure in the form of an externally brokered arrangement with Egypt and Sudan over the Nile waters. Ethiopia also continued to deal with regional security issues in a tripartite arrangement with Eritrea and Somalia.

Besides engaging Eritrea as an active participant in hostilities, the conflict in Tigray also gave Sudan an opportunity to reopen the issue of Sudanese land in the al-Fashaga Triangle, occupied for generations by Ethiopian farmers. This resulted in a number of limited clashes between Ethiopian and Sudanese security forces in the Triangle. While both governments seemed keen to avoid major conflict over al-Fashaga, the issue remains very sensitive on both sides and the possibility of unintended conflict cannot be ruled out.

Conflict Outlook

Political scenarios

Despite the continuing small-scale conflicts across the country, and the economic impact of the coronavirus pandemic, Abiy succeeded in maintaining momentum for change, as of February 2021.

The conflict in Tigray is likely to continue to be Abiy's greatest challenge. To restore lasting peace in Tigray, a first step must be the withdrawal of Eritrean forces from Ethiopian soil, or at least to a similar buffer zone to the one in place from 2000 to 2018.

The Amhara seizure of large parts of western and southern Tigray challenged the constitutional and political governance of Ethiopia's regions. It is likely that a new constitutional process may be required and potentially even a reorganising of the regions. To be successful, a similar process to the 1991–94 one that formulated the current constitution will be needed. However, such a national dialogue will require a stable and legitimate government, making it highly dependent upon the outcome of the 2021 national elections.

Risks to the success of those elections include pre-electoral violence by groups in Oromia whose leaders have been jailed or whose parties are not able or choose not to participate in the election. Deficiencies in the electoral process, such as the inability of parties to register candidates and the inability to establish polling stations due to insecurity and low voter registration, could cause the outcome to be challenged, making post-electoral violence a major risk. Although a complex undertaking, some degree of constitutional reform seems essential for Ethiopia to move past its divisive version of ethnic federalism.

Escalation potential and conflict-related risks

The continuing risk of exponential conflict escalation was demonstrated by the speed and spread of ethnic violence following the death of Hachalu Hundessa in June 2020 and by the rapid progress of the Tigray conflict between November 2020 and March 2021. In early 2021, widespread internal ethnic conflict in Amhara, Benishangul-Gumuz, Gambella and Oromia highlighted the danger of simultaneous conflicts between multiple ethnic groups and across multiple regions of Ethiopia, drawing in local security forces and

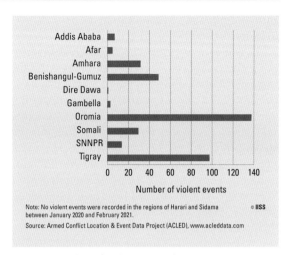

Note: No violent events were recorded in the regions of Harari and Sidama between January 2020 and February 2021. ©IISS
Source: Armed Conflict Location & Event Data Project (ACLED), www.acleddata.com

Figure 1: Number of violent events by region, January 2020–February 2021

challenging the already overstretched federal security forces.

Prospects for peace

An inclusive political settlement and sufficient economic growth to boost employment will be important preconditions to overcome the conflict drivers in Ethiopia. The prospects for an inclusive political settlement will depend on the outcome of the 2021 elections and the process that is put in place to make domestic politics and governance more representative of the diverse demands and opinions across the country. Maintaining economic growth is a priority for the government, as shown by continued legislative change designed to reduce barriers to investment. Ethiopia's 24 August 2020 accession to the 1958 UN Convention on the Recognition and Enforcement of Foreign Arbitral Awards and the commencement of trade under the African Continental Free Trade Area on 1 January 2021 illustrate the priority that the government gives to the economy and its importance for the country's peaceful future. The short-term economic outlook for the country is positive, with the real GDP rate forecast to average 8.5% in 2022–25.[28] This will help to create jobs and provide some of the economic solutions to conflict.

Strategic implications and global influences

The stability of all countries in the Horn of Africa depends, to differing degrees, on the success and stability of Ethiopia, as the conflict in Tigray demonstrated by sparking conflict and hindering development elsewhere. Equally, however, Ethiopia's growth and development can act as a catalyst for similar progress in the immediate region and farther afield. Maintaining Ethiopia's political and economic trajectory will require its partners to critically support the country's reform and development over the coming five-year window of opportunity between the 2021 and the 2026 elections.

In 2021, Ethiopia is likely to face renewed international attention, which may bring with it competing international interests. The GERD filling and the Nile will continue to be Ethiopia's greatest strategic challenge, engaging not only regional rivals, Egypt and Sudan, but also their international supporters.

Notes

[1] Samuel Gebre, 'Ethiopian Group Seeks Probe of Violence after Musician's Killing', Bloomberg, 1 January 2021.

[2] 'Ethiopia's Tigray Crisis: The Long, Medium and Short Story', BBC News, 17 November 2020.

[3] Author's own research for report on Ethiopian Special Police.

[4] From an Ethiopian security source.

[5] Aaron Maasho, 'Factbox: Ethiopia's Main Ethnic Groups', Reuters, 16 February 2018.

[6] 'Oromo Regional State Added Thousands of Special Forces to Its Security Apparatus', borkena, 10 March 2020; and Desta Gebremedhin, 'Why There Are Fears that Ethiopia Could Break Up', BBC News, 5 September 2020.

[7] See 'The Mighty Tigray Defense Force Shows Military Parade at the Celebration of Lekatit 11', Tigray Center of Excellence and Intelligence, YouTube, 24 February 2020.

[8] See Oxford Analytica, 'Ethiopia Term Extension Will Escalate Domestic Tension', Expert Briefings, 12 June 2020.

[9] 'Ethiopia's Tigray Region Holds Vote, Defying Abiy's Federal Gov't', Al-Jazeera, 9 September 2020.

[10] The EDF's assistance was only acknowledged by Abiy in an address to parliament in March 2021.

[11] See 'AR2 300mm MRL in Ethiopia Service', China Defense Blog, 6 November 2020; and Wim Zwijnenburg, 'Are Emirati Armed Drones Supporting Ethiopia from an Eritrean Air Base?', Bellingcat, 19 November 2020.

[12] 'News: Number of Civilians Killed in Recent Violence in Konso Reaches 66; 39 Injured and More Than 130,000 Displaced', Addis Standard, 2 December 2020.

[13] Samuel Gebre, 'Ethiopia Arrests al-Shabaab and ISIS Suspects Planning Attacks', Bloomberg, 14 November 2020.

[14] 'Egypt: We'll Use 'All Means' to Defend Nile Interests', Associated Press News, 29 February 2020.

[15] Salma Ismail, 'Thousands Flee Tigray Region to Sudan', UNICEF, 10 March 2021.

[16] 'Sudan Taking Control of Land on Border with Ethiopia – Minister', Reuters, 26 December 2020.

[17] See Internal Displacement Monitoring Centre (IDMC), '2020 Internal Displacement', Global Internal Displacement Database. See also 'Ethiopia's Tigray Crisis: UN 'Alarmed' by Treatment of Eritrean Refugees', BBC News, 11 December 2020.

[18] Simon Marks, 'EU Suspends Nearly €90m in Aid to Ethiopia Over Internal Conflict', Politico, 16 December 2020.

[19] 'Ethiopia Rights Commission Confirms Eritrean Soldiers Massacred Civilians in Axum, Calls for Comprehensive Investigation in Tigray', Addis Standard, 24 March 2021.

[20] United Nations High Commissioner for Refugees, 'Ethiopia – Planning Figures', March 2021.

[21] Food and Agriculture Organization of the United Nations, 'Ethiopia – Humanitarian Response Plan 2021', 11 March 2021.

[22] The new media laws enabled the media and the media's own institutions, such as associations for journalists, editors and media owners, to take responsibility for influencing and regulating the media's framework conditions, media ethics, education and general strengthening of the sector financially and qualitatively. See 'New Liberal Media Law in Ethiopia', IMS (International Media Support), 4 February 2021.

[23] Police ena Hibreteseb [Police and Society], Ethiopian Broadcasting Corporation, January 2021.

[24] United Nations Office for the Coordination of Humanitarian Affairs, 'Humanitarian Needs Overview – Ethiopia', 5 March 2021.

[25] African Development Bank Group, 'Ethiopia Economic Outlook', 2021.

[26] International Monetary Fund, 'World Economic Outlook Database', April 2021.

[27] 'Ministry, UN Sign 7.1 Bln USD Dev't Cooperation Framework Agreement', Ethiopian News Agency, 9 September 2020; and 'Ethiopia Unveils 10-Year Development Plan', Ethiopian Monitor, 11 June 2020.

[28] 'Ethiopia: Growth Rate of the Real Gross Domestic Product (GDP) from 2015 to 2025', Statista, October 2020.

Sub-Saharan Africa

SOMALIA

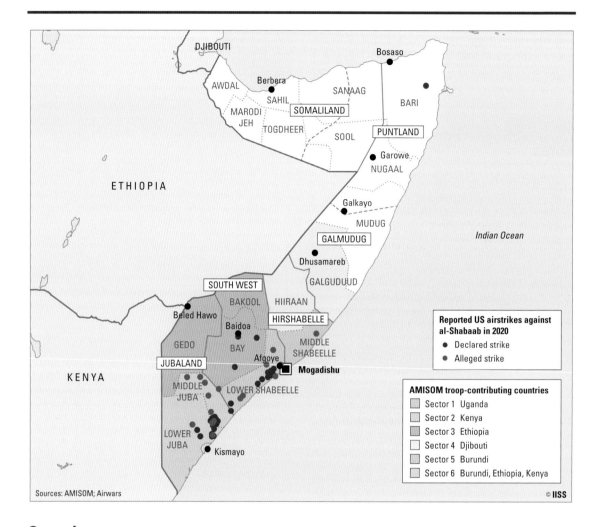

Sources: AMISOM; Airwars

© IISS

Overview

At the heart of the Somali conflict is a struggle between the federal government and the insurgency presently known as al-Shabaab. The latter had inherited the legacy of the Union of Islamic Courts (UIC), a system of Islamist rule that restored order in Mogadishu in the mid-2000s after a decade-long civil war. International suspicion that the UIC was in the grip of al-Qaeda led to an invasion by neighbouring Ethiopia in 2006, supported by the United States. The UIC collapsed, but its enforcement wing regrouped and joined other militia groups to form al-Shabaab in 2006. A Transitional Federal Government (TFG) was established in 2004, until a constitutionally

backed federal government assumed power in 2012. Yet its weak legitimacy and reliance on foreign patrons have hampered its ability to fight the insurgents.

After more than a decade of civil war, al-Shabaab is far from defeated. In 2020, attacks claimed by al-Shabaab targeted government figures and army posts across the country and spilled over to neighbouring Kenya, where militants raided a military base housing Kenyan and US troops. The group retained control over large swathes of central and southern Somalia and continued raising estimated revenues that match those of the country's authorities.[1] Even amid the outbreak of the coronavirus

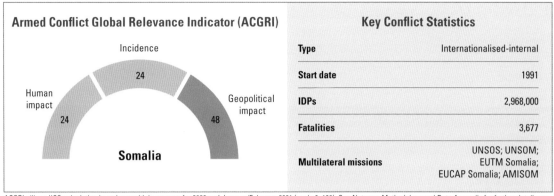

ACGRI pillars: IISS calculation based on multiple sources for 2020 and January/February 2021 (scale 0–100). See Notes on Methodology and Data Appendix for further details on Key Conflict Statistics.

pandemic, al-Shabaab was reported to provide a superior degree of governance and security for the population than the federal government. Authorised in 2007, the African Union Mission in Somalia (AMISOM) continued to support the ill-equipped Somali National Army (SNA) in counter-insurgency efforts. However, maintaining control remained a challenge: AMISOM and SNA troops are thinly stretched across the territory, so once they withdraw to their operating bases from retaken areas, al-Shabaab rapidly re-enters the territory to re-establish control.

Additionally, disputes between the Somali government and the federal member states (Galmudug, Hirshabelle, Jubaland, Puntland and South West, plus the de facto independent Somaliland) continued to undermine the functioning of the political system. Struggles over government interference in local elections and the allocation of powers and resources escalated in the run-up to the parliamentary elections, initially scheduled for December 2020 but with a new date yet to be set at the time of writing. Opposition leaders accused Somali President Mohamed Abdullahi Mohamed, popularly known as 'Farmaajo', of delaying the elections to seek political gains, and ceased to recognise his authority after his constitutional term expired in February 2021. Against a backdrop of protracted political crisis and armed conflict, Somalia continued to be plagued by chronically weak institutions, widespread poverty and low human-development measures, as well as by environmental factors that drive land degradation and exacerbate communal conflict and displacement.

Conflict Parties

Somali National Army (SNA)

Strength: 19,800 personnel. 3,000 additional troops under the Puntland government and an unspecified number of militias.

Areas of operation: Galmudug, Hirshabelle, Jubaland, Puntland and South West (excluding self-declared independent Somaliland).

Leadership: General Odawaa Yusuf Rageh (army chief of staff).

Structure: The SNA is divided into four command divisions and spread across Somalia's operational sectors. It has associated special-forces units such as the US-trained Danaab.

History: Efforts to build the SNA began in 2008. After two decades of state collapse, the SNA had to be built through both new recruitment and the incorporation of existing armed actors such as clan militias. These efforts were challenged by the lack of coordination among international partners, internecine clan fighting and the ongoing al-Shabaab insurgency. As a result, the SNA continues to suffer from deep-seated internal cleavages and cohesion problems.

Objectives: Secure the territorial authority of the federal government of Somalia, primarily through the defeat of al-Shabaab.

Opponents: Al-Shabaab, the Islamic State (also known as ISIS or ISIL) in Somalia, militias and criminal actors.

Sub-Saharan Africa

Somali National Army (SNA)

Affiliates/allies: AMISOM, the European Union, Turkey, the United Kingdom, US.

Resources/capabilities: The SNA suffers from severe shortages of resources – particularly of small arms – amid widespread internal corruption, which sees soldiers selling their arms (including to al-Shabaab) to make up for irregular and low salaries.

Harakat al-Shabaab al-Mujahideen (al-Shabaab)

Strength: Active fighting force of an estimated 5,000 to 10,000 militants, not including fighters' families, networks and those living in their controlled areas.[2]

Areas of operation: Strongest in southern Somalia (Jubaland, Hirshabelle and South West). Presence is more limited in Galmudug and Puntland. No full control over any areas of Mogadishu, but the city's northern peripheries and economic hotspots (e.g., Bakara Market) are subject to al-Shabaab authority.

Leadership: Ahmad Umar Diriye, better known as Abu Ubaidah, is the current leader, or emir.

Structure: A consultative council (*majlis al-shura*) is the group's central decision-making body, although regional political and military authorities enjoy considerable autonomy. Al-Shabaab's military wing is divided into six regional fighting units. An intelligence wing with a transnational reach (*Amniyat*) oversees a large security apparatus through which the group curtails dissent and maintains internal cohesion.

History: Emerged in December 2006 after breaking away from the UIC, which had offered little resistance against the Ethiopian invasion of Somalia. Over more than a decade later, al-Shabaab has evolved into a highly effective insurgent group, which appeals to nationalist sentiments to boost recruitment and can challenge the authority of the federal government.

Objectives: Defeat the federal government and establish Islamist rule in Somalia.

Opponents: Federal government, SNA and ISIS Somalia.

Affiliates/allies: Opportunistic alliances with militias and organised-crime syndicates.

Resources/capabilities: Al-Shabaab has benefitted from access to several sources of income, including checkpoint taxation, extortion, kidnappings, illicit trade, revenues from piracy and funding from transnational Islamist groups.

ISIS Somalia

Strength: Between 250 and 300 fighters.

Areas of operation: Based in the Galgala mountain region of Puntland, but periodically conducts targeted attacks in Bosaso and Mogadishu.

Leadership: Believed to be led by Abd al-Qadir Mumin, who was reported killed in an airstrike in March 2019. Later video footage, however, suggests he is still alive and remains leader.[3]

Structure: Little is known about its internal structure but given the group's small size and the regular targeting of senior figures by both Somali and US forces, it is likely to be relatively decentralised.

History: Mumin broke away from al-Shabaab with a small group of fighters in October 2015 and pledged allegiance to ISIS. Al-Shabaab has vowed to eliminate the rival group.

Objectives: Expand its influence by spreading ISIS's ideology within Somalia and neighbouring countries, such as Ethiopia, and attract broader support.

Opponents: Al-Shabaab, Somali and Puntland security forces.

Affiliates/allies: Believed to have connections with other Islamic State affiliates in Yemen and, more recently, Central Africa.

Resources/capabilities: Small arms.

African Union Mission in Somalia (AMISOM)

Strength: 19,626 troops.[4]

Areas of operation: The five troop-contributing countries (TCCs) are Burundi, Djibouti, Ethiopia, Kenya and Uganda. Their forces are each responsible for a sector in central and southern Somalia, including Banadir and Lower Shabelle (Uganda), Lower and Middle Juba (Kenya), Bay, Bakool and Gedo (Ethiopia), Hiiraan and Galguduud (Djibouti), and Middle Shabelle (Burundi).

Leadership: Burundian Lieutenant General Diomede Ndegeya (force commander), appointed in August 2020. Yet there is no centralised command-and-control structure, which makes coordinating operations difficult. Each sector's forces operate under their own command and are ultimately responsible to their own governments.

Structure: AMISOM contingents function as conventional militaries.

African Union Mission in Somalia (AMISOM)

History: The UN authorised the African Union to deploy a peacekeeping mission in February 2007 to support the TFG. The mission had a six-month mandate and was allowed to use force only in self-defence. In the following years, the situation failed to stabilise, and the UN agreed to boost AMISOM troops and extend the mission's mandate and scope.

Objectives: Defeat al-Shabaab, retake its territory and protect the federal government of Somalia.

Opponents: Al-Shabaab.

Affiliates/allies: Supported by numerous international governments and periodically by military contingents from allied countries, which deliver training, including the EU, Turkey, the UK and the US.

Resources/capabilities: Lacks critical resources such as air assets, but its key challenge is the unpredictability of donor funding, which makes strategic planning difficult.

The United States

Strength: Approximately 700 troops, mostly redeployed to military bases in neighbouring Kenya and Djibouti.[5]

Areas of operation: Details of ground operations rarely disclosed. Drone strikes predominantly target areas of central and southern Somalia controlled by al-Shabaab.

Leadership: US Africa Command (AFRICOM) oversees most military operations in Somalia. General Stephen J. Townsend (AFRICOM commander); Major-General Lapthe Flora (head of the Combined Joint Task Force-Horn of Africa).

Structure: US troops in Somalia operate under AFRICOM's component commands. These include US Army Africa, the Combined Joint Task Force-Horn of Africa, Joint Special Operations Command and a Mogadishu-based Military Coordination Cell tasked with coordinating operations between US forces and AMISOM.

History: The US began targeting al-Shabaab in January 2007 under president George W. Bush, with military operations significantly expanding during the Obama administration. In November 2020, president Donald Trump announced a plan to withdraw ground troops from Somalia, which became effective in January 2021.

Objectives: Defeat al-Shabaab as part of the US war on terror and support the federal government of Somalia in retaking territory.

Opponents: Al-Shabaab.

Affiliates/allies: The federal government of Somalia, AMISOM and the UN.

Resources/capabilities: MQ-9 *Reaper* drones are commonly used to conduct airstrikes in Somalia. US troops have also provided military advice and training to AMISOM and Somali military forces, especially the elite Danaab Brigade of the SNA.

Conflict Drivers

Political

Weak state capacity and limited governance:
Plagued by years of conflict, the federal government suffers from poor political legitimacy, widespread corruption and weak institutions. Above all, its long-standing inability to provide security and public services has prevented the government from exercising its authority outside Mogadishu. Rural Somalis rarely interact with representatives of the state other than the SNA, which has a poor reputation among the population. Meanwhile, al-Shabaab's hold over rural southern Somalia allows the group to provide basic services, including justice mechanisms and Koranic education.

Clan politicisation:
Somali clans challenge all political structures designed to transcend their authority. In fact, the politicisation of clan identities has contributed to the initiation of violent conflicts in Somalia. Clan loyalties can fracture political arrangements or beget unstable, exclusionary relationships, while clan competition inhibits the development of a functioning political system. Competition among Somalia's four major clans – Darod, Dir, Hawiye and Rahanweyn – is regulated through a '4.5' power-sharing system, which stipulates that political appointments are divided equally among the clans and the myriad sub-clans. However, rather than fostering clan inclusion, the system has reinforced and politicised clan identities.

Economic and social

Increasing appeal of Islamist ideology:
The spread of violent Islamist ideology was also key to the rise of al-Shabaab. Amid the collapse of state institutions and weak rule of law, Islamist groups succeeded in responding to popular grievances over justice and socio-economic inequalities. Lately, al-Shabaab has incorporated nationalist tones about

Sub-Saharan Africa

global jihad into its propaganda, in an attempt to widen its appeal among the general Somali population.

Environmental factors:
Environmental factors play a major role in exacerbating conflict in Somalia through land degradation and extreme weather conditions. Rainfall seasons are shortening and becoming increasingly unpredictable, with floods and droughts undermining the livelihoods of rural communities. Communal conflicts over scarce resources, such as water and fertile land, are increasingly common, particularly between farmers and herders, and overlap with clan and sub-clan dynamics. Environmental pressures have contributed to significant refugee outflow during the last decade and to rural-to-urban forced migration into Mogadishu and Baidoa. Food insecurity is also pervasive.

International
Regional and wider influences:
International involvement in Somalia has undoubtedly helped contain al-Shabaab's insurgency, but has also stoked domestic tensions. Ethiopia and Kenya have long been involved in Somalia's domestic affairs, providing political and financial assistance to allied Somali elites and intervening in cross-border clan conflicts. Notably, Qatar, Saudi Arabia, Turkey and the United Arab Emirates (UAE) have increasingly engaged in security and financial operations in Somalia, where their support for clan and local militia groups has exacerbated tensions between the centre and the periphery. Additionally, the large Somali diaspora exercises disproportionate influence in the country's politics through its considerable private capital and investment. Members of the diaspora have occasionally channelled resources to clans and other armed groups, including al-Shabaab.

Political and Military Developments

Growing tensions between the federal government and the federal states
Relations between the Somali central government and the federal member states remained strained in 2020, with unresolved disputes over the holding of the parliamentary elections and the succession to President Farmaajo. Ahead of the parliamentary elections initially scheduled for December 2020, a proposal to move away from indirect voting stoked tensions between Farmaajo and the opposition, including the presidents of Puntland and Jubaland. In February, federal meddling in the Galmudug local elections triggered clashes with Ahlu Sunna Wal Jamaa (ASWJ), a Sufi group whose militants were integrated into Galmudug's security forces after battling with al-Shabaab. Jubaland President Ahmed Madobe, backed by Kenya and a vocal critic of Farmaajo, threatened to annul parliamentary elections if the federal government did not withdraw its troops from Gedo region ahead of the vote.

Fears that Farmaajo would delay the vote and abuse his presidential prerogatives to remain in power after the end of his term drew criticism from the opposition. In July, the Somali parliament ousted prime minister Hassan Ali Khayre, who was at odds with the president over the latter's intention to delay the ballot. Despite reaching a consensus to keep the indirect voting system in September, the parliamentary elections were postponed to February 2021, with the Somali election body citing concerns over security and the coronavirus pandemic. After Farmaajo's term expired in February 2021 without a clear electoral time frame, opposition candidates ceased recognising the president and called for a peaceful transfer of power.

Al-Shabaab's insurgency
Al-Shabaab confirmed its ability to launch high-profile attacks against government targets. Suicide bombers killed the governors of Nugaal and Mudug provinces in March and May respectively, while an explosion in December 2020 targeted the newly appointed Prime Minister Mohamed Hussein Roble. Other attacks were directed at military targets, including the Army Chief of Staff General Odawaa Yusuf Rageh, who survived a vehicle-borne improvised explosive device (VBIED) attack in Mogadishu's Hodan district.

Al-Shabaab regularly attacked SNA and AMISOM military bases, convoys and patrols in rural areas across central and southern Somalia. In the early months of 2020, an increase in mortar attacks on Mogadishu revealed the difficulty facing security forces in expelling al-Shabaab from the areas surrounding the capital and the nearby Afgoye district. Al-Shabaab has increasingly shifted its operations northwards since ASWJ's demise; in Puntland, it launched hit-and-run attacks on military posts and assassinated several security personnel, politicians and civil servants. As much as 25% of Somali territory is estimated to be under the control of al-Shabaab, which collected an estimated US$13 million through extortion and taxes in 2020 alone.[6] Al-Shabaab also confirmed its significant transnational reach. In January 2020, the group staged an attack on Manda airstrip in Camp Simba, a military base situated in Kenya's Lamu County that houses US and Kenyan troops.

Developments in counter-insurgency operations

During 2020, AMISOM and US forces continued to provide critical assistance to the SNA in its fight against al-Shabaab. Despite the withdrawal of some US special forces from Somalia, an estimated 72 counter-terrorism operations – 54 of which have been confirmed by AFRICOM – were conducted on Somali soil, the second-highest number since the first reported strikes in 2007.[7] AMISOM supported Somali troops in the battle of Janaale, which they recaptured from al-Shabaab in March 2020. In May, the United Nations Security Council (UNSC) passed Resolution 2520, which confirmed the deployment of 19,626 personnel until February 2021, stating that 'the situation in Somalia continues to constitute a threat to international peace and security'.[8] Yet a drawdown of 1,000 troops in February 2020, and the additional withdrawal of 200 Ethiopian troops in November 2020, foreshadowed the planned transfer of security responsibilities from AMISOM to the SNA at the end of 2021. Additionally, Somalia's diplomatic turbulences with Djibouti and Kenya injected further instability into AMISOM.

Key Events in 2020–21

POLITICAL EVENTS

20 February 2020
Farmaajo signs the new electoral bill to end indirect voting into law, triggering protests from the opposition.

18 March
Somalia's federal government introduces a ban on international flights, two days after confirming the country's first COVID-19 case.

29 May
The UNSC passes Resolution 2520 confirming the deployment of AMISOM troops until February 2021.

25 July
Somalia's federal parliament passes a motion of no confidence against prime minister Hassan Ali Khayre.

20 August
Somalia's political leaders agree on adopting indirect voting in the upcoming parliamentary elections.

23 September
The Somali parliament unanimously confirms the appointment of Mohamed Hussein Roble as prime minister.

1 December
A deadline to hold parliamentary elections is missed.

MILITARY/VIOLENT EVENTS

8 February 2020
Clashes between the SNA and Jubaland security forces take place in Beled Hawo, Gedo region.

27 February
Dozens are killed in heavy clashes between the SNA and ASWJ fighters in Galmudug.

29 March
The governor of Nugaal province is killed in an al-Shabaab suicide attack in Garowe.

17 May
An al-Shabaab suicide bomber kills the governor of Mudug province and three bodyguards in Galkayo.

13 July
Army General Odawaa Yusuf Rageh survives a suicide car-bomb attack in Mogadishu's Hodan district.

16 August
Al-Shabaab attacks an upscale hotel in Mogadishu, killing at least 16 people.

18 November
Hundreds of Ethiopian peacekeepers from Tigray region are disarmed over security concerns.

Sub-Saharan Africa

15 December	18 December
Somalia cuts diplomatic ties with Kenya, accusing its neighbour of interfering in its domestic affairs.	Al-Shabaab claims responsibility for a suicide attack targeting Somali Prime Minister Mohamed Hussein Roble in Galkayo.
8 February 2021	**18 February 2021**
Opposition leaders announce they no longer recognise President Farmaajo.	Government forces and opposition supporters clash in Mogadishu.

Impact

Human rights and humanitarian

Armed violence continued to exact a high civilian toll in 2020. Around 750 civilians were estimated to have died between January 2020 and February 2021 because of armed violence, with al-Shabaab responsible for nearly half of these deaths.[9] The humanitarian crisis in Somalia remained alarming, with approximately 5.9m people in need of humanitarian assistance.[10] Heavy fighting in Gedo and Jubaland caused the displacement of roughly 60,000 internally displaced persons (IDPs) during the first half of 2020 and by the end of the year there were an estimated 293,000 new conflict IDPs across the whole country.[11] Additionally, the coronavirus pandemic, desert locusts and floods exacerbated the humanitarian situation. In particular, concerns arose that the spread of new infectious variants of the coronavirus could lead to a surge in COVID-19 cases, especially given the country's fragile healthcare system. Flooding displaced over half a million Somalis and affected an estimated 1.3m people across 39 districts, contributing to the spread of waterborne diseases such as cholera and acute diarrhoea.[12]

Political stability

Disputes over the upcoming presidential and parliamentary elections dominated Somalia's political landscape. These tensions sparked an outbreak of inter-clan clashes across Somalia and antagonised some of the government's allies – such as the ASWJ – in the fight against al-Shabaab. Notably, al-Shabaab took advantage of these fissures to enhance its propaganda and recruitment.[13] The stand-off between President Farmaajo and the opposition over the electoral law ended in September 2020 following agreement to retain the current indirect voting system for the December 2020 parliamentary elections. However, the postponing of the ballot ignited new tensions between the government and the opposition.

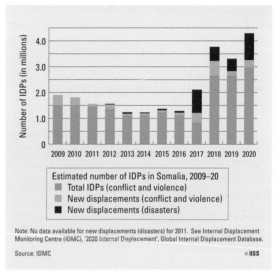

Estimated number of IDPs in Somalia, 2009–20
■ Total IDPs (conflict and violence)
■ New displacements (conflict and violence)
■ New displacements (disasters)

Note: No data available for new displacements (disasters) for 2011. See Internal Displacement Monitoring Centre (IDMC), '2020 Internal Displacement', Global Internal Displacement Database.

Source: IDMC   © IISS

Figure 1: Estimated number of IDPs, 2009–20

Economic and social

The combined effect of the pandemic, flooding and a locust infestation caused an estimated 1.5% GDP contraction in 2020, down from a forecasted growth of 3.2%.[14] The recession is largely the result of an estimated 40% drop in remittances, and a concurrent fall in the export of livestock.[15] In March, the IMF and the World Bank announced Somalia would be eligible to receive debt relief under the enhanced Heavily Indebted Poor Countries initiative, restoring the country's access to regular financing. In June, the World Bank approved a US$55m emergency package to support Somalia's ailing economy. The package provided critical supplemental financing to the 2020 budget, sustaining service delivery in the face of considerable revenue shortfall.

Years of conflict have had devastating social effects. Approximately 69% of the population lives in poverty, with an even higher incidence rate among IDPs.[16] An estimated 30% of children aged six to 17 were enrolled in school as of 2020, with strong disparities between urban and rural areas and between boys and girls.[17] Additionally, the combination of heavy flooding and below-average rainfall seasons negatively affected crop and livestock production, leaving over 2.5m people acutely food insecure.[18]

Relations with neighbouring and international partners and geopolitical implications

Somalia was also caught in the midst of broader regional turbulences in 2020. Rivalries among Gulf countries continued to play out in the country, with Qatar and the UAE vying for influence and Turkey remaining one of Farmaajo's most trusted allies. The conflict in Ethiopia's Tigray region also had wider implications for Somalia. The Ethiopian government redeployed an estimated 3,000 troops from Somalia to Tigray and disarmed an additional 200 Tigrayan soldiers serving in AMISOM.[19] These

withdrawals have sparked concerns that AMISOM-backed Somali troops will be more vulnerable to al-Shabaab.

In December, relations between Kenya and Somalia deteriorated after the Somali government accused its neighbour of meddling in its domestic affairs. Hours after Kenyan President Uhuru Kenyatta welcomed President Muse Bihi Abdi of Somaliland in Nairobi on 14 December, Somalia cut diplomatic ties with Kenya. The crisis represented the culmination of years of simmering tensions between the two countries, which have escalated over Kenya's involvement in AMISOM, unresolved trade issues, maritime-border disputes and alleged breaches of Somalia's sovereignty. Subsequently, the Somali government dismissed as 'biased' the results of a fact-finding mission mandated by the Intergovernmental Authority on Development to investigate the maritime-border dispute with Kenya.[20]

Conflict Outlook

Political scenarios

The turbulent run-up to the elections strained relations between the Somali federal government and the member states. Farmaajo's nationalist platform antagonised influential clan leaders, including the presidents of Puntland and Jubaland. In these regions, the deployment of the SNA occasionally ignited clashes with local security forces. Inadequate measures to ensure widespread public confidence in the electoral process and its eventual outcome could provoke a violent backlash from the federal states and the opposition. The ongoing dispute with Kenya over the demarcation of the maritime boundary – with a postponed adjudication date of March 2021 at the International Court of Justice (ICJ) – is also likely to have a significant impact on Somalia's domestic politics, not just on regional relations. A ruling favouring Somalia could lead the federal government to begin oil explorations off the coast of semi-autonomous Puntland, potentially igniting new disputes with the regional government over how to distribute oil revenues.

Escalation potential and conflict-related risks

AMISOM is set to transfer security responsibilities to the Somali government by the end of 2021. Yet

tensions involving AMISOM's TCCs represent a significant conflict-related risk. The crisis in Tigray already triggered a redeployment of Ethiopian forces in 2020 – both those under AMISOM and independent troops – from Somalia to the domestic front. If the Tigray conflict escalates or stretches out further into 2021, the Ethiopian government may be forced to withdraw additional troops from Somalia.

The potential of rising regional tensions between Kenya and Somalia – should either one of them ignore an unfavourable ICJ ruling – may also negatively affect AMISOM. Changes in the current size and composition of AMISOM may induce other TCCs, including Burundi, Djibouti and Uganda, to reconsider their participation in the mission: a threat Burundi and Uganda already made in 2019 after a proposed drawdown of military personnel. Cracks within AMISOM are likely to benefit al-Shabaab, as previous Ethiopian and Kenyan troop withdrawals saw the group increase attacks and quickly retake territory. With the SNA still ill-equipped to assume security responsibilities, AMISOM may continue to take a leading security role beyond the end of 2021.

Sub-Saharan Africa

Prospects for peace

The 2021 parliamentary and presidential elections represent an important inflection point for the country. Broad acceptance of election results could improve the relations between the federal government and the member states. However, this is contingent on the Somali political and security elites making a general commitment to the electoral process, which proved the major obstacle throughout 2020. A contested ballot could trigger a political crisis with broader regional ramifications. Political developments in early 2021, including the opposition ceasing to recognise Farmaajo and the violent repression of an opposition march in February, suggest that tension is likely to increase in the absence of a clear and mutually agreed electoral time frame.

Additionally, the prospects of a negotiated settlement with al-Shabaab remain thin. Over the years, calls to review the current strategy to fight al-Shabaab acknowledged the low probability of success by military force alone. Yet the protracted military stalemate between the federal government and al-Shabaab, along with the uneasiness among powerful regional actors over the situation, makes it unlikely that official negotiations will begin any time soon.

Strategic implications and global influences

The strategic value of the coastline along the Red Sea and the Horn of Africa leaves Somalia vulnerable to foreign meddling. Both Gulf and neighbouring African countries have taken advantage of the ambiguous status of federal states to bypass the central government's approval of infrastructure projects. The UAE has established close relations with the federal member states, antagonising the central government. Although Farmaajo banned Dubai's DP World from operating in Somalia and despite the rejection of a late-2019 UAE plan to build a military base in Berbera, the company successfully won 30-year concessions to develop the port of Berbera in Somaliland and the port of Bosaso in Puntland. In Puntland, the UAE were reported to have sponsored regional militias hostile to Mogadishu.[21] Farmaajo has found two close allies in Ethiopian Prime Minister Abiy Ahmed and Eritrean President Isaias Afwerki. However, a conflict between Mogadishu and the federal states could force Abiy and Isaias – both aligned with the UAE – to abandon Farmaajo, plunging Somalia into further fragmentation. The consequences of regional turbulences and shifting alliances in the Horn are therefore likely to reverberate widely across Somalia.

Notes

1   Hiraal Institute, 'A Losing Game: Countering Al-Shabab's Financial System', October 2020.

2   Security Council Report, 'August 2019 Monthly Forecast', 31 July 2019.

3   Christopher Anzalone (@IbnSiqilli), tweet, 21 July 2019.

4   United Nations Security Council, 'Security Council Reauthorizes Deployment of African Union Mission in Somalia, Unanimously Adopting Resolution 2520 (2020)', S/RES/2520, 29 May 2020, p. 4.

5   'Trump Orders Withdrawal of US Troops from Somalia', BBC News, 5 December 2020.

6   United Nations Security Council, 'Report of the Panel of Experts on Somalia Submitted in Accordance with Resolution 2498 (2019), S/2020/949', 28 October 2020, p. 8.

7   Airwars, 'US Forces in Somalia', 1 February 2021.

8   United Nations Security Council, 'The Situation in Somalia. Letter from the President of the Council on the Voting Outcome (S/2020/459) and Voting Details (S/2020/466)', 29 May 2020, p. 8.

9   Armed Conflict Location & Event Data Project (ACLED), www.acleddata.com.

10 United Nations Office for the Coordination of Humanitarian Affairs, 'Global Humanitarian Overview 2021', 1 December 2020, p. 10.

11 See Internal Displacement Monitoring Centre (IDMC), '2020 Internal Displacement', Global Internal Displacement Database.

12 United Nations Security Council, 'Situation in Somalia. Report of the Secretary-General, S/2020/798', 13 August 2020, p. 11.

13 United Nations Security Council, 'Letter Dated 21 January 2021 from the Chair of the Security Council Committee Pursuant to Resolutions 1267 (1999), 1989 (2011) and 2253 (2015) Concerning Islamic State in Iraq and the Levant (Da'esh), Al-Qaida and Associated Individuals, Groups, Undertakings and Entities Addressed to the President of the Security Council', S/2021/68, 3 February 2021, p. 11.

14 International Monetary Fund, 'World Economic Outlook: A Long and Difficult Ascent', October 2020, p. 146.

15 International Organization for Migration, 'Expected 40 Percent Drop in Remittances Threatens Somalia's Most Vulnerable', 15 June 2020.

16 World Bank Group, 'Somali Poverty and Vulnerability Assessment', April 2019, p. 126. Poverty in this assessment was defined as living off less than US$1.90 per day.

17 United Nations Office for the Coordination of Humanitarian Affairs, 'Humanitarian Needs Overview: Somalia', January 2021, p. 68.

18 Famine Early Warning System Network, 'Somalia Food Security Outlook, October 2020 to May 2021', 15 November 2020.

19 Colum Lynch and Robbie Gramer, 'U.N. Fears Ethiopia Purging Ethnic Tigrayan Officers from Its Peacekeeping Missions', *Foreign Policy*, 23 November 2020.

20 Magdalene Mukami, 'Somalia Rejects Probe Report on Tiff with Kenya', Anadolu Agency, 27 January 2021.

21 Vanda Felbab-Brown, 'What Ethiopia's Crisis Means for Somalia', Brookings Institution, 20 November 2020.

DEMOCRATIC REPUBLIC OF THE CONGO

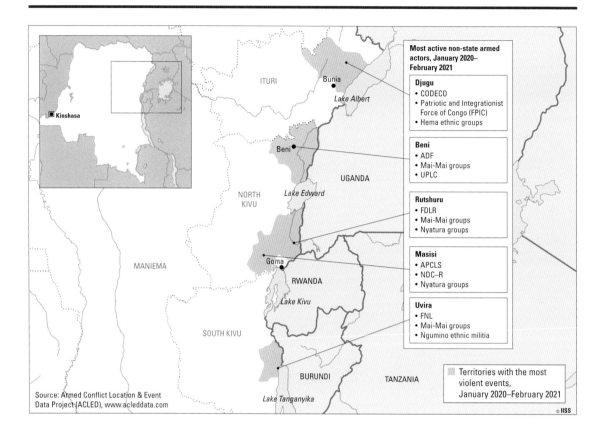

Source: Armed Conflict Location & Event Data Project (ACLED), www.acleddata.com

Most active non-state armed actors, January 2020–February 2021

Djugu
• CODECO
• Patriotic and Integrationist Force of Congo (FPIC)
• Hema ethnic groups

Beni
• ADF
• Mai-Mai groups
• UPLC

Rutshuru
• FDLR
• Mai-Mai groups
• Nyatura groups

Masisi
• APCLS
• NDC–R
• Nyatura groups

Uvira
• FNL
• Mai-Mai groups
• Ngumino ethnic militia

▨ Territories with the most violent events, January 2020–February 2021

© IISS

Overview

Over a hundred different conflicts plague the Democratic Republic of the Congo (DRC). State and non-state armed groups fight over land, minerals and identity, compounded by competing international interests. The distinction between state and non-state is blurred: the Armed Forces of the Democratic Republic of the Congo (FARDC) is one of many armed groups and it allows certain other actors to control territory and state institutions.

Foreign insurgent activity has also shaped the country's modern history. Rwanda continues to conduct military operations against Hutu rebel groups, who have operated in eastern DRC provinces since the Rwandan genocide of 1994. Ugandan insurgencies have also made use of the DRC–Uganda borderlands to escape Kampala's reach. Insecurity in the DRC and its high-value natural resources have long incentivised foreign-military activity in the country, either through the deployment of troops or by backing local armed groups. These ongoing dynamics have caused much bloodshed and left a legacy of suspicion of foreign intervention which still drives militarisation among communities in eastern DRC.

Violence escalated in 2020–21, with an increasing number of attacks on civilians and clashes between armed groups. Armed groups frequently attacked, abducted, burned, pillaged, murdered and committed sexual violence, leading to large displacements of people. Armed-group violence targeting civilians caused an estimated 2,702 fatalities in 2020–21 compared to 2,203 in the same period from 2019–20. The Allied Democratic Forces (ADF), an armed group from Uganda with obscure ties to the Islamic State (also known as ISIS or ISIL), was responsible for 49.5% of these killings. Furthermore, violence against and carried out by ethnic Banyamulenge groups continued to grow, more than doubling from 2019.[1]

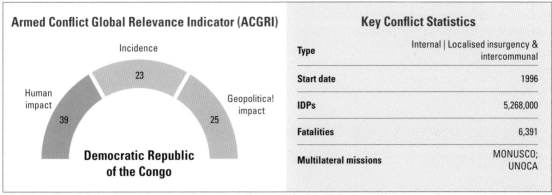

Armed Conflict Global Relevance Indicator (ACGRI)		Key Conflict Statistics	
Incidence 23		**Type**	Internal | Localised insurgency & intercommunal
Human impact 39	**Geopolitical impact** 25	**Start date**	1996
		IDPs	5,268,000
Democratic Republic of the Congo		**Fatalities**	6,391
		Multilateral missions	MONUSCO; UNOCA

ACGRI pillars: IISS calculation based on multiple sources for 2020 and January/February 2021 (scale 0–100). See Notes on Methodology and Data Appendix for further details on Key Conflict Statistics.

Eastern provinces of the DRC continued to be the most unstable in 2020–21. Violence rose in Ituri, fuelled by long-standing tension between the Lendu and Hema ethnic groups over political power, land and identity.[2] These tensions were complicated by ethnic recruitment by larger armed groups, such as Lendu recruitment by the Cooperative for the Development of the Congo (CODECO). The Nduma Defence of Renovated Congo (NDC–R), an armed group historically linked to mining areas, expanded its operations further into North Kivu, seizing control of territory previously held by other armed groups. Importantly, CODECO and NDC–R both experienced internal splintering following the death of CODECO leader Justin Ngudjolo and NDC–R leadership divisions.

In 2020–21, foreign-military operations, regional trade relations and cross-border travel were complicated by the outbreak of the coronavirus pandemic, with domestic-policy responses including border closures, travel restrictions and limitations on gatherings.

Conflict Parties

The Armed Forces of the Democratic Republic of Congo (FARDC)

Strength: 134,250.

Areas of operation: Across the country in 11 military regions, but mainly focused on North and South Kivu and with increased activity in Ituri in 2020.

Leadership: Lieutenant-General Célestin Mbala Munsense (chief of the general staff).

Structure: The FARDC is very large but poorly structured, with perhaps as many as 65% of its troops being officers, 26% of whom are high-ranking.[3] This is partly the result of a regular practice of awarding officer positions to defecting rebels.

History: The FARDC was created by the 2003 Sun City Agreement, which stipulated that all parties to the conflict contributed troops to the national army, an integration process known as *brassage*. Despite international efforts at security-sector reform, the FARDC remains a mix of feuding militias.

Objectives: While formally the FARDC fulfils national-security objectives, many officers and soldiers pursue their own agendas, seeking wealth particularly through illicit trade and mining, or enacting the violent demands of political patrons.

Opponents: The majority of armed groups in the DRC (except those with which the FARDC has an alliance of convenience).

Affiliates/allies: Frequently uses armed groups to do its fighting and sometimes allies with them for political and economic opportunities.

Resources/capabilities: Suffers from chronic resource shortages (including for salaries) amid widespread corruption, resulting in weak and ineffective operations. It is predominantly armed with small arms and light weapons, but also has artillery, 430 armoured fighting vehicles, anti-aircraft guns and surface-to-air missiles.

Cooperation for the Development of Congo (CODECO)

Strength: Most reports estimate 2,350 people, but these draw on self-reporting from within the group.[4]

Areas of operation: Djugu, Mahagi and Irumu territories in Ituri province.

Leadership: The assassination of Ngudjolo in March 2020 resulted in the splintering of CODECO into competing factions. Recent groups to emerge include Union of Revolutionaries for the Defence of the Congolese People (URPDC), led by Charité Nguna Kiza; CODECO Alliance for the Liberation of the Congo, under the leadership of Justin Maki Gesi; and CODECO Sambaza, whose leadership is uncertain.

Structure: Some factions and splinter groups accepted the 2020 disarmament process while others continued fighting.

History: CODECO formed in the 1970s, originally as a farming collective of primarily ethnic Lendu groups, which developed both spiritual and militant dimensions over time. It has since engaged in numerous bouts of violence against the Hema.

Objectives: While CODECO's objectives appear to be ethnic violence against the Hema population, ethnicity is not the main driver, and conflict is tied to political circumstances. Some factions have expressed willingness to enter a peace process, with better food provision for their areas one of the conditions for their participation.

Opponents: Individual and self-defence Hema groups, FARDC.

Affiliates/allies: CODECO is believed to have links with the Iturian groups Nationalist and Integrationist Front (FNI) and Ituri Patriotic Resistance Force (FPRI).

Resources/capabilities: Much of CODECO fighting is done with bladed weapons or small arms and light weapons.

Allied Democratic Forces (ADF)

Strength: Likely around 700–1,000, although not all its personnel are combatants.[5]

Areas of operation: Beni territory (particularly Beni town), Eringeti, Mbau and increasingly Kamango, close to the border with Uganda.

Leadership: Seka Musa Baluku (emir of the ADF and its most senior leader).

Structure: Divided between several main camps, each of which houses between 150–200 fighters.[6] Each camp has recognised military leaders and ranks, although it is unclear if the ranks follow a conventional military structure.

History: Created in 1995 from a merger between Ugandan Tabliqh Islamists and the remnants of a Ugandan secessionist movement in the DRC–Uganda border area. Over time the group has increasingly adopted jihadist rhetoric and ideology. It has referred to itself as Madina al-Tauheed wa Mujahedeen, and in April 2019 official ISIS media began claiming some of its attacks.

Objectives: The ADF regularly attacks and kills civilians in the Beni area, but expresses no clearly articulated political plans other than vague Salafi-jihadist statements. While ISIS has claimed credit for its attacks, it has not expressed specific plans in relation to the DRC.

Opponents: FARDC and United Nations Organisation Stabilisation Mission in the Democratic Republic of the Congo (MONUSCO).

Affiliates/allies: The ADF has been known to form temporary alliances or bargains with local armed actors, including elements of the FARDC and Mai-Mai groups.

Resources/capabilities: The ADF is well integrated into the borderland landscape and can draw on several sources to sustain itself, including agriculture and illicit trade. While it is armed largely with light weapons, ISIS media has regularly claimed that the group steals weapons from the FARDC.

Resistance for the Rule of Law in Burundi (RED Tabara)

Strength: Unclear, but RED Tabara claimed in 2017 to have 2,000 recruits.[7]

Areas of operation: Uvira territory and the Ruzizi plain.

Leadership: 'General' Birembu Melkiade, also called Melchiade Biremba, is the recognised leader of RED Tabara, but is currently believed to be in the custody of the DRC government. 'Colonel' Raymond Lukondo is Melkiade's deputy and the interim military leader.

Structure: Unclear, but presence of designated ranks suggests the group is mimicking a conventional military structure.

History: RED Tabara is believed to be the military wing of the Movement for Solidarity and Democracy (MSD) party led by Alexis Sinduhije, which was formed in opposition to the extension of term limits by Burundian President Pierre Nkurunziza in 2015.

Objectives: Overthrow the Nkurunziza regime in neighbouring Burundi.

Opponents: The Burundian National Defence Forces (FDN) and Imbonerakure, a militant youth wing of the ruling political party in Burundi, have made several incursions into DRC territory, resulting in several clashes with RED Tabara.

Affiliates/allies: Other Burundian opposition groups, including the National Forces of Liberation (FNL) and the National Council for Renewal and Democracy (CNRD).

Resources/capabilities: The group is believed to receive some funding from the Burundian diaspora, as well as some support from Burundi.

Raia Mutomboki

Strength: As a decentralised franchise rather than a single armed group, it is not possible to give clear numbers, though there are likely several thousand Raia Mutomboki affiliates across several dozen groups. However, many of these individuals only take up arms at specific times.

Areas of operation: Raia Mutomboki have been historically based in South Kivu and are still most active in the Kabare, Kalehe, Mwenga, Shabunda and Walungu territories, as well as in Kahuzi-Biega National Park.

Leadership: Raia Mutomboki groups have proliferated since the original group formed in 2005, each with different leadership structures. After dozens of fighters surrendered in March 2020, FARDC arrested one of the major leaders, Juriste Kikuni, in October 2020.

Structure: Groups are largely informally structured given their ideological foundation as citizens' movements. Efforts by some individuals to structure and lead them are usually transient.

History: Formed in 2005 to combat violence committed by the Democratic Forces for the Liberation of Rwanda (FDLR) but also as a form of protest against state violence and neglect. The name Raia Mutomboki means 'angry citizens', and the groups largely continue to style themselves as grassroots defenders.

Objectives: The political demands vary from group to group. Broadly, they aim to fight the FDLR, counter state violence and advocate for better access to public services for residents in their area. They also function as local defence militias.

Opponents: FDLR, FARDC.

Affiliates/allies: Alliances tend to be localised and short-term, but they often fight alongside Mai-Mai groups and other Raia Mutomboki factions.

Resources/capabilities: Raia Mutomboki largely draw on the same revenue sources as ordinary people, including agriculture and artisanal mining. Their weapons are limited to small arms and bladed weapons.

Mai-Mai (Mayi-Mayi) groups

Strength: There are over 50 known Mai-Mai groups in North and South Kivu. Some groups have formed large coalitions of several hundred fighters (such as the Mai-Mai Mazembe or Yakutumba), but most groups tend to comprise fewer than 200 fighters.

Areas of operation: Present in most of North and South Kivu.

Leadership: Each group has its own leadership arrangements, with some groups more centralised around a single leader, while others are less defined.

Structure: Largely informal and non-hierarchical.

History: Mai-Mai groups mostly formed as self-defence militias. A majority have anti-Tutsi or anti-Rwandan sentiments and see themselves as indigenous defenders against Rwandan foreigners.

Objectives: While the groups are styled as community-protection groups, usually around a particular ethnicity and locality, they often collaborate with each other, or with larger armed actors for both defensive and opportunistic reasons.

Opponents: Typically, groups considered to be 'non-local', such as people viewed as Rwandan or Banyamulenge. However, localised territorial struggles are also common.

Affiliates/allies: Alliances of convenience are periodically formed, including between Mai-Mai groups.

Resources/capabilities: Mai-Mai weapons are usually limited to small arms or machetes and other bladed weapons. Some groups take part in artisanal mining and periodically exercise control over mining sites.

The Democratic Forces for the Liberation of Rwanda (FDLR)

Strength: While the FDLR was believed to number 6,500 combatants in 2008, many fighters demobilised in 2018. In 2020, estimates range from 500 to 1,000 fighters.[8]

Areas of operation: Operates primarily in Bwito with limited operations in surrounding areas in North Kivu and into South Kivu.

Leadership: In 2019 the FDLR's most senior leaders passed away, with Ignace Murwanashyaka dying from natural causes and the FDLR's military commander Sylvestre Mudacumura killed by the FARDC. Two leaders, called Omega and Gaby Ruhinda, took over leadership of the group.

Structure: The FDLR mimics a conventional military structure, with specialised units for particular missions. However, the reduction in numbers and loss of long-standing leaders may prompt a gradual informalisation of the group.

History: Former officers from the army of Rwandan president Juvénal Habyarimana fled to the DRC (then known as Zaire) after the 1994 genocide and remobilised in refugee camps. The group changed its name to the FDLR in 1999. Individuals involved in the genocide are still believed to be with the movement. Operations in Rutshuru and other areas frequently result in clashes with state and non-state armed groups, the abduction of civilians to raise money and attacks against the local population.

Objectives: Ideologically divided between those desiring the repatriation of Rwandan refugees displaced during the genocide and others aiming to overthrow the government of President Paul Kagame in Rwanda.

Opponents: The government of Rwanda, the Nduma Defence of Renovated Congo (NDC–R), local Mai-Mai groups.

Affiliates/allies: Mai-Mai Nyatura, Collective of Movements for Change (CMC).

Sub-Saharan Africa

The Democratic Forces for the Liberation of Rwanda (FDLR)

Resources/capabilities: Funding comes from the trade of local goods, agriculture and looting. The group also trades cannabis and charcoal, and oversees the exploitation of gold and tin mines. Moreover, it receives funding from the Rwandan diaspora.

Patriotic Union for the Liberation of Congo (UPLC)

Strength: Around 400 to 500 fighters.[9]

Areas of operation: Beni territory (South Kivu province) with a primary base in Kalunguta.

Leadership: The current commander is Kambale Mayani, after Kakule Liso was removed from leadership and killed by local vigilantes in January 2021.

Structure: Formed from Mai-Mai Kilalo. Leadership comprised of former military and non-state armed groups.

History: Created in 2016 from Mai-Mai Kilalo, founded by Katembo Kilalo and Mambari Bini Pélé. The group has carried out operations against MONUSCO, ADF and FARDC in the Beni area, often partnering with other Mai-Mai groups.

Objectives: Stated goal is to defend ethnic Kobo, Nande and Piri from ADF and FDLR attacks and end the FDLR operations in Lubero territory.

Opponents: ADF (though some reports suggest ADF and UPLC have also partnered to fight against FARDC), FARDC, FDLR, MONUSCO.

Affiliates/allies: Various Mai-Mai groups, including precarious relations with Mazembe, Nguru, Kabidon, Ngolenge; may occasionally collaborate with FARDC.

Resources/capabilities: Controls some mining sites and collects fees from miners operating around its area of control near Beni town. Draws on forced community labour and a vast network of Mai-Mai affiliated groups and uses abducted children for forced labour and military operations.

The Nduma Defence of Renovated Congo (NDC–R)

Strength: While consisting of a couple of hundred fighters when it split from its parent Mai-Mai Sheka group in 2014, it has grown with the absorption of small groups and the conquest of new territory and mining sites. Estimates from fighters in 2020 suggest a total strength of 5,000.[10]

Areas of operation: Lubero, Masisi, Rutshuru and Walikale territories in North Kivu.

Leadership: The NDC–R split in July 2020, with one faction led by Guidon Shimiray Mwissa, former deputy commander of Mai-Mai Sheka, and the other faction led by Gilbert Bwira and Mapenzi Likuhe.

Structure: Unclear following the split. Previously the NDC–R had a hierarchical, military-style structure with contingents distributed in numerous bases and officers in charge of different political, economic and social relations.

History: The NDC–R splintered from the Mai-Mai Sheka group in 2014.

Objectives: The NDC–R claims to be a necessary counter to FDLR activity in the area and has contributed to pushing both the FDLR and its splinter group, the CNRD, out of the areas of Masisi, Rutshuru and Walikale. However, the NDC–R has also fought for control of mining sites in the area, particularly gold.

Opponents: The FDLR and the Mai-Mai Nyatura and Mazembe factions.

Allies/affiliates: The FARDC and numerous temporary alliances with local Mai-Mai factions.

Resources/capabilities: Draws income from its control over gold, tin and tungsten mines. Also has an extensive tax and forced-labour system in the areas that it controls. It is known to have procured light weapons from the FARDC and other armed groups.

United Nations Stabilisation Mission in Congo (MONUSCO)

Strength: 16,215 troops from 46 countries. (Additionally, there are 1,605 police and 2,970 civilian staff.)[11] While most MONUSCO troops do not have an offensive mandate and are tasked with the protection of civilians, the mission also has a Force Intervention Brigade (FIB) that is allowed to act against armed actors.

Areas of operation: The mission headquarters and the political unit are based in Kinshasa. MONUSCO's military component is predominantly concentrated in North and South Kivu, though it has a presence in Kasai and increased its presence in Ituri province in 2020.

Leadership: Lieutenant-General Ricardo Augusto Ferreira Costa Neves is MONUSCO's Force Commander, while Leila Zerrougui is the Special Representative of the UN Secretary-General.

Structure: The contingents are spread out over a number of (sometimes temporary) bases and operate in clusters of forces, with units from several contingents per base.

History: MONUSCO replaced the United Nations Organisation Mission in the Congo (MONUC) in July 2010 with an enhanced peacekeeping mandate that allowed the protection of civilians. The FIB was mandated in 2013 with strengthening peacekeeping operations.

United Nations Stabilisation Mission in Congo (MONUSCO)	
Objectives: Stabilise the situation in the DRC and improve governance.	**Resources/capabilities:** Relatively well equipped and has air assets (including four combat jets and seven helicopter gunships), as well as armoured personnel carriers and artillery. However, intermittent donor funding complicates its ability to resource its operations effectively.
Opponents: Non-state armed groups in its areas of operation.	
Affiliates/allies: Periodically conducts joint operations with the FARDC, but relations are often tense.	

Other conflict parties	
In addition to the conflict parties above, foreignstate armed forces affected the conflict dynamics in the DRC in 2020–21 by conducting strategic military operations through its porous borders. Some foreign militaries fought alongside the FARDC, such as the military forces of Rwanda, which conducted operations against non-state armed groups that opposed the Rwandan government like the FDLR. Other militaries operated	against the FARDC, such as those from Angola, South Sudan and Zambia. Additionally, other military forces from Burundi operated in the DRC with the ruling party of Burundi's youth militia, the Imbonerakure, to eliminate Burundian opposition groups, such as RED Tabara. Lastly, Ugandan military forces operated in the DRC to protect fishing interests in North Kivu.

Conflict Drivers

Political

Ethnicity and land:

The legacy of the DRC's colonial past is a lasting driver of conflict. Under the Congo Free State (1885–1908), the administration and division of territory solidified loose ethnic groupings. This approach consisted of administering particular groups via their own customs and 'traditional leaders', but the system left some ethnicities effectively stateless and created a legacy of land conflict. Groups viewed as 'indigenous' gained priority, while non-indigenous groups saw their citizenship and landholdings questioned. Some ethnic groups, such as the Banyamulenge, are viewed as non-indigenous because their ancestors had migrated from outside the DRC.[12]

Colonial ethnic divisions intensify current conflicts between groups over land, water and other natural resources. Land conflicts arise and are exacerbated by multiple and conflicting legal systems, a decrease in readily available resources and poor public services. Unable to rely on state forces for protection, rival communities arm themselves to ensure their security and their control of local resources critical for their survival. Long-standing rivalries also initiate conflicts between pastoralists and arable farmers, such as those between Lendu and Hema groups in Ituri.

Deep-rooted institutional weaknesses:

Violence has continued long after the peace process that followed the end of the Second Congo War in 2003, in large part because of the utility of armed groups in helping achieve the political ends of local and national political elites and the FARDC. This has undermined the public credibility of the FARDC, lowering its reputation to just another armed actor that frequently engages in human-rights abuses. At the national level, violence has served to divide communities and prevent them from forming coherent opposition fronts. More broadly, local people (particularly in North and South Kivu) feel both forced and incentivised to form their own militias.[13]

Security

Failed demobilisations:

More than 150,000 combatants have undergone disarmament, demobilisation and reintegration (DDR) since 2003, with limited success in ending violence.[14] While DDR is necessary in conflict resolution, demobilisation incentives provided to combatants have inspired new recruits, who may misinterpret them as meaning that violence ultimately leads to rewards. Likewise, poorly managed reintegration processes have failed to prevent former combatants from returning to arms. Both of these measures have served to perpetuate armed conflict in the DRC. Chronic shortages of resources caused by embezzlement and corruption have also plagued the DDR process.

Sub-Saharan Africa

International

Foreign intervention and mineral interests:
The interests of foreign-state and non-state actors intersect on eliminating opposition groups, exploiting mineral rights and supporting specific ethnic groups. Some foreign-military operations in the DRC, such as those of Angola, Burundi and Rwanda, have been conducted alongside the FARDC with the government's official or unofficial approval. These relations are often fragile, with multiple and conflicting motivations. Foreign governments often attempt to end non-state-armed-group operations on DRC soil, like RED Tabara or the FDLR, but simultaneously conduct their own activities that extract mineral wealth in the eastern part of the country.

Other foreign-state and non-state groups operate without official approval from Kinshasa, controlling mines and resource flows for their own benefit.

Political and Military Developments

Shifting the balance of power

Slow and growing pressure throughout 2020 led to a shift in political power dynamics with the dissolution on 6 December of the power-sharing parliamentary agreement between the Common Front for Congo (FCC), aligned with former president Joseph Kabila, and Heading for Change (CACH), a coalition which includes the Union for Democracy and Social Progress (UDPS) party of the current president, Félix Tshisekedi. Protests by UDPS party supporters against the dismissal of the national parliament's vice-president and the end of the FCC–CACH ruling coalition spread to many cities.

The end of the FCC–CACH coalition was the culmination of a series of strategic decisions by Tshisekedi to remove his predecessor's influence, including instating Albert Yuma Mulimbi as the head of the state-owned copper and cobalt enterprise Gecamines, replacing seven senior magistrates allied to Kabila and suspending Delphin Kahimbi, the military-intelligence chief.[15] Tshisekedi also made controversial appointments to the Constitutional Court, installing judges viewed as sympathetic to him and reducing the influence of those allied to Kabila.

Regional tensions and cooperation

The presence and operations of foreign militaries in the DRC continued to increase in 2020–21, destabilising local populations and resulting in numerous casualties. For example, South Sudanese military forces attacked civilians and looted properties in Ituri, subsequently clashing with the FARDC. Zambian military forces also crossed into Tanganyika province on 13 March and clashed with the FARDC. Other operations were more complex, such as those with Burundian and Rwandan military forces, which partnered with the FARDC to eradicate non-state armed groups operating in eastern DRC amid tense relations between Kigali, Gitega and Kinshasa.[16]

Expanded ADF operations

While the ADF continued to focus operations within North Kivu, by the end of 2020 it had also become the second-most active and deadly non-state armed group in Ituri, second only to CODECO. ADF activities in Ituri took place in the southern part of the province in Mambasa and Irumu. By May 2020, around 4,000 ADF fighters had set up multiple bases in the chiefdom of Walese Vonkutu, partnering with Mai-Mai Kyandenga and Mai-Mai Simba. This shift in operations resulted from increased FARDC

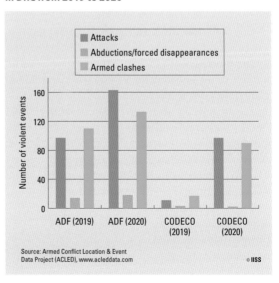

Figure 1: Increase in violence involving ADF and CODECO in DRC from 2019 to 2020

Source: Armed Conflict Location & Event Data Project (ACLED), www.acleddata.com   © IISS

pressure on the ADF in North Kivu and the capture of numerous ADF bases in Beni throughout 2020.

Violence in Ituri

Violence escalated in Ituri in the first half of 2020. Since 2017, CODECO has increasingly mobilised Lendu groups with an ethnic rhetoric against the Hema.[17] Equally, Hema groups have armed themselves and retaliated against Lendu communities. The FARDC's retreat in early February 2020 from several positions around Djugu also allowed Lendu armed groups to take control of dozens of villages in the region. Violent events against civilians in Ituri nearly doubled from the previous year, with events increasing by 84.3% and fatalities increasing by 42.7%.[18] After various peace agreements

with CODECO in August 2020, violence began to decrease but has far from ceased completely.

DDR failures

Several armed grouped entered DDR programmes in 2020, with varied success. In February 2020, for example, the Front for Patriotic Resistance (FRPI) agreed to a ceasefire and reintegration, but some of its fighters continued to commit acts of violence. Deserters of the DDR process often cited insufficient resources and ineffective implementation. More troubling was the trend towards the surrendering and splitting of larger groups, like CODECO, leaving local power vacuums that were filled by defecting factions and other armed groups.

Key Events in 2020–21

POLITICAL EVENTS

7 February 2020
Tshisekedi replaces seven senior magistrates, including allies of former president Kabila.

28 February
The FRPI and the government sign a peace deal, with the latter agreeing to integration into the FARDC.

24 March
A state of emergency and border closures are announced due to the coronavirus pandemic.

8 April
Authorities arrest Vital Kamerhe, Tshisekedi's former chief of staff, on embezzlement charges, prompting both demonstrations and counter-demonstrations.

4 May
CODECO leadership calls for the FARDC to negotiate a ceasefire in order to allow peace talks.

15 June
The ADF establishes three new bases near Eringeti, despite FARDC operations in the region.

24–25 June
The UDPS holds widespread demonstrations against a series of judicial changes proposed by the FCC.

MILITARY/VIOLENT EVENTS

9 January 2020
The FARDC engages in operations against the ADF, taking back Madina in Beni.

2 February
The ADF shifts operations from North Kivu to Ituri, with numerous attacks on civilians.

25 March
Ngudjolo is killed during a military operation in Walendu Pitsi, Ituri.

24 April
Police arrest Bundu dia Kongo leader Ne Muanda Nsemi, resulting in clashes with supporters.

26 April
The Burundian military, the FDLR and the Mai-Mai clash with RED-Tabara in South Kivu.

25 May
FARDC overthrows a strategic CODECO stronghold in the Djugu territory of Ituri.

8 July
The NDC–R announces disarmament plans and demotes Guidon Shimiray from his role as commander, leading to a split and fighting between factions.

16 July
The Banyamulenge clash with the Mai-Mai in Kipupu, resulting in sexual violence, multiple fatalities and mass displacement.

4 August
US Africa Command resumes strategic military cooperation with the FARDC.

Sub-Saharan Africa

8 October

Tshisekedi announces a temporary suspension of Minembwe commune and the creation of a commission to investigate.

14 November

Thousands of Tshisekedi supporters gather in Kinshasa to demand the end of the coalition with the FCC.

6 December

Tshisekedi announces the end of the ruling coalition with former president Kabila's FCC party, vowing to seek a new majority in parliament.

15 February 2021

Tshisekedi appoints Jean-Michel Sama Lukonde Kyenge as the new prime minister.

8–10 September

58 Hutu civilians are killed in attacks in Irumu territory, attributed to the ADF.

20 October

The ADF attacks Kangbayi prison and a nearby military base in Beni, freeing 1,300 prisoners.

16–17 November

ADF militants kill 14 civilians during raids in villages throughout Beni.

22 February 2021

The Italian ambassador to the DRC, Luca Attanasio, and the World Food Programme security escort, Vittorio Iacovacci, are killed during an abduction attempt in North Kivu.

Impact

Human rights and humanitarian

Human-rights violations in eastern DRC continued in 2020, with both state and non-state armed groups committing violent attacks against civilians. Violence by armed groups targeting women increased in 2020, with the majority of these attacks occurring in North Kivu. Use of excessive force against protesters by police and the military had fallen since Tshisekedi took office in 2019, but many demonstrations continued to be banned or dispersed, with journalists targeted in particular. Coronavirus containment measures were used by police to bar demonstrations. Human-rights advocates, lawyers and political-party members continued to face threats, violence and imprisonment for voicing critical views towards those in power.[19]

Violence in the DRC has led to 5.2 million internally displaced persons and just under 950,000 refugees and asylum seekers, primarily in Burundi, Rwanda, Tanzania and Uganda.[20] New refugees also arrived into the DRC from destabilised environments in Burundi, the Central African Republic (CAR) and South Sudan.[21] The DRC now hosts over half a million refugees from neighbouring countries.[22] Humanitarian responses struggled amid the coronavirus pandemic, funding shortages and violence against aid workers in Ituri, North Kivu and South Kivu. This increased the number of people in the DRC experiencing acute food shortages to 21.8m, exacerbating malnutrition rates among children and making the DRC home to the second-largest hunger crisis globally after Yemen.[23]

Economic and social

The DRC faced severe health concerns surrounding an Ebola outbreak during 2020. Although the government officially declared the end of the Ebola outbreak on 18 November 2020, its actual endpoint is uncertain.[24] Limited testing in much of the country made the exact spread and impact of the pandemic since March 2020 difficult to ascertain. Outside of Kinshasa, the conflict-affected eastern provinces were the most severely affected.[25] By the end of February 2021, 25,913 cases had been confirmed and 707 deaths recorded, although actual figures may have been much higher.[26] Coronavirus lockdown measures impacted school children across the country, who lacked the technology to continue their studies virtually. Workers in sectors such as mining faced harsh conditions of confined work environments. Conflict-induced displacement and the pandemic also compounded poverty. Many civilians, especially displaced people with already limited resources, faced indiscriminate looting, destruction of property and deterioration of local public services.

The coronavirus pandemic and subsequent lockdown measures did not affect all economic sectors equally. Compared to the previous year, mineral and rare-earth exports, especially copper and cobalt, increased in production in 2020, due to continued demand and mining companies' practice of confining workers to job sites.[27] Increased production helped alleviate drops in mineral prices.[28] Contact-intensive jobs were more severely hit, particularly those in the informal market, such as small traders, taxi drivers and vendors. The IMF estimated that the economy of the DRC contracted by 0.06% in 2020.[29]

Relations with neighbouring and international partners and geopolitical implications

Relationships with some international partners markedly improved in 2020, with Tshisekedi gaining the trust of the United States and the rein-statement of the African Growth and Opportunity Act (AGOA), which allows sub-Saharan African nations duty-free access to the US market. The DRC government also secured loans from the IMF and the World Bank to handle the coronavirus pandemic and mitigate its economic fallout.[30] Insecurity and violence in the borderlands continued to drive pre-existing regional tensions that stemmed from both the DRC government and neighbouring countries. Groups such as the Alliance of Patriots for a Free and Sovereign Congo (APCLS), FDLR and RED Tabara continued to operate freely and threatened cross-border attacks into Rwanda and Burundi from their bases in the DRC. Foreign militaries from Angola, Burundi, Rwanda, Uganda and Zambia carried out ongoing operations in the DRC, sometimes clashing with the FARDC and keeping diplomatic relations tense throughout the year.

Conflict Outlook

Political scenarios

The ability or inability of Tshisekedi to win political allies and navigate dissent from FCC supporters will shape short-term politics in the DRC. Shortly after the FCC–CACH coalition ended, a Constitutional Court ruling removed a floor-crossing ban in par-liament, which allowed some opposition MPs to support Tshisekedi.[31] The president could also decide to dissolve parliament and hold elections.[32] Kabila and the FCC still have deep ties within the country through FCC-appointed governors and could leverage these for political gain. The unfold-ing of these political dynamics will influence the government's ability to drive development projects forward, deal with the spread of COVID-19 and influence which conflicts to focus on. The leadership of Tshisekedi, together with economic opportunities gained through the AGOA and loans from interna-tional institutions, may prove to be the necessary measures for recovery.

Escalation potential and conflict-related risks

The break-up of the FCC–CACH coalition may divide the interests of and the support for oppos-ing armed groups. The FARDC has previously partnered with groups like the NDC–R to govern areas in eastern DRC, but FCC support for oppos-ing rebel groups could lead to further violence. The NDC–R split will likely lead to fighting between these groups as they try to control local institu-tions and resources. The growing conflict in Ituri displaced tens of thousands of people in 2020 and may escalate further in 2021. Instability and violence may lead to further displacement of DRC citizens to fragile neighbouring countries. These hostilities challenge efforts to contain the spread of COVID-19 and stimulate economic recovery. While the mining industry has been resilient to the global recession, conflict and contestation over the control of mining sites continue to suppress the benefits this industry could bring to the DRC.

Prospects for peace

A majority government for Tshisekedi removes political stalemates and allows for better security-policy implementation across the country, pro-vided they are not disrupted by Kabila and other FCC-backed actors. Agreements with CODECO reduced its violent acts in Ituri by the end of 2020, but this opened up local power vacuums that could be filled by other groups and caused infight-ing among defectors. The break-up of the NDC–R also created local power shifts, where previously the FARDC had often partnered with the NDC–R and permitted the group a level of integration into state institutions. The break-up of the NDC–R could allow the FARDC to control more territory, especially with more effective policy implementa-tion by Tshisekedi. Long-term solutions are likely only if there is further funding and changes to the DDR process, given the high desertion rates due to the lack of supplies, food and opportunities. The fracturing of armed groups also complicates the DDR processes. Instead of negotiating peace deals with a few major actors, there are now multiple groups with differing agendas. A peace deal with one group offers another group opportunities to control territory and populations. As in previous years, the solution to the DRC's conflicts continues to lie primarily in sustaining ongoing peace agreements rather than constructing new ones.

Strategic implications and global influences

Fragile relations between Burundi, Rwanda and Uganda and the ongoing support provided by these states to competing armed groups in eastern DRC make an immediate solution to the violence in the area unlikely.

Rwandan President Kagame warned of potential further military action against external threats, and Burundi will likely retaliate against RED Tabara for its incursions into Burundi during the second half of 2020.[33]

The porous borders used by actors in the Great Lakes region are a point of growing concern, given the highly destabilised situations of the CAR and South Sudan. This poses the additional threat of attacks on civilians by state and non-state armed groups from these countries. MONUSCO continued a drawdown of troops from the DRC, but its mandate was renewed for another year. The ongoing military operations between the FARDC and MONUSCO, along with Tshisekedi's improved relations with international actors, may provide further leverage and financing to handle instability in eastern DRC while managing the country's response to the coronavirus pandemic.

Notes

[1]   All fatality and event data taken from the Armed Conflict Location & Event Data Project (ACLED), www.acleddata.com.

[2]   International Crisis Group, 'DR Congo: Ending the Cycle of Violence in Ituri', 15 July 2020; and Kivu Security Tracker, 'La Cartographie des Groupes Armés dans l'Est du Congo' [The Cartography of Armed Groups in Eastern Congo], February 2021.

[3]   James Barnett, 'DR Congo in Crisis: Can Kabila Trust His Own Army?', African Arguments, 20 September 2016.

[4]   For example, see 'DRC: A New Conflict in Ituri Involving the Cooperative for Development of the Congo (CODECO)', Geneva Academy, 2021; and International Crisis Group, 'DR Congo: Ending the Cycle of Violence in Ituri'.

[5]   Estimate based on collective estimates of ADF personnel from camps listed on pp. 7–8 of the UNSC 2019 report and accounting for growth since 2019. See United Nations Security Council, 'Final Report of the Group of Experts on the Democratic Republic of the Congo', 7 June 2019, pp. 7–9.

[6]   Ibid.

[7]   Elsa Buchanan, '"We Are Ready for War" – Burundi's Rebel Groups and How They Plan to Topple President Nkurunziza', International Business Times, 2 March 2017.

[8]   Kivu Security Tracker, 'Armed Groups', 7 May 2021.

[9]   Asylum Research Centre, 'Democratic Republic of the Congo (DRC): The Situation in North Kivu, South Kivu, and Ituri', 2019, pp. 46–7.

[10]   United Nations Security Council, 'Final Report of the Group of Experts on the Democratic Republic of the Congo', p. 7.

[11]   United Nations Peacekeeping, 'MONUSCO Fact Sheet', March 2021.

[12]   Kivu Security Tracker, 'Atrocities, Populations Under Siege and Regional Tensions: What Is Happening in Minembwe?', 29 October 2019.

[13]   See Kasper Hoffmann and Judith Verweijen, 'Rebel Rule: A Governmentality Perspective', African Affairs, vol. 118, no. 471, April 2019.

[14]   United Nations Peacekeeping, 'MONUSCO–Activities–DDR–RR'.

[15]   Stephanie Wolters, 'DRC: What Now That President Tshisekedi Has Taken Control?', African Arguments, 15 December 2020.

[16]   International Crisis Group, 'Éviter Les Guerres par Procuration dans l'Est de la RDC et les Grands Lacs' [Avoiding Proxy Wars in Eastern DRC and the Great Lakes], 23 January 2020.

[17]   International Crisis Group, 'DR Congo: Ending the Cycle of Violence in Ituri'.

[18]   Armed Conflict Location & Event Data Project (ACLED), www.acleddata.com.

[19]   Human Rights Watch, 'DR Congo: Authorities Foundering on Rights', 22 July 2020.

[20]   See Internal Displacement Monitoring Centre (IDMC), '2020 Internal Displacement', Global Internal Displacement Database. See also Human Rights Watch, 'Democratic Republic of Congo Events of 2020', February 2021.

[21]   United Nations High Commissioner for Refugees, 'DR Congo Emergency', 14 February 2021.

[22]   United Nations Refugees, 'Democratic Republic of the Congo Refugee Crisis Explained', 14 February 2021.

[23]   World Food Programme, 'Democratic Republic of the Congo Emergency'.

[24]   World Health Organization, 'Ebola Virus Disease – Democratic Republic of the Congo', 18 November 2020.

[25]   United Nations High Commissioner for Refugees, 'Réponse du HCR au COVID-19 en RDC' [HCR Response to COVID-19 in DRC], 9 November 2020.

[26]   Center for Systems Science and Engineering (CSSE) at Johns Hopkins University, 'COVID-19 Data Repository', 28 February 2021.

27 Jean Pierre Okenda, 'Democratic Republic of the Congo (DRC): Updated Assessment of the Impact of the Coronavirus Pandemic on the Extractive Sector and Resource Governance', Natural Resource Governance Institute, 2 December 2020.

28 Michael Kavanagh, 'IMF Considers $365 Million Loan to Congo Battling Multiple Epidemics', Bloomberg, 15 April 2020.

29 International Monetary Fund, 'World Economic Outlook Database', April 2021.

30 'The World Bank Group Provides $47 Million to Support the Democratic Republic of Congo's Response to the Coronavirus Pandemic', World Bank, 2 April 2020; and 'IMF Approves US$363.27 Million Disbursement to the Democratic Republic of Congo to Address the COVID-19 Pandemic', IMF, 22 April 2020.

31 David Zounmenou, 'The Jury's Out on DRC's "Sacred Union"', Institute for Security Studies, 2 February 2021.

32 'Félix Tshisekedi Moves to Take Charge', Institute for Security Studies, 14 December 2020.

33 International Crisis Group, 'Éviter Les Guerres Par Procuration Dans L'est De La RDC Et Les Grands Lacs' [Avoiding Proxy Wars in Eastern DRC and the Great Lakes].

Sub-Saharan Africa

MOZAMBIQUE

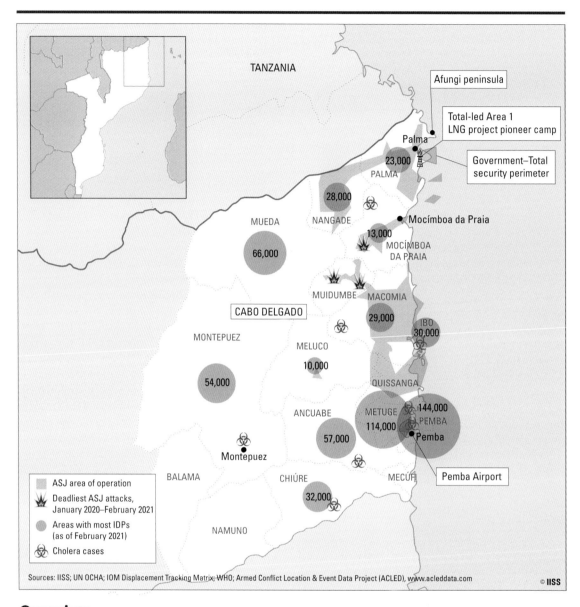

ASJ area of operation

Deadliest ASJ attacks, January 2020–February 2021

Areas with most IDPs (as of February 2021)

Cholera cases

Sources: IISS; UN OCHA; IOM Displacement Tracking Matrix; WHO; Armed Conflict Location & Event Data Project (ACLED), www.acleddata.com

© IISS

Overview

The insurgency in northern Mozambique's Cabo Delgado province originated in a schism between young hardline Salafist Islamists and the more traditional Sufi Islamic clergy which dates back to about 2007. Long-standing grievances fuelled the conflict, particularly around widespread corruption, rising criminality, lack of economic opportunities and domination by a small elite affiliated with the ruling party, Mozambique Liberation Front (commonly known as Frelimo).[1] The global-jihadi discourse and influx of extremists from other East African countries had also promoted radicalisation in Cabo Delgado, eventually leading to the formation of the non-state armed group (NSAG) Ahlu al-Sunnah wal-Jamaah (ASJ), locally known as 'al-Shabaab' and affiliated to the Islamic State (also known as ISIS or ISIL).

In its first attack in October 2017, ASJ targeted three police stations in Mocímboa da Praia

Armed Conflict Global Relevance Indicator (ACGRI)

Incidence

5

Human
impact

6

Geopolitical
impact

4

Mozambique

Key Conflict Statistics

Type	Internal | Localised insurgency
Start date	2017
IDPs	676,000
Fatalities	1,874
Functioning of government (0–10)	1.43

ACGRI pillars: IISS calculation based on multiple sources for 2020 and January/February 2021 (scale 0–100). See Notes on Methodology and Data Appendix for further details on Key Conflict Statistics.

where several of its members were being held.[2] An under-funded security apparatus and a slow, and largely inadequate, government response allowed the insurgency to expand. The government also remained ambivalent towards receiving foreign counter-terrorism assistance, instead relying on support from private military companies (PMCs). ASJ significantly scaled up its capabilities in the past four years, with recent attacks using AK-type assault rifles, rocket-propelled grenade (RPG) launchers and mortars.

Since being incorporated into the Islamic State's Central Africa Province (ISCAP) in 2019, ASJ has grown more ambitious and strategic, and demonstrated a willingness to hold territory, in line with the ISIS narrative of *tamkin* (or 'consolidation' through territorial control). The militants repeatedly seized towns like Mocímboa da Praia and Quissanga, but also knew when to withdraw.

2020 marked the deadliest year yet since the insurgency began, accounting for over half of the approximately 2,500 casualties caused by the conflict to date.[3] ASJ continued to expand north and south along the Cabo Delgado coast, even staging its first attack in the south of Tanzania. In late March 2021, the insurgents conducted one of their boldest attacks yet, launching a complex assault on the town of Palma, killing an unknown number of expatriate workers and local residents, and forcing tens of thousands to flee. Planned construction of facilities and infrastructure to extract offshore natural gas on the Afungi peninsula, just over ten kilometres southeast of Palma, was brought to a halt following the March attack on the town.

Conflict Parties

The Mozambican Defence Armed Forces (FADM)

Strength: 11,200 active military personnel (air force: 1,000; army 9,000–10,000; navy: less than 200).

Areas of operation: Northern (Cabo Delgado) and north-central (Manica, Sofala, Tete and Zambezia) Mozambique.

Leadership: Joaquim Rivas Mangrasse (chief of staff) since March 2021. He succeeded Eugénio Mussa, who suddenly died of illness on 8 February 2021.

Structure: Consists of infantry forces, a navy and an air force. Together with the Police of the Republic of Mozambique (PRM) they form the so-called Defence and Security Forces (FDS).

History: Formed following Mozambique's war of independence in 1975 but reached its current form at the end of the civil war against the Mozambican National Resistance (Renamo) in 1992. A third peace agreement between Frelimo and Renamo in 2019 provided for the disarmament, demobilisation and integration of Renamo combatants into the FADM ranks.

Objectives: Protect Mozambique's territorial integrity against foreign and domestic enemies. Assist in periods of high civil unrest and insecurity, such as during states of emergency.

Opponents: ASJ, the Renamo Military Junta (RMJ).

Affiliates/allies: PRM, local self-defence militias, Tanzanian armed forces, PMCs, United States, Portugal, the Southern African Development Community (SADC), the European Union.

Resources/capabilities: Mozambique's defence budget for 2020 was US$133 million (0.92% of GDP), up from US$126m in 2019.

Sub-Saharan Africa

The Police of the Republic of Mozambique (PRM)

Strength: Unknown.

Areas of operation: Nationwide. Four special operational zones/theatres have also been established, to which concentrations of FDS forces are deployed.

Leadership: Bernardino Rafael (commander-general). António Bachir is the first deputy commander of the Afungi operational zone, established in March 2021, which seeks to create a 25-km security perimeter around Afungi, the site where major liquefied natural gas (LNG) projects will be established.

Structure: Operates under the Ministry of Interior and consists of multi-level police units, including a tactical Rapid Intervention Force (FIR) deployed during times of major security crises and civil unrest.

In Cabo Delgado, counter-terrorist efforts over the first three years of the insurgency were mainly conducted by the PRM, with support from foreign-owned PMCs to ensure security. But the FADM increased its deployment in the region following the March 2021 Palma attack.
Together with the FADM they form the FDS.

History: Replaced the Popular Police force of Mozambique (PPM) in 1992, incorporating members of both Renamo and Frelimo.

Objectives: Enforce laws and regulations and ensure public security.

Opponents: ASJ, RMJ.

Affiliates/allies: FADM, local self-defence militias, PMCs, Tanzanian armed forces.

Resources/capabilities: Unclear.

Ahlu al-Sunnah wal-Jamaah (ASJ), also known as al-Shabaab[4]

Strength: Estimates vary from 350 to 2,000 fighters.[5]

Areas of operation: Cabo Delgado (particularly the districts of Macomia, Mocímboa da Praia, Muidumbe, Palma and Quissanga).

Leadership: Abu Yasir Hassan, also known as Abu Qassim.

Structure: Unclear.

History: Formed between 2015 and 2017; launched its first attack in 2017. In April 2019, ISIS formally recognised it as part of ISCAP.

Objectives: No specific dogma or strategy has been announced. Anecdotal evidence indicates its intention to combat security forces and replace the Mozambican government's presence with an ultimate aim of establishing an Islamic state in Cabo Delgado based on sharia law and a Salafi interpretation of Islam.

Opponents: FDS, PMCs, local self-defence militias, Tanzanian armed forces, gas companies, Makonde/Christian communities.

Affiliates/allies: ISIS, ISIS Somalia, ISIS West Africa Province.

Resources/capabilities: Unclear but likely growing as evidenced by increasing sophistication of modus operandi and weapons used.

Conflict Drivers

Political

Governance flaws:

State institutions in Cabo Delgado have been weakened by long-lasting corruption and organised crime, as well as a lack of investment, and exacerbated by an influx of foreign capital and investment to the region – including in timber, ruby mining and natural-gas extraction – since about 2010, which has increased criminal opportunities.

Frelimo loyalists have benefitted the most from the promise of future rents, obtaining key roles in government agencies and winning public tenders for their companies amid little oversight, in a context of poor or lacking public services. While Frelimo holds a significant majority in the provincial government, credible allegations point to the party's use of fraud in several provinces to retain power in the 2019 general elections.[6]

Economic and social

Poverty, marginalisation and radicalisation:

The insurgency is rooted in socio-economic grievances and ethno-political tensions. Cabo Delgado is among Mozambique's poorest provinces, with about half its population living below the World Bank's poverty line.[7] A core grievance stems from the perceived marginalisation of the Mwani and Makua communities (who are predominantly Muslim or animist) to the advantage of the Makonde group (predominantly Christian), which has strong associations to Frelimo and the southern-based government in Maputo. This animosity builds on decades of north–south tensions; the long-standing perception of the south as the primary beneficiary of the country's resources fuels the impression that strongmen (often Makonde) that operate in Cabo Delgado amass wealth thanks to their political connections in the south. President Filipe Nyusi is himself Makonde and hails from Cabo Delgado. Makonde members are also regularly promoted to senior positions within the security forces and government bodies and own businesses in the mining and energy sectors in the province.

Early ASJ leaders capitalised on those grievances, denouncing the marginalisation of the Mwani, with some indications of greater targeting of Makonde communities in their attacks. In parallel, they also criticised their Muslim elders and the country's Islamic council for their lack of orthodoxy and for submitting to the control of the Maputo government.

Informal revenue streams through illicit activities and taxation:
Corruption and organised crime have provided the insurgency with important revenue streams. A widespread informal economy operates in Cabo Delgado, through the trade in wildlife, rosewood, gemstones, drugs and human trafficking. Although ASJ may not be directly involved in any of these specifically, indications suggest that several of its early leaders ran small and informal businesses that involved some criminal activity. Some wealthier members also offered small-business loans or jobs to individuals as a recruitment tactic.

International
Influence of global jihad and shared regional history:
From approximately 2007, radical Islamists, many inspired by the teachings of radical Kenyan cleric Aboud Rogo, migrated from other East African countries, including Kenya, Somalia, Tanzania and Uganda, to Cabo Delgado and began radicalising the population there.[8] The first training camps in Mozambique began emerging in 2015. At the time, Cabo Delgado was likely perceived as a safe haven, given the relative absence of state security forces and the concurrent crackdown by authorities in Tanzania against Islamist extremism. Warnings by local Muslim clerics about the radicalisation went largely unheeded by the Mozambique authorities. Since then, many Islamist migrants have embedded themselves into local communities through marriage.

High-profile gas investments and foreign capital:
Foreign financial flows have fuelled underlying friction and resentment. Foreign investment concentrated around the timber and mining industries and commercial development of LNG and ruby deposits increased markedly following a series of discoveries of major deposits of rubies and offshore natural gas from 2010.[9] These gas deposits, totalling around 160 trillion cubic feet, discovered between 2010 and 2014, have the potential to transform Mozambique into a major LNG producer, delivering more than 60m metric tonnes annually once production reaches its full potential.[10] Multinational energy giants, including Total, Eni and ExxonMobil, are looking to invest a combined US$50 billion over the next few years.

However, it may take nearly a decade before financial benefits trickle down to the local population. Gas production was due to commence in 2024, but this will almost certainly be delayed following the Palma attack and Total's subsequent *force majeure* declaration.[11] Meanwhile, the government has amassed huge sums of debt to finance LNG projects. Public debt surpassing 113% of GDP in 2020 and 2021 will reduce the fiscal space for counter-cyclical policies in the event of exogenous shocks, such as a decline in natural-gas prices.[12]

Political and Military Developments

Escalating attacks
Overall, the number of ASJ attacks has increased exponentially since 2017. By early 2021, insurgent violence had affected 11 out of 16 districts in Cabo Delgado. Macomia, Mocímboa da Praia and Muidumbe experienced the largest number of attacks since 2017. However, in relative terms, Quissanga and Nangade saw the largest increases in 2020, while the number of attacks in Palma – containing the Afungi peninsula – increased marginally but remained consistent with previous years. In 2020 the conflict also spilled over the border with Tanzania, with attacks in the southern region of Mtwara. In January and February 2021,

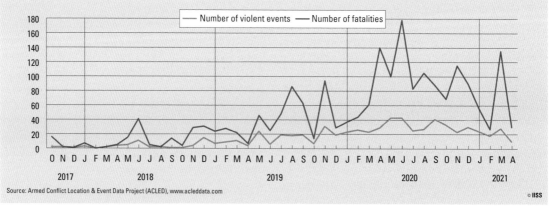

Figure 1: Number of violent events perpetrated by the Islamist insurgency and the total number of fatalities in Mozambique, October 2017–April 2021

there were 39 reported attacks and 72 fatalities, broadly in line with the trend seen over the same period in 2020.[13]

ASJ violence has followed an annual pattern, with spikes occurring in May and just preceding the rainy season – usually between December and April – before a lull when rainfall and periodic flooding restricts overland mobility and depletes food and other essential resources.

ASJ's early attacks in 2017 and 2018 mainly used bladed weapons, arson, kidnappings and rape, and primarily targeted civilian communities. However, attacks between 2018 and 2020 increasingly used assault rifles, RPGs, and during the assault on Palma also used mortars. They also made more use of military vehicles and equipment often seized in attacks on security forces, which have increased in parallel to growing counter-terrorism efforts.

Tactics and strategic thinking also appeared to have improved, with the militants able to conduct near-simultaneous attacks in multiple locations and engage in protracted clashes with the security forces over several days. As a result of their improved capabilities, the number of victims also increased exponentially: while the number of attacks in 2020 increased by 110%, the number of fatalities increased by 128%.[14]

Ineffective public and private security-force responses

A reshuffling of the military's command structure in January 2021 signalled Nyusi's growing focus on the insurgency threat. Nevertheless, multiple sources complained about the relative absence of the FADM, although deployment to the region reportedly increased following the March 2021 Palma attack. The security forces continued to lack adequate resources and training amid issues of low morale.

Counter-insurgency operations were increasingly supported by foreign PMCs: by Russia's Wagner Group between September and November 2019 and reportedly from around April 2020 by South Africa's Dyck Advisory Group (DAG), which both had contracts with the Ministry of Interior. Wagner left the country after a series of setbacks in late 2019, while DAG's contract with the authorities concluded in April 2021 and was not renewed. DAG's contract had included the use of combat helicopters, and its exit from the region will likely undermine the capabilities and efficacy of future state security responses. The South Africa-based Paramount Group became the latest PMC market entrant in Mozambique. In December 2020, the company began deploying materiel, including armoured personnel carriers and combat helicopters, as part of a contract with the Ministry of Defence.

Key Events in 2020–21

POLITICAL EVENTS

July 2020
ISIS makes first threat against gas exploration in Cabo Delgado.

24 August
Total and the Mozambican government sign security pact over Afungi.

4 January 2021
Total evacuates some of its staff and suspends construction of LNG facilities at Afungi in response to ASJ attack on the nearby resettlement village Quitunda.

14 January
President Nyusi reshuffles the army command and appoints Eugénio Mussa as chief of staff.

15 March
US embassy in Maputo confirms a two-month US training mission of Mozambican marines.

12 March
Nyusi appoints Joaquim Mangrasse as new chief of staff to succeed Mussa, who died of illness in February.

24 March
Total announces plans to progressively resume construction of LNG facilities at Afungi.

26 March
Total evacuates all staff and suspends construction work of LNG facilities at Afungi, following assault on Palma. Most other companies and public institutions present in the town also evacuate staff to Pemba.

6 April
DAG contract with Mozambican government expires.

8–9 April
SADC holds extraordinary summit to discuss coordinated response.

MILITARY/VIOLENT EVENTS

23 March 2020
ASJ militants seize Mocímboa da Praia for one day.

10 April
DAG helicopter is shot down.

27 June
ASJ targets Mocímboa da Praia in major assaults and retains control for three days, with a high number of Christian Makonde civilian fatalities recorded.

27 June
Eight workers of subcontractor Fenix Construction Services are killed by presumed ASJ militants.

5–12 August
ASJ militants seize Mocímboa da Praia and armed clashes with the FDS continue for several days. 60–90 members of the security forces are killed.

24 September
200 people are kidnapped in Bilibiza, Quissanga district.

14 October
ASJ conducts its first attack in Tanzania, in the southern town of Kitaya.

6 November
ASJ launches a three-day attack on Muatide, Muidumbe district, beheading over 50 people.

1–2 January 2021
ASJ targets Quitunda village near the Afungi peninsula.

24 March
ASJ stages a complex assault on Palma, 12 km from Afungi, killing scores of local residents and expatriate workers.

26 March
ASJ militants ambush a convoy of more than 185 people attempting to flee the Amarula Lodge in Palma.

Sub-Saharan Africa

Impact

Human rights and humanitarian

Violations of human rights have increased over the past three years as the insurgency has intensified, with abuses committed by ASJ militants and government forces alike. Evidence from 2020 shows that ASJ militants raped, kidnapped and harassed members of local communities, driving some from their homes.[15] Security forces were regularly accused of forced disappearances, arbitrary arrests, theft and murder or extrajudicial killings of presumed militants or informants.[16] In March 2021, allegations were also made against DAG.[17]

The humanitarian impact of the conflict worsened dramatically in the period from the start of 2020 to the end of April 2021, with more than 2,000 fatalities.[18] The number of internally displaced persons (IDPs) climbed from 110,000 in 2019 to over 676,000 in 2020.[19] The areas with the largest number of departing IDPs and with impeded access to humanitarian relief were Mocímboa da Praia, Muidumbe, Macomia, Meluco and Quissanga, while the district with the highest proportion of incoming IDPs was Palma-Metuge. The vast majority of IDPs (90%) stayed with hospitable families in neighbouring districts, though often in cramped and squalid conditions.[20]

Poor accessibility to the worst-affected areas restricted humanitarian aid, as did a general lack of funding, slow processing of visas for humanitarian workers, government restrictions due to the coronavirus pandemic and the insurgency, and militant attacks on transport, including humanitarian cargo. Cholera cases also increased, surpassing 4,900 confirmed cases and 55 deaths by February 2021, although the actual number is thought to be higher. There was no functional healthcare facility in the districts of Macomia, Mocímboa da Praia, Muidumbe or Quissanga, while access to water and sanitation was generally poor, and nine out of 16 districts experienced crisis levels of food insecurity.[21]

Political stability

In 2020–early 2021, the sub-national conflict did not significantly threaten Frelimo's one-party rule in the country. It continued to control Cabo Delgado, having garnered a majority of provincial-assembly seats in the 2019 general elections. Nevertheless, some reports suggested that Nyusi was losing support, including within Frelimo, in part due to the Cabo Delgado crisis. However, his role as defence minister during the 2016 'hidden debt' scandal and his ostensible resistance to launching credible investigations and prosecuting implicated officials, as well as his inability to fully disarm the RMJ – a dissident faction of Renamo – following the 2019 peace agreement were other pre-existing causes of frustration.[22]

Economic and social

The insurgency adversely affected development, local livelihoods and foreign direct investment. It complicated and disrupted logistics and hampered construction of LNG production facilities, which were scheduled to be finalised in 2024. The March 2021 assault on Palma, a key logistical hub housing many expatriate workers, marked a turning point, and prompted most companies to evacuate their staff. The US oil and gas multinational ExxonMobil, which had repeatedly delayed its final investment decision, did so again in March 2021, with the situation unlikely to change until security conditions improve. Total, which has the largest cohort of workers in the area, also delayed construction plans after the Palma attack. The company had planned to progressively resume operations from April, but this remained unlikely in the short term. The continued expansion of ASJ's operational zone also threatened gemstone-mining operations in the southwestern district of Montepuez. The large influx of IDPs also raised concerns among some commercial operators over illegal mining activities.

Poor provision of basic services in the province pre-existed the insurgency but 2020's marked escalation of violence further deteriorated the situation. ASJ's repeated targeting of humanitarian convoys further hampered response efforts and drove up inflation in the price of basic goods, leaving local populations nearly entirely dependent on foreign aid. The economic impact of the coronavirus pandemic globally compounded the dire situation, with GDP shrinking by 0.5% in 2020.[23]

Relations with neighbouring and international partners and geopolitical implications

The government appeared reluctant to invite foreign-military presence into the country, fearing it could endanger national sovereignty, and opted instead to use PMCs.

Military and logistical support was offered by multilateral institutions and bilateral partners, including the EU, the SADC, Portugal and the US, but deployment was slow and limited. However, the Palma attack prompted an apparent shifting of the government's stance, with US and Portuguese training missions launched in mid-March and mid-April 2020. On 8 April, an SADC extraordinary summit in Maputo discussed possible responses to the Cabo Delgado crisis and expressed willingness to deploy a technical mission to assess the security situation, and potentially troops.

Conflict Outlook

Political scenarios

Government stability is unlikely to be challenged in 2021, despite continued frustration with Nyusi and his government's inability to contain the insurgency. Frelimo is likely to remain the dominant political force in the near future.

Nevertheless, government finances face growing pressure due to the impact of the coronavirus pandemic, with high levels of public debt. Although economic growth is forecast to increase to 2.1% in 2021, risks are on the downside amid a very slow vaccine roll-out.[24] The mid-term positive outlook for the global natural-gas market, with solid demand in China, India and the Middle East, makes natural gas a continued strategic asset and means combatting the insurgency in Cabo Delgado is a top priority.

The likely highly lucrative Afungi concession remains central to Total's growth strategy, as apparently confirmed by its reported contingency plans to use the island of Mayotte – more than 550 km east of Palma – as a rear base for its Mozambican operations. Nevertheless, the cost of such solutions combined with parallel increased spending on physical security may further delay production. ExxonMobil's investment looks less certain, while planned LNG production by the Italian energy giant Eni – the third-largest energy company in the province – may also be delayed by the Palma assault.

Escalation potential and conflict-related risks

It is likely that the Cabo Delgado conflict will continue to escalate within the same broad parameters in the coming year. The government implicitly confirmed this with its acceptance of bilateral and multilateral military and political support, its security agreement with Total, and by its establishment of a 25-km security perimeter around the Afungi peninsula and an FADM Afungi operational command.

Despite the government claiming a series of counter-terrorism successes from the end of December 2020, the tempo of ASJ attacks remained largely consistent with the previous year. Despite a months-long lull in attacks and claims by ISIS, the Palma attack clearly demonstrated the extent of the insurgent threat and its willingness to target key economic sectors. The government's narrow focus on counter-terrorism efforts also fails to address some of the underlying causes of the conflict, making it more protracted.

Prospects for peace

The government demonstrated little willingness to negotiate with the insurgents or to address the conflict's root causes of marginalisation, corruption, organised crime and radicalisation. Furthermore, many of the government's actions since 2017 appear contingent on LNG operations commencing fully by 2024. The government therefore likely sees the insurgency as a real threat to future rents and will attempt to quash it over the coming year or at least to create a perception that it is regaining control, particularly in Palma. Meanwhile, ASJ's unclear command structure and demands will undermine any serious attempt to reach a negotiated solution.

Strategic implications and global influences

With Africa accounting for the bulk of Islamic State operations in 2020–early 2021, the Islamist extremist network is likely to continue to promote the activities of its West and Central African *wilayats*, including ASJ.

Furthermore, the growing presence of Western interests in Cabo Delgado, including French and US companies, could make strikes to personnel and assets symbolically important to ASJ and elevate its notoriety among ISIS branches. This would send a strong signal to the West that ISIS still poses a relevant threat to their citizens, while also demonstrating ASJ's growing capabilities and its ability to strike more fortified facilities, despite significant efforts to secure the area.

Awareness of the insurgency and the humanitarian situation has led to mounting international political pressure, making further military intervention highly likely. Such support may come both from regional PMCs, as well as from bilateral and multilateral partners; an assumption supported by the series of high-level meetings that followed the Palma attack. Nevertheless, capacity-building of local authorities is likely to be prioritised over military deployment.

Sub-Saharan Africa

Notes

1   Frelimo, in power since independence in 1975, maintains an overwhelming majority in the national legislature and provincial assemblies. It was re-elected in 2019, amid widespread claims of fraud. These were particularly serious in Cabo Delgado, with reports of vote-buying and ballot-stuffing by Frelimo officials and ghost voters on the electoral roll.

2   'Cinco Mortos em Ataques a Postos de Polícia no Norte de Moçambique' [Five Killed in Attacks on Police Stations in the North of Mozambique], Diario de Noticias, 5 October 2017.

3   Armed Conflict Location & Event Data Project (ACLED), www.acleddata.com.

4   There is disagreement about the name of the group. While many international organisations and commentators appear to use ASJ, many local sources refer to the insurgency as 'al-Shabaab'. This is likely in reference to the Arabic term for 'youth' rather than a specific reference to the Somalia-based non-state armed group Harakat al-Shabaab al Mujahideen, although there are some circumstantial links. To date there has been no claimed or proven operational links between the two groups. A factor that weighs against any formal link is the Somalia-based group's rejection of ISIS, and the purging of ISIS sympathisers from its ranks over the years.

5   Eric Morier-Genoud, 'Mozambique's Own Version of Boko Haram Is Tightening Its Deadly Grip', The Conversation, 11 June 2018; and Emilia Columbo and Austin C. Doctor, 'Foreign Fighters and the Trajectory of Violence in Northern Mozambique', War on the Rocks, 13 April 2021.

6   See Centro de Integridade Pública [Public Integrity Centre], 'General Elections 15 Oct 2019 Final Report', 26 January 2020.

7   World Bank Group (Poverty department), 'Strong but Not Broadly Shared Growth – Mozambique: Poverty Assessment', April 2018.

8   Saide Habibe, Salvador Forquilha and João Pereira, 'Islamic Radicalization in Northern Mozambique: The Case of Mocímboa da Praia', Cadernos IESE, no. 17E, 2019.

9   Simone Haysom, 'Where Crime Compounds Conflict: Understanding Northern Mozambique's Vulnerabilities', The Global Initiative Against Transnational Organized Crime, October 2018.

10 United States Energy Information Agency, 'Mozambique' (Country Report), July 2020; Mozambique LNG, 'About the Project'; and eni.com, 'Our Work in Mozambique'.

11 'Total Declares Force Majeure on Mozambique LNG Project', Total, 26 April 2021.

12 International Development Association and International Monetary Fund, 'Republic of Mozambique Joint World Bank–IMF Debt Sustainability Analysis', April 2020.

13 ACLED, www.acleddata.com.

14 Estimates based on the author's own calculation of the escalation.

15 See Human Rights Watch, 'World Report 2021: Mozambique', 2021.

16 Ibid.; and 'Mozambique: Video Showing Killing of Naked Woman Further Proof of Human-rights Violations by State Armed Forces', Amnesty International, 15 September 2020.

17 Amnesty International, 'What I Saw Is Death: War Crimes in Mozambique's Forgotten Cape', 2 March 2021.

18 ACLED, www.acleddata.com.

19 See Internal Displacement Monitoring Centre (IDMC), '2020 Internal Displacement', Global Internal Displacement Database. See also 'Worsening Islamist Insurgency Drives Mozambique Humanitarian Crisis', Reuters, 20 January 2021; and United Nations High Commissioner for Refugees, 'Operational Data Portal – Mozambique: IDPs in Northern Mozambique Caused by Conflict', 31 January 2021.

20 United Nations High Commissioner for Refugees, 'Mozambique Update: Cabo Delgado Situation, 16 January 2020–02 February 2021', 2 February 2021.

21 United Nations Office for the Coordination of Humanitarian Affairs, 'Mozambique: Cabo Delgado, Nampula & Niassa Humanitarian Snapshot, February 2021', 23 February 2021.

22 In April 2016, the government admitted that it had hidden US$1.4bn in debt from the IMF and bilateral donors, a move which prompted creditors to suspend disbursement until further investigations were completed. The undeclared loans had been established with the assistance of foreign financial institutions in Switzerland and Russia to help the government set up three state-owned enterprises: a tuna-fishing fleet, a maritime-security company and an asset-management company.

23 International Monetary Fund, 'World Economic Outlook Database', April 2021.

24 Ibid.

Sub-Saharan Africa

NIGERIA

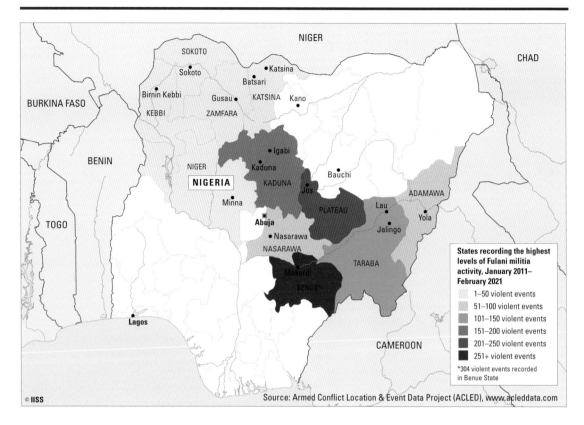

Source: Armed Conflict Location & Event Data Project (ACLED), www.acleddata.com

Overview

The Fulani pastoral-transhumant group controlling the livestock economy and the sedentary grain producers have a long history of peaceful coexistence in northern Nigeria. For centuries, Fulani pastoralists from the semi-arid Sahel region drove their cattle in Nigeria's far north, only occasionally clashing with local farmers. However, from the 1980s, intermittent violence between Fulani pastoralists and farmers swept across Nigeria's North West and Middle Belt regions, driven by rising inequalities and corruption; competition over scarce resources exacerbated by the consequences of climate change; the proliferation of small arms and the militarisation of local communities, especially in response to increasing cattle rustling and banditry; and divisive national and local politics. Disputes between semi-nomadic and settled communities increasingly exacerbated social divisions, often resulting in mobilisation along religious or ethnic lines. Between 1980 and 2011, a series of deadly riots and

retaliatory sectarian violence involved the Muslim and Christian communities in Nigeria's North West. Over the past decade, the introduction of anti-open-grazing laws preluded a significant violent escalation.

Central and northern Nigeria is riven by tension between armed Fulani pastoralists and bandits on one side, who engage in cattle rustling, kidnappings for ransom and indiscriminate killings, and by predominantly Hausa farmers and state-sponsored vigilante groups recruited to protect local communities on the other. Increasingly, violent jihadist organisations – including Ansaru (an al-Qaeda-linked group that broke away from Boko Haram), the Islamic State in West Africa Province (ISWAP) and Jama'atu Ahlis Sunna Lidda'awati wal-Jihad (JAS) led by Abubakar Shekau – have taken advantage of these tensions to expand their presence beyond their traditional strongholds in northeastern Nigeria (see Lake Chad Basin chapter). Federal and

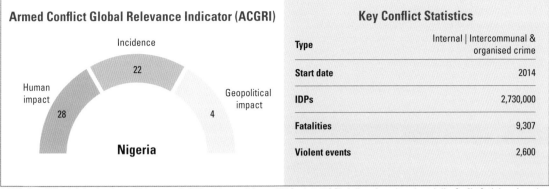

Key Conflict Statistics	
Type	Internal | Intercommunal & organised crime
Start date	2014
IDPs	2,730,000
Fatalities	9,307
Violent events	2,600

ACGRI pillars: IISS calculation based on multiple sources for 2020 and January/February 2021 (scale 0–100). The indicator's results and certain Key Conflict Statistics refer to the country as a whole rather than the specific conflict. See Notes on Methodology and Data Appendix for further details on Key Conflict Statistics.

state forces have responded to the conflict escalation by seeking cooperation with neighbouring Niger, launching disarmament initiatives and large-scale anti-banditry operations and empowering community militias and vigilante groups known as *yan sa kai* (volunteer guards).[1] In fact, the sponsoring of vigilantes has arguably contributed to the militarisation of local communities and the escalation of the violence.

Overall, violence between farmers and pastoralists in Nigeria continued to claim thousands of casualties in 2020. Violence often manifests as a series of attacks and retaliatory killings over a short period, resulting in spiralling insecurity and rapidly mounting fatality numbers. According to the Armed Conflict Location & Event Data Project (ACLED), armed conflict reportedly killed over 4,000 people, including combatants and non-combatants, across the North West and Middle Belt regions from 1 January 2020 to 25 February 2021.[2] Likewise, an Amnesty International report estimated that over 1,100 civilians died from violence in central and northwestern Nigeria between January and June 2020.[3] Earlier estimates by Amnesty International

and the International Crisis Group indicated that at least 8,000 people were killed between 2011 and 2019, mostly over the past five years.[4] These figures are likely to be significant underestimates, however, as violence takes place in hard-to-access rural areas and the central government has strong incentives to downplay its impact. In terms of domestic and international attention, the conflict also remained somewhat in the shadow of the Boko Haram insurgency, despite its continued deadliness and potential regional repercussions.

The North West states of Katsina and Kaduna witnessed a dramatic increase in armed violence, almost tripling the number of reported fatalities in 2020 from the previous year.[5] Regular fighting between Hausa and Fulani militias occured in both states, as well as attacks and counter-attacks by heavily armed criminal gangs and vigilante groups. State security forces also stepped up their activity following a spate of retaliatory killings in late 2019. The violence precipitated a humanitarian crisis in northwestern Nigeria, with over 30,000 civilians seeking refuge in Niger's Maradi region between April and June 2020.[6]

Conflict Parties

Nigerian armed forces

Strength: 143,000 military personnel, including 100,000 army personnel. Paramilitary forces number approximately 80,000 troops.

Areas of operation: Benue, Kaduna, Katsina, Nasarawa, Plateau, Taraba and Zamfara states.

Leadership and structure: Nigerian President Muhammadu Buhari (commander-in-chief of the armed forces); Major-General Ibrahim Attahiru (army chief of staff, since January 2021).
The Nigerian armed forces comprise the army, the air force and the navy.

Objectives: Establish and/or maintain security across Nigeria.

Nigerian armed forces

Opponents and affiliates/allies: Opponents include violent pastoralist and farmer communities, bandits and Boko Haram. Allies include France, the United Kingdom and the United States. Nigeria also participates in the Multinational Joint Task Force against Boko Haram along with Benin, Cameroon, Chad and Niger. Some vigilantes also work with the army on intelligence gathering.

Resources/capabilities: Heavy and light weaponry in land, air, sea and cyber spheres. The resources and capabilities of the military (including the air force and the Cyber Warfare Command) have significantly improved over the past five years. However, poor equipment and training in the army remain areas of concern.

Pastoral Fulani

Strength: Not known.

Areas of operation: Adamawa, Benue, Kaduna, Katsina, Nasarawa, Plateau, Sokoto, Taraba and Zamfara states and some parts of Kebbi and Niger states.

Leadership and structure: No formal leadership. Fulani groups include both (semi-)nomadic pastoralists and settled communities in urban and rural areas. Pastoralist communities are highly decentralised, divided into clans (*lenyi*) and sub-clans. Individuals have significant autonomy over whether to fight or retaliate for perceived wrongs, decisions that may be made without community leaders knowing. For some conflicts, mobilisation occurs along ethnic and kinship lines.

Objectives: To protect their traditional 'cattle culture' from banditry and cattle rustling.

Opponents and affiliates/allies: Opponents include sedentary farmer militias and government forces. Allies include herder-allied bandits.

Resources/capabilities: AK-47s, G3s, Mark 4 rifles, locally made single-barrel shotguns (Dane guns), 'Lebanons' (double-barrel shotguns) and a variety of other locally made guns.

Farmers, ethnic militias and vigilante groups

Strength: Not known.

Areas of operation: Adamawa, Benue, Kaduna, Katsina, Nasarawa, Plateau, Sokoto, Taraba and Zamfara states and some parts of Kebbi and Niger states.

Leadership and structure: Within several communities in the conflict areas, active mobilisations are mainly driven by traditional rulers and local community leaders. Farming communities mobilise on an ethnic basis, but, unlike Fulani combatants, in some cases they also form alliances across ethnic lines, using a Christian religious identity. Farmers hail predominantly from the Adara, Berom, Tarok, Tiv and other local ethnic groups.

Objectives: To protect against raids by Fulani pastoralists and bandits.

Opponents and affiliates/allies: Opponents include Fulani pastoralists and bandits. Allies include government forces.

Resources/capabilities: Especially reliant on locally made weapons.

Armed bandits and cattle rustlers

Strength: The number of bandit gangs decreased from 60 in 2018 to 35 in 2019 (most recent data available) due to several peace and dialogue initiatives by state governments and continued military operations in the affected areas. Zamfara State authorities reported in 2019 that an estimated 10,000 bandits operated across eight major local camps, yet it remained unclear whether they were herder-allied or operated independently.[7]

Areas of operation: Most prevalent in Kaduna, Katsina, Sokoto and Zamfara states in the North West. Operational presence also reported in the Middle Belt.

Leadership and structure: No generally recognised leader and formal structure.

Objectives: Rustling is a criminal syndicate involving different ethnic groups and nationalities. Cattle-rustling attacks are sometimes justified as reprisals against vigilante groups.

Opponents and affiliates/allies: Opponents include Hausa sedentary farmers and vigilante groups. Allies include herder-allied Fulani pastoralists and bandit groups operating in other Nigerian states as well as in Niger and Mali.

Resources/capabilities: Due to their financial resources from cattle rustling, pillaging and kidnapping, bandits can purchase more sophisticated weaponry, including small arms and light weapons. They often carry out attacks while riding motorbikes.

Conflict Drivers

Political

Breakdown of farmer–pastoralist arrangements:
Historically, disputes between farmers and herders over access to grazing land, farm destructions and transhumance were resolved through mutually beneficial rules and local mediators. This system began declining in the 1970s with the active involvement of the police, army and lower courts, which the communities perceived as corrupt and lacking the moral justification to settle such disputes. State institutions frequently turned out to be agents of coercion and exploitation, often criminalising small-scale Fulani pastoralists and forcing them to sell their cattle to pay bribes. This resulted in many pastoralists across Nigeria's North West becoming destitute.

Economic and social

Increasing competition over land and water:
Climate change and decades of sustained population growth have driven increasing competition for land and water. High demand for cultivation and increased pressure on the pastoralists' grazing areas has led to land traditionally assigned to grazing being used instead for agricultural production. Grazing reserves established in the 1960s were lost, with land often appropriated by traditional leaders, politicians and other influential elites.[8] As a result of shrinking grazing land accessible for cattle, pastoralists have increasingly moved to Nigeria's central and southern areas, where traditional grazing reserves did not exist. Some herders settled permanently, igniting tensions with farmers mainly due to the issue of livestock damaging crops.

Security

Insecurity and militarisation:
Widespread insecurity has exacerbated tensions between farmers and pastoralists. In central and northern Nigeria, many Fulani pastoralists seeking new sources of profit turned to 'rural banditry', targeting farmers, other Fulani herders and the wider civilian population. Cattle rustling, revenge killings and violence resulting from Boko Haram's activities in the Lake Chad Basin have also led to the establishment of state-sponsored vigilante groups. Amidst a lack of state intervention, the militarisation of local communities has bred further prejudice and animosity along ethnic and religious lines.

Sub-Saharan Africa

Key Events in 2020–21

POLITICAL EVENTS

28 February 2020
Nigerian authorities report the first case of COVID-19 in sub-Saharan Africa.

9 March
The Kano state governor deposes the Emir of Kano Sanusi Lamido Sanusi.

17 April
Abba Kyari, the influential chief of staff of President Buhari, dies of COVID-19.

MILITARY/VIOLENT EVENTS

14 February 2020
Armed gangs attack two villages in Batsari Local Government Area (LGA), Katsina State, killing 30 people.

1 March
Bandits attack several villages in Igabi LGA, Kaduna State, killing an estimated 50 people.

13 April
An estimated 19 people are killed amid ongoing inter-ethnic violence in Lau LGA, Taraba State.

13 May

President Buhari names former diplomat Ibrahim Gambari as his new chief of staff.

17 July

Local authorities in Zamfara State announce a new disarmament initiative to halt attacks by bandits.

5 September

Local communities in Kaduna State sign a peace agreement to end violence in the area.

27 May

Gunmen attack five villages near the Nigerien border in Sokoto State, killing 74 people.

6 July

Clashes between communal militias and Nigerian soldiers kill 61 people in Batsari LGA, Katsina State.

6 August

Suspected Fulani herders kill at least 21 villagers in a predominantly Christian district of Kaduna State.

29–30 October

Revenge violence by suspected bandits results in the killing of 21 people in Katsina State.

23 November

The Nigerian armed forces conduct airstrikes targeting militia hideouts in Katsina and Zamfara states.

26 January 2021

Nigeria's four military chiefs resign and retire from service.

2 March

279 schoolgirls kidnapped by armed gunmen in Jangebe, Zamfara State, are released.

Conflict Outlook

Political scenarios

Buhari's second term in office did not radically change the government's security response to the conflict. Despite pledges to tackle the roots of insecurity, the federal government was unable to systematically engage with pastoralist and farmer communities to induce them to buy into the government's proposed modernisation programme. The implementation of the ten-year National Livestock Transformation Plan, which, among other measures, plans to turn grazing reserves into ranches to promote sustainable development in agro-pastoral communities, will be key to curbing competition over land and water in rural areas. Yet it may face some challenges, as state governors have occasionally resisted the establishment of ranches.

Escalation potential and conflict-related risks

The activation of state-sponsored vigilante groups embedded violence in local communities and community relations and led to a proliferation of armed militias in large parts of Nigeria's North West and Middle Belt regions. These developments, along with the coexistence of communal and bandit communities in local conflict spaces, heighten the potential for a violent escalation, especially in

areas where revenge feuds and ethnic mobilisation overlap with competition over access to land and water. Additionally, concern is growing that Fulani pastoralists and bandits may coordinate with jihadist militant organisations. While bandits have largely been non-ideological, the increasing presence of Ansaru, ISWAP and others in the North West could potentially lead to tactical alliances between these groups.

Prospects for peace

Regional governments and traditional authorities have occasionally spearheaded local peace initiatives to defuse intercommunal tensions. These have included peace and disarmament agreements as well as local development programmes targeting vulnerable communities in the North West and Middle Belt. Yet problems in local-authority coordination and the increasing militarisation of community relations continue to hamper any coherent response to resolve the conflict. The persistent cycle of attacks and counter-attacks has created a legacy of animosity between farmers and pastoralists that will be difficult to defuse, especially in the context of a climate of widespread impunity and government inaction.

Strategic implications and global influences

The implications of the crisis have extended to the wider Lake Chad Basin. In the North West, Nigerian citizens displaced by the conflict have sought refuge in Niger's Maradi region. Home to their own large pastoralist communities, Nigeria's neighbouring countries – Cameroon, Chad and Niger – are also vulnerable to tensions between herders and farmers who clash over land and/or water. Furthermore, jihadist militant organisations from the wider region, including the Sahel, may increasingly look towards northern Nigeria as a fertile ground for engagement and tactical alliances with bandit groups.

Notes

[1] International Crisis Group, 'Violence in Nigeria's North West: Rolling Back the Mayhem', Report no. 288, 18 May 2020.

[2] Armed Conflict Location & Event Data Project (ACLED), www.acleddata.com.

[3] Amnesty International, 'Nigeria: Government Failings Leave Rural Communities at the Mercy of Gunmen', 23 August 2020.

[4] International Crisis Group, 'Violence in Nigeria's North West: Rolling Back the Mayhem'.

[5] Armed Conflict Location & Event Data Project (ACLED), www.acleddata.com.

[6] Sélim Meddeb Hamrouni, 'More Than 30,000 Refugees Flee Violence in Northwestern Nigeria in Last Two Months Alone', United Nations High Commissioner for Refugees, 26 June 2020.

[7] Isa Isawade, 'Zamfara Under Pressure From Bandits for More Than 10 Years — SSG', PM News, 25 April 2019.

[8] International Crisis Group, 'Herders against Farmers: Nigeria's Expanding Deadly Conflict', Report no. 252, 19 September 2017.

Sub-Saharan Africa

CAMEROON

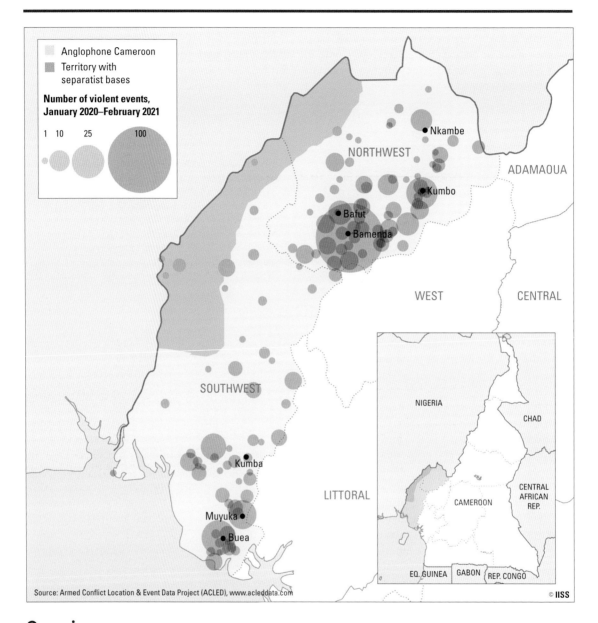

Source: Armed Conflict Location & Event Data Project (ACLED), www.acleddata.com

© IISS

Overview

The conflict in anglophone Cameroon (the Northwest and Southwest regions) began in late 2016, with a series of protests by civil-society organisations against perceived economic, political and cultural discrimination against the anglophone population (approximately 20% of the total), dating back to the abolishment of federalism in 1972.[1] Grievances levelled against the majority francophone government included neglecting development of the anglophone regions, disregarding English and bilingual opportunities in the education and public sectors and the lack of a bench for Common Law at the Supreme Court. Protester demands varied from self-determination (in the form of an independent nation called 'Ambazonia') to a return to federalism. As demonstrations escalated, violence developed and

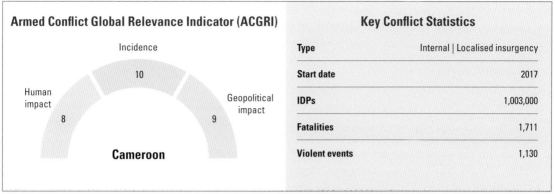

Armed Conflict Global Relevance Indicator (ACGRI)	Key Conflict Statistics	
Incidence: 10	Type	Internal | Localised insurgency
Human impact: 8	Start date	2017
Geopolitical impact: 9	IDPs	1,003,000
Cameroon	Fatalities	1,711
	Violent events	1,130

ACGRI pillars: IISS calculation based on multiple sources for 2020 and January/February 2021 (scale 0–100). See Notes on Methodology and Data Appendix for further details on Key Conflict Statistics.

Cameroonian security forces clashed with separatist groups.

An armed secessionist movement developed by October 2017, with two rival political organisations competing for leadership: the Interim Government of Ambazonia (IG) and the Ambazonia Governing Council (AGC or AGovC). The IG began to coordinate the Ambazonia Self-Defence Council (ASDC), uniting several local self-defence groups. In January 2018, the IG's first president, Sisiku Julius Ayuk Tabe, was arrested with other top leaders and extradited from Nigeria. The AGC, in turn, established a military wing called the Ambazonia Defence Forces (ADF). Several smaller militias also emerged, further fragmenting the secessionist movement. These groups used guerrilla tactics to attack government forces and intimidate citizens into boycotting commerce and education. Many groups also kidnapped citizens for ransom as a way of raising funds.

The Cameroonian government deployed parts of its elite force, the Rapid Intervention Battalion (BIR), to fight the secessionist movement, with ensuing violence taking a significant human and economic toll on civilians. However, a growing Boko Haram presence in the north of the country diverted resources and political focus from the military response in the anglophone region. For example, in 2015, the governments of Benin, Cameroon, Chad, Niger and Nigeria agreed to revive the Multinational Joint Task Force (MNJTF) to support counter-terrorism operations against Boko Haram (see Lake Chad Basin chapter). The joint conflicts with Boko Haram in the Far North and separatists in anglophone regions revealed deep fractures in the Cameroonian state. The removal of many Muslim and anglophone Cameroonians from state and military institutions and the poor access of these groups to public services have fuelled distrust and created barriers to conflict resolution.

Conflict continued throughout 2020 amidst a fracturing of separatist groups and the spread of COVID-19. Some separatist groups held peace talks with the government of President Paul Biya, but violence continued to occur in the Northwest and Southwest regions, concentrated around Bamenda. Unmet separatist demands, infighting and state forces' inability to control critical areas of disputed territory led to further political instability. Separatist groups also increasingly accused civilians of being traitors, attacking and abducting local chiefs.

The coronavirus pandemic complicated the conflict as the government closed borders, shut down schools and set curfews for public venues to curb the spread of the virus. Separatist groups split over issues such as the handling of the pandemic, the decision to disrupt upcoming parliamentary and municipal elections, and the targeting of aid workers. Following the United Nations' call for a global ceasefire, the Southern Cameroons Defence Force (SOCADEF) declared a ceasefire while the larger ADF and Cameroonian armed forces continued fighting.[2] Conflict in the anglophone region had also damaged 115 hospitals and other key public infrastructure necessary for handling the pandemic.[3]

The 2020 peace talks with fractured secessionist groups followed legislation in late 2019 granting special status to the Northwest and Southwest regions and provisions for anglophone schools and judiciary.[4] As part of the new special status and concessions towards the anglophone region, the country's first regional elections for 900 local council positions were held in December 2020. The ruling party, Cameroon People's Democratic

Sub-Saharan Africa

Movement (RDPC), captured a vast majority in the elections, winning nine of ten administrative regions.[5] This sweeping victory came amidst an official boycott of the elections by two opposition parties, the Movement for the Rebirth of Cameroon and the Social Democratic Front, though some opposition councillors defied party orders to cast their votes.[6]

Between January 2020 and February 2021, the separatist conflict caused around 1,700 fatalities, including almost 800 civilians.[7] Violence targeting civilians also increased significantly from 2019.

Separatists increased usage of improvised explosive devices (IEDs) in 2020 – concentrated in the Fako and Mezam areas, with Bamenda being a particular hotspot – following a rise in imported weapons and local manufacturing of small arms in the Northwest region.[8] Since fighting began in 2016, total fatalities of the separatist conflict have reached around 4,000 and just short of 59,000 refugees have fled across the border to Nigeria.[9] As of the end of 2019, the number of internally displaced persons (IDPs) across the country had reached almost 997,000, preventing over 850,000 children from attending school.[10]

Conflict Parties

Cameroonian armed forces

Strength: Approximately 25,400 regular military personnel and 9,000 paramilitaries. The scale of deployment in anglophone Cameroon is unclear but consists of elements of the military police (the gendarmerie) and the elite military force, the BIR.

Areas of operation: Northwest and Southwest regions, in a military region designated RMIA 5.

Leadership and structure: RMIA 5 is led by General Agha Robinson Ndong but the president is commander of the armed forces.
The BIR has no general staff and is under the authority of the chief of staff of the army. The gendarmerie is under the authority of the secretary of state in the Ministry of Defence.

Objectives: Counter-insurgency against separatist groups in Northwest and Southwest regions and restoration of the regular flow of commerce disrupted by separatist groups.

Opponents and affiliates/allies:
Opponents: IG, ASDC, AGC, ADF, various smaller militias.
Affiliates/allies: Receive military assistance from France, Israel and the United States.

Resources/capabilities: Much of the equipment inventory is ageing, but infantry fighting vehicles and protected patrol vehicles have been acquired from China and South Africa and gifted by the US. The armed forces are improving their intelligence, surveillance and reconnaissance capabilities with fixed-wing aircraft and small uninhabited aerial vehicles.

Interim Government of Ambazonia (IG) / Ambazonia Self-Defence Council (ASDC)

Strength: The ASDC consists of several local self-defence groups including the Ambazonia Restoration Army (ARA), the Manyu Ghost Warriors, the Red Dragons, the Seven Karta Militia, SOCADEF and the Tigers of Ambazonia. Collectively the ASDC can draw on some 1,000 to 1,500 fighters.[11]

Areas of operation: The ASDC operates throughout Northwest and Southwest regions. The ARA and SOCADEF operate in most divisions in Northwest and Southwest regions. The Seven Karta is primarily present in Mezam division, the Tigers in Manyu and Meme divisions, the Ghost Warriors in Manyu and the Red Dragons in Lebialem.

Leadership and structure: The IG leadership is fractured between Tabe and Samuel Ikome Sako, following the former's arrest and the latter's election as interim president. The links between the IG and the various groups within the ASDC are often tenuous. Leadership of many of the individual groups is also unknown. The ARA is led by Paxson Agbor, SOCADEF by Nso Foncha Nkem, and the Red Dragons by Lekeaka Oliver. Since May 2019, there have been significant disputes between the IG wings loyal to Tabe and those associated with Sako, as well as between the IG and the ASDC.

The IG operates a government structure that includes an executive and a legislative body. The ASDC lacks a centralised command structure. The structure of the several localised self-defence organisations that compose it is unclear, yet many leaders are titled 'general'.

Objectives: Ambazonia's independence through a strategy of increased international pressure on the Cameroonian government and disruption of commerce.

Opponents and affiliates/allies:
Opponents: Cameroonian armed forces.
Affiliates/allies: The IG coordinates with other groups through the Southern Cameroons Liberation Council (SCLC), and at times coordinates with the AGC/ADF.

Resources/capabilities: Makeshift weaponry and some imports of small arms from neighbouring Nigeria. Financing of the IG comes primarily from the Cameroonian diaspora. The ASDC recur to kidnapping for ransom as a means of funding their operations.

Ambazonia Governing Council (AGC) / Ambazonia Defence Forces (ADF)

Strength: Estimated between 200 and 500 fighters.[12]

Areas of operation: Throughout Northwest and Southwest regions, parts of Littoral region.

Leadership and structure: The AGC is led from abroad by Lucas Cho Ayaba, while the chairman of the ADF council is Benedict Kuah.
The AGC operates a government structure that includes an executive and a legislative branch. Various leaders in the ADF have the title of 'general'.

Objectives: Ambazonia's independence through a strategy of insurgency and disruption of commerce. The AGC's goal is to make the anglophone territory ungovernable and thus compel the Cameroonian government to concede.

Opponents and affiliates/allies:
Opponents: Cameroonian armed forces.
Affiliates/allies: At times interacts with groups in the ASDC and coordinates with SOCADEF. It has a loose relationship with the IG.

Resources/capabilities: Makeshift weaponry and some imports of small arms from neighbouring Nigeria. Financing for the organisation comes primarily from the Cameroonian diaspora as well as ransoms from kidnapping activities.

Southern Cameroons Defence Forces (SOCADEF)

Strength: Approximately 400 members.[13]

Areas of operation: Meme division, Southwest region.

Leadership and structure: Led from abroad by Ebenezer Derek Mbongo Akwanga.
While SOCADEF is ostensibly the armed wing of the African People's Liberation Movement (APLM), the degree of coordination between the two is unclear. SOCADEF's organisation on the ground is unknown.

Objectives: Independence for Ambazonia through a strategy of insurgency and disruption of commerce.

Opponents and affiliates/allies:
Opponents: Cameroonian armed forces.
Affiliates/allies: Maintains a loose alliance with the AGC/ADF. In March 2019, its parent organisation, the APLM, joined the Southern Cameroons Liberation Council.

Resources/capabilities: Makeshift weaponry and some imports of small arms from neighbouring Nigeria.

Various small militias

Strength: Unclear, but approximately 100–150 members in total across nearly a dozen militias, including the Vipers, often operating under the generic term 'Amba Boys'.

Areas of operation: Northwest and Southwest regions.

Leadership and structure: Unknown.

Objectives: Independence for Ambazonia through insurgency, but many groups also seem to seek short-term material gains from the conflict and are responsible for many of the kidnappings for ransom in the region.

Opponents and affiliates/allies:
Opponents: Cameroonian armed forces.
Affiliates/allies: The Vipers coordinate with the ADF and SOCADEF on an ad hoc basis.

Resources/capabilities: Makeshift weaponry and small arms imported from Nigeria.

Conflict Drivers

Political

Long-standing perceptions of discrimination:
The conflict's root causes date back to the colonial history of Cameroon and its division under French and British rule. After independence in the early 1960s, the country operated as a federation, consisting of a larger francophone territory and a smaller anglophone region. However, in 1972, a referendum abolished federalism and created a unitary state under single-party, francophone rule. This led to the perception of government neglect of the development, cultural recognition and political freedoms of anglophone Cameroonians. Tensions led to widespread anti-government demonstrations in 2016. The aggressive government response to the protest movement created a dynamic of mutual escalation. Negotiations eventually collapsed, with separatists coordinating wider-scale strikes and many calling for secession. In response, the government framed the anglophone issue as a direct security threat and made only conciliatory concessions.

Patronage, corruption and weak democratic accountability:
Rampant corruption and weak democratic accountability have elevated the anglophone sense of alienation. The office of the presidency has distributed patronage to francophone supporters and the ruling RDPC party dominates the Cameroonian political system. Gerrymandering of voting districts and a disproportionate electoral system have increasingly disadvantaged opposition parties, leading to calls for President Biya's resignation. The December 2020 regional elections offered some concessions, but the ruling RDPC won nine of ten seats amidst allegations of voter fraud and intimidation.[14] The perception of an entrenched status quo and the powerful elite have pushed many anglophones to consider full autonomy as the only solution.

International

Regional dynamics:
The armed conflict in Cameroon critically intersects with the broader regional dynamics, including widespread insecurity, a counter-insurgency campaign against Boko Haram and conflict spillover across international borders. Cameroon plays an important stabilising role against insecurity caused by Boko Haram in its Far North region. The lack of international pressure on the Biya government for peace initiatives with separatist groups must be understood in this context. International allies are hesitant to create political and military instability in Cameroon given the country's strategic role in curbing Boko Haram's further expansion.

Key Events in 2020–21

POLITICAL EVENTS

9 February 2020
Parliamentary and municipal elections are held, including in the anglophone region, where low turnout is reported.

17 March
Cameroon closes borders and schools and establishes curfews to curb the spread of COVID-19.

22 March
Reorganised partial legislative elections are held in the Northwest and Southwest regions, resulting in a major victory for the ruling RDPC.

26 March
SOCADEF declares a 14-day ceasefire to curb the spread of COVID-19.

7 April
The Cameroonian government announces a reconstruction plan for the anglophone region.

3 July
The Cameroonian government holds peace talks with Tabe, one of the IG leaders.

7 September
President Biya schedules inaugural regional elections for 6 December, with regional councils indirectly elected by local councils.

MILITARY/VIOLENT EVENTS

23 January 2020
Military forces carry out clearing operations in Ekondo Titi subdivision, killing around 14 civilians.

14 February
Military forces and a pro-government militia attack Ngarbuh village resulting in around 22 fatalities, including many children.

21 March
Ten Ambazonian camps are destroyed by military forces, with around 24 separatist fatalities in Ngo-ketunjia division.

30 March
Military forces clash with and kill more than 50 Ambazonian separatists in the Southwest region.

2 May
Week-long clashes with military forces lead to the death of separatist commander General Alhaji in Bafut.

19 June
Army forces kill General Obi, a separatist leader, in Ashum village, Mamfe area.

12 July
Ambazonian separatists kidnap at least 63 people in the village of M'Muock-Mbie.

5 September
Luca Fonteh, a separatist military leader, is killed by BIR forces in Bamenda.

27 October

Michelle Bachelet, the UN High Commissioner for Human Rights, calls for dialogue between separatists and the government.

24 October

An unidentified armed group kills at least eight students at a school in Kumba city.

5 November

Separatists kidnap Cardinal Tumi, the traditional chief of Nso, and 11 civilians in Bui division.

6 December

Regional elections are held in all ten regions, with the ruling party winning nine of ten regions.

6 December

During regional voting, separatists kill the municipal councillor in Alabukam and wound others near Akum.

17 February 2021

Hundreds participate in demonstrations in Yaoundé against the ongoing killing of chiefs in the anglophone region.

10 January 2021

The Cameroonian armed forces kill at least nine civilians and loot homes in Mautu, Southwest region.

Conflict Outlook

Political scenarios

The first talks between the Yaoundé government and separatists took place in 2020, along with the inaugural regional elections for 90 councillors with authority on certain local issues. Of these, 20 positions are filled by representatives of traditional chieftains, an influential position increasingly targeted through attacks and abductions by separatist groups. However, after boycotts by several opposition groups and the ruling party's victory in nine of the ten regional seats, this limited decentralisation is unlikely to satisfy separatist demands for independence or a return to federalism. The fracturing of separatist groups, with some entering peace negotiations while others continue fighting for independence, will continue to weaken their political leverage over the Biya government.

Escalation potential and conflict-related risks

The fractured opposition may result in further violence as competing separatist groups clash with one another, leaving civilians caught in the crossfire. Targeted violence by separatists against an increasingly disillusioned population (especially local leaders suspected of not supporting separatist causes) may also escalate further. The frequent use of indiscriminate violence in military-clearance operations will risk further weakening the legitimacy of the Biya government and encourage anglophones to join armed separatist groups.

Prospects for peace

Tabe's willingness to hold peace talks may point towards some 2021 resolution with those groups that are loyal to him. This will, however, create local power vacuums which will likely be filled by other separatists who wish to continue fighting. Indeed, the fracturing of separatist groups and their diverse demands make the prospect of sweeping universal peace arrangements very unlikely. Those left out of negotiations will continue using insurgency tactics.

Strategic implications and global influences

Boko Haram's operations in northern Cameroon reduce the likelihood of international pressure being applied on the Biya regime for any significant political changes. The country's strategic position as a backstop for Boko Haram's expansion gives the international community little appetite for regime change and potential resultant political instability in Cameroon. Major political changes may affect military operations and create opportunities for Boko Haram to broaden its reach.

Sub-Saharan Africa

Notes

1   International Crisis Group, 'Cameroon's Anglophone Crisis at the Crossroads', Report no. 250, 2 August 2017; Richard Moncrieff, 'Cameroon's Anglophone Crisis Is Escalating. Here's How It Could Be Resolved', African Arguments, 27 September 2017; and Laura-Stella Enonchong, 'The Problem of Systemic Violation of Civil and Political Rights in Cameroon: Towards a Contextualised Conception of Constitutionalism', PhD Dissertation, University of Warwick, January 2013.

2   Adam Miller, 'Call Unanswered: A Review of Responses to the UN Appeal for a Global Ceasefire', Armed Conflict Location & Event Data Project (ACLED), 13 May 2020, https://acleddata.com/2020/05/13/call-unanswered-un-appeal/.

3   Home Office, 'Country Policy and Information Note Cameroon: North-West/South-West crisis', December 2020.

4   R. Maxwell Bone and Akem Kelvin Nkwain, 'Cameroon Grants "Special Status" to Its Restive Regions. They Don't Feel Special', African Arguments, 13 January 2020; and Maxwell Bone, 'Ahead of Peace Talks, a Who's Who of Cameroon's Separatist Movements', New Humanitarian, 8 July 2020.

5   Moki Edwin Kindzeka, 'Cameroon's Ruling Party Scores Landslide Victory in Regional Elections', Voice of America, 11 December 2020; see also R. Maxwell Bone, 'Paul Biya Is Offering Cameroon's Anglophones Too Little, Too Late', Foreign Policy, 21 November 2020.

6   'Cameroon: SDF Councillors Defy Party Orders, Vote at Regional Elections', journalducameroun.com, 7 December 2020.

7   Armed Conflict Location & Event Data Project (ACLED), www.acleddata.com.

8   'Cameroon: Anglophone Crisis Dragging on Due to Illegal Manufacturing, Sale of Arms – NW Governor', journalducameroun.com, 24 November 2020.

9   International Crisis Group, 'Cameroon', 30 March 2021; and Cameroon Intelligence Report, 'Ambazonia Refugee Situation Update: UN Says 58,415 Are Now Registered in Nigeria', 31 December 2020.

10 See Internal Displacement Monitoring Centre (IDMC), '2020 Internal Displacement', Global Internal Displacement Database; and UNICEF, 'More than 855,000 Children Remain Out of School in North-West and South-West Cameroon', 5 November 2019.

11 Institute for Peace and Security Studies, 'Cameroon Conflict Insight', Peace and Security Report, vol. 1, March 2020, p. 8.

12 International Crisis Group, 'Cameroon's Anglophone Crisis: How to Get to Talks?', Report no. 272, 2 May 2019, p. 32.

13 Ibid.

14 Kindzeka, 'Cameroon's Ruling Party Scores Landslide Victory in Regional Elections'; Bone, 'Paul Biya Is Offering Cameroon's Anglophones Too Little, Too Late'.

SUDAN

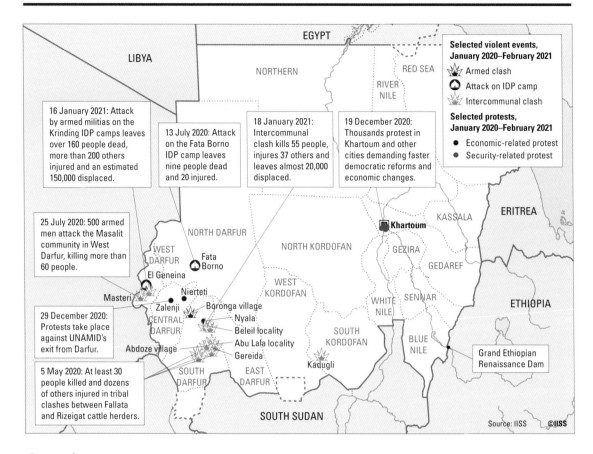

16 January 2021: Attack by armed militias on the Krinding IDP camps leaves over 160 people dead, more than 200 others injured and an estimated 150,000 displaced.

13 July 2020: Attack on the Fata Borno IDP camp leaves nine people dead and 20 injured.

18 January 2021: Intercommunal clash kills 55 people, injures 37 others and leaves almost 20,000 displaced.

19 December 2020: Thousands protest in Khartoum and other cities demanding faster democratic reforms and economic changes.

Selected violent events, January 2020–February 2021
- Armed clash
- Attack on IDP camp
- Intercommunal clash

Selected protests, January 2020–February 2021
- ● Economic-related protest
- ● Security-related protest

25 July 2020: 500 armed men attack the Masalit community in West Darfur, killing more than 60 people.

29 December 2020: Protests take place against UNAMID's exit from Darfur.

5 May 2020: At least 30 people killed and dozens of others injured in tribal clashes between Fallata and Rizeigat cattle herders.

Grand Ethiopian Renaissance Dam

Source: IISS   ©IISS

Overview

In Sudan, conflict and violence has besieged the states of Blue Nile and South Kordofan – commonly referred to as the Two Areas – and the region of Darfur for nearly two decades. Fighting in Darfur started in 2003, when several insurgent forces – mainly the Sudan Liberation Movement (SLM) and the Justice and Equality Movement (JEM) – took up arms to fight the marginalisation of minorities by the government of Omar al-Bashir. In 2005, the violence escalated, killing and displacing thousands as government-backed militias targeted civilians. On the other hand, prior conflict in South Kordofan and Blue Nile had subsided following the signing of the Comprehensive Peace Agreement in 2005, but intensified again in 2011 around the independence of South Sudan due to several factors, including the government's attempt to forcefully disarm groups such as the Sudan People's Liberation Movement/Army–North (SPLM/A–N).

In 2013, the main armed forces in Darfur and the Two Areas came together under the umbrella of the Sudanese Revolutionary Front (SRF) and declared war on the central administration. Khartoum responded by deploying the Sudanese Armed Forces (SAF) and other paramilitary forces, mainly the Rapid Support Forces (RSF), resulting in severe humanitarian suffering, mass killings of civilians and widespread displacement.

These challenges were further compounded by a deteriorating economic crisis which triggered mass protests across the country and resulted in the ousting of Bashir in April 2019. A transitional government, established with both civilian and military components, engaged the dominant forces from Darfur and the Two Areas to find a durable political solution to the crisis. A cessation of hostilities agreement was signed in 2019 and clashes

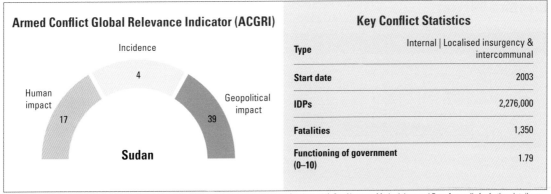

ACGRI pillars: IISS calculation based on multiple sources for 2020 and January/February 2021 (scale 0–100). See Notes on Methodology and Data Appendix for further details on Key Conflict Statistics.

involving government and rebel groups significantly declined.

However, violence picked up throughout 2020 and early 2021 and the security situation in Sudan remained tense, with widespread intercommunal clashes and violence against civilians in Darfur and the Two Areas.

In Darfur, the security situation was marked by recurrent intercommunal clashes in various localities (South, North and Central) and intermittent fighting between the government and forces from the Sudan Liberation Movement/Army–Abdel Wahid al-Nur (SLM/A–AW), as well as internal bickering among the latter's factions. Between January 2020 and February 2021, there were 284 violent incidences in the region resulting in 922 fatalities, compared to 383 deaths in 2019.[1] The rise in intercommunal clashes was particularly stark in the region in the second half of the year, with an 87% increase between July and December compared to the same period in 2019.[2] In July 2020 alone, several violent attacks in Darfur targeting civilians and camps for internally displaced persons (IDPs) killed more than a hundred people.[3] Intercommunal clashes also affected communities in Blue Nile and South Kordofan, escalating towards the end of 2020 with several incidents reported in December.

This violence produced an increased number of IDPs, with an estimated 35,000 new conflict-induced displacements across the country in the first half of 2020 alone and around an additional 25,000 people in Central and South Darfur between September and October.[4] Intercommunal conflict in January 2021 between Massalit and Arab communities also displaced over 180,000 people in North, South and West Darfur.[5]

However, 2020–21 saw a reduction in clashes between government and rebel forces – with the exception of sporadic clashes with the SLM/A–AW – partly due to the signing of a ceasefire pact and more significantly due to the signing of the Juba Peace Agreement in October 2020 between the transitional government, the SRF and the Sudan Liberation Movement/Army–Minni Minnawi (SLM/A–MM). This agreement arguably represented the most notable achievement of the year. After 13 years of operations, the United Nations–African Union Hybrid Operation in Darfur (UNAMID) ended its mandate in December 2020, handing over the role of ensuring security and civilian protection to the Sudanese government.

Nevertheless, civil unrest flared up in Sudan, triggered by a deteriorating economic situation and a resulting rise in living costs. The country's inflation rate reached 330.78% in February 2021, the highest in decades.[6] From July 2020, Sudan also endured unprecedented floods that destroyed houses, farms and livelihoods, with Darfur and Blue Nile among the worst-affected areas.[7] These floods and the implementation of lockdown measures in response to the coronavirus pandemic pushed the country's already weak economy to its breaking point. An estimated 7.1 million people (or 16% of the population) were projected to face high levels of acute food insecurity between October and December 2020 in the country.[8]

On the regional front, the century-old border conflict between Ethiopia and Sudan escalated into a full-fledged military stand-off in 2020–21. This, coupled with the ongoing dispute over the Grand Ethiopian Renaissance Dam (GERD), posed a danger to Sudan and regional peace and stability.

Sub-Saharan Africa

Conflict Parties

Sudanese Armed Forces (SAF)

Strength: 104,300 active military personnel (100,000 army, 1,300 navy, 3,000 air force), with 20,000 active paramilitary and 85,000 reserve paramilitary. These numbers are expected to grow over the next three years as fighters from various non-state armed groups are integrated into the national army as part of the Juba Peace Agreement.

Areas of operation: Across Sudan, including the restive Darfur and Two Areas.

Leadership and structure: Lieutenant-General Abdel Fattah Al-Burhan (commander-in-chief and chairman of the transitional Sovereignty Council).

Objectives: Suppress rebel insurgencies and their supporters in Darfur and the Two Areas.

Opponents and affiliates/allies: Opposes several armed groups based in Darfur and the Two Areas.
Allied with other elements of the state security apparatus, including the National Intelligence and Security Service and other paramilitary forces, such as the Popular Defence Forces (now called the Reserve Department), the Border Guards and the RSF.

Resources/capabilities: Acquires its military equipment – including ammunition, small arms and armoured vehicles – from a mix of domestic and international manufacturers financed by the state. Allegedly controls a vast number of commercial companies in several sectors, including gold mining and agricultural production, which provides an additional resource base.

Rapid Support Forces (RSF)

Strength: Estimated 30–40,000.[9]

Areas of operation: Deployed throughout Sudan to stop violence and tribal clashes.

Leadership and structure: General Mohamed Hamdan Dagalo, commonly known as 'Hemeti' (current Deputy Chairman of Sudan's Sovereignty Council). He was one of the most powerful figures during Bashir's era.
The RSF was to integrate into the SAF under the Constitutional Document signed in August 2019.

Objectives: Provide support and assistance to the SAF and other regular forces in the execution of its mission of defending the country from internal and external threats. During the Bashir era, the force was deployed in Darfur and the Two Areas to repress dissent.

Opponents and affiliates/allies:
Opponents: Various armed groups across the country.
Allies: SAF and local militias; its leader also maintains a strong relationship with United Arab Emirates and Saudi leaders.

Resources/capabilities: Primarily funded by the state as part of the state security apparatus. Also mobilises resources from its participation in mercenary activities in Libya and Yemen.

Sudan Liberation Movement/Army–Abdel Wahid al-Nur (SLM/A–AW)

Strength: 100–150 men moving between Darfur and Libya.[10]

Areas of operation: Maintains presence in Darfur, controlling pockets of the Jebel Marra Mountains and South Darfur.

Leadership and structure: Abdel Wahid al-Nur (founder and current leader).

Objectives: Previously to overthrow Bashir's regime and address the root causes of conflict (including issues around land rights) in the Darfur region, particularly for his Fur supporters. After Sudan's political transition, the group remained outside of the negotiation process and subsequent peace deals.

The group calls for the prioritisation of security (including the disarmament of Janjaweed militias) before peace talks and for the negotiation process to address the underlying conflict drivers, involve all necessary stakeholders involved and take place within Sudan. The group is reportedly working on an initiative for internal Sudanese dialogue.

Opponents and affiliates/allies: As one of the holdout rebel groups that did not sign the Juba Peace Agreement, the SLM/A–AW clashed with government forces throughout 2020.

Resources/capabilities: Bolstered its military capability by acquiring weapons and ammunition using income generated from gold-mining operations and taxation of controlled territories in the Jebel Marra area and IDP camps.

Sudan Liberation Movement/Army–Minni Minnawi (SLM/A–MM)

Strength: Over 1,000 combatants in Libya.[11]

Areas of operation: Active in Libya (and South Sudan) since it lost its foothold in Darfur in 2014.

Leadership and structure: Minni Minnawi.

Objectives: During Bashir's regime, the main objective of SLA–MM was to fight the Janjaweed militias. Following the formation of the transitional government in Sudan, the group was one of the first to sign the Juba Agreement. The group now calls for an inclusive national reconciliation process.

Sudan Liberation Movement/Army–Minni Minnawi (SLM/A–MM)

Opponents and affiliates/allies: Opposes the SAF, the RSF and the SLM/A–AW.
Affiliated with the SRF (although later broke away from it).
Fights alongside the Libyan National Army in Libya.

Resources/capabilities: Generates income from its mercenary activities in Libya.

Justice and Equality Movement (JEM)

Strength: Between 100 and 200 combatants and an additional 100 combatants in South Sudan.[12]

Areas of operation: Although JEM is a Darfur-based rebel movement (primarily in West Darfur), it no longer actively operates in the area. Its remaining small contingent relocated to South Sudan following its defeat in 2015. It, however, maintains a small presence in Blue Nile and South Kordofan.

Leadership and structure: Gibril Ibrahim (chairman since 2012).

Objectives: To fight marginalisation, bring about regime change and national reform in Sudan (by establishing a federal and democratic government of national unity). The group signed the Juba Agreement following the formation of the transitional government and joined the new Sudan cabinet.

Opponents and affiliates/allies: Opposes the SAF and the RSF in Darfur.
Joined the SRF in November 2011. It also has close links with the Libyan National Army.

Resources/capabilities: Said to receive financial support for its activities from South Sudanese and Ugandan governments and its Islamist diaspora supporters. Previously gathered support primarily from Chadian and Libyan governments.

United Nations–African Union Hybrid Operation in Darfur (UNAMID)

Strength: Consisted of 4,005 military personnel drawn from several troop-contributing countries (TCCs).[13]

Areas of operation: Headquartered in Central Darfur, the mission operated in all five states/regions of Darfur.

Leadership and structure: Jeremiah Mamabolo served as the Head of Mission/Special Representative from April 2017, appointed by the AU and UN.

Objectives: Mandated to protect civilians, facilitate humanitarian assistance, reduce intercommunal conflicts and improve security. The mission completed this mandate on 31 December 2020.

Opponents and affiliates/allies: Opposed armed forces in the Darfur region.
Allied with the government of Sudan and those of TCCs.

Resources/capabilities: Primarily financed by the UN. The approved mission funding for the period from July 2019 to June 2020 was US$257.97 million.

Conflict Drivers

Economic and social

Marginalisation and divisive policies:
The political and economic marginalisation of the periphery has been a primary driver of violence in the country. The ensuing socio-economic disparity gave rise to discontent and deep-seated resistance against the government, which manifested in persistent intercommunal disputes and rebel–government violence. These challenges have been exacerbated by the regime's Islamisation policy, which effectively discriminated against other communities, and the politicisation and exploitation of ethnic cleavages, which further polarised communities and led to the proliferation of secessionist and armed movements. The government's highly militaristic approach further aggravated some of these tensions.

Deteriorating economic conditions:
The loss of 75% of Sudan's oil revenue and around half of its national income due to the 2011 South Sudan secession was a major shock to the country's economy, considering its heavy reliance on oil.[14] Other factors, such as environmental degradation and recurrent droughts,

economic mismanagement and long-standing US sanctions (lifted in 2017) further compounded Sudan's financial woes. Distressing economic hardship triggered frequent waves of protests across the country, including the 2019 protest that brought the transitional government to power.

International

Regional disputes:
Border disputes, in varying times and degrees, have erupted between Sudan and neighbouring countries, notably Egypt, Ethiopia and South Sudan. The century-old border dispute with Ethiopia transformed into a full-fledged military stand-off in November 2020 over the Sudanese agricultural area known as the al-Fashaga Triangle. While the two countries share a long boundary, no clear demarcation exists. The situation was further exacerbated by continued disagreements between the two countries over the GERD. While the trigger for November's escalation was not clear, the relations between the two countries began to turn following the involvement of other/external parties in the GERD mediation process and the first-round filling of the GERD reservoir by Ethiopia. The two sides entered talks in December 2020 to settle the border dispute. With both countries in the midst of fragile political transitions, military conflict would have serious ramifications for regional security.

Key Events in 2020–21

POLITICAL EVENTS

9 January 2020
Hamdok visits Kauda, the SPLM/A–N al-Hilu's stronghold.

3 June 2020
UNSC Resolution 2524 is adopted, establishing the UN Integrated Transition Assistance Mission in Sudan (UNITAMS).

17 August
The Sudanese government and the SPLM/A–N Agar sign a security-arrangements protocol in Juba, agreeing on merging forces in Blue Nile and South Kordofan.

31 August
A comprehensive peace agreement is signed between the transitional government, the SRF (including the JEM and the SPLM–N Agar) and the SPLM/A–MM.

3 September
A joint agreement on principles for maintaining the cessation of hostilities is signed between the transitional government and the SPLM–N al-Hilu.

3 October
The Juba Peace Agreement between the Sudanese government and rebel groups is signed.

18 October
The Constitutional Document is amended, incorporating the Juba Agreement as an integral part.

23 October
Sudan agrees to normalise relations with Israel.

MILITARY/VIOLENT EVENTS

9 March
An attack by herders on Beleil locality in South Darfur kills at least 12 people.

5 May
At least 30 people are killed and dozens injured in tribal clashes between Fallata and Rizeigat cattle herders in South Darfur.

14 May
An attack by RSF militiamen in the Kadugli area, South Kordofan, kills at least five and displaces close to 2,000 people.

13 July
An attack on the Fata Borno IDP camp in North Darfur leaves several people dead or wounded.

23 July
Gunmen attack Abdoze village in South Darfur, killing around 20 people.

25 July
500 gunmen attack the Masalit community in Masteri, West Darfur, killing more than 70 people.

2 August
An attack in Boronga village kills an RSF officer and displaces at least 3,000 people.

24 October

A US$370m grant agreement is signed between Sudan's government, the World Bank and the European Union as part of Sudan's Family Support Programme.

12 November

General Abdel Fattah al-Burhan grants a general amnesty to people who fought in Sudan's armed conflicts, excluding those with an International Criminal Court arrest warrant.

16 November

The SLM/A–AW accepts an invitation to negotiate peace with the Sudanese government.

14 December

Sudan is officially removed from the United States' list of state sponsors of terrorism.

22 December

The UNSC adopts Resolution 2559 which ends UNAMID's mandate on 31 December 2020.

22 December

Sudan and Ethiopia hold border-demarcation talks.

31 December

UNAMID's mandate officially ends.

8 February 2021

Hamdok announces a new cabinet, integrating former rebel leaders.

December

A series of protests takes place in South Darfur against UNAMID's exit.

26 December

Tribal fighting between Masalit farmers and Fallata herders in South Darfur kills at least 15 people and injures 34.

28 December

The SAF claims to have taken control of territories in border areas with Ethiopia.

28–30 December

Tribal clashes between the Fallata and the Rizeigat tribes in South Darfur kill at least ten people and wound several others.

16 January 2021

An attack by armed militias in El Geneina, West Darfur, kills 48 people and injures 97 others.

18 January

An intercommunal clash kills 55 people, injures 37 others and displaces close to 20,000 people in South Darfur.

24–31 January

A series of attacks in the Jebel Marra area in North Darfur displaces 22,000 people.

Conflict Outlook

Political scenarios

The signing of the Juba Peace Agreement by the Sudanese government and rebel groups from Darfur and the Two Areas in October 2020 creates an opportunity to address the root causes of conflict and deliver durable peace. Although the deal is expected to improve the security situation in conflict-affected areas, it faces several implementation challenges, not least the non-inclusion of certain relevant rebel groups, including the SLM/A–AW. Communities in the eastern part of the country also opposed the deal, claiming that it excluded dominant forces in the region.

The inclusion of former rebel members in the newly appointed cabinet can be seen as an essential step in implementing aspects of the Juba Agreement. However, much remains to be done to (re)build confidence among the government and signatory parties/former armed groups to ensure that the promised reforms are realised. This is especially true given some parties' dissatisfaction with the limited progress in implementing elements of the agreement, such as the facilitation of security arrangements.

Sudan's removal from the US list of countries supporting terrorism will provide support to the government's own efforts to stimulate economic growth. Despite years of contraction, with upcoming international support and possible debt relief, the country's economic outlook is expected to improve in 2021.

Escalation potential and conflict-related risks

The spike in intercommunal violence in Darfur and the Two Areas in late 2020 and early 2021 underlined the government's failure to protect civilians by filling the gap left by the UNAMID's withdrawal, prompting calls for improved security. Unlike UNAMID, the mandate of the UN Integrated Transition Assistance Mission in Sudan (UNITAMS) is to provide political rather than security support to the transition process. This leaves the provision of

Sub-Saharan Africa

security and civilian protection entirely in the hands of government security forces, who have themselves been repeatedly implicated in atrocities in Darfur and other areas.

The humanitarian situation in Darfur and the Two Areas remains severe due to the continued intercommunal clashes and resulting displacements. An additional 4.1m people will need humanitarian assistance in 2021, taking the total to an unprecedented 13.4m, with Darfur and the Two Areas among the most affected areas.[15] Furthermore, with Sudan already hosting over one million refugees and asylum seekers, including over 60,000 from Ethiopia's Tigray region, any further displacement caused by the conflict there would stretch the country's already scarce resources.[16] While the Juba Peace Agreement is expected to facilitate humanitarian access across Sudan, including Darfur and the Two Areas, the increased violence in late 2020 and early 2021 continued to disrupt humanitarian activities.

Prospects for peace

Reaping the dividends of the Juba Peace Agreement will require the government to address its implementation challenges by involving the remaining holdout armed groups – particularly SLM/A–AW – improving relations between the civilian and military components of the transitional government and mobilising the required resources. The government will also need to step up civilian-protection efforts and ensure improved security in conflict-affected areas as part of its commitment under the national plan in the wake of UNAMID's departure.

Notes

[1] Armed Conflict Location & Event Data Project (ACLED), www.acleddata.com.

[2] United Nations Office for the Coordination of Humanitarian Affairs, 'Situation Report – Sudan: Inter-communal Violence Increased in Darfur During the Second Half of 2020', 17 January 2021.

[3] 'UN Condemns Deadly Violence in Sudan's North Darfur', Al-Jazeera, 15 July 2020; 'Dozens Killed in Renewed Violence in Sudan's Darfur: UN', Al-Jazeera, 27 July 2020; and 'Gunmen Kill At Least 22 Villagers in South Darfur, Locals Say', Reuters, 25 July 2020.

[4] Internal Displacement Monitoring Centre, 'Internal Displacement 2020: Mid-year Update', 23 September 2020, p. 15; United Nations Security Council, 'Report of the Secretary-General on the Situation in Sudan and the Activities of the United Nations Integrated Transition Assistance Mission in Sudan', S/2020/1155, 17 September 2020; and United Nations Security Council, 'Report of the Secretary-General on the Situation in Sudan and the Activities of the United Nations Integrated Transition Assistance Mission in Sudan', S/2020/1155, 1 December 2020.

[5] 'Burst of Violence in Darfur Triggers Sudan's Highest Number of Conflict Displacements in Six Years', Internal Displacement Monitoring Centre, 18 February 2021.

[6] Mohammed Amin Yassin, 'Sudan's Annual Inflation Jumps to Record Level', Asharq Al-Awsat, 12 March 2021.

[7] The floods affected an estimated 650,000 people – including refugees and IDPs – leading the government to declare a three-month state of emergency. See United Nations Office for the Coordination of Humanitarian Affairs, 'Sudan: Floods Situation Report', 14 September 2020.

[8] Integrated Food Security Phase Classification, 'Sudan: Acute Food Insecurity Projection Update October–December 2020'.

[9] Central Intelligence Agency, 'The World Factbook: Sudan', 4 May 2021.

[10] European Asylum Support Office, 'Country of Origin Information: Sudan', 13 October 2020.

[11] Ibid.

[12] Ibid.

[13] 'United Nations, African Union Reiterate Commitment to Sudan, as Joint Mission Ends Operations', UN News, 31 December 2020.

[14] World Bank, 'Sudan Country Economic Brief', Issue no. 2012-02, December 2012.

[15] United Nations Office for the Coordination of Humanitarian Affairs, 'Humanitarian Needs Overview: Sudan', December 2020.

[16] United Nations High Commissioner for Refugees, 'Sudan: Population Dashboard – Overview of Refugees and Asylum-seekers in Sudan (as of 31 March 2021)', 26 May 2021; and United Nations Office for the Coordination of Humanitarian Affairs, 'Situation Report: Sudan – Refugee Influx from Tigray Continues', 24 March 2021.

5 Asia

Rohingya refugees from Myanmar on an island in northern Sumatra, Indonesia

Overview

South and Southeast Asia play host to a number of long-standing armed conflicts. Three of them – the civil war in Afghanistan,[1] Pakistan's struggle with ethnic insurgency and anti-state terrorist groups, and the dispute over Kashmir – have a significant impact on both regional and global security, primarily due to the transnational actors involved and the potential of the Kashmir dispute to escalate into conventional war between nuclear powers India and Pakistan. The region's other conflicts are more localised with a lower impact on regional dynamics. These are the struggle between Myanmar's military and ethnic armed organisations (EAOs), which has also included severe persecution of ethnic minorities; the Malay Muslim ethno-nationalist autonomy movement and insurgency in Thailand; the Philippines' two conflicts with the New People's Army (NPA) and Moro rebels and Islamist terrorist groups; and India's Maoist insurgency and conflict in the Northeast.

The United States' 2001 invasion of Afghanistan marked the latest phase of a four-decade civil war that has involved many third parties. The conflict has significant international implications, especially as US and NATO forces withdraw from the country in mid-2021.[2] Regional countries including China, India, Iran, Pakistan, Russia and also the US would prefer state stability rather than civil war; none favour a return to the Taliban's former Islamic Emirate. However, the US, India and Pakistan have different priorities, as New Delhi and Islamabad compete for influence and play out their strategic

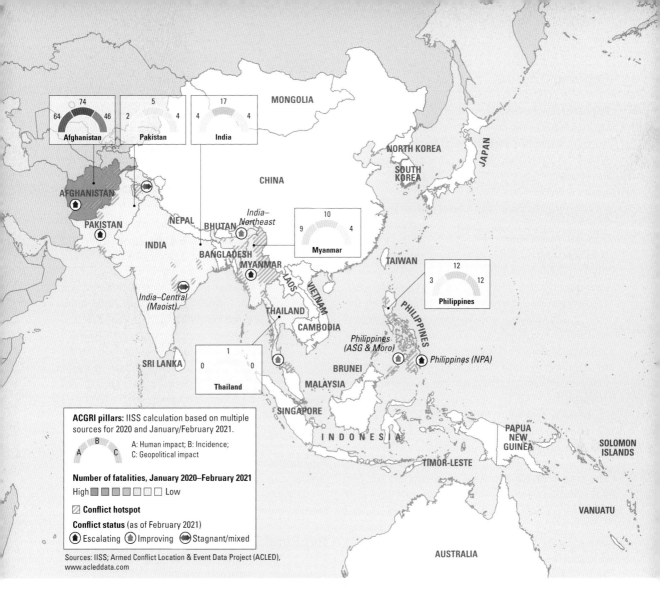

ACGRI pillars: IISS calculation based on multiple sources for 2020 and January/February 2021.

A: Human impact; B: Incidence; C: Geopolitical impact

Number of fatalities, January 2020–February 2021
High ■■■■□□□ Low

▨ **Conflict hotspot**

Conflict status (as of February 2021)
Escalating Improving Stagnant/mixed

Sources: IISS; Armed Conflict Location & Event Data Project (ACLED), www.acleddata.com

rivalry, partly fuelled by the Kashmir dispute. While Pakistan would ultimately prefer a stable state, it would be deeply concerned by an Afghanistan closely aligned with India. Therefore, tensions between India and Pakistan, and the latter's internal conflicts, affect each country's calculations regarding Afghanistan, particularly vis-à-vis Pakistan's support for the Taliban. These tensions risk prolonging the conflict.

The conflict along the Line of Control (LoC) demarcating Indian-administered and Pakistan-administered Kashmir saw raised levels of violence but lower than the highs of the mid- and late-1990s. New Delhi's controversial decision in August 2019 to end the 'semi-autonomous' constitutional status of the Indian state of Jammu and Kashmir led to tensions with China, Nepal and Pakistan. There was

also a significant uptick in the number of annual ceasefire violations across the LoC.

A coup by the Myanmar military (Tatmadaw) in February 2021 received global attention. The armed forces seized power from the civilian government following a manufactured political crisis over the results of the November 2020 elections, which had produced a landslide win for the National League for Democracy (NLD) party. A massive popular uprising in Myanmar's urban centres was quickly met with a bloody crackdown and mass arrests by the Tatmadaw. In response, the United Nations Security Council and the Association of Southeast Asian Nations (ASEAN) called for a return to the status quo and an end to the violence. The US, United Kingdom and European Union imposed sanctions on Myanmar and suspended aid.

Regional Trends

Persistence of internal conflict

South and Southeast Asia's conflicts are primarily internal, with the exception of Kashmir. The war in Afghanistan is an internal conflict that has become internationalised by notable third-party intervention. The Taliban remains backed by Pakistan, while Kabul relies heavily on US aid and has a close relationship with India. China, Iran and Russia have periodically supported both sides and vie for influence using political, security, economic and ethnic levers. Terrorist groups operating in the border areas between Pakistan and Afghanistan also affect and are affected by the war in Afghanistan and Pakistan's own internal conflict. For example, the virulently anti-Pakistan Tehrik-e-Taliban Pakistan (TTP) has taken refuge in Afghanistan and is escalating attacks inside Pakistan after reabsorbing splinter groups throughout 2020.

India's conflict with CPI–Maoist is largely localised; so too are the Philippines' conflicts with the NPA and Moro Muslim rebels, and the Malay Muslim ethno-nationalist insurgency in Thailand. The conflict in Myanmar is primarily internal but has resulted in approximately 855,000 Rohingya refugees in Bangladesh.[3] India's conflict in the northeast is also affected by insecurity across the border, with Naga, Assamese and Manipuri armed groups utilising disrupted but still-intact sanctuaries in Myanmar.

The influence of transnational jihad

The rise of the Islamic State (also known as ISIS or ISIL) has impacted the conflicts in Afghanistan and Pakistan, as well as the Philippines' fight against the Islamist Abu Sayyaf Group (ASG). The ISIS affiliate in Afghanistan and Pakistan, Islamic State in Khorasan Province (ISIS–KP), primarily recruits former TTP members and claimed responsibility for some of the most brutal attacks against ethnic and religious minorities in the region in 2020. In the Philippines, ASG, Ansar Khalifah Philippines and Bangsamoro Islamic Freedom Fighters maintained their allegiance to ISIS. Notably, the ethno-nationalist insurgency in southern Thailand has remained centred on regional identity and demands for an independent state, having resisted influence from transnational jihadist groups.

Peace processes make progress

In 2020, some gradual progress was made in peace processes in the Philippines, Thailand, and between India and Pakistan, but without any permanent settlements. Most positively, a joint statement by India's and Pakistan's Directors General of Military Operations agreed to a ceasefire along the LoC – the site of frequent artillery exchanges between the two countries. Dialogue stalled between the Communist Party of the Philippines and its armed wing (the NPA) on the one hand, and the strongman president of the Philippines Rodrigo Duterte on the other. In December 2020, Duterte declared that peace talks had been halted due to NPA attacks and forbade the agreement of local ceasefires. Elsewhere in the Philippines, a three-year extension of the transition period for the Bangsamoro Autonomous Region in Muslim Mindanao (BARMM) was backed by the BARMM chief minister and Philippines government, allowing a relative peace to prevail between Manila and the Moro Islamic Liberation Front despite delays to the latter's disarmament. In 2020, the Thailand National Security Council's Peace Dialogue Panel met with the Patani Malay National Revolutionary Front (BRN) separatists in a formal setting for the first time. The BRN unilaterally ceased hostile activities to better enable the government's response effort to the coronavirus pandemic.

Regional Drivers

Political and institutional

The most active conflicts in the region are rooted in the ethnic, religious, irredentist and centre–province tensions that emerged in newly formed post-colonial states. The 1909 Anglo-Siamese Treaty demarcated the border between what later became modern Thailand and Malaysia, splitting the historical Muslim sultanate of Patani and laying the groundwork for the Malay Muslim ethno-nationalist autonomy movement that drives insurgency in southern Thailand. In 1947, the last Hindu ruler of the princely state of Jammu and Kashmir opted to join the Indian Union rather than Pakistan, effectively splitting Kashmir between India and Pakistan and giving rise to the current conflict. Baloch insurgency and insecurity in Pakistan's Pashtun tribal areas stem partly from questions over the Durand Line as the legitimate border between Afghanistan and Pakistan, as well as a post-colonial order that split Pakistan into two wings – West Pakistan, which resembles today's borders, and East Pakistan, which is majority Bengali – following partition. This post-colonial order, followed by the secession of East Pakistan to become Bangladesh, gradually led to ethnic resentment as the Punjab province came to dominate others. Myanmar's independence from British rule in 1948 placed numerous ethnic minorities under the control of the Bamar majority, a circumstance which set in motion the current conflict.

Very often, this post-colonial legacy has combined with issues of identity, lack of political representation and the search for autonomy to drive many Asian conflicts, particularly in Kashmir, Pakistan (especially among Baloch separatists), India (the Communist Party of India–Maoist (CPI–Maoist)), Myanmar, the Philippines (ASG and Moro rebels) and Thailand. States have responded harshly to non-state actors' efforts for greater autonomy with military measures and restrictions. These have often targeted civilian populations that have ethnic or religious affiliations to non-state actors, impacting citizens' daily lives and thereby serving as an additional conflict driver. Myanmar's multiple internal armed conflicts are largely driven by EAOs' struggles for greater autonomy in remote borderlands, with efforts to demarcate territory by force ahead of peace negotiations leading to fighting between armed groups.

Central governments have tended to conflate demands for greater civil liberties and limited autonomy with violent separatist movements, as seen in Pakistan's suppression of the Pashtun Tahaffuz Movement (PTM) in Khyber Pakhtunkhwa, which demands greater civil rights for Pashtuns and uses anti-state rhetoric but is distinguishable from violent groups like the TTP. Jammu and Kashmir's integration with the Indian Union in August 2019 was a key driver of the Muslim-majority population's intensified political resistance against New Delhi. Government measures to prevent violent protests – including curfews, internet shutdowns and the deployment of additional Indian paramilitary and army personnel – fuelled resentment, whereas the contrasting government approach in areas with CPI–Maoist presence, focusing on service provision, alleviated conflict drivers. Long-lasting insurgencies, such as the Afghan Taliban and the Philippines' NPA, have also been enabled by their strong ideological unity and cohesion, and at times their decentralisation.

Economic and social

Socio-economic inequalities are root causes of the insurgencies in India, Pakistan and the Philippines. Poverty and lack of economic opportunities in parts of the Philippines continue to provide recruits for both Moro Muslim rebel groups and the NPA. India's CPI–Maoist has long tapped into sentiments of disenfranchisement in impoverished rural populations. Similarly, the conflict between Pakistan and Baloch insurgents is partially fuelled by economic inequality, seen most recently in the distribution of economic benefits derived from natural-resource extraction and the China–Pakistan Economic Corridor (CPEC) traversing Balochistan. In Myanmar, Pakistan and the Philippines, insurgents have cited internal migration of majority ethnic and religious groups to minority areas, or the entry of multinational (especially Chinese) firms, as key motivators for continued fighting. Projects like CPEC and the China–Myanmar Economic Corridor (CMEC) simultaneously motivate resistance and incentivise groups to consolidate control over future development zones so they can engage in rent seeking.

Illicit trade and informal taxation are also powerful economic drivers of conflict. The cultivation and export of illicit narcotics play a central role in Afghanistan, while illicit trade in narcotics, gems, timber and people fuels the conflict in Myanmar's periphery. Civilian populations often find themselves caught between heavy-handed insurgencies and coercive state security forces; they are sometimes punished by both for perceived cooperation with the other.

Geopolitical

The conflicts in Afghanistan, disputed Kashmir, Pakistan and the Philippines have strong international drivers that often perpetuate violence by altering power dynamics on the ground. For example, the long-standing presence of US and NATO troops, regional support for the Taliban and other forms of covert and overt intervention in Afghanistan's civil war are key drivers of conflict. The Taliban's primary objective is the withdrawal of foreign forces followed by the overthrow of the government, which it views as an extension of foreign influence. The Taliban is enabled by a diverse group of foreign donors and sponsors that has at times included Iran, private Gulf donors and – most importantly – Pakistan. The Taliban also relies on safe havens in Pakistan and coordinates its operations through leadership councils in Quetta. Similarly, Islamabad often attributes terrorist violence in Pakistan to the safe havens found by militants in Afghanistan.

The spread of transnational jihadism in South and Southeast Asia – with various groups in the region pledging allegiance to ISIS since 2014 – also shapes the conflicts by radicalising populations and spawning new non-state actors that may derail ongoing negotiations between the original conflict parties.

Regional Outlook

Prospects for peace

Prospects for sustainable peace are slim in the short term, with some limited exceptions. In India's Northeast, a final peace deal could be agreed with Naga armed groups in 2021–22. The largely observed ceasefire along the LoC may reduce violence in Kashmir, though further progress is needed for a political resolution of the conflict. India and Pakistan's announcement of a renewed ceasefire along the LoC – initiated through 'back channel' talks – raised the prospects of a potential thaw in relations. If the back-channel talks progress successfully, they could lead to more normalised diplomatic relations, confidence-building measures and the resumption of official bilateral peace talks. However, it is too early to assess the opportunity this may present for a durable reduction in tensions.

The conflicts in Afghanistan, Kashmir, Myanmar and Pakistan have the greatest implications for continued regional and international insecurity. The withdrawal of foreign troops from Afghanistan in 2021 marks an inflection point for outside intervention in the country and region. Kabul remains almost entirely reliant on outside assistance; continued aid from donor countries will likely require the government and Afghan National Defence and Security Forces (ANDSF) to remain cohesive and intact. While the troop withdrawal will satisfy a key Taliban objective and justification for its activities, the development is unlikely to lessen the Taliban's

determination to seize additional territory by force, overrun military outposts and wear down the ANDSF. The Taliban is likely to continue limited peace talks to justify the operation of its diplomatic office in Qatar, while making demands for new prisoner releases and the removal of UN sanctions. However, it is unlikely to engage in substantive negotiations or the compromise necessary to reach a political settlement with the Afghan government without substantial pressure from the international community and its regional backers, including Pakistan.

The February 2021 coup made Myanmar's peace process under the Nationwide Ceasefire Agreement framework appear defunct. The Fourth Union Peace Conference of August 2020 was more symbolic than substantive; several notable signatories suspended their involvement. Though some EAOs may seek stability in their areas of operation by maintaining old ceasefires or upholding informal truces, these are now less likely to be honoured by either side.

Escalation potential and spillover risks

Attacks by Pakistan-based terrorist groups against Indian military targets in India-administered Kashmir in 2016 and 2019 led to brief conventional conflicts that included artillery exchanges, airstrikes and dogfights between fixed-wing aircraft. The unlikely but catastrophic potential for one of these episodes to spark a nuclear exchange is a perennial escalation risk.

In Afghanistan, violence levels are likely to spike after the US and NATO withdrawal as the Taliban seeks to gain territory, while ISIS–KP may attempt to remain relevant by staging large-scale terrorist attacks in urban centres. Afghanistan's increased instability is likely to spill over into Pakistan, as the TTP and ISIS–KP become emboldened.

Myanmar could develop into a multi-front civil war in the borderlands and an armed resistance in urban areas. The Tatmadaw is likely to continue crackdowns in urban centres and attacks on civilian populations in rural areas inhabited by ethnic minorities. Large numbers of refugees are likely to enter Bangladesh but the conflict itself should remain contained, as should low-intensity conflicts including India's CPI–Maoist insurgency and the separatist movements in southern Thailand and the Philippines.

Geopolitical changes

The role of external powers is likely to become more regionalised in the short term as the US and NATO withdraw from Afghanistan. Eurasian powers, including China, India and Russia, will likely be forced to play a larger role in supporting efforts to establish and maintain regional stability, including in Afghanistan and Myanmar. Chinese investment projects across the region, especially in Pakistan's Balochistan province, will continue to encounter attacks from separatist groups and perhaps increasingly from terrorist groups. Despite their mediation efforts, regional and international powers are unlikely to play a major role in Kashmir. Although the coup in Myanmar was broadly condemned by the international community, Russia and China blocked the imposition of UN sanctions against the military government, meaning the country's political and military conflicts have continued to play out in relative isolation.

The geographies of transnational militant groups are also changing: they are likely to increase their operations in South Asia following the withdrawal of US and NATO forces from Afghanistan, while reducing their presence in Southeast Asia, including in the Philippines, where the number of foreign terrorist fighters is ebbing.

Notes

[1] The dramatic developments in the Afghanistan conflict in mid-2021, which culminated with the Taliban's takeover of Afghanistan in August, are not covered in the Regional Analysis. See addendum to the Afghanistan chapter for a brief analysis of these developments.

[2] NATO, 'Nato and Afghanistan', 9 June 2021.

[3] United Nations High Commissioner for Refugees, 'UN Appeals for US$877 Million for Rohingya Refugee Response in Bangladesh', 3 March 2020.

AFGHANISTAN

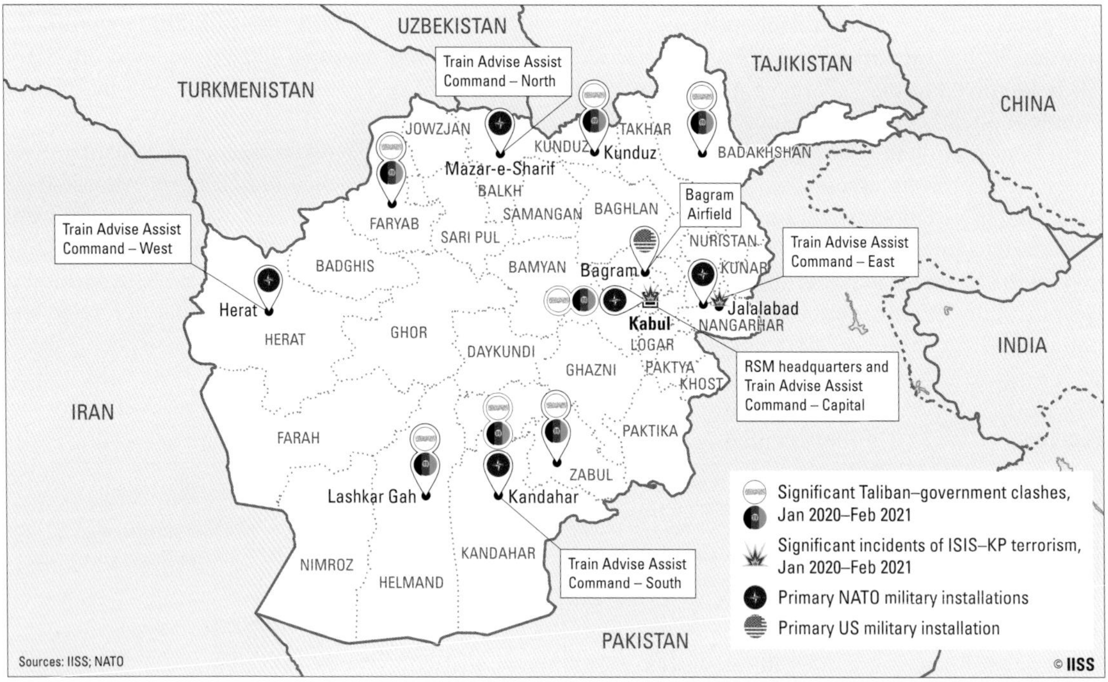
UZBEKISTAN
TURKMENISTAN
TAJIKISTAN
CHINA
IRAN
INDIA
PAKISTAN
Train Advise Assist Command – North
Train Advise Assist Command – West
Train Advise Assist Command – East
Train Advise Assist Command – South
RSM headquarters and Train Advise Assist Command – Capital
Bagram Airfield
JOWZJAN
KUNDUZ
TAKHAR
BADAKHSHAN
BALKH
SAMANGAN
BAGHLAN
FARYAB
SARI PUL
NURISTAN
KUNAR
BADGHIS
BAMYAN
HERAT
GHOR
DAYKUNDI
LOGAR
NANGARHAR
GHAZNI
PAKTYA
KHOST
PAKTIKA
FARAH
ZABUL
NIMROZ
HELMAND
KANDAHAR
Mazar-e-Sharif
Kunduz
Herat
Bagram
Kabul
Jalalabad
Lashkar Gah
Kandahar
Significant Taliban–government clashes, Jan 2020–Feb 2021
Significant incidents of ISIS–KP terrorism, Jan 2020–Feb 2021
Primary NATO military installations
Primary US military installation
Sources: IISS; NATO
© IISS

Overview

The four-decade conflict in Afghanistan has experienced multiple phases, including the 1979–89 Soviet–Afghan War which was fought between the former Soviet Union and a group of Afghan militias collectively referred to as the mujahideen and the 1992–96 Afghan Civil War, in which the Taliban consolidated its hold on power in the country. The latest phase began with the United States' invasion of Afghanistan in October 2001, which followed the 9/11 terrorist attacks. At its outset the invasion set out to destroy the al-Qaeda terrorist organisation. However, the objective expanded to include the overthrow of the Taliban regime after its then-leader Mullah Omar refused to hand over the al-Qaeda founder, Osama bin Laden, to the US. In November 2001, using a combination of special forces and conventional units and a strategic partnership with the Northern Alliance (an anti-Taliban group formed in 1996), the US-led operation removed the Taliban regime from power. As a result, the Taliban's structure and leadership quickly dissipated. In December 2001, the Bonn Conference set the groundwork for a new government of Afghanistan headed by Hamid Karzai and led to the creation of the International Security Assistance Force (ISAF) by the United Nations Security Council to train and assist the newly formed Afghan National Defence and Security Forces (ANDSF).

The first three years after the invasion passed relatively smoothly and presidential elections on 9 October 2004 confirmed Karzai as president by a large margin. However, during this period, the low levels of US security presence – which made up the majority of ISAF – and the nascent ANDSF had left space for local strongmen and militia leaders – sometimes backed by US forces – to fill the power vacuum, and also allowed for the Taliban to reconstitute and reorganise in Pakistan. By 2005 Taliban fighters had begun conducting more significant operations in Afghanistan, with violence increasing every year up to 2010. In response, coalition forces began increasing troop numbers and expanding their presence throughout the country. By 2006, ISAF operated in all regions of Afghanistan. The US security personnel deployed in Afghanistan peaked with more

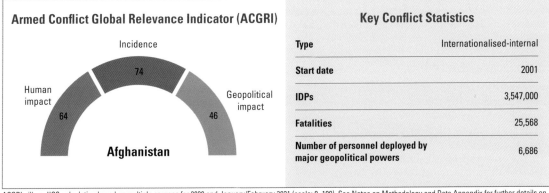

Armed Conflict Global Relevance Indicator (ACGRI)

Incidence

74

Human impact

64

Geopolitical impact

46

Afghanistan

Key Conflict Statistics

Type	Internationalised-internal
Start date	2001
IDPs	3,547,000
Fatalities	25,568
Number of personnel deployed by major geopolitical powers	6,686

ACGRI pillars: IISS calculation based on multiple sources for 2020 and January/February 2021 (scale: 0–100). See Notes on Methodology and Data Appendix for further details on Key Conflict Statistics.

than 100,000 in 2010–11 as part of then-president Barack Obama's surge strategy before falling again to approximately 9,000 by the end of his term.[1] The surge strategy inflicted high costs on the Taliban but a significant number of districts remained contested or fell as foreign troop numbers withdrew from more remote outposts.

In autumn 2018, then-US president Donald Trump appointed Zalmay Khalilzad as Special Representative for Afghanistan Reconciliation. On 28 January 2019, Khalilzad announced that the Taliban and the US had agreed, in principle, to the framework of a deal, which was signed on 29 February 2020. The deal called for the release of up to 5,000

Taliban prisoners held by the Afghan government, the eventual removal of US and UN sanctions on the Taliban, and the gradual reduction of US forces stationed in the country leading to a full withdrawal by May 2021. In exchange, the Taliban agreed to release 1,000 Afghan prisoners, participate in negotiations with the Afghan government and provide counter-terrorism assurances. However, contested election results and a dispute over prisoner releases delayed the start of intra-Afghan negotiations from March until September 2020. As of February 2021 these remained ongoing without reaching a political settlement. The Taliban maintained high levels of violence until the end of 2020.

Conflict Parties

Afghan National Defence and Security Forces (ANDSF)

Strength: 270,400, including 178,800 under the Afghan National Army and the Afghan Air Force, and 91,600 paramilitary and Afghan National Police.

Areas of operation: Operates in all 34 provinces but with more limited freedom of movement in areas controlled or contested by the Taliban. The government controls 133 districts, where 85.9% of the population lives, and the Taliban contests 187 and controls 75 (mostly rural) districts.[2]

Leadership: President Ashraf Ghani (commander-in-chief), Asadullah Khalid (minister of defence) and General Mohammad Yasin Zia (chief of general staff).

Structure: Organised under the minister of defence and the chief of general staff with five regional commands (or corps) – the 201st in Kabul, the 203rd in Gardez, the 205th in Kandahar, the 207th in Herat and the 209th in Mazar-e-Sharif. Separate commands exist for the Kabul military training centre, the military academy and the general staff college.

History: Established in 2002 following the collapse of the Taliban regime. Slow initial growth with only 27,000 troops by 2005, but increased after the Taliban resurgence. New commandos began training and entered service in 2007. Took full responsibility for security in Afghanistan in 2015 after the official end of combat operations by coalition forces in 2014. In practice, the ANDSF is still highly dependent on foreign aid, training, and direct and indirect operational support.

Objectives: (Aspires to) control all districts within Afghanistan without any challenge from non-state actors.

Opponents: The Taliban, Islamic State in Khorasan Province (ISIS–KP) and other anti-government forces.

Affiliates/allies: Relies on US support through the Bilateral Security Agreement of 2014. The US continues to pay salaries for the security forces.

Afghan National Defence and Security Forces (ANDSF)

Resources/capabilities: The US spent an estimated US$4.2 billion directly on Afghan security forces in 2020 and requested US$4bn for 2021.[3] The ANDSF has 174 aircraft (including fixed-wing platforms and helicopters), artillery, mortars, armoured vehicles and drones. However, it lacks the human resources needed to maintain and operate its aircraft and is therefore reliant upon support from foreign advisers.[4]

The Taliban

Strength: 60,000 core fighters (estimate).[5]

Areas of operation: Maintains 'shadow governments' in the districts it controls throughout the country and has named shadow provincial governors in all 34 provinces. As of January 2021, the group continued to carry out large-scale attacks in major cities and controlled an estimated 75 districts while contesting a further 187 districts.

Leadership: Led by Mullah Haibatullah Akhundzada. Together with deputies Sirajuddin Haqqani (leader of the Haqqani network) and Mullah Mohammad Yaqoob (son of Taliban founder Mullah Mohammad Omar), he heads the Quetta Shura, which directs the military campaign against the Afghan government and coalition forces.

Structure: Formally, the Taliban consists of the leader and deputy leaders, executive offices, a shura (leadership council) and 12 commissions covering military affairs, political affairs, economic affairs, education, prisoners, martyrs and disabled members, as well as the Council of Ulema (Council of Senior Religious Scholars). The organisation is historically polycentric, but power is increasingly concentrated in the Quetta Shura and among the top leaders.

History: The Taliban (translated as 'the students') movement began in the Afghan refugee camps of Pakistan following the 1979 Soviet invasion and occupation of Afghanistan. Under Mullah Omar, the group entered the Afghan Civil War in 1994 with the capture of Kandahar city. Taliban fighters quickly conquered other areas of Afghanistan and it officially ruled as an Islamic emirate from 1996 to 2001, though it never controlled the whole country.

Objectives: Since the US invasion in 2001, its main goal is the expulsion of foreign troops, the overthrow of the Kabul government (considered a foreign puppet), the dissolution of the 2004 Afghan constitution and a return to a strict Islamic government modelled on an emirate.

Opponents: US and NATO-led forces, the Afghan government and ISIS–KP.

Affiliates/allies: Connections of varying formalities with a variety of other non-state armed groups in South Asia, including al-Qaeda, the Haqqani network, the Islamic Movement of Uzbekistan and the Tehrik-e-Taliban Pakistan (TTP).

Resources/capabilities: Estimates of the Taliban's annual revenue range from US$300 million to US$1.6bn.[6] Much of this revenue comes from the group's involvement in the drug trade, extortion practices or from taxes collected in the territory it controls. However, projected figures for the group's revenue vary, especially that which is gained from the drug trade.[7] Interviews with current and former fighters have shown that donations from Persian Gulf charities and wealthy individuals have increased significantly in recent years.[8] The Taliban has local and expeditionary units that use small arms, mortars, improvised explosive devices (IEDs), vehicle-borne IEDs (VBIEDs) and unencrypted communications equipment. It also benefits from equipment lost or sold by, or stolen from, the ANDSF, including night-vision goggles, armoured vehicles and weapons optics.

Islamic State in Khorasan Province (ISIS–KP)

Strength: 2,500–4,000 (estimate).[9]

Areas of operation: Primarily confined to a small region of Nangarhar province in eastern Afghanistan but has also had small presences in Helmand, Jowzjan, Kunar and Zabul provinces.

Leadership: Led by Shahab al-Muhajir. The original leader, Hafiz Saeed Khan (previously head of the TTP Orakzai faction), was killed in a US drone strike in July 2016. Successive leaders were also either killed in US strikes or arrested.[10]

Structure: An Islamist militant organisation, formally affiliated with the larger Islamic State, also known as ISIS or ISIL, of which it is the Central and South Asia branch.

History: Formed and pledged loyalty to then-ISIS leader Abu Bakr al-Baghdadi in October 2014. The initial membership primarily comprised disgruntled and estranged members of the TTP.

Objectives: Similar to ISIS, ISIS–KP maintains both local and global ambitions to establish a caliphate in Central and South Asia to be governed under a strict Islamic system, modelled after the group's own interpretation of a caliphate.

Opponents: Mainly focuses on fighting the government in Kabul and international forces in Afghanistan, but also frequently clashes with the Taliban and Pakistani security forces.

Affiliates/allies: ISIS.

Resources/capabilities: Since its founding in 2014, ISIS has invested in improving ISIS–KP's organisation and capabilities. However, with the decline of its territory in Iraq and Syria, ISIS has fewer resources to invest in foreign networks and therefore its investment in ISIS–KP has declined. ISIS–KP relies on small arms, IEDs and VBIEDs.

Al-Qaeda

Strength: 400–600 fighters in Afghanistan.[11]

Areas of operation: The mountainous region between Afghanistan and Pakistan.

Leadership: Led by Ayman al-Zawahiri since 2011.

Structure: Below Zawahiri and his immediate advisers, maintains a shura council and committees for communications, finance and military operations.

History: Created as a broad alliance structure by Arab fighters who travelled to Afghanistan and Pakistan to fight against the Soviet invasion in the 1980s. The organisation (officially formed in 1988) was initially led by Osama bin Laden, who envisioned it as a base for a global jihadist movement to train operatives and to support other jihadist organisations throughout the world. The group was responsible for a number of high-profile terrorist attacks against the US, including the 9/11 attacks. Bin Laden was killed in a US special-operations raid in Abbottabad, Pakistan, in 2011.

Objectives: Focus has always been to fight the 'far enemy' (the West) and particularly the US, which supports current Middle Eastern regimes, and bring about Islamist governance in the Muslim world. Its affiliate groups often pursue local objectives independent of the goals and strategy of the central organisation.

Opponents: US and other Western countries supporting non-Islamic regimes.

Affiliates/allies: Currently maintains an affiliation with five groups: al-Qaeda in the Islamic Maghreb (AQIM) in North Africa, al-Qaeda in the Arabian Peninsula (AQAP) in Yemen, al-Qaeda in the Indian Subcontinent (AQIS) in South Asia, Jabhat Al-Nusra in Syria and al-Shabaab in Somalia. As of 2020, it still maintains a strong relationship with the Taliban.[12]

Resources/capabilities: Capable of engaging in complex terrorist attacks on hard and soft targets. It has also provided military advice to the Afghan Taliban.

Resolute Support Mission (RSM), including *Operation Freedom's Sentinel*. Formerly International Security Assistance Force (ISAF) and *Operation Enduring Freedom*

Strength: NATO countries and partners contribute 9,592 personnel to the *Resolute Support Mission* (RSM), including 2,500 US troops as part of *Operation Freedom's Sentinel*. After the US, the four countries contributing the most troops are Germany (1,300), Italy (895), Georgia (860) and the United Kingdom (750).[13]

Areas of operation: *Operation Freedom's Sentinel* conducts counter-terrorism missions throughout the country and the RSM maintains a central command in Kabul, with supporting commands in Mazar-e-Sharif, Herat, Kandahar and Laghman.

Leadership: General Austin Scott Miller (commander of both US forces and the NATO mission in Afghanistan since September 2018).

Structure: Coalition forces in Afghanistan are divided into two missions: US forces focusing on counter-terrorism under *Operation Freedom's Sentinel* and NATO forces focusing on training and advising under the RSM.

History: Coalition forces entered Afghanistan in 2001 and ISAF was created in accordance with the 2001 Bonn Conference. With the official conclusion of offensive combat operations by foreign forces in 2014, ISAF became the RSM and US forces transitioned from *Operation Enduring Freedom* to *Operation Freedom's Sentinel*.

Objectives: Continue supporting the government in Kabul in the country's democratisation and development. Prevent the rise of transnational terrorist organisations that might use Afghanistan as a base to plan and coordinate international attacks.

Opponents: The Taliban insurgency (although the ANDSF are the primary actors engaging the Taliban) and terrorist groups including al-Qaeda and ISIS–KP.

Affiliates/allies: 36 countries participate in various missions in Afghanistan through the RSM. The UN also maintains a mission in the country to promote peace and stability, the UN Assistance Mission in Afghanistan (UNAMA).

Resources/capabilities: The US has spent nearly US$2 trillion on the conflict in Afghanistan. The estimated annual budget for all US operations, including reconstruction efforts, is approximately US$50bn. The NATO-led mission has sophisticated aircraft, artillery, mortars, High Mobility Artillery Rocket Systems (HIMARS), surveillance drones, armoured vehicles and advanced communications technology.

Conflict Drivers

Political

Democratic legitimacy and governance flaws:
Weak governance and widespread corruption continue to plague Afghanistan. The 2014 presidential election required US-led and UN-backed mediation to resolve the contested results. The 2019 election was also contested and required closed-door negotiation to reach a political settlement, which in turn delayed the beginning of intra-Afghan peace negotiations.

Between May 2009 and 31 December 2019, the Special Inspector General for Afghanistan Reconstruction found US$19bn in waste, fraud and abuse.[14] 95% of respondents to the 2020 Asia Foundation survey stated that corruption was a major problem in Afghanistan.[15] Faith in institutions is also lacking, with only 53.9% of Afghans believing that the Afghan National Police improves security in the country, although this represents a notable increase from 36.4% in 2019.[16]

Economic and social

Ideological and subnational divisions:

Ideological and ethnic divisions are a major driver of violence and have fuelled conflict in Afghanistan over the past 43 years. The country has at least 14 ethnic groups and is divided along urban–rural and sectarian lines. The ethnic dimension of the conflict stems from the fact that the Afghan government comprises stakeholders from multiple ethnic groups, including Pashtuns, while the Taliban is a Pashtun-dominated insurgency, although it does have members from other groups. While the ethnic component of the conflict should not be exaggerated, ethnic polarisation is indeed a major obstacle to consensus building that inhibits the agreement of a political settlement. Loyalty to ethnicity and patronage networks often rivals national identity and polarisation is further fuelled by the perception that foreign aid is both misallocated and distributed unequally across regions and social classes. Low economic development, which leads to aid dependency, also fuels corruption.

Liberal democracy, civic liberties and women's rights were difficult to reconcile with the Islamist form of governance pursued by the Taliban in the 1990s and which it is seeking to restore. Opportunities for upward economic mobility are rare in Afghanistan, especially for women, as shown by the country's rank (169th out of 189) in the UN Development Programme's Gender Inequality Index.[17]

International

Third parties' involvement:

The continued presence of coalition troops, regional support for the Taliban and other forms of covert and overt intervention in Afghan domestic affairs are key drivers of the conflict. The Taliban's primary goal remains the withdrawal of all foreign troops followed by the overthrow of the Afghan government. The Taliban is enabled by a diverse group of foreign donors and sponsors which have included China, private Gulf donors, at times Iran, and most importantly Pakistan. The Taliban also relies on safe havens in Pakistan and coordinates its operations through leadership councils in Quetta. Pakistan's primary interest in supporting the Taliban is to prevent Afghanistan from aligning with India. While Iran and the Taliban were historic enemies, the former's Islamic Revolutionary Guard Corps has periodically provided financial support and training to the latter to encourage their opposition to and harassment of US troops.

Without external funding, the Taliban's fighting capacity would be significantly diminished. The ANDSF funding model also relies completely on foreign aid, almost entirely from the US, and its combat capabilities depend largely on direct and indirect US operational support. One analysis concluded that if US troops were to leave Afghanistan, 'the Taliban would enjoy a slight military advantage that would increase in a compounding manner over time.'[18]

Political and Military Developments

The US–Taliban agreement

On 29 February 2020, the Taliban and the US signed the Agreement for Bringing Peace to Afghanistan ('US–Taliban agreement').[19] This agreement called for the release of up to 5,000 Taliban prisoners by the Afghan government, the eventual removal of US and UN sanctions on the Taliban, and the gradual reduction of US forces towards a full withdrawal by May 2021. In exchange, the Taliban agreed to participate in intra-Afghan negotiations with the Afghan government, work towards a ceasefire and a political settlement, and prevent any group (including al-Qaeda) from using Afghan soil to threaten the security of the US and its allies.

Challenging intra-Afghan negotiations

Intra-Afghan negotiations did not begin in March 2020, as originally outlined by the US–Taliban agreement, due to delays in prisoner releases and a dispute between President Ghani and his political rival Abdullah Abdullah over the 2019 election results. The Trump administration threatened to withhold US$1bn in aid to the Afghan government, which prompted some compromise between the two politicians.[20] Intra-Afghan negotiations finally began on 12 September 2020 but were marred by a Taliban offensive on the outer areas of the capital of Helmand province, Lashkar Gah. The two sides did not reach an agreement on rules and procedures for negotiating substantive questions until 2 December 2020. Shortly after this breakthrough, the Afghan government and the Taliban announced a 22-day recess from negotiations. Negotiations briefly resumed in January 2021 and then abruptly ended as Taliban leaders visited foreign countries, including Iran and Russia, to bolster regional support. Talks resumed once again in late February 2021.

Continued Taliban violence

The dynamics of the conflict in Afghanistan changed significantly once the Taliban and the Afghan government initiated intra-Afghan negotiations. Nevertheless, the Taliban continued to maintain high levels of violent activity, seeing it as its primary source of leverage over the US and the Afghan government. The Afghanistan National Security Council reported that the Taliban conducted 2,804 attacks between 1 March and 19 April 2020, which it claimed violated the US–Taliban agreement.[21] Ghani views a ceasefire as a necessary precondition to peace talks, but this has been rejected by the Taliban. However, the US–Taliban agreement significantly lowered the levels of violence faced by coalition troops. Four US combat deaths occurred in January and early February of 2020 and as of 8 February 2021, the US had gone a full year without suffering a single combat death in Afghanistan.[22] This reduction in US fatalities was the combined result of both the US–Taliban agreement and the decline in US operational tempo. Other NATO troops also benefited from the reduction in violence aimed at foreign troops but were already largely disengaged from active combat operations prior to the US–Taliban agreement. ISIS–KP faced considerable pressure from both the Taliban and US and Afghan government forces in 2020, resulting in a significant decrease in its territory. However, the organisation still remained capable of carrying out attacks against US and Afghan forces.

Key Events in 2020–21

POLITICAL EVENTS

29 February 2020
The US and the Taliban sign the Agreement for Bringing Peace to Afghanistan.

9 March
Ashraf Ghani and Abdullah Abdullah both take the oath of presidential office following a dispute over the 2019 election results.

17 May
Ghani and Abdullah sign a power-sharing agreement to end the election dispute. Ghani remains president.

26 May
The Afghan government releases 900 Taliban prisoners.

MILITARY/VIOLENT EVENTS

8 February 2020
Last two US service members killed in combat prior to the signing of the US–Taliban agreement.

22 February
Ahead of the signing of the US–Taliban agreement, a seven-day 'reduction in violence' begins.

22–28 March
Taliban attacks ANDSF positions in Zabul province, killing 37, and initiates assaults in Kunduz, Faryab and Badakhshan.

25 April
The Afghanistan National Security Council reports that the Taliban conducted 2,804 attacks between 1 March and 19 April.

12 May
An unclaimed attack on a Kabul maternity ward kills 24 people.

18 June
The US reports a reduction in its troop levels to 8,600, in compliance with the US–Taliban agreement.

14 July
The Pentagon announces that US forces have withdrawn from five of their bases in Afghanistan to comply with the US–Taliban agreement.

Asia

31 July

The Taliban and ANDSF begin a three-day ceasefire for Eid al-Adha.

2–3 August

ISIS–KP attacks a prison in Jalalabad and kills 29 people.

3 September

The Afghan government agrees to release 5,000 Taliban prisoners to begin intra-Afghan negotiations.

9 September

In an unsuccessful assassination attempt, Afghan First Vice-President Amrullah Saleh's convoy is targeted with a roadside-bomb attack that leaves ten dead.

10 September

US secretary of defense Mark Esper announces that US troop levels in Afghanistan will fall below 5,000 by the end of November.

12 October

The Taliban launches an offensive on the provincial capital of Helmand province, Lashkar Gah.

24 October

ISIS–KP kills 24 people in Kabul in a suicide-bomb attack.

24 November

Donor countries pledge US$12bn in aid to Afghanistan for the period 2021–24, with at least US$3.3bn to be distributed in the first year.

2 November

ISIS–KP storms Kabul University and kills 22 people.

2 December

The Afghan government and the Taliban reach agreement on procedures to discuss substantive issues during intra-Afghan negotiations. The Taliban announces a 22-day recess shortly after.

17 November

US acting secretary of defense Christopher Miller announces that US troop levels in Afghanistan will decrease to 2,500.

December

The Taliban attacks checkpoints in districts surrounding Kandahar city.

5 January 2021

Negotiations between the Taliban and the Afghan government resume but quickly lose momentum.

15 January 2021

US Department of Defense announces that US troop levels have dropped to 2,500.

26–28 January

Taliban delegations travel to Iran and Russia to seek regional support for their negotiating positions.

Impact

Human rights and humanitarian

While UNAMA reported a 15% decrease in civilian casualties in 2020 compared to 2019 and the total fell below 10,000 for the first time since 2013, the 3,035 Afghans killed and 5,785 injured over the year was still significant. There was an uptick in civilian casualties between October and December 2020 compared to the rest of the year, caused, in part, by the breakdown in intra-Afghan negotiations and by high rates of Taliban-led violence and unclaimed terrorist attacks. Civilian casualties during this three-month period increased by 45% compared to the same period in 2019.[23] Targeted killings of Afghan journalists, academics and activists increased in

2020, as did the opacity of the conflict since many of these attacks went unclaimed. Conflict-induced displacements decreased in 2020, with 404,139 internally displaced persons (IDPs) recorded by the UN compared to 460,603 in 2019,[24] which is consistent with the slight reduction in overall violence inflicted on civilians. In contrast, 2021 is on track to be one of the deadliest years in the history of the war.

Political stability

The Afghan government's hold remained relatively stable in the areas under its control, including Kabul and the majority of provincial capitals in 2020, despite patterns of violence targeting members of

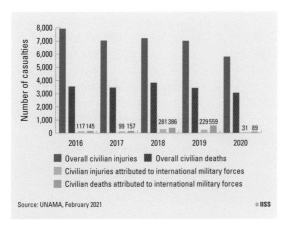

Figure 1: Trends in civilian casualties in Afghanistan, 2016–20

US$12bn in aid to the country over a period of four years, but with strict governance conditions attached.[26]

Relations with neighbouring and international partners and geopolitical implications

Intra-Afghan negotiations and the announcement that the US intends to withdraw all remaining troops from Afghanistan were by far the most impactful developments of the conflict in 2020 and early 2021. As October 2020 marked the 19-year anniversary of the US involvement in Afghanistan, the Trump administration prioritised efforts to withdraw US troops from the country, making its partnership with the Afghan government and the ANDSF increasingly tense. In March 2020, the Trump administration threatened to withhold US$1bn in aid to the Afghan government to break the stalemate between President Ghani and his political rival Abdullah Abdullah that was obstructing the intra-Afghan negotiations aimed at ending the war. Following Joe Biden's election in November 2020, the Taliban leadership engaged in diplomatic outreach to gain regional support from its allies both for its continued use of violence during negotiations with the Afghan government and for its aim to initiate new military operations against NATO troops should they remain in Afghanistan beyond the May 2021 withdrawal deadline. In December 2020, a Taliban delegation visited Islamabad to meet with Prime Minister Imran Khan and later with Pakistan's foreign minister, Shah Mahmood Qureshi, who expressed implicit support for the Taliban's position that successful negotiations must precede a ceasefire. A Taliban delegation also travelled to Iran and Russia in early 2021, and Russian Special Envoy for Afghanistan Zamir Kabulov publicly supported the Taliban's position that the US should adhere to the May withdrawal deadline.

Afghan civil society and government figures. Such incidents included an assassination attempt on First Vice-President Amrullah Saleh in September 2020, and the targeted killing of Yousuf Rashid, who headed the Free and Fair Election Foundation of Afghanistan, in December 2020. As of February 2021, uncertainty over the potential withdrawal of US troops, rising levels of violence and the targeting of officials had fuelled public debate over the long-term viability of the Afghan government, though the immediate stability held firm.

Economic and social

Afghanistan entered the coronavirus pandemic with an already floundering economy. The IMF estimated that Afghanistan's real GDP shrank by 5% in 2020, but it is predicted to recover by 4% in 2021.[25] As a result of the pandemic, tax revenue from the sales of goods declined and cross-border trade was disrupted, especially with Pakistan. Afghanistan remained dependent on foreign assistance and at a Geneva meeting in November 2020, a number of international donor countries pledged a combined

Conflict Outlook

Political scenarios

The US remains the most consequential foreign actor affecting Afghanistan's short-term trajectory, given its position as the primary source of ANDSF military support and given the Taliban's explicit objective for their troop withdrawal. In April 2021, the Biden administration announced its intention to withdraw

the remainder of US troops from Afghanistan by no later than 11 September 2021.

This date will keep US and NATO troops in Afghanistan beyond the May 2021 withdrawal deadline included in the US–Taliban agreement. However, so long as the Taliban determines a level of active engagement by the US and NATO in troop withdrawal, the trend of low US combat deaths will likely continue. While violence between the Taliban and foreign troops is likely to remain low, clashes between the Taliban and the ANDSF, as well as incidents of targeted killings and terrorism, are likely to remain high and even increase, particularly during the warm spring and summer months. The Taliban will attempt to consolidate territorial gains. Without the presence of foreign troops also fighting the Taliban, the latter will have little incentive to participate meaningfully in negotiations with the Afghan government since it calculates that it has the military advantage. In the absence of a negotiated political settlement, the Taliban would likely gradually capture provincial capitals and may eventually gain control of Kabul. In this scenario, the US and other international actors would likely attempt to use airstrikes, international aid, sanctions relief and global recognition as leverage to induce the Taliban to return to the negotiating table with the Afghan government. The success of such a strategy would depend on how much value the Taliban assigns to establishing its own international legitimacy and the continued cohesion of the Afghan government.

The Taliban's targeting of ANDSF, Afghan government officials, journalists, academics, civil society and especially women in public roles is likely to continue. The Taliban is also very likely to conduct assaults on provincial capitals. The success of ANDSF attempts to repel these Taliban attacks and to regain control over urban centres already held or subsequently captured by the Taliban will likely depend on the availability of continued foreign air support and cohesion within ANDSF units. If NATO troops were still present in Afghanistan at this point, calls for increased deployment could arise. However, Washington would likely continue back-channel diplomacy with the Taliban during this period in order to restart negotiations toward a political settlement.

Whether or not foreign troops remain in the country, a negotiated political settlement to end the conflict in Afghanistan seems unlikely. The US–Taliban agreement was not fully implemented because both the Taliban as a party to the agreement, and the Afghan government as a reluctant beneficiary, applied a maximalist interpretation in their own favour. For example, the Taliban interpreted the clause calling for the release of 'up to five thousand (5,000) prisoners' to mean no less than 5,000. While not a party to the agreement, the Afghan government also applied a broad interpretation of its obligations to the Taliban, which obstructed the subsequent intra-Afghan negotiations. Notably, the US–Taliban agreement did not explicitly condition the US troop withdrawal on the successful completion of a political settlement between the Taliban and the Afghan government.

Escalation potential and conflict-related risks

A collapse of the Islamic Republic of Afghanistan in the short term is improbable. However, levels of violence are likely to rise regardless of developments with the peace negotiations. The most likely near-term outcome, leaving aside the US troop withdrawal, is an escalation in clashes between the Taliban and the ANDSF outside major urban centres, combined with targeted killings and terrorism inside Afghanistan's cities.

Prospects for peace

Prospects for peace in 2021 are limited. The Taliban's vision of governance and for a new constitution for Afghanistan, based on its version of Islam, is incompatible with the liberal-democratic model of an Islamic republic embraced by the post-Bonn political order.[27] Those who have benefited from the established system will not want to alter it or to relinquish power to the Taliban, as already evidenced by Ghani's resistance to the proposal of an interim government. Some actors within the Afghan government view the inclusion of the Taliban in the country's political system as an existential threat. Meanwhile, the Taliban is unlikely to accept a power-sharing agreement with the sitting Afghan government especially given its military advantage over the ANDSF.

Strategic implications and global influences

Regional powers, Afghanistan's immediate neighbours and factions within Afghanistan have all expressed support for a political settlement to end the conflict. However, there is little consensus over how to successfully negotiate such a settlement and what the acceptable terms of a peace deal and the model for a future government might be. The failure of the intra-Afghan negotiations to reach a compromise on substantive issues and the Taliban's ongoing high levels of violence diminish the chances of reaching a durable negotiated settlement that could be successfully implemented. The lack of a willing and neutral third party to monitor and enforce a potential negotiated settlement also lowers any chance of long-term durability. An increasingly unstable Afghanistan that descends into civil war could attract regional actors to back local proxies, thus plunging the country deeper into conflict.

Afghanistan Conflict Report – August 2021 Addendum

Several deeply significant events took place in Afghanistan in July and August 2021, including the withdrawal of most foreign troops, the collapse of the Afghan government and Afghan National Defence and Security Forces (ANDSF), and the expansion of Taliban territorial control across most of Afghanistan, including Kabul.

The Taliban made rapid gains throughout July in northern Afghanistan, taking dozens of districts.[28] Some poorly supplied ANDSF outposts fell with little to no resistance and elite units became increasingly overstretched.[29] The Taliban engaged in information operations to demoralise the ANDSF rank and file, spreading images of surrendering units.[30] It also used local elders and powerbrokers to facilitate surrenders. On 25 June, President Ashraf Ghani met with US President Joe Biden in the White House to secure continued American support for his administration and to convince Biden to partially reverse his decision to withdraw all US troops by 31 August.[31] The Biden administration remained steadfast in its commitment to withdraw troops but did provide some air support to the ANDSF in July.

In August, the Taliban rapidly seized border posts and provincial capitals, eventually capturing major cities such as Herat. On 15 August, the Taliban entered Kabul without a fight and Ghani and other senior Afghan officials fled. Prominent militia leaders Ata Noor and Abdul Rashid Dostum also fled the country following fighting in the north.[32] A potential meeting between remaining Afghan leaders and the Taliban to establish an interim government never occurred and the Taliban declared an Emirate. As of late August, the US has deployed approximately 6,000 troops to Kabul's Hamid Karzai International Airport (along with troops from other NATO members) to facilitate the mass evacuation of remaining US citizens, former interpreters and Afghans admitted on humanitarian grounds.

Although the withdrawal of foreign troops and rapid increase in the Taliban's territorial control suggest overall violence levels will decrease in Afghanistan, pockets of anti-Taliban resistance may still occur, especially in the Panjshir Valley. Incidents of targeted killings and violence against civilians by the Taliban will also likely continue, as will terrorist attacks by groups such as the Islamic State in Khorasan Province. Risks to regional and international stability also loom.

The latest developments will be covered in depth in *The Armed Conflict Survey 2022*, which will have a reporting period of March 2021–March 2022.

Notes

[1] Special Inspector General for Afghanistan Reconstruction, 'Quarterly Report to the United States Congress', 30 April 2018, Figure 3.32, p. 90.

[2] Bill Roggio, 'Mapping Taliban Control in Afghanistan', *FDD's Long War Journal*.

[3] United States Department of Defense, 'Defense Budget Overview: United States Department of Defense Fiscal Year 2021 Budget Request', 13 May 2020, p. 64.

[4] Jonathan Schroden, 'Afghanistan's Security Forces Versus the Taliban: A Net Assessment', *CTC Sentinel*, vol. 14, no. 1, January 2021, pp. 20–9.

[5] *Ibid.*

[6] *Ibid.*

[7] David Mansfield, 'Understanding Control and Influence: What Opium Poppy and Tax Reveal About the Writ of the Afghan State', Afghanistan Research and Evaluation Unit, August 2017.

[8] Antonio Giustozzi, *The Taliban at War, 2001–2018* (London: Hurst, 2019).

[9] United Nations Security Council, 'Twenty-fourth Report of the Analytical Support and Sanctions Monitoring Team Submitted Pursuant to Resolution 2368 (2017) Concerning ISIL (Da'esh), Al-Qaida and Associated Individuals and Entities', S/2019/570, 15 July 2019, p. 15.

[10] Andrew Mines and Amira Jadoon, 'Can the Islamic State's Afghan Province Survive Its Leadership Losses?', Lawfare, 17 May 2020. See also Amira Jadoon and Andrew Mines, 'Broken, but Not Defeated: An Examination of State-led Operations

Against Islamic State Khorasan in Afghanistan and Pakistan (2015–2018)', Combating Terrorism Center, March 2020.

11 United Nations Security Council, 'Twenty-sixth Report of the Analytical Support and Sanctions Monitoring Team Submitted Pursuant to Resolution 2368 (2017) Concerning ISIL (Da'esh), Al-Qaida and Associated Individuals and Entities', S/2020/717, 23 July 2020, p. 15.

12 Asfandyar Mir, 'Afghanistan's Terrorism Challenge: The Political Trajectories of Al-Qaeda, the Afghan Taliban, and the Islamic State', Middle East Institute Policy Paper, October 2020.

13 North Atlantic Treaty Organization, 'Resolute Support Mission (RSM): Key Facts and Figures', February 2021.

14 Special Inspector General for Afghanistan Reconstruction, 'Quarterly Report to the United States Congress', 30 October 2020, p. 25.

15 The Asia Foundation, 'Afghanistan Flash Surveys on Perceptions of Peace, COVID-19, and the Economy: Wave 1 Findings', 23 November 2020, p. 71.

16 Ibid., p. 37.

17 United Nations Development Programme, 'Human Development Report 2020', 15 December 2020, p. 363.

18 Schroden, 'Afghanistan's Security Forces Versus the Taliban: A Net Assessment', p. 27.

19 US Department of State, 'Agreement for Bringing Peace to Afghanistan Between the Islamic Emirate of Afghanistan Which Is Not Recognized by the United States as a State and Is Known as the Taliban and the United States of America', 29 February 2020.

20 Pamela Constable and John Hudson, 'U.S. Vows to Cut $1 Billion in Aid to Afghanistan as Political Crisis Threatens Peace Deal', Washington Post, 23 March 2020.

21 Khaled Nikzad, 'Taliban Initiated 2,804 Attacks Post-peace Deal: Official', Tolo News, 25 April 2020.

22 Phillip Walter Wellman, 'US Goes One Year Without a Combat Death in Afghanistan as Taliban Warn Against Reneging on Peace Deal', Stars and Stripes, 8 February 2021.

23 United Nations Assistance Mission in Afghanistan, 'Afghanistan Protection of Civilians in Armed Conflict: Annual Report 2020', February 2021, p. 11–12.

24 United Nations Office for the Coordination of Humanitarian Affairs, 'Afghanistan – Conflict Induced Displacements in 2020', March 2021; and United Nations Office for the Coordination of Humanitarian Affairs, 'Afghanistan – Conflict Induced Displacements in 2019', March 2020.

25 International Monetary Fund, 'World Economic Outlook Database', April 2021.

26 'Foreign Aid to Afghanistan Could Reach $12 Billion Over Four Years, Some with Conditions', Reuters, 24 November 2020.

27 This consisted of developments which followed the 2001 Bonn Conference, including the establishment of the transitional government, the elevation of certain political elites, the new 2004 Afghanistan constitution and the 2004 presidential elections.

28 Thomas Gibbons-Neff and Najim Rahim, 'Taliban Enter Key Cities in Afghanistan's North After Swift Offensive', New York Times, 6 August 2021; and Susannah George, 'Taliban's Rapid Advance Across Afghanistan Puts Key Cities at Risk of Being Overtaken', Washington Post, 7 July 2021.

29 Thomas Gibbons-Neff and Najim Rahim, 'Elite Afghan Forces Suffer Horrific Casualties as Taliban Advance', New York Times, 7 July 2021.

30 Benjamin Jenson, 'How the Taliban Did It: Inside the "Operational Art" of Its Military Victory', Atlantic Council, 15 August 2021.

31 US, White House, 'Statement by White House Spokesperson Jen Psaki on the Visit of President Ashraf Ghani of Afghanistan and Dr. Abdullah Abdullah, Chairman of the High Council for National Reconciliation', 20 June 2021; and White House, 'Remarks by President Biden on the Drawdown of U.S. Forces in Afghanistan', 8 July 2021.

32 'Afghan Militia Leaders Atta Noor, Dostum Escape "Conspiracy"', Reuters, 14 August 2021; and Ata Mohammad Noor (@Atamohammadnoor), tweet, 14 August 2021.

PAKISTAN

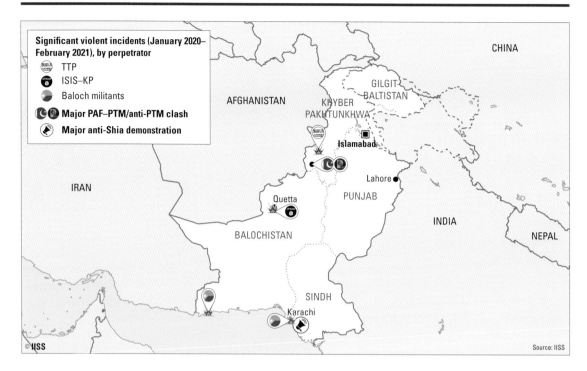

Significant violent incidents (January 2020–February 2021), by perpetrator
- TTP
- ISIS–KP
- Baloch militants
- Major PAF–PTM/anti-PTM clash
- Major anti-Shia demonstration

Overview

Since its formation in 1947, Pakistan has struggled with ethnic and centre–province tensions stemming from the perceived marginalisation of the Baloch, Pashtuns and Sindhis by the Punjabi majority. The secession of East Pakistan to form Bangladesh in 1971 enhanced this dynamic, as it made Punjab the majority province in terms of population.[1] Mass migrations due to the partition of British India had also stoked ethnic tensions, as Urdu-speaking migrants, or Mohajirs, emigrated from present-day northern India to Pakistan's Sindh province. This historical context means that the Pakistani state conflates demands for greater civil liberties and provincial autonomy with violent separatist insurgent movements, primarily in Balochistan and Khyber Pakhtunkhwa (KP).

There is a long history of Baloch insurgency against the state in pursuit of greater autonomy or the outright secession of Balochistan, including campaigns waged in 1948, 1958, 1962 and 1973. The return to violence in 2003 started the phase of the insurgency that continues today. Baloch armed groups have split on several occasions and some

splinter organisations have demobilised. However, since 2018, these groups have partially set aside their differences to form a coalition with the Baloch Republican Army (BRA) under the banner of the Baloch Raaji Ajoi Sangar (BRAS).

Groups originating in KP, particularly Swat district, and Pashtun tribal areas (formerly known as the Federally Administered Tribal Areas, FATA) have also taken up arms against the state and the Shia religious minority. An uptick in Pakistani incursions into the then-FATA to target al-Qaeda members following the 9/11 terrorist attacks stoked animosity, and militant groups coalesced to form what is often referred to as the Pakistani Taliban, which in due course became the Tehrik-e-Taliban Pakistan (TTP). Pakistani forces began a counter-insurgency campaign against the TTP in 2009 but initially lacked a coherent strategy. The December 2014 TTP attack on the Army Public School in Peshawar marked an inflection point and prompted the government to draft its first counter-terrorism policy, the National Action Plan (NAP). *Operation Zarb-e-Azb* and *Operation Radd-ul-Fasaad*, launched

Armed Conflict Global Relevance Indicator (ACGRI)

Incidence

5

Human impact

2

Geopolitical impact

4

Pakistan

Key Conflict Statistics

Type	Internal | Localised insurgency
Start date	2003
IDPs	104,000
Gini index (0–100)	31.6 (2018)
Functioning of government (0–10)	5.36

ACGRI pillars: ISS calculation based on multiple sources for 2020 and January/February 2021 (scale: 0–100). See Notes on Methodology and Data Appendix for further details on Key Conflict Statistics.

in 2014 and 2017 respectively, led to a significant decrease in insurgent attacks.

2020 saw an uptick in insurgent activity in Balochistan province and along Pakistan's western border with Afghanistan. The TTP grew in strength in the former FATA, particularly Waziristan, and attacked military and civilian targets, reversing some of the gains made by Pakistani forces by 2019. The slow progress of reforms following the 2018 merger of the former FATA into KP strained relations between Pashtun tribes and state authorities. The Pashtun Tahaffuz Movement (PTM) continued to stage protests against alleged abuses of Pashtuns' human, civil and political rights. Clashes between the movement and Pakistani forces in 2020 were less common than in 2019 but senior PTM members continued to face harassment from the state.

The spread of COVID-19 reawakened centre–province tensions between the federal and provincial governments over the 2010 18th Amendment of Pakistan's constitution, which had vested significant authority in provincial governments. Prime Minister Imran Khan and Minister for Planning, Development and Special Initiatives Asad Umar argued that it limited the federal government's ability to respond to the pandemic, among other things. However, provincial governments and opposition political parties largely saw their comments as a blatant attempt by the federal government to reduce provincial autonomy.

Conflict Parties

Pakistan Armed Forces (PAF)

Strength: 651,800 active military, 291,000 active paramilitary.

Areas of operation: Deployed throughout Pakistan (particularly along the Line of Control with India) and against insurgent groups in Balochistan and KP (including the former FATA).

Leadership: General Qamar Javed Bajwa (chief of army staff); Admiral Muhammad Amjad Khan Niazi (chief of naval staff); Air Chief Marshal Mujahid Anwar Khan (chief of air staff); Lieutenant-General Faiz Hamid (Director-General, Inter-Services Intelligence (ISI)). ISI falls outside the military command structure but its leaders are drawn from the military and have significant oversight over some operations.

Structure: The PAF consists of nine 'Corps' commands, an Air Defence Command and a Strategic Forces Command. *Operation Radd-ul-Fasaad* involves an array of PAF units that support the police and the Pakistani Civil Armed Forces (PCAF) in counter-terrorism operations.

History: The ongoing *Operation Radd-ul-Fasaad* succeeded the 2014–17 *Operation Zarb-e-Azb*. It was launched in response to a resurgence in attacks by TTP splinter group Jamaat-ul-Ahrar. *Operation Khyber-4* was launched in 2017 under *Operation Radd-ul-Fasaad* with the goal of eliminating terrorists in what is now Rajgal valley, Khyber district.

Objectives: Eliminate insurgent groups that threaten the Pakistani state.

Opponents: TTP, Balochistan Liberation Army (BLA) and other Baloch separatist groups, ISIS–KP.

Affiliates/allies: PCAF, Pakistani police.

Resources/capabilities: Well-resourced with an array of weapons systems and equipment. The defence budget for 2020 was US$9.3 billion.

Asia

Pakistani Civil Armed Forces (PCAF)

Strength: Unknown.

Areas of operation: Throughout Pakistan but most active fighting is against insurgent groups in Balochistan and KP.

Leadership: Funded by the Interior Ministry, although most divisions are commanded by officers seconded from the PAF.

Structure: The main divisions of the PCAF involved in conflict with insurgent groups and participating in the PAF-led *Operation Radd-ul-Fasaad* are the Frontier Corps (Frontier Corps KP and Frontier Corps Balochistan), the Frontier Constabulary, the Sindh Rangers and the Punjab Rangers. Each group's authority is limited to its respective geographic area.

History: Contributed to *Operation Radd-ul-Fasaad* since its establishment in 2017 and to the Special Security Division since 2016. Some outfits within the PCAF, such as the Frontier Corps, have their origins in the period of British colonial rule.

Objectives: Eliminate insurgent groups that threaten the Pakistani state.

Opponents: TTP, BLA and other Baloch separatist groups, ISKP.

Affiliates/allies: PAF, Pakistani police.

Resources/capabilities: Primarily equipped with small arms and light weapons, with some shorter-range artillery and mortars.

Tehrik-e-Taliban Pakistan (TTP)

Strength: Circa 6,000 in Afghanistan, where the majority of TTP fighters are currently based.[2] Strength in Pakistan unknown; recent analysis suggests several thousand.

Areas of operation: Balochistan, KP.

Leadership: Mufti Noor Wali Mehsud (emir and overarching leader), supported by a central shura council.

Structure: Divided by locality into factions, or constituencies, each of which is led by a local emir and supported by a local shura council, which report to the central shura council. Each faction has a *qazi* (judge) to adjudicate local disputes.

History: Following the 2001 US-led invasion of Afghanistan, al-Qaeda and Taliban militants sought haven in the tribal areas of Pakistan. Operations by the Pakistani – and later by US – forces against al-Qaeda led several groups to form a loose coalition known as the Pakistan Taliban. In 2007, some of these factions unified as the TTP under the leadership of Baitullah Mehsud who was killed in a US airstrike in 2009. A TTP shura elected Hakimullah Mehsud as the organisation's second emir, but internal divisions grew under his leadership

over legitimate targets for attacks and peace talks with the government and worsened under Fazal Hayat (Mullah Fazlullah) between 2013 and 2018, causing several factions to break away, including leaders that formed ISIS–KP in 2014. The 2014 TTP attack on the Army Public School in Peshawar triggered a major PAF counter-offensive, which further weakened the group. Following Hayat's death in 2018, the leadership reverted to the Mehsud clan under Mufti Noor Wali who sought to reunite and rebuild the group. In 2020, this process culminated with the reintegration of the Hizb-ul-Ahrar, Jamaat-ul-Ahrar and Amjad Farouqi groups and the Hakimullah Mehsud faction into the TTP fold.

Objectives: To defend and promote a rigid Islamist ideology in KP, including in the former FATA.

Opponents: PAF, PCAF.

Affiliates/allies: Afghan Taliban, al-Qaeda.

Resources/capabilities: Has access to small arms and improvised explosive devices (IEDs).

Baloch Raaji Ajoi Sangar (BRAS, an alliance that includes the Balochistan Liberation Army, BLA; the Baloch Republican Army, BRA; and the Baloch Liberation Front, BLF)

Strength: Unknown.

Areas of operation: Balochistan.

Leadership: BLA: leadership contested between Hyrbyair Marri and Bashar Zaib; BRA: Brahumdagh Bugti; BLF: Allah Nazar Baloch.

Structure: An alliance of the BLA, BRA and BLF. The BLA is divided into different factions. Pakistan's government alleges that several factions of the BLA exist and are led by different individuals. The insurgency is deeply divided, with different groups, infighting and fragmentation.

History: The alliance was formed in 2018. The BLA is the largest group and was formed in 2000 under the leadership of Afghanistan-based Balach Marri, who was subsequently killed in an airstrike in Helmand in 2007. Its leadership since then has been subject to additional deaths and significant internal contestation. In July 2019, the US State Department listed the BLA as a Specially Designated Global Terrorist organisation.

Objectives: Seeks independence for the region of Balochistan as a solution to perceived discrimination against the Baloch people. Opposes the extraction of natural resources in Balochistan by Pakistani and foreign actors, especially China, due to the implications of the China–Pakistan Economic Corridor (CPEC) for Baloch aspirations.

Opponents: PAF, PCAF.

Affiliates/allies: None.

Resources/capabilities: Attacks by BRAS members have involved small arms and IEDs, including suicide vests and car bombs.

Islamic State in Khorasan Province (ISIS–KP)[3]

Strength: Unclear.

Areas of operation: Balochistan, KP, Afghanistan.

Leadership: Shahab al-Muhajir (emir of ISIS–KP).

Structure: Poorly understood organisational structure. It is likely hierarchical, with an emir at the head, above provincial-level commanders and a shura council, in turn above district-level commanders and local commanders.

History: The Islamic State (also known as ISIS or ISIL) announced the establishment of the ISIS–KP in 2014 by former members of TTP to conduct operations in Afghanistan and Pakistan. Its first four emirs were all killed in US airstrikes in Afghanistan.

Objectives: Like all ISIS factions, ISIS–KP seeks to establish a caliphate and introduce its rigid version of Islamist governance at a local and ultimately regional and national levels. To this end, it seeks to delegitimise the Pakistani state and expel religious minorities from Pakistan.

Opponents: PAF, PCAF.

Affiliates/allies: None.

Resources/capabilities: ISIS–KP attacks have involved small arms and IEDs, including suicide vests.

Conflict Drivers

Political

Ethnic grievances:

Politically mobilised segments of Pakistan's ethnic minorities accuse the government, the army and the police of targeting them with a campaign of violent repression and marginalisation, with dissidents sometimes facing arbitrary detention, extrajudicial killings and enforced disappearances. Some groups also accuse the government of depriving them of their fair share of economic resources.

The PTM emerged in its current form in January 2018 to protest the extrajudicial killing of a Pashtun youth by the Karachi police, and its rallies attracted tens of thousands of attendees in 2019. The PTM calls for investigations into forced disappearances, an end to profiling by security services and greater civil liberties for tribal Pashtuns and migrants – positions which have garnered some support outside the movement. Protests were scaled back in 2020 due to pressure from Pakistani authorities and the coronavirus pandemic.

Economic and social

Economic grievances:

Baloch groups allege that the government violates their civil, political and human rights, but also object to Islamabad's distribution of economic benefits resulting from the extraction of natural resources in Balochistan. CPEC, part of China's Belt and Road Initiative (BRI), is often referred to as the latter's pilot project and includes the construction of power plants, mines, highways, railways and improvements to a warm deepwater port in Gwadar. Baloch groups question whether the Baloch people will

profit from CPEC or if benefits will instead accrue to China and its partners in the Pakistani government. Baloch insurgents' strategy of attacking Chinese targets threatens not only CPEC's progress but also Pakistan's most important bilateral relationship.

Religious divisions:

Pakistan's population is 96.28% Muslim according to the country's Bureau of Statistics, but it does not delineate by sect.[4] Estimates suggest that the Sunni population comprises 85–90% and the Shia 10–15%.[5] Pakistan's Sunni Muslims are primarily divided among the Barelvi and Deobandi subsects with a growing Ahl-e-Hadith community. Mainstream Islamist parties and movements representing both Deobandis and Barelvis are united in their support for blasphemy laws, which criminalise acts or statements perceived to malign Islam, particularly the Prophet Muhammad. However, the issue of blasphemy – a chief cause advocated by Barelvi militants and hardliners – has become a driver of radicalisation and violence among Pakistan's Barelvi Sunnis, which is the largest Sunni subsect in the country.

International

Instability along Pakistan's borders with Afghanistan and Iran:

Insurgent and terrorist groups have utilised Pakistan's porous borders to regroup and conduct operations. Baloch separatist groups have previously launched attacks against Iran's security forces from Pakistan. Cross-border attacks have therefore strained relations between the two countries. The TTP was able to retreat into Afghanistan and the majority of TTP fighters are currently based there. Pakistan has benefitted indirectly from US drone strikes that have killed a number of mid-level and senior TTP commanders in Afghanistan. However, a US withdrawal may limit this capability. Islamabad identifies the safe haven for terrorist groups in Afghanistan as one of the primary drivers of terrorist violence against Pakistan and evidence of Kabul's complicity. However, this is due more to Kabul's lack of control over parts of the country's southeastern provinces, than any sponsor–proxy relationship.

Political and Military Developments

Slow progress towards formalising FATA and KP merger

Attempts to formalise the *de jure* merger of the administrative and security apparatuses of the former FATA into KP, which began in 2018, continued to move at a slow pace. In 2018, the federal government announced a ten-year development plan for the former FATA, but lawmakers reported that less than 10% of the US$540 million allocated for development in FATA was actually spent in 2019–20.[6]

The aggressive military and police response to the PTM also undermined progress towards addressing the political and economic marginalisation of the former FATA. The PTM is unpopular among large segments of Pakistan's population; Pakistani politicians and the military use the ongoing conflict in the former FATA to discredit such movements and suggest the PTM is sponsored by external actors and an enabler of TTP terrorism.

Blasphemy as rallying cry for Islamist groups

In 2020, Islamist groups continued to use the issues of sect and blasphemy to mobilise members and exert power. Islamist political parties in Karachi organised large protests against Shia Muslims in September 2020. Amnesty International reported an uptick in blasphemy accusations, primarily lodged against members of the Shia, Ahmadi and Christian faiths.[7] Religious parties continued to actively defend blasphemy laws, particularly the hardline Islamist party Tehreek-e-Labbaik Pakistan (TLP). In November 2020, the TLP organised a mass protest in Islamabad over anti-Muslim cartoons that appeared in the French press. The protest prompted Pakistan's government to sign an agreement with the TLP to boycott French products and delegate to parliament the decision to expel the French ambassador, following a non-binding resolution by the National Assembly to recall Pakistan's envoy to France in October.

Foreign pressure to step up counter-terrorism measures

In 2018, the intergovernmental organisation, the Financial Action Task Force (FATF), placed Pakistan on its 'grey list' of states with structural deficiencies in anti-money laundering (AML) and countering the financing of terrorism and issued a 27-point improvement plan for Pakistan. In the reporting period, the government focused on law-enforcement operations to seize property, regulatory frameworks for AML and legislation but failed to confront certain terrorist groups. Some progress was made throughout 2020; Pakistan had complied with 14 of the 27 points by February 2020, 21 points by October 2020 and 24 points by February 2021.[8]

Violence in Balochistan and the former FATA

Insurgent activity and violence increased significantly in Balochistan province and particularly along its western border with Afghanistan compared to the general downward trend observed since 2015.[9] With the insurgents aiming to deter or disrupt Chinese investment through attacks, Pakistan remains the most dangerous posting for overseas Chinese workers, straining economic cooperation. Frequent attacks on military outposts in Balochistan occurred throughout spring and summer 2020, leading to dozens of security-personnel casualties.

The TTP grew in strength in the former FATA – reabsorbing formerly splintered militant groups – and conducted attacks on military and civilian targets.[10]

Key Events in 2020–21

POLITICAL EVENTS

8 March 2020

Pakistani authorities prevent PTM leaders from travelling to the inauguration of Afghanistan President Ashraf Ghani.

29 July

Tahir Naseem, a US citizen accused of blasphemy, is murdered during his court hearing in Peshawar.

11–12 September

Large anti-Shia sectarian protests attract thousands of demonstrators in Karachi.

12 September

Intra-Afghan negotiations between the Afghan Taliban and Afghan government begin in Doha, Qatar, partly due to the intervention of Islamabad.

17 October

Via video-link from London, former Pakistani prime minister Nawaz Sharif addresses anti-government protests organised by the Pakistan Democratic Movement (PDM).

MILITARY/VIOLENT EVENTS

10 January 2020

An attack on a mosque in Quetta kills 15 civilians. ISIS–KP claims responsibility for the attack.

29 June

BLA militants attack the Pakistan Stock Exchange in Karachi, killing two guards and a police officer.

6 July

The Hakimullah Mehsud faction rejoins TTP.

30 July

The Amjad Farouqi militant group rejoins TTP.

17 August

The Jamaat-ul-Ahrar and Hizb-ul-Ahrar militant groups rejoin TTP.

15 October

Baloch militants attack a convoy of a state-run oil and gas company travelling from Gwadar district, Balochistan, to Karachi, killing seven Frontier Corps soldiers and seven private-security personnel.

27 December

Baloch militants attack a Frontier Corps post and kill seven security personnel.

3 January 2021

11 coal miners who were members of the minority ethnic and predominantly Shia Hazara community are killed in Balochistan by ISIS–KP.

Impact

Human rights and humanitarian

There were 319 terrorism-related deaths in Pakistan in 2020, an increase of 11% compared to 2019.[11] Citizens in Balochistan and KP (including the former FATA) continued to suffer from insurgent violence, terrorist attacks, military checkpoints, forced disappearances, arbitrary detentions, arrests on dubious charges and restriction of movement. These regions have continued to suffer from chronic underinvestment and high rates of poverty since Pakistan's formation. General security in Pakistan's major cities has increased over the last decade but dangers remain for members of certain minority groups. In particular, the Hazara, a minority ethnic group that is predominantly Shia, face high levels of violence in Balochistan at the hands of groups such as ISKP.

Political stability

Pakistan's civilian government and military establishment remained relatively stable despite large protest movements and continued conflict in Balochistan and the former FATA. The military ranks remained cohesive with very low risk of fragmentation and minimal insider attacks or defections to insurgent and terrorist movements.

Economic and social

Pakistan's economic woes remain primarily structural rather than conflict driven. The country suffered from high inflation, a decline in real incomes, low exports relative to other regional countries and a depreciating currency. This economic malaise was partly due to low investment as a result of the security situation – as terrorism and insecurity continued

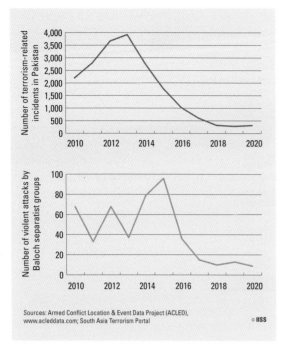

Sources: Armed Conflict Location & Event Data Project (ACLED),
www.acleddata.com; South Asia Terrorism Portal   © IISS

Figure 1: Trends in terrorism incidents in Pakistan,
2010–20

real GDP shrank by 7.7% in 2020, whereas Pakistan's shrank by 0.4%.[12] Pakistan's avoidance of a severe economic downturn can be explained partially by the US$23.13bn in remittances received from overseas Pakistanis during 2019–20. The country's continued presence on the FATF grey list has not directly affected the economy apart from deterring foreign investment. However, a future blacklisting could prevent Pakistan from receiving assistance from the World Bank, IMF and Asian Development Bank.

Relations with neighbouring and international partners and geopolitical implications

Pakistan's relations with the West improved slightly in 2020 following Islamabad's role in pressuring the Taliban to attend intra-Afghan negotiations with the aim of resolving the conflict in Afghanistan, which is deeply intertwined with insecurity in the former FATA. Relations with India remained tense partly due to an uptick in violence perpetrated by Baloch separatist groups, which Pakistan views as receiving support from the Indian government. China–Pakistan relations remained strong in 2020 despite the growing threat posed by the insurgency in Balochistan to Chinese investment. China also supported Pakistan by voting against its inclusion on the FATF blacklist along with Malaysia and Turkey.

to deter foreign investment – but a bigger factor has been the economic mismanagement of successive governments. The coronavirus pandemic negatively impacted Pakistan's economy but less so than other regional countries. The IMF estimated that India's

Conflict Outlook

Political scenarios

Religious parties and protest movements such as the TLP are poised to continue to influence Pakistan's laws and aspects of foreign policy. Religious parties perform poorly at the polls but have a successful track record of extracting concessions from the government through large-scale street protests. This dynamic continued in 2020 with the TLP-led protest against the French government. Ethnic protest movements like the PTM are unlikely to gain widespread traction among Pakistan's population, influence a change in policies or threaten government institutions. However, the marginalisation of Pashtuns in the former FATA and migrants in urban centres increases the risk of future social unrest.

Escalation potential and conflict-related risks

Since 2014, the PAF's selective strategy against insurgent groups, targeting those that directly threaten the Pakistani state, such as the TTP, but largely ignoring Pakistan-based groups that primarily target Afghanistan and India, has led to a significant reduction in violence in much of the country, particularly in urban centres. These overall gains are likely to continue in the short term, albeit with localised upticks in violence in Waziristan (part of the former FATA) and Balochistan, particularly in regions with high Chinese investment, such as Makran.

Terrorist violence in Pakistan is unlikely to return to the peak it reached in 2013. However, the underlying political and economic drivers of violence in Balochistan and the former FATA persist:

both regions face chronic underinvestment, heavy-handed security responses and insecure borders, making continued violence at current levels, or a slight increase, likely. Except for Quetta, Pakistan's provincial capitals were relatively secure in 2020 and will likely remain so. Both the TTP and ISKP may try to engage in urban terrorism if the opportunity presents itself but neither group is particularly strong outside of KP.

Strategic implications and global influences

Insurgent violence in Pakistan's tribal areas will affect its political calculation vis-à-vis Afghanistan and the Afghan Taliban. Islamabad may prefer an unstable Afghanistan to one that adopts a foreign policy inclined towards India, but it likely calculated the Taliban are the ascendant political force anyway. Its continued support for the Afghan Taliban despite rising violence from similar militant groups inside Pakistan may stem from the inflated perception that groups like the TTP are local agents of foreign actors rather than a home-grown phenomenon.

The uptick in insurgent violence in Balochistan is unlikely to significantly alter bilateral ties between China and Pakistan, which are security based. However, if Pakistan loses control of the violence in Balochistan, Chinese investment in the region may decline significantly. The ability of Islamist political parties to influence Pakistan's foreign policy through large protests will strain bilateral relations, but groups like the TLP are still likely to stop short of engaging in anti-state violence or attacking foreigners.

Notes

[1] Michael Kugelman and Adam Weinstein, 'In Pakistan, a Tale of Two Very Different Political Movements', Lawfare, 4 January 2021.

[2] Asfandyar Mir, 'Afghanistan's Terrorism Challenge: The Political Trajectories of Al-Qaeda, the Afghan Taliban, and the Islamic State', Middle East Institute, 20 October 2020; US Department of Defense Office of Inspector General, 'Operation Freedom's Sentinel: Lead Inspector General Report to the United States Congress', 21 May 2019, p. 25; and Daud Khattak, 'The Pakistan Taliban is Back', Diplomat, 9 March 2021.

[3] The Islamic State–Pakistan Province (IS–PP) is a less relevant splinter of ISKP that is sometimes referenced in media or used interchangeably with ISKP.

[4] See Pakistan Bureau of Statistics, 'Population by Religion', 2020. It records the Ahmadi sect separately since the group is not recognised as Muslim by the government.

[5] US Commission on International Religious Freedom, 'Pakistan: USCIRF-recommended for Countries of Particular Concern (CPC)', Annual Report, April 2020, p. 33.

[6] Abubakar Siddique, 'Pakistan's Tribal Areas Caught in Limbo Awaiting Integration', Gandara, 16 January 2020.

[7] Amnesty International, 'Pakistan: Accusations of Blasphemy Continue to Endanger Lives', 25 August 2020. Individuals accused of blasphemy are sometimes killed extrajudicially and on 29 July 2020, a US citizen of Pakistani origin was murdered inside a Pakistani courtroom while sitting trial for blasphemy charges.

[8] 'Jurisdictions under Increased Monitoring – February 2021', Financial Action Task Force, 25 February 2021.

[9] Ashik KC, 'Rising Organized Political Violence in Balochistan: A Resurgence of Baloch Separatism?', Armed Conflict Location & Event Data Project.

[10] The group splintered partly due to disagreements over whether civilians are legitimate targets and methods such as kidnappings. According to Noor Wali's 2018 guidelines, legitimate targets include the Pakistani state, militias that support the state and so-called non-believers (including Shia and Ahmadi Muslims, Westerners and NGOs). He ruled that other civilian deaths should be avoided, and suicide attacks reserved for high-value targets. Noor Wali reintegrated splinter factions into the TTP throughout 2020. He has also sought to re-establish a strongly hierarchical structure in the TTP following years of infighting.

[11] 'Number of Terrorism Incidents Year Wise', South Asia Terrorism Portal, Institute for Conflict Management.

[12] International Monetary Fund, 'World Economic Outlook Database', April 2021.

Asia

KASHMIR

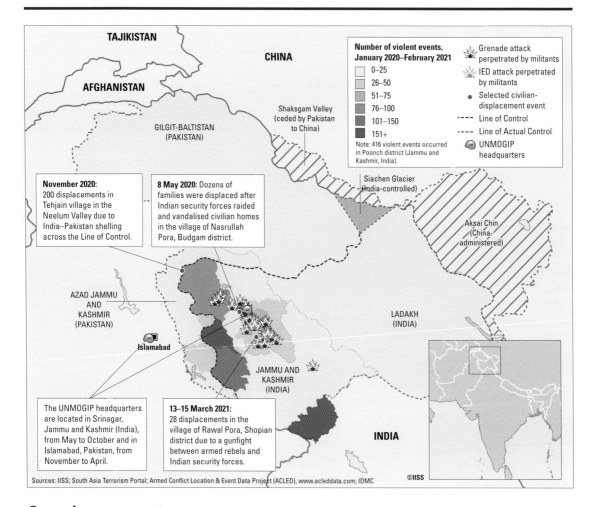

Number of violent events, January 2020–February 2021
- ☐ 0–25
- ☐ 26–50
- ☐ 51–75
- ☐ 76–100
- ☐ 101–150
- ☐ 151+

Note: 416 violent events occurred in Poonch district (Jammu and Kashmir, India).

- Grenade attack perpetrated by militants
- IED attack perpetrated by militants
- Selected civilian-displacement event
- - - - Line of Control
- - - - Line of Actual Control
- UNMOGIP headquarters

TAJIKISTAN

CHINA

AFGHANISTAN

Shaksgam Valley (ceded by Pakistan to China)

GILGIT-BALTISTAN (PAKISTAN)

Siachen Glacier (India-controlled)

Aksai Chin (China-administered)

November 2020: 200 displacements in Tehjain village in the Neelum Valley due to India–Pakistan shelling across the Line of Control.

8 May 2020: Dozens of families were displaced after Indian security forces raided and vandalised civilian homes in the village of Nasrullah Pora, Budgam district.

AZAD JAMMU AND KASHMIR (PAKISTAN)

LADAKH (INDIA)

Islamabad

JAMMU AND KASHMIR (INDIA)

The UNMOGIP headquarters are located in Srinagar, Jammu and Kashmir (India), from May to October and in Islamabad, Pakistan, from November to April.

13–15 March 2021: 28 displacements in the village of Rawal Pora, Shopian district due to a gunfight between armed rebels and Indian security forces.

INDIA

Sources: IISS; South Asia Terrorism Portal; Armed Conflict Location & Event Data Project (ACLED), www.acleddata.com; IDMC   ©IISS

Overview

The conflict in Kashmir is a long-standing militarised dispute between India and Pakistan over sovereignty in the Himalayan Muslim-majority region of Jammu and Kashmir (India), comprising an area of 220,000 square kilometres. In 1947, the region's last Hindu ruler provisionally acceded to the Indian Union after the British Raj ended. Pakistan contested the accession, triggering the outbreak of war between India and Pakistan (1947–48). In 1949 the United Nations brokered a ceasefire, dividing the formerly independent kingdom into India-administered and Pakistan-administered regions. The UN Security Council (UNSC) passed a raft of resolutions and established a three-member UN Commission for India and Pakistan (UNCIP)

tasked with holding a 'free and impartial plebiscite' in Kashmir.

Following the failure of bilateral talks and unsuccessful mediation efforts by world powers, including the United States and the Soviet Union, India and Pakistan fought two more wars over Jammu and Kashmir (J&K) in 1965 and 1999.[1] However, the status quo persisted and India retained the most prized part of the disputed region. Successive Indian governments' denial of the plebiscite produced popular discontent in the region and in the late 1980s Kashmiri dissidents started an anti-India armed movement with Pakistan's assistance. New Delhi sent thousands of troops to the region and launched widespread

Armed Conflict Global Relevance Indicator (ACGRI)

India

B
17

A
4

C
4

Pakistan

B
5

A
2

C
4

Key Conflict Statistics

Type	Inter-state
Start date	1947
Fatalities	India: 1,046; Pakistan: 900
Multilateral missions	UNMOGIP
GDP per capita, PPP (current international $)	India: 6,461; Pakistan: 5,150

ACGRI pillars: IISS calculation based on multiple sources for 2020 and January/February 2021 (scale: 0–100). A: Human impact; B: Incidence; C: Geopolitical impact. The indicator's results and certain Key Conflict Statistics refer to data for the whole of either India or Pakistan, rather than the specific conflict covered in this chapter. See Notes on Methodology and Data Appendix for further details on Key Conflict Statistics.

security crackdowns resulting in severe human-rights violations.

India and Pakistan began a peace process in 2003 that resulted in a number of confidence-building measures. Annual fatalities gradually decreased from over 3,000 in 2002 to approximately 500 in 2008.[2] However, no major political breakthrough was achieved on the core issue of Kashmir. Mass anti-India uprisings erupted between 2008 and 2016, catalysing a 'new-age militancy' that was further boosted by social media. India continues to see Pakistan as the main actor controlling armed groups in the region. It also faces hostility from local Kashmiris, most of whom seek either autonomy, independence or a merger with Pakistan.

In August 2019, India's Bharatiya Janata Party (BJP) government revoked Article 370 of the Indian constitution – which had safeguarded J&K's limited autonomy since 1949 – and divided the disputed region into two federally controlled 'Union Territories' – Jammu and Kashmir, and Ladakh. The BJP has long been opposed to Article 370, with claims suggesting it favours altering J&K's demographic composition as a final solution to the conflict. This desire is shared by BJP's Hindu-nationalist parent organisation, Rashtriya Swayamsevak Sangh (RSS), which exerts considerable influence on Prime Minister Narendra Modi's domestic policies. Direct central rule has allowed Modi to introduce new laws and policies in J&K with far-reaching implications for residents. New Delhi changed J&K's domicile law in March 2020 and amended its land laws in October, creating fears of 'demographic flooding' of non-Kashmiris into the region. The government also floated new political parties and actors to reconfigure J&K's political landscape and undermine the influence of the major regional parties that opposed the abrogation of Article 370, such as the Jammu and Kashmir National Conference (JKNC) and the People's Democratic Party (PDP). By delaying elections to the J&K Legislative Assembly the BJP seeks to increase the number of constituencies in Jammu – its election stronghold – through gerrymandering. Increased seat shares in the future elected assembly would allow the BJP to maintain its influence in J&K.

Conflict Parties

Indian armed forces

Strength: Approximately 500,000 Indian security personnel, including over 200,000 army soldiers; 58,000 infantry troops within the Rashtriya Rifles (RR), the special counter-insurgency unit; 128,000 paramilitary personnel of the Central Reserve Police Force (CRPF), Border Security Force (BSF), Indo-Tibetan Border Police (ITBP), Sashastra Seema Bal (SSB) and Central Industrial Security Force (CISF); around 100,000 personnel of the J&K Police (JKP); 30,000 Special Police Officers (SPOs); and personnel within various intelligence wings.

Areas of operation: All districts of J&K (India) and along the Line of Control (LoC). The CRPF's Jammu and Kashmir Zone Srinagar Sector covers Budgam, Ganderbal and Srinagar districts, its Kashmir Operations Sector covers Anantnag, Awantipora and Baramulla districts, and its Jammu Sector covers the Jammu region.

Asia

Indian armed forces

Leadership: Indian troops in the region are under the Northern Command based in Udhampur (Jammu and Kashmir Union Territory) and led by Lt-Gen. Yogesh Kumar Joshi. The CRPF, the primary paramilitary force, is under the Ministry of Home Affairs. A special director general has overall command of the CRPF in J&K, while inspectors general command the respective sectors.

Structure: The Northern Command is composed of seven divisions, three corps and one brigade. The RR has 65 battalions, each comprising six infantry companies, and five headquarters.

History: A heavy troop presence has been maintained along the LoC since 1949. Thousands of troops were used to crush an anti-India armed rebellion in the late 1980s. Initially, paramilitary and regular army troops fought the Pakistan-backed insurgents. In 1994 the RR was introduced, which coordinates with other security agencies, including the Special Operations Group (SOG), a JKP counter-insurgency unit.

Objectives: Guard the LoC and defeat armed opposition.

Opponents: Armed groups (Hizbul Mujahideen, HM; Lashkar-e-Taiba, LeT; Jaysh-e-Mohammad, JeM; The Resistance Front, TRF; Ansar Ghazwat-ul-Hind, AGH) and Pakistan Armed Forces.

Affiliates/allies: Village Defence Committees, volunteer state-armed groups concentrated in hilly and border areas with sizeable Hindu populations (Doda, Kathua, Kishtwar, Poonch, Rajouri, Ramban and Reasi districts).

Resources/capabilities: Ministry of Defence and Ministry of Home Affairs budgetary funds, web-based public donations through portals like 'Bharat Ke Veer' (India's Bravehearts) and the National Defence Fund, and government contracts under *Operation Sadhbhavana*.[3]

Pakistan armed forces

Strength: In total, Pakistan has some 650,000 total active military personnel and 291,000 total active paramilitary personnel across the country. The approximate strength of I and X Corps, the Pakistan Army's forces in Azad Jammu and Kashmir (Pakistan), is unknown.

Areas of operation: All districts of Azad Jammu and Kashmir and along the LoC.

Leadership: Pakistani troops in the region are under I and X Corps of the Pakistan Army. I Corps is based in Mangla (Azad Jammu and Kashmir) and led by Lt-Gen. Shaheen Mazhar Mehmood. X Corps is based in Rawalpindi (Pakistan) and led by Lt-Gen. Azhar Abbas. The Mujahid Force, a paramilitary unit, is headquartered in Bhimber (Azad Jammu and Kashmir) and works under the National Guard of Pakistan, which is controlled and commanded by the chief of army staff based in General Headquarters in Rawalpindi.

Structure: Division/brigade breakdown unknown.

History: Pakistan has maintained a heavy troop presence along the LoC since 1949. The Azad Army, an anti-Maharaja militia composed of ex-servicemen of the British Indian Army, captured the main districts of Muzaffarabad and Mirpur before the Pakistan Army officially entered Jammu and Kashmir in May 1948 to take control and consolidate the territorial gains. The Pakistan Army has not faced any insurgency within Azad Jammu and Kashmir; its operations are directed at Indian forces and the LoC.

Objectives: Guard the LoC and China–Pakistan Economic Corridor (CPEC).

Opponents: Indian armed forces.

Affiliates/allies: Anti-India armed groups based in Azad Jammu and Kashmir (Pakistan).

Resources/capabilities: Ministry of Defence budgetary funds, arms exports, government contracts and commercial ventures under army-controlled charitable foundations, such as Fauji Foundation and Army Welfare Trust.

Hizbul Mujahideen (HM)

Strength: Approximately 100 members active in Jammu and Kashmir (India) and over 1,000 members based in Azad Jammu and Kashmir (Pakistan). Additional overground workers – a term used by Indian security forces for people supporting insurgents and insurgent sympathisers – provide logistical support and information.[4]

Areas of operation: Concentrated in Anantnag, Kulgam, Pulwama and Shopian districts, with marginal presence in northern Kashmir districts.

Leadership: Headed by Mohammad Yusuf Shah (alias Syed Salahuddin). Zubair Ahmad Wani is the chief commander in the Kashmir Valley – the epicentre of the low-intensity armed conflict – below whom there are area commanders for each district.

Structure: Headquarters in Muzaffarabad, Azad Jammu and Kashmir (Pakistan). Cadres comprise mostly local Kashmiris who receive rudimentary arms training from senior members. Divisional commanders work under a semi-autonomous structure, but also receive instructions from across the LoC via satellite communication and encrypted messaging apps.

History: Indigenous armed group with a pro-Pakistan ideology, founded in September 1989 by Mohammad Ahsan Dar, a former member of the pro-independence organisation Jammu Kashmir Liberation Front (JKLF) and Jamaat-e-Islami affiliate, a pro-Pakistan religio-political organisation in J&K. Many JKLF members joined HM after 1994, when the former suffered heavy losses and voluntarily quit the armed conflict to pursue non-violent means.

Hizbul Mujahideen (HM)

HM recruitment of local Kashmiri youth also surged after the death of its young commander Burhan Muzaffar Wani in July 2016. Despite suffering heavy losses between 2017 and 2020, HM survived by procuring funds and weapons locally.

Objectives: Dislodge Indian rule in Kashmir and merge the region with Pakistan through a war of attrition. The group has stated that it would support negotiated settlement through dialogue under certain circumstances.[5]

Opponents: Indian government.

Affiliates/allies: LeT, JeM and TRF.

Resources/capabilities: Resources (including weapons and improvised explosive devices (IEDs)) procured locally by associates and sympathisers. Funding channels from charities, mosque-based donations across Pakistan and the Pakistani military establishment.

Lashkar-e-Taiba (LeT)

Strength: Second-largest armed group in Kashmir in 2020 after HM.

Areas of operation: Across the Kashmir Valley, but mostly active in the northern districts of Baramulla, Bandipora and Kupwara.

Leadership: Hafiz Muhammad Saeed. Overall command is in the hands of a divisional commander, who is often a non-Kashmiri.

Structure: Headquarters in Muridke, Punjab province, Pakistan. Valley-based cadres are mostly Pakistani nationals working under district commanders and trained in camps.

History: Founded in the late 1980s by Pakistan-based cleric Hafiz Muhammad Saeed, who also heads the missionary organisation Jamaat-ud-Dawa (JuD). Since LeT entered Kashmir in the early 1990s, it has carried out several deadly attacks against Indian armed forces and political workers.

Despite losing its commanders in quick succession since the launch of the Indian Army's *Operation All Out*, the group has survived and has recruited increasing numbers of local youth, particularly in the last two years.

Objectives: Merge Kashmir with Pakistan. The group has supported efforts to achieve a peaceful resolution to the conflict.

Opponents: Indian government.

Affiliates/allies: HM, JeM, TRF, Al-Badr. Though banned by the Pakistani government in 2002, LeT is believed to maintain connections to Pakistani intelligence agencies.

Resources/capabilities: Fundraising through charities in Pakistan (e.g., JuD and Falah-e-Insaniyat), which receive government and public contributions, and social networks in Pakistan and Afghanistan. Funds also raised through collection and selling of sacrificial-animal skins on Eid.

Jaysh-e-Mohammad (JeM)

Strength: Third-largest armed group in Kashmir in 2020. Indian security forces killed 22 JeM militants between January and July 2020.[6]

Areas of operation: Conducts attacks mainly in southern Kashmir.

Leadership: After the Indian security forces killed its Kashmir chief, Qari Yasir, on 25 January 2020, a new chief operational commander has not been appointed.

Structure: Headquartered in Bahawalpur, Punjab province, Pakistan. JeM is Pakistan-based and its members are mostly Pakistanis. Divisional commanders work under the chief operational commander based in Kashmir.

History: Founded by Pakistani Masood Azhar in 2000. JeM entered Kashmir in the early 2000s and introduced suicide attacks. The Pakistani government banned the group in 2002. After a period of dormancy, JeM re-emerged in 2017 with an attack on a paramilitary camp in Pulwama.

Objectives: Merge Kashmir with Pakistan.

Opponents: Indian government.

Affiliates/allies: HM and LeT. Believed to have ties to the Taliban in Afghanistan.

Resources/capabilities: The most powerful insurgent group in Kashmir, with highly trained cadres and better resources than other insurgent groups. Fundraising through seminaries, mosques (e.g., Binori Town Mosque) and charities in Pakistan (e.g., Al Rashid Trust) and donation appeals published in magazines and pamphlets. Money also raised through legal businesses operating in Pakistan and funds allegedly received from political (e.g., Jamiat-e-Ulema-e-Islam) and other militant organisations in Pakistan.

The Resistance Front (TRF)

Strength: The TRF is the largest recruiter after HM, LeT and JeM.

Areas of operation: Has carried out attacks in northern, central and southern districts of Kashmir Valley.

Leadership: No central leadership.

Structure: Composite organisation without defined structure. JKP claims that the TRF is a hybrid militant outfit composed of cadres from existing armed groups such as LeT and HM. TRF militants killed by Indian security forces and arrested TRF sympathisers have been identified as native Kashmiris.

The Resistance Front (TRF)

History: Founded after the abrogation of Article 370 in August 2019, the TRF started by lobbing grenades in Srinagar in late 2019. The group has used social media to publish statements and claim attacks.

Objectives: Dislodge Indian rule in Kashmir and deter (through violence) potential settlers from mainland India.

Opponents: Indian government.

Affiliates/allies: Believed to have ties with LeT.

Resources/capabilities: Unknown.

United Nations Military Observer Group in India and Pakistan (UNMOGIP)

Strength: 40 observers from Croatia, the Philippines, South Korea, Sweden, Thailand, Switzerland, Uruguay, Chile, Italy, Mexico and Romania (in descending order of troop numbers). 68 civilian staff, including Pakistanis, Indians and international members.[7]

Areas of operation: UN field stations: six based in Azad Jammu and Kashmir (Pakistan) and four based in J&K (India). The Sialkot field station in Pakistan monitors the working boundary, which is the international border between Punjab province, Pakistan, and the disputed territory of Jammu and Kashmir.

Leadership: Maj.-Gen. José Alcaín from Uruguay (chief military observer and head of mission); Nester Odaga-Jalomayo from Uganda (chief of mission support).

Structure: UNMOGIP is mandated by UNSC Resolution 91. Headquarters alternates between Islamabad in November–April and Srinagar in May–October.

History: In January 1948, UNCIP was created under UNSC Resolution 39. In January 1949, the first team of unarmed military observers arrived to supervise the ceasefire between India and Pakistan. Under UNSC Resolution 91 of March 1951, UNCIP was replaced by UNMOGIP. After UNSC Resolution 307 (1971), India and Pakistan made minor adjustments to the ceasefire line and in 1972 established the LoC to be supervised by UN military observers.

Objectives: As a neutral observer, monitor, investigate and report ceasefire violations along the 770-km LoC and working boundary between India and Pakistan. Receive petitions from political groups within Kashmir on the situation at the LoC and submit findings to both India and Pakistan and the UN Secretary-General.

Opponents: N/A.

Affiliates/allies: UN departments of Peace Operations and Operational Support.

Resources/capabilities: UN approved budget: US$10,519,800 for January 2021– December 2021.

Conflict Drivers

Political

Indian and Kashmiri self-determination:
The origins of the Kashmir conflict lie in the controversial 1947 accession, supported by the JKNC but vehemently opposed by many Kashmiris who favoured accession with Muslim-majority Pakistan. New Delhi sought to win over Kashmiris by agreeing to substantial autonomy (with a separate constitution and flag) under Article 370 of the Indian constitution, which exempted the state from the full applicability of Indian laws. Unrest soon followed when New Delhi arrested the popular J&K prime minister Sheikh Muhammad Abdullah in 1953 on charges of conspiring to declare independence. JKNC's cadres formed the Plebiscite Front, mobilising Kashmiris around the demand for self-determination until New Delhi co-opted Abdullah under the 1975 accord. This was strongly opposed by pro-plebiscite groups, who went on to launch an armed struggle in the late 1980s.

India has consistently refused to recognise Kashmiri demands for self-determination outside the framework of the Indian constitution, creating a fundamental discord. Kashmiris perceive that their political identity and group security are threatened by India's centralising policies, which have systematically eroded J&K's autonomy. Forcible integration of the disputed region with India has prompted the Muslim-majority population in J&K to intensify its political resistance against New Delhi's policies.

BJP ethno-nationalism:
The removal of Article 370 has long been an ideological concern of the BJP, which believes in the political creed of *Hindutva* (Hindu ethno-nationalism) and seeks to establish *Akhand Bharat* (a supposed undivided India that includes much of South Asia) by incorporating areas bordering India, including Azad Jammu and Kashmir (Pakistan).

With firmer control over the state now, the Modi government has initiated a slew of policies that are viewed with increased suspicion by J&K's political parties and local population. The March and October 2020 amendments to domicile and land laws in J&K paved the way for 'non-permanent' residents to acquire domiciles in the region and apply for public-sector jobs previously reserved for local residents of J&K under Article 370 and 35A of the Indian constitution. The Union Territory of Jammu and Kashmir Reorganisation (Adaptation of Central Laws) Third Order, 2020, promulgated on 26 October, gave New Delhi sweeping powers to acquire land and evict the population in order to establish industrial centres and designate strategic areas for 'direct operational and training requirements' of the army. J&K's Muslim population view these policies as a strategy to alter the region's demography and in the long term dispossess them of their land and resources. Regional parties have declared their opposition to these policies while armed groups have vowed to target Indian settlers.

International
Regional geopolitics:
Pakistan asserts its claim on Kashmir based on the 'two-nation' doctrine, which had been the basis for the partition of British India into two (religiously defined) separate states (India and Pakistan). Over the years, Pakistan has deployed different military and diplomatic tactics to weaken India's control over J&K, including funding the Kashmiri insurgent groups that intensified the armed conflict and increased acrimony between the two countries. Kashmir's abundant water resources, which feed vast agricultural lands in Pakistan and generate more than 2,000 MW of electricity for India's government-owned National Hydroelectric Power Corporation, makes it an important strategic concern for both New Delhi and Islamabad.[8] Pakistan's formal military alliance with China provides balance against India.

Political and Military Developments

Release of J&K political leaders
The Modi government released three former J&K chief ministers between March and October 2020 amid reports that detained former legislators and politicians were being forced to sign a bond declaring that they would 'not make any comment(s) or issue statement(s) or make public speech(s)' or 'hold or participate in public assembly(s) related to recent events in the state of Jammu and Kashmir'.[9] After JKNC patron Farooq Abdullah announced an alliance with other regional parties on 15 October and declared that they would 'struggle for restoration of what was snatched from Jammu Kashmir and Ladakh', he was immediately summoned by the Enforcement Directorate (a federal financial-investigation agency) in relation to a case registered against him in 2018 involving alleged financial irregularities in the Jammu & Kashmir Cricket Association. New Delhi used the same pressure tactic with some other influential J&K political leaders.

Modi's experimentation in J&K
The absence of an elected executive in J&K allowed the Modi regime to experiment and implement its policies there through a bureaucratic structure controlled by New Delhi. The BJP seeks to use the delimitation commission – responsible for periodically redrawing Indian electoral constituencies – to add seven or more seats to the J&K Legislative Assembly by 2022 and increase the seat share of Jammu province to at least 44, thereby increasing the likelihood that the party will be able to form the region's next government.

Reconfiguration of the local political landscape and District Development Council elections
Many independent councillors joined the Jammu and Kashmir Apni Party (JKAP), a new political party created by former PDP politician and J&K minister Altaf Bukhari on 8 March 2020, which included legislators that defected from the PDP, JKNC and the Indian National Congress (INC). In public statements the JKAP aligned itself with the BJP's stance that the abrogation of Article 370 is a fait accompli and that political parties should instead strive for the restoration of J&K's statehood without autonomy.

The first District Development Council (DDC) elections were held in J&K in November and December 2020. Nearly 68% of registered voters in

Asia

the Jammu region and 35% of voters in the Kashmir region cast their ballot.[10] Introduced by New Delhi, the DDC undermines the influence of the two major regional parties, the JKNC and PDP. By creating 280 DDC constituencies (each district comprising 14 constituencies), political power is dispersed among different political parties and councillors.[11]

For example, the People's Alliance for Gupkar Declaration (PAGD) – an alliance of six parties formed in October 2020 that calls for Article 370's restoration – won 110 DDC seats. However, cross-voting (which the PAGD blamed on horse-trading and arm-twisting of the elected DDC members by the BJP-controlled administration) meant the alliance secured the chairmanship of only five DDCs.[12] The exit of the Jammu and Kashmir People's Conference (JKPC) from the PAGD in January 2021 further weakened the alliance's position in northern Kashmir, a JKPC stronghold.

Violence along the Line of Control (LoC)

Indian and Pakistani forces continuously exchanged artillery fire along the LoC in 2020 and early 2021, leading to a substantial increase in violations of the 2003 ceasefire agreement and many civilian casualties. Amid heightened clashes, the Indian and Pakistani governments summoned the chargés d'affaires of each other's High Commissions in November and December 2020 respectively to register protest over the ceasefire violations.

China–India clashes in Ladakh region

On 15–16 June 2020, China–India border skirmishes that first erupted 5 May in Ladakh escalated when their militaries clashed in Galwan Valley, with casualties on both sides. The crisis forced India to relocate some military units from the western front at the LoC to the northern front at the Line of Actual Control (LAC), a poorly demarcated 3,488-km line that divides Chinese- and Indian-held territories in J&K.

The border stand-off generated much interest among J&K residents, including former chief minister Farooq Abdullah, in the widespread expectation that a potential China–India war would herald a breakthrough on the Kashmir issue or pressure India to restore Article 370. Many analysts attributed China's military posturing at Ladakh to India's August 2019 reorganisation of J&K which had carved out Ladakh as a separate 'Union Territory' directly administered by New Delhi. On 11 February 2021 China and India announced disengagement plans to de-escalate tensions along the LAC.

India–Pakistan de-escalation measures

In a major development, India's and Pakistan's directors general of military operations (DGMO) made a surprising joint statement on 25 February 2021 announcing that they had agreed 'for strict observance of all agreements, understandings and cease firing' along the LoC and 'all other sectors'.[13]

Key Events in 2020–21

POLITICAL EVENTS

12 Jan 2020

16 foreign delegates, including the US ambassador to India, attend a tour of Kashmir. The US State Department states: 'We remain concerned by detention of political leaders and residents, and Internet restrictions.'

26 February

New Delhi approves the application of 37 central laws under the concurrent list to Jammu and Kashmir (India) under Section 96 of the Jammu and Kashmir Reorganisation Act, 2019.

8 March

Former PDP politician and J&K education minister Altaf Bukhari launches the JKAP.

13 March

Former J&K chief minister and JKNC leader Farooq Abdullah is released from prison.

MILITARY/VIOLENT EVENTS

12 January 2020

Senior HM commander Umar Fayaz Lone (alias Hamad Khan) is killed in a gunfight with Indian forces in the Tral area of Pulwama district.

24 March

Former J&K chief minister and JKNC leader Omar Abdullah is released from prison.

31 March

New Delhi announces amendments to laws concerning domicile rules in J&K.

2 June

The J&K government approves the 'Media Policy 2020', empowering authorities to penalise media outlets publishing 'anti-national' content.

29 June

Influential separatist leader and Tehreek-e-Hurriyat founder Syed Ali Shah Geelani resigns from the All Parties Hurriyat Conference (APHC) over an internal feud within the separatist coalition.

12 July

JKP arrests the chairman of Tehreek-e-Hurriyat and book him under the Public Safety Act (PSA).

7 August

Manoj Sinha takes office as lieutenant governor of Jammu and Kashmir (India).

22 August

Seven political parties, including the INC, sign the second Gupkar Resolution reiterating their demand for the restoration of J&K's autonomous status under Article 370.

13 October

Former PDP leader and J&K chief minister Mehbooba Mufti is released from prison following a 14-month detention.

15 October

Six political parties in J&K form the PAGD. The INC later distances itself from the PAGD.

26 October

The Modi government amends 14 laws related to Jammu and Kashmir and repeals 12 others, including the landmark Big Landed Estates Abolition Act, 1950.

25 November

President of the PDP youth wing, Waheed Para, is arrested by the National Investigative Agency (NIA) over alleged links to a separatist armed group.

28 November–19 December

The first DDC elections take place.

7 January 2021

Lieutenant Governor Manoj Sinha announces the Industrial Development Package for J&K, worth over US$3.8 billion. It is later designated the Jammu and Kashmir Industrial Policy 2021, with funds to be distributed 2021–30.

19 January

The JKPC exits the PAGD.

5 February

4G high-speed internet is restored in J&K following an 18-month ban.

3 May

Five Indian security personnel and two militants are killed in a clash in Chanjmulla village, Kupwara district. At least six civilians are injured in a separate incident after an explosive detonates in nearby Ahgam village.

6 May

Indian security forces kill HM's chief operational commander, Riyaz Ahmad Naikoo, in Beighpora village, Pulwama district. At least 16 civilians are injured in clashes with Indian security forces.

19 May

Two HM militants, including the son of Tehreek-e-Hurriyat chairman Mohammad Ashraf Khan, are killed in a gunfight with Indian security forces in Nawakadal locality, Srinagar.

15–16 June

Chinese and Indian forces clash in Ladakh region, J&K.

8 July

Militants kill local BJP leader Sheikh Waseem Bari, his brother and father in Bandipora district, J&K. The TRF claims responsibility for the attack.

29 October

The TRF kills three BJP workers in Kulgam district, J&K.

1 November

HM's chief operational commander Saif-ul-Islam Mir is killed in a gunfight with Indian security forces in the Rangreth area of Srinagar.

18 November

New Delhi deploys circa 25,000 paramilitary personnel to Jammu and Kashmir to secure the DDC elections.

19 February 2021

A militant kills two policemen in the Baghat area of Srinagar.

Asia

Impact

Human rights and humanitarian

The Modi government's hardline Kashmir policy during its second term had a significant impact on human rights in the region. The authorities launched a sustained crackdown against the separatist movement and criminalised the propagation of the separatist narrative. Measures included the Media Policy-2020 and 18-month-long internet restrictions (the government viewed social media as a security challenge because it was being used by separatist groups for political mobilisation). Freedom House dropped its designation of Kashmir from 'Partly Free' in 2019 to 'Not Free' in 2020 and 2021, citing deteriorating civil liberties and the dissolution of locally elected institutions.[14]

Throughout 2020, New Delhi frequently deployed the PSA's stringent anti-terror law and the Unlawful Activities Prevention Act (UAPA) against Kashmiri dissidents and suspected separatist activists. Restrictions on Kashmiri civil society remained in place, while human-rights defenders and journalists were targeted by the NIA. In October 2020, the NIA raided the offices of the Association of Parents of Disappeared Persons (APDP), English daily newspaper *Greater Kashmir*, Srinagar-based non-governmental organisation Athrout and the Jammu Kashmir Coalition of Civil Society (JKCCS). These raids and the NIA's confiscation of hard drives prevented the JKCCS from publishing its comprehensive yearly report on human rights in Kashmir.

Continuing with its hardline counter-insurgency strategy, in 2020 the Indian Army destroyed dozens of civilian homes where militants had taken cover during gunfights or were suspected to be hiding. As a result, several families were made homeless and pushed into poverty, particularly in south Kashmir. While several political prisoners were released in 2020, many remained in detention, though India's official statements on the exact number of persons detained and released since the August 2019 clampdown showed discrepancies.[15]

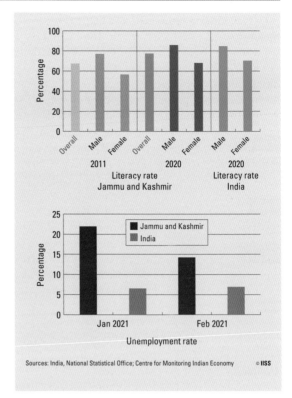

Sources: India, National Statistical Office; Centre for Monitoring Indian Economy   © IISS

Figure 1: Literacy and unemployment rates in Jammu and Kashmir (India)

Economic and social

The Modi regime encouraged Indian corporations and industrialists to establish their businesses in Kashmir with a view to using an economic approach to resolving the political issue of Kashmir.[16] However, Indian industrialists' entry has affected small local enterprises. In February 2020, most of the successful bids for extraction of mineral blocks in Kashmir went to non-local bidders. Concurrently, the J&K administration continued to ban stone quarrying in 2020, affecting the livelihoods of thousands of families associated with the industry across Kashmir.

Conflict Outlook

Political scenarios

The BJP government's hardline policies in J&K have constrained separatist organisations' ability to mobilise support. The crackdowns on dissenting voices and entities, arbitrary arrests, prohibition on public assembly and the censorship of local media through the Media Policy-2020 precluded any effective mobilisation against New Delhi's controversial policies in the reporting period. The expansion of surveillance architecture and an increased security presence on streets and roads also helped New Delhi to control the restive population. The three separatist leaders – Syed Ali Shah Geelani, Mirwaiz Umar Farooq and Mohammad Yasin Malik – remained in custody or under house arrest. New Delhi also exerts increased pressure on local newspapers to ensure they do not carry press statements of separatist organisations, which has further undermined the latter's political reach. The BJP government will continue with its hardline policy to prevent a conflict relapse into the political unrest that marked the decade prior to 2019. Strikes organised by the local population in February 2020 indicate that political resistance is still alive in Kashmir, although mass anti-India street protests (seen in 2008, 2009, 2010 and 2016) are also less likely to occur given India's repressive measures and crowd-control tactics. This context may create the conditions for increased militant violence.

Escalation potential and conflict-related risks

Beyond the aforementioned risk that India's repressive measures to curtail street protests could create the conditions for increased militant activity, since the abrogation of Article 370, armed groups have diversified and adopted new tactics to gain greater international legitimacy, including increased sophistication of their online content. Insurgent groups are likely to continue targeting non-locals to instil fear among possible Indian settlers.

Prospects for peace

The February 2021 India–Pakistan ceasefire agreement heightened prospects for the resumption of bilateral dialogue, which has been suspended since 2013. However, the BJP government has tried to delink the Kashmir issue from its discussions with Pakistan about other issues; it would be unwilling to explicitly include it in the agenda of talks at the ministerial level.

There are incentives for both countries to sustain the ceasefire. Although diplomatic efforts to resolve the Kashmir dispute have suffered regular setbacks, military confrontation has not changed the status quo either. Resumed bilateral dialogue could help sustain the February ceasefire, which, at the least, will provide respite from the violence for the residents living along the LoC.

If the ceasefire has a positive impact on the political situation within the Kashmir Valley, then New Delhi could consolidate its changes implemented in Kashmir following the abrogation of Article 370. With the border situation stabilised, India could redeploy some of its troops in the hinterlands of the Kashmir Valley and intensify counter-insurgency operations.

Pakistan's options to confront India are limited due to its sluggish economy and overreliance on foreign aid and loans. Improved relations with India could help Pakistan's economy. Pakistan has reportedly shown its willingness to resume dialogue with India provided J&K's statehood is restored and Kashmiri voices are included (likely via the APHC). An India–Pakistan dialogue on J&K could pave the way for a wider engagement on other bilateral issues. The BJP government has already publicly pledged to reinstate J&K's statehood at an 'appropriate time'.[17]

Strategic implications and global influences

Although US President Joe Biden has pledged to put human rights and democracy at the core of his foreign policy, at present there is no real external pressure on India with respect to Kashmir. Instead, Biden has underlined India's importance to the US foreign-policy goal of strengthening security in the Indo-Pacific, to counter the increasing challenge posed by China in the region. India's position as a strategic partner in the Quadrilateral Security Dialogue (featuring Australia and Japan in addition to the US) will temper Biden's response to Modi's domestic policy.

Beijing is likely to continue applying pressure along the LAC to discourage New Delhi from actively participating in Washington's policy of containment against China and targeting Azad Jammu and Kashmir (Pakistan), through which the CPEC (part of China's Belt and Road Initiative) passes.[18] Meanwhile, the US exit from Afghanistan and a likely return of the Taliban to power will give Islamabad greater influence. This context will encourage anti-India armed groups in Kashmir and affect India's access to mineral-rich Central Asia. New Delhi may therefore find that it is preferable to normalise its relationship with Pakistan to agree a deal on Afghanistan (concerning access to its mineral resources and security issues). In return, Pakistan would likely push for Kashmir-centric initiatives and confidence-building measures.

Notes

1   When referring to developments before 15 August 2019, the acronym 'J&K' refers to the state of Jammu and Kashmir (including Kashmir, Jammu and Ladakh regions, which India controls). For developments after the abrogation of Article 370 and the bifurcation of J&K in 2019, J&K refers to the Union Territory of Jammu and Kashmir (including Jammu and Kashmir regions, which India controls).

2   See 'Yearly Fatalities', Datasheet – Jammu & Kashmir, South Asia Terrorism Portal.

3   The Indian Army's Northern Command launched *Operation Sadhbhavna* in 1998 as a public-outreach programme that built civilian infrastructure and provided some public services. According to official estimates, Northern Command has spent over US$70 million on the operation since 1998. See Indian Army website, 'Operation Sadhbhavana'.

4   Data on the number of active militants in Kashmir is provided by the J&K Police. Membership estimates for individual groups are not officially available. However, based on the pattern of fatalities suffered by each armed group in previous years, it is widely believed that HM is the largest armed group, followed by LeT and JeM. In 2020, the three major armed groups had 86, 35 and 43 fatalities respectively. The remaining fatalities are attributed to smaller groups, such as TRF, Al Badr and Ansar Ghazwat-ul-Hind.

5   Shujaat Bukhari, 'We Are Not Against Dialogue: Hizb Chief', *Hindu*, 15 December 2016.

6   Azaan Javaid, '118 Militants, 11 of Them Pakistanis, Killed in 6 Months, 48% Dip in Recruitment: J&K Police', *ThePrint*, 1 July 2020.

7   'UNMOGIP Mission Fact Sheet', United Nations Peacekeeping, 21 January 2020.

8   See 'Power Stations' on NHPC website. See also 'Kashmir and the Politics of Water', Al-Jazeera, 1 August 2011.

9   'In Kashmir, Bonds Prohibit Detainees from Holding Meetings or Speaking About Article 370', *Scroll.in*, 21 October 2019.

10 Press Trust of India (PTI), 'J&K DDC Polls Conclude with Voter Turnout of 51%; Counting on Tuesday', *Business Standard*, 19 December 2020.

11 See 'J&K District Council Polls Soon', *Hindu*, 21 October 2020.

12 Naveed Iqbal and Arun Sharma, 'Upsets Later, DDC Tally: BJP 6 in Jammu, Gupkar 5 in Kashmir', *Indian Express*, 14 February 2021.

13 India, Ministry of Defence, 'Joint Statement', 25 February 2021.

14 Freedom House, 'Freedom in the World 2020', 5 February 2020.

15 On 5 February 2020, the Indian government claimed that 6,605 people had been detained in J&K since 5 August 2019, of which 437 were still detained. Of the 444 detained under the PSA during this period, 389 were still in custody. However, on 4 February 2021, the government stated that 613 people had been detained since August 2019, of which 430 were released and 183 were still in detention in J&K. Yet on 9 March, it stated that 627 people had been detained since August 2019, of which 454 had been released while 173 were still in custody. See Ananya Bhardwaj, '389 People Detained in J&K Under Public Safety Act Since Article 370 Was Scrapped: Govt', *ThePrint*, 5 February 2020; 'Jammu and Kashmir: 183 People Still Under Detention, Centre Tells Parliament', *Scroll.in*, 4 February 2021; and PTI, '173 People, Detained When Article 370 Was Abrogated in J&K, Still Under Custody: Govt', *Greater Kashmir*, 9 March 2021.

16 New Delhi views development as a corrective measure that can address the alienation of Kashmiri youth, who are at the forefront of street protests and drive the new-age militancy.

17 PTI, '"Centre Will Grant Jammu and Kashmir Statehood at an Appropriate Time": Amit Shah', *Wire*, 14 February 2021.

18 Top policymakers in the BJP government and the Indian army chief have previously given statements advocating seizing Azad Kashmir as the next step after the abrogation of Article 370. See 'India–Pakistan (Kashmir)', in IISS, *Armed Conflict Survey 2020* (London: IISS, 2020), p. 269.

Asia

MYANMAR

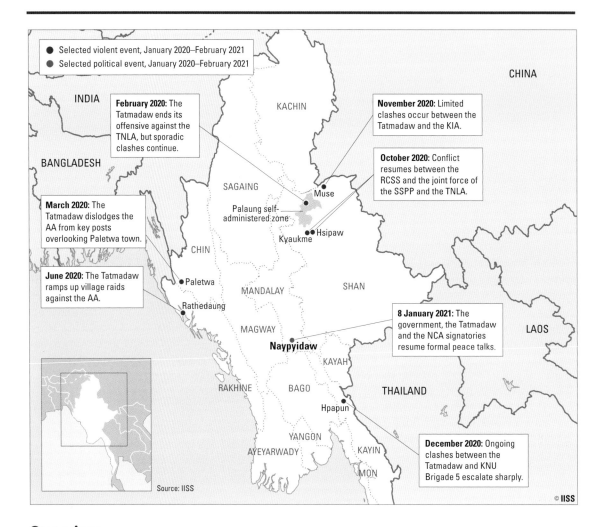

Selected violent event, January 2020–February 2021
Selected political event, January 2020–February 2021

CHINA

INDIA

KACHIN

February 2020: The Tatmadaw ends its offensive against the TNLA, but sporadic clashes continue.

November 2020: Limited clashes occur between the Tatmadaw and the KIA.

October 2020: Conflict resumes between the RCSS and the joint force of the SSPP and the TNLA.

BANGLADESH

SAGAING

Muse

Palaung self-administered zone

March 2020: The Tatmadaw dislodges the AA from key posts overlooking Paletwa town.

Hsipaw

Kyaukme

CHIN

June 2020: The Tatmadaw ramps up village raids against the AA.

Paletwa

MANDALAY

SHAN

Rathedaung

MAGWAY

8 January 2021: The government, the Tatmadaw and the NCA signatories resume formal peace talks.

LAOS

Naypyidaw

KAYAH

RAKHINE

BAGO

THAILAND

Hpapun

December 2020: Ongoing clashes between the Tatmadaw and KNU Brigade 5 escalate sharply.

YANGON

KAYIN

AYEYARWADY

MON

Source: IISS

© IISS

Overview

A long-running war has been waged by the Myanmar military, or the Tatmadaw, against a wide and dynamic array of ethnic armed organisations (EAOs) that arose in resistance to central control by the ethnic Bamar majority, following the country's independence in 1948. In 1962, General Ne Win staged a *coup d'état* before intensifying efforts to incorporate Myanmar's ethnic areas by force. The Tatmadaw has also worked tirelessly to crush democratic movements in Myanmar's Bamar-dominated centre. The democratic uprising of 1988, which saw the rise of Aung San Suu Kyi and the National League for Democracy (NLD), triggered a decades-long struggle for control of the central government among Bamar elites.

After drafting a new constitution in 2008, the Tatmadaw formulated a new approach to managing both ethnic armed opposition and elite-power competition. In October 2015, eight EAOs signed the Nationwide Ceasefire Agreement (NCA), marking the beginning of a formal peace process. Less than a month later, the NLD won open elections by a landslide, ushering in an era of hybrid rule between the military and the civilian-elected government. Fraught civil–military relations, stumbling peace talks and escalating conflict between the Tatmadaw

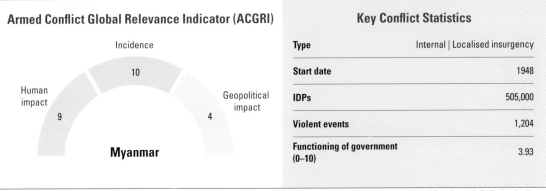

Armed Conflict Global Relevance Indicator (ACGRI)	Key Conflict Statistics	
Incidence: 10	Type	Internal | Localised insurgency
Human impact: 9	Start date	1948
Geopolitical impact: 4	IDPs	505,000
Myanmar	Violent events	1,204
	Functioning of government (0–10)	3.93

ACGRI pillars: IISS calculation based on multiple sources for 2020 and January/February 2021 (scale: 0–100). See Notes on Methodology and Data Appendix for further details on Key Conflict Statistics.

and non-ceasefire EAOs characterised the period between 2015 and 2020.

Myanmar experienced at least 1,205 conflict events in the period between 1 January 2020 and 25 February 2021, including 539 battles between armed actors, driven by four important conflicts.[1] In the west of the country, the Arakan Army (AA) fought for a permanent foothold in Rakhine State. In the east, the Tatmadaw and the Ta'ang National Liberation Army (TNLA) clashed regularly. Towards the end of 2020, a frozen conflict also re-ignited between the TNLA and its rival, the Restoration Council of Shan State (RCSS). Finally, fighting continued between the Tatmadaw and Brigade 5 of the Karen National Liberation Army (KNLA) over a military road project near the Thai border in Myanmar's southeast.

Though the overall pace of the conflicts involving the AA and TNLA slowed in 2020, those with the KNLA and RCSS, the two most influential signatories to the NCA, experienced greater fluctuation. On 8 January 2021, both groups resumed formal peace talks but the coronavirus pandemic soon thwarted what limited progress had been made and the KNLA–Tatmadaw confrontation deteriorated, while sporadic but intense clashes between the Tatmadaw and RCSS also accelerated. On 1 February 2021, the Tatmadaw seized power from the civilian government after manufacturing a political crisis over the results of the November 2020 elections, catapulting Myanmar into an intensified degree of violent turmoil.

Conflict Parties

Myanmar armed forces (Tatmadaw)

Strength: 406,000 active military and 107,000 active paramilitary.

Areas of operation: Operates nationwide. Headquarters in Naypyidaw.

Leadership: Senior-General Min Aung Hlaing (commander-in-chief), who assumed the role of Chairman of the State Administration Council following the 1 February 2021 coup.

Structure: Six Bureaus of Special Operations with 14 regional military commands. It also fields ten light infantry divisions, elite units tasked with spearheading offensives.

History: First seized power in 1962 and ruled via several successive regimes until 2011 when it initiated a process of democratisation, continuing nevertheless to reserve 25% of parliamentary seats, as enshrined in the 2008 constitution.

Objectives: Preserve the union, quell ethnic and political dissent, maintain political power, conduct Bamar-centric state building, modernise the military and secure international credibility.

Opponents: More than 20 EAOs, National Unity Government (NUG) and various 'people's defence forces'.

Affiliates/allies: Has integrated various armed organisations into its command under the People's Militia Force and Border Guard Force (BGF) schemes.

Resources/capabilities: Likely self-sufficient in the production of small arms and munitions. Increasingly reliant on airpower, it possesses new MiG-29 and Yak-130 aircraft and Mi-17 and Mi-24 helicopters from Russia and China. It has demonstrated joint naval, air and land operations and is capable of mounting major operations on multiple fronts.

Asia

Arakan Army/United League of Arakan (AA/ULA)

Strength: Up to 10,000 fighters, the majority of which are deployed in Rakhine State.[2]

Areas of operation: Most active in northern and central Rakhine State as well as southern Chin State. Limited operations in Kachin State, northern Shan State and possibly Bangladesh.

Leadership: Twan Mrat Naing (founder and commander-in-chief); Nyo Twan Awng (vice deputy commander).

Structure: Top commanders direct operations from headquarters in either Kachin State or Shan State. Regular fighters operate from villages, jungle hideouts and fixed positions.

History: Founded in 2009 in Kachin State under the tutelage of the Kachin Independence Army (KIA), the group began to build a presence in Rakhine State as early as 2013.

Objectives: Establish autonomous control over Rakhine State and liberate the Rakhine people.

Opponents: The Tatmadaw and the former NLD-led civilian government.

Affiliates/allies: Member of the Federal Political Negotiation Consultative Committee (FPNCC), a 'political' alliance of EAOs outside of the NCA. It is also a member of two military alliances, the Northern Alliance and the Brotherhood Alliance.

Resources/capabilities: Capable of mobilising large contingents of fighters to stage frontal assaults on military and police positions. Fields small arms, mortars, improvised explosive devices (IEDs), 107mm surface-to-surface rockets, and satellite-communications equipment. Wields some administrative control in Rakhine State and has strong support from the local population.

Kachin Independence Army/Kachin Independence Organisation (KIA/KIO)

Strength: Up to 10,000 regulars.

Areas of operation: Kachin State (where it controls static positions across wide territories) and northern Shan State (where its units are more mobile). The Tatmadaw does not recognise its presence in Shan.

Leadership: General N'Ban La heads the KIO and is the senior commander of the KIA.

Structure: Divided into ten brigades.

History: Formed in 1961. Signed a written ceasefire in 1994 which later broke down in 2011. The KIA founded the Northern Alliance in 2016 before launching a major joint offensive against the Tatmadaw.

Objectives: Seek Kachin autonomy within a federal democratic union.

Opponents: The Tatmadaw.

Affiliates/allies: Member of the FPNCC and leader of the Northern Alliance.

Resources/capabilities: Generates income through formal and informal activities. Likely manufactures or assembles small arms and ammunition in its area of control. Possesses 107mm unguided rockets. Demonstrated ability to overrun Tatmadaw positions and downed one helicopter in 2021.

Karen National Liberation Army/Karen National Union (KNLA/KNU)

Strength: Between 4,000 and 5,000 fighters.

Areas of operation: Military operations in Bago region, Karen State, Mon State and Tanintharyi region.

Leadership: General Saw Mutu Sae Poe (chairperson); Padoh Saw Kwe Htoo Win (vice chairperson); Padoh Saw Tadoh Moo (general secretary).

Structure: The KNLA is formed of seven brigades.

History: The KNU was established in 1947. That same year, it formed the Karen National Defence Organisation (KNDO), a collection of local armed units that later evolved into the KNLA. The KNLA/KNU organisation signed a ceasefire with the Tatmadaw in 2012 before signing the NCA in 2015. It served as the leader of the Peace Process Steering Team (PPST) until 2018.

Objectives: Seek Karen self-determination within a federal democratic union.

Opponents: The Tatmadaw and some elements of the BGF.

Affiliates/allies: Member of the PPST as a signatory to the NCA.

Resources/capabilities: Primarily fields small arms including leftover US-made Vietnam-era M-16s. Also has rocket-propelled grenades and landmines.

Myanmar National Democratic Alliance Army/ Myanmar National Truth and Justice Party (MNDAA/MNTJP)

Strength: Between 3,000 and 4,000 fighters.

Areas of operation: Kokang self-administered zone (SAZ), northern Shan State.

Leadership: Peng Deren (commander-in-chief), Yang Wenzhou (deputy commander).

Structure: Three brigades: 211st, 311th and 511th.

Myanmar National Democratic Alliance Army/ Myanmar National Truth and Justice Party (MNDAA/MNTJP)

History: Formed in 1989 by Peng Jiasheng as a breakaway of the Communist Party of Burma. Suffered an internal split in 2009 after Peng refused to transform the group into a border guard. A subsequent Tatmadaw offensive expelled Peng from Laukkai, and an MNDAA bid to retake it in 2015 ultimately failed.

Objectives: Liberate the Kokang people, oppose authoritarianism.

Opponents: The Tatmadaw.

Affiliates/allies: Member of the FPNCC, the Northern Alliance and the Brotherhood Alliance.

Resources/capabilities: Fields small arms including AK pattern rifles, RPGs, mortars and landmines. Often operates in combined units with the TNLA.

Shan State Army–North/Shan State Progress Party (SSA–N/SSPP)

Strength: Between 3,000 and 4,000 fighters.

Areas of operation: Military operations in northern Shan State with some possible unarmed activities in neighbouring Mandalay region.

Leadership: Lieutenant-General Pang Fa (commander of the SSA–N and chairperson of the SSPP).

Structure: Three brigades split into nine battalions.[3]

History: The SSPP signed a ceasefire with the government in 1989. It maintains an intense rivalry with the RCSS.

Objectives: Seek Shan unity and self-determination within the multi-ethnic Shan State.

Opponents: The Tatmadaw and RCSS.

Affiliates/allies: Member of the FPNCC and military partner to the TNLA in its fight against the RCSS.

Resources/capabilities: Relies heavily on the United Wa State Army (UWSA) for small arms and support.

Shan State Army–South/Restoration Council of Shan State (SSA–S/RCSS)

Strength: Between 8,000 and 10,000 fighters.

Areas of operation: Headquartered at Loi Tai Leng in southern Shan State. Began operations in northern Shan State as early as 2011, with further expansion there after 2015.

Leadership: Yawd Serk (founder and chairperson).

Structure: Ten brigades.

History: The SSA–S was formed by a breakaway faction of the Mong Tai Army in 1996 after refusing to surrender to the government. The RCSS, the group's political wing, was then established in 1999. The RCSS/SSA–S signed an initial ceasefire with the government in 2011 before joining the NCA in 2015.

Objectives: Shan self-determination within a federal democratic union.

Opponents: The Tatmadaw, TNLA and SSPP.

Affiliates/allies: Member and acting leader of the PPST as a signatory to the NCA.

Resources/capabilities: Fields small arms, landmines, RPGs and mortars.

Ta'ang National Liberation Army/Palaung State Liberation Front (TNLA/PSLF)

Strength: Between 8,000 and 10,000 fighters, including irregulars.

Areas of operation: Strongest presence in the Palaung self-administered zone but operates in nearly every Palaung area in northern Shan State.

Leadership: Tar Aik Bong (chairperson); Tar Ho Plan (commander-in-chief); Tar Bone Kyaw (first secretary-general).

Structure: Mobile command structure drawing on both regular and irregular fighters.

History: Its predecessor, the Palaung State Liberation Army (PSLA), signed a ceasefire in 1991 before disarming in 2005. Former PSLA cadres re-armed and formed the TNLA/PSLF in 2009. The TNLA leads the Brotherhood Alliance together with the AA and MNDAA. It spearheaded a major offensive along the primary overland trade corridor linking Myanmar with China in 2019.

Objectives: Liberate ethnic Palaung people and form an autonomous Palaung state within a federal union.

Opponents: The Tatmadaw and RCSS.

Affiliates/allies: Member of the FPNCC, the Northern Alliance and leader of the Brotherhood Alliance.

Resources/capabilities: Capable of conducting large-scale offensive operations in areas of government control. Demonstrated coordinated military action with alliance partners. Fields small arms, mortars, landmines and 107mm surface-to-surface rockets. Relies heavily on 'taxation' for income generation.

Asia

United Wa State Army/United Wa State Party (UWSA/UWSP)

Strength: Up to 30,000 fighters.

Areas of operation: Wa State, an autonomous enclave in eastern Shan State.

Leadership: Bao Youxiang (president of Wa State and top political and military leader of the UWSA/UWSP); Xiao Minliang (vice-president).

Structure: Five divisions along the Myanmar–Thailand border and four divisions in the Wa Hills.

History: The UWSA arose from the Communist Party of Burma in 1989 and immediately signed a ceasefire with the government, which it maintains today. It captured additional territory along the Thai border in the 1990s and built a large drug empire based on opium and later methamphetamine to fund its operations.

Objectives: Preserve autonomy over Wa State, maintain buffer forces through proxy allies, possibly seek vision of a Myanmar confederation rather than federation.

Opponents: The Tatmadaw.

Affiliates/allies: Leader of the FPNCC.

Resources/capabilities: Fields advanced equipment such as Chinese-made drones, a helicopter, armoured vehicles, anti-aircraft guns and FN-6 man-portable air-defence systems (MANPADS). Manufactures small arms like the Type-81 assault rifle.

Conflict Drivers

Political

Marginalisation of ethnic groups:

Myanmar's internal armed conflicts have been driven largely by a struggle for greater autonomy among the numerous ethnic groups that inhabit the country. Common grievances have been influenced by a history of neglect and abuse by successive Bamar-dominated governments that have extracted wealth from ethnic areas since independence in 1948.

In principle, most of Myanmar's EAOs agree that the formation of a federal union would provide a political solution to enduring conflict. However, climate change and natural disasters continue to drive migration from the central dry lands and Irrawaddy delta inhabited by the socio-politically dominant Bamar majority. Internal Bamar migration to the fertile highlands inhabited by Myanmar's ethnic populations complicates a potential political solution based on ethnic federalism.

Economic and social

Illicit economies:

Revenue generated from the production and trafficking of illicit narcotics has played a central role in Myanmar's conflict by funding the continuation and expansion of armed activity. Armed groups have profited from every aspect of such illicit trade, including the import of precursors, renting of land to producers and taxation of shipments. State security forces conducted a crackdown on manufacturers in northern Shan State in the first half of 2020, likely to deny income to armed groups.

State-backed development projects:

Development linked to the China–Myanmar Economic Corridor, which includes plans for a high-speed rail link with Mandalay, is expected to exacerbate conflicts as groups vie to consolidate control of territories slated for development, with a future eye towards rent seeking. For example, some observers see the RCSS's expansion into northern Shan State – which has driven conflict with the TNLA and SSPP – as economically motivated. In addition to related environmental and social concerns, armed groups have also alleged that the Tatmadaw have used hydropower projects to justify further militarisation.

Security

Ceasefire and state expansionism:

In 2019 the Tatmadaw demanded that the TNLA limit its movement within the Palaung SAZ and that the AA vacate Rakhine, demands that were fundamentally at odds with the TNLA's wider fight for ethnic interests and the AA's aim to seek a permanent presence in Rakhine. Such efforts to demarcate territory by force ahead of ceasefire discussions propelled fighting in 2019 and 2020.

The Tatmadaw has also used ceasefires to extend its control into ethnic areas, which has driven conflict in Hpapun township, Kayin State, where its ongoing road building has spurred sporadic fighting with the KNLA since March 2018 and which worsened in 2020. The KNLA, Karen civil-society organisations and the local population oppose the project, interpreting construction as an effort to 'Burmanise' the area.

Political and Military Developments

Peace negotiations

After 15 months of stalled talks, the government, the Tatmadaw and ten EAO NCA signatories resumed formal peace negotiations at the Joint Implementation Coordination Meeting (JICM) on 8 January 2020. All parties agreed to hold the 4th Union Peace Conference (UPC), the premier peace summit meant for key agreements on a federal solution, but the coronavirus pandemic soon halted this limited momentum. As the already cumbersome pre-negotiations moved online, the government's attention was diverted by the Rohingya genocide case brought against it by the Gambia at the International Court of Justice. Though the 4th UPC eventually convened in August 2020, the agreement reached was mostly symbolic, with key points recycled from the NCA and a document drafted at a previous UPC.

The Rakhine conflict

Fighting in Rakhine and Chin states intensified in the first half of 2020 as the Tatmadaw moved to retake control of the strategic Paletwa township. By mid-2020, the Tatmadaw had largely dislodged the AA from its fixed positions throughout the eastern half of the theatre. With a full river and land blockade in place, the Tatmadaw spent the monsoon months of May to September conducting village raids against AA supporters and operatives. By November 2020 the Tatmadaw appeared poised for a new offensive, but the fighting abruptly stopped as both parties entered into negotiations to hold elections in formerly disenfranchised constituencies.

Instability in northern Shan State

In northern Shan State, a limited Tatmadaw offensive to target TNLA weapons caches and outposts ended in February 2020. After declaring a unilateral ceasefire on 9 May 2020, Tatmadaw pressure on the TNLA eased, creating a vacuum that helped re-ignite a dormant conflict between the RCSS and a coalition formed by the TNLA and SSPP that continued into 2021.

Worsening of Hpapun conflict

Towards the end of 2020, ongoing conflict over the Tatmadaw road project between the Tatmadaw and the KNLA's Brigade 5 continued to worsen in the remote township of Hpapun, exacerbated further by the coronavirus pandemic. Although the Joint Ceasefire Monitoring Committee (JMC) had stalled in 2019, civilian delegates had managed to mediate the conflict through informal channels, but this became impossible due to pandemic-related restrictions. A major confrontation was already brewing before the coup of 1 February 2021.

General elections and *coup d'état*

General elections on 8 November 2020 were won by a landslide by the incumbent NLD, prompting the military to claim as many as 8.6 million voter irregularities, a figure widely dismissed by observers.[4] An acute political crisis emerged in the final days of January 2021 as last-ditch efforts to mediate an agreement between the NLD and Tatmadaw failed. On 1 February 2021 the military staged a *coup d'état*.

Post-coup resistance and repression

The Tatmadaw's initial response to nationwide resistance to its 1 February 2021 coup featured mass arrests, internet shutdowns and the use of less-lethal crowd-control measures. However, as protests and civil disobedience persisted, it deployed elite military units into major urban areas and began a campaign of mass killing, beatings, torture and terror. As of 30 April 2021, the regime had killed at least 759 civilians in its crackdown.[5]

Asia

Key Events in 2020–21

POLITICAL EVENTS

8 January 2020

The government, the Tatmadaw and NCA signatories restart formal peace process at the JICM.

2 February

NCA signatories hold a working meeting on the implementation of the eight-point JICM agreement.

23 March

Myanmar confirms its first cases of COVID-19. Ad hoc restrictions are applied until a general lockdown comes into effect on 10 April.

23 March

The government declares the AA a terrorist organisation in step with the Tatmadaw's policy preference.

27 April

The President's Office forms a joint committee with EAOs to formulate responses to the coronavirus pandemic in ethnic areas.

10 May

The Tatmadaw commander-in-chief meets with UWSA leaders, offers relief supplies to tackle the coronavirus pandemic in sign of steadily improving relations.

14 June

The government extends a ban on visas and inbound international flights after confirming a string of imported COVID-19 cases.

7 July

Joint Ceasefire Monitoring Committee–Union Level convenes for the first time since 2018.

19 August

The government, the Tatmadaw and EAOs convene the 4th UPC. No substantive agreement is reached.

September

Bangladesh Prime Minister Sheikh Hasina condemns Myanmar for the Rohingya crisis at the United Nations General Assembly. Myanmar responds by accusing Bangladesh of harbouring rebel fighters.

October

NCA signatories hold a series of internal coordination and working meetings.

8 November

The NLD wins the 2020 general elections by a landslide, prompting the military to issue unfounded claims of widespread election fraud.

1 January 2021

The government announces new plans to restructure its peace-process architecture.

1 February

The Tatmadaw seizes legislative, executive and judicial power, prompting nationwide protests.

MILITARY/VIOLENT EVENTS

January 2020

The Tatmadaw launches a renewed offensive to dislodge AA positions in northern Rakhine and southern Chin states.

February

The Tatmadaw completes a limited offensive against the TNLA in northern Shan State.

20 April

A World Health Organization driver is killed in Minbya township, Rakhine State.

May

The AA issues an ultimatum for the government and Tatmadaw to vacate Rakhine State. The Tatmadaw deploys additional units into Hpapun township, Kayin State, amidst ongoing clashes with the KNLA.

June

The Tatmadaw and RCSS clash over territorial disputes in Hsipaw and Kyaukme townships, northern Shan State.

16 July

Two Tatmadaw privates murder Mu Naw, a local Karen woman in Hpapun township. Her death further galvanises public opposition to the Tatmadaw's presence in the area.

3 August

The AA responds to accelerated Tatmadaw raids in Rathedaung township, Rakhine State, with a major attack, demonstrating its continued ability to conduct large-scale operations.

September

The Tatmadaw launches a limited pre-election offensive against Northern Alliance outposts in northern Shan State to push fighters away from polling stations. The KIA and TNLA retaliate with ambushes.

14 October

The AA abducts three NLD candidates during election campaigns.

November

The Tatmadaw and AA abruptly enter into a de facto ceasefire in Rakhine State after more than two years of uninterrupted fighting.

December

The Tatmadaw pulls back its forces in Shan and Rakhine states while unrelated fighting with the KNLA accelerates in Kayin State.

March 2021

Security forces conduct a major nationwide crackdown with widespread arrests, killings, internet blackouts and generalised violence against civilians.

Impact

Human rights and humanitarian

Human-rights abuses remained widespread in 2020. In Rakhine, arbitrary detention, targeted killings, arson and torture were widely reported. The Tatmadaw's use of heavy firepower also drove high displacement. By March 2021, more than 99,300 people remained displaced by the Rakhine conflict.[6]

In Shan State, armed groups targeted civilians with forced recruitment, extortion and kidnapping, and renewed inter-EAO fighting near populated areas drove high displacement. Up

Figure 1: Civilians in protracted displacement settings (as of 25 March 2021)

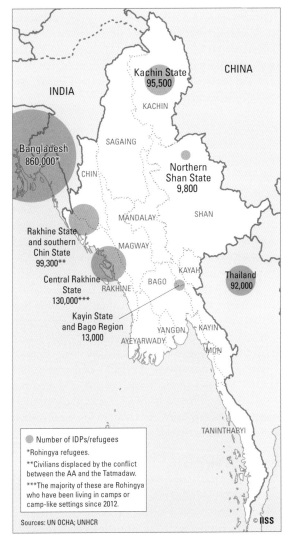

Number of IDPs/refugees

*Rohingya refugees.

**Civilians displaced by the conflict between the AA and the Tatmadaw.

***The majority of these are Rohingya who have been living in camps or camp-like settings since 2012.

Sources: UN OCHA; UNHCR

© IISS

to 3,900 people fled clashes between the TNLA and RCSS in the period between 27 December 2020 and 15 January 2021 alone.[7] In southeastern Myanmar, intensified fighting between the KNLA and the Tatmadaw displaced up to 4,000 people in December 2020.[8] Human-rights groups in Kayin State documented numerous incidents of Tatmadaw violence against civilians, including the indiscriminate shelling of villages, as the Tatmadaw continued to use collective punishment as a form of 'counter-insurgency'.

As of January 2021, up to 855,000 Rohingya refugees remained in temporary camps in Bangladesh, with virtually no progress made towards their voluntary and dignified return in 2020.[9]

Political stability

The elite power struggle between the Tatmadaw and NLD-led government was the most destabilising factor in Myanmar's political landscape. In response to the NLD's landslide victory in the November 2020 elections, the Tatmadaw manufactured a political crisis with unsubstantiated allegations of irregularities and demanded the government dissolve the Union Election Committee. A crisis was clearly emerging by early 2021, yet heavily deteriorated civil–military relations precluded efforts towards a mediated compromise. The NLD's unwillingness to concede to the Tatmadaw's demands was used as the pretext for the 1 February 2021 coup.

Armed conflict also strained socio-political relations. For example, the conflict between the RCSS and SSPP, two Shan EAOs, and which involved the TNLA, disrupted the Committee for Shan State Unity, a coalition of Shan political parties, civil-society organisations and EAOs. It also exacerbated tensions between Ta'ang and Shan constituents, with alleged RCSS intimidation against the ethnic Ta'ang National Party (TNP) leading to the cancellation of elections for nearly 60,000 people.[10]

Economic and social

The coronavirus pandemic and related lockdown measures led to the closure of businesses, the disruption of trade and labour supply and a reduction in remittances. According to the IMF, real GDP growth dropped from 6.8% in 2019 to just 3.2% in 2020. Already reeling from the pandemic slowdown, the February 2021 coup prompted the emergence of the Civil Disobedience Movement (CDM), a popular revolt that brought the country's key economic sectors to a three-month standstill. An updated IMF forecast showed an 8.9% contraction of Myanmar's GDP in 2021.[11]

Relations with neighbouring and international partners and geopolitical implications

In 2020, regional interests in Myanmar were complicated most by the continued instability in Rakhine, which delayed progress on India's Kaladan Multi-Modal Transit Transport Project that aims to link Kolkata with Sittwe and by threatening Chinese interests on Ramree Island, which houses the pipeline terminus connecting the Shwe gas field in the Bay of Bengal to Yunnan province. The conflict also prevented any progress towards facilitating the safe and voluntary return of the Rohingya, thereby continuing to strain Myanmar's relations with Bangladesh, with a diplomatic row ensuing at the UN General Assembly in September 2020.

Conflict Outlook

Political scenarios

The February 2021 coup thrust Myanmar into its worst political crisis since 1988. Though the military regime initially articulated a plan to hold new elections in 2022, it later threatened to to delay the elections and thereby extend its control. Any future elections organised by the regime will lack credibility, especially given the detention of many of the country's leading political figures, including Aung San Suu Kyi.

In opposition to the new regime, in April 2021 ousted members of the civilian government formed the National Unity Government (NUG), a parallel body claiming legitimate control over Myanmar, and announced plans to raise a 'people's defence force'. At present, the NUG commands strong public support, but it lacks a tangible way to exercise its mandate and will likely struggle to raise an effective fighting force.

Irrespective of the NUG's performance, the Tatmadaw will likely face prolonged opposition from the general public, not least from the CDM. The siege mentality adopted by the Tatmadaw to quell post-coup protests only hardened public attitudes against it. Neither side is likely to back down easily, making continued volatility in Myanmar highly probable.

Escalation potential and conflict-related risks

Myanmar's long-running internal armed conflicts are at stark risk of further escalation and intensification. At worst, the volatility seen in 2020 and early 2021 could develop into a multi-front war in the borderlands alongside armed resistance in urban areas. Any scenario will likely involve continued attacks on the civilian population in both urban and ethnic areas.

Two ongoing armed conflicts accelerated immediately after the coup. A fresh KIA offensive in February 2021 marked the return of open conflict to Kachin State for the first time in 36 months. Having vowed to protect civilians in its area, the KNLA overran a Tatmadaw border post on 27 March 2020 and the Tatmadaw responded with regular airstrikes, displacing as many as 40,000 civilians by 23 April 2021.[12]

On 30 March 2021, the Brotherhood Alliance, which includes the AA, TNLA and MNDAA, threatened to 'join hands' with the nationwide resistance movement that emerged following the coup if the regime continued its attacks on civilians. Though military action by the alliance could strain the Tatmadaw by creating a de facto unified front among the most important EAOs, the AA has expressed reluctance to resume fighting after more than two years of punishing warfare.

Armed resistance among the Bamar majority was also growing, with reports that thousands had left Myanmar's cities to seek military training from EAOs, while community-organised 'self-defence' brigades have already mobilised in urban areas.[13] Extreme violence against civilians – of the type used to quell protests in the industrial city of Bago on 9 April, which killed 82 civilians – will likely prompt resistance in the form of bomb attacks and armed clashes in major cities like Mandalay and Yangon.[14]

Prospects for peace

Myanmar's peace process under the NCA was predicated on the pursuit of a democratic federal union, which has been shattered by the Tatmadaw's blatant diversion from that path. The coup also forced a seismic realignment of Myanmar society. Driven by intense hatred for the regime, the Bamar majority began to champion the cause of the EAOs, which may embolden some groups to intensify their military opposition. Although other armed groups may seek stability in their areas by maintaining old ceasefires or informal truces, any formal agreement with the current regime will be considered unsavoury politically, reducing its likelihood.

Strategic implications and global influences

The international community's response to the attempted coup largely consisted of inaction and deference, except for Russia, which expressed an explicit desire to deepen ties with the Tatmadaw in a March 2021 visit. China appeared to have adopted a laissez-faire approach to the unrest, maintaining its traditional line of 'non-interference', though it would likely block any response by the UN Security Council. Though some members of the Association of Southeast Asian Nations (ASEAN) condemned the coup and crackdown, the bloc appeared reluctant to take substantive diplomatic action to confront the crisis. For the most part, Myanmar's political and military conflicts will likely continue to play out in isolation.

Notes

1   Armed Conflict Location & Event Data Project (ACLED).

2   Estimates of strength numbers for all EAOs in this chapter are taken from Stein Tønnesson, Min Zaw Oo and Ne Lynn Aung, 'Pretending to Be States: The Use of Facebook by Armed Groups in Myanmar', *Journal of Contemporary Asia*, 4 May 2021.

3   Interview with Francesco Buscemi, Researcher, Sant'Anna School of Advanced Studies, 27 May 2021.

4   AFP, 'Tatmadaw Raises Prospect of Coup After Voter-fraud Claims', *Frontier Myanmar*, 27 January 2021.

5   Assistance Association for Political Prisoners, 'Daily Briefing in Relation to the Military Coup', 30 April 2021.

6   United Nations Office for the Coordination of Humanitarian Affairs, 'Myanmar Humanitarian Update No. 5', 25 March 2021.

7   United Nations Office for the Coordination of Humanitarian Affairs, 'Myanmar Humanitarian Update No. 3', 27 January 2021, p. 2.

8   *Ibid.*

9   Inter Sector Coordination Group, 'Rohingya Humanitarian Crisis Joint Response Plan 2020 Funding Update as of 2020-01-31', 11 February 2021.

10   Zaw Ye Thwe, 'Parties Protest Cancelation of Vote in Mong Kung', Myanmar Now, 2 November 2020.

11   International Monetary Fund, 'World Economic Outlook Database', April 2021.

12   United Nations Office for the Coordination of Humanitarian Affairs, 'Myanmar Humanitarian Update No. 6', 30 April 2021.

13   'Dissidents Fleeing Myanmar Junta Find Shelter and Support with Ethnic Armed Groups', *Irrawaddy*, 23 March 2021.

14   'Reports: Myanmar Forces Kill 82 in Single Day in City', Associated Press, 11 April 2021.

Asia

INDIA–NORTHEAST

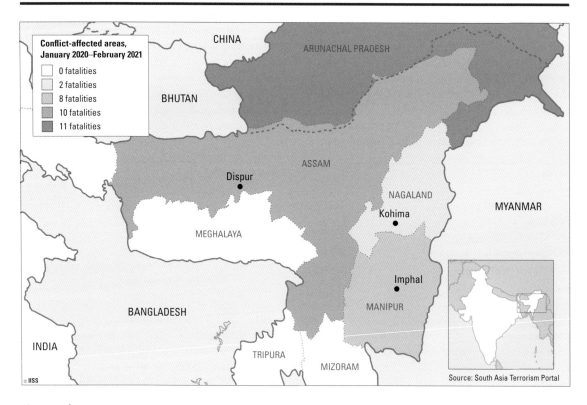

Conflict-affected areas,
January 2020–February 2021

0 fatalities
2 fatalities
8 fatalities
10 fatalities
11 fatalities

CHINA

ARUNACHAL PRADESH

BHUTAN

ASSAM

Dispur

NAGALAND

Kohima

MYANMAR

MEGHALAYA

Imphal

BANGLADESH

MANIPUR

INDIA

TRIPURA

MIZORAM

© IISS

Source: South Asia Terrorism Portal

Overview

Over 100 non-state armed groups have operated in Northeast India since India's independence in 1947. These groups have mobilised around identity-based fears of exploitation or cultural assimilation by a defined 'other' and around competition over access to socio-economic resources granted by New Delhi.

The longest-running and most politically significant of these is the Naga insurgency, which broke out in the Naga Hills during the 1950s when the Naga National Council (NNC) – increasingly anxious about the prospect of cultural assimilation by India – established a parallel government and began attacking Indian security forces. Several failed negotiation efforts – including the 1975 Shillong Accord – have intersected with intra-factional politics to fragment the Naga movement into several subgroups. These include the National Socialist Council of Nagalim–Isak Muivah faction (NSCN–IM) and the National Socialist Council of Nagaland–Khaplang (NSCN–K), which violently separated from one another in 1988. The NSCN–IM entered into a ceasefire with the Indian government in 1997, which still stands though remains fragile. Although a 2015 Framework Agreement aimed to accelerate the peace process, ongoing tensions and unresolved issues hampered a final resolution, making stand-offs and armed clashes a common feature of the ceasefire landscape.[1] New Delhi attempted to impose a negotiation deadline of 31 October 2019, leading to another stand-off, however subsequent climbdowns have returned the status quo of armed coexistence. The NSCN–K had signed its own ceasefire with New Delhi in 2001, but this was terminated as armed operations resumed in 2015. The group has since split three times into pro- and anti-talks factions. Several smaller fragments from both NSCN factions and the remnants of the NNC formed the Working Committee (WC) in 2016. Now made up of seven factions, this umbrella coalition has engaged in its own peace talks with the Indian government with demands distinct from those made by the NSCN–IM, leading to tensions between the two parallel peace processes.

Armed Conflict Global Relevance Indicator (ACGRI)	Key Conflict Statistics	
	Type	Internal | Localised insurgency
Incidence	**Start date**	1956
17	**IDPs**	473,000
Human impact · Geopolitical impact	**Fatalities**	1,046
4 · 4	**Violent events**	2,002
India		

ACGRI pillars: IISS calculation based on multiple sources for 2020 and January/February 2021 (scale: 0–100). The indicator's results and certain Key Conflict Statistics refer to the country as a whole rather than the specific conflict covered in this chapter. See Notes on Methodology and Data Appendix for further details on Key Conflict Statistics.

Other pro-independence insurgencies arose in Mizoram State, following a devastating famine in the Mizo Hills, and in the former princely state of Manipur during the 1960s. The late 1970s also saw the emergence of insurgent groups from the radical fringes of anti-migration movements in the states of Assam and Tripura. Although the anti-migration movements campaigned for concessions that would protect communities against unchecked illegal migration, their armed components took more radical stances; for example, the United Liberation Front of Asom (ULFA) fought for Assamese sovereignty. Few indigenous armed groups have emerged from the state of Arunachal Pradesh, but the region has served as an important access corridor for Naga armed groups and others from their camps in neighbouring Myanmar, as well as in Bangladesh and Bhutan. These access routes have grown increasingly important since Indian counter-insurgency successes from the 1990s onwards have reduced the available operating space for armed groups inside Northeast India itself. However, they have been threatened by cross-border diplomacy, cooperation and military operations. In 2019 in particular, Myanmar military operations targeted Indian insurgents, disrupting the network of camps on the Burmese side of the international border that had been used to launch strikes into India.

Sustained counter-insurgency, protracted peace talks and large-scale surrenders have all caused violence levels to decline significantly since 2010. However, several lingering conflict drivers continued to sustain the conflict, albeit at a low level, during 2020.[2] According to partial data from the South Asia Terrorism Portal, annual insurgency-related fatalities totalled just 27 in 2020 (with four further fatalities recorded to 1 March 2021), a decrease from 34 in 2019, and a vast drop from the 1,059 recorded in 2008.[3] Furthermore, the total number of insurgency-related incidents declined from 640 in 2019 to 389 in 2020 (with 74 further incidents until 1 March 2021).[4] However, while the 2020 reduction in fatalities continues the trend over recent years of weakening insurgent capabilities and the growing ascendancy of the Indian state, the decline in the overall number of incidents (including arrests, minor clashes, reported incidents of extortion and otherwise) reflects the dampening impact that the coronavirus pandemic has had on insurgency in the region.

January 2020 saw the final collapse and demobilisation of the remnants of the formerly anti-talks National Democratic Front of Bodoland–Saoraigwra (NDFB–S), as its remaining cadres surrendered and signed the third Bodo Accord, which incorporated a number of Bodo armed groups and expanded the administrative and financial powers of the Bodoland Territorial Region. The NDFB–S had faced sustained pressure from counter-insurgency operations since Indian government forces launched *Operation All Out* in December 2014, and was further crippled in 2019 by the Myanmar military (Tatmadaw) operations against Indian insurgent camps within its borders. By bringing together four rival Bodo factions, the final accord appeared to overcome the failures of previous accords, which had dealt with individual factions and thus led to violent outbidding. Although little headway was made in the peace processes with the region's other pro-talks armed groups (such as the ULFA–Pro Talks Faction (ULFA–PTF), NSCN–IM and the WC), the end of 2020 saw surrenders from key hardline anti-talks leaders. These

Asia

included Drishti Rajkhowa, the deputy commander-in-chief of ULFA–Independent (ULFA–I), Nyemlang Konyak, formerly with the NSCN–Khaplang/Yung Aung (NSCN–K/YA) and a number of militants from each group.[5] This indicated that a combination of sustained counter-insurgency operations within India, Myanmar military operations during 2019, and the destabilising impact of the coronavirus pandemic had pushed a number of hard-core militants into revoking their armed struggle.

Conflict Parties

Indian armed forces

Strength: 1,395,100.

Areas of operation:
III Corps: Responsible for operations in:
- Nagaland
- Manipur
- parts of Assam and Arunachal Pradesh.
IV Corps: Responsible for operations in:
- Assam
- parts of Arunachal Pradesh.

Leadership and structure: Zonal command structure subdivided into Corps commands.

Objectives: Counter-insurgency, border defence.

Opponents and affiliates/allies: Opposes armed groups. Cooperates with other state forces, although challenges exist around intelligence sharing, overlapping jurisdictions and operational coordination.

Resources/capabilities: The most suitably equipped and trained to operate in the difficult, rugged terrain of Northeast India, drawing upon logistics and airpower to supply distant outposts. Heavy weaponry is rarely deployed to counter-insurgency operations, though there have been exceptions.

Assam Rifles

Strength: 65,143.[6]

Areas of operation: Arunachal Pradesh, Assam, Manipur, Nagaland.

Leadership and structure: Led by a director general, typically a military officer of lieutenant-general rank.
Organised into 46 battalions officered by army personnel. It is under the jurisdiction of the Ministry of Defence, but as a central paramilitary force is answerable to the Ministry of Home Affairs.

Objectives: Counter-insurgency, border defence.

Opponents and affiliates/allies: Opposes armed groups. Cooperates with other state forces, although challenges exist around intelligence sharing, overlapping jurisdictions and operational coordination.

Resources/capabilities: Battalions are typically equipped to the same standard as an Indian Army infantry battalion, with small arms and mortar capabilities.

State Police

Strength: n/a.

Areas of operation: All states in Northeast India.

Leadership and structure: Led by Director General of Police, answerable to state government.

Objectives: Law and order, limited counter-insurgency.

Opponents and affiliates/allies: Opposes armed groups. Cooperates with other state forces, although challenges exist around intelligence sharing, overlapping jurisdictions and operational coordination.

Resources/capabilities: Police face logistical challenges in navigating the treacherous terrain and fair-weather roads, as well as deficiencies in firearms, including reliance on old, colonial-era rifles.

Main armed groups in talks/ceasefires with the Indian government

National Socialist Council of Nagalim–Isak Muivah (NSCN–IM)

Strength: 5,000.[7]

Areas of operation: Nagaland, Naga-inhabited areas of Arunachal Pradesh, Assam and Manipur.

Leadership and structure: Led by its 'general secretary' Thuingaleng Muivah.
Organised centrally but demographically dominated by the Tangkhul tribe of Manipur.

Objectives: Sovereign 'Nagalim' through shared, but separate, sovereignty with the Indian government.

National Socialist Council of Nagalim–Isak Muivah (NSCN–IM)

Opponents and affiliates/allies: Opposes state forces, NSCN–K, Zeliangrong United Front (ZUF), Kuki armed groups, WC.
Limited, tacit cooperation with security forces, as well as allied civil-society bodies (e.g., Naga People's Movement for Human Rights, United Naga Council Manipur).

Resources/capabilities: One of the largest and best-equipped groups in the region, with access to AK-series rifles, light machine guns, mortars and rocket-propelled grenades (RPGs).

Working Committee (WC)

Strength: Umbrella organisation – N/A.

Areas of operation: Nagaland, Arunachal Pradesh, Manipur.

Leadership and structure: A conglomerate of smaller armed groups.[8]

Objectives: Solution within Indian constitution.

Opponents and affiliates/allies: Opposes NSCN–IM. Allied with constituent members.

Resources/capabilities: Varied across membership.

National Democratic Front of Bodoland–Saoraigwra (NDFB–S)

Strength: Unknown.

Areas of operation: Bodo areas of western Assam, Myanmar.

Leadership and structure: Led by B. Saoraigwra until demobilisation in 2020.

Objectives: Formerly sovereign Bodoland; surrendered and incorporated into peace accord along with other pro-talks NDFB factions in January 2020.

Opponents and affiliates/allies: Until January 2020, opposed pro-talks Bodo groups.

Resources/capabilities: Operationally weak since 2016, surrendered and demobilised January 2020.

United Liberation Front of Asom–Pro Talks Faction (ULFA–PTF)

Strength: In transition to civil-society movement.

Areas of operation: Assam.

Leadership and structure: Functions as a civil-society movement, campaigns for welfare of surrendered ULFA cadres.

Objectives: Address implementation of the Assam Accord, issues related to illegal migration and rights of former combatants.

Opponents and affiliates/allies: Opposes ULFA–I. Allied with Assamese civil-society organisations (e.g., All Assam Students Union).

Resources/capabilities: Uses peaceful means.

Main armed groups not in talks/ceasefires with the Indian government

United Liberation Front of Asom–Independent (ULFA–I)

Strength: 250.[9]

Areas of operation: Assam, Arunachal Pradesh, Myanmar, China (Yunnan province).

Leadership and structure: Paresh Baruah (commander-in-chief).
Small outfit focused on cross-border strikes.

Objectives: Sovereign Assam.

Opponents and affiliates/allies: Opposes ULFA–PTF. Allied with Coordination Committee (CorCom), NSCN–K/YA.

Resources/capabilities: Improvised explosive devices, grenades, RPGs, rifles including HK-33s, AK-56s, INSAS, MQ-81s, M-22s.

National Socialist Council of Nagaland–Khaplang/Yung Aung (NSCN–K/YA)

Strength: Unknown.

Areas of operation: Myanmar (Sagaing); Nagaland, Arunachal Pradesh, Manipur.

Leadership and structure: Led by Burmese Naga Yung Aung after death of S.S. Khaplang in 2017. Split in 2016 (pro-talks NSCN–Reformation), 2018 (pro-talks NSCN–Khango Konyak), 2020 (anti-talks NSCN–Nyemlang Konyak, which has since been renamed to NSCN–K/Nikki Sumi).

Objectives: Sovereign independent Nagaland through armed struggle, cross-border strikes.

Opponents and affiliates/allies: Opposes state forces, NSCN–IM, other rival NSCN factions.
Leading member of the United National Liberation Front of Western South East Asia (UNLFWESEA); allied with CorCom.

Resources/capabilities: No information.

Coordination Committee (CorCom)

Strength: Umbrella organisation – N/A.

Areas of operation: Arunachal Pradesh, Manipur.

Leadership and structure: Umbrella organisation of Manipuri armed groups.[10]

Objectives: Sovereign Manipur.

Opponents and affiliates/allies: Opposes state forces, rival anti- and pro-talks Manipuri armed groups.
Allied with UNLFWESEA

Resources/capabilities: Varied across membership. People's Liberation Army (PLA) and United National Liberation Front (UNLF) are the best equipped and best trained of the six outfits.

United National Liberation Front of Western South East Asia (UNLFWESEA)

Strength: Umbrella organisation – N/A.

Areas of operation: Wide membership in Northeast India.

Leadership and structure: Umbrella organisation incorporating numerous anti-talks armed groups.

Objectives: Sovereign Northeast India.

Opponents and affiliates/allies: Opposes state forces. Allied with CorCom.

Resources/capabilities: Varied across membership.

Manipur Naga People's Front (MNPF)

Strength: Unknown.

Areas of operation: Manipur.

Leadership and structure: Small armed group coordinating with key anti-talks groups such as PLA and ULFA–I. Formed out of merger between Manipur Naga Revolutionary Front and United Naga People's Council (2013).

Objectives: Naga sovereignty.

Opponents and affiliates/allies: Opposes state forces, NSCN–IM. Allied with anti-talks outfits from CorCom, UNLFWESEA.

Resources/capabilities: Unknown.

Other conflict parties

The above is a non-exhaustive summary of the main state and insurgent conflict parties in Northeast India relevant to developments in 2020, as well as new organisations.[11] Foreign-state armed forces have also affected the conflict dynamics in Northeast India. The Myanmar military launched a number of operations during 2019 against insurgent groups camped along the border areas of Sagaing, Myanmar, coordinating with the Indian Army on the Indian side of the border. This disrupted armed group activity, however the 2021 military coup in Myanmar raised concerns that Indian insurgent groups could regroup amid renewed pressure on the Tatmadaw elsewhere in the country.

Conflict Drivers

Economic and social

Coronavirus pandemic's disruptions:
Regardless of their ceasefire status with the Indian government, all insurgent groups rely on extensive taxation networks in strategic locations such as Dimapur and Kohima in Nagaland, the city of Imphal in Manipur and the highways connecting it to the rest of the region, and the tea gardens of Upper Assam. This lucrative political economy of insurgency has long shaped regional patterns of violence against civilians, as armed groups seek to force through their demands during negotiations with businesses, politicians and civilians.

However, rebels' ability to collect taxes was hampered by coronavirus lockdowns in 2020. In Nagaland, for example, armed-group taxation during India's national lockdown (from March to May) fell to approximately 20% of prior levels, creating considerable financial pressures.[12] The need to maintain social distancing and protect cadres from infection also led to camp lockdowns, which further reduced armed groups' ability to collect taxes from local populations and instead drove them to self-sustenance and farming.[13] After lockdown ended, attempts to increase taxation to make up the shortfall received hostile reactions from civilians and businesses who were themselves still reeling from the economic impact of the pandemic.[14] This arguably created opportunities for Nagaland Governor R.N. Ravi to condemn the activities of 'armed gangs' in the state; the public backlash forced groups such as the NSCN–IM to reduce their tax rate, demonstrating the impact of the pandemic on armed-group legitimacy.[15]

International

Impact of the India–China territorial stand-off:

The territorial stand-off between India and China during the spring and summer of 2020 re-ignited concerns that China might exploit Northeast India's porous borders to aid insurgent groups in the region. Chinese support to Northeast insurgents dates back to the 1960s and 1970s, when China offered arms and training to rebels from Manipur and Nagaland. Today, the leadership of the Assamese ULFA–I is based in Yunnan province, China, and its actions and statements in 2020 continued to reflect pro-Chinese positions. On 6 July 2020, the group released a video on its YouTube channel declaring support for China in its ongoing terri-torial stand-off with India.[16] After a joint team of ULFA–I, PLA and MNPF militants killed three soldiers in Manipur on 29 July, a statement claiming responsibility for the ambush lauded efforts to counter Indian 'expansionism', and paraphrased a declaration from Prime Minister Narendra Modi – widely thought to have been issued in response to the India–China stand-off – that the 'era of expansionism is over'.[17] However, while insurgents continued to conduct low-level cross-border raids and launch attacks on state forces from their sanctuaries in Myanmar – which had been disrupted but remained intact – there was little evidence to suggest that external pressure had ratcheted up insurgent activity in the region. In fact, most data pointed towards a reduced ability of armed groups to operate as a result of the corona-virus pandemic.

Key Events in 2020–21

POLITICAL EVENTS

27 January 2020

The Indian government signs the third Bodo Accord with the members of the four main Bodo factions. Includes provisions to strengthen the autonomy of the Bodoland Territorial Region.

February

The NSCN–IM and the Indian government's interlocutor R.N. Ravi trade accusations of insincere behaviour following failures to break the deadlock in peace talks.

March

In response to the coronavirus crisis, the NSCN–IM locks down its general headquarters at Camp Hebron, Dimapur, and introduces preventative and hygiene measures for its cadres.

April

Indian security sources suggest that the national lockdown may have incited civilian anger against paying taxes to armed groups.

19 May

The Manipur government complains of unauthorised NSCN–IM camps within the state; the NSCN–IM retorts that its ceasefire covers all Naga areas.

June

Critical comments from Ravi on armed-group taxation spark condemnation from the Naga armed groups in talks with New Delhi.

MILITARY/VIOLENT EVENTS

5 and 15 January 2020

Security forces kill two NDFB–S militants during separate operations in the districts of Chirang and Kokrajhar, Assam.

21 February

Unidentified assailants shoot and kill a Bodoland People's Front worker in Udalguri district, Assam.

13 March

One ZUF militant is killed following clashes with NSCN–IM militants in Tamenglong district, Manipur.

24 April

Unidentified assailants kidnap a former Dima Halam Daogah militant from Dima Hasao district, Assam. His body is recovered on 30 April.

16 May

One civilian is killed in the crossfire between security forces and NSCN–IM militants in Longding district, Arunachal Pradesh.

23 June

Police kill one individual collecting taxes in the name of NSCN–K/YA in Dimapur, Nagaland.

29 July

The NSCN–K/Nyemlang faction breaks away from the NSCN–K/YA after accusing the incumbent leadership of running a 'drug empire'.[18]

16 August

The NSCN–IM releases two copies of the 2015 Framework Agreement, accusing Ravi of doctoring the agreement.

23 September

NSCN–K/Nyemlang faction leader Nyemlang Konyak joins NSCN–R and therefore the WC.[19] Konyak surrenders before security forces four days later.

16 October

The NSCN–IM says it will not compromise on its demand for a separate flag and constitution.

11 November

ULFA–I deputy commander-in-chief Drishti Rajkhowa surrenders to security forces.

December

63 militants from Assam and 52 NSCN–K/YA militants surrender.

26 January 2021

Ravi says that the peace process has stalled because of an unwillingness to forsake 'gun politics'.[20]

17 February

The People's Democratic Council of Karbilongri (PDCK) declares a unilateral ceasefire and says it is ready to enter into talks with the Indian government.

29 July

PLA, MNPF and ULFA–I militants ambush Assam Rifles soldiers in Chandel district, Manipur, killing three soldiers.

4 August

NSCN–KK militants kill one of their own senior militants in Tuensang district, Nagaland.

10 September

Security forces kill one NSCN–K/Nyemlang militant in Zunheboto district, Nagaland.

21 October

NSCN–IM militants kill one Assam Rifles soldier during a clash in Tirap district, Arunachal Pradesh.

8 November

Manipur police clash with NSCN–IM militants in Senapati district, Manipur. No injuries are reported.

8 and 14 December

Two grenade blasts take place outside the residences of forest officers in Imphal East district, Manipur. No injuries are reported.

23 January 2021

One civilian is killed in Tengnoupal district, Manipur, after suspected militants shoot at a motorcycle-repair workshop.

12 February

Police rescue three individuals kidnapped by Kuki militants following a gun battle in Thoubal district, Manipur.

Conflict Outlook

Prospects for peace

The extent to which security forces can utilise coronavirus lockdowns to disrupt taxation dynamics between armed groups and local populations may significantly affect the conflict in the year ahead. If rebels are further separated from the population, they may resort to increasingly desperate measures to regain lost taxation revenues, such as grenade attacks and kidnapping, and therefore increase violent incidents. However, in the longer term, damaging rebel-group legitimacy and perceptions of their capacity may produce significant counter-insurgent opportunities to isolate both pro- and anti-talks groups from local populations, particularly if the state is able to provide increased services to civilians in response to the pandemic.

This may, in turn, have a bearing on the Naga peace process with the NSCN–IM in particular. It has long been suggested that the Indian government's strategy has been to wear down armed groups through protracted peace processes that wed militants to a 'new normal' of ceasefire, thereby reducing the space for an ageing leadership to threaten a credible return to violence.[21] Indeed, the impact of the pandemic and subsequent lockdowns on the finances of powerful groups such as the NSCN–IM and the legitimacy of their taxation practices may further weaken their negotiating position with New Delhi. Having already secured compromises on key issues such as sovereignty and its proposal to incorporate Nagas beyond Nagaland into one territorial entity, New Delhi will probably seek to push the NSCN–IM into closer alignment with the WC to force through a final peace deal. Alternatively, it could simply leave the continuing pandemic to further weaken the NSCN–IM in 2021.

Strategic implications and global influences

India's support for the development of democracy in Myanmar meant it responded to the February 2021 military coup in that country with 'deep concern'.[22] In recent years, India had considerably improved its ties with the Tatmadaw, most notably culminating with the 2019 series of coordinated operations in which the Tatmadaw targeted Indian insurgent camps within Myanmar, while the Indian Army secured key areas on the Indian side of the border. With the continued presence of Indian insurgents along the India–Myanmar border in Sagaing region, and the possibility that armed groups may regroup in this isolated borderlands region, it clearly remains in New Delhi's interests to maintain cooperative military-to-military partnerships with the Tatmadaw throughout 2021, particularly given the latter's scepticism of Beijing.[23]

Notes

1 Alex Waterman, 'Ceasefires and State Order-making in Naga Northeast India', International Peacekeeping, 16 September 2020.

2 Alex Waterman, 'Normalcy Restored? The Lingering Drivers of Insurgency in Northeast India', in Raymond Izarali and Dalbir Ahlawat (eds), Terrorism, Security and Development in South Asia: National. Regional and Global Implications (Abingdon: Routledge, Forthcoming).

3 'Yearly Fatalities – Insurgency North East', South Asia Terrorism Portal, Institute for Conflict Management, accessed 16 March 2021.

4 'Number of Terrorism-related Incidents Year Wise: Insurgency North East', South Asia Terrorism Portal, Institute for Conflict Management, accessed 1 March 2021.

5 Amlan Jyoti Das, 'Chose Life over Death, Says Top ULFA (I) Commander Drishti Rajkhowa', EastMojo, 21 December 2020; Abhishek Saha, 'Wanted ULFA–I Deputy Commander-in-Chief Drishti Rajkhowa Surrenders', Indian Express, 13 November 2020; and 'Nagaland: 52 NSCN (K-YA) Militants Surrender in Phek District', NORTHEAST NOW, 27 December 2020.

6 Ministry of Home Affairs, Government of India, 'Annual Report 2019–2020', p. 124.

7 Rituparna Bhattacharyya and Venkat Pulla, 'The Nagas Saga and an Uncertain Future? Nagas after Nehru to Modi', in Venkat Pulla, Rituparna Bhattacharyya and Sanjai Bhatt (eds), Discrimination, Challenge and Response: Mapping Global Racisms (Cham: Palgrave Macmillan, 2020), pp. 141–59.

8 Including NSCN–Kitovi-Neokpao/Unification (NSCN–KN/U), NSCN–R, NNC/Federal Government of Nagaland (NNC/FGN), NNC–Parent, National People's Government of Nagaland/Naga National Council–Non-Accord (NPGN/NNC–NA), Government of the Democratic Republic of Nagaland/Naga National Council–Non-Accord (GDRN/NNC–NA), NSCN–K/Nikki Sumi (formerly NSCN–Nemlyang Konyak).

9 Justice Prasanta Kumar Deka, State of Assam, and Union of India, 'Unlawful Activities (Prevention) Tribunal: In the Matter of United Liberation Front of Asom (ULFA)', 24 December 2019, p. 16.

10 Including People's Liberation Army (PLA), People's Revolutionary Army of Kangleipak (PREPAK), United National Liberation Front (UNLF), Kanglei Yawol Kanna Lup (KYKL), PREPAK–Progressive (PREPAK–Pro), Kangleipak Communist Party (KCP).

11 See IISS, Armed Conflict Survey 2020 (Abingdon: Routledge for the IISS, 2020), pp. 254–8, for a comprehensive breakdown of both main and smaller armed groups.

12 Karishma Hasnat, '"Armed Gangs" Resume "Extra Tax" Collection as Curbs Ease in Nagaland, Guv Wants End of Parallel Govt', News18, 26 June 2020.

13 Prasanta Mazumdar, 'Naga Rebels Get COVID-19 Relief, Encouraged to Do Farming in Lockdown', New Indian Express, 9 May 2020.

14 Hasnat, '"Armed Gangs" Resume "Extra Tax" Collection as Curbs Ease in Nagaland, Guv Wants End of Parallel Govt'.

15 'NSCN (IM) Reduces Its "Tax" Rate from 5% to 3% in View of the "Prevailing COVID-19 Pandemic Crisis"', Hindu, 5 July 2020.

16 'Ulfa Releases Video Backing Chinese, Alleges PM Modi Responsible for Assam's Corona Spread', INSIDENE, 7 July 2020.

17 Arindam Das, 'Militant Groups MNPF, PLA and ULFA-I Claim Ambush on Assam Rifles Team in Chandel District', Times Now, 30 July 2020.

18 'NSCN (K) Led by Nyemlang Konyak Makes Criminal Accusations against Yung Aung', Morung Express, 2 August 2020.

19 'Nyemlang in NSCN (R) Camp: Akato', Nagaland Post, 23 September 2020.

20 Bikash Singh, 'Nagaland Suffering Due to "Gun Politics" by Some People: Governor', Economic Times, 26 January 2021.

21 Alex Waterman, 'India's Counterinsurgency in the Northeast Challenges the Relationship Between Time and Insurgent Success', Eleventh Column, 30 October 2018.

22 Kallol Bhattacherjee, 'India Expresses "Deep Concern" over Military Coup in Myanmar', Hindu, 1 February 2021.

23 Sreemoy Talukdar, 'Rather than "Setback", Myanmar Coup Leaves India on Firmer Geopolitical Footing with Tatmadaw', Firstpost, 4 February 2021.

INDIA–CENTRAL (MAOIST)

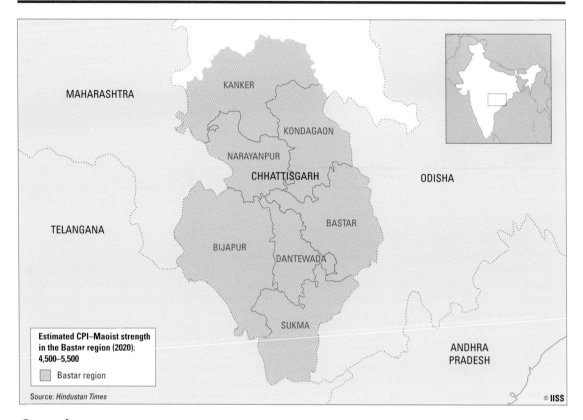

Estimated CPI–Maoist strength
in the Bastar region (2020):
4,500–5,500

☐ Bastar region

Source: *Hindustan Times*

© IISS

Overview

Communist insurgencies seeking to overthrow feudal structures and impose a new socialist economic order in India date back to the Telangana peasant rebellion (1946–51), the 1967 Naxalbari uprising which gave rise to the 'Naxalite' Maoist movement in West Bengal and a revived Naxalite movement from the 1970s to the 1990s. Counter-insurgency campaigns suppressed each of these movements, however fragments of the Naxalite movement remained.

The most recent manifestation of communist insurgency began in 2004 when a number of disparate factions of the Naxalite movement from across the states of Bihar, Chhattisgarh, Jharkhand and Andhra Pradesh merged to form the Communist Party of India–Maoist (CPI–Maoist). By the late 2000s and early 2010s, CPI–Maoist had consolidated control over large swathes of territory in what became known as the 'Red Corridor', spanning Bihar, Chhattisgarh, Jharkhand, Maharashtra and West Bengal. At its peak, the insurgency affected over 200 districts, causing over 1,000 conflict-related deaths per year in 2009 and 2010, and was labelled India's 'single biggest internal security challenge' by then-prime minister Manmohan Singh.[1] On 6 April 2010, CPI–Maoist militants killed 76 members of the Central Reserve Police Force (CRPF) in one of the single most deadly insurgent attacks on Indian security forces since independence.[2] However, since 2014 counter-insurgency operations have yielded successes, securing key surrenders and increasingly limiting CPI–Maoist's ability to hold on to key strongholds in outlying areas. Of the 91 districts affected by broader Naxalite violence in 2019, only seven were deemed to be 'highly affected', while 37 were deemed 'moderately affected' and 47 'marginally affected'.[3] According to the Indian Ministry of Home Affairs, just 30 districts accounted for 83% of Naxalite violence during 2019, reflecting the concentration of Naxalite violence around key hotspots.[4] On

Armed Conflict Global Relevance Indicator (ACGRI)

Incidence

17

Human
impact

4

Geopolitical
impact

4

India

Key Conflict Statistics

Type	Internal | Localised insurgency
Start date	2004
IDPs	473,000
Fatalities	1,046
Violent events	2,002

ACGRI pillars: IISS calculation based on multiple sources for 2020 and January/February 2021 (scale: 0–100). The indicator's results and certain Key Conflict Statistics refer to the country as a whole rather than the specific conflict covered in this chapter. See Notes on Methodology and Data Appendix for further details on Key Conflict Statistics.

11 February 2020, Minister of State for Home Affairs G. Kishan Reddy said that CPI–Maoist violence and its geographical spread had declined continuously and considerably since 2017.[5]

In 2020–21, the coronavirus pandemic had a mixed impact on the conflict dynamics in the Red Corridor. Hopes for a coronavirus ceasefire in response to calls from the United Nations for a global ceasefire were short-lived. On 5 April 2020, the CPI–Maoist's Malkangiri-Koraput-Visakha Border (MKVB) division committee – which operates in the border regions between Odisha, Andhra Pradesh and Telangana – announced that it had 'decided against carrying out any kind of attack on the security forces during this period'. However, this unilateral announcement, which gave a five-day deadline for a government response, was issued only by this local branch of the CPI–Maoist organisation. Thus, the ceasefire was neither endorsed by the CPI–Maoist's central leadership nor heeded by New Delhi or any of the state governments in the MKVB's areas of operation.[6]

As the Indian government imposed its national lockdown between March and May 2020, reports emerged that CPI–Maoist militants in the Bastar region – comprising seven districts of Chhattisgarh State (Bastar, Dantewada, Bijapur, Narayanpur, Sukma, Kondagaon and Kanker) – were struggling to maintain their supplies.[7] At the same time, it was reported that CRPF and state police forces were focusing on enforcing lockdown measures, while supply-shortage concerns arising from the pandemic had reduced the number and intensity of security-forces operations.[8] This, in turn, created opportunities for CPI–Maoist to reinforce south Bastar using militants from Andhra Pradesh,

Telangana, Maharashtra, Jharkhand, Odisha, West Bengal and Nepal.[9]

Conflict-related fatalities in the Red Corridor in 2020 remained relatively high vis-à-vis areas of India affected by non-Naxalite insurgencies, but nonetheless declined for the third year running, from 302 in 2019 to 239 in 2020, with a further 30 fatalities taking place up to 1 March 2021.[10] The 2020 fatality figures marked the lowest number of insurgency-related fatalities in the CPI–Maoist conflict since the party was formed in 2004. However, the violence that did occur continued to be concentrated in key CPI–Maoist strongholds such as the Bastar region, where police estimate up to 4,500–5,500 CPI–Maoists reside, including militants and political cadres.[11] The Bastar region has long accounted for the majority of insurgency-related violence in Chhattisgarh and continued to do so during 2020, representing 127 out of a total of 135 insurgency-related fatalities.[12] In Bijapur district, fatalities doubled from 20 in 2019 to 40 in 2020, with a similar increase in Sukma district from 33 in 2019 to 62 in 2020.[13] These localised increases reflected security forces' efforts to suppress CPI–Maoist activity in *Operation Prahar 2020*. Involving 2,500 police and paramilitary troops, the operation was launched in February 2020 in an attempt to anticipate the annual CPI–Maoist Tactical Counter Offensive Campaign (TCOC) that usually precedes the monsoon each year and exploits the summer months between March and June.[14] In 2020, however, CPI–Maoist initiated the TCOC early and divided it into two phases (from January to March and from April to June) in a bid to surprise security forces.[15]

Security forces yielded some successes, particularly in Dantewada district, where 196 of the total 352 CPI–Maoist-related surrenders of 2020 took place.[16]

However, security forces sustained heavy losses during CPI–Maoist's surprisingly early TCOC, particularly in Sukma and Bijapur. In one major incident on 22 March, 350 CPI–Maoists ambushed a group of 100 security-forces personnel in Sukma, killing 17.[17] Seemingly in response to the uptick in CPI–Maoist violence in these two districts, the Ministry of Home Affairs said it would deploy five additional battalions of CRPF personnel to Sukma and Bijapur.[18] On 9 October, CPI–Maoist announced that its 'people's court' had executed 25 alleged police informers in Bijapur district, indicating increasing strain on the group's ability to maintain support from the local population.[19] All of the above indicated that security forces – although achieving mixed successes across the districts – had placed significant pressure on and provoked resistance from CPI–Maoist in their strongholds within the Bastar region.

Conflict Parties

Central Reserve Police Force (CRPF)

Strength: Approximately 92 battalions deployed.

Areas of operation: Deployed across central and eastern India. Key states include Andhra Pradesh, Bihar, Chhattisgarh, Jharkhand, Maharashtra and Odisha.

Leadership and structure: CRPF battalions are central-government forces but are deployed to state governments to assist in law-and-order activities. CRPF forces are designed to augment existing state police forces to combat CPI–Maoist insurgents across the Red Corridor. The central government is responsible for deploying CRPF forces and for coordinating with individual state governments.

Objectives: Support state-level law enforcement in counter-insurgency duties.

Opponents and affiliates/allies: Opposes CPI–Maoist, and periodically small Naxalite splinter groups such as the People's Liberation Front of India (PLFI). Deployed in support of state police forces.

Resources/capabilities: INSAS/AK-series rifles. Forces are vulnerable to improvised-explosive-device (IED) attacks when travelling in unprotected vehicles. Some units have anti-mine vehicles; however, these are rare.

State police forces

Strength: n/a.

Areas of operation: Individual states across central and eastern India.

Leadership and structure: All 'Naxal-affected' states have built up their own anti-Naxalite paramilitary forces/armed police units. For example, Maharashtra's C-60 commandos have challenged CPI–Maoist forces without CRPF support. All states additionally have 'India Reserve Battalions' of armed police.

Objectives: Maintain law and order, perform counter-insurgency duties.

Opponents and affiliates/allies: Opposes CPI–Maoist, and periodically small Naxalite splinter groups such as the PLFI. Coordinates with central security forces such as the CRPF, as well as the police forces of neighbouring states.

Resources/capabilities: Unknown.

Communist Party of India–Maoist (CPI–Maoist)

Strength: Estimates of CPI–Maoist strength in the Bastar region, Chhattisgarh are around 4,500–5,500 political and military cadres.[20]

Areas of operation: Andhra Pradesh, Bihar, Chhattisgarh, Jharkhand, Kerala, Madhya Pradesh, Maharashtra, Odisha, Telangana, West Bengal. Hotspot of CPI–Maoist activity in the Bastar region of Chhattisgarh.

Leadership and structure: Nambala Keshav Rao (alias 'Basavraj') has led the Central Committee (CC) since 2018. The CC was reorganised in early 2020. Notably, ten of the 21 committee members were from Telangana, four from Jharkhand, two each from Andhra Pradesh, Maharashtra and West Bengal, and one from Bihar.[21] Local command structures include 'zonal' commanders (broadly approximate to district level) and local 'area' commanders under sub-committees.

Objectives: Seeks to overthrow Indian parliamentary democracy in favour of a communist regime through rural insurgency. Attempts to mobilise a power base by tapping into marginalised communities in India's hinterlands. Deploys hit-and-run attacks against Indian security forces.

Opponents and affiliates/allies: Primarily targets Indian federal and state security forces, as well as harassing/killing civilians suspected of collaborating with security forces. Other rivals/opponents include smaller splinter factions such as the PLFI.
Seeks to cultivate alliances with disempowered local civilians.

Resources/capabilities: Primarily arms itself with home-made firearms, although its elite fighting units wield AK-47s and semi-automatic weapons seized from police. The group also makes frequent use of IEDs.

Communist Party of India–Maoist (CPI–Maoist)

Strength: 150–300.[22]

Areas of operation: Jharkhand, Odisha.

Leadership and structure: Founded by Dinesh Gope. Local command structures include 'zonal' commanders (broadly approximate to district level) and local 'area' commanders under sub-committees.

Objectives: Unclear. The group emerged out of rivalries within CPI–Maoist stemming from the collection of extortion revenue.

Opponents and affiliates/allies: Rival of CPI–Maoist. Generally avoids direct engagement with security forces. Has links with organised crime and tacit associations with local politicians.

Resources/capabilities: Generally uses small arms, with limited use of explosives/IEDs.

Conflict Drivers

Political

Declining popular support:

CPI–Maoist continued to tap into its support base in the isolated rural hinterlands during 2020. The group, for example, attacked infrastructure projects, such as the Taliperu road project in Telangana, which are viewed with suspicion by local communities as attempts to extract resources and compound inequalities.[23] However, counter-insurgency operations, combined with the impact of the coronavirus pandemic, have complicated its relationship with local populations. The coronavirus lockdown between March and May severely reduced economic activity, which CPI–Maoist relies on for extortion revenues, and forced the closure of several local weekly markets that are vital for the group's supplies. This led to increased CPI–Maoist pressure on rural civilians, for example forcing village headmen to arrange supplies and diverting rations from families living below the poverty line.[24] In addition, CPI–Maoist's public declaration that it had executed 25 police informers in Bijapur appeared to mark a warning to the population against collaborating with the police, suggesting that its popular support in the area was facing increasing pressure.[25]

Economic and social

Community grievances:

CPI–Maoist insurgents in central and eastern India have long tapped into the grievances of marginalised, landless communities, particularly in the isolated tribal hinterlands. These communities – which have experienced sharp socio-economic inequalities as a result of caste and class dynamics as well as resource-extraction projects – have been targeted by CPI–Maoist as a support base, particularly since the early 2000s. Responding to these grievances, CPI–Maoist has used a combination of limited governance, service provision, rebel justice and the coercion and taxation of perceived class enemies to secure recruits, food, shelter, information and taxation revenue. However, in recent years government shifts towards service provision have helped to reduce conflict drivers and have placed CPI–Maoist under increasing pressure, forcing it to target state welfare projects and execute suspected collaborators.

Asia

Key Events in 2020–21

POLITICAL EVENTS

29 January 2020

CPI–Maoist reorganises the CC with 21 members. Ten of these are from Telangana, while none are from Chhattisgarh.

18 March

Eight CPI–Maoist militants surrender to police in Malkangiri, Odisha.

6 April

CPI–Maoist MKVB division unilaterally calls for a coronavirus-related ceasefire. State forces ignore the deadline.

16 April

Reports indicate that CPI–Maoist exploited lockdown pressures to reinforce south Bastar with militants from Andhra Pradesh, Telangana, Maharashtra, Jharkhand, Odisha, West Bengal and Nepal.

18–20 June

Around 10,000 people attend a three-day programme organised by CPI–Maoist in Sukma district, Chhattisgarh.

11 July

The Odisha state government declares that Angul, Boudh, Sambalpur, Deogarh and Nayagarh are now Naxal-free.

20 July

CPI–Maoist establishes 12 new area committees and reconstitutes its state committee.[26]

17 August

Telangana State renews its ban on CPI–Maoist for another year, amid attempts by the group to re-establish its presence in the state.

2 December

CPI–Maoist says it will conduct a 'year-long action' to celebrate the 20th anniversary of the formation of its armed wing. The group vows to regain its footing and strength.

13 February 2021

Maharashtra Deputy Inspector General of Police for Gadchiroli range says that CPI–Maoist is attempting to exploit the tri-junction between Maharashtra, Madhya Pradesh and Chhattisgarh to revive its activities in the region. Police establish an outpost in the area.[27]

MILITARY/VIOLENT EVENTS

25 January 2020

Civilians in Malkangiri district, Odisha, kill one armed CPI–Maoist and injure another after the militants had attempted to intimidate them and prevent them from supporting road construction in the area.

February

Security forces launch *Operation Prahar 2020* in the Bastar region, Chhattisgarh.

22 March

CPI–Maoist militants kill 17 CRPF personnel in Sukma district, Chhattisgarh.

4 April

Security forces kill three CPI–Maoist militants in West Singhbhum district, Jharkhand.

8 May

Police and CPI–Maoist militants exchange fire in Rajnandgaon district, Chhattisgarh. Four militants and one police officer are killed.

June

Police in Dantewada district, Chhattisgarh, launch *Lon Varratu* (return to your village) initiative offering financial support to CPI–Maoist rebels who surrender.

30 June–9 July

53 CPI–Maoist militants surrender to security forces as a result of the *Lon Varratu* initiative in Dantewada district, Chhattisgarh.[28]

12 August

Security forces kill four CPI–Maoist militants in Sukma district, Chhattisgarh.

3–4 September

CPI–Maoist militants kill six civilians suspected of being police informers in separate locations in Bijapur district, Chhattisgarh.

18 October

Anti-Naxal police commandos in Gadchiroli district, Maharashtra, kill five CPI–Maoist militants.

16 November

The central government agrees to deploy five new CRPF battalions to the Bastar region, Chhattisgarh.

21–22 December

A PLFI 'area commander' and a PLFI 'zonal commander' are killed by security forces in Ranchi and Khunti districts, Jharkhand.

30 January 2021

CPI–Maoist militants kill two civilians suspected of being police informants in Kandhamal district, Odisha.

13 February

Police kill two CPI–Maoist militants from Chhattisgarh in Mandla district, Madhya Pradesh.[29]

Conflict Outlook

Political scenarios

Telangana has faced low levels of CPI–Maoist activity since the state, which borders Chhattisgarh and Maharashtra, was formed in 2014. However, a number of events during 2020 suggest that the group may attempt to expand its activities within this former CPI–Maoist stronghold. When the CPI–Maoist CC was reorganised at the beginning of 2020, ten out of the 21 nominees were from Telangana State.[30] State intelligence sources were quoted as suggesting that a number of CPI–Maoist squads had entered into Telangana through rivers and forests with a mandate to regain the support of the Adivasi (tribal) population in the rural hinterlands.[31] In July 2020, militants twice clashed with police in the border areas separating Telangana from Chhattisgarh and Maharashtra, further pointing towards CPI–Maoist activity along the state's periphery.[32] Rather than limited forays, these clashes appeared to be part of a concerted effort to refocus on Telangana. Also in July, CPI–Maoist appeared to be laying the administrative and political framework for expansion into Telangana, by establishing 12 new area committees and reconstituting its state committee.[33] In 2020 ten militants and two civilians were killed in the state, surpassing its total annual fatalities for every year except 2017.[34] This spike in CPI–Maoist activity throughout 2020, combined with the political reorganisation of both the CC and the local committees within the state, suggest that CPI–Maoist is likely to enhance the intensity and scope of its efforts further in 2021 to regain a foothold in Telangana.

Escalation potential and conflict-related risks

The central government's decision to deploy five battalions of CRPF personnel to advanced positions within the CPI–Maoist hotspots of Bijapur and Sukma districts in the Bastar region of Chhattisgarh represents a clear attempt to take the fight to CPI–Maoist in one of its remaining stronghold areas. As in 2020 when the group reinforced the region, during 2021 CPI–Maoist is likely to resist these advanced CRPF deployments with violence and will also likely target civilians who are suspected of collaborating with security forces. Thus, while CPI–Maoist-related violence is likely to continue to decline overall elsewhere, the struggle for the Bastar region will probably intensify during 2021, particularly during the annual TCOC.

Notes

1   'Yearly Fatalities – Maoist Insurgency', South Asia Terrorism Portal, Institute for Conflict Management, accessed 31 December 2020; and Niranjan Sahoo, 'Half a Century of India's Maoist Insurgency: An Appraisal of State Response', Observer Research Foundation, *Occasional Papers*, 13 June 2019.

2   '76 Security Men Killed by Naxals in Chhattisgarh', NDTV, 7 April 2010.

3   The term 'Naxalite' is commonly used to describe the Maoist-inspired insurgency in central India, owing its historical roots to the 1967 Naxalbari revolt in West Bengal. The term captures broader Maoist violence rather than a specific organisation (i.e., CPI–Maoist). See 'Maoist Insurgency: Assessment 2020', South Asia Terrorism Portal, Institute for Conflict Management, accessed 31 January 2021.

4   Ministry of Home Affairs, Government of India, 'Annual Report 2019–2020', p. 11.

5   Ministry of Home Affairs, Government of India, 'Reduction in Incidents of Naxal Violence in the Country over a Period of Three Years Due to Resolute Implementation of National Policy and Action Plan', 11 February 2020.

6   Mohua Chatterjee, 'Days After Killing 17 Troopers, Maoists Offer Covid Ceasefire', *Times of India*, 7 April 2020.

7   Ejaz Kaiser, 'Maoists Seek Share in Govt Ration from Villagers as Lockdown Cuts Supply Chain', *New Indian Express*, 15 April 2020.

8   Ritesh Mishra, 'Amid Lockdown, Chhattisgarh Police Re-calibrate Anti-Maoist Ops in Bastar', *Hindustan Times*, 5 April 2020.

9   'Maoist Groups Using Lockdown to Regain Strength', *Outlook India*, 16 April 2020.

10 'Yearly Fatalities – Maoist Insurgency', South Asia Terrorism Portal, Institute for Conflict Management.

11 Ritesh Mishra, 'Maoists Organise Meeting in Chhattisgarh, 10,000 People Attend', *Hindustan Times*, 26 June 2020; and Mishra, 'Amid Lockdown, Chhattisgarh Police Re-calibrate Anti-Maoist Ops in Bastar'.

12 'Yearly Fatalities – Chhattisgarh', South Asia Terrorism Portal, Institute for Conflict Management, accessed 1 March 2021.

13 'Yearly Fatalities – Bijapur (Chhattisgarh)' and 'Yearly Fatalities – Sukma (Chhattisgarh)', South Asia Terrorism Portal, Institute for Conflict Management, accessed 31 December 2020.

14 Ritesh Mishra, 'Security Forces in Chhattisgarh's Bastar Intensify Anti-Maoist Ops', *Hindustan Times*, 22 February 2020.

15 Ritesh Mishra, 'Maoists Preponed Tactical Counter-offensive Campaign in Chhattisgarh', *Hindustan Times*, 7 July 2020.

16 'Yearly Surrender – Maoist Insurgency' and 'Yearly Surrender – Dantewada (Chhattisgarh)', South Asia Terrorism Portal, Institute for Conflict Management, accessed 31 December 2020.

17 Bibhu Prasad Routray, 'Maoist Attack in Chhattisgarh: The Devil Is in the Details', Institute of Peace and Conflict Studies, Red Affairs, 31 March 2020.

18 Ritesh Mishra, 'Centre Agrees to Deploy 5 New CRPF Battalions in Maoist-hit Bastar in a "Bold" Move', *Hindustan Times*, 16 November 2020.

19 'Naxals Claim They Have Killed 25 Informers in Chhattisgarh's Bijapur', *New Indian Express*, 10 October 2020.

20 Mishra, 'Maoists Organise Meeting in Chhattisgarh, 10,000 People Attend'; and Mishra, 'Amid Lockdown, Chhattisgarh Police Re-calibrate Anti-Maoist Ops in Bastar'.

21 Amarnath K. Menon, 'Return of the Maoists', *India Today*, 3 August 2020.

22 Deepak Kumar Nayak, 'Jharkhand: PLFI: Declining Impact', *South Asia Intelligence Review*, vol. 18, no. 49, 1 June 2020.

23 'Telangana: Maoists Trigger IED Blast at Cherla in Kothagudem', *Telangana Today*, 7 September 2020.

24 Rajbala Rana and Mathew Sinu Simon, 'COVID-19: Impact on Left Wing Extremism in India', *IDSA Comment*, 28 April 2020.

25 'Naxals Claim They Have Killed 25 Informers in Chhattisgarh's Bijapur', *New Indian Express*.

26 '12 New Maoist Committees Formed in Telangana', *New Indian Express*, 20 July 2020.

27 'Armed Outpost in Gondia to Help Curb Naxal Activity: Maha DIG', *Outlook India*, 13 February 2021.

28 Indrajit Sharma, 'Chhattisgarh: Dantewada: Maoists' "Homecoming"', *South Asia Intelligence Review*, vol. 19, no. 4, 20 July 2020.

29 'Two Naxals from Chhattisgarh Killed in MP's Mandla District', *Outlook India*, 13 February 2021.

30 Menon, 'Return of the Maoists'.

31 S. Harpal Singh, 'The Return of the Maoists in Telangana', *Hindu*, 8 August 2020.

32 Menon, 'Return of the Maoists'.

33 '12 New Maoist Committees Formed in Telangana', *New Indian Express*.

34 'Yearly Fatalities – Telangana', South Asia Terrorism Portal, Institute for Conflict Management, accessed 1 January 2021.

THAILAND

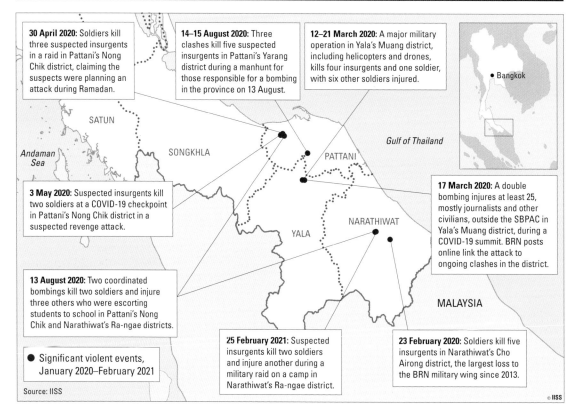

30 April 2020: Soldiers kill three suspected insurgents in a raid in Pattani's Nong Chik district, claiming the suspects were planning an attack during Ramadan.

14–15 August 2020: Three clashes kill five suspected insurgents in Pattani's Yarang district during a manhunt for those responsible for a bombing in the province on 13 August.

12–21 March 2020: A major military operation in Yala's Muang district, including helicopters and drones, kills four insurgents and one soldier, with six other soldiers injured.

• Bangkok

SATUN

Andaman Sea

SONGKHLA

Gulf of Thailand

PATTANI

3 May 2020: Suspected insurgents kill two soldiers at a COVID-19 checkpoint in Pattani's Nong Chik district in a suspected revenge attack.

NARATHIWAT

YALA

17 March 2020: A double bombing injures at least 25, mostly journalists and other civilians, outside the SBPAC in Yala's Muang district, during a COVID-19 summit. BRN posts online link the attack to ongoing clashes in the district.

13 August 2020: Two coordinated bombings kill two soldiers and injure three others who were escorting students to school in Pattani's Nong Chik and Narathiwat's Ra-ngae districts.

MALAYSIA

• Significant violent events, January 2020–February 2021

Source: IISS

25 February 2021: Suspected insurgents kill two soldiers and injure another during a military raid on a camp in Narathiwat's Ra-ngae district.

23 February 2020: Soldiers kill five insurgents in Narathiwat's Cho Airong district, the largest loss to the BRN military wing since 2013.

© IISS

Overview

The decades-long conflict in southern Thailand is based on a regional Malay Muslim ethno-nationalist autonomy movement that has been alienated from the central state. The armed insurgency, which represents a small fraction of the population in the three southern provinces of Narathiwat, Pattani and Yala, as well as four districts in Songkhla, has historically resisted influence from transnational jihadist groups and focused on regional identity and autonomy. Malay Muslims represent about 85% of the population[1] in the region, compared to only 4.3% at the national level[2] – which contributes to centre–periphery tensions between the central government and the Malay–Muslim population.

The Anglo-Siamese Treaty of 1909 demarcated the border between the then-kingdom of Siam and colonial Malaysia, dividing the historical sultanate of Patani, the reference point for the regional identity held by civil-society groups and the insurgents. The first phase of the armed conflict began in the

mid-1960s, based on an independent Patani regional movement comprising disparate and sometimes conflicting insurgent groups, the largest of which was the Patani United Liberation Organisation (PULO). By the mid-1990s violence had effectively ceased, following counter-insurgency operations and nationwide amnesty initiatives.

Although the conflict re-ignited in 2001 with sporadic attacks, the government of then-prime minister Thaksin Shinawatra did not recognise the violence as an insurgency until January 2004, when an insurgent raid on a military base in Narathiwat province killed four soldiers and seized light weapons.[3] In April and October that same year, the storming of the Krue Se Mosque by security forces and the Tak Bai massacre became powerful rallying points for the insurgency. The Patani Malay National Revolutionary Front (BRN) emerged as the most effective combatant force on the ground in 2005.

Armed Conflict Global Relevance Indicator (ACGRI)	Key Conflict Statistics	
	Type	Internal | Localised insurgency
	Start date	2001
	Gini index	34.9 (2019)
	GDP per capita 2020, PPP (current international $)	18,236.4
	Functioning of government (0–10)	5

Armed Conflict Global Relevance Indicator (ACGRI)

Incidence

1

Human impact

0

Geopolitical impact

0

Thailand

ACGRI pillars: IISS calculation based on multiple sources for 2020 and January/February 2021 (scale: 0–100). The indicator's results and certain Key Conflict Statistics refer to the country as a whole rather than the specific conflict covered in this chapter. See Notes on Methodology and Data Appendix for further details on Key Conflict Statistics.

Militant violence peaked in May 2007, when an average of four people were killed each day.[4] Militant attacks, which had traditionally targeted government officials and Buddhist civilians, have shifted over the past five years to include Muslim civilians and local army 'collaborators', as well as security personnel and paramilitary soldiers. There were also high levels of internal forced migration, particularly of Buddhist civilians, to safer areas, including Hat Yai in Songkhla province. Militant attacks and total fatalities have declined since 2016, but an attack on a checkpoint in Muang district in Yala province in November 2019 killed 15 security personnel and civilians, the highest number of fatalities in decades.[5]

In 2020, the number of attacks and fatalities was the lowest since 2004, amid COVID-19 restrictions, as well as the military's operational strategy targeting insurgent camps and networks, peace negotiations and elements of the BRN favouring talks. Thai authorities attributed some violent incidents to revenge attacks, including the double bombing outside the Southern Border Provinces Administrative Centre (SBPAC) during a COVID-19 summit on 17 March, which injured at least 25 people, including journalists and other civilians.[6] Security forces also conducted relatively large-scale military operations against insurgents suspected in previous attacks, including a number of encounters lasting several days.

In January 2020, the National Security Council's (NSC) Peace Dialogue Panel, led by former NSC chief Wanlop Rugsanaoh, engaged in formal talks for the first time with the BRN's negotiating team, led by Anas Abdulrahman, supported by Malaysia's lead facilitator Abdul Rahim Bin Mohd Noor and including Swiss and Thai observers. The talks excluded Majlis Syura Patani (MARA Patani), the umbrella insurgent

group that had conducted intermittent negotiations for the past four years but does not represent a significant faction of combatants. A second round of talks in March focused on administrative issues and prospects for a reduction in violence, but subsequent rounds were postponed due to the coronavirus pandemic and renewed violent incidents. Virtual technical-level talks were held in February 2021 with a focus on guidelines for future negotiations.

In early April 2020, the BRN announced a unilateral 'halt of activities' because COVID-19 was 'the main enemy'. The armed forces' Internal Security Operations Command (ISOC) responded that the BRN statement was 'irrelevant' and authorities would continue to enforce the law, with security forces killing three insurgents in Pattani's Nong Chik district at the end of the month.[7] The BRN denounced the incident as taking advantage of the pandemic and killed two paramilitary soldiers in the same district in an attack in early May.[8] Violence continued into 2021, with two soldiers killed in late February during a raid on a suspected insurgent camp in Narathiwat's Ra-ngae district.[9]

At the national level, anti-government protests, centred in Bangkok, continued throughout the year, with some civil-society leaders highlighting the militarisation of the southern region. Protester demands included the resignation of Prime Minister Prayuth Chan-o-cha, amendment of the constitution and an unprecedented call for reform of the monarchy, strongly resisted by the royal palace–military coalition. As a response to the protest movement, authorities continued to detain students and other leaders, including on charges of *lèse-majesté* and sedition, while enforcing cyber-crime laws against political speech.

Asia

Conflict Parties

Royal Thai Army – Fourth Army Area

Strength: Unknown.

Areas of operation: Headquartered in Nakhon Si Thammarat province, the Fourth Army is responsible for Thailand's southern region.

Leadership and structure: General Narongpan Jittkaewtae (commander-in-chief of the Royal Thai Army); Lieutenant-General Kriangkrai Srirak (commander of the Fourth Army). The SBPAC, operating under the Ministry of Interior, oversees security and development in the region, reporting to the military-dominated ISOC operating under the Prime Minister's Office, which has extensive powers since the 2017 coup.

Objectives: The military seeks to preserve the current political order, increasingly under the control of the monarchy. In southern Thailand, pacification is its primary goal.

Opponents and affiliates/allies: The BRN is the main insurgent group in the field. The military's opponents in politics and civil society include human-rights groups criticising military actions in the region, opposition party Pheu Thai, members of the now-dissolved Future Forward Party and the loosely organised protest movement. The military is closely aligned with the monarchy and controls the ruling Palang Pracharath Party, which leads a coalition of 19 parties and enjoys the support of the country's richest family-run conglomerates.

Resources/capabilities: Equipped with light arms purchased from the United States, other NATO member states and Israel. Aircraft, including attack helicopters, and armoured vehicles are principally sourced from the US.

Royal Thai Border Police

Strength: Unknown.

Areas of operation: Forces are stationed along national borders nationwide, including in southern Thailand, where they operate across the region.

Leadership and structure: Police Lieutenant-General Wichit Paksa (commissioner). The police and subsidiary forces are legally under the Ministry of Interior, but in practice they are subordinate to the military and the ISOC. The police coordinate paramilitary forces including *thahan phran* (hunter/soldier) rangers and the *or sor* (Volunteer Defence Corps).

Objectives: Trained to protect Thailand's borders against illegal entry, drugs and other trafficking.

Opponents and affiliates/allies: Counter-insurgency efforts in the south are linked to drugs and weapons trafficking by criminal networks.
Allied with the Royal Thai Armed Forces.

Resources/capabilities: Paramilitary platoons have heavy-weapons teams and aerial units at the regional level. The force also received counter-insurgency training from US special forces.

Village Defence Volunteers (*chor ror bor*) and Village Protection Volunteers (*or ror bor*)

Strength: Unknown.

Areas of operation: Locally recruited to serve in their own communities.

Leadership and structure: Village militias are commanded by officers from the police or military. Supervision is often poor. They are organised in squads of about ten volunteers stationed at village checkpoints, often alongside regular police personnel.

Objectives: Provide local security support (for which militia volunteers are paid a small monthly stipend).

Opponents and affiliates/allies: Opposes the BRN and Runda Kumpulan Kecil (RKK).
Support military and police forces in the region.

Resources/capabilities: Volunteers are typically more lightly armed than other forces, in some cases with shotguns, and undergo about ten days of training.

Patani Malay National Revolutionary Front (BRN)

Strength: Approximately 3,000.[10]

Areas of operation: Narathiwat, Pattani and Yala provinces, as well as the four southeastern districts of Songkhla province. More infrequent attacks have targeted Bangkok and tourist centres in the south.

Leadership and structure: Led by an executive council, known as the Dewan Pimpinan Parti. Sama-ae Kho Zari succeeded Dulloh Waemanor as secretary-general in 2019. A network of religious teachers leads the BRN and recruits from *pondok* Islamic religious schools. Five organisational units cover political work and recruitment, economic and financial affairs, women's affairs, youth (*pemuda*), and the armed groups,

known as the Pejuang Kemerdekaan Patani (Patani Freedom Fighters) who are organised in a loose, cell-like structure.

Objectives: The long-term goal is the independence or self-determination of the historical kingdom of Patani. The short-term tactic is to make the region ungovernable.

Opponents and affiliates/allies: Opposes the Royal Thai Army, associated security forces and 'collaborators' in the region. Political elements of the BRN have allied with PULO and other groups under MARA Patani and previous coalitions.

Resources/capabilities: Light weapons including assault rifles such as M16s, often stolen from security forces, and small- to medium-sized improvised explosive devices (IEDs).

Patani Malay National Revolutionary Front (BRN)

Strength: Unknown.

Areas of operation: Narathiwat, Pattani and Yala provinces, as well as the four southeastern districts of Songkhla province. More infrequent attacks have targeted Bangkok and tourist centres in the south.

Leadership and structure: Organised in a cell-like structure (consisting of five to ten members in a village) loosely subordinate to the BRN.

Objectives: The long-term goal is independence. The short-term tactic is to make the region ungovernable.

Opponents and affiliates/allies: Opposes the Royal Thai Army, associated security forces and 'collaborators' in the region. Tactical arm of the BRN.

Resources/capabilities: Light weapons and small to medium-sized IEDs.

Conflict Drivers

Political

Malay ethno-nationalist identity:
Insurgent demands have traditionally centred on the establishment of an independent state in southern Thailand, although the historical kingdom of Patani also included areas of present-day Malaysia.

While the pragmatic reality of establishing such a state remains questionable, the appeal continues to act as a rallying cry, with the call for an independent Patani, or 'Patani Merdeka', invoked in propaganda materials. Islamic religious identity is also integral to conceptions of Patani-Malay ethnicity across the region, giving threats to regional identity an additional perceived religious dimension and triggering a religious obligation to resist assimilation policies pursued by various governments in Bangkok and implemented over decades, including the promotion of Buddhism as the state religion and the state-sponsored migration of Thai-Chinese to the southern region.

Economic and social

Economic and political marginalisation:
Insurgent spokespeople and Malay Muslims consistently explain their grievance as stemming from alienation from the state, discrimination by local governments – particularly in education and employment opportunities – and other social problems. Muslim residents in the region are on average significantly poorer than Thai Buddhists in the same area and populations in nearby provinces, and the three southern provinces of Narathiwat, Pattani and Yala lag behind the rest of the country in several socio-economic indicators. For example, Pattani and Narathiwat are currently the two poorest provinces with poverty rates of approximately 34%.[11] Government-school curricula have been traditionally taught in Thai rather than the native Malay. Student achievements in the south consistently fall short of national standards, with many students attending *pondok* Islamic religious schools rather than government schools.

Security

Militarisation of the region:
Strict military measures in the region continue to affect daily life, particularly for Muslim civilians, including security checkpoints, detentions under martial law, harassment of civil-society leaders and insurgent family members, and the stationing of military outposts near and in schools. Human-rights advocates criticise the government for allegedly failing to implement international agreements banning torture and enforced disappearances, as well as to transparently investigate extrajudicial killings.

The government has also strengthened surveillance and cyber-security measures across the country and in the region, including the October 2020 formation of the new CyberCrime Investigation Bureau to monitor social media. The military's registration of SIM cards and collection of DNA, as well as alleged social-media disinformation campaigns and CCTV surveillance, are widely resented in the region.

Asia

Key Events in 2020–21

POLITICAL EVENTS

15 January 2020
The BRN signs a unilateral Deed of Commitment with the non-governmental organisation Geneva Call, pledging the protection of children.

20 January
Thailand's NSC delegation and the BRN's political faction meet for first round of formal talks in Kuala Lumpur hosted by Malaysian negotiators.

2–3 March
The NSC chief negotiator Wanlop Rugsanaoh and the BRN, led by Anas Abdulrahman, conduct a second round of talks.

3 April
The BRN announces a unilateral pledge to 'cease activities' due to the coronavirus pandemic. Thai authorities dismiss the declaration as 'irrelevant'.

1 May
The BRN condemns the killing of three insurgents, claiming that the military took advantage of the pandemic to conduct the attack.

14 September
Muslim representatives from the region meet Thai authorities in Pattani's Nong Chik district, asking for Friday to be designated as a holiday, Muslim pilgrimage management and Malay as an official language.

20 November
Human-rights advocates file a legal suit against the Prime Minister's Office and the ISOC, alleging that information and disinformation operations have targeted civil-society groups.

15 December
The cabinet re-extends the state of emergency in most of Narathiwat, Yala and Pattani until 19 March.

21 December
The director of the Centre for Conflict Studies and Cultural Diversity at Prince of Songkhla University, Associate Professor Srisompob Jitpiromsri, calls on the government to allow observers from other countries, in addition to Malaysia, to facilitate the peace process.

5 January 2021
Police in Yala's Muang district join an imam in enforcing sharia rules governing young people's mixed-gender interactions in public.

3 February
Wanlop and BRN representatives meet virtually due to social-distancing restrictions, focusing on the pandemic response and increased participation in talks.

MILITARY/VIOLENT EVENTS

23 February 2020
Soldiers kill five insurgents in Narathiwat's Cho Airong district, the largest loss to the BRN military wing since 2013.

24 February
A motorcycle bomb injures ten people, including an assistant district chief and three students, in Songkhla's Saba Yoi district, in what is believed to be a revenge attack after the killing of the five insurgents in Narathiwat.

12–21 March
A major military operation in Yala's Muang district, including helicopters and drones, kills four insurgents and one soldier, with six other soldiers injured.

17 March
A double bombing injures at least 25, mostly journalists and other civilians, outside the SBPAC in Yala's Muang district, during a COVID-19 summit. BRN posts online link the attack to ongoing clashes in the district.

30 April
Soldiers kill three suspected insurgents in a raid in Pattani's Nong Chik district, claiming the suspects were planning an attack during Ramadan.

3 May
Suspected insurgents kill two soldiers at a COVID-19 checkpoint in Pattani's Nong Chik district in a suspected revenge attack.

14–15 July
Two separate bombings in Pattani's Mae Lan and Panare districts, targeting officials, kill one soldier and wound ten civilians, including two children.

13 August
Two coordinated bombings kill two soldiers and injure three others who were escorting students to school in Pattani's Nong Chik and Narathiwat's Ra-ngae districts.

14–15 August
Three clashes kill five suspected insurgents in Pattani's Yarang district during a manhunt for those responsible for a bombing in the province on 13 August.

10 September
A paramilitary soldier is arrested after firing shots at a school bus at a military checkpoint in Pattani's Yaring district, which he claimed was an accident.

25 February 2021
Suspected insurgents kill two soldiers and injure another during a military raid on a camp in Narathiwat's Ra-ngae district.

Conflict Outlook

Political scenarios

In 2020 ongoing protests demanding political, constitutional and monarchical reforms reached an impasse with the military-dominated government, especially as a reshuffle of senior positions in the armed forces in October further consolidated power among loyalists with connections to King Maha Vajiralongkorn. The goals of southern insurgents and civil-society groups include some form of autonomy in the region and recognition of the Malay Muslim identity, with implications for the 2017 constitution that enshrines Thailand as an 'indivisible Kingdom' and the monarch as head of state. Both points are intractable in future negotiations.

The consolidation of power within the military and government could provide greater consistency in the Peace Dialogue Panel's negotiating strategy, which has historically been interrupted by coups and changing administrations. Conversely, some signs point to disunity on the insurgent side, with the exclusion of MARA Patani from current talks and lack of cohesion within the BRN between the executive council, political faction and combatants on the ground, leading to questions about the durability of the potential agreements to reduce violence.

Escalation potential and conflict-related risks

The probability of the conflict escalating to previous levels of violence remains low, given the increase in security and surveillance measures, continuing COVID-19 restrictions and the possibility of more inclusive talks. The pattern of violence over the past year suggests a continued strategy on the part of military-led forces of targeting insurgent camps, with insurgent revenge attacks mostly but not exclusively targeting security personnel. The continued lack of investigation and accountability for extrajudicial killings, including of suspected insurgents killed in conflicts with authorities, will also impede efforts to reduce violence in the short term.

The military strategy of suppression has broadly succeeded over the past three years. At the same time, groups within the BRN have advocated engaging in peace talks, while attacks on civilian targets have reduced, contributing to lessening violence overall. Neither development, however, provides for long-term peace in the region without addressing the underlying drivers of the conflict.

Strategic implications and global influences

The conflict remains deeply rooted in regional identity and resistant to transnational jihadist influences. As the stalemate is prolonged, however, the evolving jihadist movements in the region and proliferation of extremist materials online may gain more traction in Thailand, which so far has been extremely limited.

As an intermediary in talks, Malaysia is also an interested party in the conflict, conducting law-enforcement operations in its own territory and pressuring BRN leaders to join negotiations by monitoring and detaining its members. A more transparent and credible peace process would require the inclusion of more impartial foreign observers and adherence to international norms.

Notes

1   Matthew Wheeler, 'Behind the Insurgent Attack in Southern Thailand', International Crisis Group, 8 November 2019.

2   See 'Executive Summary', National Statistical Office, 27 December 2016.

3   'No One Is Safe: Insurgent Attacks on Civilians in Thailand's Southern Border Provinces', Human Rights Watch, 27 August 2007.

4   Zachary Abuza, 'The Ongoing Insurgency in Southern Thailand: Trends in Violence, Counter-insurgency Operations, and the Impact of National Politics', Institute for National Strategic Studies, September 2011, p. 4.

5   Muhammad Ayub Pathan and Abdullah Benjakat, 'Insurgents Attack Security Checkpoint in Yala, 15 Killed', *Bangkok Post*, 6 November 2019.

6   'Thailand: Insurgents Bomb Government Agency in South', Human Rights Watch, 17 March 2020.

7   Mariyam Ahmad and Nontarat Phaicharoen, 'COVID-19 Pandemic Adds Hardship to Insurgency-hit Thai Deep South', BenarNews, 16 April 2020; and Jack Burton, '3 Suspected Insurgents Killed in Pattani', Thaiger, 2 May 2020.

8   Anthony Davis, 'COVID-19 Moment of Truth for Peace in Thailand', Asia Times, 27 May 2020.

9   Matahari Ismail and Mariyam Ahmad, 'Thailand: 2 Soldiers Killed, 1 Injured in Deep South Attack', BenarNews, 25 February 2021.

10 Srisompob Jitpiromsri, Napisa Waitoolkiat and Paul Chambers, 'Special Issue: Quagmire of Violence in Thailand's Southern Borderlands Chapter 1: Introduction', *Asian Affairs: An American Review*, vol. 45, no. 2, 28 April 2019.

11 Judy Yang, 'Reducing Poverty and Improving Equity in Thailand: Why It Still Matters', World Bank, 17 October 2019.

Asia

PHILIPPINES (NPA)

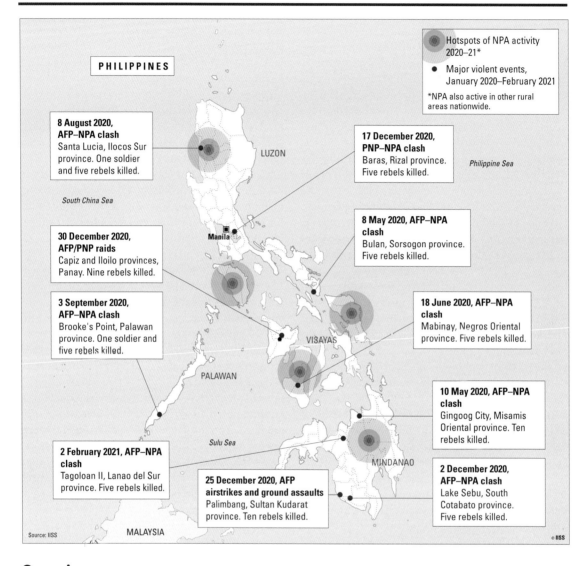

Hotspots of NPA activity 2020–21*

● Major violent events, January 2020–February 2021

*NPA also active in other rural areas nationwide.

PHILIPPINES

8 August 2020, AFP–NPA clash
Santa Lucia, Ilocos Sur province. One soldier and five rebels killed.

17 December 2020, PNP–NPA clash
Baras, Rizal province. Five rebels killed.

30 December 2020, AFP/PNP raids
Capiz and Iloilo provinces, Panay. Nine rebels killed.

8 May 2020, AFP–NPA clash
Bulan, Sorsogon province. Five rebels killed.

3 September 2020, AFP–NPA clash
Brooke's Point, Palawan province. One soldier and five rebels killed.

18 June 2020, AFP–NPA clash
Mabinay, Negros Oriental province. Five rebels killed.

10 May 2020, AFP–NPA clash
Gingoog City, Misamis Oriental province. Ten rebels killed.

2 February 2021, AFP–NPA clash
Tagoloan II, Lanao del Sur province. Five rebels killed.

25 December 2020, AFP airstrikes and ground assaults
Palimbang, Sultan Kudarat province. Ten rebels killed.

2 December 2020, AFP–NPA clash
Lake Sebu, South Cotabato province. Five rebels killed.

LUZON

Philippine Sea

South China Sea

Manila

PALAWAN

VISAYAS

Sulu Sea

MINDANAO

MALAYSIA

Source: IISS

© IISS

Overview

The post-independence Maoist rebellion in the Philippines began in 1969 with the founding of the New People's Army (NPA) as the armed wing of the Communist Party of the Philippines (CPP). Student activist Jose Maria Sison had established the CPP a year prior as a successor to the Hukbalahap communist movement, which had fought against both Japanese occupation of the Philippines during the Second World War and the independent Philippine state itself from 1946 onward. Inspired by Marxist–Leninist ideology and Sison's writings, the NPA has waged a guerrilla-style insurgency in rural areas across the Philippines for over five decades, with the aim of overthrowing the government in Manila and replacing it with a socialist political system led by the working class.

The NPA was at its strongest in the 1980s during the dictatorship of Ferdinand Marcos (1965–86), when its membership swelled to around 26,000 fighters. The majority of fighting took place across mountainous terrain and in countryside villages, although Special Partisan Units operated in towns

Armed Conflict Global Relevance Indicator (ACGRI)		
	Incidence	
	12	
Human impact		Geopolitical impact
3		12
	Philippines	

Key Conflict Statistics	
Type	Internal | Localised insurgency
Start date	1969
IDPs	153,000
Fatalities	1,687
Violent events	1,451

ACGRI pillars: IISS calculation based on multiple sources for 2020 and January/February 2021 (scale: 0–100). The indicator's results and certain Key Conflict Statistics refer to the country as a whole rather than the specific conflict covered in this chapter. See Notes on Methodology and Data Appendix for further details on Key Conflict Statistics.

and cities with the task of assassinating high-profile targets. In the post-1986 democratic era, public support for the NPA declined and the intensity of conflict reduced. Intermittent talks between Manila and the CPP–NPA – represented by the National Democratic Front of the Philippines (NDFP) which formed in 1973 – have failed to end the insurgency under six successive administrations led by Corazon Aquino, Fidel V. Ramos, Joseph Estrada, Gloria Macapagal Arroyo, Benigno Aquino III and Rodrigo Duterte.

After Duterte's election in 2016, the Armed Forces of the Philippines (AFP) and the NPA declared unilateral ceasefires, and several rounds of peace talks followed in Oslo, Rome and Amsterdam. Talks collapsed within a year amid a cancelled prisoner amnesty and fresh rebel attacks, prompting Duterte to terminate all dialogue between Manila and the NDFP in November 2017. Violence soon rebounded, with the NPA active in rural parts of Mindanao, the Visayas and northern Luzon. In 2019, Duterte formed the National Task Force to End Local Communist Armed Conflict (NTF–ELCAC) to coordinate local-level talks with NPA commanders, bypassing the CPP–NDFP leadership. Using this strategy, the government now no longer seeks a national peace accord, but aims to reduce the NPA's influence in local settings while also undermining the authority of its national-level political bodies, the CPP and the NDFP.

Fighting has persisted at approximately the same level since peace talks collapsed in 2017. In 2020, the NPA remained strongest in Mindanao, but Samar, Mindoro, Negros Island and northern Luzon also saw frequent rebel attacks. In line with its historical tactics, the NPA ambushed AFP soldiers

and Philippine National Police (PNP) officers from the roadside during these attacks, while using rifles and improvised explosive devices (IEDs) to target vehicle convoys. On occasion, passing civilians were also caught in the crossfire. Violence spiked at the end of the year, in the absence of the usual joint 'holiday ceasefire' covering Christmas and New Year which was scrapped by Duterte in 2020–21. On 25 December 2020, AFP airstrikes and artillery offensives in Palimbang killed ten suspected insurgents,[1] while on 30 December a further nine alleged rebels were shot dead in a series of coordinated AFP–PNP raids on Panay Island.[2] These pre-planned offensive operations reflected a shift toward a more proactive counter-insurgency strategy by the AFP, in line with its target to 'destroy' the NPA by 2022.[3]

In its rural areas of influence, the NPA continued to collect 'revolutionary taxes' from firms, subjecting non-compliant businesses to thefts and arson attacks which saw equipment and premises burned. In December, Secretary of National Defense Delfin Lorenzana described such extortion as 'the main source' of NPA financing, alleging that the group amasses PHP1 billion (US$20.65 million) annually in Mindanao alone, with large telecommunications firms, mining companies and banana producers serving as primary targets.[4] The NPA continued to use the tactics of fear and intimidation to ensure compliance of communities, assassinating local opponents such as tribal leaders and village chiefs, with indigenous rural populations often coming into conflict with the group.

With regard to the peace process, Duterte appeared to angle for a return to high-level dialogue at the start of 2020, asking Sison to return to the Philippines from his exile in the Netherlands for a one-on-one meeting, as a precursor to reviving formal talks.[5] However, Sison refused, arguing that the offer was a pretext for his arrest. The government's relationship with the CPP soured on 21 April after NPA rebels killed two AFP soldiers delivering aid in Aurora, ending a brief truce that had been announced on humanitarian grounds amid the coronavirus pandemic.[6] Duterte responded by ruling out future talks, and by the end of 2020 described the peace process as 'dead' and banned localised ceasefires.[7] The government continued its increasingly hostile stance toward the insurgency and provoked vigilante violence by 'red-tagging' civil-society groups that it claimed had ties to the rebel movement.[8] On 9 December, the CPP–NPA was designated a 'terrorist group' by the newly created Anti-Terrorism Council.

Conflict Parties

Armed Forces of the Philippines (AFP)

Strength: 143,100 regular combatants across the army, navy and air force, with a reserve force of 131,000, including 50,000 reservists serving in the paramilitary Citizen Armed Force Geographical Units.

Areas of operation: Operates nationwide. Headquarters, Camp Aguinaldo, is in Quezon City, Metro Manila. Large deployments to tackle the NPA across Mindanao and the Visayas.

Leadership and structure: Led by Chairman Lt-Gen. Cirilito Sobejana, who was appointed in January 2021. Divided into six area unified commands, including the Eastern Mindanao Command which is responsible for combating the NPA in its southern heartlands, and the Central Command in the Visayas.

Objectives: Defeat the NPA militarily by 2022, while supporting the NTF–ELCAC in its efforts to engage rebel commanders and encourage local-level defections.

Opponents and affiliates/allies: Opposes the NPA. Assisted by the PNP in anti-NPA operations. Cooperates with Revolutionary Proletarian Army–Alex Boncayao Brigade (RPA–ABB) rebels against the NPA and has trained RPA–ABB members as local defence forces.

Resources/capabilities: Access to combat tanks and armoured trucks. The army uses rifles and artillery in anti-NPA operations such as ground patrols and raids. The air force carries out airstrikes with rapid-attack aircraft, and provides further support in the form of transport planes and helicopters.

New People's Army (NPA)

Strength: Around 4,000 fighters nationwide (AFP estimate).[9] Despite significant annual losses, its strength has remained constant over the last decade due to ongoing recruitment efforts. However, its membership has declined significantly from the 26,000 it numbered in the 1980s during the Marcos dictatorship.

Areas of operation: Most active in its traditional stronghold of eastern Mindanao, though NPA activity has expanded further west. Present in rural areas nationwide, with hotspots of activity in 2020–early 2021 including northern Luzon, Mindoro, Negros Island and Samar.

Leadership and structure: Led by its founder, Jose Maria Sison, from self-imposed exile in the Netherlands. The NDFP peace-negotiation panel is chaired by Julie de Lima, Sison's wife. Both have little influence over the day-to-day conflict, which is overseen by a network of ground commanders. The NPA is the armed wing of the CPP, which is represented in peace talks by the NDFP. NPA rebels operate through small, closely knit fighting units.

Objectives: Ideology has remained unchanged since the 1960s. The NPA is fighting what it calls a 'Protracted People's War' to overthrow the Philippine state and replace it with a socialist system. It does not hold or govern territory but exercises de facto control in rural strongholds through extortion and intimidation. Launches ambushes against AFP troops, aimed at diminishing morale, using rifles and IEDs.

Opponents and affiliates/allies: Opposes the AFP and the PNP. Targets the RPA–ABB (which consists of former NPA rebels) in attacks as it considers the group to have betrayed the communist cause.
No known affiliates. In its early years, the NPA received funds and weapons from China and like-minded Maoist insurgent groups based abroad.

Resources/capabilities: High-powered rifles looted from AFP and PNP bases, and other firearms seized from private security guards during raids on businesses. Also deploys IEDs.

Revolutionary Proletarian Army–Alex Boncayao Brigade (RPA–ABB)

Strength: Estimated to have fewer than 500 members and is largely inactive.

Areas of operation: In the late 1990s, the RPA–ABB operated in Manila and in cities across Luzon, Negros Island and the Visayas. The group is currently present in the Western Visayas. In 2020, several incidents involving the RPA–ABB took place in Iloilo province.[10]

Leadership and structure: As the former urban-assassination squad of the NPA, the ABB's members operated in units of up to four snipers. It broke away from the NPA and merged with the RPA – a splinter group of the CPP – in 1997. The group was led by Nilo dela Cruz and Arturo Tabara when it signed a peace deal with the government in 2000. Tabara died during a clash in 2004. Current leadership and structure are unknown.

Objectives: While under NPA command, the ABB was tasked with assassinating AFP soldiers, PNP officers and state officials in urban areas. After merging with the RPA, the group espoused a Maoist ideology similar to that of the NPA, but now has no apparent overarching aim or strategy.

Opponents and affiliates/allies: Opposes the NPA, which considers the RPA–ABB an enemy for having signed a peace deal with the government and abandoning the Maoist cause. Has cooperated with the government since 2000 and some RPA–ABB rebels have received AFP training to defend their camps from NPA attacks.

Resources/capabilities: Retains access to a limited cache of rifles and other light weapons for defensive purposes.

Conflict Drivers

Political

CPP–NPA ideological unity:
A high degree of ideological unity within the CPP–NPA and minimal splintering or factionalism has prolonged the insurgency and enabled the group to endure for over five decades. The CPP founder Sison outlined his anti-capitalist and anti-imperialist stance in *Philippine Society and Revolution* (1970) and remains the group's primary leadership figure. The CPP–NPA's refusal to compromise on its demand to replace the government with a socialist system has blocked progress in peace talks under multiple administrations.

Duterte–Sison animosity:
As a former university student of Sison in the 1960s and as the first Mindanaoan to be elected president, Duterte began his term in 2016 with the hope of establishing peace with the CPP–NPA. However, after talks faltered, a public war of words with Sison ensued, and the cycle of mistrust that had developed between the group and previous Manila administrations returned. In 2020, Sison labelled Duterte 'mentally, politically and morally deranged' and the CPP called Duterte a 'demagogue' after he characterised the NPA as a greater security threat to the country than jihadist groups in the south.[11] The NDFP indicated in September 2020 that it foresees a resumption in peace talks with the government after Duterte's term ends in 2022.[12]

Economic and social

Geographical advantages:
In recent years, the NPA has been active in at least 69 of the Philippines' 81 provinces, while still operating no fewer than 54 rebel fronts.[13] In an expansive maritime nation of more than 7,000 islands, a group which boasts broad geographical presence is almost impossible to defeat through conventional military means. NPA fighters operate in densely forested, mountainous and inaccessible terrain, which was a strategic choice on the part of Sison, who outlined the need for decentralisation and guerrilla tactics in *Specific Characteristics of Our People's War* (1974). Rebels are hard to track as they operate in small groups and move between temporary camps.

Asia

Rural economic hardship:
Economic marginalisation in the countryside fuels anti-state grievances and aids NPA recruitment efforts. In Mindanao, a lack of access to land and natural-resource revenue, along with limited job opportunities, drives support for an array of armed groups which thrive in a climate of weak governance. According to data from the Philippine Statistics Authority (PSA), 24.5% of rural residents were living in poverty in 2018 compared to 9.3% of urban Filipinos.[14] At 31.6%, the poverty incidence among farmers was the highest of any occupation included in the PSA data.[15] Many vulnerable young recruits are also attracted to the NPA, which provides them with financial support.

Key Events in 2020–21

POLITICAL EVENTS

10 January 2020

Duterte states that a new negotiating panel is ready to revive talks with the NDFP, on the condition that Sison return to the Philippines for a one-on-one meeting.

13 March

NDFP peace consultant Julius Soriano Giron is killed during a joint AFP–PNP raid in Baguio city, Benguet province.

27 April

Duterte confirms that peace talks with the CPP NPA will not resume, citing rebel attacks on government troops during a coronavirus ceasefire.

28 April

Sison labels Duterte 'politically and morally deranged' and alleges that Duterte has 'never been interested' in serious dialogue with the NDFP.

23 July

Fidel Agcaoili, chair of the NDFP peace-negotiating panel, dies of natural causes aged 75 while in exile in the Netherlands.

10 August

NDFP peace consultant Randall Echanis is killed in Quezon City, Metro Manila. A CPP statement alleges government involvement.

19 September

Julie de Lima states that the NDFP is preparing to resume peace talks after Duterte leaves office in 2022.

27 November

NDFP peace consultants Benito and Wilma Tiamzon are sentenced to reclusion perpetua or up to 40 years in prison for the abduction of AFP troops in 1988.

MILITARY/VIOLENT EVENTS

15 January 2020

NPA insurgents ambush members of the RPA–ABB in Alimodian, Iloilo province, firing on vehicles and detonating a landmine.

18 March

Duterte declares a unilateral AFP ceasefire with the NPA until 15 April, to focus on containing the coronavirus pandemic.

24 March

Sison declares a ceasefire amid the coronavirus pandemic until 15 April – later extending it until 30 April – ordering the NPA to 'refrain from launching tactical offensives'.[16]

21 April

NPA rebels ambush AFP personnel delivering humanitarian aid in Maria Aurora, Aurora province, killing two government troops.

30 April

As the ceasefire ends, the CPP instructs NPA rebels to 'transition from an active defense posture to an offensive posture'.[17]

10 May

AFP soldiers clash with the NPA in Gingoog City, Misamis Oriental province, leaving ten insurgents dead.

8 August

AFP troops encounter NPA rebels in Santa Lucia, Ilocos Sur province, leaving one soldier, one civilian and five insurgents dead.

3 September

AFP troops clash with the NPA in Brooke's Point, Palawan province. One soldier and five rebels are killed.

14 October

The CPP orders the NPA to attack Chinese firms, citing a 'violation of Philippine sovereignty' in the South China Sea.[18]

25 November

Police shoot dead two NDFP peace consultants, Eugenia Magpantay and Agaton Topacio, during a raid in Angono, Rizal province.

7 December

Duterte proclaims the peace process to be 'dead' and states that there will be no ceasefire with the NPA for the remainder of his term.

9 December

The Anti-Terrorism Council designates the CPP–NPA as a 'terrorist group', under the Anti-Terrorism Act of 2020.

5 February 2021

Duterte grants amnesty to RPA–ABB rebels for politically motivated crimes but does not extend the offer to the NPA.

7 December

Duterte confirms that the annual ceasefire between the AFP and the NPA over the Christmas and New Year period will not take place in 2020–21.

25 December

Ten suspected NPA insurgents are killed during AFP airstrikes and artillery offensives on rebel positions in Palimbang, Sultan Kudarat province.

30 December

Joint AFP–PNP raids kill nine suspected NPA insurgents in the provinces of Capiz and Iloilo, on Panay Island.

1 January 2021

The CPP directs the NPA to revive its 'Special Partisan Units', tasked with assassinating government personnel in major cities.

Conflict Outlook

Political scenarios

Localised peace dialogues, which form part of what Duterte terms a 'whole-of-nation' approach to tackling the NPA conflict, have had minimal impact, and though rebels continue to surrender through the Enhanced Comprehensive Local Integration Program – which offers housing, livelihood assistance and skills training to former insurgents – the NPA has been able to continually replenish its ranks, making peace an unlikely prospect.[19] In 2020, the armed forces claimed that 7,615 NPA rebels had surrendered that year.[20] The figure is, however, a gross misrepresentation as the majority were villagers or supporters in areas of NPA influence, rather than armed rebels.[21]

In the absence of formal peace talks, the use of social media to spread online propaganda continued to feed an information war and widened existing divisions between the two sides. The proliferation of red-tagging – a practice historically associated with the Marcos dictatorship whereby political opponents were labelled as communists – has been a growing concern under Duterte's administration. The NPA insurgency has become deeply politicised as senior figures in the government and the armed forces have publicly accused universities, activists, human-rights lawyers, journalists and politicians from the left-wing Makabayan bloc of supporting or aiding the rebel cause.[22] This climate of suspicion and fear makes the conflict a hot-button issue that will likely broaden current political divisions between pro-Duterte and opposition lawmakers.

Escalation potential and conflict-related risks

Given the AFP's aim to 'destroy' the NPA by the end of Duterte's presidency in 2022, military operations are expected to increase in intensity in 2021. The NPA shows little sign of ending its campaign of guerrilla warfare in the countryside and may escalate its attacks against AFP troops in response to government operations. The NPA was increasingly active in western areas of Mindanao in January 2020–February 2021, and further activity in that region is likely as it seeks to escape military pressure in its eastern strongholds. Rebel attacks may also spread to towns and cities after the CPP ordered the NPA to revive its Special Partisan Units in early 2021.[23]

Amid the hostile environment created by red-tagging, targeting of non-combatants by security forces and vigilante groups is likely to become more frequent in 2021. The killing of four NDFP peace consultants – Julius Soriano Giron, Randall Echanis, Eugenia Magpantay and Agaton Topacio – in AFP–PNP raids and attacks by unidentified assailants in 2020, is evidence of this concerning trend.[24]

Strategic implications and global influences

While local grievances primarily drive the NPA, the group has a record of attacking multinational firms in Mindanao, particularly in the mining sector. It believes that these firms are causing environmental harm while garnering profits from the country's natural resources. Chinese firms may be at particular risk, as in October 2020 the CPP ordered the NPA to attack Chinese companies involved in infrastructure projects in the Philippines, citing the 'plunder and destruction of Philippine marine resources' and alleging 'violations of Philippine sovereignty' by China in the South China Sea.[25] Should the NPA act on this, likely in the form of thefts and arson attacks, it could discourage Chinese investments in eastern Mindanao where the NPA is strongest.

Notes

1 Edwin O. Fernandez, '10 Suspected NPA Rebels Killed as Army Thwarts Holding of CPP Anniversary Rites in Sultan Kudarat', INQUIRER.net, 26 December 2020.

2 Nestor P. Burgos, Jr, '9 IP Villagers in Panay, Tagged as Reds, Killed in 1-Day Police, Military Operation', INQUIRER.net, 30 December 2020.

3 Martin Sadongdong, 'AFP Chief: NPA "Totally Destroyed" by End of Duterte's Term in 2022', *Manila Bulletin*, 12 December 2020.

4 Jeanette I. Andrade, 'Lorenzana: NPA Rebels Amass P1B Yearly from Extortion', INQUIRER.net, 14 December 2020.

5 Michael Hart, 'Duterte's Peace Overture to the NPA: Another false Dawn?', Geopolitical Monitor, 27 January 2020.

6 'Army: Rebels Attack Soldiers Guarding Aid Distribution, 2 Killed', CNN Philippines, 22 April 2020.

7 Daphne Galvez, 'No Ceasefire with Communist Rebels "Ever Again Under My Term" – Duterte', INQUIRER.net, 8 December 2020; and Eimor Santos, 'Palace: No Localized Ceasefire with Reds Too', CNN Philippines, 8 December 2020.

8 Amnesty International, 'Philippines: End Deadly Practice of Red-tagging', 2 November 2020.

9 Kristina Maralit, 'AFP: CPP–NPA Weak Force', *Daily Tribune*, 9 January 2021.

10 Gail Momblan, '"Reds" Attack RPA–ABB in Iloilo Anew', Philippine News Agency, 16 January 2020.

11 'Joma Sison: Duterte Needs Peace Talks More than Reds', GMA News, 29 April 2020; and Gabriel Pabico Lalu, 'CPP: Duterte is PH's Biggest Terrorist; Palace: "They're Not Worth Responding To"', INQUIRER.net, 23 June 2020.

12 Eimor Santos, 'Communist Rebels Eye Talks with Robredo for "Post-Duterte" Resumption of Peace Negotiations', CNN Philippines, 19 September 2020.

13 Priam Nepomuceno, 'AFP Chief Seeks to Dismantle All Communist Fronts This Year', Philippine News Agency, 17 January 2021.

14 Philippine Statistics Authority, 'Farmers, Fisherfolks, Individuals Residing in Rural Areas and Children Posted the Highest Poverty Incidences Among the Basic Sectors in 2018', 3 June 2020.

15 *Ibid.*

16 Karlos Manlupig, 'Joma Sison Now Open to Truce with Gov't in Response to UN Call for "Global Ceasefire"', INQUIRER.net, 24 March 2020.

17 'No Truce Extension: CPP Tells NPA to Shift from Defense to Offense', *MindaNews*, 30 April 2020.

18 Nonoy Espina and Jojo Rinoza, 'Philippine Communist Leadership Orders Guerrillas to Go After Chinese Firms', BenarNews, 14 October 2020.

19 Michael Hart, 'Collapsed Talks Lead Philippines to Seek New Approach with NPA', *Asia Sentinel*, 11 April 2019.

20 'With Over 200 Rebels Killed in 2020, Military "Close" to Eradicating NPA by End of Duterte's Term – AFP Chief', CNN Philippines, 12 December 2020.

21 Disputes over figures issued by both sides have long been a feature of the conflict. The strength of the NPA is estimated to have remained consistent at around 4,000 fighters, despite reports of thousands of rebels having surrendered to the AFP each year. A very small proportion are thought to be armed NPA rebels, with the majority being alleged supporters of the communist movement or members of the NPA's 'Militia ng Bayan' (People's Militias).

22 Phil Robertson, 'Philippine General Should Answer for "Red-tagging"', Human Rights Watch, 10 February 2021.

23 Jeoffrey Maitem and Mark Navales, 'Philippine Communist Guerrillas Say They Will Revive Urban Hit Squads', BenarNews, 4 January 2021.

24 'NDFP Slams Duterte Gov't Over Killing of 2 Peace Negotiators in Angono', GMA News, 2 December 2020. This trend is also exemplified by the killing of nine labour activists by police in March 2021, after Duterte had ordered authorities to 'finish off' communist rebels and 'forget about human rights'. See Nonoy Espina and Jojo Rinoza, 'Philippines Rights Groups: 9 Activists Killed in "Bloody Sunday" Raids', BenarNews, 7 March 2021; and Ted Regencia, '"Kill Them": Duterte Wants to "Finish Off" Communist Rebels', Al-Jazeera, 6 March 2021.

25 Espina and Rinoza, 'Philippine Communist Leadership Orders Guerrillas to Go After Chinese Firms'. In 2012, the Philippine government formally designated the waters to its west, within its 200 nautical-mile exclusive economic zone, the 'West Philippine Sea'.

Asia

PHILIPPINES (ASG & MORO)

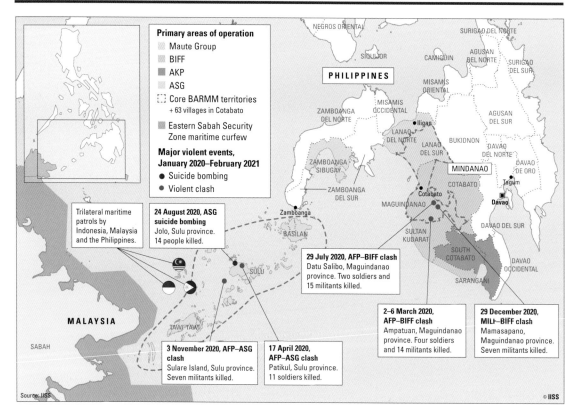

Primary areas of operation
- Maute Group
- BIFF
- AKP
- ASG
- Core BARMM territories + 63 villages in Cotabato
- Eastern Sabah Security Zone maritime curfew

Major violent events, January 2020–February 2021
- Suicide bombing
- Violent clash

Trilateral maritime patrols by Indonesia, Malaysia and the Philippines.

24 August 2020, ASG suicide bombing
Jolo, Sulu province. 14 people killed.

29 July 2020, AFP–BIFF clash
Datu Salibo, Maguindanao province. Two soldiers and 15 militants killed.

2–6 March 2020, AFP–BIFF clash
Ampatuan, Maguindanao province. Four soldiers and 14 militants killed.

29 December 2020, MILF–BIFF clash
Mamasapano, Maguindanao province. Seven militants killed.

3 November 2020, AFP–ASG clash
Sulare Island, Sulu province. Seven militants killed.

17 April 2020, AFP–ASG clash
Patikul, Sulu province. 11 soldiers killed.

Source: IISS

© IISS

Overview

After earlier armed uprisings by Moro Muslim rebels in western Mindanao and the Sulu islands against Spanish and American colonisers, the modern-day Moro conflict began in 1972 with the formation of the Moro National Liberation Front (MNLF). The Jabidah massacre of Moro army recruits by government forces in March 1968 had sparked revived secessionist activities, with the MNLF leading an armed campaign against the Philippine state fuelled by political, economic and cultural oppression. Several peace deals were signed over the next two decades between the MNLF and the government, but most of them either failed or were not fully implemented. The 1976 Tripoli Agreement under the dictatorship of Ferdinand Marcos collapsed, while the creation of the Autonomous Region in Muslim Mindanao (ARMM) in 1989 failed to stem the violence or resolve grievances.[1] MNLF founder Nur Misuari served as ARMM governor for five years after his group signed a final peace agreement,

the Jakarta Accord of 1996 – a deal that is yet to be fully implemented.

In the 1990s, the MNLF declined in strength and was overtaken as the main actor in the conflict by a splinter group: the Moro Islamic Liberation Front (MILF), which had broken away in 1977 under the leadership of founder Hashim Salamat. The MILF clashed regularly with the national armed forces in the jungles of western Mindanao in the 1990s and 2000s, while simultaneously engaging in talks with Manila from 1996 onwards. This eventually led to the signing of a Comprehensive Agreement on the Bangsamoro (CAB) in 2014 and the Bangsamoro Organic Law (BOL) in 2018, under the administration of President Rodrigo Duterte. The BOL legislated for self-governance in exchange for disarmament.[2] The law was ratified via a referendum in early 2019, thus creating the new Bangsamoro Autonomous Region in Muslim Mindanao (BARMM). MILF chairman Al Haj Murad Ebrahim was appointed to lead the

Armed Conflict Global Relevance Indicator (ACGRI)

Incidence

12

Human impact

3

Geopolitical impact

12

Philippines

Key Conflict Statistics

Type	Internal | Localised insurgency
Start date	1972
IDPs	153,000
Fatalities	1,687
Violent events	1,451

ACGRI pillars: IISS calculation based on multiple sources for 2020 and January/February 2021 (scale: 0–100). The indicator's results and certain Key Conflict Statistics refer to the country as a whole rather than the specific conflict covered in this chapter. See Notes on Methodology and Data Appendix for further details on Key Conflict Statistics.

interim Bangsamoro Transition Authority (BTA), with governing powers over the region until the first BARMM parliamentary elections, which were originally scheduled for 2022.

While the MNLF and MILF no longer fight government forces, several armed Islamist groups continue to oppose the peace process. The Abu Sayyaf Group (ASG), established in 1991, is notorious for kidnappings, piracy attacks and beheadings. In May 2017, the ASG joined forces with three ISIS-aligned groups – the Maute Group, the Bangsamoro Islamic Freedom Fighters (BIFF) and the Ansar Khalifah Philippines (AKP) – to seize the city of Marawi for five months. Daily battles with government forces displaced 350,000 residents and prompted Duterte to declare martial law in Mindanao, which remained in place until the end of 2019.[3] Since the siege of Marawi, the ASG has carried out a string of suicide bombings in the maritime provinces of Basilan and Sulu. The strength of the Mautes, the BIFF and the AKP has declined due to bombardments by the Armed Forces of the Philippines (AFP), but cells remain present in western Mindanao.

The BARMM transition progressed in 2020, though the coronavirus pandemic delayed both the approval of priority legislation and the disarmament of MILF rebels. Appointments to the 80-member BTA were completed by 28 February 2020, with 41 members selected by the MILF and 39 appointed by the government. The interim BARMM parliament was suspended from 2 April until 16 June amid rising COVID-19 cases, with half of lawmakers attending via video link once sessions resumed.[4] After parliament returned, the BARMM Administrative and Civil Service codes were approved while deliberations began on the Local Government code.[5] This

key legislative framework, along with other legislation on elections and the region's revenue, were still to pass as of February 2021.

Citing delays in approving key legislation, in November 2020 BARMM Chief Minister Ebrahim backed a three-year extension of the transition period, which would postpone the first BARMM parliamentary elections to 2025. Ebrahim argued that more time was needed to develop structures for a 'higher level of good governance' in the region.[6] Duterte also supported the proposal.[7] By 31 December, three bills had been filed in the House of Representatives on the proposed BARMM transition extension, to be deliberated during 2021.[8] The slow disarmament of MILF rebels added to the need for an extension. Phase Two of the disarmament process was completed in March 2020, with 12,000 MILF fighters and at least 2,100 weapons decommissioned in accordance with the terms of the Annex on Normalization in the 2014 CAB.[9] Phase Three aims to disarm a further 35% of the 40,000-member MILF, but as of January 2021 only 1,500 of these rebels had surrendered their arms.[10]

Spoilers to the BARMM peace process remained active in 2020–21. The ASG posed the greatest risk, clashing regularly with the military in their island strongholds of Basilan, Sulu and Tawi-Tawi. The group was also active on the Zamboanga peninsula and maintained ties with Islamist cells in Malaysia's Sabah State. Kidnappings by the ASG in the Sulu Sea also threatened shipping routes, while in Basilan, the group was forced to retreat after its leader, Furuji Indama, was killed by the AFP in September 2020.[11] AFP offensives targeted BIFF hideouts in the marshlands of central Maguindanao and Maute Group cells in Lanao del Sur, while AKP remnants in South Cotabato were subject to law-enforcement operations.

Asia

Conflict Parties

Armed Forces of the Philippines (AFP)

Strength: 143,100 regular combatants across the army, navy and air force, with a reserve force of 131,000, including 50,000 reservists serving in the paramilitary Citizen Armed Force Geographical Units.

Areas of operation: Operates nationwide. Headquarters, Camp Aguinaldo, is in Quezon City, Metro Manila.

Leadership and structure: Led by Chairman Lt-Gen. Cirilito Sobejana who was appointed in January 2021. Divided into six area unified commands, including the Western Mindanao Command. AFP battalions are usually 500-strong.
It is supported in gun battles and law-enforcement raids by the Philippine National Police (PNP).

Objectives: Defeat ISIS-affiliated groups in western Mindanao and the Sulu islands. Conducts routine patrols in areas of militant activity, often over difficult terrain.

Opponents and affiliates/allies: Opposes ISIS-affiliated groups: the AKP, the ASG, the BIFF and the Maute Group. Allied with the MILF and the MNLF, which provide intelligence support.

Resources/capabilities: Access to combat tanks and armoured trucks. The army uses rifles and artillery in operations against militant groups and is assisted by air-force rapid-attack aircraft, helicopters and transport planes. Naval assets are deployed in the Sulu Sea.

Abu Sayyaf Group (ASG)

Strength: 300 active members (estimate).

Areas of operation: Maritime provinces of Basilan, Sulu and Tawi-Tawi. Limited presence along the coast of the Zamboanga peninsula. Active presence in the Sulu and Celebes seas, with ASG militants engaged in hostage-taking off the coast of Malaysia's Sabah State.

Leadership and structure: Hatib Hajan Sawadjaan and Radullan Sahiron lead ASG factions in Sulu province.[12] The ASG leader in Basilan province, Furuji Indama, was killed in September 2020 by the military.
No centralised command structure. The group is composed of a network of cells, arranged according to clan affiliation and family ties.

Objectives: Re-establish an Islamic sultanate in the Sulu islands. In 2014, then-leader Isnilon Hapilon (now deceased) declared allegiance to ISIS and sought the creation of a caliphate.[13] ASG links with ISIS are now limited.

Opponents and affiliates/allies: Opposes the AFP, the MILF and a faction of the MNLF led by Muslimin Sema. An MNLF faction based in Sulu, commanded by Nur Misuari, is more tolerant of the ASG.
Allied loosely with other ISIS affiliates in Mindanao: the AKP, the BIFF and the Maute Group. The group has ties with Islamist militant cells in Sabah State, eastern Malaysia.[14]

Resources/capabilities: Uses high-powered rifles and improvised explosive devices (IEDs) to attack AFP troops. Deploys speedboats in maritime kidnap-for-ransom operations and has used firearms and knives to kill hostages. The group has carried out suicide bombings since mid-2018.[15]

Ansar Khalifah Philippines (AKP)

Strength: Fewer than 50 active fighters (estimate).

Areas of operation: Southern Mindanao provinces of Sarangani and South Cotabato. In 2020, the group was most active in Polomolok municipality.

Leadership and structure: Salahuddin Hassan. AKP sub-faction leader Jeoffrey Nilong was killed by the AFP in September 2020.[16]
The group has no formal structure, with AKP remnants being divided into small cells.

Objectives: Establish an Islamic caliphate in Mindanao.

Opponents and affiliates/allies: Opposes the AFP and the PNP. The MILF and the MNLF are also opposed to the AKP but operate in separate parts of Mindanao.
Cooperates with the BIFF. Allied to the ASG and the Maute Group through a shared affiliation with ISIS, but without direct cooperation.

Resources/capabilities: Small firearms. The AFP classifies the AKP as a local criminal actor rather than a major jihadist threat. The AKP engages in gun battles with both the AFP and the PNP, and has perpetrated IED attacks such as the September 2018 bombing in General Santos city.[17] It is unclear whether the AKP still retains its bomb-making capabilities. The AKP is also involved in car-napping, robberies, the illegal drugs trade and gun-for-hire activities.

Bangsamoro Islamic Freedom Fighters (BIFF)

Strength: More than 900 members (according to BARMM Chief Minister Ebrahim in January 2021).[18] Previous AFP estimates suggested that the BIFF had 300–400 active members in recent years.

Areas of operation: Most active in an area known as the 'SPMS box' (encompassing the towns of Shariff Aguak, Pagatin, Mamasapano and Datu Salibo) in central Maguindanao province. Also operates in the provinces of North Cotabato and Sultan Kudarat.

Leadership and structure: Divided into three factions, led by Esmael Abdulmalik (alias 'Abu Toraife'), Ismael Abubakar (alias 'Imam Bongos') and Ustadz Karialan (alias 'Imam Minimbang') respectively. Though it has no centralised leadership, factions of the BIFF cooperate in a tactical alliance against the AFP.

Objectives: Establish an independent homeland for the Moro people. Pledged allegiance to ISIS in 2014 and has since fought to establish an Islamic caliphate in Mindanao.

Opponents and affiliates/allies: Opposes the AFP and the MNLF. Despite being its parent group, the MILF is also opposed to the BIFF and has, alongside the military, attacked BIFF militants.
Allied to Mindanao's other ISIS affiliates: the AKP, the ASG and the Maute Group.

Resources/capabilities: Uses high-powered rifles in battles with government troops. Retains the ability to construct powerful IEDs, evidenced by the discovery in 2020 of rudimentary bomb-making factories operated by the BIFF in Maguindanao province. Targets the AFP with roadside ambushes and IED attacks and has occasionally bombed civilian targets in major urban centres.

Maute Group

Strength: Fewer than 25 active fighters (AFP estimate) but recruitment activities reportedly continue. The Maute Group used to number up to 1,000 members, but most of its fighters were killed by the AFP during the 2017 Marawi siege.

Areas of operation: Active on the northern side of Lake Lanao in the provinces of Lanao del Sur and Lanao del Norte. Operates primarily in rural and mountainous areas.

Leadership and structure: Faharudin Hadji Satar (alias 'Abu Bakar') is the de facto leader. The previous leader Owaida Marohombsar (alias 'Abu Dar'), who was also 'emir' of ISIS in Southeast Asia, was killed in a military offensive in March 2019.[19] Founders Abdullah and Omar Maute were killed in the 2017 Marawi siege.[20]
No defined structure and only small cells remain.

Objectives: Through seizing and holding territory it aims to forge an ISIS-style caliphate in southeast Asia centred on Mindanao.

Opponents and affiliates/allies: Opposes the AFP and the MILF.
Pledged allegiance to ISIS, though its relations with the AKP, the ASG and the BIFF have been limited since 2017.

Resources/capabilities: Thought to possess only a small cache of rifles. The group no longer has the capability to seize and hold territory or launch attacks on the scale of the Marawi siege.

Moro Islamic Liberation Front (MILF)

Strength: 26,500 active members serving in its Bangsamoro Islamic Armed Forces (BIAF), down from 40,000 in 2019 as 13,500 have since been demobilised. The entire force is set to be disarmed by 2022 under the terms of the 2014 CAB.[21]

Areas of operation: Western Mindanao. Most fighters remain encamped in a network of MILF bases and no longer fight AFP troops, but sometimes clash with ISIS-affiliated militant groups. The group's headquarters, Camp Darapanan, is situated in Maguindanao province.

Leadership and structure: Led by chairman Al Haj Murad Ebrahim, who also serves as Chief Minister of the BARMM. The group operates as a conventional armed force with a centralised leadership body. It is in the process of transitioning from a rebel group to a political party and has formed the United Bangsamoro Justice Party to contest future BARMM elections.

Objectives: Initially advocated for an independent Moro state, launching ambushes and bomb attacks targeting the AFP. From the late 1990s it began peace negotiations with Manila, seeking autonomy via political dialogue. The MILF no longer fights AFP troops and is committed to peace, having signed peace deals in 2014 and 2018.

Opponents and affiliates/allies: Opposes the AKP, the ASG, the BIFF and the Maute Group. However, the MILF initiated a dialogue with these ISIS-aligned groups in 2020 to persuade them to support the BARMM. The group clashes occasionally with rival MNLF factions, but fighting is often short-lived and localised in nature.
Formally allied to the AFP.

Resources/capabilities: Access to high-powered automatic rifles and grenade launchers, but these will be decommissioned by mid-2022.

Asia

Moro National Liberation Front (MNLF)

Strength: Fewer than 10,000 active fighters. The MNLF's strength has declined since the 1970s when it had 30,000 members.

Areas of operation: Western Mindanao and the Sulu islands. Most MNLF fighters are encamped and rarely engage in fighting aside from localised inter-factional and clan disputes.

Leadership and structure: MNLF founder Nur Misuari is still an influential figure and leads a 3,000-strong faction in Sulu. Muslimin Sema became chairman of the larger, more moderate MNLF faction in 2020 after the death of former leader Yusop Jikiri.[22]
Initially a centralised organisation, the MNLF splintered after signing a peace agreement with the government in 1996.

Objectives: No longer advocates for full Moro independence and was broadly supportive of the government–MILF peace process that produced the BARMM. However, Misuari remains a vocal critic and Duterte has sought to engage him amid fears that his faction could yet prove disruptive.

Opponents and affiliates/allies: Opposes the AKP, the BIFF and the Maute group. The MILF is a rival, but the two sides rarely resort to violence.
Formally allied to the AFP since the 1996 peace deal. However, tensions remain, as evidenced by the 2013 siege of Zamboanga. The Misuari faction retains kinship – but not operational – ties to the ASG.

Resources/capabilities: The group no longer engages in major fighting with AFP soldiers. However, it remains a powerful, dormant actor in the conflict with access to rifles and a wide network of bases.

Conflict Drivers

Economic and social

Repression of Islam and Moro culture:
The roots of separatism lie in the oppression of Moro Muslims, who account for approximately a quarter of total residents on the Catholic-majority southern island of Mindanao.[23] Despite being present in western Mindanao since the arrival of Arab traders in the Sulu islands in the early 14th century, the Moros have been denied an independent homeland. Moro rebels battled Spanish and American colonial forces before taking on Philippine troops post-independence in 1946. One major cause of resentment among the Muslim population is the flow of Christian migration southward through the country which, they believe, has eroded traditional Moro culture and identity. Duterte vowed to correct 'historical injustices' upon taking office, but not all Moros are satisfied with the control over BARMM land and resources granted to them under the BOL.[24] ASG followers in Sulu still feel aggrieved and harbour ambitions of reviving a historic Islamic sultanate.

Economic marginalisation and poverty:
Poverty and underdevelopment have long been drivers of recruitment for Moro rebel groups. The five provinces that make up the core BARMM region – Basilan, Lanao del Sur, Maguindanao, Sulu and Tawi-Tawi – are among the most deprived in the Philippine archipelago, despite being rich in fertile soils, natural resources such as timber, gold and mineral deposits, and the renewable energy resource of hydropower. The central government and large multinational firms have accrued most resource profits, while poor infrastructure and inadequate public services have restricted development. In 2018, 61.3% of the population in the BARMM were unable to meet basic food and non-food needs and 2.5 million people were living in poverty.[25] In Sulu, the poverty rate is highest, at 74.3%.[26] A lack of livelihood opportunities has made separatism a credible alternative path for many young Moro men.

International

Transnational jihadism in Southeast Asia:
From the 1970s onward, a fracturing of the separatist movement – which was then simply a local affair – served to prolong the conflict, as the MNLF spawned the MILF amid personality clashes and divergent ideological views. In more recent times, transnational jihad has had a

similar effect on the movement. The AKP, the ASG, the BIFF and the Mautes all pledged allegiance to ISIS after its emergence in Syria in 2014, and Islamism became a primary motivator for violence as these forces battled to forge a regional caliphate. The Marawi siege of 2017 and a number of suicide bombings followed, while foreign jihadis from Malaysia, Indonesia and as far afield as Egypt travelled to Mindanao to join ISIS affiliates, posing a challenge to the dominance of the MILF and the BARMM peace process.

Key Events in 2020–21

POLITICAL EVENTS

1 January 2020

Martial law ends in Mindanao after having been in place since the outbreak of the Marawi siege in May 2017.

11 March

Phase Two of the MILF decommissioning process is completed.

22 July

Three priority codes – the Administrative, Civil Service and Local Government codes – are filed for deliberation by lawmakers in the BARMM parliament.

12 October

A midterm review recommends extending the BARMM transition – originally set to end with elections in 2022 – by three years to 2025.

17 October

MNLF chairman Yusop Jikiri dies of bone cancer at the age of 66.

28 October

BTA lawmakers approve the BARMM Administrative Code, enacting the proposed governance structures for the region into law.

11 November

Muslimin Sema becomes the new MNLF chairman and pledges support for the government–MILF peace process.

12 November

MILF chairman and BARMM Chief Minister Al Haj Murad Ebrahim supports the recommendation of extending the BARMM transition to 2025.

MILITARY/VIOLENT EVENTS

16 January 2020

ASG militants kidnap five Indonesian fishermen from a vessel off the coast of Sabah State, Malaysia.

2–6 March

An AFP offensive targeting the BIFF in central Maguindanao province leaves 14 militants and four soldiers dead.

17 April

ASG militants ambush AFP troops in Patikul, Sulu province, killing 11 soldiers and leaving 14 others injured.

22 April

A firefight in Patikul, Sulu province, kills six ASG militants and injures eight AFP troops.

4 June

AFP soldiers kill five and capture 14 BIFF militants amid gun battles in Lambayong, Sultan Kudarat province.

5 June

ASG militants kill four AFP Special Forces troops during an ambush in Patikul, Sulu province. Two militants are also killed.

29 July

AFP troops clash with BIFF militants in Datu Salibo, Maguindanao province, leaving 15 militants and two soldiers dead.

31 July

Six ASG militants and three AFP soldiers are killed during gun battles in Patikul, Sulu province.

24 August

Two ASG suicide bombers kill 14 people and wound 75 in Jolo, Sulu province.

6–9 September

ASG sub-leader Furuji Indama is among five militants killed in clashes with the AFP in Zamboanga Sibugay province.

9 September

AKP sub-leader Jeoffrey Nilong is killed in a clash with AFP soldiers in Surallah, South Cotabato province.

3 November

AFP forces attack a speedboat off Sulare Island, Sulu province, killing seven members of an ASG cell notorious for kidnapping people for ransom.

Asia

1–7 December
Lawmakers file three bills in the Philippine House of Representatives seeking a three-year extension to the BARMM transition.

20 January 2021
Governor of Sulu province Abdusakur Tan claims that his constituents are opposed to postponing the BARMM elections which are scheduled for 2022.

13 November
AFP troops and PNP officers clash with the AKP in Polomolok, South Cotabato province, killing six militants.

3 December
BIFF militants attack an AFP base and shoot at houses in Datu Piang, Maguindanao province, but are repelled by AFP forces.

29 December
MILF rebels kill seven militants after blocking a BIFF attack on an AFP base in Mamasapano, Maguindanao province.

Conflict Outlook

Political scenarios

Through 2021, deliberations on postponing the first BARMM parliamentary elections from 2022 to 2025 will take centre stage. The bills looking to extend the transition period require congressional approval, and if granted, the rule of the MILF-controlled BTA would be prolonged by three years. An extension may risk undermining public support for the peace process and delays to the democratic process may frustrate the MNLF, a historical rival of the MILF. Yet thus far, the MNLF has not proved to be disruptive. Duterte has initiated ongoing dialogue with Misuari to ensure that his Sulu faction does not harm peace efforts, while new chairman of the larger MNLF faction Sema has asserted that 'the MNLF is at one with the MILF in securing lasting peace' and backs an extension to forge a 'durable governance foundation'.[27] A strong and transparent public bureaucracy to underpin the BARMM is key to avoiding a repeat of the corruption and inefficiency problems that beset the ARMM, and an extended transition period would afford the BTA more time to implement policy in this effort.

Escalation potential and conflict-related risks

In western Mindanao, the remnants of ISIS-aligned groups pose a continued risk. However, their strength and capabilities have declined significantly since the 2017 Marawi siege, amid continued AFP bombardments. Having banded together in past years, militants are now geographically dispersed and operate as a loose network of cells rather than as an alliance of coherent, organised groups. While the BIFF remains resilient in its rural strongholds in central Maguindanao, the group is effectively penned in and unable to expand. The AKP, particularly the Nilong faction, suffered significant

losses in 2020 and survives only as a local bandit-type organisation in South Cotabato. Similarly, the Maute Group in Lanao del Sur has lost members and resources in recent years, operating with no clear structure. The ASG represents the largest threat. In Basilan its strength has declined, but the Sawadjaan faction in Sulu remains resilient. It has been able to withstand military operations and resist infiltration by recruiting through family connections.[28] ASG suicide attacks and kidnappings will pose a continued risk to civilians over the coming years, while clan disputes or *ridos* – which occasionally involve MILF and MNLF rebels along with private armies – represent another ongoing threat to security in some localities.[29]

Strategic implications and global influences

Since the territorial defeat of ISIS in Syria and Iraq, financial and material support for its affiliates in the Philippines has reduced, as has the number of foreign fighters joining Mindanao-based groups. The route which militants would usually take – coming across the Sulu Sea from Sabah State – has become difficult to navigate due to trilateral naval patrols carried out since mid-2017 by Indonesia, Malaysia and the Philippines. The patrols, initiated in response to an influx of foreign fighters to Mindanao ahead of the 2017 Marawi siege, are designed to police porous shared sea borders and prevent the transit of jihadist fighters by sea. A dusk-to-dawn curfew for civilian vessels imposed off Sabah State by the Malaysian authorities aids these efforts.

The ongoing threat of terrorism provides an incentive for the Philippines and the United States to renegotiate the Visiting Forces Agreement (VFA), which allows for US troops to be stationed in the country in line with the 1951 Mutual

Defense Treaty. Duterte, a long-standing critic of US military presence in the Philippines, had initially pledged to terminate the VFA in February 2020 before pausing his plan to allow for further debate.[30] Keeping the VFA in some form would aid efforts in tackling ISIS-aligned groups as the VFA not only enables bilateral military exercises, but also facilitates US training, intelligence, surveillance and reconnaissance support for AFP forces based in Mindanao.

Notes

[1]   Michael Hart, 'Deciphering the Jihadist Threat to Mindanao's Moro Peace Process', International Institute for Strategic Studies, 20 May 2019.

[2]   Congress of the Philippines, 'Republic Act No. 11054, Bangsamoro Organic Law', 27 July 2018.

[3]   United Nations Office for the Coordination of Humanitarian Affairs, 'Philippines Humanitarian Bulletin', Issue 6, July 2017.

[4]   Albashir Saiden, 'BARMM Parliament Resumes Session, Tackles COVID-19 Response', Philippine News Agency, 17 June 2020.

[5]   Bangsamoro Information Office, 'BTA Approves Bangsamoro Administrative Code', 28 October 2020; and Edwin Fernandez, 'BARMM Parliament Approves Civil Service Code', Philippine News Agency, 25 February 2021.

[6]   Taj Basman, 'Bangsamoro Chief Minister Backs Extending Transition by 3 Years', Rappler, 15 November 2020.

[7]   Pia Ranada, 'Duterte Backs Extension of Bangsamoro Transition Period to 2025', Rappler, 26 November 2020.

[8]   Julie M. Aurelio, '3 Bills to Postpone First BARMM Elections', INQUIRER.net, 15 December 2020.

[9]   Bong Sarmiento, '12,000 MILF Fighters Deactivated', INQUIRER.net, 25 March 2020.

[10] Katrina Domingo, 'Some Abu Sayyaf Members Seek to Join Bangsamoro Decommissioning: BARMM Chief', ABS-CBN, 29 January 2021.

[11] 'Abu Sayyaf Leader in Basilan Killed, Philippine Military Says', BenarNews, 30 October 2020.

[12] On 11 July 2020, the AFP said senior ASG leader in Sulu Hatib Hajan Sawadjaan was still alive and 'very active', despite reports that he had been killed during an encounter with government troops in Patikul earlier that month. However, rumours of his death or incapacitation through injury persisted. See, for example, Ellie Aben, 'Philippine Military Says Abu Sayyaf Leader Still Alive', Arab News, 11 July 2020.

[13] 'Marawi: DNA Test Confirms Death of Isnilon Hapilon, One of FBI's Most Wanted Terror Suspects', ABC News, 22 October 2017.

[14] 'Terror Group with Partners Active in Sabah: Azis', Daily Express, 28 January 2020.

[15] Michael Hart, 'Philippines' Abu Sayyaf Terrorists Turn to Suicide Bombing', Asia Sentinel, 24 April 2020.

[16] Bong S. Sarmiento, 'Alleged Leader of Islamic State-inspired Group, Brother Slain in South Cotabato', INQUIRER.net, 10 September 2020.

[17] Richelyn Gubalani, 'Suspect in 2018 GenSan Bomb Blast Slain in SoCot Encounter', Philippine News Agency, 20 July 2020.

[18] Eimor Santos, 'Hundreds of BIFF Fighters "Willing to Rejoin" MILF, Work with Gov't', CNN Philippines, 22 January 2021.

[19] Carmela Fonbuena, 'DNA Test Confirms Death of Abu Dar, Last Surviving Maute Leader', Rappler, 14 April 2019.

[20] Raul Dancel, 'Philippines Security Forces Kill Two Top Terrorists, Including ISIS Chief in South-East Asia', Straits Times, 16 October 2017.

[21] President of the Philippines, 'Executive Order No. 79: Implementing the Annex on Normalization Under the Comprehensive Agreement on the Bangsamoro', 24 April 2019.

[22] Asangan T. Madale, 'Sema New MNLF Chairman', Manila Times, 15 November 2020.

[23] Philippine Statistics Authority, 'Factsheet on Islam in Mindanao', 28 September 2017.

[24] Jonathan de Santos, 'Duterte: Correct Historical Injustice, Pass Bangsamoro Law', Philippine Star, 25 July 2016.

[25] Nash B. Maulana, '61% of BARMM Families Poor', Manila Standard, 27 February 2020.

[26] Ibid.

[27] John Unson, 'MNLF Leader Backs Term Extension for Bangsamoro Transition Authority', Philippine Star, 26 November 2020.

[28] Michael Hart, 'Family Ties and New Recruits: Abu Sayyaf Proves Hard to Dislodge in the Philippines', Geopolitical Monitor, 2 November 2020.

[29] International Crisis Group, 'Southern Philippines: Tackling Clan Politics in the Bangsamoro', Report No. 306, 14 April 2020.

[30] Department of Foreign Affairs of the Republic of Philippines, 'Statement of Foreign Affairs Secretary Teodoro L. Locsin, Jr. on VFA Extension', 11 November 2020.

Asia

Data Appendix

Number of fatalities due to conflict events, by country, 1 January 2020 to 25 February 2021
Number of reported fatalities due to violent events (defined by the Armed Conflict Location & Event Data Project (ACLED) as battles, explosion/remote violence or violence against civilians) from 1 January 2020 to 25 February 2021. If no exact number is stated a conservative estimate has been used. This estimate depends on the parties involved and whether the event was a significant attack, or occurred within a war zone.
Source: ACLED, www.acleddata.com/

	Number of fatalities
Afghanistan	25,568
Yemen	22,986
Mexico	9,915
Nigeria	9,307
Syria	9,303
Nagorno-Karabakh*	6,706
Democratic Republic of the Congo	6,391
Brazil	5,877
Somalia	3,677
Ethiopia	3,606
Mali	3,169
Iraq	3,027
South Sudan	2,640
Burkina Faso	2,509
Mozambique	1,874
Cameroon	1,711
Philippines	1,687
Libya	1,495

	Number of fatalities
Sudan	1,350
Niger	1,304
India	1,046
Colombia	961
Pakistan	900
Honduras	778
Chad	767
Myanmar	714
Egypt	703
Central African Republic	590
Turkey	559
El Salvador	385
Ukraine	121
Thailand	107
Israel–Palestinian Territories*	33

*The figure represents the sum of fatalities for the two parties involved in the conflict. For the Nagorno-Karabakh conflict it represents the sum of fatalities for Armenia and Azerbaijan.

Number of refugees (total), by country of origin, as of 31 December 2020

Number of refugees, specifically those in a refugee-like situation under the mandate of the United Nations High Commissioner for Refugees (UNHCR), and Palestinian refugees recorded by the UN Relief and Works Agency for Palestine Refugees (UNRWA).

A refugee is someone who is unable or unwilling to return to their country of origin owing to a well-founded fear of being persecuted for reasons of race, religion, nationality, membership of a particular social group or political opinion (as per the UNHCR 1951 Refugee Convention). In the case of Palestinian refugees, these are persons whose normal place of residence was Palestine during the period 1 June 1946 to 15 May 1948, and who lost both home and means of livelihood as a result of the 1948 conflict.

Data from UNHCR is updated to 31 December 2020 and released by UNHCR as full-year figures in June 2021. The UNRWA data is from June 2021.
Source: UNHCR, www.unhcr.org/refugee-statistics/; UNRWA, www.unrwa.org/

	Number of refugees
Syria	6,689,582
Israel–Palestinian Territories*	5,703,919
Afghanistan	2,594,774
South Sudan	2,189,141
Myanmar	1,103,299
Democratic Republic of the Congo	840,449
Somalia	814,551
Sudan	787,755
Central African Republic	642,437
Nigeria	352,953
Iraq	333,418
Colombia	189,889
Mali	164,601
Ethiopia	151,336
Pakistan	133,143
Nagorno-Karabakh*	112,049
Turkey	93,738
Cameroon	78,560

	Number of refugees
El Salvador	45,640
Ukraine	35,180
Honduras	34,473
Yemen	33,369
Egypt	26,604
Niger	18,874
Libya	17,595
Burkina Faso	15,768
Mexico	15,408
India	12,428
Chad	10,488
Brazil	1,588
Philippines	490
Thailand	182
Mozambique	91

*The figure represents the sum of refugees for the two parties involved in the conflict. For the Nagorno-Karabakh conflict it represents the sum of refugees for Armenia and Azerbaijan.

Number of internally displaced persons (total), by country, as of 31 December 2020

Total number of internally displaced persons (IDPs) due to conflict and violence, to 31 December 2020.

IDPs are persons or groups of persons who have been forced or obliged to flee or to leave their homes or places of habitual residence, in particular as a result of or in order to avoid the effects of armed conflict, situations of generalised violence, violations of human rights or natural or human-made disasters, and who have not crossed an internationally recognised state border (as per 1998 UN Guiding Principles on Internal Displacement).

Source: Internal Displacement Monitoring Centre (IDMC), www.internal-displacement.org/database/displacement-data

	Number of IDPs (conflict and violence)
Syria	6,568,000
Democratic Republic of the Congo	5,268,000
Colombia	4,922,000
Yemen	3,635,000
Afghanistan	3,547,000
Somalia	2,968,000
Nigeria	2,730,000
Sudan	2,276,000
Ethiopia	2,060,000
South Sudan	1,436,000
Iraq	1,224,000
Turkey	1,099,000
Burkina Faso	1,075,000
Cameroon	1,003,000
Nagorno-Karabakh*	735,800
Ukraine	734,000
Central African Republic	682,000
Mozambique	676,000
Myanmar	505,000
India	473,000
Mexico	357,000
Chad	342,000
Mali	326,000
Libya	278,000
Niger	257,000
Honduras	247,000
Philippines	153,000
Israel–Palestinian Territories*	131,000
Pakistan	104,000
Thailand	41,000
Egypt	3,200
Brazil	0
El Salvador	0

*The figure represents the sum of IDPs for the two parties involved in the conflict. For the Nagorno-Karabakh conflict it represents the sum of IDPs for Armenia and Azerbaijan. For the Israel–Palestinian Territories conflict, it only includes Palestinian IDPs since there is no data available for Israel.

Number of conflict events, by country, 1 January 2020 to 25 February 2021

Number of violent events (defined by ACLED as battles, explosion/remote violence or violence against civilians) from 1 January 2020 to 25 February 2021.

Source: ACLED, www.acleddata.com

	Number of events
Syria	11,892
Yemen	11,199
Ukraine	9,132
Afghanistan	8,773
Mexico	7,994
Brazil	7,440
Nagorno-Karabakh*	6,231
Iraq	3,493
Somalia	2,897
Democratic Republic of the Congo	2,740
Nigeria	2,600
India	2,002
Philippines	1,451
Myanmar	1,204
Mali	1,134
Cameroon	1,130
Libya	1,107
South Sudan	919
Colombia	808
Turkey	799
Burkina Faso	751
Honduras	656
Mozambique	608
Egypt	578
Pakistan	558
Sudan	525
Niger	443
Central African Republic	405
Israel–Palestinian Territories*	387
Ethiopia	379
El Salvador	365
Thailand	143
Chad	121

*The figure represents the sum of events for the two parties involved in the conflict. For the Nagorno-Karabakh conflict it represents the sum of events for Armenia and Azerbaijan.

Number of interventions by major geopolitical powers in conflict-affected countries, by country, 2020*

Number of major geopolitical powers within the G20 group that conducted military interventions in conflict-affected countries, by country. The figures refer to G20 countries deploying unilaterally or as part of a coalition (other than a mission under the aegis of an international organisation).

Source: IISS calculations based on Military Balance+ data collected in April 2021, milbalplus.iiss.org

	Sum of interventions	Intervening countries
Iraq	7	Australia Canada Germany Italy Turkey UK US
Niger	4	France Germany Italy US
Syria	4	France Russia Turkey US
Ukraine	4	Canada Russia UK US
Afghanistan	2	India US
Libya	2	Italy Turkey
Mali	2	France UK
Philippines	2	Australia US
Somalia	2	Turkey UK
Nagorno-Karabakh**	1	Russia
Burkina Faso	1	France
Cameroon	1	US
Chad	1	France

	Sum of interventions	Intervening countries
Colombia	1	US
El Salvador	1	US
Honduras	1	US
Nigeria	1	UK
Yemen	1	Saudi Arabia
Brazil	0	
Central African Republic	0	
Democratic Republic of the Congo	0	
Egypt	0	
Ethiopia	0	
India	0	
Israel–Palestinian Territories	0	
Mexico	0	
Mozambique	0	
Myanmar	0	
Pakistan	0	
South Sudan	0	
Sudan	0	
Thailand	0	
Turkey	0	

*The indicator covers only interventions related to the specific conflict (i.e., the deployed military forces are conflict parties and/or the deployment has an explicit mandate to assist the conflict parties with training and capability building). The US interventions in Thailand and Turkey are not considered conflict-related and are not included in the indicator calculation for either country.
**The figure represents the sum of interventions in Armenia–Azerbaijan.

Number of personnel deployed by major geopolitical powers in conflict-affected countries, by country, 2020*

Total number of military personnel deployed into conflict-affected countries by major geopolitical powers within the G20 group (including unilaterally, as part of a combat coalition or a mission under the aegis of an international organisation).

Source: IISS calculation based on Military Balance+ data collected in April 2021, milbalplus.iiss.org

	Number of personnel deployed
Syria	8,059
Afghanistan	6,686
Iraq	5,208
Democratic Republic of the Congo	4,308
Nagorno-Karabakh**	4,117
South Sudan	3,767
Mali	3,510
Ukraine	3,403
Yemen	2,500
Niger	1,695
Chad	1,500
Libya	902
Egypt	614
Burkina Faso	400
Somalia	390
Sudan	388
Honduras	370
Philippines	309
Cameroon	300
Central African Republic	298
Nigeria	80
Colombia	70
India	10
Pakistan	10
Brazil	0
El Salvador	0
Ethiopia	0
Israel–Palestinian Territories**	0
Mexico	0
Mozambique	0
Myanmar	0
Thailand	0
Turkey	0

*The indicator covers only deployments related to the specific conflict (i.e., the deployed military forces are conflict parties, and/or the deployment has an explicit mandate to assist the conflict parties with training and capability building). The US deployments in Thailand and Turkey are not considered conflict-related and are not included in the indicator calculation for either country.
**The figure represents the sum of deployments in Armenia and Azerbaijan.

Number of UNSC resolutions concerning conflict-affected countries, by country, 2020

Number of resolutions announced by the UN Security Council (UNSC) in 2020 concerning the country. Countries for which no resolution was announced receive a value of 0.

Source: UN Security Council, www.un.org/securitycouncil/content/resolutions-adopted-security-council-2020

	Number of resolutions
South Sudan	8
Sudan	8
Somalia	6
Libya	5
Afghanistan	3
Central African Republic	3
Syria	3
Yemen	3
Iraq	2
Mali	2
Colombia	1
Democratic Republic of the Congo	1
Israel–Palestinian Territories	1
Nagorno-Karabakh	0
Brazil	0
Burkina Faso	0
Cameroon	0
Chad	0
Egypt	0
El Salvador	0
Ethiopia	0
Honduras	0
India	0
Mexico	0
Mozambique	0
Myanmar	0
Niger	0
Nigeria	0
Pakistan	0
Philippines	0
Thailand	0
Turkey	0
Ukraine	0

Number of peacekeeping and other multilateral missions present in conflict-affected countries, by country, 2020*

Number of multilateral peacekeeping, special political missions and other multilateral political presences under the aegis of international organisations present in a country. These include missions undertaken by the UN, regional organisations or ad hoc groups formed in response to UN sanctions/UNSC resolutions or endorsed by UN and other international organisations. Missions that work in conflict prevention and assist in peacebuilding or conflict-related political, training or capability building are counted.

Sources: IISS calculations based on Military Balance+ data; the Stockholm International Peace Research Institute (SIPRI), www.sipri.org; and data from the UN, European Union, regional organisations and ad hoc coalitions

	Number of missions	Names of missions
Mali	6	African Union Mission for Mali and the Sahel (MISAHEL) EU Training Mission Mali (EUTM Mali) EU Capacity Building Mission Sahel Mali (EUCAP Sahel Mali) G5 Sahel Joint Force (FC-G5S) UN Office for West Africa and the Sahel (UNOWAS) UN Multidimensional Integrated Stabilization Mission in Mali (MINUSMA)
Central African Republic	5	AU International Support Mission in Central Africa (MISCA) AU Observer Mission to the Central African Republic (MOUACA) EU Training Mission in the Central African Republic (EUTM RCA) EU Advisory Mission in the Central African Republic (EUAM RCA) United Nations Multidimensional Integrated Stabilization Mission in the Central African Republic (MINUSCA)
Somalia	5	AU Mission in Somalia (AMISOM) EU Training Mission Somalia (EUTM Somalia) EU Capacity Building Mission in Somalia (EUCAP Somalia) UN Support Office in Somalia (UNSOS) UN Assistance Mission in Somalia (UNSOM)
Ukraine	5	EU Advisory Mission Ukraine (EUAM Ukraine) EU Border Assistance Mission to Moldova and Ukraine (EUBAM Moldova and Ukraine) Joint Control Commission (JCC) OSCE Observer Mission at Russian Checkpoints Gukovo and Donetsk OSCE Special Monitoring Mission to Ukraine (SMM)
Israel–Palestinian Territories	4	EU Border Assistance Mission for the Rafah Crossing Point (EUBAM Rafah) EU Police and Rule of Law Mission for the Palestinian Territory, EU Coordinating Office for Palestinian Police Support (EUPOL COPPS) Office of the UN Special Coordinator for the Middle East Peace Process (UNSCO) UN Truce Supervision Organization (UNTSO)
Iraq	3	EU Advisory Mission in support of Security Sector Reform in Iraq (EUAM Iraq) NATO Mission Iraq (NMI) UN Assistance Mission for Iraq (UNAMI)
Libya	3	AU Mission in Libya EU Border Assistance Mission in Libya (EUBAM Libya) UN Support Mission in Libya (UNSMIL)
Niger	3	EU Capacity Building Mission Sahel Niger (EUCAP Sahel Niger) G5 Sahel Joint Force (FC-G5S) UN Office for West Africa and the Sahel (UNOWAS)
Sudan	3	UN Integrated Transitional Assistance Mission in Sudan (UNITAMS) UN–AU Hybrid Operation in Darfur (UNAMID) UN Interim Security Force for Abyei (UNISFA)
Afghanistan	2	NATO Resolute Support Mission (RSM) in Afghanistan UN Assistance Mission in Afghanistan (UNAMA)
Burkina Faso	2	G5 Sahel Joint Force (FC-G5S) UN Office for West Africa and the Sahel (UNOWAS)
Colombia	2	OAS Mission to Support the Peace Process in Colombia (MAPP/OEA) UN Verification Mission in Colombia (UNVMC)
Democratic Republic of the Congo	2	UN Regional Office for Central Africa (UNOCA) UN Organization Stabilization Mission in the Democratic Republic of the Congo (MONUSCO)
South Sudan	2	IGAD Ceasefire & Transitional Security Arrangements Monitoring & Verification Mechanism (CTSAMVM) UN Mission in the Republic of South Sudan (UNMISS)
Syria	2	Office of the Special Envoy of the Secretary-General for Syria UN Disengagement Observer Force (UNDOF)
Yemen	2	Office of the Special Envoy of the Secretary-General for Yemen UN Mission to Support the Hudaydah Agreement (UNMHA)

	Number of missions	Names of missions
Nagorno-Karabakh**	1	Personal Representative of the Chairperson-in-Office on the Conflict Dealt with by the OSCE Minsk Conference
Cameroon	1	UN Cameroon–Nigeria Mixed Commission (CNMC)
Chad	1	Multinational Joint Task Force (MNJTF)
India	1	UN Military Observer Group in India and Pakistan (UNMOGIP)
Mozambique	1	Personal Envoy of the Secretary-General for Mozambique
Myanmar	1	Office of the Special Envoy to the Secretary-General on Myanmar
Pakistan	1	UNMOGIP
Philippines	1	International Monitoring Team (IMT)
Brazil	0	
Egypt	0	
El Salvador	0	
Ethiopia	0	
Honduras	0	
Mexico	0	
Nigeria	0	
Thailand	0	
Turkey	0	

*Multilateral operations covering regional conflicts (such as the ones in the Sahel or Lake Chad Basin) are attributed to the country in which they are primarily based. Those which are based outside of the countries involved in the conflict (such as the G5 Sahel Cross-Border Joint Force, based in Mauritania, or United Nations Office for West Africa and the Sahel (UNOWAS), based in Senegal) are counted for all the countries involved in the conflict. The UNMOGIP in Kashmir is counted for both India and Pakistan.
**The figure combines the number of multilateral missions for the conflict.

Estimates of Gini index, by country, latest available data

The Gini Index measures the extent to which the distribution of income (or, in some cases, consumption expenditure) among individuals or households within an economy deviates from a perfectly equal distribution. A Lorenz curve plots the cumulative percentages of total income received against the cumulative number of recipients, starting with the poorest individual or household. The Gini index measures the area between the Lorenz curve and a hypothetical line of absolute equality, expressed as a percentage of the maximum area under the line. Thus a Gini index of 0 represents perfect equality, while an index of 100 implies perfect inequality.
Source: World Bank, data.worldbank.org/indicator/ SI.POV.GINI?most_recent_year_desc=true. Source for Palestine: Trading Economics, tradingeconomics.com/ west-bank-and-gaza/gini-index-wb-data.html

	Gini index
Central African Republic	56.2 (2008)
Mozambique	54 (2014)
Brazil	53.4 (2019)
Colombia	51.3 (2019)
Honduras	48.2 (2019)
Cameroon	46.6 (2014)
Mexico	45.4 (2018)
South Sudan	44.1 (2016)

	Gini index
Chad	43.3 (2011)
Philippines	42.3 (2018)
Democratic Republic of the Congo	42.1 (2012)
Turkey	41.9 (2019)
Israel	39 (2016)
El Salvador	38.8 (2019)
Syria	37.5 (2003)
Somalia	36.8 (2017)
Yemen	36.7 (2014)
India	35.7 (2011)
Burkina Faso	35.3 (2014)
Nigeria	35.1 (2018)
Ethiopia	35 (2015)
Thailand	34.9 (2019)
Niger	34.3 (2014)
Sudan	34.2 (2014)
Palestinian Territories	33.7 (2016)
Mali	33 (2009)
Pakistan	31.6 (2018)
Egypt	31.5 (2017)
Myanmar	30.7 (2017)
Armenia	29.9 (2019)
Iraq	29.5 (2012)
Ukraine	26.6 (2019)
Azerbaijan	26.6 (2005)
Afghanistan	No data
Libya	No data

GDP per capita, current prices, purchasing power parity (international dollars), per country, 2020

Gross domestic product (GDP) per capita represents the total value in purchasing-power-parity (PPP) terms of final goods and services produced within a country during a specified time period divided by the average population for the same year. PPP is a theory that relates changes in the nominal exchange rate between two countries' currencies to changes in the countries' price levels. The GDP is expressed in current prices–international dollars.

Source: International Monetary Fund, www.imf.org/external/datamapper/PPPPC@WEO/OEMDC

Functioning of government, EIU Democracy Index, by country, 2020

The functioning of government, a pillar of the EIU Democracy Index, assesses the effectiveness of the system of checks and balances on the exercise of government authority as well as elements such as openness and transparency of government, public access to information, government accountability, pervasiveness of corruption, public confidence in government and political parties. The functioning of government is scored on a 0–10 scale.

Source: Economist Intelligence Unit, www.eiu.com/n/campaigns/democracy-index-2020/

	GDP per capita
Israel	40,547.288
Turkey	30,252.675
Mexico	19,130.104
Thailand	18,236.360
Brazil	14,916.285
Azerbaijan	14,430.858
Colombia	14,323.895
Armenia	13,261.333
Ukraine	13,109.593
Egypt	12,789.913
Iraq	10,002.965
Philippines	8,452.403
El Salvador	8,421.511
India	6,461.009
Libya	5,893.257
Honduras	5,449.575
Myanmar	5,241.645
Nigeria	5,186.766
Pakistan	5,150.037
Sudan	4,097.683
Cameroon	3,646.457
Ethiopia	2,908.295
Mali	2,400.817
Afghanistan	2,390.024
Burkina Faso	2,262.427
Yemen	1,927.331
Chad	1,611.004
Mozambique	1,276.615
Niger	1,258.705
Democratic Republic of the Congo	1,106.371
Central African Republic	979.403
Somalia	924.532
South Sudan	791.308
Palestian Territories	No data
Syria	No data

	Index
Israel	7.5
India	7.14
Colombia	6.43
Mexico	5.71
Brazil	5.36
Pakistan	5.36
Turkey	5.36
Armenia	5
Philippines	5
Thailand	5
El Salvador	4.29
Honduras	4.29
Myanmar	3.93
Ethiopia	3.57
Nigeria	3.57
Egypt	3.21
Azerbaijan	2.86
Ukraine	2.71
Burkina Faso	2.36
Cameroon	2.14
Sudan	1.79
Mozambique	1.43
Niger	1.14
Afghanistan	0.64
Palestinian Territories	0.14
Central African Republic	0
Chad	0
Democratic Republic of the Congo	0
Iraq	0
Libya	0
Mali	0
Syria	0
Yemen	0
Somalia	N/A
South Sudan	N/A

Data Appendix

Index